THE BLUE GUIDES

*in preparation

Temple of Hadrian, 2C AD, Ephesus.

BLUE GUIDE

TURKEY

The Aegean and Mediterranean Coasts

Bernard Mc Donagh

Maps and plans by John Flower

A & C Black
London

W W Norton
New York

First edition 1989

Published by A & C Black (Publishers) Limited
35 Bedford Row, London, WC1R 4JH

© A & C Black (Publishers) Limited 1989

Published in the United States of America by
W W Norton & Company, Incorporated
500 Fifth Avenue, New York, NY 10110

Published simultaneously in Canada by
Penguin Books Canada Limited,
2801 John Street, Markham, Ontario L3R 1B4

ISBN   0–7136–2806–5

ISBN   0–393–30489–2   USA

FOR JOHN, ELIZABETH
AND ANTHONY Mc DONAGH

After a number of years in the Civil Service **Bernard Mc Donagh**
retired in 1983 to devote himself to his two consuming passions—
writing and travelling. From editing a daily official journal and
making documentary films in Britain, from living in Kinshasa, where
he promoted British trade (honoured with the Order of Zaire by the
Congolese Government), and in Hamburg and Stuttgart, where he
was British Consul, he turned to making a detailed study of ancient
and modern Turkey. This was the natural development of his lifelong
interest in classical archaeology, which had already taken him across
Europe and North Africa. Research on this Blue Guide involved
many extended visits to Turkey, where he found his knowledge of
the language invaluable. He is the author of a children's book,
'Turkish Village', published by A & C Black.

Dr M. Naim Turfan is a lecturer at the School of Oriental and African
Studies, University of London.

Historical maps by András Bereznay

Typeset by CRB Typesetting Services, Ely, Cambs.
Printed in Great Britain by
BPCC Hazell Books Ltd
Member of BPCC Ltd
Aylesbury, Bucks, England

PREFACE

One of the most interesting developments in international tourism during recent years has been the increasing popularity of Turkey as a holiday destination. Attracted, perhaps, by its reputation for clean beaches, unpolluted seas and good food and wine, travellers have flocked there in their thousands. Many, too, have been drawn to that country by allurements of a more spiritual kind. They have sought out the fine buildings and vast ruined cities which in settings often wild and savage but almost always of great natural beauty provide such striking evidence of Turkey's rich and stormy past. This Blue Guide, the fruit of many extended journeys during recent years, aims to describe these ancient remains as well as the modern cities and towns that lie between Bursa in the north and Antakya in the south-east and, in passing, to give some account of the diverse cultures, which have combined to form modern Turkey.

It would have been impossible to write the Blue Guide Turkey without the assistance, generously given, of many friends both Turkish and British. Their comments and advice have helped to improve the text in many ways and to remove a number of erors. Any that remain are the sole responsibility of the author.

Dr Naim Turfan, whose penetrating and thought-provoking note on the development of civilisation in Anatolia makes an admirable introduction to the Guide, helped me to resolve a number of vexed points on Turkish history. I am greatly indebted to Professor Ekrem Akurgal, doyen of Turkish archaeologists, who provided invaluable advice at the planning stage of the book. Professor Cevdet Bayburtluoğlu of Ankara University generously put his extensive knowledge of Lycia at my disposal and helped me to organise my visits to the principal Lycian sites. Dr P.R.S. Moorey of the Ashmolean Museum, Oxford, very kindly cleared up some of my problems concerning the early history and archaeology of the SE Mediterranean. Bay Edip Özgür, archaeologist and Assistant at the Antalya Museum, my guide and mentor on a number of expeditions in southern Turkey, read the section on Antalya, including the guide to the Museum, and those on Lycia, Pamphylia and Cilicia and suggested some additions and clarifications.

Modern visitors to Turkey can not fail to be impressed by the accounts left by earlier travellers of their adventures in that country. The works of Lithgow, Charlemont, Beaufort, Chandler, Forbes, Spratt, Daniell, Fellows, Newton, Texier and, more recently, Freya Stark, George Bean and John Freely are eloquent reminders of dangers faced and difficulties and hardships overcome. From time to time I have taken the liberty of drawing on the experiences of some of my illustrious predecessors, *beatae memoriae*, to illustrate how much has changed in Turkish life and society and how much has remained the same.

By providing introductions to its various Regional Directors the office of the Director-General of Tourism in Ankara, greatly assisted my research in Turkey. So, too, did the Prime Minister's General Directorate of Press and Information, which arranged for me to be accompanied by charming cicerones both in the capital and in Southern Turkey. I am also very grateful to Bay Ercihan Düzgünoğlu, Culture and Information Counsellor, and Bay Ahmet Ersoy, Press Counsellor at the Turkish Embassy in London, who helped me to prepare for and plan my journeys to Turkey and who supplied me with a number of valuable introductions.

Without the assistance of the local Tourist Offices, especially those in Bursa, Çanakkale, Bergama, İzmir, Selçuk, Aydın, Bodrum, Pamukkale, Antalya, Alanya, Silifke, Mersin, İskenderun and Antakya, it would have been difficult for me to visit many of the ancient sites, which are covered in this edition of the Blue Guide. Their officers also provided much practical information on matters like hotels and transport. I would like to thank particularly Bay Nuri Toğay, Director of Tourism for İçel province, and Bay Celal Taşkırsan and Bay Hüseyin Kurt of Silifke Tourism Office, who spared no effort to assist me during my stay in their areas.

I would like to offer a special thanks to the directors of the various Regional Museums and to their staffs, who were always happy to show me the treasures under in their care and who displayed infinite patience in answering my many questions. I have particularly happy memories of the days between journeys, which I spent in the museums of İzmir, Antalya, Side, Antakya and Alanya, browsing through the galleries, reading in the library or discussing the collections with their conservators.

Despite a large increase in the number of tourists there is little evidence of a diminution in the welcome traditionally extended to the foreign visitor by Turkish hotels and restaurants. He is still treated as a *misafir*, a guest, rather than a tourist. I discovered this at first hand in establishments like the Kaptan Oteli in Alanya, the Billur Oteli and Hisar Oteli in İzmir, the İnci Oteli in Adana, the Yaka at Kızkalesi, and the Hidro Oteli in Harbiye, all of which served as my headquarters at various times. Their managements and staff did everything possible to make my stay pleasant and agreeable. While Turkish food, like good wine, needs no bush, I am glad to be able to record my appreciation of the excellent meals, which I enjoyed in the many restaurants, which I visited during my travels. The Mahperi Rstaurant in Alanya and Mola 33 at Akkum near Silifke delighted me with outstanding examples of Turkish cuisine on more than one occasion.

In Britain my researches were greatly facilitated by my being able to use the British Library, the Joint Library of the Societies for the Promotion of Roman Studies and Hellenic Studies, the Royal Geographical Society Library and Banstead Public Library. I would like to express my sincere thanks to the librarians and staff of these establishments for the efforts, which they made, to obtain so many rare and out-of-print works for my use. For new books I was able to rely on the excellent service offered to Londoners by Hatchards of Piccadilly and by the Vermilion Bookshop.

My travels in Turkey were greatly assisted by the help and advice, which I received from H.M. Consul-General in İstanbul and H.M. Vice-Consul in İzmir. I was also fortunate in being being able to draw on the encyclopaedic knowledge of the Venerable Geoffrey Evans, Archdeacon of the Aegean, who not only provided me with much useful information about some of the ancient sites in south-west Turkey, but also introduced me to a number of local experts.

Tom Neville, who was involved in the early stages of producing the Blue Guide Turkey, eased me gently into the project and helped me to master my word-processor. However, it was his successor Gemma Davies, who turned a complicated mass of typescript, maps, site plans, photographs and prints into the finished work. For her unwearying patience, unfailing kindness and helpful advice I am very grateful. I would also like to thank John Flower and András Bereznay for the great pains which they took over the preparation of the maps and site plans. Their work provides an admirable complement to the text.

During the months which it took to research amd write this book I was sustained by the help and encouragement of many friends. I am particularly grateful to Joyce and Robert Moore, Dennis and Ann Franklin, Mike Grisdale, Jim and Marian Pearce, Brian Wheeler, and Bill, Marjorie and Mike Taft, formerly of İzmir, now of Kansas City. They provided me with hospitality, tracked down sources and references and helped in innumerable other ways.

I owe a special debt of gratitude to my many Turkish friends. They opened their doors and their hearts to me, encouraged me to explore their culture and to learn their language and, above all, they shared their lives with me. I look back with a great deal of pleasure on the many months, which I spent in their company. I have particularly happy memories of my time in İstanbul and in villages like Kulaca Köyü and Çandır Köyü. If this Blue Guide helps other travellers to understand the Turkish people, appreciate their culture and enjoy their country, some of this debt may be repaid.

Bernard Mc Donagh
April 1989

Acknowledgements

For permission to reproduce the illustrations in the guide, the publishers would like to thank Bernard Mc Donagh, Godfrey Goodwin, the Trustees of the British Museum, the Trustees of the Tate Gallery and Türkiye Turing ve Otomobil Kurumu in İstanbul.

For permission to reproduce quotations grateful thanks to the following: William Heinemann Ltd, Strabo's 'Geography', Theocritus' 'The Greek Bucolic Poets'; Collins Harvill Publishers, 'On the Shores of the Mediterranean' by Eric Newby; Penguin Books Ltd, Herodotus' 'The Histories', Pausanias' 'Guide to Greece', Arrian's 'Life of Alexander the Great', translated by Aubrey de Selincourt, 'The Penguin Book of Greek Verse', edited by C.A. Trypanis; 'The Greek Anthology', edited by Peter Jay; 'The Anger of Achilles' by Robert Graves, by permission of A.P. Watt Ltd on behalf of The Executors of the Estate of Robert Graves, Macmillan Inc. in the USA; Basil Blackwell, 'Greek Religion' by Walter Burkert; John Murray (Publishers) Ltd, 'Turkey's Southern Shore' and 'Turkey beyond the Maeander' by George Bean, 'The Lycian Shore' and 'Alexander's Path' by Freya Stark; Scottish Academic Press Limited, 'The Cilician Kingdom of Armenia, edited by T.S.R. Boase; Routledge and Kegan Paul, in the USA A.M. Kelly Publishers, 'Travels in Asia and Africa 1325–54' by Ibn Battuta.

A NOTE ON BLUE GUIDES

The Blue Guide series began in 1918 when Muirhead Guide-Books Limited published 'Blue Guide London and its Environs'. Finlay and James Muirhead already had extensive experience of guide-book publishing: before the First World War they had been the editors of the English editions of the German Baedekers, and by 1915 they had acquired the copyright of most of the famous 'Red' Handbooks from John Murray.

An agreement made with the French publishing house Hachette et Cie in 1917 led to the translation of Muirhead's London Guide, which became the first 'Guide Bleu'—Hachette had previously published the blue-covered 'Guides Joanne'. Subsequently, Hachette's 'Guide Bleu Paris et ses Environs' was adapted and published in London by Muirhead. The collaboration between the two publishing houses continued until 1933.

In 1931, Ernest Benn Limited took over the Blue Guides, appointing Russell Muirhead, Finlay Muirhead's son, editor in 1934. The Muirhead's connection with the Blue Guides ended in 1963, when Stuart Rossiter, who had been working on the Guides since 1954, became house editor, revising and compiling several of the books himself.

The Blue Guides are now published by A & C Black, who acquired Ernest Benn in 1984, so continuing the tradition of guide-book publishing which began in 1826 with 'Black's Economical Tourist of Scotland'. The Blue Guide series continues to grow: there are now more than 35 titles in print with revised editions appearing regularly and many new Blue Guides in preparation.

'Blue Guides' is a registered trade mark.

EXPLANATIONS

Type. the main routes are described in large type. Smaller type is used, in general, for historical, background and practical information as well as for the description of sub-routes and diversions. Small capitals are used for ancient place names.

Abbreviations. In addition to generally accepted and self-explanatory abbreviations, the following occur in the Guide.

Bulv. *Bulvar* (Boulevard)
c *circa* (about, concerning a date)
C Century
Cad. *Cadde* (*Caddesi* in certain circumstances for grammatical purposes) (Avenue)
m metres
Meyd. *Meydan* (Square)
Rte Route
Sok. *Sokak* (Street)

Note on Spelling

Throughout the main text Greek proper nouns and place names are written, as a rule, in the familiar English or Latin forms, e.g. Cnidus rather than Knidos, Dionysus rather than Dionysos, odeum rather than odeion.

CONTENTS

MAPS AND PLANS

Historical Maps and Plans

A NOTE ON THE ANATOLIAN CIVILISATIONS

'And man does flourish but his time'
John Webster, *Vanitas Vanitatum*

by M. NAİM TURFAN

Implying as it does a sense of permanence, civilisation imbues this permanency with an achieved social order, a way of life.

Anatolia (Anadolu) has for the last 9000 years been the homeland of many distinct civilisations. They have each left their trace on its terrain; they have all contributed to developments in world history—developments much to do with highly evolved urban order and economy.

The huge 13-hectare neolithic settlement of Çatalhöyük near Konya, dating from the seventh millennium BC, provides one of the earliest patterns of urbanisation and perhaps the highest level of continuous organic association of specific types of craftsmanship—in a word, culture. With its elaborate wall-paintings, its sophisticated jewellery and weapons, its extensive agriculture and stock-breeding and its identification of property-ownership by use of seals, Çatalhöyük is striking as a pioneer of civilisation in Anatolia.

Between 1800 and 1200 BC the Hittite civilisation, as it came to be known, directly affected its successors—the late Hittite principalities, the Urartians of eastern Anatolia, the Hellenes and the Etruscans. For example, ancient Greek religion and mythology, no less than the Urartian, were strongly influenced by their Hittite precursors.

By the 6C BC, western Anatolia emerged as the home of philosophy, with the appearance of Thales, Anaximander and Anaximenes, all natives of Miletus (Balat), who established Anatolia as the cultural heart of the world's landscape. Yet Anatolia was also to become the home of epic and myth, witness Homer's 'Iliad' and 'Odyssey' centred on Troy (Hisarlık) and the return of Odysseus after the Trojan War, together with the much-fabled Midas (725–696? BC) and Croesus (560–547/6 BC), kings of Phrygia and Lydia.

The middle of the 4C BC heralded the thrust of the accumulated Anatolian civilisation of the classical period throughout the surrounding regions of the Near East and the Mediterranean until blocked by the advent of Rome over 200 years later. For the eastward conquest of Alexander of Macedon (336–323 BC) prompted the mutual accommodation of the cultures of the Asian and European continents, giving rise to the development of the earliest urban centres of the age—western Anatolian cities such as Pergamum (Bergama), Ephesus (Selçuk), Priene (Güllübahçe), Miletus and Didyma (Yenihisar). The art that developed here had a direct and important influence on Roman civilisation, and established these western Anatolian cities as the cultural equals of Rome in its heyday.

In view of the variety of languages and civilisations covering the same area (and often the same sites), and confusion persisting even in the scholarly literature, place names will normally accord with their contemporary usage, where known (except that Roman spellings will be used throughout instead of Greek in accordance with the editorial decision), with modern equivalents provided in brackets on first mention. Otherwise, modern Anatolian Turkish nomenclature will be used, usually with a suitable alternative where I feel it helpful to the reader. In the case of Anadolu, the more familiar Anatolia is used throughout.

Indeed, right up to the acme of the Byzantine period, in the 10th and 11C AD, the Eastern Roman pre-eminence in architecture, sculpture and painting rested on the prowess of her core Anatolian domains in these fields.

After this, the scene began to be dominated by the Selçuks, masters of the art of building *medreses* (Islamic institutes of higher education), hospitals, observatories, bridges and *kervansarays* (caravanserais)—not to mention the other crafts, notably carpet-weaving.

From the 13C to the 20C one of the world's most durable imperial dynasties, the Ottoman (Osmanlı), impressed its own seal on the culture of Anatolia in its entirety. The Ottomans created a vast territorial empire, based on the strength and integrity of the cultural resource base that was Anatolia.

So this is Anatolia, a land rich in heritage, home through the ages to peoples of diverse origins, diverse lives, diverse contributions—all preserved under its custodians of the last millennium, the Muslim Western Turks.

I. Prehistoric Anatolia

The living conditions of the earliest-known inhabitants of Anatolia depended upon their ability to hunt and gather edible plants. Their sanctuaries from wild animals and inclement weather took the form of rock shelters and caves; and they moved on whenever food resources became scarce. Their artefacts were related to their specific needs. Hence we find around their settlements flint hand-axes and scrapers and, with the refinement of flaking techniques, a wider range of later tools from types of points and perforators to cutters, chisels and a variety of microtools, all characteristic of the period known as the Palaeolithic (or Old Stone) Age. Yet, the evidence of the material activities of these people is complemented by their cultural attainments, particularly painting—a clear indication of their spiritual aspirations. For the inhabitants of Anatolia frequently decorated the walls of their cave and rock dwellings with depictions of their everyday lives and of the magical aspects of activities relating chiefly to fertility and the hunt. The reasoning, as it were, behind their hunting was reflected in this revelation—the depiction of the animal hunted—from which we may infer a holism in early man's view of life and perception of the cosmos. Evidence of Palaeolithic man in Anatolia is spread across various provinces, notably in the caves of Beldibi, Karain, Belbaşı, Öküzini and Kumbucağı, in and around Antalya; the caves called Kadıini in Alanya, Kapalıin in İsparta, Mağaracık in Hatay and Palanlı in Adıyaman. And the growing expertise and increasingly concerted effort in man's activities continued through the Mesolithic (or Middle Stone) Age until the advent of what is known as the Neolithic Revolution.

The start of the Neolithic (New Stone) Age was marked by the decisive step of man taking advantage of his environment through the deliberate cultivation of plants previously gathered wild and the domestication of animals previously acquired through skill in hunting. This active production of a more or less stable supply of food necessitated a more permanent relationship with the specific tracts of land, the plains, upon which all depended. Clearly, caves and rock dwellings on high ground, though secure, were no longer suitable

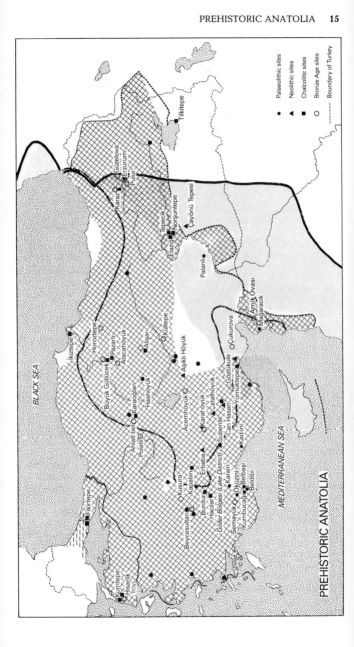

PREHISTORIC ANATOLIA

•	Palaeolithic sites
◄	Neolithic sites
■	Chalcolithic sites
○	Bronze Age sites
-----	Boundary of Turkey

BLACK SEA

MEDITERRANEAN SEA

Tilkitepe

Güzelova
Karaz
Erzurum
Pulur

Tepecik
Norşuntepe
Elazığ
Çayönü Tepesi

Palanlı

Sakçagözü Ovası
Mağaracık

İkiztepe
Horoztepe
Büyük Güllücek
Pazarlı
Alacahöyük
Alişar
Kültepe

Aşıklı Höyük

Çukurova

Karaoğlan
Hashöyük

Acemhöyük
Karahöyük
Çatalhöyük
Göztükule
Yumuktepe

Ahlatlıbel
Polatlı

Kuşura
Suberde
Can Hasan
Kadıni

Kapalın
Etibaba
Karaın

Beycesultan
Burdur
Hacılar
Göller Bölgesi (Lake District)
Semayük
Kumbucağı
Belbaşi
Beldibi
Okuzini

Fikirtepe
Kumtepe
Hisarlık
Troy

and man was obliged to construct his own shelter where he wished it, not to take shelter where he happened to find it.

Undoubtedly, Anatolia is now generally regarded as the most advanced centre of neolithic culture in the Near East. And by far the most important site is that of Çatalhöyük, lying about 50km SE of Konya and prominent between approximately 6500 and 5500 BC. The significance of the site chosen for settlement may not immediately be apparent to the modern visitor, who sees a vast dry plain covered with wheat and a few grazing herds but completely devoid of woodland. But in the 16th millennium BC the entire Konya basin was one lake, and by the time of the Çatalhöyük settlement this had drained to form a rich alluvial plain, with fertile grazing land and marshes in the east and thick forest to the west and south—an ideal source of timber for constructing dwellings.

The settlement presents a fairly uniform style of architecture, with rectangular single-storeyed houses built of mud-bricks supported internally by wooden beams and buttresses, grouped around courtyards and rising in terraces up the slope of the mound on which they were built. The flat-roofed houses had no doors but were entered through apertures in their roofs, reached by ladders, so that not only did the settlement present a solid blank wall to the outside as defence but the flat roofs served both as working space and as passageways from house to house, in many respects like villages of the region today. Inside were raised platforms or benches made of clay-brick for sitting and sleeping, and under these—as well as in separate shrines—were buried the dead, after excarnation (removal of the flesh). Indeed, the presence of over 40 shrines in the Çatalhöyük settlement offers us an insight into neolithic Anatolian religion. For, in addition to various statuettes of male deities, the presence of numerous stone and clay female figurines, often flanked by wild animals, indicates the prominence of the cult of the mother goddess, symbol of fertility and fecundity. We shall come across this cult of the mother goddess, and her association with wild beasts such as the leopard, again and again; for what originated here at Çatalhöyük was to dominate Anatolian religious belief through subsequent millennia. And the carving of bulls in association with the mother goddess in wall reliefs forms our first encounter with the popular bull cult, whose symbol endured through the Hittite period and beyond, most notably in the Urartian.

But perhaps the most striking characteristic of the shrines and houses of Çatalhöyük is the spectacular wall-paintings—possibly the oldest paintings to be found on man-made walls as opposed to natural cave walls. At Çatalhöyük, the walls are lavishly and artistically decorated with paintings of a religious nature, often scenes of death or excarnation, and plaster reliefs pertaining to a fertility cult. Other paintings depict most vivid naturalistic scenes—hunting, running and dancing, flowers, butterflies and bees—even the view of a town and a volcano in eruption, probably Çatalhöyük and the nearby, then volcanic, mountain, Hasan Dağı. There are also the numerous drawings and imprints of hands, crosses, stars and other symbols with, presumably, a magical and protective significance. And of particular interest are the intricate geometrical patterns closely resembling the bright geometrical Anatolian *kilims* (woven carpets) of today; in some instances even the stitched borders of the kilims are depicted, suggesting that these were copies of, rather than models for, the woven materials.

Other crafts practiced in Çatalhöyük included very fine obsidian and flint work in the preparation of weapons and mirrors, coloured-bead jewellery of various designs, fine woollen textiles and, in particular, wooden vessels and basketry showing a skill and sophistication unrivalled in the neolithic Near East.

Economy was based on agriculture, stock-breeding of sheep and goats and hunting of wild cattle, deer, boar, asses and leopards. A wide range of crops was cultivated—including varieties of grains—vegetable oil was used and very likely hackberry wine, if not beer, drunk. Indeed, the Çatalhöyük diet—the most varied known from any Near Eastern neolithic site—was a balanced one, as is evinced by the well-preserved teeth of the skeletons. Trade flourished, with what seems to have been a monopoly on the production and export of obsidian along the eastern Mediterranean (Akdeniz) in return for flint for weaponry, seashells for bead-making and a variety of stones for the manufacture of stone vessels, stone beads, cult statuettes and domestic utensils. A number of local raw materials, including ochres and other paints, greenstone, copper and iron ores and fossil shells, were also used in Çatalhöyük.

There is no doubt that the influence of Çatalhöyük as an important cultural 'hearth' spread far beyond Anatolia geographically and far into the future chronologically, to the extent that it is evident in aspects of village culture in Anatolia today.

In addition to Çatalhöyük, other major neolithic settlements flourished across Anatolia, notably the *höyüks* (barrows) of Gözlükule (Tarsus), Yümüktepe (Mersin) and the Amik plain of Hatay in the SE, of Erbaba and Suberde in the Lake District (Göller Bölgesi) and of Aşıklı Höyük and Can Hasan in central Anatolia. The earliest-known neolithic settlement, that of Çayönü Tepesi, near Diyarbakır in eastern Anatolia, dates from about 7000 BC.

About 5700–5600 BC, approximately 300km W of Çatalhöyük, near the town of Burdur, a settlement known as Hacılar became the most prominent and advanced culture of the late Neolithic/early Chalcolithic (Copper Stone) Age. Remarkable architectural developments include an increase in size—the houses were often two-storeyed and with flights of mud-brick steps connecting the lower and upper floors—and, more importantly, the arrangement of the houses in blocks with wide double doorways at ground level entered from narrow streets.

Interestingly, the disappearance of male deity statuettes at Hacılar is offset by the increase in the number of baked-clay figurines of female deities representing the mother goddess but modelled in a more stylised way than at neolithic sites like Çatalhöyük. The fertility cult is no longer confined to elaborately decorated shrines, as at Çatalhöyük, but has become domesticated, with the statuettes to be found in nearly every dwelling.

What is perhaps of particular interest at Hacılar is the gradual rise in importance of pottery manufacture alongside the decline of stoneware. And the extremely high standard of technique was more than matched by the rich geometrical painted designs for which Hacılar was unsurpassed throughout the Near East and the Mediterranean. The creativity in pottery decoration equals that of Çatalhöyük in wall-painting, an art that disappeared in Hacılar with the decline of hunting. For Hacılar was a mainly agricultural economy; teeth deteriorated as gritty cereal foods replaced the earlier balanced diet. The range of crops was still wide and a continuation of that of Çatalhöyük with some additions, such as chick-peas. Trade seems to have been as important, particularly the import of red and yellow ochres, haematite and white marble, obsidian and pumice. And, besides the spectacular painted pottery-ware, local bone and polished stone, textile and kilim-weaving industries flourished.

Towards the end of the early Chalcolithic period Hacılar, like other settlements, met with violent upheaval and came to an end with the burning and abandonment of the site. And yet elsewhere, notably in the Konya region of central Anatolia, the middle to late Chalcolithic period (early fifth to late fourth millennium BC) maintained its development. Indeed, a site like Can Hasan, south-east of Konya, displays all the stages of the Chalcolithic Age, during which copper was really discovered and utilised for the first time. For example, at Beycesultan (near Denizli) has been found a small hoard of copper objects—bars, needles, drills, a sickle, a fragment of a dagger (and a silver ring)—illustrating the use of this once rare and precious metal in ordinary household activities, and thus, by inference, the growing prosperity, based on industry and trade, of Anatolia generally during the Chalcolithic Age. By now, settlements were springing up all over Anatolia, from İstanbul (Fikirtepe) and Çanakkale (Kumtepe) to Samsun (İkiztepe) in the north, across central Anatolia (Karaoğlan, Hashöyük, Alişar, Pazarlı, Büyük Güllücek) and stretching far into the east and south-east (Karaz, Tilkitepe, Tepecik, Norşuntepe, Elazığ, Yümüktepe). And it was during the Chalcolithic Age that people seem to have begun to feel the need to surround their settlements not simply with walls but with fortifications (of which notable examples include the later Hacılar, Yümüktepe and the second town of Troy) and the urge to enlarge their lands through competition with other groups; although otherwise elements of customs and traditions of earlier ages tended to persist, with modifications. The characteristic building of the period comprised a unit of a single room with a hearth and grain store, made of mud-brick on a rectangular plan and entered through a fore-court, or vestibule—an innovation that proved durable and came to be known in western Anatolia and the Aegean world as the *megaron* (hall-and-porch) style. The dwelling was long and narrow, never expanded sideways or connected with others, more similar dwellings being built alongside if additional accommodation was required. There is no evidence to date of separate shrines, but in the later stages a distinctive marble statuette of a deity makes its appearance. In pottery, the most notable feature is the clear break from the sophisticated Hacılar tradition, with the predominance of a heavier and coarser ware.

As the Chalcolithic Age passed smoothly into the Bronze Age, c 3200 BC, a flourishing metallurgy developed in Anatolia. This development is attested mainly by the absence of stone artefacts rather than by the presence of quantities of metal ones, since metals such as gold and silver were continually recycled and have thus rarely survived. Moreover, the stone and pottery artefacts that exist tend to be imitative of metalware either in their design or in their metallic glaze. As the metal industry and trade progressed, it gave rise to specialised professions, the division of labour and hence a more complex lifestyle. The obvious prosperity of the region seems to have been based chiefly on the exploitation of its rich metal resources and the establishment of its position as the central metal market for trade eastward with Syria and Mesopotamia and westward with the Mediterranean and Balkans. Major urban communities and city-states organised under kings now began to emerge out of the traditional agriculturally-based economies. Plentiful evidence of this political organisation of Anatolia by the mid Bronze Age (second millennium BC) is available from royal tombs and fortresses and from the numerous city sites covering Anatolia, bearing in mind that not all shared the same speed or characteristics of development. The most important settlements of the period included, to the west, Troy and its environs; to the south, Semayük, Karahöyük and other *höyüks* in the Konya area; in the centre, notably Ahlatlıbel, Polatlı, Büyük Güllücek, Alişar, Alacahöyük, Kültepe and Acem-höyük; to the south-east, Çukurova and the Amik Ovası (Plain); to the east, the Malatya and Elazığ areas, Erzurum, Karaz, Pulur and Güzelova; and to the north, the Samsun and Sinop regions.

But the great advance in metallurgy is chiefly evident from such sites as the Alacahöyük burial chambers in north-central Anatolia, with their extraordinarily rich collections of gold, silver, bronze and copper artefacts—vessels, jewellery, bull and stag statuettes, ritual standards, sun-dials and musical instruments such as the sistrum with its tinkling bell-like sound. The wealth displayed here and in sites such as Troy II and Yümüktepe leaves no doubt of the standing of such people and of the prosperity of the small independent city-states. The palace complex at Troy, for example, features megaron-style buildings for the rulers. Evidence of the religious beliefs of the period is readily available as shrines are numerous. Beycesultan, for example, reveals both male and female deities with sacrificial containers before them and hearths nearby. And the shrines of Beycesultan, like Çatalhöyük, contain altars in the form of rams' horns and stylised bulls' heads—the bull comprising, as we have noted, a significant link between the neolithic and Hittite religions. Thus, the roots of Hatti and later Hittite religious belief may be inferred as extending as far back as the Neolithic Age in Anatolia. In addition, Anatolian neolithic influences on the Minoan civilisation of Crete are striking, most prominently in the cult of the mother goddess as Mistress of Beasts and her association with the leopard (among other animals), the worship of the bull and the sport of bull-leaping—depicted in one of the Çatalhöyük wall-paintings and very often represented in Minoan art.

Relations with the Balkan and Aegean regions may also be adduced from the ceramic styles, architectural designs and building techniques of the Bronze Age Anatolian city-states. The precious metal artefacts, also, of Alacahöyük and Horoztepe resemble items from a *kurgan* (burial mound or barrow) to the north-east at Maikop in the Kuban region of Caucasia. The implications of this similarity are several: that the craftsmen were natives of Anatolia; that the rulers of Alacahöyük and Horoztepe, in whose graves the artefacts have been found, were Caucasian in origin and brought their knowledge with them; or that the craftsmanship was derived through trade. Although the answer is as yet unknown, my own belief, until evidence is provided to the contrary, is that knowledge spread through trade.

However, towards the end of the third millennium BC there occurred an outbreak of destruction and conflagration throughout central, western and southern Anatolia, and evinced not only at the major sites of Troy II, Beycesultan, Kusura, Ahlatlıbel and Polatlı, but also at hundreds of lesser settlements across the region. Indeed, the majority of sites were deserted and never reoccupied. To judge from the occurrence of similar upheaval and destruction over the whole of the Near East at about the same time, it would seem that the area was undergoing widespread movement of population, a conclusion supported by certain cleavages in the cultural continuity of Anatolia and innovations of a type not necessarily local. Yet this period of disturbance served to usher in the enduring empire of intermingled peoples—indigenous Hattis and incoming Hittites.

II. The Hittites

Even the most cursory discussion of the Hittite civilisation that developed in late Bronze Age Anatolia between 1900 and 1200 BC must involve a prior look at the indigenous culture with which the invading peoples intermingled, and which lent their very name to the capital, Hattusha (Boğazköy), of the Hittite Empire—the Hattis.

This entails retracing our steps to the early Bronze Age, to the latter part of the third millennium BC, and to the region centring on Kültepe (Hattian Kanesh; N of Kayseri) in central Anatolia. Kültepe was the capital of one of the numerous independent city-states, the Hattian kingdom of Kanesh, prominent and prosperous by virtue of its position at the centre of the Assyrian trading network in Anatolia of that era, known as the Assyrian Colonial Trade period and controlled, as its name implies, from Assur (Assyria) rather than by any local state. Significantly, it was through the mainly Hatti trade connections with the literate Assyrian merchants that Anatolia entered the written historical records and thus began the short passage from prehistory to history, a process completed by the Hittites' rapid adoption of a new cuneiform script, to become the first known literate civilisation of Anatolia. Thenceforth, our knowledge rests not on the interpretation of material culture alone, but is complemented by written records. For at Kültepe, and to a lesser extent at Alişar and Boğazköy, thousands of clay tablets inscribed in Assyrian cuneiform bear witness to the commercial activities of the Assyrian merchants in the Hatti and neighbouring kingdoms. Yet despite the mutual cultural, and particularly artistic, influences arising out of these prolonged trade relations, the Hatti language seems to have remained intact, unaffected by the presence of the Assyrian merchant network with its settlements and economic domination of the region. For as soon as the merchant settlements broke up and disappeared their language faded away, never having been adopted by the local populace.

The Hattis' lack of a native written tradition cannot diminish the richness and sophistication of their own Anatolian culture. In pottery, for example, the Hattis are credited with the development of the so-called Cappadocian ware—whose origin was long in doubt—into true polychrome pottery; evidence of all phases in its development are present at the Kültepe site. And architecture became monumental, with 60 rooms being counted on the ground level of a palace at Kültepe. But perhaps most important, the complexity of the Hatti cosmic views—of the relationships between the solar and lunar systems and the planets—may be cited as an example of the high level reached by an indigenous Anatolian civilisation. The bronze Hatti sun-disc, with its radial lobes representing the planets, seems to have been an important temporal and religious symbol, and figurines of bulls and stags—sacred symbols of the Hatti religion—attest the strong line of continuity from the Neolithic and Chalcolithic Ages which was to extend through the Hittite period. Particularly significant is the worship of the goddess Kubabat, Mistress of Beasts, so often referred to in the letters of the Assyrian merchants—the Mother Goddess of prehistoric Anatolia who was worshipped under variations

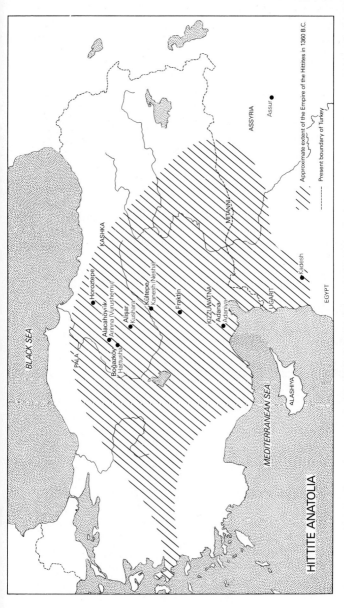

Approximate extent of the Empire of the Hittites in 1360 B.C.

Present boundary of Turkey

ASSYRIA

Assur

KASHKA

MITANNI

BLACK SEA

PALA

Horoztepe

Alacahöyük

Arinna (Vurushemu)

Boğazköy (Hattusha)

Alişar

Kushar

Kültepe

Kanesh (Neshar)

Fraktin

Kadesh

KIZZUWATNA

Adana

Adanya

UGARIT

EGYPT

MEDITERRANEAN SEA

ALASHIYA

HITTITE ANATOLIA

of this name until she was transformed into the Hellenistic Artemis throughout Anatolia. Indeed, many elements of Hatti civilisation persisted through the succeeding Hittites, as the Hattis gave way to superior Hittite strength but absorbed their conquerors into their own culture.

Nowhere is this more immediately apparent than in the Hittite label 'Land of the Hatti' for their own state, even though they spoke not the indigenous Hatti tongue but an inflective language of the Indo-European group which they called 'the language of Nesha' or Neshian, after their first capital city, Kanesh or Nesha (Kültepe). I would argue here that such adoptions—and they were numerous in all aspects of culture as well as in terminology—are not to be explained in terms of any great tolerance by the conquering Hittites, but more logically in terms of their meeting a much higher level of civilisation than their own; and over the 600 years of their empire the Hittites continued this habit of borrowing from wherever it suited them.

The outbreak of destruction and conflagration across Anatolia c 2000 BC, referred to at the end of Section I, marked the arrival of the Hittite peoples on the Anatolian scene, although it took another 200 years for them to establish themselves as a fully-fledged empire. Whence the Hittites came is still not universally agreed. But in view of the general displacement of population from eastern and central Anatolia westwards about the turn of the third/second millennia, as indicated by the archaeological evidence, and the known arrival of the Hittites in Hatti central Anatolia at about the same time, the argument in favour of Hittite immigration from the east or north-east, probably eastern Caucasia (Derbent Kapıları), is to my mind wholly convincing.

Anitta, king of Kushara (possibly Alişar?) in the 18C BC, is now generally taken as being the founder of the Hittite state. He, according to eight cuneiform tablets containing, in three languages, what is known as the Anitta Text and found among a collection of nearly 30,000 tablets at Boğazköy (Hattusha), transferred his capital to Nesha (Kanesh; Kültepe) which had been conquered by his father, and from there captured and overran a succession of neighbouring kingdoms. Of particular interest is his destruction of the city of Hattusha and cursing of any future king who might attempt to rebuild the city. For ironically, in the 17C BC, one of his own successors, Labarna, moved the capital back from Nesha to Hattusha, which he rebuilt and refortified; and it remained the capital throughout the Hittite period—the Old Kingdom, up to c 1450 BC, and the subsequent Empire period, up to c 1200 BC. Indeed, the later Hittites, according to the major inscription on which our scanty knowledge of the early Hittites is based—the constitutional decree of Telepinu (Telipinu; c 1525 BC), counted Labarna and his queen, Tawannanna, as the true founders of the dynasty, to the extent that a special sanctity seems to have been accorded to their very names which were assumed, like titles, by every reigning couple from Telepinu on and held for life.

Hattusha was most probably selected and maintained as the Hittite capital for strategic reasons, as forming an easily defendable (and strongly fortified) mountain stronghold on the northern periphery of the empire, poised against external danger which tended to threaten most from the Kashka state to the north and east. But such a site could not have proved the best choice administratively as from the earliest days the Hittite state established a policy of expansion southwards over the more prosperous regions of central and south-east Anatolia and northern Syria—chiefly, we assume, in order to increase its economic power.

The peak of the Hittite Empire lay in the period from about 1375 BC when Shupiluliuma succeeded to the throne and founded a new Hittite state after a long period of disruption and oblivion in the 16th and 15C BC, with migrations of new tribes and displacement of peoples all over the Near East. But even at its zenith, the Hittite Empire was never a single, cohesive, political unit—imperial in the sense that we understand it today. Central Anatolia continued to consist, as in the previous period, of numerous largely self-contained communities, but with the difference that local rulers were generally eliminated, local government to varying extents in the hands of groups of Elders, and overall suzerainty possessed by their Hittite overlords. Such a loose confederation of different peoples, with their own customs, traditions and even languages (of which there are thought to have been over 20 in Anatolia during this period) proved durable, and enabled the ruling dynasty to incorporate and absorb elements from their subject peoples that served to strengthen and enrich the civilisation of Hittite Anatolia.

As an example of this Hittite characteristic, I would cite the evidence of Hurrian influence. This derived from the Hurrian state of Mitanni (also known as Hanigalbat) on the W bank of the river Firat (Euphrates) and its north-western neighbour, the Hurrian Kizzuwatna. The independent Mitanni state tended to maintain its position in the regional balance of power by marriage treaties with the Hittite and Egyptian empires, between which it formed a buffer-state, from time to time falling under the domination of one or the other, or of Assyria. Kizzuwatna likewise—a buffer kingdom between Mitanni and the Hittites, with its capital at Adaniya (Adana)—was culturally dominated by the Mitanni but tended to fall periodically under Hittite political domination. The Hurrians, with their distinctive language—its agglutinative character so different from both the Hatti and the Indo-European Hittite—were throughout to play a leading part in Hittite cultural history. The geographical location of the two Hurrian states established them as a natural channel not only for Hittite military expansion towards northern Syria and Mesopotamia but, more importantly, for the cultural communication of the Mesopotamian civilisations, themselves possessing large Hurrian populations, to the Hittite. Indeed, Hurrian culture, which extended in a broad swathe from Erzurum and Lake Urmia in the north to as far south-west as Palestine, paved the way for the passage of certain mythical and religious elements through the Hittite and into the Hellenistic civilisations. It is known that whenever the Hittites returned from successful campaigns against neighbouring states they carried back with them the effigies and standards of the indigenous deities and incorporated them into their own pantheon. In the early stages of the empire, the names of the Hittite gods were nearly all Hatti (with only one known Hittite). But as time passed we find an increasing number of Hurrian names among the Hittite pantheon, and Hurrian cults seem to have abounded. Similarly, while the royal names of the Hittites are almost all Hatti, the personal names of later kings, queens and princes have been found often to be Hurrian, replaced on their accession to the throne by Hittite (that is to say, Hatti) throne names. Indeed, scribes and officials of all ranks bore Hurrian names. On a more practical level, it has been argued that the proficiency of Hittite chariot-warfare lay in the rigorous training of their horses—following the regulations of one Kikkuli, a Hurrian.

Before embarking on an examination of the various aspects of

Hittite statecraft and culture, it is useful to note the actual records on which, apart from archaeological evidence, our entire knowledge of the Hittites rests. This material is composed of a vast array of baked-clay cuneiform tablets, surviving in a number of sites across Hittite Anatolia, but chiefly in the important sites of Kültepe and Alişar and, most prominently, Boğazköy (the capital, Hattusha), where a 'state archive' of over 25,000 tablets has been discovered. The Kültepe archives, relating largely to the Assyrian Trade Colony period, were found mainly in tradesmen's houses, often on wooden shelves in rooms set aside for their collection. But where they were kept in the living quarters, they appear to have been held in chests, baskets or clay containers modelled like decorative dolls' houses, about 20 to 30cm high.

The cuneiform adopted by the Hittites was not that used by the Assyrian traders but an Old Babylonian cuneiform, possibly already existing in parts of Anatolia or else developed by Babylonian scribes taken in the northern Syrian campaigns who were directed to write down the Hittite language. The dimensions of the early tablets—flat-faced, sometimes waxed, and convex behind—ranged from hand-sized to over 30cm in height, and contained up to three columns of inscription. An incised line separated the text from the colophon which recorded a description of the contents, the number in the series—if the document extended over more than one tablet—and the name of the scribe. Tablet catalogues—some by author, others by subject—provided information on the contents of the tablets, the number making up the series and sections that were missing, lost or transferred. There were also tiny tablets, no more than about 5cm by 7cm, kept on each shelf and giving in brief the contents of the tablets on that shelf, thus saving time and effort in searching for material.

These highly advanced libraries of the Hittite capital were evidently under the supervision of the Chief Scribe, the head of what must have been the most learned and intellectual section of society. In addition to their archival work, the scribes were prominent in diplomatic affairs, writing correspondence and preparing and transcribing treaty agreements. They were trained in special schools to become proficient not just in Hittite, but also in the major Hittite languages of Pala, Luwian, Hurrian and some Hatti, and especially in Sumerian and Akkadian—the diplomatic languages of the time. They must have been heavy users of the three-language Sumerian/Akkadian/Hittite tablet dictionaries that have so often come to light!

A class apart from these palace, cuneiform scribes were the hieroglyph scribes who appear to have been less intensely educated and were available for more popular work. This can be inferred from the existence of hieroglyph inscriptions, usually in the more generally-known Luwian language, on most rock reliefs, some seals and some ceramic cups. It is likely that these were public scribes employed in work relating to or for the general population and in people's transactions, mostly on perishable materials such as wooden tablets which have not survived.

This, then, accounts for a large proportion of our knowledge of the Hittite Empire and the Hittite way of life. Documents of state or of public concern have survived in large quantities, probably the most famous being the bilingual Treaty of Kadesh between the Hittite and Egyptian Empires c 1270 BC—the first recorded international treaty we know of. But of the populace at large, their concerns and business affairs, almost nothing can be gleaned. Yet in the complexity and organisation of its archives, the Hittite state reveals itself as singularly advanced and sophisticated.

The development of the role of the Hittite royalty can be traced as it progressed from that of a petty local princedom through the stage of what may be termed a 'constitutional' monarchy to become, like other contemporary rulers of the Near East, an absolute monarchy supported by the gods. But although the Hittite kings were deified after their death, they were never god-kings during their lifetime and were never incorporated into the pantheon. As the vice-gerent of the gods, the king had a dual role as head of state, with all the temporal duties and responsibilities arising out of this, and as High Priest, with his possibly even more important duties, for the entire statecraft of the empire was imbued with a deeply religious hue. Indeed, the Hittite rock reliefs always depict the king in priestly garb, with a tall cap (akin to the *terlik* worn in south-east Anatolian traditional costume and known in archaeology as the 'Phrygian cap'), long robes, a curved staff and curling, pointed shoes (similar to what are known in Anatolia today as *çarıks*). The duty of the king to conduct ceremonies in the capital—Hattusha—on the holy days of particular deities was one that was taken extremely seriously—to the extent that the travels of the royal family were carefully arranged around these days and the king would even leave a campaign in order to attend them. But generally the summer months were reserved for military campaigns and the winter given over to ceremonies and religious functions. Neglect of his religious duties was so serious as to draw down the wrath of the gods on the entire populace.

One of the most striking aspects of the king's position as High Priest was the requirement that he be protected at all times from defilement and impurity, for the purpose of showing respect to the gods and, at the same time, defending him from sorcery. The care with which the purity of the king was maintained can be judged, for example, from the existence of regulations requiring those employed in the palace kitchen to swear every month that the water they gave to the king was pure—if even a single hair was found in the royal bath-water, the penalty was death—and requiring royal shoemakers and leatherworkers to use only leather provided by the palace. To the enquiring mind, these might suggest protective measures against disease, an all-too-common cause of death and one to be deflected at all costs from the person on whom the stability of the state depended.

Yet for all the personification of royal authority, the early Hittite king was not a despot. He ruled in accordance with recognised laws and with the assistance and advice of a council, or *panku*—although the influence of this institution varied, as is natural, in inverse proportion with the strength of the king; and the panku was eventually abolished. During the early stages, in the Old Kingdom, the panku (meaning 'all' or 'whole') was theoretically open to all citizens who could bear arms but seems in practice to have been composed of prominent civil and military personnel, a tendency that grew more pronounced as the size and population of the state increased, and the number of eligible candidates necessarily decreased.

At the capital, the influence of the king's mother (normally, although by no means always, the widowed queen of his predecessor) and his wife was considerable. The queen herself had a prominent religious function, as can be understood, for example, from the Fraktin (SE of Kayseri) rock reliefs depicting Queen Puda-Hepa as offering sacrifice to a deity. It was the queens Puda-Hepa and Ashmunika who left the greatest number of documents, and we know of the existence of a 'queen's palace'—probably a separate building in the palace complex at Hattusha to which widowed queens withdrew.

In the patriarchal social organisation of the Hittites, the king had numerous wives in addition to his queen, and his children all played their part in the administration of the state—sons becoming priests, army commanders, even rulers of dependent princedoms, and daughters acting as instruments of policy through marriage alliances with foreign powers. The patriarchal system appears to have been in strong contrast with the matriarchal tendencies of earlier Anatolian culture in which, through her symbolising of fecundity and productivity, the place of woman was higher. But we can understand the increasing importance of the man in the Hittite period, with the value placed on the bearing of arms for Hittite expansionist policies. Indeed, at the highest level, patrilineal succession was the norm from the earliest days of the Hittite state, the king choosing his successor from among his own sons. But the confusion in the kingdom arising out of the frequent fratricidal strife led to the regulation by Telepinu of the succession to the first-born son. While history reveals that this law was by no means adhered to throughout the Hittite period, deviation from it seems to have been held always as a great crime.

Of the administrative organisation clearly required to run such an extensive and complex empire as the Hittite, very little of substance is yet known. The state was evidently based on a kind of fief-system, whereby newly-conquered lands were administered by princes who then owed certain obligations to the central authority, obligations of which the most important would have been military service through the provision of foot-soldiers and chariots on request. Vassal kingdoms, judging from the evidence of signed treaties, also pledged similar obligations in return for a Hittite guarantee of their sovereignty. Apart from these, there were a number of provinces, such as Pala and Kizzuwatna. But it is impossible, on the basis of the still scanty evidence, to be certain of the division of labour of the closely inter-related military, religious and administrative duties of the large bureaucracy.

According to Hittite laws, society was divided into two levels—the free people and the slaves. But the distinction is not altogether clear in the case of every social group, and it is certain that the institution of slavery by no means resembled the modern understanding of it. Free citizens included, in theory, farmers, artisans, tradesmen and petty officials. But farmers, in an empire heavily dependent on agricultural produce, were closely bound to the state and burdened with the heaviest taxes; while artisans, although possessing property rights and able to sell their produce, were probably in many cases employed directly by the state (for example in religious sanctuaries). In contrast, slaves could be bought and sold, but they had rights, such as of property and marriage, which were protected and regulated by the state; for example, the value of a slave was half that of a freeman, but so was his punishment. Once again, the archives of the Hittites have so far revealed little on the origin of slavery or who became slaves. Prisoners of war, brought back as booty, formed an entirely separate group known by their Sumerian name as *nam.ra*, and were put to work on the land, much as prisoners of war this century, and used to repopulate deserted regions. They had no freedom of movement, but probably as time passed they mixed and merged with the local populace. Thus, we can confidently admit nam.ras as another group of people who contributed to the cultural synthesis that was created in Anatolia, even though not recognised in Hittite law as a separate class, as were freemen and slaves.

We do know, however, of the existence of a shadowy group of people, neither free nor slave, who could own land and could not legally be bought or sold but by marrying whom women lost their free status. Were these an early form of 'untouchable' class, so low racially that they were kept apart? We just don't know.

An all-important pillar of the Hittite state was the military. That the Hittites were possessed of a strong and well-organised military structure is evinced by their achievement in extending their territories in the face of constant attacks by the Kashkas from the north and incessant attempts at secession from the Empire by vassal states in the west and by Kizzuwatna in the south-east. At the same time, foreign policy dictated the maintenance of buffer kingdoms between themselves, the Mitanni, Egyptian and Assyrian states. As summers were taken up with campaigns and winters with the preparation for campaigns, we can infer that there was a standing army. The king, as Commander-in-Chief, had his personal troops. In addition, troops were forthcoming under the various treaty obligations of vassal states, under the command of their respective local rulers, and some mercenary troops were also available. The basic strength of the armies consisted in their foot-soldiers, but mobility was provided by the charioteers, depicted in Egyptian reliefs. The three-man chariot of the Hittites, providing full protection for the driver, must have given a distinct advantage over the Egyptian two-man chariot. Chariot-fighting required long and careful training, and horses were imported from Babylon to improve the stock, according to a surviving letter of Hattushili III. As for the numerical strength of the Hittite forces, this increased from a mere 1400 foot-soldiers and 40 chariots in the 18C BC to 17,000 foot-soldiers and 3500 chariots on the Hittite side at the battle of Kadesh in 1285 BC. Tactically, surprise or night attacks were preferred and, if these failed, siege warfare. It is clear from archaeological and philological evidence that the Hittites attached great importance to their own frontier defences—their massive fortifications being best observed at Hattusha.

On the other hand, the Hittites were not generally a sea-faring people and were cut off from the coast until the conquest of Kizzuwatna with its Mediterranean shore, when maritime relations were established with Ugarit and Alashiya (Cyprus). But there is documentary evidence of a naval battle off Cyprus during the reign of Shupiluliuma II (c 1210–1200 BC) in about 1200 BC.

Of the economic basis of the state, again available documentation offers scanty information. The land belonged primarily to the gods, and after them to the king who could dispose of land at will in return for obligations and services. As in previous eras, agriculture and animal husbandry formed the mainstay of the state economy, with a variety of grains—among them chiefly wheat and barley—from which different kinds of bread were made. Beer and wine were produced, pulses and fruits cultivated and, in some areas, olives and olive oil. Yet harvests varied and periods of famine have been recorded, particularly in later years, with references to wheat imported from abroad to meet the needs of the people. There was an abundance of animals, from which meat, milk, wool and leather were obtained; and the place of honey in the economy may be gauged from the numerous regulations on bee-keeping. Metals included copper and bronze, as well as silver and gold. However, what characterises the Hittite in comparison with earlier periods is the development of the iron-smelting industry—in an area where iron-ore was plentiful. The military successes of the Hittites have been attributed largely to their use of iron weapons and to their control of the production and the export of iron implements. Silver was used as a form of currency, in bar or disc shape, and the originally Babylonian weights, though varying according to time and country, were strictly regulated.

An intriguing aspect of land trade lies in its general reduction after the Assyrian Trade Colony era, in conjunction with the growth of state monopolies excluding foreign traders, and the less experienced native entrepreneurs tending to utilise members of conquered populations as agents for the import of desired materials. Frequent foreign campaigns also ensured the acquisition of goods from abroad, while the increase in domestic manufacture and craftsmanship to serve the growing state restricted the availability of raw materials for export. Maritime trade also began to develop along the northern Syrian coast and in the Aegean, likewise under the detailed jurisdiction of the central authority.

In the field of art, Hittite craftsmanship may be characterised as an amalgamation of contributions by the various ethnic groups of the Empire, an amalgamation in which it is impossible to determine the specific elements. From the artefacts found in the royal tombs of Alacahöyük and Horoztepe, we know of the sophistication of late Bronze Age art; and in architecture, with the growing Mesopotamian influence of the Assyrian Trade Colony period, the Kültepe site may be cited as an example of urban civilisation comparable with the best of Mesopotamia and Syria. Moreover, the close cultural relations of Anatolia at this time with northern Syria and beyond to Egypt is shown in all the archaeological evidence.

All this, then, was available for the Hittites to draw on and develop. We see in Hittite pottery monochrome and geometrical polychrome ware, both showing great skill in shape and proportion, particularly in their animal designs. Ceramic rhytons in the form of stylised lions, antelopes, birds and snails were used in religious ceremonies to pour libations to the gods. Stylised animal motifs recur on seals and as cups shaped in the form of animal-heads, whereas cups shaped as complete animals and small clay bull figures (about 70cm high) are beautifully modelled in a lively, naturalistic way. It could be argued that ceramic art was the most developed of the Hittite arts, but if that is so then stonemasonry was not far behind. It has been said that all imperial Hittite sculpture was subservient to architecture. Yet although the massive and spectacular monumental rock reliefs to be found as far as the empire extended and the free-standing reliefs (orthostats) along the exterior walls of the Hattusha palaces did not reach the level of fully-dimensional statuary, they are fine examples of stone-carving as a craft in its maturity; and the tiny but delicately-carved stone figurines, probably worn as amulets, and seals—both pictorial and inscribed—give us an idea of how the reliefs must have looked in their prime.

As far as other art forms are concerned, of the documented statues of deities in precious metals unfortunately nothing remains, but bronze figurines of the early period have been found. An extant example of incised bone from Kültepe, depicting the Tree of Life, dates from the first half of the second millennium BC. One interesting development in ceramic art which deserves mention is that of narrative art—which appears on pottery reliefs and on seals.

Architectural design was not rigidly uniform. The foundations of the normally detached houses were of stone, with mud-brick walls and flat roofs—the like of which may be seen throughout rural Anatolia today. The size of the houses and the internal division and size of rooms seem to have varied, with extra rooms added as required. The houses were separated from one another by paved alleys through which ran a regular, and clearly communal, sewage system. Monumental architecture, such as the temples, palaces and massive fortresses of the later, imperial, period rather than the more humble dwellings of the populace, has often been preserved intact or excavated—notably at Boğazköy, Alacahöyük and Yazılıkaya.

As for the regulation of people's lives, two tablets providing part of a codex of laws offer some insight into the complexities of men's actions and transactions in the Hittite period. Of these two tablets, one regulates individuals' rights and proprietorship and the other relates to ownership of property and agricultural implements, including prices of goods, and to crimes of morality. That the laws were not immutable but could be altered as the society developed can be deduced from four clear stages in the style of writing, the syntax and the grammar of the inscriptions between the reigns of Murshili I (c 1620–1590 BC) and Tuthaliya IV (c 1250–1220 BC). These reveal a clear progression from the simple compilation of traditions and customs, through the gradual replacement of torture to the forfeiture of animals as punishment, the restricting of the death penalty alongside the increase of material penalties to reductions in fines. These quite advanced laws, with the extensive use of indemnities or compensation payments, are evidently based on the principles of rectification and retribution rather than revenge. By its peak, the Hittite state seems to have exacted the death penalty only for sexual offences, sorcery and treason. The lack of a preamble to the codex prevents proper understanding of the ethical foundation of the legal system, but it is clearly religious in essence—the justice of the gods encompassing the entire human and animal kingdom and dispensed by their vice-gerent on earth, who was Chief Justice as well as High Priest.

The religion of the Hittites, like most of their culture, reveals multiple origins and, in the face of complete inability to force its own cultural traits on the natives of Anatolia, an astonishing capacity for cultural absorption. Indeed, the expansion of the empire was matched by an expansion in number, in function and in ethnicity of its pantheon, which seems to have reflected the mixed composition of the Hittite population. The deities are readily identifiable since their names are listed in treaties, and other documents describe religious ceremonies, indicating the languages of hymns sung by the priests and giving the names of the deities in their own languages. What is significant here is that the Hittites accepted foreign influences without altering them beyond recognition, as if they followed a deliberate policy of integration based on respect for the character or ethnicity of their subject peoples.

The pantheon of the Hittites illustrates their deification of aspects of nature, with certain deities holding a special place, notably the Storm-God (whose Hatti name was Taru) and his wife, the Sun-Goddess of the city of Arinna (Hatti name, Vurushemu). Much information can be gleaned from rock reliefs such as that of the religious sanctuary at Yazılıkaya ('Inscribed Rock', near Boğazköy) which depicts what is thought to be the full assemblage of gods and goddesses, although their precise identification has not been easy as the inscribed names have worn away. Apart from these monumental reliefs, very few statues have survived, the metal ones—like other metal artefacts—having been lost through re-cycling.

On the Hittite views of death and burial customs, we find cremation and inhumation practised, both side by side and separately, with different styles of inhumation in different cemeteries. It appears that cremation was more common for monarchs, but which was the real Hittite tradition cannot yet be determined. What is particularly interesting is the evidence that people were buried with their animals, most notably with their horses—in striking parallel with the well-known later *kurgan* tradition of the horse-dominated Turkish and Mongolian autochthonous societies that originated and spread in all directions from their Central Asian heartlands.

As in religion, so Hittite literature reflects the multiplicity of languages and cultures of the Empire. Of the wide corpus of its literature—including historical texts, prayers and hymns, fortune-telling and predictions, as well as the purely creative and artistic poetry—what is perhaps of particular interest here is Hittite myth and epic. The Hittites seem to have been as lacking in originality in this area as in so many others, and to have incorporated wholesale from existing Anatolian societies with their well-developed religious, philosophical and cosmological speculations. Indeed, the majority of Hittite myths tend to be of ancient Sumerian or Old Babylonian origin, acquired via Hurrian influences, while a number of others reveal northern Syrian strains, via Kizzuwatna. For example, the epics and myths originating from northern Syria include many Luwian words, which indicates their entry into the Hittite corpus through the cosmopolitan Kizzuwatna, with its predominant Hurrian and Luwian languages and its geographical suitability as a channel of communication with northern Syria. Yet the Hittite lack of originality did not extend to lack of creativity and spontaneity. They never adopted foreign epic or mythical traditions in their entirety but simply reduced or omitted irrelevant or uninteresting parts, expanded those more to their taste, and altered the names of heroes to suit their own linguistic preference. Often, as in the case of the Sumerian epic of Gilgamesh, the Akkadian version would be used as a set text in the scribes' schools while abridged Hittite and Hurrian versions circulated among the people.

What can, however, be stated with some certainty, is that the myths and epics borrowed by the Hittites from outside, particularly Babylon, also travelled through other cultures all over the ancient Near East, from the Sumerians in Mesopotamia right up to the Hellenistic period of western Anatolia and the Aegean. This is perhaps sufficient to show that the various civilisations cannot really be treated as entirely separate entities but together formed inter-related parts of a single whole.

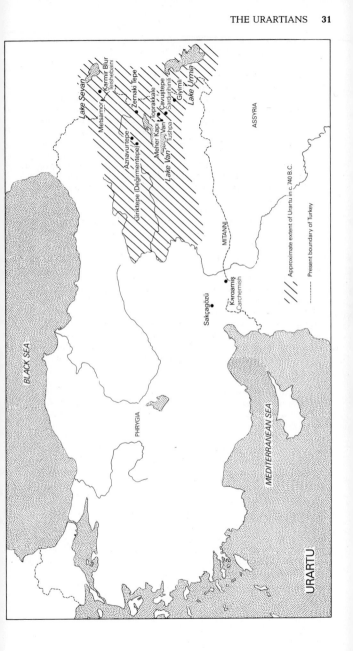

III.   The Urartians

With the collapse of the Hittite Empire in the face of the eastward invasions of Aegean peoples, generally known as the 'Peoples of the Sea', in about 1200 BC, and with the break-up of its dominions into small independent principalities of more or less Hittite character, there arose in the east of Anatolia a new power—Urartu. With its centre around Van Gölü (Lake Van), the heartland of this state comprised that area of mountains and high plateaux bordered by three other lakes—Çıldır, Gökçe (Sevan) and Urmia—but during its peak extended far beyond, into Transcaucasia (Kafkasötesi) in the north, into north-western Iran in the east, up to the Malatya region in the west and down as far as Şanlıurfa (Urfa) in the south. And for 300 years, from the 9th to the 6C BC, Urartu was a formidable regional power, rivalling Assyria in Mesopotamia and competing constantly with her Assyrian foe for complete hegemony over eastern and south-eastern Anatolia.

Yet for all this, the name of Urartu rapidly fell into desuetude on its decline—though it appears in the Old Testament as Ararat—as the sources of antiquity and the Middle Ages attributed the culture of the Van area to Assyrian civilisation. It was not until the 19C AD that this even began to be questioned, and the latter half of the 20C that the Urartian state was finally recognised as a civilisation in its own right, with excavation and research in the three countries comprising the region covered by the Urartians—the Soviet Union, Turkey and Iran.

While the early existence of the confederation of small states from which the larger unit known as Urartu was to develop in the 9C BC is poorly documented, the most recent archaeological research has proved that there was, from the third millennium BC, a strong cultural union in this wide geographical area between Caucasia and northern Syria, the Malatya region and Lake Urmia. Moreover, its peoples were of Hurrian stock, sharing a language structure with morphology, phonology, syntax and vocabulary that can be classified as Asiatic due to its agglutinative character. Indeed, the Urartian language, in possessing this capacity for creating new words by adding suffixes to a given root is similar to the branch of languages known as Ural-Altaic—of which the closest, geographically, today is Turkish, spoken in its various dialects from western Anatolia and parts of eastern Europe across the mountains and plateaux of eastern Anatolia, Caucasia and Soviet Central Asia as far as Chinese Turkistan (Xinjiang).

Archaeological excavations have revealed relations with, among other neighbouring regions, the Mitanni state in SE Anatolia during the 15th and 14C BC and, on their fall to the Hittites, directly with the Hittite Empire itself—relations which evidently played an important role in the cultural and economic development of the high plateau societies of eastern Anatolia. With the collapse of the Hittite Empire about 1200 BC these societies formed a loose defensive confederation against the northward expansion of Assyria. The first documentary information on them is found in an inscription of the Assyrian king Salmanassar I (1272–1243 BC), referring to Uruatri as one of the countries with which Assyria had hostile relations and claiming to have conquered eight kingdoms bearing the collective name of Uruatri. Subsequent Assyrian records refer to the high plateau lands as the land of the Nairi, and indeed the Urartians themselves always used the term Nairi or Biaini (Viaini) to refer to their lands and peoples (the modern name Van is thought to have derived from the latter). But from the reign of the Assyrian king Asurnasirpal II (883–859 BC), the name Urartu comes to be used synonymously with Nairi in the Assyrian annals which, after all, form the bulk of the documentary evidence concerning Urartu and the basis of our knowledge.

One of the most important and informative early Assyrian records is located at a temple on Balawat Hill, near Nineveh. The lintels of its huge bronze gates (the Balawat Gates) are covered with reliefs depicting the victory of Salmanassar III (858–824 BC) over the Urartians at a time when they were beginning to merge, in the face of the number and ferocity of the Assyrian attacks, into a unified state.

The name of Aramu (or Arame, 850–840 BC) emerges as the first leader of the united Urartian peoples, but the real founder of the state of Urartu is generally held to be Sarduri (or Seduri) I (840–830 BC), who built Tushpa (near Lake Van) as the Urartian capital, with the massive fortress of Van as its citadel. The first written sources of Urartu itself belong to Sarduri I whose inscriptions, in the Assyrian language and script, detail the achievements of his reign and describe himself in Assyrian terms as the 'King of the Nairi lands'. Thus the extent of Assyrian cultural influence over the early state can be guessed at. The oldest inscriptions in the Urartian language date from 824 BC and belong to Sarduri I's son and successor, Ishpuini (830–810 BC). Yet, as the primitive hieroglyphic Urartian script appears to have become by this time insufficient for a rapidly developing state, he adopted a modified version of Assyrian cuneiform for state purposes, while the native Urartian hieroglyphs continued to be used for religious and commercial purposes.

It was under Ishpuini and his son (and joint ruler) Menua (810–786 BC) that Urartian expansion really began, in conjunction with a massive construction programme, a dual policy continued by successive Urartian kings who matched their military successes with the building of roads, fortresses, towns (located centrally and in frontier areas), canals and aqueducts, temples and shrines, vast granaries, cisterns and wine cellars, together with monumental inscriptions to record for their populace and for posterity the great achievements of their reigns. Menua is credited with being the first monarch in Western Asia to adopt a policy of conquest through building systematically planned lines of fortresses, a strategy later to be revived by the Romans. Indeed, major construction projects were carried out by Urartian rulers right up to the collapse and destruction of the state at the hands of invading Cimmerians and Scythians, autochthonous peoples moving westward from Central Asia and sweeping all before them.

The expansionist policies, in every direction, of Ishpuini and Menua were continued by Argishti I (786–764 BC), one of whose inscriptions (at Van Castle) is the largest Urartian inscription found to date. It describes in great geographical detail his numerous conquests and establishment of strong military bases as springboards for future campaigns, including his efforts to reach the Mediterranean and take over control of the major Assyrian trade routes.

The reigns of Argishti I and Sarduri II (764–735 BC) formed the zenith of Urartian dominion in extent, prestige and power, and no less in its architectural, cultural and artistic activities—activities which retained their high standard despite Sarduri II's ignominious defeat by the Assyrian Tiglatpileser (Tiglath-Pileser) III (744–727 BC) in 742 BC, which marked the beginning of a gradual but by no means steady decline from the Urartian position as one of the two dominant regional powers of the Bronze Age Near East.

One characteristic act of Urartian monarchs was the building of new settlements bearing their own names or names of deities; and Sarduri II's foundation of Sardurihinili (Çavuştepe), 24km SE of Van, in the Gürpınar plain, is one of the most striking examples of the high level of development achieved in Urartian architecture. The lower of the two fortresses contained a depot, various workshops and other rooms, a shrine and a palace complex, while the upper fortress seems to have been used only for religious purposes, containing a shrine dedicated to the god Haldi. Along the top of the massive walls were a number of two-storeyed buildings featuring at least five blind windows in basalt. In the huge depots over a hundred wine containers—some holding over a thousand litres of wine—remain half buried. Three cisterns supplied the magnificent three-storeyed palace, so the castle could evidently withstand a siege. But perhaps most striking is the palace lavatory with its septic tank and sewage canal passing beyond the outer walls, indicating the level of Urartian advancement in comparison with other contemporary cultures. Of particular historical interest are the layers of destruction by fire and the thousands of Scythian-style arrow-heads in front of the fortress walls and inside the fortifications, vividly attesting the siege and destruction of the fortress by the Scythians at the end of the 7C BC. (Probably the most important later Urartian settlement from the point of view of its rich archaeological revelations is Rusa II's (685–645 BC) city of Teishebaini [Karmir Blur, near Erevan in the Soviet Union].)

It was Menua who seems to have been the most prolific builder, with over 120 inscriptions describing his various achievements and the bulk of the Urartian roads to his credit. Indeed, the road system was extremely advanced, facilitating economic development and fostering cultural relations. It seems to have been a continuation of earlier Hurrian policy, utilising to best advantage the natural passes and routes to the difficult mountainous terrain of the eastern Anatolian high plateau land with its extremes of climate, and underpinning the conscious development and expansionist policies of the Urartian kings—as evinced by the spread of the road network from the heart of the kingdom, around Lake Van. Indeed, the two major caravan highways across Asia that have been used by mankind through the centuries pass through the eastern Anatolian high plateaux near Van, and their utilisation by the Urartians is known from the discovery of carbonised remains of silk at Toprakkale—the second capital of the Urartians founded near Tushpa by Rusa II (735–714 BC)—which can only have come from China.

Among the most notable constructions of Menua's reign, mention should be made of the Aznavurtepe castle and shrine to the NE of Lake Van, which is the only known example in Urartian architecture of outer walls with watch-towers. A large reservoir was constructed at the foot of the hill to meet the water needs of the inhabitants. The shrine, thought to be the oldest found to date, was built according to the standard Urartian design of a square-shaped single room resting on a basalt foundation, with limestone walls covered with frescoes and four cuneiform inscriptions. Despite plunderings over the course of time, a number of valuable bronze lion statues and gold and silver artefacts were discovered inside. Also attributed tentatively to Menua is a palace at Giriktepe (or Değirmentepe), near Aznavurtepe. Here, excavation has so far revealed a two-storeyed building with two kitchens, a throne-room and various other rooms. But its most interesting architectural feature is that of mud-brick, instead of the usual timber, columns resting on stone foundations; these survived the destruction of the palace by fire at the end of the 8C BC, by Cimmerian or Scythian invaders, as the mud-brick baked hard. In the centre of the palace is a beautifully constructed stone well, 12m deep, at the bottom of which were found tools such as axes and bronze artefacts probably thrown down there for safety during the attack. And even more fascinating is the discovery of 37 skeletons, fossilised by fire, in one room. Mostly women, they must have been put in here for shelter during the attack, along with a quantity of elaborate gold and silver jewellery found buried in the same room.

Menua was also responsible for the construction of a canal extending over 51km from the Gürpınar plain to the Van plain, over aqueducts where the terrain necessitated, complete with 14 inscriptions along its length. This canal, known today as the Şamram Canal, was a remarkable feat of engineering and is still in use. The construction of lesser canals was part of a continuing Urartian policy of extending animal husbandry and agriculture by means of an irrigation network.

As will have become quite apparent by now, apart from archaeological evidence, the vast bulk of our information about the Urartians comes from two main sources—the monumental rock and stone inscriptions of the Urartian monarchs and, particularly for the earlier period before these were initiated, the annals of the Assyrian kings. Compared with the wealth of Hittite clay tablets that have come to light, those of the Urartians to date number only 15 and thus cannot be said to constitute a major documentary source! The Assyrian royal archives stored at Nineveh and Kalah (Nimrud) include many intelligence reports covering the period from the late 8C BC when, as far as we can ascertain, the Urartian royal annals are incomplete, if not entirely missing, so that isolated inscriptions comprise our only indigenous source to date. The Assyrian reports are most detailed and informative, and reveal the extent and reliability of their espionage system; but problems in dating and sequence are manifold as many of the reports are undated or damaged.

The Urartian royal inscriptions, however, to be found on cliff faces and on the walls of palaces, fortresses, temples, shrines and tombs, provide a valuable and often very detailed source of information chiefly relating to military campaigns and construction work, although much incidental knowledge may also be gleaned from them. For example, the fact that most of the inscriptions begin by addressing a god indicates the place held by religion in Urartian society, while the deity whose name appears most frequently—the god Haldi—may be taken as the most important. Dates and names of rulers may be established fairly accurately by a comparison of Urartian with Assyrian annals, as well as isolated comments which throw light on aspects of administrative organisation.

Concerning the Urartian administration, we can see a clear development from the early confederation of—at the risk of anachronism—'feudal' principalities, whose rulers seem to have been relatively free in internal affairs while paying some kind of central tax or tribute to a fully-centralised monarchal state with control over provincial as well as central units of administration. Once again, we must look to Menua as the first Urartian monarch to take steps in the realisation of the religious and economic continuity, consistency and inviolability of the state. It was evidently in pursuance of this aim that

Menua set about the dam-building and irrigation works that extended state authority over the fertile plateaux; and these, alongside his massive programme of road construction, served to exert central control over the 'feudal' lords who gradually subsumed themselves under the name of their rulers. It is noteworthy that Menua's innovation of appointing governors over subject territories—a vital factor in the centralisation of the kingdom—was not only continued by his successors but adopted by the Assyrian king Tiglatpileser III in place of the traditional Assyrian system of inherited governorships.

Royal succession passed from father to son. Ishpuini established a form of joint rule with his son and successor, Menua, which in terms of military and building achievements seems to have been quite workable. But Menua ousted his own eldest son from sharing his throne and abolished the system of dual rulership together with the passage of succession specifically to the eldest son.

In the absence of detailed legal and economic documentation, the role and duties of provincial governors are not clear. We infer from the Assyrian cuneiform inscriptions of Sargon II (722–705 BC) that Urartian nobility and royalty were quite distinct from one another and that ownership of land was quite separate from administrative responsibility for the same land. Sargon II refers to Rusa I's brothers as owning seven cities which also have appointed provincial governors over them.

A central administration was essential for the development of an efficient and extensive irrigation network, in its turn vital for a well-founded agricultural system, which the Urartians developed to exploit the rich pasture lands of the eastern Anatolian high plateaux for animal husbandry. This emphasis on agriculture, with the establishment of agricultural centres in the heart of the kingdom as well as in the provinces, combined with rapid development in metallurgy, required human labour—a requirement that was met by the enforced settlement of huge numbers of captives brought back from frequent and regular compaigns for the purpose of populating and working new land. The numbers involved were colossal; Argishti I, for example, was responsible for the resettlement on the land of nearly 300,000 people. But these people were not like slaves who had no rights and were employed in heavy manual labour such as massive construction projects. These resettled people had certain obligations, including military service, to the state but considerable freedom in their everyday lives. Nor were they harshly treated: each family was allotted a standard dwelling with doors that were closed and locked from the inside and, judging from the animal bones found in their kitchens, they were free not merely to rear their own stock but also to hunt wild animals.

But apart from such isolated items of information as these, and in the absence of sufficient written documents, it is premature to speculate very far on the contractual relations between rulers and ruled. Yet we can be sure of the existence of a flourishing trade, based on the twin pillars of a sound agriculture, comprising crops and livestock, and a booming industrial development deriving from the rich supply of metals in Urartian territories: gold, silver, copper and iron. At Metsamor, near the Aras river, were huge smelting sites for bronze and iron; and glass was manufactured here where the main ingredients, including zinc and manganese, were all available. Iron and soft steel were also imported from Colchis, and metal artefacts exported all over the Near East and beyond; for example, the famous bronze cauldrons found throughout the Mediterranean, as far as Etruria in Italy, have been attributed to Urartu.

Similarly, our knowledge of the religious life and beliefs of the Urartian people is restricted by reliance on written sources—namely inscriptions—that concentrate on military campaigns and construction programmes, albeit including religious constructions, while ignoring the social aspects. Thus we derive the bulk of our scanty knowledge from rock and stone reliefs, paintings and architecture. By far the most important source for Urartian state religion and its close links with state organisation is the rock relief and inscription of Meher Kapı, 5km NE of Van Castle, built in the reign of Ishpuini and Menua at the end of the 9C BC and dedicated to Haldi. The cuneiform has twice been renewed—an indication of its importance to contemporaries—and the entire pantheon of 79 deities is depicted, standing on their respective sacred beasts with their own sacrificial animals according to their level in the hierarchy. The number and breed of animal to be sacrificed to each is clearly indicated, but not the occasion or frequency of sacrifice. The huge totals give us some indication of the extent and importance of animal husbandry and stock-breeding in the kingdom and the evident link between these and the requirement to dedicate and sacrifice animals to the gods, quite apart from the desire to propitiate the gods in the hope of averting natural calamity or inducing success in enterprise. The essential place of animals in the society is also evident from the Urartians' twice-yearly campaigns, coinciding with the breeding season, which doubled up as raids into regions such as Transcaucasia to obtain the maximum number of animals possible. In view of all this, it is unlikely that the Urartians would have jeopardised the basis of their prosperity and security by slaughtering too frequently the large numbers of beasts specified in the Meher Kapı inscription, as some scholars have argued.

We can be certain that the Urartian religion was closely linked with those of Anatolia (Hurrian and Hittite), Mesopotamia (Assyrian and Babylonian) and Iran. The Hurrian influence is particularly noticeable in the names of deities. For example, the chief god, Haldi, known to be of Hurrian origin, was worshipped in all the states of the early Urartian confederation of the 13th to the 11C BC, and as the most prominent deity was adopted in the 9C as the head of the official pantheon. The second god in the hierarchy, Teisheba, was the God of the Storm and Thunder, identifiable as the Hurrian Storm-God, Teshup (Hittite name, Taru); his wife, Huba, matches the Hurrian Hepat. The third god, Shivini, the Sun-God, was the equivalent of the Hurrian Sun-God, Shimigi.

The Urartian state religion was evidently created in what seems to have been a deliberate policy of 'Urartification' which took place as an integral part of the centralisation of the provinces. And the incorporation into the official pantheon of local deities, as had been done by the Hittites before them, was probably a policy designed by the Urartian kings to avoid alienating their subject populations. This policy is also apparent in connection with the lingering of a strong animist tendency, especially in the provinces—a tendency shorn, however, of its totemistic and dangerously separatist elements by the inclusion of animist deities like Ebani, the Earth God, and Suinin, the Water- and Sea-God, in the state pantheon without their totems. The consequent abandonment of totems by the subject peoples could only serve to strengthen the centralising policy of 'Urartification'.

Shrines were important for economic as well as for religious reasons. Economically, they disposed of considerable wealth in that they owned large flocks and herds as well as tracts of land and vineyards, all dedicated to the gods. Religiously, they were the scenes of rituals and ceremonies, including the dedication and the sacrifice of animals. The open-air shrine in the centre of Van Castle is of particular interest for the continuity of its tradition of sanctity right up to the present day. During the Ottoman (Osmanlı) period, an Islamic shrine (*türbe*) was constructed beneath the stone platform on which the Urartian rituals were performed. Even now, sacrifices are made on Thursdays—the meat subsequently dispersed as charity amongst the poor—by those who believe a wish has been fulfilled. And young men, unlucky in love, believe that by sliding through the ancient drainage-hole of the sacrificial platform, their wishes will be granted and wives found. Thus traditional folkways live on, despite changes in interpretation.

The banishment of totems by the Urartian state religion was not matched by the complete eradication of popular cults with their primitive baked-clay idols, especially in the more outlying areas; nor by a corresponding disappearance of animist beliefs. Indeed, spring waters, caves, mountains, trees and rocks, considered holy by the Urartian people, are venerated to this day in parts of Anatolia and Central Asia. Curious stone effigies of fish found in spring pools in Kars and Transcaucasia attest the sanctity of such springs; caves were held to be the gateways to the underworld and had been holy from prehistoric times, as had certain rocks; and rocks generally symbolised strength and protection—the Urartians believed their rock inscriptions would last forever (as indeed they look set to do!). False stone doors carved into walls and rocks, an architectural form and religious belief peculiar—in Anatolia—to the Urartians, were venerated as holy, and as doors by which the gods would enter the world. An example is Meher Kapı, known locally as Kör Kapı (Blind Door) or Yalancı Kapı (False Door). Some locals still believe that these doors open on particular days of the year.

The significance of trees and the symbolism of the Tree of Life, depicted on virtually all Urartian artefacts, lies in the dynamism of trees through seasonal renewal. The involvement of the Tree of Life in a variety of ceremonies indicates more than a merely ornamental function; indeed the religious and particularly protective function is evinced by its appearance on all kinds of Urartian weaponry (including their elaborately decorated bronze belts), dedicated in secret cult ceremonies invoking the Tree of Life before setting out on campaign. And elsewhere in Anatolia at about this time depictions of the Tree of Life, carved in stone, were also being made—flanked by bulls on a monumental wall ('Herald's Wall') at Kargamış (Carchemish) in the 9C BC, and flanked by deities on both sides of the entrance to the Palace at Sakçagözü in the late 8th–early 7C BC. The universality of the Tree of Life in Near Eastern societies, dating from the Sumerian of c 3000 BC—and most likely brought by them from their Central Asian homeland—suggests its symbolising of immortality in the face of man's fear of death and spiritual uncertainty.

As for the after-life, the Urartians clearly believed in it. They buried their dead in tombs shaped like rooms or even houses, with their possessions beside them. Both cremation and inhumation were widely practised among all strata of society, but with only archaeological evidence to guide us we can but speculate as to Urartian views on death and burial. Tombs are similar in character to shrines, possibly the most important, architecturally, being the sumptuous royal tombs at Van Castle with their elaborate design and valuable artefacts inside. Ordinary graves were much simpler and poorer; so we can surmise that social differentiation in life continued in death.

In art, as in religious practice, a clear division beween 'palace' art and folk art is readily discernible. Palace art was, certainly during the earlier period, not dissimilar to that of the Assyrian court and, indeed, was long thought to be a branch of Assyrian art. This resemblance is understandable given the extent of Assyrian political and cultural influence in the 9C BC and the early Urartian rulers' aspirations to the Assyrian ideal—for example their adoption of cuneiform script and the diplomatic Akkadian language, their use of clay tablets and of Assyrian ideograms for the names of the same deities, their adoption of Assyrian royal titles and terms for military ordnance, and their painting of frescoes with Assyrian animal and flower motifs. Yet, from the point of view of style, form and tradition—for example, the motifs of the lion, the bull, the Tree of Life and the winged sun-disc—the origins of Urartian palace art go back beyond the Assyrian to the older Mesopotamian and Egyptian civilisations and reveal a multiplicity of influences from preceding and neighbouring cultures, including Hurrian and Hittite. And it is impossible to disentangle strands of individual societies from the general web of interrelated cultures of the whole broad region of the ancient Near East, for the continuity and spread of art, especially that expressed in animal motifs, should not be sought in the aesthetic nature of their work but in its being rooted in the commonality of people's belief. However, this is not to deny Urartian (or any) artistic endeavour its own character and style, developed through drawing on a wide cultural heritage.

Perhaps the most strikingly original Urartian artistic representations were their fantastic creatures composed of parts of different animals, such as bull- or goat-headed birds with the legs of lions, bird-headed men with fish bodies, bird-women, lion-headed bulls and lion-griffons. Can these be interpreted as forming part of the state policy of extending and justifying its sovereignty over its peoples, emphasising simultaneously the power and protective role of the state, both in a political and a religious sense, through such symbolism of uniqueness? My answer would be yes.

The well-known huge mixing-bowls and cauldrons of beaten bronze, produced from the 8C BC, bore four finely-cast handles—initially in the form of birds with human heads and extended wings, with evidently a magical symbolism. With the passage of time, the handles came to be shaped as griffons' or lions' heads on bird-figures, and eventually as bulls' heads. In Lycia (SW Anatolia), bird-figures such as these were associated with a cult of the dead. We can speculate on similar Urartian associations and their possible connection with an earlier Hittite cult of Ereshkigal, the Sun-Goddess of the Underworld, and later sacrificial rites in Homeric Greek culture.

The monumental palace art of rock reliefs, frescoes, seals and, especially, bronze artefacts share the characteristic of a wholly stylised and uniform representation of the deities, maintaining constancy of proportion regardless of the nature or size of the material; even the miniature figures depicted on thrones, weapons, the famous bronze belts of the warriors, seals, and necklaces reveal the same attention to detail. It is in such aspects that the remarkable quality of Urartian monumental art lies.

And it is such aspects that are entirely absent from the folk art of the Urartians—an art that seems to have shown its face whenever central authority slackened and to have flourished as the state declined from its position as a great regional power. The most important example of folk art yet found is a hoard of bronze plaques, embossed and engraved, from a small local shrine at Giyimli (76km SE of Van). The motifs of bull, lion and eagle, or mythical multiple-beasts, with their symbolism of state power, do not appear in these folk reliefs, probably as the artists were free to create their own representations, not of an imposed state tradition but of aspects of daily life—with the assistance, naturally, of religion and magic. The depictions are coarse and primitive but clearly aim to represent the human figure with all its fallibility, not the stylised ideal that officialdom continually strove to impose upon its subjects.

Thus in art, as in religion, we see the dichotomy of the Urartian, or any other, state with the centralising tendency of its rulers in constant opposition to the separatist tendencies of its constituent parts—the subject peoples. Yet the three centuries of Urartian dominance witnessed a flowering of art and culture which ran parallel with its economic and political power—an achievement that should not have deserved the prolonged oblivion into which it so rapidly fell.

IV.   The Phrygians

Turning back to central and western Anatolia, the rising star of Phrygia flared brightly from the early 8C BC until the westward advance of the Cimmerians extinguished its dominance abruptly in 676 BC. In its prime, this powerful state extended from its capital at Gordion (Yassıhöyük—near Polatlı) over the high plateau of central Anatolia beyond the Kızılırmak (Halys River) and into the Konya region as far as Tuz Gölü (Salt Lake).

Yet the origins of the Phrygian people are obscure, as are also the questions of when and to which parts of Anatolia they originally migrated. It is generally agreed that the Phrygians were among those migrating peoples known loosely as the 'Peoples of the Sea' who were responsible for the final destruction of a Hittite Empire already weakened by Kashka attacks from the north. And certainly major Phrygian settlements include, besides the cities of Midas and Gordion, a number of prominent Hittite centres such as Boğazköy, Pazarlı, Alişar, Alacahöyük and Kültepe. Moreover, in the excavations at Boğazköy and Alişar, for example, layers of ash demonstrate that the destruction wreaked by the invading peoples was complete, with Phrygian buildings—quite distinct in design and character—lying on top of or in close proximity to earlier Hittite buildings. The most plausible explanation, based on the writings of Greek and Lydian historians and archaeological evidence—particularly from Troy—establishes the Phrygians as migrants from the Danube (Tuna), first to Thrace (Trakya) where they seem to have settled for some time, thence migrating during the later 13C BC via the Çanakkale Boğazı (Çanakkale Straits; Hellespont) into north-western Anatolia and settling in and around Troy; here they were soon 'Anatolised', adopting, for instance, local styles of ceramic design. From the 12C BC they seem to have spread rapidly over the

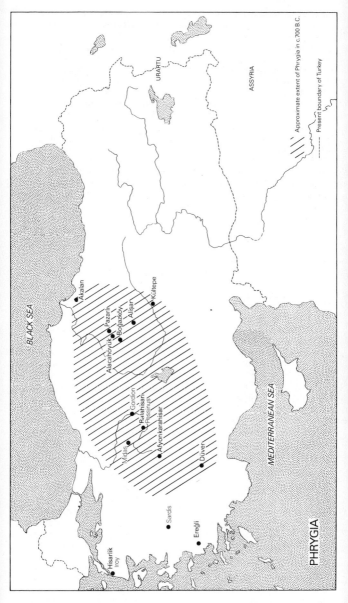

URARTU

ASSYRIA

Approximate extent of Phrygia in c.700 B.C.

Present boundary of Turkey

BLACK SEA

Alaalan

Pazarlı

Boğazköy
Alişan

Kültepe

Alacahöyük

Gordion

Balahisar
Pessinus

Midas

Afyonkarahisar

Düver

MEDITERRANEAN SEA

Sardis

Eregli

Hisarlık
Troy

PHRYGIA

whole of western Anatolia, pushing the older inhabitants of the area—chiefly Luwians—well beyond the Toros Dağları (Taurus Mountains). Moreover, the little that can be determined of the Phrygian language indicates a tongue of the Indo-European type with vocabulary deriving from Slavic, Aramaic and Hittite.

Part of the problem related to tracing Phrygian origins lies in the varied names applied to tribes or peoples who may have been Phrygians or who may have been related to them. Such is that of the Mushki, recurring in Assyrian annals, often in connection with the Tabal, and long assumed to have been Phrygians. It is most probable, although not wholly certain, that the Phrygian kingdom which emerged as a major power in the later 8C BC comprised a confederation of peoples, including Mushkis and Tabals, under the rule of King Midas (Mita in Assyrian sources), united against the assertive policies of Assyria in much the same way as the early Urartian confederation in 9C eastern Anatolia. And, from the beginning of the 7C, with a balance of power established in Anatolia and to the east, Phrygian attention was directed westward, to the Aegean and Greece.

Among the kings of Phrygia we know almost nothing of Gordios, the first king of this western Anatolian kingdom and the founder of its capital, Gordion, but more about his son and successor, Midas. Herodotus claims the latter as being of Macedonian origin, yet he was undoubtedly Anatolian, as was also his name, Mita, which appears in this form not only in Assyrian sources but also in Hittite documents of c 1400 BC in eastern Anatolia and in inscriptions written in Hittite hieroglyphs—and is thus not an 8C importation.

Midas (725–696? BC), whose name is synonymous with riches, was the wealthy ruler of a prosperous kingdom, strategically situated on the crossroads of the ancient Anatolian trade routes from Meso-potamia, northern Syria and eastern Anatolia to the Aegean coast. In a period when the export of goods from north-western Iran, eastern and central Anatolia and Caucasia by sea from northern Syrian ports to the west had become virtually impossible, the rise in importance of the land routes must have been a great advantage to Phrygia. In addition, the kingdom possessed its own abundance of natural resources, notably its animal husbandry, producing excellent wool (and, in particular, that of its Angora—or Ankara—goats); its thick forests yielding timber for housing, furniture and tombs; and its silver, lead and haematite deposits and seams of crystal, onyx and mica. Trade in its own products and its central position in transit trade clearly accounted in large measure for Phrygian economic and political prominence.

Midas' interest in Aegean affairs and good relations with the western Anatolian Greek city-states is indicated by his being the first Anatolian to offer gifts to Greek oracles, impressing the historian Herodotus with his wealth (according to Herodotus' own account) when he dedicated his throne at the Delphic shrine of Apollo, and by his marriage to the daughter of Agamemnon, king of Kyme (Cyme; near İzmir). Moreover, Midas' name has been perpetuated in Greek epics; for example the stories of how he became king and how his Gordion knot was untied (or rather cut through) by Alexander of Macedon, and how his ears were transformed into those of a donkey and the rumour of this spread by the whispering grass.

Yet on the actual working of the Phrygian state, there is very little solid documentation apart from archaeological evidence. The earliest depictions of Phrygians appear in the Assyrian reliefs of Tiglatpileser III in his palace at Nimrud and the polychrome frescoes of Tel Ahmar palace in northern Syria—men with curled hair and short beards, wearing round earrings, long robes decorated with tasselled bands, and high boots. On baked-clay tablets in Phrygian Pazarlı and on wooden painted panels in Tatarlı barrow near Afyonkarahisar are found illustrations of Phrygian foot-soldiers with their short tunics and knee-length socks, helmets protecting their cheeks and with horse-hair crests, and carrying short spears and shields. Women and cavalry are also depicted in relief and frescoes.

Phrygian architecture was well developed, with the megaron style of a room with a hearth entered through a vestibule—an architectural feature familiar in western Anatolia since the Chalcolithic Age. Houses were built of timber, with thatched roofs of mud and rushes, although examples of stone houses exist in late 8C to mid-6C Gordion and Pazarlı. (Interestingly, in both places roof tiles have been found depicting the Tree of Life flanked by goats.) The general style of building the walls around a supporting framework of timber uprights and horizontal beams was both sturdy and aesthetically pleasing. As for the outer appearance of Phrygian houses, evidence from excavation is complemented by numerous sacred monuments carved in rocks, which display the same gabled roofs as the wooden-framed houses, in addition to the common flat-roofed houses of much of Anatolia. A most interesting innovation was that of decorating the floors of houses with pebble mosaics, for example, in a geometrical pattern of red or dark blue on a white background, as seen in Troy and Gordion, or with painted baked-clay nail mosaics, for example, in a geometrical pattern in black and cream in Pazarlı. Geometrical patterns particularly popular among Phrygians included the swastika, the winding meander motif and parallelograms.

From the mid 6C BC, Phrygian houses were ornamented externally, in addition to carved wooden doors, by the application to walls of polychrome baked-clay decorative panels with animal or human figures and geometrical designs. This geometrical ornamentation seems to have been specific to Iron Age Phrygia, spreading from Akalan (near Samsun on the Black Sea—Karadeniz coast) down to Düver (near Burdur) and becoming most prevalent during the period of Lydian domination of Phrygia about the mid 6C, with similar designs found in Sardis, the Lydian capital.

In sum, Phrygian architecture occupied an important place in western Anatolian architectural development, with its blend of Anatolian (megaron plan) and Thracian/Balkan (timbered housing with pitched roofs) elements.

Of the ceramic arts, not a great deal is known, beyond the division of what might loosely be called the central Anatolian Iron Age ceramics into two broad divisions: the eastern and south-eastern, approximating roughly to the old Hittite area, with its emphasis on patterns of stylised stag motifs and geometrical concentric circles, and the western, with its grey or red monochrome—a developed version of Thracian coarse and primitive ceramics found at Troy after its invasion and destruction in c 1200 BC.

In metallurgy, however, the Phrygians excelled, with their bronze vessels, fibulae (clasps) and ladles renowned as far away as Assyria in the east and Greece in the west, and their *phyales*—used for pouring libations to the mother-goddess, Kubile, and identical with the modern Turkish *hamam tası*, used when bathing—exported along the Aegean coast and to Greece. Some of the Urartian-style bronze cauldrons on tripod bases found in Greece may well have been made in Phrygia. But this thriving export of bronze and other metal artefacts from

Phrygia to Greece, attested by finds in Delphi, Olympia, Perachora, Argos, Heraion, Ithaca, Sparta, Mitylene (Midilli; Lesbos), Rhodes and Ephesus, was not matched by the import of Greek products. Hence, the contribution of Anatolian Phrygia to Greek art and craft seems to have been considerable.

In weaving, Phrygia was also renowned, with the best example of decorated Phrygian material being the dress of the Tabal king Urpalla (Warpalawa) on the İvriz rock monument relief at Ereğli. Embroidery in gold thread was a particular speciality, from which derives the Latin *phyrgio*, 'an embroiderer', while the famous Phrygian kilims known as *tapates* survive in the French *tapis* (carpet).

The carpentry of this timber-producing country was well made and artistic. Phrygian carpenters made furniture without the use of nails, and often contrived contrasting colours through the use of different woods. In addition to painted decoration, ivory inlay was a popular craft and evidently developed quite independently of the contemporary Assyrian and northern Syrian workshops.

All in all, Phrygian art, from their mosaics to their stone-and woodcarving, from their bronze-ware and geometrically decorated ceramics to their textile- and kilim-weaving, reveals a distinctive creativity and originality. That their textile techniques and designs and their woodcarving directly affected early Greek art is attested by 7C BC eastern Greek painted vases. Moreover, Greek authors attributed such musical instruments as the cymbal, flute, triangle and syrinx (Pan-pipes) to Phrygians. Clearly, such cultural influence must have derived from some historical factors. Notable among these would be that as the Greeks established, for economic reasons, trading colonies in the Aegean and eastern Mediterranean, they met societies with a rich cultural heritage and an advanced artistic tradition, which inspired the further development of their own artistic style. Thus the hitherto principally abstract geometric forms of the Greek city-states were intermixed with elements from Urartian and Phrygian bronze-work, human figures and stylised animal motifs such as sphinxes and griffons. The role of Phrygia as a channel transmitting Near Eastern and Anatolian culture westward into Greece and beyond may also be perceived in its writing. The Phrygians used an alphabet, similar to that of the Greeks, which was fairly easily read if not easily understood. This alphabet originated in Phoenicia, but, eventually, it was desseminated across the Mediterranean—a dessemination in which the Phrygians, as evident from the inscriptions in tombs excavated in Gordion, played a vital role.

Similarly, the Phrygian (and deeply Anatolian) cult of the mother-goddess was transmitted into Greek religious belief. For this, the oldest and the most predominant Phrygian cult, centred on the worship of a mother-goddess, Kubile, or Matar Kubile, known to the Greeks as Kybile (or Cybele) and worshipped as Kubaba by the Luwians and as Kybele or Kybebe by the Lydians. Often identified with Agdistis by Phrygians, she is believed to have been transformed in some Anatolian cities into the Greek goddess Artemis, and had been worshipped under various names in Anatolia for 7000 years, since the neolithic cultures of Çatalhöyük and Hacılar.

This fertility cult was based at the holy city of Pessinus (Balahisarı) where an effigy of the goddess in black stone (probably a meteorite) was supposed to have fallen from the sky, and the cult was apparently dependent upon the myth of Kubile and her beloved, the beautiful young Atys (Attis). A number of versions of this myth exist, most of them involving self-castration—either of Atys or of the hermaphrodite Agdistis (Kubile's rival where not identified with Kubile herself)—the loss of Atys through his untimely death and the apparent symbolism of man, who must fertilise and then perish, for the planting of the crops and nature's retreat during winter. Around the Pessinus shrine and its High Priest, known as Atys, there were held fairs and religious celebrations, most prominent being the orgiastic spring festivals at which young men would castrate themselves in an extreme of spiritual fervour, imitating the self-castration of Kubile's consort, Atys; they were then accepted as subordinate priests (*galli*; the secondary meaning of *gallus* is eunuch). This annual ritual of passionate lamentation, self-mutilation and castration was believed to resuscitate Atys and thus revive the flagging forces of nature. Such was the importance of this cult, according to which Phrygians maintained that the entire state was the property of Kubile of Pessinus, that even after the destruction of the kingdom Phrygian worshippers apparently maintained its practice and spread it from town to town across a wide swathe of central and western Anatolia during the Lydian era; passing thence to Rome in 204 BC, this cult of the mother-goddess was to continue in importance. Indeed, the associations with the orgiastic cult of the Bacchae, women who followed Bacchus (deriving from the Lydian God of Wine, Baki, also known as Dionysus), as well as with the all-female Amazons, are striking.

Throughout the mountainous areas of Phrygia were to be found stone shrines to Kubile, represented in her shrine of Arslankaya, for example, standing between two lions, especially near mountain springs, ravines and precipices—places the goddess was believed to inhabit. It is significant that the Homeric epithets for Artemis included Mistress of Beasts and Lady of the Wilds—epithets that cannot be wholly coincidental in their aptness for Kubile. Prominent among these shrines is the Midas Mezarı (Midas Tomb), not in fact a tomb but a place of prayer, bearing the name of Midas (Midai) in its Phrygian cuneiform inscription. Other shrines are carved into the rock face in the form of stone stairs leading to a ledge or seat, either symbolising the goddess' throne or used as a sacrificial platform.

Important Phrygian citizens were customarily buried in rock tombs or in barrows. The rock tombs having been robbed over the centuries, most available information derives from the less vulnerable barrows, the majority of which are located just outside Gordion, the capital. Of these hundred or so, by far the largest—in a system where the height of the mound directly reflected the importance of the deceased—is the Büyük Tümülüs (Great Tumulus), believed to be of either Gordios or, more probably, Midas. Few of the Phrygian barrows have yet been excavated, but these conform to a pattern in that the body is laid out (uncremated until the 7C BC, from which time the body was cremated beforehand) on a wooden couch inside a finely constructed wooden room with a variety of artefacts as gifts on tables and hanging on the walls. The tomb is covered with earth or gravel to form a large mound. The size and careful construction of the Büyük Tümülüs is in striking contrast with the total lack of gold and silver artefacts inside. This may indicate that it was not customary among Phrygians to offer such gifts for tombs. On the other hand it fits in with the tradition that Midas committed suicide by drinking bulls' blood after his humiliating defeat by the Cimmerians in c 696 BC, who then sacked and burned the city of Gordion and devastated the Phrygian state. Possibly Midas died after an early defeat and was interred as honourably as his subjects could manage after the sacking of the city, with the main invasion and evacuation of the city following later. In any event, the Phrygian state did not completely cease to exist after the death of Midas, but never again possessed any political importance.

V.   The Lydians

As the dominance of the Phrygian kingdom waned in the 7C BC, it was succeeded in western Anatolia by the Lydian state under its Mermnad dynasty with their expansionist policy and avowed intent to establish Lydia's place in the balance of power in the Near East and the Mediterranean world. From its original base in western Anatolia, squeezed between the city-states of Aeolia, Ionia and Caria on the coast and Phrygia to the east, the kingdom was to extend at its peak, under the legendary king Croesus, from the shores of the Greek city-states to the bend of the Kızılırmak (Halys) in central Anatolia—the old Phrygian border—and from the Propontis Sea (Marmara Denizi) in the north to the Lycian coast in the south. In other words nearly half of Anatolia was to come under Lydian hegemony. Moreover, the physical geography of the Lydian home-land fitted her for regional dominance—with rich natural resources of water, forests, agricultural and pasture land and ample mineral deposits including, most importantly, the abundant gold from the rich alluvial plain of the Paktolos (Pactolus) River (Sartçay). Such natural fertility and prosperity was enhanced by Lydia's strategic and commercial position.

Yet the origins of the Lydians, as of so many other peoples in Anatolia, are not easy to disentangle, although it is known that an indigenous population had been settled in this area since the Chalcolithic Age. The most convincing theory argues, partly on the basis of the close connection between the Lydian and Hittite languages and cuneiforms, that the Lydians entered Anatolia from the east or north in the later part of the third millennium BC. As for more recent Lydian history, Herodotus provides a detailed (if not entire reliable!) account of their three dynasties, the Atyads, the Heraclids—Tylonids in Lydian terminology—and the Mermnads, who between them ruled from about 2000 BC to 547/6BC. Archaeological evidence, including a cuneiform inscription of the Hittite king, Tuthalia IV (1250–1220 BC), confirms his dating of the early Atyad dynasty; and the period of the later Mermnads, especially Croesus, is amply documented by Greek and Roman authors.

The Lydian capital, Sardis (Sartmustafa), according to the findings of excavations, was in the Bronze Age a village of wholly Anatolian character but possessing cultural links with Greece, as we see from ceramic pieces discovered there. After total destruction in the wave of migrations of about 1200 BC, along with most of the rest of Anatolia, the Thracian-origin Heraclid/Tylonid dynasty is said by Herodotus to have continued for 22 generations, over a period of 505 years from 1185 BC. The last king, called in Greek Mursylos, was known in the Lydian language as Kandaules (Candaules), also the name of a Lydian god—meaning 'dog-strangler'; indeed, excavation has revealed the remains of a ritual feast given in honour of the god

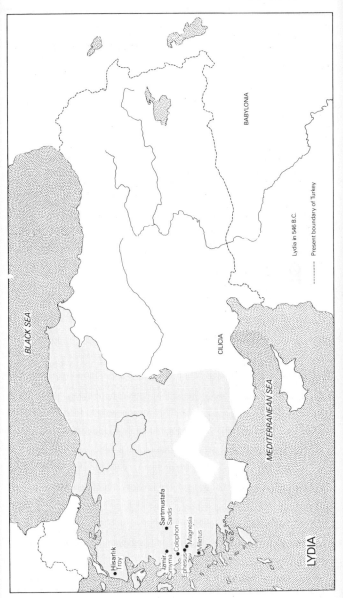

BLACK SEA

BABYLONIA

Lydia in 546 B.C.

------ Present boundary of Turkey

CILICIA

MEDITERRANEAN SEA

Hisarlık
Troy

Sartmustafa
Sardis

Izmir
Smyrna
Colophon
Ephesus
Magnesia
Miletus

LYDIA

Kandaules which included the skeletons of a number of new-born puppies, strangled, sacrificed and very likely consumed.

On the accession of Gyges (c 687–652 BC), the first of the Mermnads, the historians Herodotus, Nicolaus of Damascus and Plato agree that he killed Kandaules with the help of a woman, possibly Kandaules' queen, and then took over both throne and queen. From this time, Lydia and its capital, Sardis, took the names by which they have been known since, in place of Maionia and Hyde respectively, as Homer knew them. And until its destruction in 547/6 BC, Sardis assumed the position of the richest, most powerful and most influential city of ancient Anatolia.

During the reign of Gyges, Lydia rose from obscurity to the status of a great power alongside Egypt, Assyria and Babylonia. After his internal administrative and, particularly, military reforms to counter the Cimmerian threat that engulfed Phrygia, Gyges subjugated the northern city-state of Troy and the major Ionian cities of Magnesia ad Sipylum (Manisa), Miletus, Smyrna (İzmir) and Colophon (near Değirmendere) and thus established Lydian control of the western trade centres. He is acknowledged by Herodotus as being the first barbarian king after Midas to send gifts to the Oracle at Delphi—a policy clearly designed to ingratiate himself with the Greek market, and one continued by his successors. However, unable to maintain his initially successful resistance against the Cimmerians, he succumbed to them in a battle during which the city of Sardis, but not the impressively fortified acropolis, was sacked and destroyed.

Under Gyges' son, Ardys (c 652–629 BC), Sardis underwent a second sacking before the Cimmerians moved on to the shores of the Aegean and thence down the Mediterranean coast until they settled in Cappadocia. Ardys was able to re-establish Lydia and build on his father's policy of expansion.

This episode tells us much about the strength of the Lydian economy at this time, which was able to withstand the sacking and destruction of its capital twice in rapid succession. Founded on trade and prosperity in natural resources, the state could be restored as long as the acropolis survived; for this defensive bastion, with its palace complex, contained the core of Lydia's political, administrative and military power, and served as a protection and refuge for Sardis' lower town. However, the Cimmerian invasions of the late 8th and early 7C BC thoroughly disrupted the balance of power so painstakingly constructed after the Hittite collapse; with the precarious position of Urartu and the complete collapse of Phrygia in her prime, the Near East was in a state of chaos.

Under Alyattes (c 610–560 BC), the fourth Mermnad king and apparently the most able, Lydia reached its greatest territorial extent, reasserting its sway over Priene, Caria and the Ionian cities and arranging marriage alliances with Ephesus and with the Medes of Persia—a great power in Anatolia after the Assyrian Empire had fallen to the combined onslaught of the Medes and Scythians, and from 585 BC (on the conclusion of a five-year war with Lydia) the neighbours of Lydia across the Kızılırmak. Thus a short-lived balance of power among Media, Lydia, Babylonia and Cilicia was achieved—to be destroyed by the rise of the Persian Empire in 547/6 BC, with the conquest of Lydia.

In view of the strength of this new Near Eastern power in Anatolia, Media, it is no wonder that Alyattes attended so assiduously to affairs in the west and concentrated on developing relations with Greece—building shrines in Miletus, sending gifts to the Delphic Oracle, improving relations with Corinth and inviting Greek sculptors and artists to his capital. It is from Alyattes' reign that Hellenic influence really begins to become evident in western Anatolia.

Alyattes' son, Croesus (560–547/6 BC), inherited a prosperous state, and it was during his reign that it reached its zenith in wealth, cultural development and political influence. His is the best-known name of the Mermnads among the early Greek and Roman authors, who praised his wealth and generosity; and his name has continued to be synonymous with extreme wealth, the expression 'Karun gibi zengin' ('As rich as Croesus') still current in Turkey and elsewhere. A great patron of the arts, he established Lydia as the centre of ancient eastern Greek art. Using his wealth, he brought Ephesus under Lydian domination and financed the re-building of the city, including its temple to Artemis—which acknowledges his donation in its inscription—after its destruction by the Cimmerians. Croesus soon held sway over the Greek city-states, all of which paid him taxes (an important source of Lydian wealth) except the privileged Miletus. Yet these city-states, despite Croesus' assistance, must have remained vulnerable to external attack, for they never organised themselves as a defensive confederation and so lost their independence one by one when Lydian protection was no more.

An example of Lydian commercial development is the prominent trading port of Smyrna once it had recovered from the sacking of Alyattes in 600 BC—which is supposed to have rendered it uninhabitable for 30 years. Excavation has turned up innumerable native lydion vases, made in Sardis. These, used as containers for the much-prized Lydian cosmetic creams, were exported all over the western Anatolian coast, Greece and even Italy; but since their form and workmanship is far inferior to contemporary Greek ware, we may infer that they merely comprised the packaging, as it were, and were not valued in themselves as works of art. We know that Lydia was famous for its perfumes and cosmetic creams—as indeed is that region of western Anatolia today.

The people of Sardis are credited with the development of the marketplace during the late 7th and early 6C BC, with its one-roomed shops collected together along with places of refreshment and brothels. Herodotus' description of the marketplace at Sardis has been borne out by excavations and his epithet of *kapeloi* (thought to mean retail-traders, also huckster) for the Lydians seems most apt. Finds of ceramics from the Greek city-states of the Aegean coast, figurines in bronze and ivory from Phrygia, carvings from the Scythians, beads from Phoenicia and glazed ceramics from Assyria indicate the extent of the trading network that converged at Sardis. But most important to Lydia's economy was the rich gold resource of the Paktolos (Sartçay) valley. It is interesting to note that the gold-working and industrial area of Sardis was well distant from the acropolis. This, combined with historical references to wealthy individuals who were able to loan large sums even to royalty, implies the existence of a moneyed class independent of the king, and would distinguish the Lydian monarchy from the absolute monarchies of the east.

The invention of the coin was undoubtedly Lydia's most significant contribution to human history. For as a natural result of this invention, trade by barter came to be replaced by a money economy, and commercial and business development was accelerated. The use of precious metal as a unit of value had been practised in a primitive way since the end of the third millennium BC, most notably in the

Babylonian system based on silver weights. But this cumbersome arrangement by weight impeded transport of valuable goods and was virtually inaccessible to villagers and small artisans who were unable to obtain the ingots of gold or silver for use as a measure. The Lydian invention, then, of small and easily portable coins made of electrum (a natural mixture of gold and silver) for use in exchange for goods facilitated and regularised commercial transactions. In addition, with each coin being guaranteed by the stamping of an official inscription on it, the need for more general literacy and for good scribes provided the initiative for the creation of a simple alphabet that could readily be understood. The new Lydian coinage quickly caught on, and every important trade centre in western Anatolia was before long issuing its own coins. The spread of money from there and its important contribution to the development of civilisation since requires, I think, no further explanation here.

Yet, despite the great reputation of Croesus in particular among the contemporary Greeks, he may not have been a ruler with such business acumen at they maintained. Historical evidence does not show that he increased the wealth of his extremely prosperous inheritance by very much. On the contrary, it may be argued that the profits from the developing Lydian industry and trade were used, not productively, but in military campaigns—for which the Lydians consistently utilised paid soldiery—and in conspicuous consumption. Thus, the economic base of the society (and its purchasing power) did not increase, making the collapse of the kingdom, when it came, very sudden. So sudden, indeed, was the fall of Croesus, his capital and his kingdom to the forces of the Persian king Cyrus in 547/6 BC that the shock spread right through the Near East, affecting most of all the ancient Greek world which seems to have taken its Lydian protector very much for granted.

The conspicuous consumption of the Lydians is most evident in their architecture, in their sculpture and in their jewellery, as may be seen from archaeological research. Jewellery, particularly gold jewellery, was evidently much in demand among wealthy Lydians, to judge from the quantity of earrings, headbands, rings and necklaces found in their tombs. Yet there is no trace of the large-scale gold artefacts referred to in the historical sources—no doubt too valuable to remain unscathed for long. But it was Lydia's school of sculpture and its works in marble and ivory that set it at the centre of early eastern Greek art. And in this respect mention must be made of a small marble model belonging to a shrine of Kybele (Kubile) found in the agora in Sardis. This beautifully carved and decorated model, with a figurine of Kybele in the doorway, quite clearly establishes the original character of the Lydian school of sculpture and its role in the creation of the Ionian style, a style of sculpture which blends the Ionian delicacy with the power and vivacity of eastern art.

Architecture, on the other hand, falls into two distinct groups—the poor housing of the citizens of Sardis (for of the rest of the country there is virtually no archaeological evidence as yet) and the magnificent tombs of their aristocracy and royalty. The humble inhabitants of Sardis lived mostly in one- or two-roomed houses of rough stone and rubble, topped with clay-brick and roofed with thatched mud and rushes, with a hard floor of compressed clay and containing a hearth and two bins or pits—for storage and for rubbish. Some of them inhabited wooden-framed houses covered with painted mud-brick. However, it is likely that the houses were supplied with both plain and painted pottery and they may have been decorated with carpets, screens and curtains, like modern Turkish village houses. They were constructed in terraced rows, often around courtyards, and tended to burn down easily. Indeed, Herodotus tells of an Ionian revolt (499–494 BC) in which the attackers were totally unable to loot the town of Sardis because it was so rapidly swept through by fire; a great contrast to the marble and limestone splendour of its noble tombs. It has also been suggested that the Lydian love of outdoor games of dice, knucklebones and gambling was related to their eagerness to keep outside their miserable dwellings as much as possible. Be that as it may, Sardis was sacked and burned at least twice during the Mermnad period before its destruction by Cyrus of Persia in 547/6 BC, and there may well have been a disinclination to build and rebuild housing of quality at the lower end of the town away from the protection of the acropolis. Yet the superb craftsmanship and excellent material so evident in the construction of tombs for the rich and powerful can leave us in no doubt about Lydian social division. The burial chambers themselves are all of about the same size, and constructed of elaborately carved marble or limestone to form a dwelling in which the deceased were evidently expected to continue their existence. Over the chambers were built barrows, the size of which attested the importance of the individual within. The royal cemetery of Lydia, on the shores of the Marmara Gölü (Gygaean Lake) north of Sardis, is situated in the area called Bintepe ('A Thousand Hills') where there are about 100 such barrows, of which a number are particularly large and thought to belong to the Mermnad kings Gyges, Ardys and Alyattes. Not many have yet been excavated, and that of Alyattes, for example, was found to have been stripped completely bare by ancient grave-robbers. In the valley of the Küçük Menderes river, on either side of the İzmir–Ankara highway, the plain is dotted with small barrows—a parallel burial tradition dating from the Mermnads. Ordinary folk were interred in rock-cut chamber tombs.

Regarding the religious beliefs of the Lydians, not a great deal is known beyond the continuation of the cult of Kybele (Agdistis). Artemis too was worshipped—indeed throughout the Hellenistic period ranked as the major divinity of Sardis—and reference is made to a god, Kandaules, possibly related to the Greek Hermes. Euripides, the dramatist, claimed that the god Bacchus came to Greece from his homeland in Lydia—a claim now generally accepted. Certainly, what is known of Lydian religious ceremonies, with the long-haired eunuch-priests screaming themselves to a high pitch of frenzy and dedicating locks of their hair, tambourines and whips to the goddess, fits in broadly with ceremonies associated with the Bacchic cult, whether in Greece or in western Anatolia. Later Greek and Roman inscriptions in Sardis reveal the growing importance of Greek deities such as Athena, Apollo, Dionysus, Zeus and Hermes, and it is possible to view the Lydian rulers as increasingly under the influence of the Greek religion. But this is not entirely to deny the existence of a popular Lydian religion, which I would designate as the cult of Kybele, especially in view of the spread of the Lydian kingdom over the precise territory occupied by the Phrygian state, whose well-attested and certainly popular devotion to the goddess is known to have continued after the collapse of Phrygia as a political entity.

Music—by reputation often high-pitched and wild—played an important part in Lydian life, especially religious life, and the Lydians are credited with the invention of the 'Lydian mode' and a number of instruments, such as the 20-stringed harp, the *paktis* (lyre), the *megadis* (a lower-pitched lyre) and the *barbitos*—invented to create sound harmony with the paktis. According to Herodotus, the armies of Alyattes went into battle to the sound of pipes, horns, harps and flutes.

In music, as in so many other fields, Lydians set the fashion for numerous urban centres in the area. For example, Lydian love of purple cloth, of scents and saffron, of finely-carved ivory and other luxuries such as carpets and fine woollen and mohair textiles, spread rapidly through the Mediterranean coastal towns. But visual beauty ranked higher than aural for the Lydians, as may be inferred from their patronage far more of sculpture and architecture than of music and poetry. There is no evidence, to date, of any great literary achievement, and very few Lydian tablets. Most examples of Lydian inscriptions are on steles at tombs, in the Lydian alphabet. The language itself appears to be related to Hurrian and Luwian, identifying it, therefore, as an Anatolian language with Indo-European affinities.

Yet, in sum, the 6C BC, and particularly the reign of Croesus, saw a flowering of Lydia as a major centre of art, particularly in sculpture and architecture. And the characteristic and original Lydian blend of Anatolian and Greek elements, attributable to the patronage of its Lydian kings, served as an important phase in the development of the coming Hellenistic era.

VI.   Hellenistic Anatolia

Anatolia came under Persian domination in 547/6 BC when Cyrus II of Persia defeated Croesus of Lydia and imposed two centuries of Achaemenid rule. During this period, the Persians exerted military and administrative control by appointing satraps, recruiting mercenaries and levying taxes. But perhaps their most memorable achievement, and the one by which they maintained their dominance for so long, was their construction of a vast and efficient network of roads throughout their empire, including the famous Royal Road across Anatolia which linked the Aegean with the heartland of Persia from Sardis along a route roughly through Phrygia, across the Kızılırmak, via Tokat, Sivas and Malatya, over the Fırat and Dicle (Tigris), and through Nineveh to Susa. Indeed, it was said by Herodotus to take 90 days to travel from end to end on foot—a distance of over 2500km. Yet culturally Persia was not a dominating force, except at what might be called the 'palace' level of monumental art, and the Hellenistic inclination evident under the Lydian kings continued to exert its sway. This process was further strengthened in 334 BC with the conquest of first the Anatolian portion and then the rest of the Persian Empire and beyond by Alexander of Macedon, best known as Alexander the Great. And what is generally called—since the 19C—the Hellenistic period dates from Alexander's death in 323 BC to the assumption by Octavian as 'Augustus' of the Roman Consulship in 27 BC. It is to the civilisation of Anatolia in this period that we now turn.

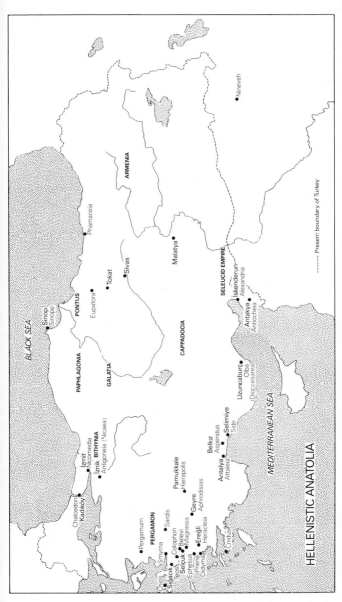

Nineveh

ARMENIA

Pharnaceia

Malatya

PONTUS

Eupatora

Tokat

Sivas

SELEUCID EMPIRE

İskenderun
Alexandria

Sinop
Sinope

PAPHLAGONIA

CAPPADOCIA

Antakya
Antiocheia

------- Present: boundary of Turkey

BLACK SEA

GALATIA

Uzuncaburç
Oba
(Diocaesarea)

İzmit
Nicomedia

İznik BITHYNIA
Antigoneia (Nicaea)

MEDITERRANEAN SEA

Belkız
Aspendus

Antalya
Attaleia

Selimiye
Side

Pamukkale
Hierapolis

Chalcedon
Kadıköy

Pergamum   PERGAMON

Sardis

Geyre
Aphrodisias

Smyrna

Teos   Colophon
Çeşme

Selçuk   Belevi
Magnesia

Ephesus   Ereğli
Priene   Heracleia
Didyma

Chios

Sığacık

Cnidus

HELLENISTIC ANATOLIA

The sudden death of Alexander with no heirs other than a mentally disturbed half-brother and a posthumous son caused serious dynastic problems whose immediate settlement by the administrative division of his empire among a number of military commanders proved but temporary. The internecine strife into which these *Diadochi* (Successors)—as they have passed into history—rapidly fell initiated the almost continuous warfare that was to characterise the Hellenistic period. The three major monarchies that emerged out of the Wars of the Diadochi (323–280 BC)—Macedonia under the dynasty of Antigonus, Egypt under that of Ptolemy, and Anatolia and the rest of the Asian provinces under that of Seleucus—were unable to maintain their respective frontiers unopposed, the most fluid being those of the Seleucid dynasty. Indeed, Anatolian political history was at its most confused after its fall to Seleucid domination, with the almost immediate rise of independently ruled and mutually antagonistic local kingdoms in Pontus, Bithynia, Pergamum, Cappadocia and Armenia. Of these, the western Anatolian kingdom of Pergamum under the Attalid dynasty became most prominent after Attalus I's defeat of the Celtic Galatians in 240 BC, expanding its borders from the Thracian coast in the north to the Mediterranean shore near Antalya. With the Ptolemaic kingdom of Egypt, Pergamum dominated the Aegean and eastern Mediterranean, but was able to maintain its ascendancy only by reliance on Roman support; and the last king of the Attalid line, Attalus III (139–133 BC) bequeathed the kingdom and treasury of Pergamum to Rome on his death.

By this time, the Romans were already a dominating power in the Hellenistic world and a force to be reckoned with by all who sought to acquire or preserve political power of any dimension. The precarious balance of power—at times hardly discernible—of the 2C BC had thus been heavily distorted, for whereas in the previous century cities and local kingdoms could play off one power against another, now all looked to Rome. And its peaceful acquisition of Pergamum in 133 BC established western Anatolia as a Roman province—from 129 BC the Roman Province of Asia.

Yet the lack of central authority so evident in Anatolia, as elsewhere, during the greater part of the Hellenistic period seems to have proved fertile ground for a flourishing of the arts and sciences in numerous urban centres. For out of political faction and misrule emerged, by the middle of the 2C BC, the cultural homogeneity of Hellenistic rule.

Probably the most obvious and important characteristic of the Hellenistic period was the city—a tradition long established in Anatolia where, especially in the western regions, cities had long occupied a considerable position in economic and cultural, as well as political, life. Yet now new cities were founded all over the Hellenistic world, taking their names from their founders and often maintaining a close connection with them and their successors. Alexander, entering Anatolia in 334 BC, himself added to the numerous cities already existing in the hinterland by founding one of his many Alexandrias, the modern city of İskenderun—whose continuing importance today as a thriving port attests the perspicacity and care with which the site was chosen. The founding of cities, a policy particularly applied by the Seleucids, was not always the establishment of a completely new site or community. It could be, and often was, done by revitalising an existing town through changing its name, bringing in colonists and giving special concessions in order to stimulate trade and production. Alexander favoured the re-establishment of Smyrna, and although this was only begun by one of the Diadochi, Antigonos, and completed by another, Lysimachos, the city maintained its founding links with Alexander well into the 2C AD. Antigonos himself founded the city of Antigoneia (near İznik Gölü, Lake İznik), later to change its name to Nicaea (İznik), and Lysimachos transferred the city of Ephesus to its present location at the foot of Bülbül Dağı—Ephesus being but one of a number of cities, particularly ports, that changed their location for one reason or another. The Seleucids founded many cities, mostly inside areas of mixed ethnicity and usually near great roads or rivers and shores suitable for harbours. Seleucus I Nicator (321–280 BC), for example, built one of his 16 Antiocheias on the south-eastern Anatolian coast—Antakya, in the province of Hatay—in a strategically important position for the eastern trade routes. And the local kingdoms of Anatolia themselves adopted this policy of establishing such cities. For example, Attaleia (Antalya) was founded in the kindgom of Pergamum by Attalus II, Pharnaceia and Eupatora in the kingdom of Pontus and Nicomedia in Bithynia. These cities, too, became important cultural centres.

The general policy behind this widespread construction of cities across the Hellenistic world was partly to prompt the economic development that would support, through taxation and gifts, the lavish expenditure of their rulers. But more than this, they were to serve as oases of Hellenistic culture in a world of diversity and strangeness—particularly in the Asian provinces to the east. Even close at hand, such as in Anatolia, the Hellenistic culture of this period seems to have affected only a minority of the population—the urban and the educated; those living outside the cities largely maintained their own folkways and beliefs. As in previous periods of Anatolian history, while the areas of confrontation, as it were, and especially now the regions along the Aegean and Mediterranean coasts, naturally evolved in conjunction with the changing circumstances, in the hinterland Hellenism exerted far less influence. The cities of the Hellenistic period, then, were founded and populated with immigrant Greeks and Macedonians alongside native people sympathetic to Hellenism. These communities were granted a certain degree of autonomy in their internal affairs. Thus, they could, as in the classical city-state, organise their own administrative institutions, pass their own laws and elect their own administrators. The new cities developed rapidly with their economic concessions, and often grants, and grew into centres of culture maintaining their own existence quite separate from the kingdoms inside whose territories they were located. Yet unlike the city-state, or *polis*, of the classical period, these cities did not possess the characteristics of a state. They were the property of kings and their citizens the dependants of these kings. Thus, they were obliged to pay taxes like any other city. But, as I have pointed out, they had special privileges and, since the administrators within the cities tended to be drawn from the population and were therefore close to them, the oppression so apparent in much of the Hellenistic world was probably somewhat reduced in these cities.

All the cities resembled one another in the urban planning techniques associated with Hippodamos of Miletus in the 5C BC, an architect and philosopher who planned the organisation of cities upon the basis of the rationalisation of public life, geometrical theory and simplicity of layout. The older, unplanned settlements which had grown up around the acropolis had arisen out of the earlier tradition of the western Anatolian city-states where the populace took refuge in the acropolis in times of danger and later gradually rebuilt haphazardly downwards. What is known as the Hippodamian plan was a systematic division of the city into zones, based on a regular gridiron of roads intersecting at right angles and centring on the *agora* (market place) and other public and administrative buildings— a design that provided for the efficient and logical organisation of the expanding functions and services of the city. We know that this design was implemented in a number of prominent cities such as Heracleia (Ereğli) and Cnidus, and for the new sites of cities like Priene, Colophon, Smyrna and Ephesus which shifted their locations; indeed, many settlements of the Hellenistic period were to be expanded according to this plan. Yet, while the early written sources inform us (correctly or otherwise) that this form of urban design was first applied by Hippodamos in Miletus, Rhodes and Piraeus with great success, archaeological excavations have revealed the rectangular, intersecting grid plan in the cities of Urartu (9–7C BC)—for example, at the Karmir Blur and Zernaki Tepe sites—thus indicating quite conclusively that it came from the east.

During the late 3rd and early 2C BC, the building programme of the kings of Pergamum, in their capital city, ushered in a new and striking phase in urban planning which was to be adopted in the enlarging of other Hellenistic mountain cities. This was the construction of large terraces on the slopes of the mountain to support their majestic civil and religious buildings, giving Pergamum an ordered and well-planned layout, based on a system of terracing. This period thus witnessed a further development in urban planning beyond the two-dimensional linear grid found at Miletus and elsewhere; the Pergamum school produced a design which strove for a more dynamic and monumental environment that emphasised vertical as well as horizontal composition. The result, in these terraced mountain- and hill-side cities, was a complex of porticoed public buildings—temples, shrines, public fountains, theatre, gymnasium, agora, and sometimes library as at Pergamum—attached to one another by stairs to various terraces on different levels, all designed and built together in organic coordination.

The primary role of the city during the Hellenistic period should not obscure the existence, nor importance, of the larger political entities, the kingdoms. These were carved out of territories involved in the continuous warfare among the successor-states of Alexander's empire and themselves, like the semi-autonomous cities, remained mutually antagonistic in political terms and competitive in cultural and economic.

The local kingdoms of Anatolia were ruled by absolute monarchs who each sought to expand his territory and establish a world empire on the lines of Alexander's. Taxes had to be levied for the principle objective of maintaining and enlarging the armed forces. Thus, the real burden of the incessant warfare was borne, in effect, by the people. The Seleucids adopted, in Anatolia and elsewhere, the old Persian imposition of a ten per cent tax on land and immovable property and taxed the producers of papyrus, beer and wine, while oil and salt were monopolies of the king. Other sources of income included profits from agricultural labour on royal lands, the exploitation of mineral resources, particularly of precious metals, and gifts and tribute from vassals. Often, trade was fostered by various means, including the levying of taxes on the import and export of goods. It was clearly in the pursuit of a sound economy for the perpetuation of their military and political goals that the cities were so assiduously founded and fostered.

The armies were composed of paid soldiery whose numbers could thus easily be expanded during wartime and reduced in time of peace. The foot-soldiers formed the essential strength of the forces and were complemented, as the finances of the kingdom allowed, by cavalry and elephants. Organisation was by *phalanx*, sub-divided into units of *taxeis* (singular: *taxis*) with about 1500 soldiers, armed with shield, sword and long spear, who acted as the striking force. The development of naval power was vital in a period so dependent upon commerce, for whoever commanded the seas controlled the overseas trade. It was no coincidence that Pergamum and Ptolemaic Egypt between them dominated the Aegean and Mediterranean for so long, in conjunction with the independent city-state of Rhodes, whose navy, up to the Roman occupation, was the strongest. The Hellenistic period, with its numerous sea-battles, witnessed the development of ship-building techniques from the three-decked *trireme* to the five-decked, and even the eight-decked *okter* with its 1600 oarsmen—200 on each deck—providing immense power and speed.

The administrative organisation of kingdoms in the Hellenistic period was not uniform but varied according to local conditions and traditions. Generally, however, the king ruled with the help of a council of personal advisers or 'Friends' (*Philoi*), appointed by himself and drawn chiefly but not—in the Seleucid kingdom at least—exclusively from Greek and Macedonian personnel. This mixture of immigrant and native counsellors probably provided some connection with the locality, even where the monarch himself had none, and prevented too severe tax impositions on the general populace. The Seleucids divided their territories among satrapies, each under a *strategos* who administered also the smaller units of *hyparchioi* (counties) and *toparchioi* (villages). Among the *strategoi* were two governor-generals, one for the Upper Asian and one for the Lower Asian satrapy. As for jurisdiction, judges were appointed by the king who himself held ultimate authority and could authorise executions or grant pardons.

The autocratic nature of the Hellenistic monarchy from the very start of the period found, perhaps, its roots in the reign of Alexander who, in the course of time, became increasingly authoritarian, to the extent that he not only became an object of worship in some of the lands he conquered but even came to require his long-standing supporters and companions-in-arms at court to perform obeisance to him. Yet the growing practice of the ruler-cult in the Hellenistic kingdoms was probably more closely connected with the need for legitimation of their rule by the new kings who came to succeed to portions of Alexander's empire. Each of the Hellenistic dynasties seems to have adopted a special protector-god from among the pantheon—the Seleucids, for example, claiming Apollo of Miletus as the father of Seleucus I. This practice gradually extended to the worship of first the dead and later the living monarchs as gods in some parts of the Hellenistic world, although the stages by which the full transformation took place could be long drawn out. At Troy, for instance, in 298 BC an inscription in honour of the new ruler, Seleucus, named a month in his honour, accorded him a festival and recognised Apollo as the ancestor of the dynasty, but did not go quite so far as to name him a god himself. In Anatolia, the cult of ruler-gods seems not to have impressed itself as deeply as elsewhere—

most particularly in Ptolemaic Egypt and in the more easterly Seleucid territories. The Attalids of Pergamum were not recognised as gods during their lifetime and there appears not to have been an official dynastic cult here, although many cities honoured them with cult recognition. Indeed, the initiative to deification often came from the cities and, while it may not have altered the legal relationship between king and city, the good will generated thereby must have been as useful to the city as the deification, with its reinforcement of his authority and legitimacy, to the king.

But while the adoption of patron-gods and the growth of the ruler-cult had clear political implications, there were many other reasons for new religious developments, chiefly, it appears, as a response to changes in social conditions and corresponding individual attitudes. The great mixing-up of peoples characteristic of the Hellenistic period caused a mixing of their beliefs, including a gradual decrease in the number of deities who had previously represented aspects of nature, and a perceptible tendency toward monotheistic belief. It is possible to argue that as people's understanding, through reason, of the world around them increased, their need for representative deities decreased. Such a process may be observed in the popularity of the new deity, Tyche, representing the rather abstract Fortune or Luck, announced by Seleucus I as the paramount god of the Seleucid state, and before long worshipped extensively within and without Seleucid territories. Tyche was in due course to enter the Roman pantheon as Fortuna. Yet the transfer also of the long-revered Anatolian goddess, Kybele, to Rome and the passage of the Egyptian Sarapis to Anatolia and elsewhere, alongside the growth and spread of many mystery-cults promising individual salvation through their ceremonial rites, implies the continuing need of ordinary people for more personal and comprehensible deities. Among the Hellenistic pantheon deities such as Zeus, Dionysus, Apollo and Athena, long known and worshipped in Anatolia, increased in importance. So where do we see this reduction in numbers of deities and gradual inclination toward montheism? These may be observed in the tendency of each city or kingdom to accord their own patron deity supremacy over all the rest—local and newcomer alike—and to try to combine the other deities on a single subordinate level.

In science and philosophy as in religion, the general upheaval generated by almost continual warfare and the rise and fall of states, the intermixture of peoples with their own traditions and beliefs, and the place of the cities as patrons of religious, intellectual and artistic activity led to the cross-fertilisation of ideas in conjunction with a profound doubt as to the bases and continuing security of people's way of life and most cherished beliefs. Thus we see the advance of rational enquiry blocked, as it were, by retreat in the face of adversity and change. In religious belief, the tentative acknowledgement of abstract ideas or a single, coherent plan ruling men's lives was countered by renewed interest in personality cults, whether of rulers or gods. In science, great strides were made in astronomy, mathematics, physics and anatomy as the cities offered patronage and provided superb libraries. Notable scientists of the Hellenistic period came chiefly from the schools of Pergamum and Alexandria—the astronomers Hipparchus of Nicaea, who invented trigonometry, and Apollonius of Pergamum and the physicians Herophilus of Chalcedon (Kadıköy district of İstanbul) and Erasistratus of Chios (Sakız) whose knowledge of the human body was said to be based on the practice of dissection, even of the living—of criminals obtained from prison. In the branch of mechanics and the application of technology, however, achievement was less spectacular, with only the requirements of warfare and gadgetry for the wealthy apparently being advanced. Could this deficiency and, indeed, general weakening in the rational outlook during the course of the Hellenistic period be attributable to a failure by the philosophical schools to support scientific endeavour? For the four major schools of philosophy that find their roots in this period do seem to subordinate the question of understanding the world to the aim of gaining peace of mind. The Cynical school of Diogenes of Sinope (Sinop) sought virtue and moral freedom in liberation from desire and rejected the conventions and conveniences of society; Pyrrho's Sceptics maintained that there was no rational ground for preferring one course of action to another— which in practice argued that men should, without self-doubt or recrimination, conform to whatever customs prevailed around them; the Epicurean school looked to the attainment of 'static' pleasure, as in the absence of desire or need, through moderate contentment; and the Stoics of Zeno denied the possibility of chance, positing rather that the course of nature was rigidly determined by natural laws and that a man's virtue was the sole good. Thus, the Hellenistic age may be viewed as giving birth to a general philosophy of retreat, not one that sought to grapple with the problems of society. Yet this can also be seen not so much as a failure to support the rational sciences, as I have suggested above, as perhaps a symptom of the same individual timorousness in the face of a dangerous and uncertain world. Safer indeed to be indifferent to it all and concentrate on one's own salvation.

Yet curiously enough, this intellectual dilemma is hardly apparent in the arts, so brilliantly and grandly represented in the Hellenistic cities. Architecture, sculpture and painting form the media of expression for which the Hellenistic age is particularly remembered. In architectural achievement, new temples were constantly erected during this period, with each new god being accorded his own; and the thriving cities continuously sought to outdo one another in their patronage of culture and in their monuments of artistic endeavour.

The classical Doric and Ionic orders of architecture continued into the Hellenistic period and gradually came to develop a Hellenistic character with, in particular, the spread of a new order incorporating the elegance of the Ionic and featuring the Corinthian-style capital. Indeed, the Corinthian capital, as it now developed, became particularly popular and well-known in Anatolian architecture of the period, impressive examples being found at the Mausoleum of Belevi near Selçuk. Probably the oldest surviving temple of the Corinthian order is the peripteral Temple of Zeus Olbios near Olba (Diocaesarea; Uzuncaburç, near Silifke). The rich and lively ornamentation of acanthus leaves typical of the Corinthian capital, sometimes interspersed with figural elements-human and animal, was most suitable for the growing aesthetic taste for effects in light and shade, developed also in other aspects of Hellenistic architecture. A mixture of styles may often be found within one building, as in the small Temple of Dionysus at Pergamum and in the colonnades of the Temple of Athena Polias Nikephoros there. The classical Ionic style, resting on the fame of its earlier buildings, however, showed no rapid change, as is evident in the colossal new Temple of Apollo at Didyma, begun in 310 BC on virtually the same plan as its preceding building of 540 BC; while perhaps the best example of the classical Ionic style of architecture is the Temple of Athena Polias in Priene.

But the distinctive Hellenistic character of temple architecture began to emerge about the beginning of the 2C BC with the career of Hermogenes. He was an outstanding architect and theoretician who is recorded by Vitruvius as having written his own theories on temple design, based principally on mathematical proportions and adjustments. It was he who abandoned the by now over-worked and exhausted Doric order and developed new and original techniques based on the Ionic. Perhaps Hermogenes' finest and best-known work was in relation to the introduction of the *pseudo-dipteros* to Anatolia, in which the usual inner *pteron* was omitted, allowing a spacious colonnade two spans in width around the core of the temple, pleasant to walk in and protected from sun and rain; it also created, with its deeply-incised ornamentation, a pleasing contrast of light and shadow that was wholly in accord with Hellenistic aesthetic preferences, and one in which Hermogenes was interested. A fine example of this interest—and the effect produced by the play of light and shadow from a distance—is his Temple of Artemis Leukophryene at Magnesia ad Maeandrum (near Söke). His use of a simple Attic base and Attic frieze is evident here and at the Temple of Dionysus at Teos (Sığacık). Both of these architectural devices were to become standard. Hermogenes' principle of widely spaced columns required a reduction in weight and hence the height of the frieze and supported architectural elements, again a tendency that was to be reflected in the architecture of the later Hellenistic period as architects sought to reduce the appearance of massiveness in their buildings and attain the maximum effect of lightness.

But one of the chief characteristics of Hellenistic architecture was its increasing secularisation, as we have seen in relation to urban planning, where the major municipal buildings were no longer all religious in nature. The agora, gymnasium, town hall, theatre and other public buildings were given due importance among the city's monuments. Indeed, it is still possible to see some of the best theatres of the Hellenistic world, with Roman modifications, in the Anatolian sites of Pergamum, Aphrodisias (Geyre), and Ephesus. Of particular importance in urban architectural development was the new emphasis given to planning on a central axis and the front entrance in place of the classical four-sided character of many buildings—and especially temples—and to the three-dimensional concept apparent in the multi-storeyed constructions with their monumental stairways and close attention to the problems and potential of space.

Major developments were evident in the sculpture and art of the Hellenistic period. The classical style and subtle expression of major Hellenistic sculptors created the expressive and muscular physiques that are so well-known today. Figuring prominently was the palace sculptor of Alexander, Lysippos, who introduced new 'impressionistic' proportions on the grounds, according to the written sources that have come down to us, that he wanted to represent men not as they were but as they appeared. Pliny the Elder records that Lysippos sculpted 1500 works, including portraits of Alexander, but, apart from some Roman copies, virtually none of the originals survives. Among artists, the figure most comparable to Lysippos was Apelles of Colophon who was brought up in Ephesus and became the palace artist of Alexander. Just as Alexander allowed himself to be sculpted only by Lysippos, so his portrait was only painted by Apelles. He depicted Alexander clasping lightning in one hand, lightning that was said by contemporary sources to have gleamed so brightly that it seemed almost to emerge from the picture, displayed in the Temple of Artemis at Ephesus. Many anecdotes are told of Apelles' intimacy with the monarch; for example, that Alexander used to visit the studio and talk at length about painting, only to be told by Apelles to keep his mouth shut if he did not want to be laughed at by the slaves who ground the colours.

Notable works of sculpture from the Hellenistic period include the bronze athlete found at Selçuk (Ephesus), which has been attributed to Lysippos, and the statue of Alexander found at Manisa (Magnesia ad Sipylum), on which Lysippos' influence has been perceived. After Alexander, sculptures of kings were often made, as were statues of the new deity, Tyche, who was believed to hold the fate of cities in her hands. The statue of Tyche sculpted by Eutychides (one of Lysippos' pupils) for Antiocheia and that of a boy in prayer by Boidas (a son and pupil of Lysippos) were popular enough to have copies made for Roman clients. A new and interesting depth in sculpture was achieved by Doidalsas in a bronze model of Aphrodite, in a crouching pose, for Nicomedia (İzmit) in Bithynia. But pride of place in sculpture (as well as in painting) most be accorded to the Pergamum school which flourished after Attalus I's victory over the Galatians prompted numerous victory sculptures. Of these, one of the most remarkable is that known as the 'Ludovisi Gaul'—of a Galatian who, having killed his wife, is on the point of stabbing himself with his own sword; while the great sculptural frieze on the huge altar erected in the Acropolis of Pergamum, representing a struggle of gods and giants and symbolising the victory of Pergamum over the Galatians, is among the finest examples of Hellenistic plastic art. Other schools of repute included the Tralles (Aydın) school from the 2C BC, admired for the depiction of such aesthetic details as the veins in human skin and the natural fall of silken drapery, and for the depth of expression achieved by its sculptors—who were particularly noted for their fine group statuary. The school of Rhodes was also prominent in both sculpture and painting during the 1C BC. Monumental art accounted for much sculpted decoration, with the earlier figures of deities soon replaced by expressive and vibrant human and animal forms. Best known must be the famous 'Alexander Sarcophagus' (4C), thus misnamed because although its sides are ornamented in glorious reliefs of Alexander's exploits, the sarcophagus actually belongs to one of his vassals, King Abdalonymous of Sidon (in modern Lebanon).

As for artists, whose work is familiar mainly from copies and historical sources Pliny has recorded many of their names and works, often with amusing anecdotes. For example, the artist Nealkes threw a paint-soaked sponge at a picture of a battle scene he was painting in exasperation at his inability to portray successfully the foaming mouth of a horse, and by so doing achieved the desired result. Vitruvius also narrates a story illustrating the tastelessness and dull conformity of the later Hellenistic period. The artist Apaturios of Alabanda (Araphisar) made his name by painting the stage decoration of the *ekklesiasterion* (assembly hall) at Tralles in a new and original design replacing the columns with human figures and resting the architrave on centaurs. But the mathematician Likymnios, in rebuke, likened the Tralleans to the people of Alabanda who had become a laughing-stock by putting sculptures of athletes in the agora and sculptures of orators in the gymnasium, for the unsuitable placing of statues in respect to the proper function of the places where they were displayed was held to be in very poor taste.

The standard of floor mosaics during the Hellenistic period was by no means inferior to that of painting. Found in the vestibules of numerous houses, their limitation in colour was amply compensated by their particular technique in shading. Mosaic copies of popular paintings were common, of which the most famous—although quite distant from our area—is that in the Casa del Fauno in Pompeii, depicting the defeat of Darius by Alexander. This is a copy of a late 4C painting usually attributed to Philoxenos of Eretria. Minor arts, such as ceramics and work in precious metals, continued to flourish in Hellenistic Anatolia. The production of metal, and especially silver, vessels with relief decoration greatly expanded. Yet the gold- and silver-ware created for the extravagant courts of Pergamum and elsewhere has almost entirely disappeared.

Roman Anatolia. The Hellenistic period drew to a close in the 1C BC with, as I have indicated, the steadily increasing dominance of the Romans in Anatolia. After Attalus III's bequest of Pergamum to them in 133 BC, Nicomedes of Bithynia bequeathed his own kingdom to Rome in 74 BC, and Pontus and Cappadocia were acquired by conquest. With Pompeius' (Pompey's) effective clearance of the corsairs from the Mediterranean trade routes in 67 BC, Cilicia too fell under Roman domination. In 64/63 BC came the reorganisation of Roman administration in Anatolia and the incorporation of virtually the whole of Anatolia into the Roman imperial edifice. With this came Roman culture to Anatolia; yet it might be argued that Anatolia 'hellenised' Rome while Rome colonised her, for she possessed a well-developed and creative culture whose roots stretched back thousands of years. And with the advent of the Roman imperial period, from the assumption by Augustus of the Consulship, Anatolia became increasingly important to Rome. The obvious wealth of Roman Anatolia, so apparent in the extraordinary opulence of numerous cities with their luxurious buildings from the 1C BC to the end of the 2C AD, seems to have been founded upon the twin bases of craft and commerce. The old-established Anatolian manufactures revived in prosperity under the early Roman emperors, maintaining their hold on local markets and providing some of the major centres of transit trade in the Empire, notably at Ephesus and Antioch. Anatolian wool was exported in the form of varieties of textiles, ivory and precious metals—particularly bronze—as finely worked artefacts. But it was the rich marble deposits of the Anatolian quarries that were most eagerly sought by the Romans and assured Anatolia of a prominent role in the marble trade. Along with exports of marble in block form and in semi-finished 'quarry' state went numerous skilled Anatolian craftsmen to work it in ateliers and trade centres all over the Empire.

Anatolia's flourishing economy meant that during this period many of the existing municipal mints remained active and silver coins such as the *cistophori* issued by Pergamum and Ephesus continued to exist alongside Roman coinage as a general provincial currency—the Romans making no serious attempt to impose a uniform weight on them. Successive Roman emperors visited Antatolian cities, particularly to open campaigns in the east; and their visits prompted the issuing of new coins, and the setting up of new buildings and shrines, which were usually dedicated to the Emperor in question.

The monumental architecture of the major Hellenistic cities was modified by the Romans through the introduction of the colonnaded street, crossed by colonnaded side streets and doubled or even trebled by parallel streets. This, combined with the increased construction of lavish public works, gave the urban centres a new luxurious character and revealed a new taste for ostentation. At Ephesus, provision was even made for street lighting at night. The regular urban street plan, considered monotonous, went out of fashion, and the agora took on the form of a court enclosed by four porticoes, often constructed in connected series, as at Aphrodisias. Temple architecture remained, with certain innovations and adaptations, firmly within the Hellenistic tradition, but the triumphal arch, so typical of the Roman Empire, appeared on a number of Anatolian sites, such as Ephesus, Nicaea and Diocaesarea. The theatres of Priene, Miletus, Pergamum, Aphrodisias and Ephesus, among others, were adapted according to contemporary taste, and new theatres constructed in the Roman style, for example in Aspendus (Belkız), Hierapolis (Pamukkale) and Side (Selimiye). Architectural innovations, such as the *thermae* (combined bath and gymnasium) in Ephesus, Miletus and elsewhere, and the Roman basilicas in Smyrna and Aspendus, made their appearance. Other, quite new skills were adopted in their entirety from their Italian source—roads and bridges, aqueducts, cisterns and other hydraulic works.

An interesting feature of architectural technique in Roman Anatolia was the type of building material used. In addition to the traditional dressed stone of Anatolian monumental architecture, the Roman period introduced the extensive use of kiln-fired brick—clearly evident in a number of buildings, notably at Ephesus and Pergamum—or even bands of brickwork alternating with wider bands of mortared rubble—as in the city walls of Nicaea—instead of the usual Roman concrete of mortared rubble faced with brick.

Sculpture, especially in marble, continued to thrive as a medium of artistic expression, tending to derive inspiration from the traditional Hellenistic schools of, chiefly, Pergamum and Rhodes. Workshops in centres such as Ephesus and Aphrodisias flourished, as marble votive stelae and funerary reliefs and sarcophagi were in almost as much demand as the prized sculptures and friezes that went to adorn the temples and other public buildings of the Empire as well as the homes and gardens of wealthy private citizens. Paintings, frescoes and mosaic-work continued to develop to meet a growing market, and were exported to Rome and other imperial cities where they were often copied; relatively few original examples have survived in their own settings.

The Roman Empire went through a period of crisis in the 3C, a crisis from which the western part of the Empire was to suffer disastrously. Yet the eastern part, centring on Anatolia, while experiencing severe political upheavals and economic collapse, did not suffer as massive and irreversible a decline in population or decay of city life and economy as the western, despite the drying-up of funds for lavish public works and the imposition of increasingly heavy taxes and military duties on a large proportion of the population.

Unlike the western part, the eastern Roman Empire was able to revive, indeed continued to exist for centuries to come. The cumulative effect of the old Hellenistic civilisation as it spread outward from its epicentre in the Aegean basin was not merely spatial but temporal. The cultural continuum of the Hellenistic world was to exert an undeniable influence on those who held the reins of power in Anatolia long after the fall of Rome. For it was the integration of Hellenistic culture and the new Christian religion within the Roman imperial framework that gave rise to that historical phenomenon which we know as the Byzantine Empire.

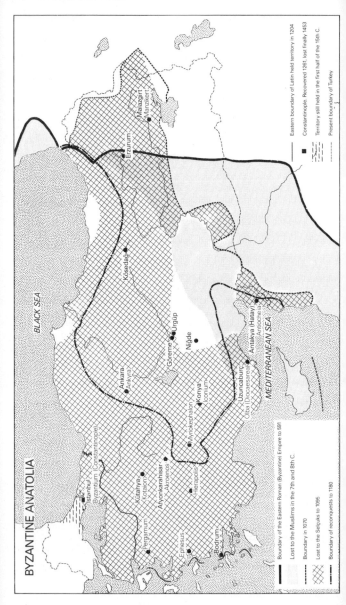

BYZANTINE ANATOLIA

BLACK SEA

MEDITERRANEAN SEA

Istanbul/
Byzantium (Constantinople)

Pergamum

Ephesus

Bodrum

Kütahya
(Kotaion)

Afyonkarahisar
Akroenos

Heraplois

Myokephalon

Ankara
Ankyra

Konya
Iconium

Göreme

Ürgüp

Niğde

Uzuncaburç
Olba (Diocaesarea)

Antakya (Hatay)
Antiocheia

Kösedağ

Erzurum

Malazgirt
Manzikert

Boundary of the Eastern Roman (Byzantine) Empire to 591

Lost to the Muslims in the 7th and 8th C.

Boundary in 1070

Lost to the Selçuks to 1095

Boundary of reconquests to 1180

Eastern boundary of Latin held territory in 1204

Constantinople. Recovered 1261, lost finally 1453

Territory still held in the first half of the 15th C.

Present boundary of Turkey

VII. The Byzantines

The Byzantine Empire, one of the longest-surviving empires the world has known, takes its name from its capital, the ancient city of Byzantium (İstanbul). Yet this is a misnomer, for the label of the 'Byzantines', like that of the 'Hittites', never really existed in their own time. The rulers and subjects of the Empire never used the term, but referred to themselves as *Romaioi* (Romans), as did their contemporaries; and they saw themselves as the legitimate successors of the Caesars. Indeed, the Eastern Roman Empire, to give its more correct title, is generally accepted as taking its foundation from AD 395, when Theodosius I (379–395) divided the Roman Empire into its Eastern and Western parts. The Eastern already possessed a capital; the old Byzantium had been renamed Constantinople on its completion as a new city in AD 330 and created as Rome's second capital by Constantine (324–337) as a deliberate and conscious 'Christian' contrast to 'heathen' Rome. And, in reality, Latin West and Hellenistic East possessed two very different world views, a divergence that widened with the spread of Christianity and thence made itself visible in the political as well as in the religious realm.

The aspect of Christianity as the official religious faith of the Eastern Romans was an important one from the foundation of Constantinople as the second, Christian, capital of the Roman Empire by the Emperor Constantine—who himself was eventually baptised on his death-bed in 337—throughout the long and turbulent history of the succeeding Eastern Roman Empire until its final displacement by that of the Ottoman Turks in 1453. Indeed, the nine principal dynasties (from that of Heraclius to that of Palaeologus) of the Eastern Romans spanned the entire Middle Ages and juxtaposed with the period that saw the rise of a newer monotheistic faith, Islam, and the competition for political domination between the adherents of the two religions. Moreover, this was a struggle in which the greatest damage was inflicted on the Byzantine Empire and especially her capital by her co-religionists during the Crusades; the wealthy city of Constantinople was sacked thoroughly over three days in 1204 by the Fourth Crusade, and up to the very eve of the Empire's demise the bishops of Constantinople adamantly opposed the reunification of the Church in return for military support, with the declaration by a high official that, 'It would be better to see the royal turban of the Turks in the midst of the city than the Latin mitre.' On the other side, Jean Gerson, Chancellor of the University of Paris, in an address to the King of France, delivered shortly after the Council of Pisa (1409), affirmed that the Byzantines 'prefer Turks to the Latins'.

The origins of such deep antagonism between eastern and western branches of the Church lie back in the years surrounding the partition of the Roman Empire between Theodosius' two sons in AD 395. The Western Roman Empire rapidly declined in the face of waves of invasions from the north and east, chiefly by the Germanic tribes, the Goths and, most importantly, the Turco-Mongolian peoples known as the Huns under Attila; and finally collapsed in 476. The Eastern Roman Empire incorporated all the old Hellenistic lands of the eastern Mediterranean, comprising arguably the most civilised part of the Roman Empire, with its ancient traditions and urban development, its rich economic resources and strategic value for political, military and economic relations to the west as well as to the east. Thus, from the earliest days, the Eastern Romans considered themselves the true successors of the Roman Empire—a conviction that persisted through change of religion from the old paganism and through change of language from Latin to Greek from the 6C.

In 451, at the Fourth Ecumenical Council in Chalcedon, Constantinople was formally recognised as the second in importance, after Rome itself, of the five Patriarchates of the Christian Church—the other three being Alexandria, Antioch and Jerusalem; this was a decision that confirmed and extended what had in effect been agreed in 381 at the Second Council in Constantinople. The eastern part of the Empire was thus well-placed to take advantage of the collapse of the western part, even though the primacy of the Patriarchate of Rome was to continue unabated. For the Patriarchates were embroiled in dogmatic controversies from the start, with the first major schism between Rome and Constantinople as early as 482 and lasting for 35 years; and the separatist, monophysite heresies of Antioch and Alexandria (condemned at the Fourth Council) were to continue unresolved until Syria and Egypt were conquered by Iran and incorporated into the Islamic world in the 7C. With these losses, despite the major territorial acquisitions of Justinian (527–565), the eastern part of the Empire was reduced virtually to the land mass of Anatolia, first referred to as Asia Minor by the Latin historian Orosius in the early 5C. Within these straitened boundaries, it assumed for the first time a fairly homogeneous form—with religious orthodoxy and Hellenistic tradition acting as the binding forces of this autochthonous Anatolian culture, compounded as it was with heavily Asiatic elements. At the same time, relations with Rome and the western lands became increasingly distant. With the contemporary Christian belief in the indivisibility of Church and State, the Pope remained theoretically the subject of the Emperor, but the strength and independent spirit of the Papacy was clearly evinced in, for example, its uncompromising rejection of Constantinople's attempt to impose its own uniform practices on all ecclesiastical ritual and discipline at the Quinisextum Council of Constantinople in 692. And the gulf between the Latin and Orthodox Churches, as they came to be known, widened still further in 800 when Pope Leo III (795–816) crowned Charlemagne (800–814) emperor in Rome—thus symbolising the divergence between the Churches as well as the political division between the now rival Empires centred on Rome (Western Roman) and Constantinople (Eastern Roman). But the final schism (Great Schism) between the Western and Eastern Churches was not to occur until 1054; and subsequent attempts at reunion—such as the Council and Union of Lyons in 1245 and of Florence in 1439—were doomed to failure.

The Eastern Roman Empire was faced with the implacable hostility of her co-religionists in the west, as perceived for example in Latin aims to acquire for themselves Muslim Syria and Palestine—once part of the Eastern Empire—and their willingness to ally with Islamic rulers against the Eastern Empire when it suited them.

In other directions, the Empire faced, during its thousand-year history, enemies on more than one front, often at the same time, and on a number of occasions Constantinople itself came under direct attack. Especially from the north, through the Balkans, came wave after wave of invasion and migration by various Turkish clans—Avars, Bulgars, Peçeneks, Uz (Oğuz), Kuman-Kıpçaks—vast numbers of whom were gradually, from the 6C onwards, converted from their 'sky-god' religion with its shamanistic accretions and relocated by the Byzantines. These Turks were settled en masse in different parts of Anatolia (including the sparsely populated border zones in the south and south-east) in the Byzantine policy of the Christianisation and repopulation of Anatolia, and were in time incorporated into the congregation of the Anatolian Orthodox Churches. Similarly, Slavic tribes headed south—in waves of invasion and migration—to add further to the racial and cultural mixture that was the Byzantine Empire. The 13C saw the establishment of the Altın Ordu branch of the Turco-Mongol Empire in Russia, with the consequent further pressure of migrating peoples south, and the conquest by the İlhanlı branch of Baghdad, successors to a long history of Muslim (and chiefly Arab) states against whom the Byzantines had intrigued and fought. The Sassanid Empire of Iran had twice advanced on Constantinople early in the 7C; and the Caliphates of first the Umayyad and then the Abbasid dynasties organised, from Damascus and Baghdad respectively, numerous Muslim armies, predominantly Turkish in composition and usually under Turkish commanders—fighting with all the zeal of the newly converted. Their advances into Anatolia included further huge influxes of Turkish settlers who were established around the border zones in south-east and east Anatolia and Azerbaycan (Azerbaijan) as a counterpoise to the Byzantine settlement policies. It was these settlers who were to bear the brunt of the Christian attacks when the Muslim armies were themselves pushed back, particularly with the onset of the Crusades from Latin Europe in 1096—Crusades which had the fundamental intention of eradicating Islam, not simply the reconquering of Jerusalem and the territories of Palestine and Syria.

From Egypt, too, came strong counter-offensives to the Crusader and Byzantine incursions, from first the Ayyubids and then their successors, the Mamluks. Yet this mutual antagonism did not prevent alliances from being concluded by the Eastern Romans with the Altın Ordu and with the Mamluks against the İlhanlıs in 1271, thus creating the short-term stablity of a balance of power.

The predominantly Christian-Turkish presence in Anatolia had existed, as we have seen, for some centuries before the Selçuk victory over the Eastern Romans at Manzikert (Malazgirt) in 1071 firmly established the Anatolian Muslim Selçuk state there, as an offshoot of the larger Selçuk Empire to the east. And the quarter-century immediately following the battle of Manzikert saw the migration of over a million people—chiefly clans of newly converted Muslim Turks spreading from Central Asia; a number thought to have exceeded the existing, depleted population and which, therefore, turned Anatolia into a virtual Turkish homeland. From then on, almost continuous migrations of mainly Turkish peoples were to stream into Anatolia from the east, under pressure from the turbulent new Turco-Mongol states forming and expanding westward from Central Asia. And in just over a hundred years the Byzantine Empire turned from an offensive to a defensive empire, with the defeat of Manuel I Comnenus (1143–80) by the Selçuk sultan, Kılıç Arslan (1156–92), at the battle of Myriokephalon (one of the passes of the Sultandağ range, possibly Karamıkbeli, north of Eğridir Gölü) in western Anatolia in 1176.

In the meantime, however, a new Mongol wave began its own occupation of eastern Anatolia from Erzurum, defeating the Selçuks at the battle of Kösedağ (east of Sivas) in 1243 and establishing İlhanlı domination. Thus it disrupted Turkish unity in Anatolia—a unity that was not to be re-established until after the emergence of a new Turkish state, the Ottoman, at the end of the 13C.

We have seen, then, the range of racial and cultural, religious and linguistic influences acting upon and inevitably being absorbed into the Empire of the Eastern Romans. And that the land mass of Anatolia was no stranger to such infiltrations is evident from its previous history and prehistory. Yet what held together this nebulous mass of humanity centred around the Anatolian heartland of the Byzantine Empire? As I have pointed out, it was the religious orthodoxy of a dogmatic and increasingly isolated centre of Christianity and the Hellenistic tradition derived from its Roman parentage. For the Roman Empire of the first three centuries AD had not simply transmitted the Hellenistic civilisation it found in Anatolia and the eastern Mediterranean; it had used what it found to develop its own traditions. And, indeed, in aspects of government, the Romans had laid down the framework of law and administrative organisation that was, in all its essential features, to maintain the Eastern Empire for the first few centuries of its existence. Yet although the Byzantine conception of its Roman ideological and political heritage was to endure, its character did alter over the course of time, due mainly to the Christian ethic of the developing Empire and its gradual imposition of this Christianity on every aspect of the society, and to the substitution, during the reign of Heraclius (610–641), of Greek for Latin as the official language. Thus, in time, a system of government evolved in response to these and other political and economic developments, which came to have very little if anything in common with that of its predecessor, the Roman Empire.

The structure of the Eastern Roman Empire was a monarchal one in that the Emperor's authority was absolute, and his temporal and spiritual roles so closely identified that he was believed to embody political legitimacy and God's will in his own person—any form of disrespect to him warranting the death penalty. Respect for the laws, a very Roman preoccupation, thus characterised also the behaviour of the Byzantine emperors, even though this might come to acquire only a formal sense. A new Emperor, for example, had to be accepted by the army, the people and the chief administrative and legislative organ—the Senate—in order to acquire legitimacy; but this procedure rapidly dwindled to the merest formality as the tradition was established that the Patriarch of Constantinople enthroned the new Emperor in the church of Haghia Sophia (or Ayasofya), thus bestowing on him the highest spiritual legitimacy. A fair exchange, it might be argued, since the Patriarch was himself selected by the Emperor. In this way developed the doctrine of the Emperor's right and duty to protect the Church and defend Christians, not only in his temporal role by maintaining and extending the territories of the Christian Empire and actively encouraging the spread of the faith (through mass conversions of subject peoples), but also in his spiritual role by ensuring the maintenance of sound doctrine and the suppression of heresy. Yet while the Emperor possessed, and indeed acted upon, this extent of authority over the affairs of the Church, the counterpart was of course that the Church developed huge power in the administration of the state and enormous influence among the imperial population as its authority was extended. This was primarily due to the intimate relationship between the foundation of the Empire and the establishment of Christianity as the state religion, as we have seen, but was compounded with the economic well-being of the Church which owned large tracts of land and much property; indeed, a wide network of monasteries covered the Empire. Yet the weakening of the Empire in its declining years was reflected in a weakening of the Church, as the loss of imperial territory involved the loss of Church territory. As the number of bishoprics reduced from 450 at their peak to 67 in the 15C, with the Empire's diminishing political dominion, it is interesting to observe that the bishoprics thus territorially reduced all retained their titles. Indeed, to this day, the İstanbul Patriarchate retains its position and continues its traditional function under the Republic of Turkey's secular government.

Succession was, in theory, hereditary and joint emperors were not unknown—the second usually a high commander or the son of the first and nominated as his successor. Throughout the millennium of the Empire, there seems never to have been any attempt to move towards a constitutional monarchy or republic; all the popular uprisings and assassinations were evidently related to specific grievances or a specific ruler, and never rejected the system itself or aimed at governing power.

The Emperor was also head of the judiciary, with all justice dispensed in his name. In the 14C the Emperor's court was the highest, with the higher officials as members, and dealt with major criminal offences as well as acting as the court of appeal for lesser crimes tried in the lower courts. The lower courts were headed by senior officials and provincial courts were maintained in the major cities. The initial severity of punishments was reduced slightly with the growing entrenchment of the official religion but increased once more under the Isaurian dynasty. For example, crucifixion was abolished but replaced by the cutting off of hands, feet or ears, and by blinding; punishments such as banishment and consignment to monasteries came to be used more extensively.

Administratively, the Empire was divided into the centre and the provinces, both with a strong military disposition. The central administration was staffed by high military and civil personnel whose rivalry was a constant source of faction and struggle for control. The highest minister, the Magister Officiorum (Master of Offices), exerted authority in domestic and foreign affairs alike: he supervised the imperial machinery, controlled the palace guards, all frontier units, communications and security, and introduced and negotiated with ambassadors. But in the course of time this central ministry was dismantled and the heads of most of its departments developed into separate officials responsible directly to the Emperor. The chief institution was the Senate, based on the Roman model, whose most important role lay in exercising its authority in the selection and recognition of the Emperor—a role that was never removed, even though reduced to a formality. The Senate, whose membership comprised the economically important land-owning aristocracy of the provinces, inevitably gained and lost influence according to the strength and power of the incumbent Emperor. The other major central institution was the Imperial Council (*Concilium Principis*; later *Sacrum Consistorium*) composed of high civil servants based at the capital, whose lack of significance may be deduced from their meetings being called *silentium* (silence) and their being expected to listen respectfully, and standing, to the words of the Emperor. The term *silentium* was later adopted as the proper name of the Imperial Council, which gradually lost its status as a permanent body, meeting only irregularly, at the behest of the Emperor. Opportunities for the Emperor to communicate directly with his subjects were provided by sessions in the Hippodrome (Sultan Ahmet Meydanı) in Constantinople.

In the provinces, the early civil and military administration was abandoned by Heraclius for a division of Anatolia into military provinces (*themes*), each under the command of a *strategus* who exercised, under the direct control of the Emperor, supreme military and civil command within his theme. The soldiers responsible for the defence of an area were given grants of land there on which to settle in return for hereditary service, and came to form the backbone of the Empire's defensive system. Over the centuries, various Slavic and Turkish populations were transplanted to parts of Anatolia by the government and settled in the themes as *stratiotai* (soldier-farmers), alongside local peasants likewise endowed with small-holdings in return for undertaking military obligations. By the 11C the old structure of the theme system had collapsed and given way to two principal types of land-holding—the large hereditary estate of the civil or military magnate and the *pronoia*. The latter was a method of tenure whereby crown land was granted to secular magnates together with its entire revenue and rights of administration, often with exemptions from taxation and other public obligations and normally in return for military service. At first granted for fixed periods and inalienable, in the course of time the pronoia became hereditary, although the obligation of service generally remained. This fief-like pronoia, which centred on the relationship between land tenure and military service, and between the peasants and the local landed lord on whom they were economically dependent, was an important factor in the process of 'feudalisation'—a process that tended to increase the power of the landed military (and even civil) aristocracy at the expense of the central administration, certainly in the later Byzantine period.

The imperial armed forces were well-trained and organised in the early period, with units maintained at the frontiers and the central army deployed wherever required. The early structure underwent considerable reorganisation in the 7C with the introduction of the theme system bringing the provincial soldiery under the command of strategi. The army was composed of foot-soldiers and cavalry, plus some irregular troops at the frontiers, armed with swords, shields, spears, battle-axes and massive catapults for siege warfare. Increasing numbers of foreign mercenaries were also employed.

Naval forces were established in the 7C in response to the establishment and successes of the navies of the Muslim states in the eastern Mediterranean. After this, the structure was reorganised from time to time, Heraclius combining all naval forces into a single theme and Leo III (717–741) dividing them into a central navy at Constantinople and provincial navy of the themes, while in the 10C they were further divided into units of three to five warships. After the 11C, the Byzantine naval forces fell into decline and were abolished by Andronicus II Palaeologus (1282–1328). With the ensuing passage of maritime superiority to Venice and Genoa, his successor, Andronicus III Palaeologus (1328–41) tried to restore the navy but without success. And on the conquest of Constantinople by the Ottomans in 1453, the Byzantine naval defence comprised five rented battleships, four of which were deployed in the Golden Horn (Haliç).

As the Eastern Roman Empire was well placed in territory that controlled the major trade routes, both land and sea, between Asia, Europe and Africa, for centuries it dominated international trade—an important source of revenue. Byzantine gold coinage appears to have been much prized up to the middle of the 11C, but then gradually lost its value as the Empire declined—indeed, in the final years, the Empire was unable to mint any gold coins at all, so desparate were its financial straits. Moreover, from the later 13C, the still-substantial trade of Constantinople was largely controlled by foreigners who enjoyed numerous privileges and were generally exempt from taxation. Principal exports were manufactured goods, all industries being organised in guilds under state control and concentrated in Constantinople. Of particular importance were the crafts in metal, glass and jewellery, but above all the textile industry in cotton, silk and linen-flax. It was during the reign of Justinian II (527–565) that two priests are reputed to have smuggled the eggs of silk-worms inside a hollow cane from China and cultivation of silk was begun in Constantinople. From this time on, the export of silk constituted a very profitable trade in addition to meeting a substantial home demand from the wealthy, the Church and the Palace. Yet the centralisation of the economy, as in most aspects of the society, is particularly evident in the contrast between the position of Constantinople as the dominant (indeed at times the only) active urban centre in the Empire with the numerous thriving cities acting as trade and cultural centres throughout Anatolia and beyond during the Hellenistic (and early Roman) period.

Meanwhile, the basis of the economy continued, as throughout Anatolian history, to be agriculture, with wheat as the staple crop, followed by fruit and cotton, and widespread animal husbandry. According to Byzantine thought, the soil belonged to God and was dispensed through the Emperor. Hence, all land belonged to the state and could be distributed in return for tax. Thus, in the early period, the nobility possessed the bulk of the land, the rest being worked by independent labourers; and later, with the introduction first of the theme and subsequently of the pronoia system, most of the land was distributed as military holdings. But throughout the Byzantine period, the most important state income was derived from the land; agriculturalists, it appears, consistently bore the greater burden of taxation.

Turning to the intellectual side of Byzantine life, education was not widespread but concentrated mostly on the sons of the well-to-do, with the aim of recruiting bureaucratic personnel—the administration, like the Church, offering suitable career prospects likely to command considerable wealth and patronage. To this end, by the 10C, there had been set up in Constantinople ten schools teaching about 200–300 boys in all. Constantinople was early established as a centre of learning as scholars from Alexandria, Antioch and Athens flocked to the new capital on its foundation; its university was established during the reign of Theodosius II (408–450) with, eventually, a total of 31 chairs—in Latin, Greek grammar, Greek science and philosophy, Latin rhetoric, philosophy, and law. Clearly, a strong classical tradition continued well into the Byzantine period. Nor were the teachers obliged to be Christians until Justinian's reign. At the height of the Iconoclastic controversy (726–843)—a long and bitter struggle between proponents of the cult of images and its opponents, eventually to be won by the former—the university was closed down, and remained closed for over 200 years until 863. After this, its fortunes waxed and waned in accordance with the interest and support of the reigning Emperor. Other centres of learning also existed, but of lesser importance and influence. And in all the schools, one might surmise that the emphasis on religious teaching and the participation of religious dignitaries as teachers increased as the Empire declined.

Intellectual life in general may be said to have been, from the first, closely connected with the inter-relations between the Christian Eastern and Western Roman and the Hellenistic worlds. It took several centuries for Christianity to establish itself thoroughly enough to permeate the whole of society. Yet the adoption of Greek as the official language of the Empire affected intellectual life in no small measure, and the Islamic conquest of Egypt, Syria and Palestine in the 7C displaced much intellectual activity towards Constantinople. However, it must be noted that such intellectual fields as astronomy, mathematics, chemistry, botany, zoology and medicine showed minimal development during the Byzantine period. At first, classical Latin and Greek texts were studied; and from the 9C, when the Empire opened up to Islamic civilisation and learning, some works were translated from Arabic. Nor was geography well studied. The few works that were written tended to concentrate on the practical aspects of travel and pilgrimage and included lists of Church dignitaries. There was no interest in cartography.

As for creative literature, the early continuance of the old pagan tradition was in time replaced by the complete domination of Christian thinking, although the classical forms were long retained. Knowledge of the Bible came to be of principal importance for Byzantine authors, whether in Anatolia, Syria, Palestine or Egypt, all of which contained, in the early period, lively centres of literature— pride of place belonging, however, to Constantinople. Poetry was the preferred genre, taking as its subject-matter the weighty themes of history, law and theology, while all kinds of prose works were converted into poetry. Some poets took mythological tales as their topics and used the classical metre. Rhythmical poetry developed steadily from the 2C, with perhaps its most important practitioner being Romanus the Melode ('Hymn-Writer'), the simple language of whose hymns (especially his 'Nativity' hymn) conveys a profundity in sense. The 'Akathistos' hymn, still in use in the liturgy of the Orthodox Church, is attributed to the 6C Byzantine Empire. Rhetoric developed as an art and as a taught subject in the various Byzantine schools from the 4C. Justinian's tutor, Agapetus, the Deacon of Haghia Sophia, wrote for him a book of 'advice literature' ('Mirrors for Princes') outlining the religion, morals and political duties of a Christian king, entitled 'Ekthesis kephalaion parainetikon pros Basilea Iustinianon' ('Advice to the Emperor Justinian'); the work found much favour and was translated into several languages.

From the 4C, the taste for religious fables and hagiography also grew, but about the middle of the 7C there set in a general stagnation of literature, as the Iconoclastic controversy decimated holy paintings and created a nervousness and timidity that was to affect intellectual pursuits in general. Only hagiography appears to have thrived, as those who suffered and died for the sake of the religious art were revered as saints by the populace, and their hagiographies, with those of priests, were much sought after.

With the re-establishment of the University of Constantinople in 863, the literary revival included a renewal of interest in classical literature. Ancient and early Byzantine works were collected, studied and summarised in encyclopaedic volumes, of which perhaps one of the best examples is Photius' (the Patriarch of Constantinople) 'Myriobiblon' ('Library'). About this time a taste for epigrams, didactic and allegorical poetry developed—a taste indulged by numerous well-known and popular authors. The famous epic tale of the

Byzantine struggles against the Muslim states, 'Basileus Digenis Akritas' ('King Digenis Akritas'), combined secular and religious themes; and the 11C also produced religious drama in verse and continued to meet the market for hagiographies. The military and political decline of the Empire juxtaposed, as is not unusual, with a revival in literature. In particular, after the Latin occupation of Constantinople from 1204, the influence of Latin literary subjects and the form of the epic, or tale in verse, popular with the Latin Crusaders, became fashionable. The kind of language used in literature began to be courtly; it is quite clear that no important literature ever appeared in the language and idiom of the people.

The two most important branches of scholarship in the Byzantine Empire were philosophy and history. Both, as with so many aspects of Eastern Roman culture and statecraft, continued the old traditions of Rome and the Hellenistic era for some centuries. Philosophy soon • became embroiled with the divergent views of Christian thinkers on the possible utilisation by Christianity of the old pagan culture in a harmonious way. Some encouraged this while others vehemently opposed it, yet, in general, one might argue that by the 9C Christian dogma dominated philosophy. Indeed, by the 11C the transfer of the products of Islamic civilisation and of ancient Hellenistic civilisation was fully realised by the Muslims of the Selçuk Turkish territories, so that the birth of the Renaissance and Reformation was chiefly assisted by the Islamic scholarship of the Selçuk period. Before the 6C, philosophy had been taught in the Christian centres of learning, often using the ancient traditions as a basis; for example, John Philoponus, teaching at Alexandria in the 6C, explained Christian belief by using Aristotelian logic and categories. This type of Christian thinking relying upon classical philosophy was long to continue; the 8C John of Damascus—one of the most outstanding Byzantine philosopher-theologians—argued that reality was revealed by God and that classical philosophy was the tool by which man might understand this revelation. Indeed, probably the most complete works of Orthodox dogma that we know is his 'Pege gnoseos' ('Fount of knowledge'). The independent philosophers gained ground from the mid 9C, their greatest representative, Michael Psellus, regarding Aristotelian logic and physics merely as a preliminary study to that of metaphysics. The independents, therefore, favoured Plato, Plotinus and Proclus over Aristotle. But orthodox Byzantine philosophy, right up to the 14C, remained largely under Aristotelian influence.

Byzantine historiography, of which probably Procopius of Caesarea and Michael Psellus are the best-known practitioners, tended to concentrate on its own history and that of the peoples with whom the Empire had relations. Thus, their histories provide much information on, for example, the Turkish clans and states of the Huns, Avars, Kuman-Kipçaks, Uz (Oğuz), Hazars, Peçeneks, Selçuks and Ottomans. The histories fall into three main categories—the 'Historia' (history), the 'Chronographia' (world history or chronicle) and the 'Ecclesiastica historia' (ecclesiastical history). But there seems to have been no major development in historiography under Byzantine rule.

As for the visual arts and architecture, the blending of the style of the preceding Roman and Hellenistic eras of Anatolia with the local traditions of far greater antiquity, within the context of an increasingly Christian interpretation, inspired that distinctive art we call Byzantine. Yet under the broad temporal and spatial umbrella of the Eastern Roman Empire there existed a number of local schools with their own, more or less differing, styles. Indeed, while Constantinople stood out as the main centre of artistic and other activities, the moving force in art remained, as always, Anatolia. The peoples of Anatolia adopted the Christianity of their rulers, and their traditions and beliefs, never totally lost, adapted to suit this new faith.

Those aspects of Byzantine art which were fairly immovable—walls, buildings, architectural sculpture and reliefs, murals and mosaics—are liberally scattered throughout the major towns and cities of Anatolia. But of the more easily transportable arts—gold and silver artefacts, ivory and enamel, materials woven in silk, illuminated manuscripts and icons—very little escaped the looting of the Crusades or the avid collecting of the Renaissance and modern periods; and a great deal is to be found gracing the museums of the European capitals—a testament to 19C imperial rivalry and imperial pomp. Indeed, that the buildings, especially those of a religious nature, still remain (a certain amount of disfiguration notwithstanding) is due only to the tolerance of the succeeding Ottoman dynasty of the Turks and of the Islamic faith, which, while they may have converted many churches into mosques, did not raze to the ground all vestiges of the alien religion as has been the case in so many countries which found themselves heirs to an Islamic society.

In Constantinople lie the remains of the Byzantine Empire's only really outstanding defensive walls—the city walls constructed under Theodosius II to contain the rapidly expanding capital, and running for over 5km from the Marmara Sea to the Golden Horn. In general, Byzantine defensive architecture was unambitious and rather undistinguished, contributing no real innovations in style or effectiveness. But central Anatolia is an interesting area for military architecture, with citadels, defensive walls and fortresses at Kotaion (Kütahya), Ankyra (Ankara) and Akroenos (Afyonkarahisar). Of other secular architecture, Constantinople is the chief source, with its magnificent triumphal arch, the Golden Gate, and various monuments such as Constantine's Hooped Column (Çemberlitaş) still standing. Of the numerous public squares and their linking colonnaded streets none remains, although the site of the famous Hippodrome—alongside Haghia Sophia and the Imperial Palace—and three of its monuments are still extant. The Palace itself comprised a huge complex of buildings that were continually improved and enlarged from the 6th to the 10C; after this, the imperial residence was transferred to the north-east of the city, the Blachernae quarter, where a sumptuous high pavilion dominated the Golden Horn. Excavation has also revealed some private palaces. But it was in the construction of aqueducts and cisterns to meet the water requirements of the capital's populace that Byzantine utilitarian architecture excelled, as evinced in the huge aqueduct of Valens (Roman Emperor in the East, AD 375—378) which extends for nearly a kilometre and the underground cistern (Yerebatan Sarayı) of Justinian with its 336 columns.

But given the religious complexion of the Byzantine Empire, it comes as no surprise that great attention was paid to church architecture, and a clear development may be discerned from the period of Justinian. It was during this time that the distinctive Byzantine style began to emerge, with the domination of the basilical form which was to become the basis of a universal church plan. This kind of longitudinal hall with central and flanking naves separated by columns directed the gaze of the congregation to the altar at one end. The earliest Christian basilicas in Anatolia include the Church of St. John Studios (Imrahor Camii) in İstanbul, the Church of the

Virgin Mary in Ephesus and some 5C churches in Pergamum and Cilicia. This basilical form gradually began to incorporate a dome over the central nave at the apse, in place of the old vaulted roof. And as the temper of religious thinking evolved to emphasise the directing upwards toward heaven of the worshippers' gaze, so the architectural tenor evolved towards a centralised structure of a square or even octagonal plan supporting a central dome. Examples of this style include the Church of SS. Sergius and Bacchus (Küçük Ayasofya Camii) in İstanbul and, most notably, the Church of Haghia Sophia, constructed during Justinian's reign by two Anatolian architects–Anthemios of Tralles and Isidoros of Miletus. The 9th to 13C, after the stagnation of the Iconoclastic period, witnessed the predominance of the cruciform style in which the central square was surmounted by a dome and surrounded by four arms forming a cross, as can be observed, for example, in the 10C Church of the Myralaion Convent (Bodrum Camii) and the Church of St. Saviour Pantepoptes (Eski İmaret Camii), both in İstanbul. After the demise of the Latin occupation of Constantinople and the accession of the Palaeologus dynasty from 1261 to the conquest of Constantinople, restoration rather than new building was the chief activity, using old building materials and cheaper, easier forms of decoration, such as fresco in place of mosaics. But the period shows much greater variety and vivacity in design and technique.

Away from the capital, every old pagan temple was converted sooner or later into a basilica as the Empire established itself. This transformation was sometimes achieved by ingenious innovations as at the Temple of Zeus Olbios at Diocaesarea (Uzuncaburç), but more often required no architectural alterations, the basilica simply being built around the existing temple, as at Side. In addition, numerous churches were built with their distinctive regional characteristics of style, technique and form. In western Anatolia, Ephesus became a prominent Byzantine city, its ancient cult of Artemis being replaced by that of the Virgin, who had her own basilica—the Church of the Virgin Mary—built and rebuilt on the remains of a huge ancient buiding. Also in Ephesus is the church built on what is said to be the tomb of St. John the Evangelist. Hierapolis became another major urban centre with a number of important buildings. Southern Anatolia, along the Mediterranean shore, holds a wealth of Byzantine monuments, for almost every ancient city became a Byzantine town of some importance, and religious and secular buildings abound. The Iconium (Konya) region of central Anatolia was the location of numerous monastic foundations including troglodyte rock churches —normally associated with Cappadocia. Ancient Cappadocia is famous for its churches, homes, chapels, hermits' cells and even convents hollowed out of the soft volcanic tufa that forms what are commonly known as 'fairy chimneys' (peri bacaları). In the eastern regions of Anatolia, around Lake Van, the Armenians developed an artistic style, particularly in architecture, so distinctive that it cannot really be included with the Byzantine.

What we know of the decorative arts of Byzantine Anatolia is, as I have pointed out, limited, but the bulk of our knowledge relates to architectural ornamentation such as frescoes and mosaics—of which numerous examples again trace a clear course through the long period of Byzantine history. As in the development of architecture, so the distinct Byzantine style of artistic decoration was evolving by Justinian's reign into low relief and rather abstract design, replacing the classical high relief and naturalistic designs. Yet the classicism of the naturalistic mosaics so well exemplified in the 5C mosaic pavements of Antioch, portraying hunting scenes, animals and trees, clearly lingered on well into the 6C, as in the mosaic pavement of the Great Palace of Constantinople with its rural scenes of hunting, fishing, playful children and various wild and domestic animals. But gradually mosaic decoration, particularly in religious architecture, was becoming more symbolic, blending into the spatial conception of the building. From about the middle of the 6C the icon, or holy personage depicted on a panel, began to dominate both art and religious devotion. The importance of the icon lay not in its symbolic or instructive purpose but in its role as representing the actual presence of the saintly personage, and it was against this aspect—the idolatrous worship of images—that the imperial Iconoclasts reacted so harshly, prompting the century-long period of Iconoclastic struggle. For this reason, little remains or is known of the art of the periods just preceding and during the century of Iconoclasm; but its final defeat in 843 on the grounds that rejection of the representation of the holy figure of Christ denied his humanity and thus made a nonsense of the Incarnation, opened the way to a flowering of Byzantine art from the 9th to the 11C.

This 'Golden Age' of Byzantine art developed most fully in wall mosaics and, in particular, the large-scale mosaic decorations created under the patronage of the court, the finest of which are to be found in Haghia Sophia. The richness and depth of the mosaics of this period can be attributed to the undulating technique combined with the mixture of reflecting glass, stone and even silver and gold pieces with matt terracotta, thus allowing light to play over the surface to give the brightly-coloured designs an effect of animation.

One of the most important regional developments in figurative art was that of the Cappadocian rock churches—the frescoes of Göreme, Ürgüp and Niğde being of particular interest for their narrative form and distinctive style and technique.

The final period of Byzantine art, dating from the regaining of Constantinople from the Latins in 1261 by the new Palaeologian dynasty until its conquest by the Ottomans, juxtaposed the severe political and economic decline of the Empire with a new humanistic vigour and creativity in the decorative arts. Among the fairly numerous works ascribed to this period, including the Deësis mosaic panel in the Haghia Sophia, probably the most outstanding is the Church of St. Saviour in Chora (Kariye Camii) in İstanbul, whose early 14C mosaics depict a series of scenes from the lives of Christ and the Virgin Mary, and whose frescoes portray scenes of the afterlife and Resurrection; all are vivid, expressive and animated in their detail, and both frescoes and mosaics have been preserved and restored to their original beauty.

In the minor arts, secular works have been discovered, or are known through historical sources. Particularly interesting are the early ivories and silver plates which bore a strong Hellenistic character as late as the 7C. Figurative sculpture, however, so prominent a genre in the Hellenistic period, seems to have sunk into a decline from the 5C, discouraged by the Church and lingering only in monuments to emperors until about the end of the 8C. Jewellery and textiles indicate closer links with eastern or pre-Hellenistic Anatolian designs, with motifs such as the lion-headed bird reminiscent of the Urartian fantastic-animal figures and the stylised tree between two birds or animals—the Tree of Life—dating back as far as the Late Hittite/Urartian period, if not further.

But in time the minor arts, particularly ivories and work in metal and enamel, came to be as preoccupied with religious themes as the other branches of art—notably miniatures and manuscript illustration—and scholarship in the Byzantine Empire. Precious materials like onyx and rock crystal were also used only for religious vessels, as was glass. Only metal and pottery seem to have been employed for household use.

Thus, the overwhelming image cast by the Byzantine Empire is one of intense, even brooding, religiosity in the arts and intellectual pursuits—but a religiosity combined, in statecraft and relations both domestic and foreign, with an overweening desire for temporal power and wealth, and a cruelty and deception astonishing even by the standards of the age. Yet these characteristics allowed the Empire to endure for nearly a thousand years and to produce a distinctive style of art and religious outlook that continues to this day in areas where the Eastern Orthodox Church survives. But despite its idiosyncratic Christianity, and conviction of its place as the legitimate successor to the Roman Empire—with Justinian's ambition in the 6C to restore the old Roman boundaries in their entirety—the sheer physical geography and ethnic composition of the Empire rooted it definitively in its Anatolian past. The Byzantine Empire, then, with its pivotal position amidst numerous cultural influences—both spatial and temporal—could never be considered a truly European state; drawing on its Anatolian heritage, the Byzantine Empire was but one in a series of Anatolian civilisations.

VIII.   The Selçuks

The arrival of the Selçuk Turks on the Anatolian scene in the 11C did not signify the arrival of the Turks in general, but rather their emergence as an organised political entity in Anatolia. Large-scale migrations of Turkish peoples from their ancestral lands, roughly between the Ural and Altay mountain ranges of Central Asia, had been occurring since time immemorial. These were chiefly due to the cyclical recurrence of climatic changes involving the progressive dessication and therefore desertification of huge areas of the arable and pasture-land on which their steppe economy depended, concomitant with increasing pressure of population over the centuries. Indeed, similar cultural elements encountered as far apart, in the Old World, as China, India, Mesopotamia, Anatolia and central Europe may be said to be located around the rim, as it were, of the cultural hub of the Central Asian steppe—a hub comprising the forefathers of the Turks. The characteristic steppe culture of the Turks derived from an admixture of sedentary and nomadic lifestyles, in varying proportions during the course of time as policy dictated. Sections of this autochthonous people, as they moved away from the ancestral homelands—simply migrating or conquering as they went—tended to call themselves, and be known by, their more immediate tribal or clan names. But this practice, natural though it may have been in territories and among peoples where the majority belonged to the same, Turkish, race, has served only to divert the attention of contemporaries, perhaps, and succeeding generations, certainly, from the actual racial unity of the apparently diverse peoples who

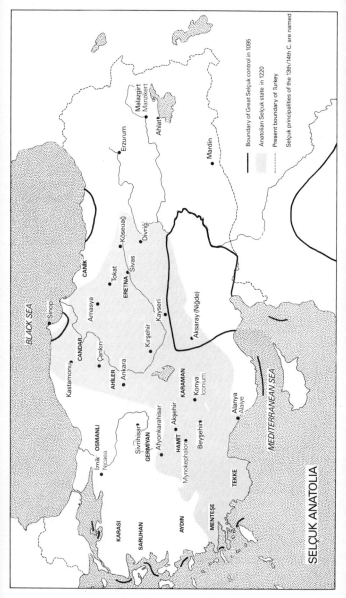

Boundary of Great Selçuk control in 1095

Anatolian Selçuk state in 1220

Present boundary of Turkey

Selçuk principalities of the 13th/14th C. are named

Malazgirt
Manzikert

Ahlat

Erzurum

Mardin

Köseuağ

Divriğ

Sinop

Tokat

Amasya

Sivas

ERETNA

Kayseri

Kırşehir

Aksaray (Niğde)

BLACK SEA

CANIK

CANDAR

Kastamonu

Çankırı

AHILER

Ankara

KARAMAN

Konya
Iconium

Alanya
Alaiye

İznik
Nicaea

Sivrihisar

Afyonkarahisar

Akşehir

Beyşehir

GERMIYAN

HAMIT

Myrokephalon

OSMANLI

MEDITERRANEAN SEA

TEKKE

KARASI

SARUHAN

AYDIN

MENTEŞE

SELÇUK ANATOLIA

have been moving west and settling in, for example, Anatolia since the beginning of recorded time.

Indeed, it was only in the 6C that the Göktürk Empire of the steppe-land west of the Orhon River, stretching from Manchuria to the shores of the Black Sea, emerged as the first state to take its name from that of the people who founded it and comprised its nucleus—the Turks. Yet it can be said with certainty that the Huns of Central Asia, as early as the first millennium BC, were among the first politically-organised groups of Turks participating in and changing written history.

Hence, we can see that the Anatolian Selçuk Turks of the 11C AD were simply the latest in a long history of Turkish migrations; for in the racial and cultural mix of historic and prehistoric Anatolia there had always been a strong Turkish, or Proto-Turkish, presence. But Selçuk is the name of the people and dynasties who directly caused the Turkish domination of the Islamic world and initiation of an entirely new age in the history of Islamic civilisation. The Selçuks comprised two main branches and ruled between the 11th and 14C in Turkistan, Harezm (Khwarizm), Horasan, Afghanistan, Iran, Iraq, Syria, Azerbaycan (Azerbaijan) and Anatolia. The parent body was that of the Great Selçuks, incorporating the Iran, Iraq and Syria Selçuks, and its offshoot comprised the Anatolian (or Rum; derived from Roman) Selçuks, both descendants of the Oğuz (Uz) Turks. The Great Selçuks' displacement of the ruling Turkish Gazneli (Gaznavid) dynasty in 1040 established their domination over the Iranian plateau territory, and from this base their ruler, Tuğrul Bey (1038–63) overwhelmed the Abbasid Caliphate of Baghdad in 1055, becoming protector of the Caliphate. In this way, the Great Selçuks became rulers of virtually the entire western region of the Islamic world from their centre of government in Iran.

It was from this foundation that the Muslim Turkification of Anatolia derived, out of which the Anatolian Selçuk State was to emerge in due course. And this Muslim Turkification—through the large-scale migration of groups of Turks (often known as Türkmens) under the leadership of their *Beys*, and their constant harassment of the Armenian and Georgian buffer-states and eastern frontiers of the Byzantine Empire—was carefully orchestrated by the dual policy of the Great Selçuk rulers. First, they found it expedient to prepare a base composed of their own kith and kin—whether Muslim or pagan—for future expansions. Secondly, with the continuous arrival of new groups of nomadic Turks from Central Asia, they needed both to ease the pressure of population and to divert these unruly nomadic clans away from the settled urban society of the Selçuks' new empire; and where better than the fertile pastures and uplands of Anatolia that so resembled the steppe country of their homeland? Thus, the migrants were controlled and encouraged to establish their own petty territories over eastern Anatolia, all later to be incorporated into the Anatolian Selçuk State. For example, the Saltuk principality (1072–c 1202) was established by Emir Saltuk, one of the commanders in the battle of Manzikert (Malazgirt) in 1071, who was duly awarded territory around Erzurum by the Sultan in return for military service; such was the normal pattern. But the main thrust of the Great Selçuk offensive under Alp Arslan (1063–72) and his son Melikşah (1072–92) was carried out by Süleyman Şah who advanced after the battle of Malazgirt right across Anatolia to take İznik (Nicaea) on the south-eastern tip of the Marmara Sea in 1078.

The absence of a united Byzantine/Latin Christian front paved the way for Süleyman Şah's expansionist policies in the 1080s, to the extent that he was soon in a position to charge customs duties on ships passing through the Bosphorus Straits (İstanbul Boğazı). Yet in the ensuing years, the partial recuperation of the Byzantine Empire, aided by disunity among the petty Turkish rulers constantly squabbling over succession and the spoils of victory, was compounded with the Crusader attacks from 1096. Then it took nearly a century to consolidate Anatolian Selçuk power and authority, if not influence— a consolidation marked by the battle of Myriokephalon in 1176. And what had long been seen by their adversaries as land under Turkish occupation now became known universally as Turkia (Turquia or Turchia)—a Turkish homeland.

Further victories, defeats and internecine strife continued, and out of this struggle the dominant Anatolian Selçuk State reached its zenith in the reign of Alâeddin Keykubad (1220–37), only to be confronted shortly afterwards with a new 'crusade', this time from the east. The Mongols (or, more correctly, Moğols), the other autochthonous people of Central Asia, had, like the Turks, their own long history of movement, migration and invasion far distant from their homeland, often in conjunction with but also without or even against their old neighbours, the Turks. The Mongols now confronted the Selçuk Turks in Anatolia, this time with an added dimension of pagan versus Muslim. And at the famous battle of Kösedağ in 1243 the Selçuks lost. Anatolia plunged once more into political turmoil. While Turkification increased with the influx of numerous Turks driven before the Mongol armies, Anatolian Turkish political unity was shattered; but its Islamisation continued unabated due to the non hostile stance of the newly-converted Mongols towards Islam.

All told, the Empire of the Great Selçuks and its branch, the Anatolian Selçuk State, comprised a harmonious blend of both Turkish and Islamic elements, a synthesis of the Islamic cultural environment with the customs and traditions—political, economic, legal, even psychological—of the Turkish steppe culture.

The most prominent feature of the state was the Turkish 'feudal' structure that had characterised it since the early, pagan, Göktürk and later, Muslim, say Karahanlı empires. According to this, the state was considered the common property of the ruling dynasty and thus the succession did not pass to a single prince but was divided up amongst them all, leading inevitably to numerous succession struggles as the multiple heirs fought for primacy. The Great Selçuks incorporated this feudal tradition into their statecraft, awarding royal princes and Turkmen beys their various rights according to the feudal hierarchy, when Tuğrul Bey himself took the Islamic title of Sultan after the battle of Dandanakan in 1040 and drew all the feudal beys under his mandate. However, the sheer power and privilege of the beys·was a major obstacle to the Selçuk attempts to unify and centralise the state, an obstacle that was reduced by the state recruitment of new Turkish emirs according to the system of patron/ client mutual obligation (kul in Turkish; cliens in Latin), according to which senior positions were filled by those who had no other source of backing except the monarch. However, the established Turkish law accepting the state as the common property of the entire dynasty was too strong to be broken, at least by the Selçuks. The new emirs rapidly accumulated local dynastic power like that of the feudal beys, and despite the title of Sultan acquiring the sense of Imperator or Hakan (Kağan) during the Selçuk period, it never represented an absolute authority on the lines of that of the Iranian Sassanid or the Byzantine emperors. Indeed, the Great Selçuk title of Sultan al-'Azam (Greater Sultan) implicitly acknowledged the existence of lesser sultans, or local rulers. And the succession struggles continued to constitute the state's greatest weakness; for example, in 1185 the Anatolian Selçuk, Kılıç Arslan II (1156–92) in his old age divided his state amongst his 11 sons, each attached directly to himself but independent of one another, but immediate strife broke out which only increased on the death of Kılıç Arslan—the exposed vulnerability at once attracting attack and invasion from Crusaders, Byzantines, Armenians of Cilicia and others who sought to take their advantage. Yet for all this, in contrast with the feudal system of contemporary Europe and the 'feudal' tendencies of later Ottoman state practice—which served to promote the stagnation of society with its excessive emphasis on a stability engendered through the succession of the first-born son regardless of talent—the Selçuk tradition, while it certainly provoked instability through internecine struggle, did ensure the primacy of merit.

Moreover, the position of primacy held by the successful prince was enhanced during the Selçuk period by the partnership of Sultan and Caliph. On the Great Selçuk Sultan, Tuğrul Bey, becoming the protector of the Caliph and being proclaimed 'World Ruler' in Baghdad in the Caliph's Palace in 1058, the Sultan was authorised to enact civil laws. This paved the way for the outstanding religious tolerance that was to mark the Selçuk period and offered support and succour to its numerous non-Muslim subjects—various Christian sects, Jews and pagans. On the fall of the Great Selçuks, the mantle of partner and protector of the Caliph was donned by the Anatolian Selçuks who continued to contain the Caliph within the bounds of religion.

Within the Selçuk state—whether Great Selçuk or Anatolian—there continued to be a special emphasis on Turkish titles in state administration and, indeed, Turkish administrative titles such as *Atabey* (Prince's tutor) and *Subaşı* (Superintendent) permeated even as far as the Delhi Sultanate in India. The Sultan normally retained his Turkish personal name and added a Muslim one—for example, 'İzz-al-Din Kılıç Arslan II—and used, after the ratification of his position by the Caliphate, Islamic titles bestowed by the Caliphate, such as Kasîm Emîr ül-Mü'minîn (Partner of the Caliphate). The *Hutbe* (Friday prayer) was read throughout the land in the name of the Sultan, and his signature adorned edicts and central government decisions.

Government was broadly administered through four separate *Divâns* (Ministries) under a *Divân-ı Vezâret* (Prime Ministry) presided over by the *Sahib Divân-ı Saltanat* or *Hâce-i Buzurg* (Prime Minister) who was second only to the Sultan in authority. The Sultan reserved certain days of the week for audience with high officials, the distribution of military 'fiefs', the ratification of the appointment of vassal rulers and, significantly, the direct reception of his subjects as suppliants. Besides the central administration, the provinces were carefully administered down to the smallest town with its locally elected head. The sophistication of the Selçuk provincial administration may be deduced from its advanced communications and intelligence systems, with fortified positions along all major routes—especially trade routes—protecting the freedom of the highways and with military stations sited along the frontiers.

The Selçuk Sultan presided over the high court in cases of treason against the state and appointed judges (*kadıs*) to the judiciary. The highest of those was the Kadı of Konya, the capital, who supervised both consuetudinary (secular; *örf*) and canonical (religious; *şeriat*) jurisdiction, the latter administered according to the Hanefi school of jurisprudence. The armed forces had their own, separate kadıs.

The armed forces were the object of one of the most important and far-reaching innovations effected by the Selçuks' Turkish/Islamic synthesis—the military/economic institution of *iktâ* ('fief'). This was a system by which the state could mobilise and maintain huge armies at minimal expense. Specific territory was allocated in lieu of salary to a state official who was responsible for its administration and for the payment of tax therefrom. This iktâ could be transferred from father to son, provided the duty was inherited, thus ensuring a long-term interest in the welfare of the land and its population. By this method the Selçuks created not only a valid form of maintenance for the Türkmens who formed the backbone of the army and state, but also a positive inducement to benevolent local administration, public works and agricultural development in that greater production increased income but extortionate policies would ruin the inheritance for the iktâ-holder's successors. For the Selçuk soldiers, who were carefully dispersed throughout the Anatolian provinces and were maintained and equipped by the land-taxes, were under the command of the *Subaşıs* who resided in the provincial centres and represented the central authority of the Selçuk state. Indeed, it might be argued that the advantage of the military iktâ system lay in the spreading in this way of Selçuk sovereignty over as wide an area as possible. The Anatolian Selçuks, unlike the Great Selçuks, did not grant huge iktâs; they were clearly aware that these would be difficult to control. A Subaşı who was also the governor of a province, was granted only a small iktâ for his personal maintenance and that of any soldiers residing on this land; otherwise he exerted only military and administrative authority over the province to which he was appointed, and could claim no right of possession over the land or the soldiers, as loss of the duty for any reason meant loss of these. While the iktâ cavalry was fundamental to the Selçuk armed forces, there were also the permanent troops maintained centrally. These comprised two groups: troops under Türkmen commanders who held centrally-located iktâs, and kuls of the Palace—salaried personnel directly attached to the Sultan, recruited from various races and educated at the Palace, serving under commanders selected for their merit and loyalty, and in permanent readiness for battle. There was also a special unit of mercenaries composed of non-Muslim Turks and Christians of various origins. The provincial and central armies, then, were the two major sources of soldiery; at their peak, the Anatolian Selçuks could mobilise 100,000 men under arms, with a central salaried force of 12,000. Clearly, the aim of minimal expenditure in maintaining as large and as well-motivated a military as possible was a valid one.

The iktâ system was as relevant to Selçuk land economy as it was to Selçuk military organisation. It was one of three main types of land dispensed by the state, to which all land belonged (as *mirî*). İktâ was granted in return for a duty and could be reclaimed if that duty were given up, although, as we have seen, provincial iktâs tended to become hereditary, as did the duty. *Vakıf* comprised land belonging to the Sultan, the taxes of which were allocated to the upkeep of institutions of learning or of social welfare. *Mülk* was land separated from that of the Sultan and granted freely and without qualification to persons of distinction or to those who had performed some outstanding service. It was often turned into vakıf on the demise of the recipient, although it was inheritable.

As for the residents of the land, these were classified according to the type of land on which they resided, and gave their service and taxes to those under whom they worked, but they were not slaves tied to the land (or serfs), and they possessed recognised rights of objection and disobedience. Our knowledge of the population on the land is derived largely from the numerous censuses of population and land, including newly conquered lands, carried out by the Selçuks whose provincial administration, as I have pointed out, was detailed and painstaking.

Economic development was paramount in the transition of the steppe Turks into a predominantly settled culture based on an urban society. A massive surge in overland trade between Anatolia and the Near East, Central Asia and eastern Europe, and in maritime trade between Anatolia and the Far East, India, the Mediterranean and the whole of Europe, was stimulated by a number of factors. Chief among these must have been the growing Selçuk political stability and centralisation of power, combined with their administrative sophistication which controlled the major trade routes under the overall protection of their vast armed forces.

Since the early Islamic period, the domination of the eastern Mediterranean trade by the Muslim states and the Christian/Muslim conflicts of the area had blocked Anatolia from the main routes of maritime trade, to the extent that the later Byzantine period of rule in Anatolia had been one of stagnation. Indeed, it is hard to find widespread material evidence of a prosperous and thriving urban society to match that of Hellenistic or Roman Anatolia, except to a limited extent in the eastern region which had long been under Islamic domination. But the impetus of the Selçuks in the 13C changed all this and opened up the international trade routes, by land and sea, between the Muslim and Christian lands, and thereby stimulated the very marked economic prosperity of the country.

The Selçuk sultans well understood the importance of the transit trade and adjusted their military and economic policies accordingly. They conquered the Black Sea and Mediterranean ports and transferred to them a Turkish population with trading skills and capital, they concluded trade agreements with the Latins, they levied low customs duties—all tactics directed towards the stimulation of trade and the economy. Perhaps most interesting was the very first appearance of a kind of state insurance which guaranteed the losses of tradesmen resulting from brigands on land or from corsairs and foreign navies at sea.

Overland trade was organised in *kervans* (caravans); and at every staging post was located a *kervansaray* (caravansarai), built to cater for all the needs of the traveller entirely free of charge. All travellers could enter and stay for up to three days with full board, medical attention for the sick and new shoes for the poor. Some even contained libraries and chess-sets (chess was a popular pastime) for the entertainment of travellers. These kervansarays were elaborately organised and often enormous, employing their own staff, including a resident doctor, running a medical unit, and a small mosque for prayers, and raising their own flocks for feeding their guests. They were run as vakıfs, of which the first, written condition was that every traveller be treated equally regardless of economic, social, religious or ethnic status. And they doubled up effectively as fortresses when necessary. For example, one kervansaray near Aksaray (Niğde) was besieged for two months by a Mongol commander and his troops when a Turkish bey took refuge with his 20,000 soldiers, but held out successfully; clearly a fully fortified and self-sufficient complex of buildings. Indeed, travellers and traders from all over the world—but most notably Marco Polo and Ibn Battuta—were full of admiration and praise for the charity, comfort and security provided to all, without any charge, on the vast road network and in the cities and towns of the Selçuk State. For, in addition to the kervansarays, the Selçuks maintained institutions such as the *misafirhâne* (guesthouse), *imâret* (charitable institution serving food to the poor) and *zâviye* (religious lodge) which welcomed freely as their guests travellers, the poor, members of learned societies and so on.

All this clearly indicates the level of benevolence of the state. Indeed, the records of these institutions show the quantities of sheep, rice, cracked wheat (bulgur), honey, oil and other foodstuffs required for their charitable activities. And the aim, above all, was the display of the munificence and beneficence of the state so as to improve and increase the people's sense of gratitude, obligation and loyalty to the central authority, possibly at the cost of their individuality. It is no wonder that all the neighbouring Turkish buffer-states also allocated substantial resources to welfare services such as these; for the wealth and magnificence of the state was measured in terms of its degree of charitable care and welfare for its subjects.

Similarly, the larger cities contained colonies for foreigners and religious minorities, notably Iranians, Arabs, non-Muslim Turks such as İdil (Volga) Bulgars and Kıpçaks, Latin and other Christians, and Jews. These had their own districts with *hans* (inns), Christian and Jewish religious sanctuaries and, in Konya and Sivas, Latin consulates to look after the special needs of their communities.

Not surprisingly, parallel with the rapid and massive development of international trade, Anatolian Selçuk cities grew in size, population and wealth, with Konya, Sivas and Kayseri achieving prominence among a range of thriving urban communities across Anatolia from the Black Sea to the Mediterranean, some newly established by the Selçuks, others given new vitality and yet others completely rebuilt and renovated after centuries of warfare, sieges and economic neglect. As international trade increased, there also grew up the huge international fairs for which Anatolia has long been well-known, mostly just outside cities and towns—that near Kayseri on the trade route between Anatolia, Syria and Iraq being considered one of the largest. In response to the development of maritime trade, dockyards were established at Sinop and Alaiye (Alanya) for the northern and southern fleets respectively.

But Anatolia was not simply a well-organised vehicle for the international transit trade under the Selçuks. Contemporary opinion attributed its great wealth not merely to its extensive trade and low customs duties but also to its high level of agricultural and industrial production, based on rich natural resources, fertile soil and abundant flocks and herds. Past history can testify to Anatolia's ever-abundant agricultural and mineral resources. In addition to extensive export of animals and grain, industries based on the extraction and export of iron ore, silver, copper, alum and salt grew up. A thriving carpet industry developed, the Selçuks introducing woven carpets to Anatolia, and the products of Selçuk Türkmen weavers were exported to Islamic and Christian countries alike. The production of mohair and silk cloth (the latter known among the Christians as Turkish silk, *seta Turchia*) as well as numerous varieties and patterns of wool, cotton and silk material, including the famous Selçuk velvet brocades, was prominent especially in Bursa and Üsküdar, and exports went all over the world. Other industries included leather, dyes, soap, oil and wax for lamps, while many cities developed their own viticulture and cultivation of medicinal plants for export. Certain luxury goods were imported, such as sugar from Egypt, furs from the northern Bulgar and Kıpçak Turks, glass from Iraq and satins from the Byzantine state. In addition, cloth of various qualities and some armaments such as helmets and ballistae were both home-produced (mainly in Sivas) and imported.

The economic prosperity of Selçuk Anatolia was reflected in the private wealth of individuals, as evinced by their conspicuous consumption, particularly in wedding celebrations, dowries and so forth. And not just entrepreneurial activity, but the extraordinarily high salaries and iktâ incomes of statesmen and senior officials provided for this kind of lifestyle. Moreover, while in the Islamic world generally it was the Jews who were the great bankers and moneylenders, in Selçuk Anatolia prominent Muslim Turkish bankers and moneylenders were also numerous. Indeed, the money economy, with its common use of money orders and bills of exchange, can be said to have been highly developed—it is possible that the English word 'cheque' derives, via Arabic and the Crusaders, from the Turkish verb *çekmek* (to draw [money]). The Selçuk rulers evidently followed a specific monetary policy as they regulated and encouraged trade, limiting the passage of cash out of the country so that the wealthy were encouraged to invest in industry and construction and other immovable property. Selçuk gold coins were in high demand elsewhere, due to careful maintenance of the standard and value of the coinage right up to the Mongol invasions.

As in their welfare policies, so the Selçuk religious stance attested their zeal in seeking to display the Islamic faith which they had so recently discovered. Thus the Selçuks in Anatolia revealed all the enthusiasm of the newly converted with a corresponding lack of profound knowledge of the faith they so ardently embraced—a combination which must surely have accounted in no small measure for their great tolerance. Indeed, the syncretic Islam of the Anatolian Turks, originating as they did from Central Asia with their own coherent religion, to this day reflects their strong tendency towards shamanistic practices, particularly in folk dances, folk music and folk customs. And the Selçuk rulers seem primarily to have sought to intensify the Islamic adherence and belief of the newly-arriving Türkmen nomads. For, as the Selçuks conquered new lands, they immediately set up religious buildings and, especially in the areas bordering Byzantine Christian territory, encouraged religious zealots and dervishes to travel there, stimulating yet further the Islamic belief of the Muslim inhabitants and settlers. Thus, the resettlement and repopulation policies of the Selçuks may be seen as running parallel with their policy of Islamisation of the Türkmens. And coupled with this, it should be borne in mind that the Selçuks, on entering Anatolia, entered a predominantly Christian land, where no doubt pronounced religious tolerance would be politically expedient in establishing an effective rule. Certainly, the whole tenor of the Selçuks' religious policy indicated their keen desire to show the supremacy of Islam in every aspect, so that there was no need for the use of force in order to convert the populace who, in turn, were able to reside and worship freely and without constraint as they wished—as is evident from the judicial records of the canonical law-courts and from local place names.

Not surprisingly, all these factors combined to produce a most syncretic Islamic belief in Anatolia—a synthesis of views and backgrounds that prepared the ground for the emergence of such humanitarian and tolerant thinkers as Mevlâna Celâleddin Rumî, Muhiddîn İbn 'Arabî and Yunus Emre. For the official Sunni orthodoxy of the state in no way debarred or discouraged Sufî mysticism, one of the main functions of which was the creating of a link between the intellectuals and the people. On the contrary it is likely that one of the factors most instrumental in the spread of *sufism* was the Mongol invasions and devastation, for the widespread spiritual crisis and despair thus created proved fertile ground for the establishment of mystic orders (*tarikats*). The Selçuks were noted for their invitations to prominent Islamic figures—be they of Turkish, Iranian or Arab origin and whether of orthodox or Sufî persuasion—and Selçuk Anatolia became a sanctuary for many of these. During this period, the most important scholars of the Islamic world dwelt in areas under Turkish domination, and particularly in the various Selçuk domains.

The policies of the Selçuks in Anatolia and elsewhere of founding throughout their lands mosques, *medreses* (Islamic institutes of higher education), libraries, medical schools, hospitals, imârets, zâviyes, and kervansarays, all deriving their income and maintenance from vakıf lands, formed one of their finest contributions to the history of civilisation. But most important was the Selçuk organisation of the medreses—previously left to private benefactors—under state patronage, maintained by vakıfs and offering free education. Allocations were usually made for teachers and students, and further incentive to scholarship came through the provision of prize money. With the Selçuk domination of the Islamic world, this state provision for medreses became widespread.

In the medrese, besides the study of Islam, philosophy, mathematics, astronomy and medicine were all taught in the larger centres, and some, if not all, in the smaller or more remote ones—depending to some extent on the degree of tolerance of the local religious hierarchy. The larger Selçuk cities, such as Konya, Kayseri, Sivas, Erzurum and Mardin, boasted several medreses each, and most towns had access to one; for example, the Caca Bey Medrese in Kırşehir, which was originally established as an observatory.

As far as the medical sciences were concerned, Selçuk Anatolia was well endowed in the 13C. Three medical schools—the Gevher Hatun Şifaîye founded in Kayseri in 1205, the İzzeddin Keykâvus Darüşşifa founded in Sivas in 1217, and the Turan Melek Darüşşifa founded in Divriği in 1228—functioned as hospitals as well as centres of learning; the İzzeddin Keykâvus Darüşşifa, for example, employed a large staff including doctors, ophthalmologists and surgeons and was financed by several vakıfs. As the 13C progressed, another hospital—the Atabeg Ferruh—was founded in Çankırı in 1235, and more medical centres at Amasya (1266), Kastamonu (1272) and Tokat (1275). Books of medicine were also written and studied.

In addition to the natural and medical sciences, other intellectual disciplines flourished in Selçuk Anatolia, not least because so many noted Sufi mystics (*mutasavvuf*) found it such a suitable environment, especially among the newly converted populace. The list is long of prominent mystics, philosophers, historians and literary figures of the Islamic world who accepted Selçuk hospitality and resided in Anatolia at some stage in their careers or, like Celâleddîn Rumî, spent their days there in tranquillity away from the turbulence of the Mongol invasions; the mystics Sadreddîn Konevî and Necmeddîn Dâye, the philosopher Şehâbeddîn Suhraverdî, the poets Yunus Emre and Nizâmeddîn Gencevî, and the historians Râvendî, İbn Bîbî, Kadı Burhâneddîn Anevî and later Kerimuddîn Aksarayî would certainly be included, along with the world-famous Nasreddîn Hoca of Sivrihisar—the ubiquitous hero of countless Sufi parables all over the Middle East to this day.

The scholars and writers of the Selçuk period preferred to use Arabic as the language of religion, Farsî (Persian) as the language of state and of literature, and Turkish as the language of business and of conversation. Thus, in the literary field, Farsî became the accepted tongue even though a number of celebrated examples show that the Turkish language could provide no less artistic a medium. The great poet, Yunus Emre, wrote indisputably the best mystical poetry of the period entirely in the most excellent Turkish, and Celâleddîn Rumî and his son, Sultan Veled, composed poetry in Turkish in addition to their usual Farsî compositions, while in Konya and in other large cities resided a number of authors and poets who wrote in Turkish—such as Ahmed Fakîh, Hoca Dehhânî, Hoca Mes'ûd and Şeyyâd Hamza. Yet, ironically, the tradition of writing in Farsî continued, most likely through some kind of intellectual snobbery, as it were, with Turkish-speaking poets boasting to one another that their Farsî was even better than that of native Iranian poets. In addition, as with the language of state, the adoption of Farsî seems to have been a deliberate choice, as a means of distancing the ruling classes from the people. Further, in the ethnic mix of Turk, Arab and Iranian at the Selçuk court, the adoption of a language other than Turkish would avoid the exclusiveness of a racially Turkish and Turkish-speaking aristocracy, while at the same time reserving Turkish as a private, and even confidential, means of communication between the royal family and their closest aides.

The flowering of the architectural and decorative arts in Selçuk Anatolia represents one of the most spectacular developments of the Islamic world during this period. The prominence of architecture obviously derives from the active construction policy undertaken by Selçuk monarchs in all spheres of life and over all parts of their territories. Konya, the capital, was a large city containing numerous public buildings including the Sultan's Palace and a Great Mosque (Alâeddîn Camii). It was enclosed by a fortified wall with, as contemporary accounts tell us, 144 towers constructed of finely cut stone and boasting antique columns decorated with lions, deer, elephants and dragons carved in relief. But most towns overspilled their fortifications and show little concern for spatial organisation or indeed any comprehensive urban planning—surprising in view of the Selçuks' acute sense of planning at the regional and state levels, as attested by their highly developed communications system.

Selçuk architecture in Anatolia derived its inspiration from a number of sources—from the tented communities of their Central Asian ancestral homeland, from the Islamic traditions of the Middle East and in particular of the Great Selçuk Empire, and from local Anatolian styles and the dictates of geography. Out of all these influences, Anatolian Selçuk architecture developed its own distinctive form, spatial organisation and decoration, to achieve a new and original style.

Apart from palaces and fortifications, of which little remains bar contemporary descriptions and some archaeological evidence, the bulk of Selçuk architectural energy was directed into religious buildings and public works of a charitable aspect funded as religious endowments. The former include mosques, *mescids* (small local mosques without a *mimber*—pulpit) and türbes. 12C mosques in eastern and central Anatolia are unrelated experiments in building rather than steps in the development of a definite style, but by the 13C the basilica style was becoming widespread with its light-wells and domes, as in the ornate Ulu Cami—the sole remaining isolated masterpiece of this style—in Divriği, or even triple domes, as in the Alâeddîn Camii in Niğde, the Ulu Cami in Sinop and, most significantly, the Gök Medrese Camii in Amasya whose series of triple-domed units has been suggested as the prototype of the multi-domed Great Mosque of the early Ottoman period.

A second major Selçuk style features numerous beautifully-carved wooden posts inside the mosque and a flat wooden roof resting on unassuming stone walls devoid of ornamentation; the pillars sometimes bear antique Hellenistic or Byzantine marble capitals and sometimes rest on them. These mosques, notably the Ulu Cami at Afyonkarahisar and the Eşrefoğlu Camii at Beyşehir, reveal a direct evolution from the portable prayer-tents with their carved wooden support-posts of the newly-converted nomadic Türkmens of Central Asia, via the mosques with carved wooden posts of 11th and 12C Central Asia and are thus an example of the direct Turkish contribution to Anatolian culture. The domed türbes, to be found all over central Anatolia, characteristically free-standing with their round or octagonal form resting on a square base, seem to hark back to Central Asian steppe traditions—the shamanistic Gök-Türks mummified the dead and kept them in a tent for six months before burying them.

In the realm of Selçuk public architecture, we find a wide variety of buildings ranging from the medreses and *hânekâhs* (dervish monasteries) to *hamams* (Turkish baths) and hospitals. Buildings were chiefly of stone, rather than the bricks of the Great Selçuk and other Muslim states' preference, and the use of this material in construction stimulated the magnificent Selçuk craftsmanship in stone-carving. Carved-stone decoration in the form of figural and abstract geometrical designs appeared on all kinds of buildings and on the stone features such as the *mihrab* (niche indicating the direction of Mecca) and mimber of the mosques. The earlier preference for geometrical patterns, angular calligraphic inscriptions, simple rosettes and *mukarnes* (stalactites) gradually altered during the course of the 13C to incorporate a more ornate, even baroque, style with delicate but richly intricate floral motifs and more cursive calligraphic border patterns. The harmony in style and form throughout Anatolia was marked, the only appreciable regional difference being that the eastern cities such as Erzurum, Sivas and Divriği favoured a very high relief, while the central Anatolian regions of Konya and Kayseri practised a low relief with very fine decorative work.

In stonework, as in other decorative forms employed by the Selçuks, figural representation, both human and animal, abounded. The characteristic human figure—occasionally a woman, but more commonly a man—was depicted sitting cross-legged holding a handkerchief or pomegranate, musical instrument or cup, and surrounded by attendants. Round faces, almond-shaped eyes and small mouths reflected the Central Asian ideal of beauty, reminiscent of Uygur-Turfan wall-paintings. Small human heads often appeared in rosettes or scattered among arabesques on Selçuk portals, mihrabs and capitals—apparently in a shamanistic usage as charms or amulets. Most remarkable, perhaps, was the existence in Konya of free-standing human statuary; the 12C Arab traveller, al-Harawî, described in detail the statues of both men and women adorning the gardens of the wealthy, while a later Arab, al-Ghazzî, commented disapprovingly during his 16C travels on the human statues at the city gates and along the city walls—so life-like 'they seemed on the verge of speech'. This representation of the human figure, even in the most religious buildings and artefacts and even in the form of sculpture-in-the-round, is yet another indication of the intellectual openness of Islam reflecting on the vibrant syncretic vigour of Selçuk Anatolia.

The real, mythical and fantastical animal depictions in all types of art similarly reveal influences from the pre-Islamic shamanism of Central Asia as well as traditional motifs of Anatolian antiquity—if indeed these were not the same thing. Lions and bulls, for example, were common in Selçuk decorative arts, as were double-headed eagles, all of which, as we have seen, recur time and again in the Anatolian civilisations. The Tree of Life appears once more as a significant ornamental element of Selçuk architecture, often in conjunction with a pair of lions or dragons or as part of the arabesque forming the background for double-headed eagles or lions. The dragon—usually depicted in pairs with entwined and knotted bodies—common to Chinese art is very differently portrayed in Selçuk decoration, yet the connection through the Türkmens' migrations across Asia over the centuries, even millennia, is quite clear. And the conjunction of many of these human and shamanistic animal figures with astrological motifs such as planets and signs of the zodiac reveal complex and interesting symbolism throughout Selçuk decorative art; as does also the more rare appearance of sphinxes, sirens, winged angels, griffons and harpies—magical creatures believed to be endowed with supernatural powers of protection. As for the natural world, all kinds of birds and animals appear and hunting scenes are especially common in non-religious architecture, for instance, on the stucco so popular in palace decoration.

Stucco held an important place in early Islamic architecture, both religious and secular. Yet in contrast to the Great Selçuk Empire where stucco was much used and developed considerably, Selçuk Anatolia, with its preference for stone-carving, reserved stucco mainly for palaces. Of these, the most interesting and important examples, portraying many of the motifs available to Selçuk artists, were in the Kubadâbâd Palace at Beyşehir and the Pavilion of Kılıç Arslan II in the Alâeddîn Palace at Konya.

Probably the most important form of Selçuk decorative art in the façades and furnishings of, particularly, religious buildings was woodwork. The style and technique of Selçuk wood-carving was remarkably developed and produced spectacular effects. It was employed on doors, window-panels, columns and capitals, pillars, beams, consoles and mihrabs, and on such furnishings as mimbers and lecterns (*rahle*). But the most outstanding achievement was arguably in the monumental wooden mihrabs and mimbers. Great skill and craftsmanship was required for the complex *kündekâri* technique based on tongue-in-groove construction whereby individually-carved units were fitted together to compose panels that created larger pieces, as can be seen in the mimbers of the Alâeddîn Camii in Konya, the Ulu Cami of Sivrihisar and the Eşrefoğlu Camii at Beyşehir. The meticulous attention and skill required for such work, however, was not always forthcoming, so that various types of false kündekâri emerged, apparently the same but in fact carved from single solid blocks subsequently attached with pins or glue to the mimber or other architectural feature to be adorned. This inferior work also tended to warp and split, unlike true kündekâri where the use of panels with the grain running at right-angles to that of the frame prevented warping. Examples of false kündekâri include the mimbers of the Alâeddîn Camii and Arslanhâne Camii in Ankara and the Ulu Cami and Huand Hatun Camii in Kayseri.

Other forms of decorative wood-carving were reliefs—deep-cut, flat or rounded—commonly used on window-panels, lecterns, daises and cenotaphs; with deep-cut rounded reliefs most popular for panels containing calligraphic inscription and arabesques. Open lattice-work was much used for the balustrades of mimbers. But pride of place went to the portable, collapsible lecterns of the Selçuk wood-carving art, for they display workmanship of an unusually fine quality. Painted and lacquered woodwork was also produced.

The third prominent type of architectural decoration for which the Selçuks were renowned in their innovation and artistic achievement was that of tiles. Anatolia was the centre for tiles in the 13C Islamic world; and these, and glazed bricks, were extensively used to adorn palaces, mosques, türbes, mescids and medreses. The first important tile-manufacturing centre was Konya, with lesser centres at Kubad-âbâd, Ahlat, Kayseri and Akşehir, all producing tiles of a remarkable consistency and uniformity in both style and subject matter. Both tiles and tile mosaics, with their brilliant colours (especially the turquoise, purple and cobalt blue), came to be widely used in Selçuk architectural decoration. Tile mosaics, which could be applied easily to curved surfaces, became very popular for decorating domes, vaults, arches and mihrabs, and were most suitable for the various rounded motifs and geometrical designs favoured by the period. In the construction of domes, a common technique was the skilful arrangement of bricks, glazed bricks and tiles or tile mosaics to form intricate geometrical patterns; and glazed monochrome tiles were also used to cover broad surfaces to great effect. But the richest and most interesting tiles were those made for the palaces, consisting mainly of star-and-cross-shaped pieces representing figural compositions such as the Sultan, the palace élite, hunting scenes and real or fantastic animals. These tiles were produced only for the palaces—structures that no longer exist and are known only through excavations.

After the outstanding quality and work in tiles, it may come as a surprise to find that Selçuk pottery reveals no really original development. Indeed, very little survives beyond the odd fragment of lustre-ware and numerous pieces of glazed slip-ware for mosque and domestic use—both in monochrome and with figural decoration of the characteristic Selçuk style. As for the Selçuk use of glassware, there is little evidence of glass manufacture in this period, although glass was certainly used in the windows of the Kubadâbâd and Alâeddîn Palaces. Excavation in Kubadâbâd has revealed fragments of coloured glass probably of cups, plates, bottles and other palace ware, and a single gilded and enamelled plate, with an inscription around the rim indicating that it was made to order for the Selçuk

Sultan Gıyaseddîn Keyhüsrev (1237–47). At this time, the centres of enamelled and gilded glass were Aleppo and Damascus.

In metallurgy, on the other hand, the Anatolian and the Great Selçuks excelled in both technique and design. In Anatolia, the metalwork showed strong regional characteristics reflecting a variety of influences in decorative motifs and technical experimentation in design. Unfortunately, few of the metal—and fewer still of the precious metal—artefacts of the Anatolian Selçuks have survived; reliance must be placed largely on the accounts of contemporary chroniclers, such as İbn Bîbî who describes the gold and silver ware used at the wedding feast of Sultan İzzeddîn Keykâvus (1211–19) and the gold artefacts stored in the Selçuk treasury, and the few extant items. Recent archaeological research has, however, unearthed more bronze, brass and silver items of Anatolian Selçuk provenance, such as mirrors, candlesticks and incense-burners, bowls, plaques, buckles, lamps and drums. Konya seems to have been the centre of production in metalwork; and the various techniques employed, such as pierced-work, inlay, cloisonné enamel, cast relief and embossing, all displaying excellent craftsmanship, indicate the advanced level reached. The decorative motifs and patterns are, as is to be expected, typical of the Selçuk decorative arts, representing all the human, animal and abstract designs, but most commonly the Anatolian motifs of double-headed eagle, lion, bull, griffon and sphinx together with magical astrological signs. Unusual is the incorporation of Byzantine themes, such as the apotheosis of Alexander of Macedon. Yet these serve to underline the rich synthesis of Anatolian craftsmanship.

First-hand evidence of Anatolian textiles in the Selçuk period is sadly lacking, comprising only two red silk pieces, probably of 13C Konya provenance, gold-brocaded, with lion, double-headed eagle and dragon's-head motifs. However, the travellers İbn Battuta and Marco Polo have much to say in praise of Anatolian silks and other fabrics, and the Kubadâbâd Palace tilework with its vivid figural representations depicts the patterned kaftans worn by the nobility.

But a far more important Selçuk contribution to Anatolian culture was their introduction of the knotted carpet—a tradition belonging to the pastoral society of their Central Asian homeland. The few surviving carpets of the Selçuk period, found in the Alâeddîn Camii in Konya, are double-knotted with the Turkish or Gordion (Gördes) knot, and feature stylised geometrical designs and motifs of natural origin in a limited range of colours (red tones, blue, dark blue, beige and yellow) and angular calligraphic borders. Once again, it is largely from contemporary sources that we derive our information—Marco Polo was much impressed with the Selçuk knotted carpets, which he tells us were sought after throughout the world.

Mention should be made, at least in passing, of the art of miniature painting, evinced in illustrated manuscripts during the Selçuk period. While a few have survived from 12th and 13C Anatolia, these reflect contemporary Islamic styles in general rather than a specifically Anatolian contribution. Nevertheless, they form a valuable historical and cultural record of the lifestyle such as tents, clothing, weapons, human types, architectural features and even mechanical devices. However, even here, elements peculiar to the Anatolian Selçuk iconography and artistic style are present; so it may be argued that within a broadly homogeneous Islamic style of miniature-painting, possibly the most original works were of Anatolian provenance.

Thus, the Anatolian Selçuks, despite the tortuous complexity of their rise and political consolidation as a major regional power by the 13C, undoubtedly proved a fertile and imaginative source of cultural and artistic endeavour. Drawing on a wide range of influences from various sources, they created more than just a synthesis—an originality in styles, in techniques, in objectives that was to characterise the entire Selçuk domain, from decorative arts to architectural innovations, from scholarly thought to a rare religious tolerance. It can be no coincidence that the unsettled politics of the time and exposure to so many antagonists stimulated an intellectual vivacity that revealed itself in the widespread search for new ideas and the hospitality accorded to visiting scholars, mystics and religious dignitaries—culminating in an environment that in turn fostered both thought and craftsmanship. And yet the seeming coincidence of cultural symbols and motifs of Anatolian history and pre-history with those brought by the Selçuks from their ancestral homelands is too striking to be accepted simply as such—leading one to speculate on the still-obscure origins of many of the peoples entering Anatolia over the millennia.

IX.   The Ottomans

The defeat of the Anatolian Selçuk Turks at the battle of Kösedağ in 1243 subjected them to the increasingly intrusive suzerainty of the Mongol İlhanlıs, ruling from Iran. And with the eclipse of the Selçuks as an independent regional power, in conjunction with the new waves of Türkmen migration, westwards from the İlhanlı base to the more loosely-controlled Selçuk/Byzantine frontier region, numerous petty independent *beyliks* (principalities) began to form in western Anatolia from the middle of the 13C. For the frontier area, adjoining as it did the rich plains of the Byzantine Empire, became a haven for those fleeing Mongol authority, indeed any who sought a new future. Thus the population increased and assembled around the many beys who were leading raids into Byzantine land under the potent banner of *gazâ* (holy war) and establishing themselves and their followers in the territories they managed to acquire there. By the end of the 13C, such raids had become so common that they seemed almost to form constituent parts of one single wave of invasion. And one particular beylik, situated furthest to the north and closest to the coveted Christian lands, besieged Nicaea (İznik) and defeated a substantial Byzantine army of some 2000 mercenaries in 1301 at the battle of Baphaeon (Koyunhisar, near Yalova)—a victory that spread the reputation of its leader, Osman Gâzî (1299?–1326), far and wide. Thenceforth, *gâzîs* (fighters of holy war) from all over Anatolia hitched themselves to Osman's rising star, following the usual custom of adopting the name of their leader and thus calling themselves Osmanlıs. More and more Turks migrated west and north to Osman Gâzî's beylik, tempted by the prospect of much booty and fresh lands in which to settle. It was thus that the Osmanlı—commonly known as Ottoman—principality established its paramountcy in western Anatolia from the beginning of the 14C, and it was from these small beginnings that the Ottoman dynasty—or dynasty of Osman, in accordance with the Arabo-Iranian (as opposed to Turkish) tradition that states and dynasties usually took the name of their founder—was to grow into a vast and durable empire, spreading over three continents by the 16C.

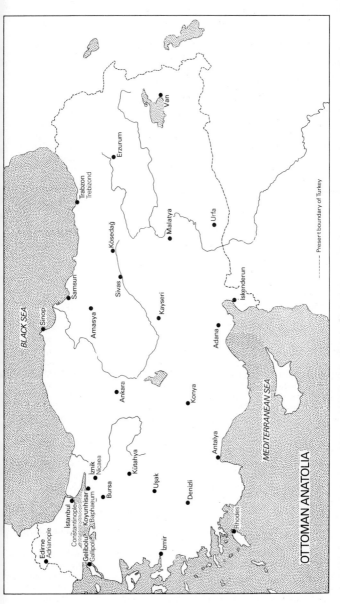

BLACK SEA

Van

Erzurum

Trabzon
Trebizond

Urfa

Malatya

Kösedağ

Samsun

Sivas

Kayseri

İskenderun

Sinop

Amasya

Adana

Ankara

Konya

MEDITERRANEAN SEA

İznik
Nicaea

Kütahya

Antalya

Bursa

Denizli
Uşak

İstanbul
Constantinople

Koyunhisar
Baphaeum

Gelibolu
Gallipoli

Edirne
Adrianople

İzmir

Rhodes

- - - - - Present boundary of Turkey

OTTOMAN ANATOLIA

The Ottoman beylik, in common with all the other frontier principalities, based its organisation on and sought its legitimation in the
ideal of gazâ—continuous expansion through the religious duty of
holy war, with the ultimate aim of achieving world empire in the
name of Islam. This ideal gradually evolved from the popular folk
tradition of heroic exploits to the more learned orthodox doctrine of
the şeriat (canonical law). Thus gazâ was intended not to devastate
but to subjugate the non-Muslim world, and the warlike raids of the
frontier gâzîs were soon succeeded by the establishment in conquered lands of the new Muslim state's protective administration,
tolerating and even guaranteeing the lives, property and religious
freedom of their non-Muslim subjects in return for loyalty. In this, as
in so many aspects of Ottoman civilisation and particularly statecraft,
the clear precedent set by their Selçuk predecessors was adopted
and developed.

It was under Osman Gâzî's son and successor, Orhan Bey (1326–62),
that an Ottoman foothold in Europe was acquired, a strategic marriage
alliance with the Cantacuzenus family—one of the claimants to the
Byzantine throne—providing the opportunity to intervene in internal
Byzantine affairs. This was an opportunity he exploited to establish a
military presence in Gallipoli (Gelibolu) and other Thracian fortresses,
advancing to capture Adrianople (Edirne) in 1361.

The pattern of Ottoman expansion set in Anatolia continued in the
Balkans (Rumelia; from Rumeli or Rum İli). The Ottomans accepted into
their service submissive local nobility and military commanders, along
with their troops, instead of killing them. Those local populations who
submitted voluntarily to the gâzîs were left unmolested, while Turkish
settlers were brought in from Anatolia to populate new villages. These
frontier villages were sited along the main avenues of the Ottoman
advance and were usually centred around zâviyes founded by ahîs,
members of a religious fraternity-cum-trade guild who played an
important role in frontier society by organising the newly-settled
communities. Thus conquest was always followed by rapid Turkish
colonisation, providing a solid foundation for the next phase of
expansion.

But the ease with which the Ottomans colonised Rumelia is partly
explained also by the state principle of protecting the peasantry against
local administrative exploitation, replacing the heavy taxes and
oppressive privileges of the old feudal overlords and the Church with
the far lighter tax and less burdensome presence of the new centralised
administration. This deliberate policy of conciliation, combined with
the Ottomans' extreme religious tolerance, meant that, in general,
while the nobility and higher religious dignitaries tended to seek
support from Latin Christendom, the Orthodox peasantry and lower
ranks of the Church sided wholeheartedly with the Muslim Ottomans—
to the extent of assisting them against their Christian overlords, thus
exacerbating yet further the deep and lasting hostility of Christian
rulers and Church. The ramifications could be discerned even as far
away as England, where a scholar like Henry Stubbe, Under-Library-
Keeper at the Bodleian, Oxford, in the mid-17C, was to assert that 'it is
indeed more the interest of the princes and nobles than of the people
which at present keeps all Europe from submitting to the Turks'.
Interestingly enough, the book could not be published, but it circulated
(possibly widely) in manuscript form.

At all times, the Ottomans tried to adhere to a policy whereby an
advance on one front was paralleled by a subsequent advance on the
other front, so the conquest of Rumelia did not distract them from

expansion in Anatolia. By the end of the 14C, then, the Ottoman domain extended from the Danube to the Fırat.

The sudden and massive Ottoman defeat in 1402 by the powerful Turkish ruler of Central Asia and Iran, Emir Timur (Tamarlane, from Timur Leng), and the imposition of Timurid suzerainty did not, however, prevent the Ottomans from re-establishing their position in Rumelia by 1415. From this time on expansion was rapid. Of particular significance was the conquest of Constantinople (İstanbul) in 1453, the last remaining Byzantine stronghold—apart from its offshoot Comnene kingdom in Trabzon (Trebizond), which was shortly to follow suit—surrounded on every side by Ottoman territories. Fâtih Mehmed II (Mehmed the Conqueror; 1451–81) now laid claim, as the legitimate successor of the Eastern Roman Empire, to all its former territories, and from his capital at İstanbul undertook an administrative policy and a series of campaigns that established a centralised empire over virtually the whole of Anatolia and Rumelia, almost as far as Belgrade. Indeed, Fâtih Mehmed may be taken as the true founder of the Ottoman Empire, for these lands, centring on Istanbul, were to constitute the Ottoman core territory for the next four centuries, and it was he who first adopted the title of 'Sovereign of the Two Lands and of the Two Seas' (Anatolia and Rumelia, and the Mediterranean and Black Seas respectively).

The reign of Selim I (1512–20) saw the defeat of the rival Turkish Mamluk state, thus adding Egypt, Syria and the Hejaz to the Ottoman domains. This was of major significance in that the Ottomans thus replaced the Mamluks as the protectors of the Caliphate and, by extension, of the Islamic world, the position of Islamic law necessarily took on a new importance in the Empire, and the world's richest centres of transit trade fell into the Ottoman orbit.

Kanûnî Süleyman I (the Law-Giver, also known as the Magnificent; 1520–66), utilising the growing capability of the Ottoman fleets, captured Rhodes—one of the most strategic strongholds of the eastern Mediterranean—from the Knights of St. John, and established control over much of the North African littoral. And 16C Ottoman naval supremacy in the Mediterranean dated from the battle of Prevesa in 1538, at which the Ottomans routed a powerful crusading fleet. On land, Kanûnî Süleyman extended the Ottomans' European frontier to incorporate Hungary and Transylvania. Certainly, up to the end of the 16C, the Ottoman Empire was involved directly or indirectly with virtually all aspects of international politics, frequently sought by France as an ally against the Holy Roman Empire of her Habsburg rivals. Ottoman policy, meanwhile, was simply to maintain Christian disunity, weaken the dominant Habsburg power and prevent a joint Christian crusade against itself. It could, for example, be argued that Ottoman pressure on the Habsburgs was an important factor in the extension of Protestantism in Europe.

In the other direction, Kanûnî Süleyman subdued and incorporated Azerbaycan, western Iran, Iraq and the Emirate of Basra, thus acquiring control over the Persian Gulf and the Red Sea and the routes to India. But 1570/71 saw the last of the great Ottoman conquests, with the capture of Cyprus, and the first of the great Ottoman defeats, at the battle of Lepanto (İnebahtı).

The later 16C was the zenith of Ottoman territorial expansion, extending as it did from central Europe to the Indian Ocean. But the Ottomans' motive force, gazâ, seemed by now to have expired, leaving a spiritual vacuum. For the Empire had long been trapped in what might be called the paradox of hegemony, by which continuous geographical expansion necessitated still further conquests to protect new frontiers and incorporate new neighbours as buffer states, vassals and, in due course, Ottoman provinces, thus creating yet more new frontiers; meanwhile the core territories of the state had to bear the increasingly massive costs and were consequently weakened and impoverished—with disaffection expressed by numerous local Anatolian uprisings. Moreover, the widespread devastation and utter destruction inflicted upon the Islamic world by the Mongols in the 13C had completed the already perceptible decline in Islamic dynamism and vigour. The rise of the Ottomans to the status of a world power had been fuelled by the continuing momentum of, as it were, the dead weight of Islamic civilisation, while Islamic intellectual vivacity and spirit of enquiry had passed to western Europe, where it was to provide the foundation for the rationalism of the Renaissance and Reformation. Yet rather than the two opposite and opposing cultures stimulating one another, the Ottoman Empire, with its indulgent religious tolerance and overweening sense of superiority that prevented it from observing (let alone learning from) the growing intellectual stature of its adversaries in western Europe, was thus possessed of a mentality wholly unconducive to the development of a new and dynamic civilisation.

However, the organisation and running of the Ottoman Empire, which was to endure for nearly 700 years, offered no grounds for supposing any such deficiency. Legitimacy, in terms of legal succession to Selçuk sovereignty, was early provided for the Ottoman dynasty by the tradition that Osman Gâzî was presented by the Selçuk Sultan with the title of Bey and the traditional symbols of authority—a robe of honour, a horse, a flag and a drum—after his capture of an important Byzantine fortress, and that it was only after the death without issue of the last of the Selçuk sultans that Osman Gâzî announced his independence by having the *hutbe* (Friday prayer) read in his own name. Osman is also credited with the support of an *ahî şeyh* (sheikh) who supposedly provided spiritual legitimacy for the dynasty by giving Osman both a gâzî's sword and his own daughter in marriage. And the growing beylik took, as the fundamental inspiration for its state organisation, the model of the Selçuk and İlhanlı states. For example, the Ottoman state concept, always based on the principle of gazâ, also incorporated the ancient Turkish principle of justice and protection of the populace from abuse and exploitation and of the distribution of largesse through acts of public welfare—so prominent under their Selçuk predecessors.

The succession of the royal family, like that of the Selçuks, tended to depend on the outcome of fratricidal struggle. But whereas the Selçuk princes were usually fairly independent regional governors based in provincial capitals, the Ottoman princes were kept under close central control; and later on, as ancient Turkish tradition faded, all but the eldest were confined to the Palace and thus easily disposed of when the eldest inherited the throne. When Fâtih Mehmed codified his body of law (*kanûnnâme*), he merely legalised long-existing practice by permitting, along with *şeriât* consent, the killing of all his brothers by the son who succeeded to the throne. Thus, the element of fratricidal strife and internal disorder on the death of the Sultan was reduced, but at a cost, as we have discussed earlier. In any case, the risk of Palace intrigue and struggle was never entirely eliminated, for various powerful factions, such as Palace cliques—usually centring on the *Vâlide Sultan* (mother of the reigning Sultan), the Grand Vizier and the *Harem Ağası* (chief black eunuch of the Palace)—the *Ulema* (doctors of theology) or the *Yeniçeris* (Janissaries), wielded much influence over the selection of the successor and often took opposing sides, supporting different candidates whom they could manipulate to their own respective advantage.

The Sultan presided over the *Divân-ı Hûmâyûn* (Imperial Council), composed of high executive, military and administrative officials and viziers (ministers), which dealt with all governmental matters—political, judicial and financial—and was supported by a vast Palace bureaucracy. But from the reign of Fâtih Mehmed, the Sultans tended to withdraw from direct participation, leaving the Grand Vizier to act as absolute deputy, but often following the proceedings from behind a small grille cut into the wall of the Council Chamber and intervening as they wished. Gradually, too, the Grand Vizier came to deputise for the Sultan as Commander-in-Chief of the armed forces on campaign. But his immense power and authority was generally kept from rivalling that of the Sultan himself by various bureaucratic checks and balances.

The Palace was held to be the centre of the Ottoman Empire and the source of all power and favour. Government was conducted here; indeed, the term *Dergâh-i Âli* or *Kapı* (Sublime Porte) for the Ottoman Government derives from the 'Gate' of the Palace (*Dersaâdet* or 'Gate of Felicity') where the Sultan received his subjects, dispensed justice and observed ceremonies. Traditionally, a new Sultan was not accepted by his subjects as legitimate until he had secured the capital which contained the seat of government. The organisation of the Palace was divided into an Inner (*Enderûn*) and Outer (*Bîrûn*) Court, connected by the Gate of Felicity where the Sultan conducted state business. The Inner Court was where the Sultan spent his private life and the Outer contained all the services and organisations that regulated his relations with the outside world.

Thus the Palace was more than a royal residence; it was the centre of government. And the foundation of the Ottoman central government organisation was the *kul* system with its practice of *devşirme*. This was a system by which, in its classical form, levies were made of the sons of Ottoman Christian villagers engaged in agriculture, excluding certain categories such as urban families, those with particular skills vital to the local economy and families with only one son. The bulk of the boys thus levied were brought up to become members of the *Yeniçeri* corps of militia. But the best were creamed off to the Palace where they received the finest education and training for recruitment into the higher ranks of the religious and civil service, or, at the least, as commanders in the cavalry of the *Kapıkulu* (élite household) forces. The aim of this policy was to create a corps of totally loyal servants of the Sultan, with no independent source of power or patronage, and provided with the best education and greatest opportunity for advancement by merit—for all these boys came from obscure village backgrounds where their prospects were minimal. For this reason, many families, especially in the poorer villages, willingly offered their sons, for whom they themselves could never afford such advantages. Indeed, in the course of time an increasing number of Grand Viziers—the highest position in the Empire after the Sultan—came to be of kul origin. Muslim Turks were exempt from this special levy for sound political reasons; they would inevitably retain family and religious links and therefore be less capable of absolute loyalty to the Sultan and likely to abuse their privileged status to further their relatives' position, thus distorting the whole, finely-tuned balance of state and economy—as indeed seems to have occurred in any case, long before the classical kul system was relaxed to include Muslim Turks.

In the provinces, the main administrative unit of the Empire was, from the start, the *sancak*; and a *beylerbeylik* or *eyâlet* (province) was comprised of groups of these, headed by a Beylerbeyi (Provincial Governor). But a system of checks and balances limited the local authority of the Beylerbeyi through the existence of two other provincial administrative units answerable to the Palace. These were the units of the Kadı, with his religious, judicial and administrative duties, and of the *Hazîne Defterdârı* (Provincial Treasurer), with his fiscal responsibilities to the Palace Treasury.

While a variety of land and taxation administrative systems operated in different parts of the Empire, the backbone of the Anatolian (and Rumelian) organisation was the *timar* system, based chiefly on the Selçuk iktâ. In this way the provinces were geared to support the huge and growing armed force required to implement the Ottoman policy of continuous expansion by military conquest, with minimal cash expenditure. The division of the populace into two broad classes, *askerî* (military, or executive) and *reâyâ* (peasantry) meant that only members of the askerî were eligible for timar, and military service was required in return. The timar was not hereditary, although sons of a deceased timar-holder (usually continuing in the askerî tradition) would be assigned new timars according to the size and value of their father's, nor did the timar-holders constitute a 'feudal class'. For under the centralised Ottoman administration it was not the land itself that was allotted as timar, but the authority to collect a fixed amount of state revenue from the resident reâyâ, and therefore certain rights over the reâyâ themselves. The reâyâ had, however, their own rights over the land, chief among which were those of inheritance and of direct recourse to the central authority, even the Sultan, against oppression and exploitation. Moreover, a timar-holding *sipâhî* (soldier) who, for example, failed to perform military service for seven years lost his timar; so clearly the system was designed to prevent, or at least reduce, the accumulation of local centres of power and autonomy. A further, and major, factor in balancing the power of the provincial timar-holders was the huge, centrally-paid standing army of the Yeniçeri corps, composed of Palace kuls and under the direct command of the Sultan, to whom they owed absolute loyalty. In short, so long as the major institutions of the highly centralised Ottoman state continued to function in an orderly way, the ruler maintained his power and any feudal tendencies were kept under control.

The distinction between the askerî and reâyâ classes could also be breached from the other direction. For while it was in the interest of the state to maintain the order and harmony of society by ensuring that each individual remained in his own class, the opportunity for individual upward mobility through merit alone provided the incentive for personal endeavour and loyalty to the Sultan. Undoubtedly, while members of the askerî class were obliged to profess Islam, and it was in the convert's interest to appear zealous in his new faith, motives for conversion and degree of faith were of less significance than was personal merit in obtaining promotion and distinction. Such tolerance and *largesse d'ésprit* was important in an extensive and heterogeneous state, not only for non-Muslim subjects but also for the reâyâ. In this way, the constant admittance of new and capable elements into the askerî class assured the vigorous survival of the society and of the Empire itself.

However, it must be said that these institutions, so efficient in the administration of the Empire in its classical period, all showed increasing signs of disorder and disability from the 16C when distortion of their original bases began to exert its influence on the imperial organisation—the period from which the Ottoman decline is generally taken as dating. For example, an increasing number of reâyâ were accepted as sipâhîs and assigned timars, thus confusing the more-or-less rigid distinction between askerî and reâyâ; Palace favourites were more and more frequently granted timars for non-military purposes, thus reducing the land and revenues supporting the essential armed forces; the Yeniçeri corps began to establish businesses and loyalties other than to the Sultan and could no longer be depended upon to act in his interest alone. The list is endless.

Ottoman law, continuing the Selçuk tradition, was divided into şeriat (canonical) and kanûn (Sultanic), of which the latter were codified by Fâtih Mehmed in two kanûnnâmes (codes of law) for the first time. Kanûn was largely, although not entirely, based on the long-established customary (consuetudinary; örf) law of the community, generally acknowledged if not approved by religious authorities. Essential to the establishment and modification of the kanûn pertaining to particular regions or social groups were the population and taxation surveys regularly carried out in precise detail. The basic principle of the kanûn-i osmanî (Ottoman kanûn) was that the land and the reâyâ belonged to the Sultan. Thus was the Sultan's absolute ownership of all land and hence absolute sovereignty in the Empire assured. This enabled the timar system to be widely established and allowed the Sultan to exercise some control over private mülk and vakıf estates. Indeed, this principle was the cornerstone of the centralised imperial organisation—although, as we have seen, the Turkish tradition of protecting the peasantry from administrative oppression and the periodic distribution of state largesse did help to offset provincial exploitation of the reâyâ. The law—both kanûn and şeriat—was administered and executed by kadıs, appointed by the Sultan, and in kanûn great importance was attached to precedent, the kadıs exercising considerable discretionary powers, so that Ottoman law was in a continuous state of development.

With regard to the international trade of the Ottoman Empire, it would be surprising if an expanding state of the territorial extent it had achieved by the end of the 16C was not intimately bound up in the trading patterns of Europe to the west, the Black Sea lands to the north, the Mediterranean and North African countries to the south and the Middle East as far as India to the east. As the Empire grew, it acquired control of traditional trade routes in all directions, both on land and by sea, as we have seen, and İstanbul and other cities such as the early capitals of Bursa and Edirne, İzmir, Antalya and the Black Sea ports became major centres of a thriving transit trade between Asia and Europe. During the 16C, Kanûnî Süleyman implemented a policy of co-operation with France against the Habsburgs, and the renewal and further grants of extensive capitulations (special trading privileges such as monopolies) to the French merchants at this time served as a model for similar agreements with England, the Netherlands and others. The political weapon used by Ottoman Sultans of capitulation agreements with western European mercantile states had the effect of turning the Empire into a European dependency, as successive Ottoman governments were obliged to admit the import of manufactured goods to the detriment of indigenous guilds and industries and gave away the profits from exports. In addition, the 16C price revolution in Europe arising out of the New World silver extended to the Ottoman Empire, flooding it with cheap silver. Internally, the frequent debasing of coinage, the drop in crop production, the growing pressure of population and the often excessive exploitation of the provincial populace by state officials were also indicative of a general economic malaise. Yet these are only some of a combination of factors, both internal and external, institutional and incidental, generally put forward as likely contributors to the crisis besetting Ottoman society from the 16C.

The Ottomans were active in building *külliye*'s (urban centres supported by vakıfs)—deriving from the early zâviyes of the ahîs—in the major cities, in order to provide public services and markets and to boost the growth of the cities. The külliye was usually a complex of religious and charitable buildings—mosque, medreses, hamam, kervansarays, water installations, roads and bridges—along with their supporting commercial establishments—market, han, mill, dyehouse, slaughterhouse or imâret—sited nearby. These külliyes were a vital part of all Ottoman towns, adding their own distinctive character, but sadly have been razed to the ground in the old Christian provinces. The great commercial and cultural complexes of the Ottoman Empire were created out of the vakıf system, every major town having its own Great Mosque (Ulu Cami) and *bedestan* (commercial centre, such as the well-known Kapalı Çarşı, or Covered Market, of İstanbul). The Ottomans, like the Selçuks before them, founded numerous charitable institutions such as medreses, libraries, hospitals, children's schools, kervansarays and public kitchens. Likewise, they were concerned to ensure the ease and safety of road travel, improving roads, building bridges and endowing charitable and fortified institutions along the routes, including also wells, fountains, places of prayer and small guesthouses.

The urban population was based mainly on the productive classes of merchants and craftsmen, as well as being divided into the two religious groups of Muslim and non-Muslim. Yet Muslim and non-Muslim members of each class enjoyed the same rights and status and were only really distinguished by their residential quarters—every city having a separate district for Muslims, Christians and Jews, each containing its own religious dignitaries and representative officials. Indeed, Fâtih Mehmed, on making İstanbul his capital, brought under Ottoman protection the Greek Orthodox and Armenian Patriarchs and the Jewish Chief Rabbi and established them in İstanbul to minister to the needs of their communities.

The basis of economic life in Ottoman cities was the craft guilds, whose members comprised a large proportion of the populace and who were extremely well organised and regulated. During the early Ottoman period these were more loosely and independently established as ahîs, but with growing Ottoman authority and centralisation they came under closer governmental control. Nevertheless, the internal arrangements of the guilds continued to be largely autonomous and long resisted official interference, while conforming to fixed rules and regulations, chiefly concerning prices, weights and measures, quality of merchandise, fraud and profiteering.

In the Ottoman Empire, as in the Selçuk and other Muslim states, the chief educational institution was the medrese where subjects included, besides the purely religious studies, branches of all the sciences—the calligraphic, oral, intellectual and spiritual, such as, Arabic language and literature, logic, natural sciences and mathematics, ethics and politics. The Ottoman Sultans established numerous medreses in their major cities and especially in İstanbul, and from these were recruited the *ulema* (doctors of Islamic theology). And during the Ottoman period it was the ulema who formed the intellectual class, for Ottoman scholarship was very much confined to the traditional Islamic concept whereby its sole aim was the understanding of Allah's word. Reason, then, served religion, and precedent was the guiding principle in all aspects of scholarship; compilation, annotation and commentary, rather than original thought, were of the essence. For the victory of orthodoxy in the 12C gradually stifled the spirit of inquiry and made authoritative opinion the test in all intellectual disciplines as well as in theology; the elaborate doctrine of *taklid*, blind and implicit obedience and imitation (in the sense in which the word is used in the 'Imitation of Christ') in matters of faith and ritual, was thus to spread like a canker from theology to all aspects of society. Yet this is not to deny the value of the Islamic scholars, for their religious discourse often touched on important topical matters of state politics or public interest, as in the treatises of İbn Kemâl; and the Ottoman ulema were renowned in jurisprudence and as encyclopaedists of Islamic learning, notable among them Molla Hüsrev, Zenbilli Ali Cemalî Efendi, Şeyh Bedreddîn and Molla Gurânî as jurists, and Molla Fanarî, Molla Lutfî, Taş-köprülüzâde and Kâtib Çelebi as encyclopaedists. The library was an important institution and from the 14C onwards many works were translated from Arabic—the language of religion and scholarship—into Turkish, including the works of history, politics, astrology, natural history and etiquette for the use of statesmen, as well as more popular works, such as the 15C Yazıcızâde brothers' poem, 'Muhammedîye' (Book of Muhammed), and prose work, 'Envâr al-Âşıkîn' (The Lights of the Lovers).

The influence of mysticism, as taught particularly by al-Ghazâlî (died IIII), was widespread in the Ottoman period, dominating scholarship to the extent that the early Ottoman medreses followed the most broad-minded intellectual traditions, on al-Ghazâlî's principle that hostility to logic and mathematics was futile as these incorporated the essential elements of all the sciences. Yet, in his reaction to Neo-Platonism, al-Ghazâlî maintained that while some sciences, such as logic and mathematics, were innocuous (or neutral) for religious belief, others, such as philosophy which could lead to free-thinking and be used against orthodoxy, should be regulated and even restricted when necessary. We can see that in the 15C, under the patronage of Fâtih Mehmed, Ottoman scholarship in mathematics and astronomy was distinguished. Most prominent among Ottoman astronomer/mathematicians were Kadızâde Mûsâ Paşa, particularly for his commentaries on Euclid and al-Çağmînî, his student, Ali Kuşçu, and the latter's students, Molla Lutfî and Mirim Çelebi. Historiography was encouraged by Murad III (1421–44, 1446–51) and Fâtih Mehmed, the most respected works including Kemalpaşazâde's 'Tarih-i Âl-i Osman' (History of the House of Osman) and Aşıkpaşazâde's 'Tevârih-i Âl-i Osman' (Histories of the House of Osman), while chronicles of note included Mustafa Ali's 'Kunh al-Ahbar' (World History). And deep-rooted attachment to music in Ottoman, as in Selçuk, society combined with the enquiring spirit of Islamic tradition during the early Ottoman period to the extent that it was even used in the care of the physically and mentally ill. As Evliya Çelebi records, at the domed hospital of the Beyazid külliye in Edirne, ten singers and musicians played music three times a week as a 'cure for the sick, a medicine for the afflicted, spiritual nourishment for the mad and a remedy for the melancholy'.

Scholastic theology—the confirmation of Islamic dogma by rational argument—also flourished, with the major theologians, Hocazâde of Bursa and Alâeddîn of Tus debating the relationship between religion and philosophy—the subject of an earlier famous disputation between al-Ghazali and İbn Ruşd; Hocazâde's defence of the şeriat against philosophical enquiry won the day.

Thus, by the end of the 15C, a more rigid interpretation of Islam was beginning to assert itself among the Ottoman ulema which opposed study of the rational sciences; this prejudice was, for example, responsible for the destruction of Murad III's (1574–95) superb observatory in 1580. Perhaps an even more graphic example is the fate of the immense library of Grand Vizier Damad Ali Paşa, whose catalogue alone comprised four volumes. After his death in battle in 1716, the imperial edict requisitioning all his books for the state libraries was modified by the Şeyh-ül-İslâm (head of the ulema) who issued a canonical judgement disallowing the donation of those books on history, philosophy and astronomy. It became more and more difficult for the Ottomans, and for the Islamic world in general, to match the scientific and technical developments of their European rivals, as the ulema and the medreses took an increasingly firm stand against innovation in the practical and rational sciences. Only in areas of obvious state importance, such as geography and medicine, were translations made, and even here copying rather than learning from new developments was the norm. Geographical and cartographical works of the standard achieved by the Ottoman admirals, Pirî Reis and Seydî Ali Reis, in the early 16C were not to be repeated. And probably the last prominent figure in Ottoman medicine, Ahî Çelebi—founder of the first Ottoman medical school—was active in the 15th and early 16C.

Ottoman creative literature, however, continued to flourish. *Divan* (Court) literature in the Ottoman Turkish (*Osmanlıca*) of the court circles, with its high content of Arabic and Farsî loan-words and phrases, was composed by poets well-versed in all three languages of Islam. Divan poetry reached its zenith in the mid 16C with poets such as Bâkî and Fuzulî, but with also the notable talents of, particularly, Nef'î and Nailî in the 17C and of Nedim and Şeyh Galib in the 18C. Popular literature—in ordinary Turkish—was chiefly expressed in the form of the secular folk-poetry of the *âşıks* (wandering minstrels), such as Köroğlu and Öksüz Dede, and the mystical poetry of the dervishes, such as Kaygusuz Abdal and Pir Sultan Abdal.

Moreover, in stark contrast to the growth of religious fanaticism from the 16C was the traditional and continuing popularity among the general populace of the mystical dervish movements—at times acting as focal points for political revolt in a society where religious and mystical thought has often provided the stimulus for social and, particularly, political action.

Turning now to the artistic expression of the Ottomans, the Anatolian heartland was not only the centre of Ottoman development, it is also the major location of Ottoman architecture and artefacts today; for the gradual disintegration and final collapse of the Ottoman rule was immediately followed by the wanton destruction of all vestiges of Ottoman civilisation, particularly in the Christian territories. In other words, the price of local nationalism was civilisation. What remains in these territories are, the vestiges of language, folkways, music, culinary traditions and other such intangible inheritances. We find in the early architecture a clear development from the Selçuk period, incorporating eastern and Islamic precepts with local Anatolian and Mediterranean construction techniques—but a development that was before long to diverge into a style and composition very much its own. During the formative period of the 14th and early 15C, the necessary pragmatic reconstruction and use of existing Byzantine buildings by Osman Gazi was transformed into a definite building programme by his successor, Orhan Bey. Like his father, Orhan established numerous zâviyes for the ahîs and frontier communities, and military fortresses; but it was he who began the construction of public buildings in İznik and Bursa and other large towns, following the Anatolian Turkish pattern of establishing mosques, medreses, imârets, zâviyes, türbes, hans and hamams. Under Orhan's successors larger and more ostentatious buildings began to be constructed, but still along more-or-less traditional lines, taking the dome as the essential element of vaulting and employing for some time Selçuk decorative techniques. Perhaps the best example of the highest stage of this development, forerunning the Ottoman style, is the Yeşil Cami (Green Mosque) at İznik with its single-domed square form within a building complex, its large porch and its architecturally integrated minaret. This 'primitive' Ottoman style evolved during the early 15C to introduce the large central dome surrounded by four small corner domes—the foundation in plan and structure of the classical Ottoman style. This was introduced in the Üç Şerefeli Cami in Edirne, together with the rectangular courtyard that was to become, with the porch, an essential feature of the Ottoman mosque.

With the conquest of Constantinople in 1453, Ottoman architecture entered its classical phase with the rationally planned külliye on a systematic geometrical and symmetrical basis and the half-dome as a major structural element in the Great Mosques. These include, notably, the Fâtih Camii, Beyazid Camii, Şehzâde Camii and Süleymaniye Camii and their külliyes, all in İstanbul. The last two—Şehzâde and Süleymaniye—were the work of the renowned Ottoman architect Sinan, who dominated 16C religious and secular architecture with several hundred constructions. He was particularly interested in the use of space, especially domed space, and in experimenting with large, structurally expressive buildings, his greatest and most spectacular achievement being generally agreed as the Selimiye Camii in Edirne. Two other notable monuments of the classical period, the Yeni Cami and Sultanahmet Camii (Blue Mosque) in İstanbul were the work of Sinan's pupils. Provincial mosque architecture of the period was very much based on the style of İstanbul, the capital setting the pattern in this as in almost all aspects of Ottoman society.

Other architectural constructions worthy of note were the Palaces, of which only the Topkapı Sarayı and a number of *köşk*s (kiosks) remain, the covered wooden bedestans, hans, medreses, türbes, libraries and bridges. Throughout, the great developments in style were founded upon a few basic elements, of which the structural clarity of the domed space was the characteristic and essential feature, by manipulation of which variations in space and external configuration were achieved. Decorative effects of stone- and marble-carving became supplementary, although the use of two-coloured stone and marble was ingenious, but from the early 18C the influence of French rococo began to extend into Ottoman architecture, which developed its own 'Turkish baroque' or rococo style and gradually adopted more and more foreign elements, blending them into a kind of 'international eclecticism', best exemplified in the Dolmabahçe Sarayı and the Yıldız Sarayı in İstanbul. Such adoptions included the penchant for immense single buildings, such as military barracks, schools, ministries, stations and palaces, quite unlike the building complexes of Ottoman tradition.

The major decorative arts of the Selçuk period underwent considerable change in emphasis as well as style during the Ottoman era. Apart from the virtual disappearance of stone-carving, the spectacular wood-carving for which the Selçuks were noted was replaced by inlay-work. This was most popular during the 16C for the decoration of mimbers, lecterns, windows, doors and drawers, with entire panels of wood being covered with inlaid mother-of-pearl, ivory, bone and jade. Ottoman art also featured painted decoration on wooden ceilings, doors and cornices as well as on furniture and mimbers. Stucco-work was comparatively rare in Ottoman architectural decoration until the baroque taste of the 18C suddenly rendered it fashionable. But frescoes, particularly of flower and leaf compositions, were popular from the start, and by the 16th and 17C covered all surfaces of buildings. With the changing tastes of the 18C, naturalistic landscapes and scenes of houses became more fashionable, and such murals adorned the private houses of many of the wealthy and the higher officials of state as well as the palaces.

One of the most spectacular developments was in Turkish tile art (but less so in tile mosaic art) which reached its peak during the Ottoman period, and was one of the most important of the architectural decorative arts. With the removal of the Ottoman capital to Bursa, nearby İznik and Kütahya replaced Konya as centres of tile and pottery-manufacturing, continuing to flourish (as indeed Kütahya flourishes today) when İstanbul became the capital. Ottoman tile decoration concentrated on internal walls rather than domes and minarets—often completely covering them—and also decorated arches, doors, windows and columns. Floral designs almost entirely replaced figural motifs; colours grew richer and more varied—to include shades of blue, turquoise, green, white, black, yellow, gilt and the brilliant *bolus* (or sealing-wax) red—and techniques of glazing and decoration more skilful up to the end of the 16C. But after this came a distinct decline in the quality of both İznik and Kütahya tiles, their lively and brilliant blues and reds fading and lighter colours becoming fainter, with smudged and running contours and poor glazing. The 18C saw the closure of the İznik workshops and the uphill struggle by Kütahya to justify its position as a worthy replacement. Ceramic-ware of the two centres flourished in parallel with the tile-ware, with similar schools of, for example, the erroniously named 'Damascus' and 'Rhodian' ware, both manufactured in İznik.

An interesting development was the institution called the *Ehl-i Hiref* (Artists and Craftsmen) attached to the Topkapı Sarayı (then called Yeni Sarayı or New Palace). Artists were divided according to their particular skills and came under the supervision of the *Hazinedâr Başı* (Chief Treasurer) for their commissioned work, their supply of materials and their salaries, although some of them also worked outside the Palace in their own ateliers and workshops. These artists formed the core of Ottoman craftsmanship, dominated the styles, motifs and designs of the provinces and exerted influence far beyond the confines of the Empire, particularly in western Europe.

The largest and most influential section of the Ehl-i Hiref comprised the painters—including brush-and-ink artists, illuminators of manuscripts, portrait-painters, miniature-painters and wall-painters. Designs created here were used by the manufacturers of İznik and Kütahya and the rug-weavers of Uşak. In effect, the Palace controlled quality, techniques and materials in all fields and, as the principal consumer, could impose its own taste in design and choice of motif.

Besides the corps of painters, there were bookbinders and calligraphers, goldsmiths and jewellers, coinsmiths, specialists in the cutting and setting of gems and in goldwork, metalworkers, textile-workers, furriers, tilemakers, wood- and ivory-carvers, cap-and tur-ban-makers, carpenters and candlestick-makers, to name but some. Prominent among Ottoman motifs were the *hayatî* (stylised blossom) and *rumî* (split leaf) themes that characterised virtually all 15C decorative art. More diversity became apparent in the 16C as these motifs developed, for example in the classical *saz* motif of hayatî blossoms combined with large twisting leaves, and new ones were introduced, especially the highly-decorative style of Iran when artists of the defeated Safavid court were brought to İstanbul by Selim I. Gradually, the more naturalistic depiction of flowers evolved, while realistic and documentary painting came to be adopted in manuscript illustration. In all fields of art, and among whatever motifs were chosen, the abundance of flowers such as roses, tulips, hyacinths and carnations and garden scenes reflected the deep and widespread love of nature of the Turks.

Ottoman fabrics, like tiles and pottery, were a particularly suitable medium for their rich designs, often decorated with a lavish profusion of flowers and leaves. Ottoman fabrics such as velvet, brocade, satin and taffeta—named according to their methods of weaving—were much admired and held as most valuable, and weaving and embroidery with gold and silver thread was intricate and rich. First Bursa and later İstanbul were the centres of weaving, including silks, cottons and wools, coloured with plant-dyes of excellent quality. But the 18C saw a lowering of the standard of textile-manufacture, and the flooding of the markets with cheap foreign fabrics.

Knotted carpets, introduced into Anatolia by the Selçuks, developed into a craft of wide international repute under the Ottomans. From the 14C, Italian and Flemish painters began to represent Turkish carpets in their pictures, known from the 15C as 'Holbein' carpets through their strong association with Hans Holbein's paintings. The rich and varied decorative themes and motifs of Ottoman carpets formed a major field of artistic design and this lively Anatolian tradition continues today.

Glass manufacture was a major Ottoman industry whose products, by their nature, have not survived well. But a variety of glass vases, decanters, glasses, lamps and other household objects were produced in İstanbul, as well as stained-glass windows—well-attested by the Süleymaniye Camii windows. In the 18C, glass manufacture was monopolised by the Tekfur Sarayı workshops in İstanbul and a very high standard set. Later, other workshops were founded in İstanbul manufacturing excellent glass- and crystal-ware; for example, in 1899 at Paşabahçe, where most of the best-known glass-and crystal-ware is still produced. But the craft did suffer acutely from the competition with cheap foreign ware imported without duty in the 19C.

The goldsmiths' and jewellers' craft was prominent in the Ottoman period but metalwork, expecially of silver, brass and tinned copper, perhaps suffered as a result of the overwhelming popularity of the highly developed and exotic ceramic art. Metal objects engraved with calligraphic inscriptions, flower designs and arabesques were produced according to a variety of techiques, prominent among them being that of encrustation with precious gems. Although numerous domestic items such as mirrors, caskets, pen-cases, lamps, candle-sticks and censers were produced, it was in military arms and armour that Ottoman metalwork excelled, with finely-executed helmets, swords and the like richly inlaid, gilded and even encrusted with jewels.

The importance of Ottoman miniatures, manuscript illumination and portraiture lies not only in their artistic development, which was considerable, but also in their unique character as a contemporary source of valuable information. The presence at Fâtih Mehmed's court of a number of foreign painters, notably the Italian Gentile Bellini, contributed to the Ottoman school of portraiture. Prominent artists included Sinan Bey—who worked for a time in Venice and painted Fâtih Mehmed seated, smelling a rose—and his pupil, Ahmed of Bursa (Şibilizâde Ahmed). A collection of drawings and miniatures in an album attributed to Fâtih Mehmed includes numerous examples of figural drawings—of people, animals and fantastic creatures—by the famous Mehmed 'Siyah Kalem' ('Black Pen') portrayed with his characteristic striking, even pitiless realism. Fâtih's immediate successors tended to patronise more the traditional Islamic school of miniature, attracting numerous Iranian and Egyptian artists to their court. And by the time of Süleyman, artists from all over the Empire were working in İstanbul—the centre of the Islamic world for any who aspired to excellence and fame in whatever field of endeavour. The outcome of such a variety of styles and influences present in the Ehl-i Hiref was a rich eclecticism and vitality, with different schools predominating at different times. Beside the highly-decorative classics in the Iranian style, there emerged campaign chronicles employing topographical sketches of military manoeuvres and expeditions by Matrakçı Nasuh, portrait studies of all the Ottoman Sultans and other dignitaries such as Admiral Barbaros Hayreddîn Paşa (Barbarossa) by, for example, Haydar Reis (Nigârî) and the charactistically Ottoman annals of the Sultans—the kind of history in which Ottoman authors excelled—with illustrations by Nakkaş Osman and others of major events, celebrations, guild processions and hunting parties. By the late 16C, the zenith in Ottoman miniature-painting, realism was firmly established, in contrast to the romanticism of contemporary Iranian schools. Another, quite different, development was that of manuscripts illustrating Islamic history and especially the life of the Prophet; while new subject-matter introduced in the 17C included illustrations from everyday life and books of fortune-telling. And Ottoman miniature-painting flourished anew in the 18C, with artists such as Levnî of Edirne, during the so-called Tulip Period (*Lâle Devri*, 1718–1830), when familiarity with art in western Europe initiated a new creativity in book illustration, indulging, for example, a taste for frivolous enjoyments and a pre-occupation, in portraiture, with dress.

In the early 19C, traditional Ottoman painting began to modify in style, adopting the three-dimensional technique with its play of light and shade. Artists such as Hüseyin Giritli, Osman Nuri and Salih Molla displayed, for all the tentative quality of their work, a striking precision in design and freshness of colour. The succeeding generation of artists, including Ahmed Ali Paşa (known for his sweet nature as 'Şeker'—'Sugar'—Ahmed), Hüseyin Zekâî Paşa, Süleyman Seyyid and Osman Hamdi, achieved a greater maturity in technique and composition, adopted new subject matter such as figures and still life, and painted more varied landscapes than the preceding artists' cultivated parks and gardens—fountains, mosques, old houses, caiques (*kayıks*) on the Bosphorus and crumbling walls and ruins. Ali Riza, for example, painted out-of-doors and is most interesting for his apt choice of colours and unpretentious style. In 1873, on the return of Şeker Ahmed Paşa from Paris, where he had long worked— influenced by the school of Gustave Courbet—he exhibited his painting at the first ever Ottoman exhibition. In 1914, a group of young artists who had been studying in Paris returned to İstanbul to enrich Ottoman painting with a new vision and a new technique, based on the 'impressionist' use of warm and cool colours for light and shade respectively. And the landscapes of İstanbul and the Bosphorus indeed lent themselves to the new 'impressionistic' style of this generation of artists, among whose names in particular those of Hüseyin Avni Lifij, Nazmi Ziya, Çallı İbrahim and Namık İsmail are prominent.

The Ottoman period in Anatolian history, then, may be seen in all its various aspects to have encompassed a huge variety of tastes, influences, traditions and developments. And the moulding of all these into an original and distinctive whole was arguably no mean achievement, indeed it was one in which the strong centralising tendency of the Ottoman system—in administrative organisation, in economic life, in political endeavour and in artistic expression— played an important role. And as I close with the Ottoman civilisation, this note on Anatolian civilisations draws also to a close—a review that looks back over the past without, I hope, sharing the lament of Fâtih Mehmed's unfortunate son, Cem Sultan, who failed to gain the Ottoman throne, that

'How good a time it was we never knew until lost without trace'.

Further Reading

The only work to date that surveys comprehensively the civilisations of Anatolia is *Anadolu uygarlıkları ansiklopedisi*. İstanbul: Görsel Yayınları, 1982; 6 vols. However, there does exist the catalogue of the Council of Europe's XVIIIth European Art Exhibition in İstanbul, 22 May–30 October 1983, entitled *The Anatolian civilizations*. (Ed.) F. Edgü. [Ankara]: Turkish Ministry of Culture and Tourism, [1983]; 3 vols, which provides an English commentary and a wealth of illustrations. As for works in English suitable for a good grounding, the following are recommended:

U.B. Alkım, *Anatolia I: from the beginnings to the end of the second millennium BC*. (Trans.) J. Hogarth. Geneva: Nagel Publishers, 1968.

E. Akurgal, *Ancient civilizations and ruins of Turkey, from prehistoric times until the end of the Roman Empire*. (Trans.) J. Whybrow and M. Emre. 6th ed. İstanbul: Haşet Kitabevi, 1985.

E. Akurgal (ed.), *The art and architecture of Turkey*. Oxford: Oxford University Press, 1980.

E. Akurgal, C. Mango and R. Ettinghausen, *Treasures of Turkey: the earliest civilizations of Anatolia, Byzantium, the Islamic period*. Geneva: Editions d'Art Albert Skira, 1966.

Cambridge ancient history. Cambridge: Cambridge University Press; espec. 3rd ed., Vols I–II (1970–75) and 2nd ed., Vol. III/1 (1982) and VII/1 (1984).

Cambridge medieval history. Cambridge: Cambridge University Press; espec. 2nd ed., Vol. IV (1967).

Cambridge history of Islam. (Ed.) P. Holt., A.K.S. Lambton and B. Lewis. Cambridge: Cambridge University Press, 1970. 2 vols.

H. Metzger, *Anatolia II: first millennium BC to the end of the Roman period*. (Trans.) J. Hogarth. Geneva: Nagel Publishers; London: Barrie and Rockliff, 1969.

Chronological table

c 10,500–7000	Cave dwellings at Karain and Belbaşı; primitive stone implements and weapons
c 7000	First settlement at Hacılar; earliest evidence of agriculture in Anatolia
c 6500–5500	Çatalhöyük becomes first cultural centre; earliest known religious shrines, pottery, frescoes and statuettes in Anatolia
c 5500	Sophisticated painted pottery and figurines at Hacılar and Çatalhöyük
c 5000–3000	First settlements at Alacahüyük, Alişar, Canhasan and Beycesultan
c 3000	First settlement at Troy
c 2500–2000	Period of Hattian culture
c 1950	Assyrian merchant-colony at Kanesh (Kültepe), first written records in Anatolia
c 1900	Founding of Hattusa by Hittites
c 1700–1450	Old Hittite Kingdom
c 1450–1200	Hittite Empire
c 1260	Fall of Troy
c 1180	Destruction of Hattusa
c 1200–1100	Foundation of Neo-Hittite states at Carchemish, Karatepe and Zincirli
c 1100–1000	Migration of Greeks to Aegean coast of Anatolia
c 900	Rise of Urartian culture in E Anatolia
c 900–800	Rise of Phrygian, Lydian, Carian and Lycian cultures in W Anatolia
c 800	Foundation of Pan-Ionic League and rise of Greek culture in W Anatolia
c 756	Foundation of Cyzicus by Miletus
c 750	Foundation of Greek trading post at Al Mina
717	Carchemish and Neo-Hittite states captured by Assyria
c 700	Cimmerians ravage cities in W Anatolia
c 700	Homer born at Smyrna
c 660	Foundation of Byzantium by Megara
c 654	Foundation of Lampsacus by Phocaea
c 640	First use of coinage in Asia Minor
c 650–600	Miletus founds colonies at Amisus and Trebizond
c 600–500	Beginning of Greek science and philosophy in Ionia
c 610	Thrasybulus tyrant of Miletus
c 600	Foundation of Massilia by Phocaea
585	Battle between Cyaxares of Media and Alyattes of Lydia
561–546	Croesus ruler of Lydia
546	Cyrus of Persia defeats Croesus, Ionia comes under Persian rule
539	Phocaea defeated by Etruscan and Carthagenian navies at Alalia (Corsica)
c 535	Phocaians found Elea (Magna Graecia)
522	Darius king of Persia
512	Darius captures Byzantium
499	Ionians revolt against Persian rule begins
498	Ionians capture and burn Sardis

494	Ionian revolt crushed (Battle of Lade) and Miletus burned
490	Persians defeated at Marathon
486	Death of Darius
481	Xerxes at Sardis
480	Xerxes invades Greece; Persians defeated at Thermopylae and Salamis
479	Persians suffer further defeats at Plataea and Mycale. Ionian cities regain their freedom
478	Ionian cities become members of the Delian League
467	Athenians defeat the Persians at the battle of Eurymedon
431	Beginning of the Peloponnesian War
410	Athens victorious at Cyzicus
409	Foundation of the city of Rhodes
408	Athens recaptures Byzantium
404	End of the Peloponnesian War
401	Xenophon and the Ten Thousand begin their expedition to Persia
400	Thibron's campaign in Asia Minor
399	Socrates put to death in Athens
395	Agesilaus lays siege to Sardis
394	Battle of Cnidus
386	King's peace. Ionia once more under Persian rule
356	Birth of Alexander the Great
336	Assassination of Philip of Macedon. Accession of Alexander
334	Alexander crosses into Asia Minor and defeats the Persians at the battle of the Granicus. Ionian cities liberated. Alexander lays siege to Miletus and Halicarnassus
334–33	Alexander conquers Lycia, Pamphylia and W Pisidia
333	Alexander conquers Cilicia. Inflicts second defeat on the Persians at the battle of Issus. Darius routed
323	Alexander dies at Babylon on 10 June at the age of 32. Outbreak of war between the Diadochi, Alexander's successors
318–17	Antigonus master of Asia Minor
305	Demetrius besieges Rhodes
301	Battle of Ipsus. Antigonus defeated and killed. Lysimachus rules Anatolia and Seleucus controls N Syria
300	Foundation of Antioch
295	Seleucus occupies Cilicia and Lysimachus Ionia
281	Battle of Corupedium. Seleucus defeats Lysimachus and becomes master of Anatolia. Death of Seleucus
278–77	Gauls come to Anatolia and are defeated by Antigonus II Gonatas
263–41	Rise of the Attalid kings of Pergamum. Reign of Eumenes I
230	Rome and Pergamum become allies. Pergamum defeats the Gauls
204	Baitylos of Pessinus taken to Rome

188	Treaty of Apamea. End of Seleucid rule in Anatolia
186	Prusias I of Bithynia attacks Pergamum
133	Death of Attalus III, last king of Pergamum. He bequeaths his kingdom to Rome
130	Roman province of Asia. Aristonicus defeated
100	Mithridates VI Eupator becomes king of Pontus
88	Mithridates VI Eupator overruns Asia Minor; Roman citizens massacred
83	End of Seleucid Empire
80	Commagene kingdom founded
78	P. Servilius campaigns against pirates in Isauria, Lycia and Pamphylia
74	Nicomedes IV of Bithynia dies and leaves his kingdom to Rome
66	Mithridatic wars end. Rome in control of most of Anatolia, including Cilicia
41	Antony meets Cleopatra at Tarsus
40	Antony and Cleopatra marry at Antioch
31	Antony defeated at Actium by Octavian
30	Antony and Cleopatra commit suicide. Octavian makes triumphant visit to Antioch
AD	
14	Death of Augustus and accession of Tiberius
18	Germanicus in Asia Minor
19	Death of Germanicus at Antioch
40–56	Journeys of St. Paul. First Christian community established at Antioch
43	Lycia becomes an imperial province
111	Pliny the Younger governor of Bithynia
117	Death of Trajan at Selinus, Cilicia
124	Hadrian visits Asia Minor
129	Galen born at Pergamum
165	Plague in Asia Minor
215	Caracalla in Antioch
303	Persecution of Christians in Nicomedia
325	Council of Nicaea
381	Council of Constantinople
392	Christianity made state religion by Theodosius the Great
395	Division of the Roman Empire
431	Council of Ephesus
527–65	Reign of Justinian the Great. Byzantine power reaches its zenith
626	Avars and Slavs besiege Constantinople
636	Byzantines defeated by Arabs at Yarmuk
677	Arab fleet attacks Constantinople
717–18	Arabs besiege Constantinople
726–80	First Iconoclastic Period
813	Bulgars besiege Constantinople
831–43	Second Iconoclastic Period
923	Bulgars take Adrianople and besiege Constantinople
963–69	Nicephorus Phocas victorious over Arabs and regains Cilicia and Cyprus
1054	Schism between Greek and Roman churches

1071	Byzantines defeated by Selçuks at Manzikert. Turks overrun Anatolia
1071–1283	The Sultanate of Rum; Selçuks dominant power in Anatolia
1096	Beginning of First Crusade. Latin armies enter Anatolia for first time
1176	Selçuks annihilate Greeks at Myriocephalon; Byzantium loses last chance to expel the Turks from Asia Minor
1203	Beginning of Fourth Crusade; Latins attack Constantinople
1204	Latins sack Constantinople; dismemberment of Byzantine Empire. Lascarids set up Byzantine capital in Nicaea. Comneni found Empire of Trebizond
1240	Ottoman Turks make first appearance in W Anatolia. Mongols invade E Anatolia
1242	Mongols defeat Selçuks at Kösedağ and destroy their power in Anatolia
1261	Michael VIII Palaeologus retakes Constantinople and restores Byzantine Empire
1324	Death of Osman Gazi, founder of Ottoman dynasty
1326	Ottomans under Sultan Orhan take Bursa and establish their first capital there
1389	Turks defeat Serbians at Kossova
1396	Beyazit I defeats Crusader army at Nicopolis
1397	First Turkish siege of Constantinople
1402	Tamerlane defeats Turks at Ankara and captures Beyazit I; Mongols overrun Anatolia
1422	Second Turkish siege of Constantinople
1439	Council of Florence. Last attempt to unite Roman Catholic and E Orthodox churches
1444	Turks crush Crusader army at Varna
1448	Turks defeat Hungarians at second battle of Kossova
1453	Turks under Mehmet II conquer Constantinople; Constantine XI, last emperor of Byzantium, dies in battle. İstanbul becomes capital of Ottoman Empire, which now comprises most of Greece, the southern Balkans and western Anatolia
1517	Selim I captures Cairo and assumes the title of Caliph. The Ottoman Empire has by now expanded into S Europe, E Anatolia, Syria, Palestine, Egypt and Algeria
1520–66	Reign of Süleyman the Magnificent. Zenith of Ottoman power
1571	Turks conquer Cyprus. Christian powers defeat Turkish fleet at battle of Lepanto
1578–1666	'The Rule of the Women'. Ineffective sultans give up control of the Empire to their women and Grand Viziers
1666–1812	Perod of intermittent wars between Turks and European powers. Ottoman Empire loses much territory in S Europe
1821	Greek War of Independence begins
1826	Mahmut II destroys Janisssary Corps

1832	Greece achieves independence. Ibrahim Paşa of Egypt invades Anatolia
1839–76	The Tanzimat Period. Programme of reform in the Ottoman Empire
1877	Establishment of first Turkish parliament. Dissolved the following year by Sultan Abdül Hamit II
1908	Constitutional rule and parliament restored
1909	Abdül Hamit II deposed
1912–13	Balkan Wars; Turks lose Macedonia and part of Thrace
1914	Turkey enters World War I as ally of Germany
1915	Turks repel Allied landings on Gallipoli peninsula
1918	Turks surrender to Allies. İstanbul occupied by Anglo-French army
1919	Sivas Congress. Atatürk leads Turkish Nationalists in beginning of struggle for national sovereignty. Greek army lands at Smyrna
1920	Establishment of Grand National Assembly of Turkey with Atatürk as President. Greek army advances into Asia Minor.
1922	Turks defeat Greeks and drive them out of Asia Minor; Sultanate abolished
1923	Treaty of Lausanne establishes sovereignty of modern Turkey, defines its frontiers and arranges for exchange of minority populations between Greece and Turkey. Establishment of the Turkish Republic with Atatürk as first President
1924	Abolition of Caliphate
1925–38	Atatürk's programme of reforms to modernise Turkey
1938	Death of Atatürk
1945	Turkey enters World War II on side of Allies
1946	Turkey becomes charter member of the United Nations
1950	Turkey enters Korean War as part of United Nations force
1973	Bosphorus Bridge built between Europe and Asia; opened on 50th anniversary of the founding of the Turkish Republic

Chronology of Kings and Emperors

The Ptolemies of Egypt

Ptolemy I Soter 305–282
Ptolemy II Philadelphus 282–246
Ptolemy III Euergetes I 246–222
Ptolemy IV Philopator 222–205
Ptolemy V Epiphanes 204–180
Ptolemy VI Philometor 180–145
Ptolemy VIII Euergetes (Physcon) 146–116

Ptolemy IX Soter II 116–107; 88–80
Ptolemy X 107–88
Ptolemy XI 80
Ptolemy XII Auletes 80–58; 55–51
Ptolemy XIII 51–47
Ptolemy XIV 47–44
Ptolemy XV (Caesarion) 44–30

The Kings of Pontus

Mithradates I c 302–265
Ariobarzanes c 265–255
Mithradates II c 255–220
Mithradates III c 220–185
Pharnaces I c 185–169
Mithradates IV Philopator
  Philadelphus 169–150

Mithradates V
  Euergetes c 150–120
Mithradates VI Eupator 120–63
Pharnaces II
  (King of Bosporus) 63–47

The Seleucids of Syria

Seleucus I Nicator 321–280
Antiochus I Soter 280–261
Antiochus II Theos 261–246
Seleucus II Callinicus 246–226
Seleucus III Soter 226–223
Antiochus III the Great 223–187
Seleucus IV Philopator 187–175
Antiochus IV Epiphanes
  175–164
Antiochus V Eupator 164–162

Demetrius I Soter 162–150
Alexander Balas 150–146
Demetrius II Nicator 146–140
              129–125
(usurper Tryphon 142–139)
Antiochus VI Epiphanes 145–142
Antiochus VII Sidetes 139–129
Seleucus V 125
Antiochus VIII Grypus 121–96
Antiochus IX Cyzicenus 115–95

The Attalids of Pergamum

Philetaerus 282–263
Eumenes I 263–241
Attalus I Soter 241–197
Eumenes II Soter 197–160

Attalus II 160–138
Attalus III 138–133
(Eumenes III = Aristonicus
  133–129)

The Kings of Bithynia

Zipoetes c 297–279
Nicomedes I c 279–255
Ziaelas c 255–228
Prusias I 228–185
Prusias II 185–149

Nicomedes II
  Epiphanes 149–128
Nicomedes III Euergetes 128–94
Nicomedes IV Philopator 94–74

Ephiphanes = God made manifest; noble, distinguished. *Soter* = Saviour.
Philopator = devoted to one's father. *Eupator* = born of a noble father.
Euergetes = Well-doer, Benefactor.

The Kings of Commagene

Ptolemaeus c 163/3–c 130
Samus II Theosebes Dikaios
  c 130–c 100
Mithridates I Callinicus
  c 100–c 70
Antiochus I Theos Dikaios
  Epiphanes Philoromaios
  Philhellen c 70–c 35

Mithridates II c 31
(Antiochus II did not reign
  died 29)
Mithridates III c 20
Antiochus III died AD 17
  (After his death, Commagene
  was annexed by Rome)
Antiochus IV AD 38–72

Roman Emperors

Augustus 27 BC–AD 14
Tiberius 14–37
Caligula 37–41
Claudius 41–54
Nero 54–68
Galba June 68–Jan. 69
Otho Jan.–April 69
Vitellius Jan.–Dec. 69
Vespasian 69–79
Titus 79–81
Domitian 81–96
Nerva 96–98
Trajan 98–117
Hadrian 117–38
Antoninus Pius 138–61
Marcus Aurelius 161–80
L. Verus 161–69
Commodus 180–92
Pertinax Jan.–March 193
Didius Julianus March–June 193
Septimius Severus 193–211
Caracalla 211–17
Geta 211–12
Macrinus 217–18
Elagabalus 218–22
Alexander Severus 222–35
Maximinus 235–38
Gordian I 238
Gordian II 238

Pupienus 238
Balbinus 238
Gordian III 238–44
Philip I 244–49
Decius 249–51
Trebonianus Gallus 251–53
Aemilian 253
Valerian 253–60
Gallienus 253–68
Claudius II 268–70
Quintillus 270
Aurelian 270–75
Tacitus 275–76
Florian 276
Probus 276–82
Carus 282–83
Carinus 282–85
Numerian 283–84
Diocletian 284–305
Maximian 286–305
Licinius 308–24
Constantine the Great 306–37
Constantine II 337–40
Julian 361–63
Jovian 363–64
Valentinian I 364–75
Valens 364–78
Gratian 367–83
Valentinian II 375–92
Theodosius I 378–95

Byzantine Emperors

Arcadius 395–408
Theodosius II 408–50
Marcian 450–57
Leo I 457–74
Leo II 474
Zeno 474–91
Anastasius 491–518
Justin I 518–27
Justinian the Great 527–65
Justin II 565–78
Tiberius II 578–82
Maurice 582–602
Phocas 602–10
Heraclius 610–41
Constantine II 641
Heracleonas 641
Constantine III 641–68
Constantine IV 668–85
Justinian II 685–95
Leontius 695–98
Tiberius III 698–705

Justinian II
  (second reign) 705–11
Philippicus Bardanes 711–13
Anastasius II 713–15
Theodosius III 715–17
Leo III 717–41
Constantine V 741–75
Leo IV 775–80
Constantine VI 780–97
Eirene 797–802
Nicephorus I 802–11
Stauracius 811
Michael I 811–13
Leo V 813–20
Michael II 820–29
Theophilus 829–42
Michael III 842–67
Basil I 867–86
Leo VI 886–912
Alexander 912–13
Constantine VII 913–59

Romanus I (co-emperor) 919–44
Romanus II 959–63
Nicephorus II Phocas 963–69
John I Tzimisces 969–76
Basil II 976–1025
Constantine VIII 1025–28
Romanus III Argyrus 1028–34
Michael IV 1034–41
Michael V 1041–42
Theodora and Zoe 1042
Constantine IX 1042–55
Theodora
(second reign) 1055–56
Michael VI 1056–57
Isaac Commenus 1057–59
Constantine X Ducas 1059–67
Romanus IV Diogenes 1067–71
Michael VII Ducas 1071–78
Nicephorus III 1078–81
Alexius I Comnenus
1081–1118
John II Comnenus 1118–43
Manuel I Comnenus 1143–80
Alexius II Comnenus 1180–83
Andronicus I Comnenus
1183–85

Isaac II Angelus 1185–95
Alexius III Angelus 1195–1203
Isaac Angelus
(second reign) 1203–04
Alexius IV Angelus
(co-emperor) 1203–04
Alexius V Ducas 1204
*Theodore I Lascaris 1204–22
*John III 1222–54
*Theodore II Lascaris 1254–58
*John IV 1258–61
Michael VIII
Palaeologus 1261–82
Andronicus II
Palaeologus 1282–1328
Andronicus III
Palaeologus 1328–41
John V Palaeologus 1341–91
John VI Cantacuzenus
(co-emperor) 1341–54
Andronicus (IV)
(co-emperor) 1376–79
John (VII) (co-emperor) 1390
Manuel II Palaeologus 1391–1425
John VIII Palaeologus 1425–48
Constantine XI
Dragases 1449–53

(* Ruled in Nicaea during the Latin occupation of Constantinople)

Ottoman Sultans

Orhan Gazi 1324–59
Murat I 1359–89
Beyazit I 1389–1403
(Interregnum 1403–13)
Mehmet I 1413–21
Murat II 1421–51
Mehmet II,
the Conqueror 1451–81
Beyazit II 1481–1512
Selim I, the Grim 1512–20
Selim II 1566–74
Süleyman I, the Magnificent
1520–66
Murat III 1574–95
Mehmet III 1595–1603
Ahmet I 1603–17
Mustafa I 1617–18
Osman II 1618–22
Mustafa I
(second reign) 1622–23
Murat IV 1623–40

Ibrahim 1640–48
Mehmet IV 1648–87
Süleyman II 1687–91
Ahmet II 1691–95
Mustafa II 1695–1703
Ahmet III 1703–30
Mahmut I 1730–54
Osman III 1754–57
Mustafa III 1757–74
Abdül Hamit I 1774–89
Selim III 1789–1807
Mustafa IV 1807–08
Mahmut II 1808–39
Abdül Mecit I 1839–61
Abdül Aziz 1861–76
Murat V 1876
Abdül Hamit II 1876–1909
Mehmet V 1909–18
Mehmet VI 1918–22
Abdül Mecit (II)
(Caliph only) 1922–24

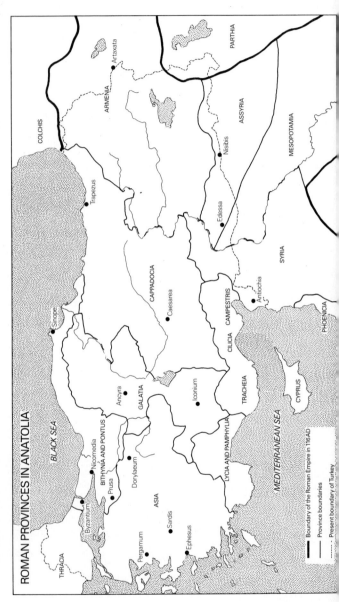

ROMAN PROVINCES IN ANATOLIA

PARTHIA

ARMENIA

Artaxata

COLCHIS

ASSYRIA

MESOPOTAMIA

Nisibis

Trapezus

Edessa

CAPPADOCIA

SYRIA

Caesarea

Antiochia

Sinope

CILICIA CAMPESTRIS

PHOENICIA

BLACK SEA

TRACHEIA

Ancyra

GALATIA

Iconium

CYPRUS

Nicomedia

BITHYNIA AND PONTUS

LYCIA AND PAMPHYLIA

Prusa

Dorylaeum

MEDITERRANEAN SEA

Byzantium

ASIA

THRACIA

Pergamum

Sardis

Ephesus

———— Boundary of the Roman Empire in 116AD

———— Province boundaries

·········· Present boundary of Turkey

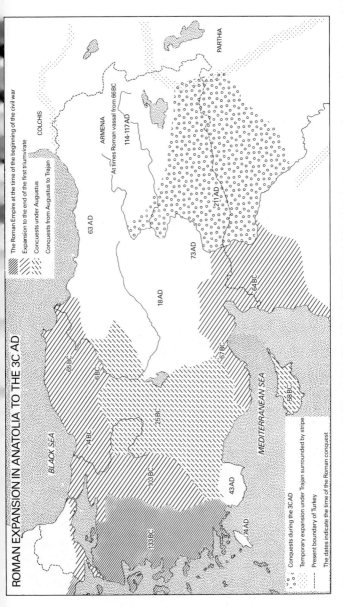

ROMAN EXPANSION IN ANATOLIA TO THE 3C AD

The Roman Empire at the time of the beginning of the civil war

Expansion to the end of the first triumvirate

Conquests under Augustus

Conquests from Augustus to Trajan

- Conquests during the 3C AD
- Temporary expansion under Trajan surrounded by stripe
- - - - Present boundary of Turkey

The dates indicate the time of the Roman conquest

COLCHIS

ARMENIA
At times Roman vassal from 66BC
114-117 AD

PARTHIA

BLACK SEA

MEDITERRANEAN SEA

133BC

74BC

103BC

65BC

6BC

25BC

18AD

63AD

73AD

64BC

67BC

58BC

43AD

74AD

21AD

THE

HUNGARY
TRANSYLVAN
WALL
SERBIA BULG
GREECE
MEDITERRANEAN SEA
ALGIERS TUNIS
TRIPOLI

 Osmanli possessions in the early 14C

Expansion to 1389

Expansion to 1481

Expansion to 1570

Expansion to 1683

Temporary expansions are surrounded by stripes

SION OF THE OTTOMAN EMPIRE UNTIL 1683

CRIMEAN KHANATE

BLACK SEA

CASPIAN SEA

ANATOLIA

PT

Persian Gulf

HEJAZ

RED SEA

YEMEN

INDIAN OCEAN

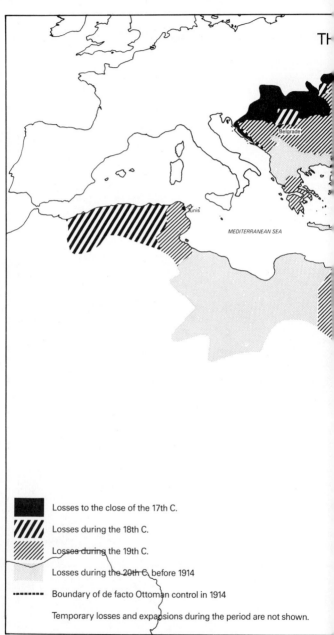

TH

Belgrade

Tunis

MEDITERRANEAN SEA

■ Losses to the close of the 17th C.

▨ Losses during the 18th C.

▨ Losses during the 19th C.

Losses during the 20th C. before 1914

-------- Boundary of de facto Ottoman control in 1914

Temporary losses and expansions during the period are not shown.

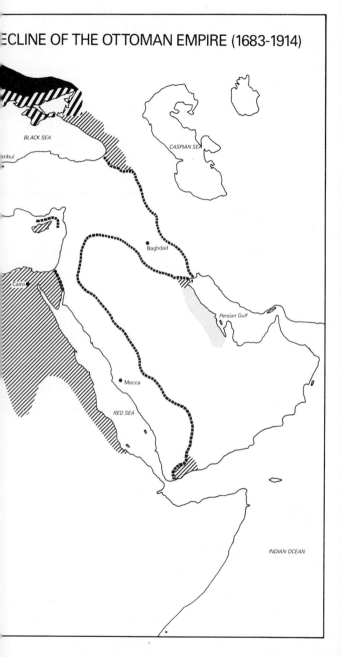

DECLINE OF THE OTTOMAN EMPIRE (1683-1914)

BLACK SEA

CASPIAN SEA

anbul

Cairo

Baghdad

Persian Gulf

Mecca

RED SEA

INDIAN OCEAN

GLOSSARY OF ARCHAEOLOGICAL AND ARCHITECTURAL TERMS

ABACUS. The upper member of a capital

ACROPOLIS. Fortified hilltop. Citadel of a city

ACROTERION (ACROTERIUM). Statues or ornaments at the apex and inner corners of a pediment

ADYTON. Inner sanctuary of a temple

AEGIS. Cuirass or shield with Gorgon's head and ring of snakes

AGORA. Public square or market-place

ALABASTRON. Jar used for ointment or oil

AMAZONOMACHIA. Combat between Greeks and Amazons

AMBO. Pulpit in a Christian basilica; facing pulpits in a church from which the epistle and gospel were read

AMPHITHEATRE. An elliptical or circular space surrounded by seats arranged in tiers; used by the Romans for gladiatorial contests

AMPHORA. Two-handled container for wine or water

ANALEMMA. Supporting wall at the side of a theatre

ANTA. Projecting pilasters ending the lateral walls of the cella of a Greek temple

ANTEFIX. Ornament on the eave or cornice of a building; a feature used to hide the end of the tiles

ANTHEMION. Flower ornament

APOTROPAION. A protective symbol to turn away evil

APSE. A semicircular recess in a wall, especially in a church or in a Roman law-court

ARCHITRAVE (EPISTYLE). A lintel or main beam resting on columns. The lowest member of the entablature

ASHLAR (MASONRY). Square cut stones and masonry constructed of these

ASTRAGAL. A moulding at the top or base of a column

ATLANTES. Columns in the form of a male figure; cf. Caryatid

ATRIUM. The court of a Roman house, roofed at the sides, but exposed to the sky in the centre or the entrance to a Byzantine church

BALLISTA. War machine which catapulted large stones; used to break down defensive walls

BAS-RELIEF. Low relief sculpture on a marble or stone slab

BASILICA. Roman exchange and court of law; building with a central hall and side halls which were lower in height

BEMA. Rostrum or a raised section of the chancel of a Byzantine church

BOULEUTERION. Meeting place of the Boule, the legislative council of a city. The city hall

CAIQUE. Small wooden trading vessel frequently found in Greek and E Mediterranean waters

CAPITAL. The topmost part of column

CARYATID. Column in the form of a female figure; cf. Atlantes

CAVEA. The auditorium of a theatre; name derived from the fact that originally it was dug out of a hill

CELLA. The great hall of a temple which contained the cult statue

CHITON. A tunic worn short by men and long by women

CHLAMYS. Light cloak worn by ephebes

CHTHONIC. Dwelling in or under the ground

CIPPUS. A small column, sometimes without base or capital, bearing an inscription. Used as a landmark or funeral monument.

COLONNADE (see also STOA and PORTICO). A row of columns which supports an entablature

COLUMNAE CAELATAE. Sculptured columns

COMPOSITE CAPTIAL. Corinthian capital with Ionic volutes, which are slightly reduced in size

CONVENTUS. Provincial court of justice

CORNICE. The upper member of the entablature

CREPIDOMA. The stepped platform on which a temple stood

CUNEUS. Wedge-shaped division in the cavea of a theatre

CYCLOPEAN MASONRY. Masonry composed of large, irregular shaped blocks laid without mortar and not in courses

DEME. A village

DIAZOMA. A horizontal passage in the cavea of a theatre (διάζωμα, a girdle)

DIPTEROS. A temple surrounded by two rows of columns

DROMOS. A long narrow entrance to a building, sometimes lined with columns or statues. Passage giving access to a tholos or beehive tomb

EGG AND TONGUE or EGG AND DART. A moulding of alternate eggs and arrowheads

ENGAGED COLUMN. Partly detached column

ENTABLATURE. The stonework resting on a row of columns, including architrave, frieze and cornice

EPHEBUS. Greek youth of 18 or over, usually undergoing training either in the army or at a university

EPISTYLE (Greek). The architrave

EROTES. Figures of Eros, the god of love

EXEDRA. Semicircular recess, usually with a seat, in a Classical or Byzantine building

FLUTES. The vertical channels cut into the sides of columns

FORUM. Roman market place

FRIEZE. The middle member of the entablature

GEISON (Greek). The cornice

GIGANTOMACHIA. War of or with the giants

HERM. Quadrangular pillar usually adorned with an erect phallus and surmounted by a bust

HEROON. Shrine or temple dedicated to a demigod or deified hero

HIERON. Temple or sacred enclosure

HIMATION. An oblong cloak thrown over the left shoulder and fastened over or under the right

HIPPODROME. A place for horse or chariot races

HOPLITE. Heavily-armed foot-soldier

HYDRA. Jar for carrying water

HYPAETHRAL. Open to the sky

ICONOSTASIS. Screen bearing icons in a Greek Orthodox church

ISODOMIC. A term applied to masonry laid in courses of equal height

KANTHARUS (CANTHARUS). Wine cup with two large curving handles, usually associated with Dionysus

KLINE. Couch, bed or bier

KOMAST. A reveller; often depicted singing or dancing at or following a symposium

KORE. Maiden. Archaic female figure. Name sometimes given to Persephone the daughter of Demeter

KOUROS. Boy. Archaic male figure

KRATER. Vessel in which wine was mixed with water

KYLIX. Shallow wine cup

LABRYS. A double-axe; religious symbol of great antiquity

MAENAD. Bacchante. A 'raver'. A female follower of Dionysus. (From the Greek Μανιάς, raving, frantic)

MEGARON. Large hall of a palace or house

METOPE. Plain rectangular panel in a Doric frieze, which was replaced in the Classical period by a sculptured relief

NAISKOS. Cella of modest proportions in a Greek temple

NAOS (Greek). A temple or sometimes the cella of a temple

NARTHEX. Narrow vestibule along the W side of a church

NAUMACHIA. A mock naval battle staged in a flooded amphitheatre

NEOCORUS. Title borne by a city which possessed a temple dedicated to the imperial cult

NYMPHAION. Sanctuary of the Nymphs with fountain or running water

ODEUM. A concert hall sometimes roofed

OIKOS. A house

OINOCHOE. Wine jug

OMPHALOS. A sacred stone marking the centre of the earth where the eagles of Zeus met

OPISTHODOMUS. The porch at the rear of a temple, which was sometimes used to store valuables

ORCHESTRA. Large circular space occupied by the chorus and actors in Greek theatres

ORTHOSTATS. Upright slabs at the base of a wall

PALAESTRA. Training area for wrestlers, boxers, etc.

PANCRATION. Athletic contest involving wrestling and boxing; everything except biting or gouging of eyes was permitted

PARODOS. Space between the cavea and the stage of a theatre

PEDIMENT. A low-pitched gable above a portico

PEPLOS. A mantle in one piece worn draped by women

PERIBOLOS. A precinct or the circuit around it

PERIPTEROS. A temple surrounded by a row of columns

PERISTYLE. A row or rows of columns surrounding a building or open court

PETASUS. Broad-brimmed hat worn by an ephebe

PHIALE. Saucer or bowl

PITHOS. Large earthenware jar used for storing oil, grain, etc.

PLINTH. A square block forming the base of a column

PODIUM. A platform, also a low wall or continuous pedestal carrying a colonnade

PORTICO. A stoa or colonnade

PRONAOS. The porch in front of a temple

PROPYLON (pl. Propyleia). Entrance gate to a temenos

PROSKENION. A raised platform in front of the stage-building used by the actors in a Roman theatre

PROSTYLOS. A building with free-standing columns in a row

PROTHESIS. Laying out of a corpse

PRYTANEION or PRYTANAEUM. The administrative building in a city. This contained an altar dedicated to Hestia, on which burned a perpetual flame

PSEUDO-DIPTEROS. A dipteral temple without the inner row of columns

PTERON (Greek). A row of columns surrounding a Greek temple

QUADRIGA. Four-horsed chariot

SATYR. Follower of Dionysus, usually depicted as half-animal, half-human with tail, hooves and permanently erect phallus

SCAENAE FRONS. Elaborately ornamented front of the scene building in a theatre

SKENE. The stage-building of a Roman theatre

SHAFT. The body of a column between the base and capital

SILENUS. An old satyr, the son of Pan or Hermes and a nymph, who reared Dionysus. Ususally depicted as a grotesque, fat drunken old man precariously balanced on the back of a donkey

SIMA. The gutter of a building

SOCLE. Projecting part of a base or pedestal

SOFFIT. The lower surface of an architectural element

SPINA. Barrier in the centre of a Roman amphitheatre.

STADIUM. Long building in which foot-races and other athletic contests were held

STELE. Narrow stone slab set upright bearing writing or a decoration. Often used as a grave stone or marker

STOA (See also COLONNADE and PORTICO). A porch or portico not attached to a larger building

STYLOBATE. The top step of a crepidoma

SYNTHRONON. Semicircular bench or benches for the clergy in the apse or in rows on either side of the Bema

TEMENOS. A sacred enclosure

TEMPLE-IN-ANTIS. Simple building in which the side walls were extended to form a porch. This had two columns between the antae

TETRASTOON. A square surrounded by four colonnades

THEATRON. At first applied to the section of the theatre occupied by the audience, later extended to the whole building. (From the Greek θέατρον or θέατρον, the seeing place; cf.

Auditorium (Latin) the hearing place)

THEME (Byzantine). A province

THOLOS. A circular building. Term sometimes applied to an underground beehive tomb

THYRSUS. Staff, wreathed with vine leaves and ivy and surmounted with a pine-cone, carried by Dionysus and his followers

TORUS. A large convex moulding, e.g. at the base of a column

TRICONCHOS. A building composed of three 'conches', i.e. of three semicircular niches surmounted by half-domes

TRIGLYPH. Part of Doric frieze bearing three vertical grooves, which alternated with the metopes

TRISKELES. Three legs radiating from a common centre

TYMPANON or TYMPANUM. The area enclosed by the mouldings of a pediment

TRIREME. Greek galley rowed by three banks of oars

VELUM. Canvas used to protect spectators in the auditorium of a Roman theatre from the sun

VOMITORIUM. Covered exit in a Roman theatre

XOANON. A primitive wooden cult statue or idol, frequently believed to have fallen from heaven

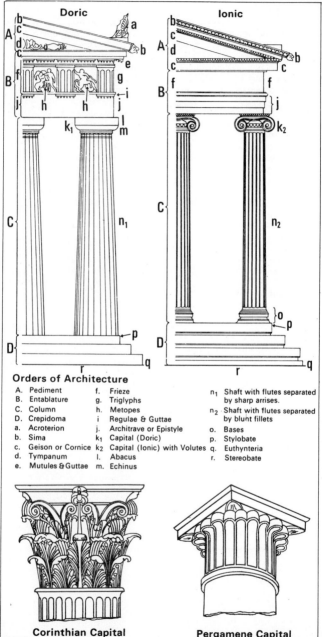

Orders of Architecture

A.	Pediment	f.	Frieze
B.	Entablature	g.	Triglyphs
C.	Column	h.	Metopes
D.	Crepidoma	i	Regulae & Guttae
a.	Acroterion	j.	Architrave or Epistyle
b.	Sima	k_1	Capital (Doric)
c.	Geison or Cornice	k_2	Capital (Ionic) with Volutes
d.	Tympanum	l.	Abacus
e.	Mutules & Guttae	m.	Echinus

n_1 Shaft with flutes separated by sharp arrises.

n_2 Shaft with flutes separated by blunt fillets

o. Bases
p. Stylobate
q. Euthynteria
r. Stereobate

Corinthian Capital

Pergamene Capital

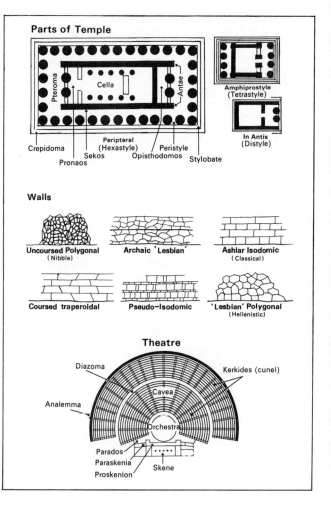

Parts of Temple

Pteroma

Cella

Antae

Amphiprostyle
(Tetrastyle)

In Antis
(Distyle)

Crepidoma

Pronaos

Sekos

Peripteral
(Hexastyle)

Opisthodomos

Peristyle

Stylobate

Walls

Uncoursed Polygonal
(Nibble)

Archaic 'Lesbian'

Ashlar Isodomic
(Classical)

Coursed traperoidal

Pseudo-Isodomic

'Lesbian' Polygonal
(Hellenistic)

Theatre

Diazoma

Kerkides (cunel)

Cavea

Analemma

Orchestra

Parados

Paraskenia

Proskenion

Skene

SELECT BIBLIOGRAPHY

Akurgal, E. *Ancient Civilizations and Ruins of Turkey*, İstanbul 6th edition 1985.

Arrian, *Life of Alexander*, trans. A. de Selincourt, London 1958.

Atvur, O. *Side*, İstanbul 1984.

Bayburtluoğlu, C. *Lycie*, n.d. Ankara.

Beaufort, F. *Karamania*, London 1817.

Bickerman, E.J. *Chronology of the Ancient World*, London 1980.

Bieber, Margarete. *The History of the Greek and Roman Theater*, Princeton 1971.

Blake, Evrett C. and Edmonds, Anne G. *Biblical Sites in Turkey*, İstanbul 1972.

Boardman, J. *The Greeks Overseas*, London 1980.

Boardman, J.; Griffin, J.; Murray, O. ed. *The Oxford History of the Classical World*.

Boase, T.S.R. ed. *The Cilician Kingdom of Armenia*, Edinburgh 1978.

Burkert, W. *Greek Religion*, Oxford 1985. *Homo Necans* trans. P. Bing, Berkeley 1983.

Charlemont Lord. *The Travels of Lord Charlemont in Greece and Turkey 1749*, ed W.B. Stanford and E.J. Finopoulos, London 1984.

Casson, L. *Ships and Seamanship in the Ancient World*, Princeton 1986.

Çelebi, Evliya. *Travels in Europe, Asia and Africa* trans. J. von Hammer 1834–1850.

Chandler, R. *Travels in Asia Minor and Greece*, 3rd edition London 1817.

Chandler, R.; Revett, N.; and Pars, W. *Ionian Antiquities*, Society of Dilettanti 1769.

Clayton, P and Price, M. *The Seven Wonders of the Ancient World*, London 1988.

Cumont, Franz. *Oriental Religions in Roman Paganism*, New York 1956. *The Mysteries of Mithra*, New York 1956.

Erim, Kenan T. *Aphrodisias. City of Venus Aphrodite*, London 1986.

Fellows, C. *Asia Minor*, London 1839. *Lycia*, London 1840.

Ferguson, J. *The Religions of the Roman Empire*, London 1970.

Fox, Robin Lane. *Alexander the Great*, London 1973. *Pagans and Christians*, London 1986.

Freely, John. *The Companion Guide to Turkey*, London 1979.

Garland, R. *The Greek Way of Death*, London 1985.

Gibbon, E. *The Decline and Fall of the Roman Empire*, London 1910.

Goodwin, Godfrey. *Ottoman Turkey*, London 1977. *A History of Ottoman Architecture*, London 1987.

Gough, Mary. *The Plain and the Rough Places*, London 1954.

Hägg, Tomas. *The Novel in Antiquity*, Oxford 1983.

Hadas, Moses. *Hellenistic Culture*, Columbia 1959.

Haynes, Sybille. *Land of the Chimaera*, London 1974.

Hamilton, W.J. *Researches in Asia Minor*, London 1842.

Haroutunian, Arto der. *A Turkish Cookbook*, London 1987.

Herodotus. *The Histories* trans. Aubrey de Selincourt, London 1955.

Ibn Battuta. *Travels in Asia and Africa 1325–1354*, London 1983. *Voyages. II. De la Mecque aux steppes russes*, Paris 1982.

Inan, Jale *Roman Sculpture in Side*, Ankara 1975.

Jones, A.H.M. *The Later Roman Empire. 284–602* 2 vols, Oxford 1986.

MacMullen, R. *Paganism in the Roman Empire*, Yale 1981.

Metzger, H. *Anatolia II*, Geneva 1969.

Newton, C.T. *Travels and Discoveries in the Levant*, London 1865.

Oberleitner, W.; Gschwantler, K.; Bernhard-Walcher, A.; Bammer, A.

Funde aus Ephesos und Samothrake, Vienna 1978.
Ovid. *Metamorphoses* trans. Mary M. Innes. London 1986.
Önen, Ü. *Lycia*, İzmir 1984. *Karien*, İzmir 1986.
Özgür, M. Edip. *Aspendos*, Antalya 1984. *Perge*, İstanbul 1988.
Parks, W. *Oracles of Apollo in Asia Minor*, Beckenham 1985.
Pausanias. *Guide to Greece* trans. Peter Levi, 2 vols, London 1984.
Pekman, Adnan *Perge Tarihi* (History of Perge), Ankara 1973.
Poliakoff, Michael B. *Combat Sports in the Ancient World*, Yale 1987.
Price, S.R.F. *Rituals and Power*, Cambridge 1986.
Radt, Wolgang. *Pergamum. An Archaeological Guide*, İstanbul 1978.
Ramsay, W.M. *Letters to the Seven Churches*, 2nd edition 1906.
Reynolds, J.M. *Aphrodisias and Rome*, London 1982.
Rosenbaum, E.; Huber, G.; Onurkan, S. *A Survey of Coastal Cities in Western Cilicia*, Ankara 1967.
Sansone, D. *Greek Athletics and the Genesis of Sport*, Berkeley 1988.
Spratt, T.A.B. and Forbes, E. *Travels in Lycia*, London 1847.
Stark, Freya. *Ionia: a Quest*, London 1954. *The Lycian Shore*, London 1956. *Alexander's Path*, London 1958.
Stoneman, R. *Land of the Lost Gods*, London 1987. *Across the Hellespont*, London 1987.
Strabo. *The Geography*, vols V and VI, London 1970 and 1928.
Taşkıran, Celal and Hüseyin, Kurt. *Kızkalesi, a guide*, Silifke 1986. *Uzuncaburç, a guide*, Silifke 1985.
Texier, Charles *Asie Minor*, Paris 1862.

Catalogues and Journals

The Anatolian Civilisations vol. II. Greek, Roman and Byzantine; vol III. Seljuk and Ottoman, İstanbul 1983.
The Proceedings of the Xth International Congress of Classical Archaeology, 3 vols, Ankara, İzmir, 23–30/IX/1973.
The Journal of Hellenic Studies. Supplements on archaeology in Asia Minor. 1960, 1964–65, 1970–71, 1971–78, 1984–85.
Anatolian Studies. Various volumes.

Detail of a page from an early guidebook to Turkey in Latin.

PRACTICAL INFORMATION

This part of the Blue Guide has been prepared with two objects in mind. It is hoped that it will assist travellers to prepare for their journey to Turkey and that, when read in conjunction with the chapters on the various routes, it will help them to have a problem-free and enjoyable visit.

Every effort has been made to ensure that the information provided is both up-to-date and accurate. Based largely on recent first-hand experience of living and travelling in Turkey, it has been compiled with the assistance of the London office of the Ministry of Culture and Tourism. While it as comprehensive as the scope of the guide permits, readers seeking additional details are advised to consult the various specialist sources which are listed under the different subject-headings.

As Turkey's tourist industry continues to expand, it is inevitable that changes will take place in that country. The publishers and the author would be pleased to hear from readers of any suggested amendments which might be considered for inclusion in future editions of the guide.

İstanbul falls outside the scope of the Blue Guide Part I. However, as it will be the entry-point for many visitors to the Marmara, Aegean and Mediterranean areas, references to the city and its services are given, where they are considered appropriate.

Sources of Information

General information on Turkey may be obtained from the offices of the *Ministry of Culture and Tourism*, which is represented in more than a dozen foreign countries. In Great Britain enquiries should be addressed to the Ministry at 170–173 (First Floor) Piccadilly, London, W1V 9DD, tel: 01–734 8681/82, telex: 8954905 TTIOFC-G, and in the United States to 821 United Nations Plaza, New York, NY 10017, tel: 212 687 2194, telex: 426428 or to 2010 Massachusetts Avenue NW Washington DC 20036, tel: 833 84 11, 429 94 44, Telex: 251544.

The Ministry produces a number of useful publications, which are available free of charge from its overseas offices. These include illustrated pamphlets on Turkey's various regions, a small folding map (produced by the London office), which is updated each year to show changes in the road system, and a booklet listing the various operators offering holidays in, and flights to, Turkey. Its offices can also supply the brochures produced by some of these companies. In addition, the Ministry's experienced staff is able to offer advice on a wide range of subjects—anything from the resort most likely to suit an individual enquirer to the best time of the year to visit a particular part of the country.

A number of the books listed in the bibliography (see p 128) provide a useful background on the country and its history. Others provide additional information on individual archaeological sites, which supplements the necessarily general accounts in the guide.

Detailed maps of Turkey are mainly confined to the western part of the country. Among the most useful are: Turkey and Western Asia and Turkey–East published by Roger Lascelles, 47, York Road, Brentford, Middlesex, TW8 OQP. The first covers Thrace and Asiatic Turkey as far east as Samsun and Antakya on a scale of 1:800,000. On the reverse it shows Turkey in relation to its neighbours on a scale of 1:2,500,000. The whole country is covered in two sheets produced by Freytag & Berndt on a scale of 1:2,000,000. These maps may be obtained from specialist shops like Edward Stanford Ltd, 12–14 Long Acre, London WC2, or ordered through booksellers. A useful road map showing western Anatolia from İzmit to Antalya on a scale of 1:800,000 and the whole country on a scale of 1:2,000,000 is produced by Ada Kitabevi, Kibris Caddesi No. 10, Kuşadası. This is available only in Turkey.

When to visit Turkey

There is no doubt that the best seasons to visit places on the Marmara and Aegean coasts and hinterland are the spring and autumn. In those areas around the middle of March the weather begins to improve dramatically. The countryside, which lay dormant during the long months of winter rain, burgeons forth in a dazzling display of colour. Farmers in the fields near Bursa, busily preparing for summer's harvest, are stalked by lines of solemn storks. Not far away at Kuş Cenneti noisy flocks of migrant birds fill the air with their cries. In the ruins of Troy, Pergamum and Ephesus lizards, warmed by the growing power of the sun, move slowly over antique walls. Carpets of anemones, which range in colour from a red so intense that it is almost black to palest white, clothe the sites of Xanthus, Tlos and Pinara. Deep in the pine woods near Fethiye asphodel, the flower of the Elysian Fields, visible reminder of the shades of ancient Telmessian heroes, nods its ghostly head.

There are few tourists at that time of year, so accommodation, particularly in the small resorts, is cheap and easy to find. As buses and trains are not crowded with foreign visitors, reservations may be made without difficulty and journeys accomplished in reasonable comfort. Visits to the ancient sites and to the museums are more pleasant in the absence of the crowds that fill them in the summer.

During the months of June, July and August a different situation prevails. Most resorts are full to bursting point and prices are at their highest. Travelling in crowded buses and trains in day-temperatures of up to 30° C is unpleasant in the extreme. Only those who have to take their holidays in mid-summer should go to Turkey then.

From the middle of September to early December the days are warm and sunny, the nights fine but cool. The debilitating heat of summer has passed and with it has gone the great mass of foreign visitors. Although the verdant hues of spring have long disappeared from the countryside, the mosaic of brown and umber, which has replaced them, has its own beauty. As at the beginning of the year prices are lower and usually it is not necessary to book accommodation in advance. Autumn days in Marmaris, Fethiye or Bodrum have their own quiet charm, as the cognoscenti will attest.

The situation on the Mediterranean coast is broadly the same. Spring and autumn in this part of Turkey are delightful. However, summers are even hotter and more exhausting than on the Aegean coast. In August a day-temperature of 40° C is not uncommon in Mersin, Adana and Antakya.

Formalities

Passports and Visas. It is necessary to be in possession of a valid passport to enter Turkey. Citizens of the United Kingdom, the United States, the Republic of Ireland, Australia, New Zealand, Canada and most countries in W Europe do not require a visa for a stay of up to three months. Nationals of other countries should ask the Turkish Embassy for information about the regulations which apply to them.

Anyone who wishes to stay in Turkey for longer than three months should make an application for a residence permit. The authorities normally require an applicant to prove that he has adequate financial means, e.g. income from a source outside the country or that he has legal employment in Turkey. However, some long-term residents, who do not wish to involve themselves in the complications of applying for a permit, leave the country before the end of each three-month period. After a few days' absence in Greece or another of Turkey's neighbours, they return and begin a further three months' stay. This practice appears to acceptable to the Turkish authorities.

Customs Regulations. Apart from the occasional spot-check, visitors to Turkey are not asked, as a rule, to open their baggage on arrival in the country. They are allowed to bring in any goods which are for their personal use. These include one camera and a reasonable quantity of film, a transistor radio, sports equipment, 400 cigarettes, 50 cigars, 1kg of coffee, 1.5kg of instant coffee and 5 (100cc) or 7 (70cc) bottles of spirit, of which no more than three shall be of the same brand. Any valuable items, including antiques, should be noted on the visitor's passport to facilitate control on departure.

Sharp instruments (including camping knives) and weapons may not be brought in without special permission.

Turkey prohibits the import, use of, and trade in narcotics (including marijuana). Offences against this law are punished by severe penalties.

Currency Regulations. Not more than $1000 worth of Turkish currency may be taken out of the country. There is no limit on the amount of foreign currency, which may be brought in. Keep all receipts obtained for the exchange of foreign currency into Turkish lira. You may have to show these when converting unused Turkish lira back into foreign currency or when taking goods purchased in Turkey out of the country.

Health Regulations. No vaccinations are required by the Turkish authorities, but see the suggestions in the section on 'Health' below.

Domestic animals, including hunting dogs, must have a rabies vaccination certificate issued 48 hours before departure. This should be accompanied by a Turkish translation provided by a Turkish Embassy or Consulate.

Motoring. Motorists should be in possession of either a Green Card International Insurance, which has been endorsed for Turkish territory in Europe and Asia or Turkish third party insurance. The latter may be purchased at the frontier posts.

Accidents, whether they involve persons or not, must be reported to the police. The Turkish Touring and Automobile Association (*Türkiye Turing ve Otomobil Kurumu*) will carry out any necessary repairs to the vehicles of motorists in possession of credit cheques issued by their national automobile associations. The bill, calculated in Swiss francs, will then be forwarded to the association concerned. Recovery and repatriation of a damaged vehicle can be arranged by the Turkish Touring and Automobile Association for a motorist, who has an AIT or FIA booklet.

Private Yachts. Yacht owners in possession of a Transit Log may keep their boat in Turkish waters for a period of not more than two years for the purpose of wintering or maintenance. Certain marinas are licenced for the berthing of yachts for a period of two to five years. Details may be obtained from the marinas concerned.

On arrival in Turkish waters the yacht owner should proceed to the nearest port of entry—Çanakkale, Bandırma, İstanbul, Akçay, Ayvalık, Dikili, İzmir, Çeşme, Kuşadası, Güllük, Bodrum, Datça, Marmaris, Fethiye, Kaş, Finike, Kemer, Antalya, Alanya, Anamur, Taşucu (Silifke), Mersin, İskenderun, Samsun, Trabzon—so that his log may be controlled.

Owners should acquaint themselves with the various regulations, which apply to those sailing in Turkish waters. Details may be obtained from Turkish Embassies or the relevant yachting associations. In particular the following should be noted:

International navigation rules should be followed at all times.
The Turkish courtesy flag should be flown between 08.00 and sunset.
Zig-zagging between Turkish and Greek waters should be avoided.
Yachtsmen should not take archaeological objects from Turkish coastal waters. The penalty for doing so is confiscation of the yacht.
Yachts should not be moored in the forbidden zones. Further information about these zones may be obtained from any Turkish Embassy or Consulate.

Travel to Turkey

Air. There are frequent flights by British Airways and Turkish Airlines (THY) from London to İstanbul, Ankara, İzmir and Antalya. From the United States of America there are good connecting flights via London or via Amsterdam with KLM.

There are bus services, for which a small charge is made, from all Turkish airports, except Dalaman, to the town terminals. Taxis are also available.

THY offers substantial reductions to students, sports groups and families. When planning a holiday, budget-conscious travellers should note that the air fare constituent in the price of a package tour is usually much less than the cost of a flight-only ticket.

Particularly attractive to students and to those who wish to limit their expenditure, are the many cheap charter flights, which operate from London during the holiday season. It should be noted that some of these restrict the visitor to a maximum stay of two weeks.

Charter flights to Dalaman in SW Turkey bring Bodrum, Marmaris, Fethiye and the small and very beautiful resorts of the Lycian coast within the reach of travellers who have only a limited amount of time at their disposal. Many of the tour companies operate special coach services from Dalaman to these resorts. Visitors unable to obtain seats on one of these coaches should take a taxi or dolmuş to Dalaman village, where they can pick up one of the regular bus or dolmuş services to their destination.

Details of charter flights to Turkey operated by companies like Regent Holidays, Shanklin, Isle of Wight are given in the brochure published by the Turkish Ministry of Culture and Tourism. (See above.) They are also frequently advertised in the holiday columns of the 'The Times', 'Sunday Times', 'The Observer', 'The Guardian', and other daily and weekly papers.

Sea. Between 4 April and 13 June there is a sailing every 15 days by the car-ferries of the Turkish Maritime Line from Venice to İzmir and İstanbul, and from 20 June to the end of October at weekly intervals to the same destinations. Costs, including sleepers or couchettes to Venice, are likely to be substantially higher than the air-fare. However, Turkish Maritime Lines offer reductions on return tickets to students, children, journalists and groups. Enquiries and bookings should be addressed to travel agents or direct to Sunquest Holidays, Aldine House, 9/15 Aldine St, London W12 8AW; 01–749 9911.

There is also the luxurious Orient Express ferry, which leaves Venice every Friday between April and October for İstanbul and Kuşadası. This is operated by British Ferries Ltd, 20 Upper Ground, London, SE1 9PF, tel: 01–928 6000. Travellers, for whom expense is not a consideration may take the revived Orient Express train from London, Victoria. This connects with the ferry in Venice.

It is also possible to travel by car-ferry from Brindisi via Patras and Piraeus to İzmir. There are night-sailings from Famagusta (Magosa) in the Turkish Republic of N Cyprus to Mersin three times each week and frequent services link the Greek islands of Lesbos, Chios, Samos, Cos and Rhodes with the Turkish mainland during the holiday season. Details of times and fares may be obtained from local travel agents.

Rail. While it is possible to travel by rail from London to İstanbul, the rigours of this journey, which can take as long as three days, are such that it will commend itself only to the most hardy travellers. The trains, which are popular with immigrant workers returning to Yugoslavia, Greece and Turkey from W Europe, are usually very crowded and the condition of the carriages, and especially of the toilets, deteriorates as the journey progresses.

The trains are subject to delays, and are slow and frequently late in arriving at their destination. Any illusions of sharing the luxury enjoyed by the characters in Agatha Christie's celebrated crime novel are quickly dispelled by a few hours in their noisy, smoke-filled compartments.

The following is a summary of the trains operating in spring 1988:

From Paris there is a daily service by the 'İstanbul Express' via Lausanne, Milan, Venice, Trieste, Belgrade and Sofia.

From Munich two daily services to İstanbul are provided by the 'İstanbul Express' and by the 'Tauern-Orient Express', which run via Salzburg, Zagreb, Belgrade and Sofia.

From Vienna there is a daily service by the 'İstanbul Express' and by the 'Balkan Express' via Graz, Zagreb, Belgrade and Sofia. From Venice to İstanbul there are daily departures by the 'İstanbul

Express' via Trieste, Belgrade and Sofia. There is a wagon-lits service twice a week on this route.

From Athens a slow, uncomfortable train, which is routed via Thessaloníki, takes 35 hours to reach İstanbul.

As the frequency and routes of these trains may change, it is advisable to check the current situation with British Rail's European Travel Centre at Victoria Station, London or with a travel agent. They should also be able to provide information about the discounts offered to students and young people under the age of 26.

Road. It is approximately 3000km from London to İstanbul. Any driver, willing to tackle this distance, must be prepared to contend with the convoys of TIR lorries which carry goods to Turkey and destinations in the Middle East. Although most of the roads *en route* are well-surfaced and well-maintained, some sections are very crowded. An additional disincentive is provided by the checks at the various international borders, which are often long-winded and time-consuming. Information about car insurance, the international driving licence, etc., may be obtained from the AA or the RAC. Both organisations can also provide their members with detailed route-maps and town-plans.

Two routes are suggested: one by Ostend, Brussels, Cologne, Frankfurt, then by Nuremberg, Linz, Vienna, Budapest and Belgrade or by Stuttgart, Munich, Salzburg, Ljubliana, Zagreb and Belgrade. From Belgrade the route is by Nis, Sofia and Edirne to İstanbul. The so-called S route is by Calais, Paris, Geneva, Venice, Ljubliana, Belgrade, Sofia to İstanbul. Travellers, who wish to shorten the length of time spent driving, may take the car-ferry from Venice to İzmir or İstanbul.

Coaches. There are frequent express coach services from Paris (connecting bus from London), Strasbourg, Munich and Vienna to İstanbul. Travellers who dislike flying will find that the coaches, which are faster, cleaner, and more comfortable than the trains, offer a suitable alternative. Non-smokers are advised to obtain seats immediately behind the driver. Discounts are offered to various categories of passenger. Details may be obtained from the various operating companies.

The service Paris–İstanbul is operated for Bosfor Turism by Tourisme Eurolines, 3–5 Avenue de la Porte de la Villette, 75019 Paris, tel: 40 34 36 67 or 42 05 12 10.

From Strasbourg the service is provided by Varan Tourism, 37, Faubourg de Pierre, 67000, Strasbourg, tel: 20 03 87.

From Munich the service is by Bosfor Turism, Seidi Str. 2.2. 8000, München 2, tel: 59 50 02 and 59 24 96.

From Vienna there are services by Bosfor Turism, 1040 Wien, Süd Bahnhof, Argentinierstr. 67, tel: 65 06 44 and 65 09 418, and by Varan Tourism, Südbahbhof, Südtiroler Platz 7, tel: 65 65 93 and 65 09 602.

Travel in Turkey

Air. Passengers arriving at the international airports of Ankara, İstanbul, İzmir and Antalya may pick up connecting flights, operated by THY, to the principal cities in Turkey. There is a free coach service between the international and domestic terminals at İstanbul airport.

Turkish Airlines offers reductions on internal flights to students, families and sports groups of five or more. Details may be obtained from any THY office.

Sea. In İstanbul a passenger and car-ferry crosses the Bosphorus every 30 minutes between Kabataş and Sirkeçi on the European side and Harem on the Asian side. From Harem coach station there are frequent services to most of the cities in Asiatic Turkey. A ferry from Karaköy on the European side provides a useful connection with Haydarpaşa, the Asian terminus of Turkish Railways.

Two excursions by boat from İstanbul are specially recommended: a cruise up the Bosphorus and a day-trip to the Princes Islands (Büyük Ada). Boats from Eminönü to Anadolu Kavağı, stop briefly *en route* at some of the small villages on both the European and Asian sides of the international waterway. From Sirkeçi there are daily services to Büyük Ada. These continue to Yalova on the S shore of the Sea of Marmara.

Many travellers from İstanbul to Bursa and points beyond prefer to take the boat to Yalova, a mere 30km drive from Bursa, to making the tedious, boring and time-consuming bus journey via İzmit. Those, who are not constrained by budget considerations, may like to consider the fast hydrofoil service from Kabataş to Mudanya, a small resort which is somewhat nearer to Bursa than Yalova.

There is a weekly ferry from İstanbul to İzmir, which departs at 15.00 each Friday throughout the year. During the summmer months there are additional services on Monday and Wednesday. These leave at 14.00.

Turkish Maritime Lines operate an Aegean and Mediterranean cruise at fortnightly intervals between the 27 May and 16 September. Lasting 10 days, this leaves İstanbul on Wednesday at 14.00 and calls at Dikili, İzmir, Marmaris, Alanya, Antalya, Fethiye, Datça, Bodrum and Kuşadası. Places are limited, so early reservation is advised. The current sailing timetable, costs and information about discounts available to children, students, journalists and groups may be obtained from TML or their agents.

Rail. During recent years the Turkish Government has spent a considerable amount of money in improving its rail-network. As a result the country now has a number of excellent trains, which are sometimes faster and are certainly more comfortable than many of the long distance coaches, which compete with them on the same routes. Unfortunately none of the crack trains run in the area covered by this Guide. The Turkish State Railways' network of c 10,000km is largely confined to the centre of the country and only a few of the places described in this book, e.g. İzmir, Mersin, Adana, Konya are served by trains.

Long Distance Buses. In Turkey most long distance journeys are made by bus. The country is covered by a network of services, operated by private companies, which compete vigorously with each other for passengers. Most of the buses in use, are modern vehicles of German manufacture—Mercedes and MAN predominate. A number have air-conditioning installed, but this may not always function. Even when it is in working-order there will always be some passenger who claims to be sensitive to draughts and who will ask to have it turned off. (The same passenger will usually ask for the roof vents to be closed, although the atmosphere is thick with cigarette smoke.) The buses are clean and well-maintained. Ticket prices are incredibly low.

Long distance services start from the *Otogar*, which is usually located on the outskirts of the town. There is often a courtesy minibus, which takes passengers from the company's town office and, in some cases from the principal hotels, to the Otogar.

With buses arriving and departing at all hours of the day and night, a Turkish Otogar is a most interesting and exciting place, a noisy bustling scene of apparently uncoordinated activity. Hucksters, shouting at the tops of their voices, attempt to attract customers to their companies, hungry passengers besiege the fast-food stands, small boys crouch on the ground, brushing energetically at dusty shoes, while waiters from nearby kahves, carrying carefully-balanced trays covered with glasses of hot, sweet tea, tread a wary path through the crowd.

To avoid being confused by all the excitement at the Otogar, it is advisable to plan bus journeys, particularly long-distance journeys, well in advance. It is suggested that you adopt the following procedure. Having decided on the time you wish to travel, find out which companies operate suitable services. Hotel clerks are usually willing to do this for you. On main routes you will generally have a choice of four or five services. It is advisable to select the most expensive—the additional cost will be negligible—as its buses are likely to be newer and more comfortable. If you are travelling during the daytime, consider the direction of your journey to ensure that you are seated on the shaded side of the bus. Do not rely on a claim that it is air-conditioned. (See above.) If travelling at night, make sure that you have reserved accommodation at your destination—particularly if your bus arrives in the small hours.

All seats on long distance buses are numbered and, providing you make your reservation sufficiently far in advance, you will be able to choose where you want to sit. As a rule Turkish travellers prefer the centre of the coach—the seats numbered 9 to 28. Seats 5 to 8 and 33 to 36 should be avoided, as they are directly over the wheels and give a very bumpy ride. Seats 37 to 43, situated at the rear of the bus, are subject to a swaying movement, which can be distinctly unpleasant. The best seats are 1 to 4. These are located just behind the driver and near the front door.

If you are a non-smoker, it is particularly important to select one of the front seats. Despite vigorous Government propaganda, the average Turkish male is likely to be a chain-smoker, so proving the truth of the Italian expression *'fuma come un Turco'*. Fresh air from the windows near the driver and from the front door, when it is opened from time to time, will help to reduce the quantity of cigarette-smoke in that part of the bus. The front seats also give the best view of the countryside.

When making a reservation, you may be surprised to find that on some occasions you will be refused the seat of your choice, even though it is shown on the chart to be free. Almost invariably the reason is that the adjoining seat has been booked by a female passenger who is travelling alone. Custom does not permit a Turkish lady to sit next to a man who is not related to her. This laudable and modest practice sometimes produces an amusing musical chairs effect, when a lady joins the bus *en route*. The male passengers then move, as necessary, to allow her to sit in splendid isolation.

Turkish bus music—sometimes called arabesque music—is something of an acquired taste. Not even all Turks enjoy it! If you think that you are likely to find it distracting, you would be well advised to bring a personal stereo and a supply of tapes. Talking books are an excellent choice for long journeys. The earphones will also save you from hearing the current Turkish Top Ten, which tend to be repeated *ad nauseam*. The writer once suffered the hit song of the moment, 'Mavi, mavi, mas mavi,' 15 times during a six hour journey!

There is quite a high incidence of bus-sickness on some routes, particularly between Demre and Antalya, Alanya and Anamur, and Anamur and Silifke. On these roads it is usually attributed to the swaying motion of the bus, which results from a combination of many sharp curves with an equally large number of steep ascents and descents.

Proprietary preparations, which help with this condition, may be obtained, without prescription, from Turkish chemist shops. Sit at the front of the bus if possible.

Long distance buses stop about every two hours at a *kahve* or *lokanta*. To make the most of these breaks on a night-journey from the Aegean or Mediterranean coast to the interior, it is advisable to have some warm clothing, as even during the summer months the temperature on the Anatolian plateau drops sharply after dark. After each stop, eau-de-cologne is offered to the passengers by the *yardımcı*, the conductor. He will also supply, without charge, bottles of cold water.

The Turks are a gregarious and friendly people and your fellow passengers will almost certainly try to engage you in conversation. Youngsters will proudly display their knowledge of English, while their elders may speak in German or more rarely in French, which they learned as guest-workers. They will offer to buy you tea at one of the various stops, an offer which it would be discourteous to refuse. They will ask for your views on their country and for your impressions of the people.

Long distance bus journeys provide an opportunity to see Turkey and to learn about Turkish life, which is denied to travellers who stick to organised tours. The journeys can be amusing and exasperating by turn. Often very tiring, they are always vastly rewarding and should on no account be missed by anyone who wishes to take more than a superficial interest in the country.

Dolmuş. The dolmuş or shared taxi is a colourful feature of Turkish life. This operates over a specified route, which is stated on a notice fixed to the windscreen or announced by a small boy who hangs precariously out of the front passenger door. In cities and towns the dolmuş is most likely to take the form of a large, much-repaired American car. In country areas it will probably be a mini-bus. It does not operate to a timetable but departs when it is full. Dolmuş means 'stuffed' or 'filled' in Turkish and as more and more people pile in, passengers begin to appreciate the aptness of its name. Sometimes they may suspect that the driver is trying to win a place for his vehicle in the Guinness Book of Records! While some drivers will take large rucksacks or heavy luggage on the roof the dolmuş is not a very suitable conveyance for travellers so burthened. They are advised to take a taxi or bus.

Taxis. Taxis in Turkey operate from ranks and rarely pick up fares while cruising. Most have meters, but these may or may not work, so it is advisable to agree a fare with the driver before starting a journey. A friendly hotel clerk will give you an idea of how much to pay.

Private Transport. Turkey has an excellent network of approximately 50,000km of well-maintained main roads. Side roads to villages are usually asphalted, but are often very narrow. Roads to the remoter archaeological sites, e.g. Tlos, Pinara, Selge, are little more than rough tracks which are impassable during bad weather.

Road signs conform to international standards. Look out for the following: DUR = Stop; DIKKAT = Caution, Take care, (often a notification of road-works); YAVAŞ = Slow; TEK İSTİKAMET = One-way street; HASTANE = Hospital; TÜNEL = Tunnel; BOZUK SATIH = Poor surface. Archaeological and historical sites are indicated by distinctive yellow signs.

In and around the larger towns and cities, where there is a high density of traffic, drivers tend to be competitive in their attitude to others and often display more spirit than skill. In the countryside, where it is possible to travel for long distances without seeing another vehicle, avoid being lulled into a false sense of safety. Around the next corner there may be a slow-moving tractor or a procession of overloaded lorries crawling along in low gear. Keep a sharp look out also for herds of grazing sheep and goats which sometimes stray across the road.

Petrol is slightly cheaper in Turkey than in most European countries. Several brands are on sale: Petrol Ofisi, Türk Petrol, BP, Mobil, Shell. While Super grade is widely available it may be difficult to obtain in some of the remoter areas. On the main roads filling stations often have adjoining service facilities, restaurants and sometimes small motels, e.g. the Karan Motel near Anamur.

There are car-rental offices in İstanbul, İzmir, Kuşadası, Antalya and Adana. In addition to Hertz, Avis, and Europcar there are many local companies. The cars usually on offer are the Murat (Fiat 124 and 131) and the Renault 12. Car-hire is not cheap in Turkey and careful calculations should be made of the final cost before making an agreement. The international companies usually accept payment by credit card. Others will expect to be paid in cash. It is sometimes cheaper to book a fly-drive package than to purchase an air ticket and rent a car on arrival.

The speed limit is 30km in towns, 90km outside. To avoid problems with the Traffic Police it is advisable to stick to these limits.

In many of the tourist resorts motorcycles and mopeds are available for hire. Crash helmets are not usually provided, so bring your own protective headgear. Bicycles may be hired in some places, but this method of transport is likely to appeal only to the very energetic.

Travellers from the British Isles should remember that traffic in Turkey, as in Europe, proceeds on the right-hand side of the road.

Accommodation

Hotels and pensions in Turkey range from luxurious establishments like the Büyük Efes in İzmir, the Talya in Antalya and the Büyük Sürmeli in Adana to simple, family-run concerns in Kaş, Kalkan and other small resorts on the Aegean and Mediterranean coasts.

Accommodation is very reasonably priced. A stay in a 5-star hotel, which provides every comfort and offers meals guaranteed to tempt the most jaded appetite, costs less than in a medium-class hotel in most European countries. For travellers on a limited budget there are rooms in small pensions or private houses for a few pounds a night—even during the holiday season. During March and April, October and November the cost will be even less.

However, Turkey has a relatively high rate of inflation, which, inevitably, will be reflected in the cost of accommodation in future years. For this reason hotel and pension prices are not given in the Blue Guide. Visitors who are making their own holiday arrangements are advised to contact the office of the Turkish Ministry of Culture and Tourism before departure. On arrival at a resort, precise details of the current prices charged by all the local hotels and pensions may be obtained from the Tourism Information Office, whose address is given at the beginning of the relevant section of the guide.

Prices of some hotels, though payable in Turkish lira, will be quoted in US $ or German Marks. As a result the cost of accommodation may vary slightly from day to day to take into account fluctuations in the rate of exchange.

Prices are reviewed annually by the Ministry of Culture and Tourism and any increases sanctioned come into effect on 1 January. This is an unfortunate arrangement, which can do little to encourage visitors to come to Turkey during the 'low' season.

The larger hotels will usually accept payment by credit card. (See also the section on 'Credit Cards'.) Smaller establishments will often take travellers' cheques. Cash is always welcomed.

Many hotels in Turkey are registered with the Ministry of Culture and Tourism. This means that they have been inspected and that they have been found to comply with standards laid down by the Ministry. These standards require the hotels to provide a certain stated range of facilities.

As an additional safeguard for visitors, registered hotels are obliged to keep a book in which complaints and suggestions may be noted. This book is examined regularly by the Ministry's inspectors. Complaints about registered hotels, which, if sustained, may result in sanctions being taken against them, may also be made direct to the Ministry.

The registered hotels are listed in a very useful publication, which may be obtained, free of charge, from any of the Ministry's offices in Turkey or overseas. In it the hotels are graded, and the services which they offer listed. An indication of the price charged by each category of hotel and pension for a double room is given.

A number of hotels, usually of the simpler kind, are registered with the municipal authorities. These also have to meet certain requirements and are inspected from time to time to ensure that they do so. Details of these establishments may be obtained from the local Tourist Office.

While the standards of service and cleanliness in the hotels registered with the Ministry of Culture and Tourism are generally excellent, some shortcomings have been noted from time to time. The following are some examples.

Many establishments rely on solar panels to heat water for baths and showers. Theoretically, there should be a back-up heating system of some kind, but this may not always work or the management may be reluctant to use it for reasons of cost. As a result at the beginning and end of the year, when the daily amount of sunshine can vary both in duration and intensity, there may be no hot water supply to the rooms or it may be available during certain hours only. Remedy: badger the management to put the matter right. If that does not succeed, make a suitable entry in the complaints' book and also report your complaint to the local Tourism Office.

The baths in some hotels do not have plugs. Remedy: complain as outlined in the preceding paragraph. However, to avoid endless frustrating arguments, which may spoil your holiday, be prepared and take a bath plug with you.

It may be possible to have breakfast and some other meals served in your room. Ask at reception. There is usually an additional charge for this service.

Motels. While a number of establishments calling themselves motels have separate chalets in a landscaped garden and some located near the sea have their own private stretch of beach, many are indistinguishable from ordinary hotels. However, their prices are often somewhat higher than hotels offering equivalent facilities. It would appear that guests pay for the name. Motels registered with the Ministry are listed in the publication mentioned above.

Holiday Villages. Along the Aegean and Mediterranean coasts there are a number of holiday villages. These vary widely in style and in the services and facilities which they offer. Some holiday villages, like the luxurious Altın Yunus at Çeşme, are expensive and cater almost exclusively for foreign visitors. Others are patronised by Turkish and foreign guests. In general they attract holidaymakers, who like all their recreations and amusements to be centralised in one location.

Private Rooms. In many resorts it is possible to get a room in a private house. Inevitably, these vary a great deal in quality. The best are very good and are on a par with those in the smaller pensions. Look out for notices, which are often in German or English, outside those houses where rooms are available. Alternatively, make some enquiries at the *Otogar*, as members of the families offering this kind of accommodation often meet incoming buses.

The cost of staying in a private house is usually very modest. Single rooms are often difficult to get and you should be prepared to share with one or more guests. (Turkish custom will ensure that only members of the same sex are involved in this arrangement.) Breakfast is often included in the cost of accommodation. If you have a bath or shower, there is usually an extra charge for this.

Youth Hostels. Students and young people, who belong to organisations like BITS, FIYTO, ISTC and who possess ISIC, INTERAIL, BIGE or YIEE cards, are entitled to stay at any of the following hostels:

Topkapı Atatürk Student Centre
Londra Asfaltı, Cevizlibağ Durağı
Topkapı, İstanbul.
This hostel has 750 beds.

Kadırga Student Hostel
Cömertler Sok. No: 6
Kumkapı, İstanbul.
This hostel has 500 beds.

Intepe Youth and Boy Scout Hostel, Güzelyalı Mevkii
Tusan Moteli Yanı, Çanakkale.

Hasanağa Youth and Boy Scout Hostel, Küçük Kumla,
Gemlik, Bursa.

Atatürk Student Hostel Inciraltı,
1888 Sok. No. 4, Inciraltı, İzmir.

Costs are very low, approximately £3 per person (£2 per person for groups).

Camp Sites. In Turkey there are a number of camp sites, which have been approved by the Tourism Ministry. In addition to those in İstanbul, and İzmir, others are located in the provinces of Adana, Antalya, Aydın, Balıkesir, Bursa, Mersin, and Muğla. An up-to-date list may be obtained from any Tourism Information office in Turkey or overseas.

All the sites are situated on or near the main roads. Some have their own restaurants and private beaches. Camping outside the registered sites is possible, but is not recommended by the authorities.

Food and Drink

Turkish haute cuisine has always been highly praised by visitors to the country. Even the French have been obliged, grudgingly, to acknowledge its merits. Based on the use of the best-quality meat, fish and vegetables, carefully prepared and served, it eschews the elaborate sauces used by cuisiniers of other nationalities to disguise the shortcomings of their less-successful offerings. Because of the uncomplicated nature of Turkish cooking even the most unpretentious establishments are usually able to provide pleasantly satisfying meals. For a list of the most popular dishes, see the reference section below.

Restaurants open early in the morning and do not close until very late at night. Customers are welcome at any hour. Even if you arrive in the middle of the afternoon, a time when you would be sent packing by European restaurateurs, you will be able to obtain a cooked meal. Service, although it may not be very quick, is always offered with a smile. The staff of most Turkish restaurants are clearly anxious to satisfy the wishes of their customers.

Restaurants in the larger towns and in the cities usually add a 10 per cent service charge to the bill. If you have been looked after very well, you may wish to give a small additional amount to show your appreciation. If a service charge is not shown, 10 per cent is usually acceptable as a gratuity.

While lapses do occur from time to time, disappointing experiences reported by foreign visitors are, almost always, due to misunderstandings arising from difficulties with the language or to a lack of knowledge of Turkish customs on the part of the diner. The following comments may help readers of the Blue Guide to avoid some of these.

Eating out in Turkey is a serious business, so be prepared to allow plenty of time for your meal. Begin by asking for a selection of *Meze*, hors d'oeuvres, and over these consider your choice of main course and of what is to follow. If, in the European fashion, you order all the courses at the beginning of the meal, they will probably all arrive at the same time—*Meze* or soup, main dish, vegetables and dessert! You will then have to chose which of the rapidly-cooling dishes you are going to eat first.

In Turkey hot dishes are not usually served at the same temperature as is customary in Europe. This is particularly true of the 'Hazır Yemek' (Fast Food) restaurants, where the dishes are prepared early in the day and kept warm in bains-maries. It is also true of the Hatay where restaurateurs are strongly influenced by the customs of their Arab neighbours.

To avoid problems say to the waiter, when you are ordering the meal, 'hepsi çok sıcak olsun', let everything be very hot. This should ensure that your nice, freshly-cooked steak does not arrive with a garnish of tepid vegetables and tired, flaccid chips.

Breakfast
(*Kahvaltı*)

Hotel and pension breakfasts usually consist of tea, fresh bread, butter, jam, sheep's cheese, olives and sometimes a boiled egg. In Marmaris instead of jam you will almost certainly be offered a portion of the delicious *Çam Balı*, pine honey, for which that region is famous.

If you tire of hotel fare, try breakfasting in a pastry-shop. Ask for *Su Böreği*. This looks like mille feuille, but contains soft white cheese sprinkled with herbs. Accompanied by a large glass of sweet, milkless tea, this makes a tasty and sustaining breakfast. The problem is to summon up sufficient will-power to stop at one slice!

Many Turks like to begin the day with a bowl of chicken soup. If you have travelled overnight by bus, try this as a restorative. During the winter months, *Salep*, a hot, sweetened milk drink made from the pounded dried tubers of certain orchidaceous plants is an excellent, if slightly exotic alternative.

As a rule coffee is not offered for breakfast in Turkey. Sachets of imported Nescafe are sometime available in the more expensive hotels, but beware, they will add a sizeable amount to your bill.

If you are unable to face the day without coffee, take a jar of your favourite instant brand with you. The waiter will gladly provide unlimited quantities of hot water. It would be a kind and much appreciated gesture, if, occasionally, you shared your coffee with him—and with any other members of the hotel staff, who have been particularly helpful during your stay.

Lunch and Dinner
(*Öğle yemeği* and *Akşam Yemeği*)

In Turkey an important part of lunch or dinner are the *Meze*, hors d'oeuvres. They are so delicious and satisfying that many diners skip the main dish altogether. In addition to *Börek*, pastry filled with cheese and herbs, you will probably be offered *Dolma*, stuffed vine leaves, Russian salad, soft white cheese, olives, excellent Turkish Rocquefort cheese, *Cacık*, yogurt flavoured with cucumber and garlic, taramasalata, and various spicy dips. Not to be missed is *Imam Bayıldı*. The name of this dish, which consists of aubergines stuffed with onions and tomatoes, means 'the Imam fainted'. Presumably he did so with pleasure, because of its delicious taste, although some say because it was so costly to prepare.

For the main course there is a wide choice of fish, beef, poultry and lamb cooked in a variety of ways. (As the vast majority of Turks belong to the Islamic faith, they do not eat pork. However, haunches of wild boar are sometimes offered for sale to visitors at the marinas on the Mediterranean coast.)

Fish (*Balık*). Some of the fish on the menu are natives of the E Mediterranean and may be unfamiliar to you. However, they are usually displayed in refrigerated cabinets in the restaurant, so you should have little difficulty in making a choice. Fish-lovers recommend *Lüfer*, blue-fish, *Levrek*, sea bass, *Palamut*, tunny, *Kalkan*, turbot and *Kılıç balığı*, sword-fish. Fish is usually grilled, *ızgara* or fried *Tava*.

In İstanbul near the Galata Bridge try the *Hamsi*, anchovies, *Uskumru*, mackerel, or *Sardalya*, sardines. Freshly grilled and pressed into a sandwich, they are delicious.

Meat (*Et*). In addition to *Bonfile*, a small filet steak, there is the ubiquitous *Kebab*, some varieties of which are named after the places where they originated—Bursa, Adana, Urfa. Rivalling the *Kebab* in popularity are *Köfte*, especially *Inegöl Koftesi*. These meatballs of minced lamb served with raw onion rings are named after a small town near Bursa.

Offal, particularly *Kara Ciğer*, liver and *İşkembe*, tripe, often appears on the menu. Try *Arnavut Ciğeri*, Albanian-style liver fried with a spicy mixture of onions, or *İşkembe Çorbası*, tripe soup. Adventurous spirits may like to sample *Koç Yimurtası*, lambs testicles. Esteemed by the Turks as a nourishing delicacy, they are often served in a mixed grill.

Vegetables (*Sebze*). A walk through the weekly market in any

Anatolian town is one of the pleasures of a visit to Turkey. There you will find great piles of locally-produced vegetables—potatoes, onions, beans, cauliflowers, aubergines, cucumbers, tomatoes—all of which are used with great skill by Turkish cooks. Sample them, when dining in one of the town's restaurants.

Dessert (*Tatlı*). Turkish meals are usually brought to a close with *Baklava*, pastry filled with almonds and pistachio nuts and soaked in syrup. This is one of the many very sweet desserts which are popular with Turkish diners. If you are not tempted by the exotically-named *Kadın Göbeği*, Lady's navel, try *Sütlaç*, cold, creamy rice pudding or end your meal with some of the excellent locally-produced fresh fruit.

Coffee (*Kahve*). Although it is possible to order Nescafe or one of its equivalents in İstanbul, İzmir and other large cities, these are poor substitutes for Turkish coffee, which provides the perfect end to a Turkish meal.

As sugar is added to Turkish coffee, while it is being prepared, remember to tell the waiter whether you want it *Sade*, without sugar, *Az Şekerli*, with a little sugar, *Orta*, with a moderate quantity of sugar, or *Çok Şekerli*, with a lot of sugar.

Do not attempt to drink all the contents of the cup. If you do so, you will get a mouthful of grounds! A little cold water added to the coffee before you begin to drink will cause the coffee-grounds to settle at the bottom of the cup.

If you have been invited by a Turkish family to dine in their home, you will be offered, and it is polite to accept, more than one cup of coffee.

Fast Food

For a quick snack go to a *Büfe*. There you can have *Börek* (see above), toasted sandwiches or *Lahmacun*, a wafer-thin pizza coated with a spicy mixture of chopped lamb and onion in a creamy tomato sauce. An excellent accompaniment to Lahmacun is *Ayran*. This is a chilled drink made from yogurt diluted with water. One of the best places for *Lahmacun* in Turkey is a *Büfe* near İstanbul's Sirkeçi Railway Station. This may be found near a flight of steps at the right-hand side of the station entrance.

A more conventional style pizza may be obtained in *Pide* restaurants. *Pide* is a thick dough base covered with either *Et*, meat, *Yumurta*, eggs or *Peynir*, cheese. As in the case of Lahmacun, Ayran goes very well with Pide.

In İstanbul, İzmir, Bursa and some other cities in Turkey there are restaurants, which serve hamburgers and European-style pizzas. Unfortunately, these are rather poor imitations of the genuine article. Travellers would be well-advised to stick to places which sell authentic Turkish food.

Alcohol

There is no ban on the sale of alcohol in Turkey and many Turks drink beer, wine or *Rakı*, an aniseed-flavoured spirit of considerable potency. Known as *Aslan Sütü*, 'lions' milk', this is a type of grape-brandy which resembles the Arab *Arrack* or the Greek *Ouzo*. As an accompaniment to a meal it is customary to mix a quantity of *Rakı* with an equal quantity of cold water. The best known brand is *Yeni*

Rakı. Like Turkish spirits and some beer and wine this is produced by the state monopoly company *Tekel*.

In addition to the beer made by *Tekel*, there are light and dark beers produced by *Efes Pilsen*. *Tuborg* is also brewed under licence in Turkey. Most towns have at least one pub, where beer only is sold.

In Anatolia to avoid offending those who follow the strict rule of Islam, which forbids the drinking of alcohol, pubs are usually tucked away in side streets. Patrons sit at small tables, where their drinks, often accompanied by appetising snacks, are brought to them. The atmosphere is decorous and relaxed. There is usually a video in one corner of the room showing a rather banal comedy film. As a rule few of the customers show much interest in this; most prefer to chat quietly over their drinks.

In İstanbul pubs are more like their European counterparts. They are often noisy, smoke-filled places with sawdust on the floor. In resorts on the Aegean and Mediterranean coasts, pubs are usually found in the areas frequented by foreign visitors. Their ambiance generally reflects their mixed Turkish and foreign clientele.

One of the results of the influx of visitors to Turkey in recent years is that Turkish wines have become much better known. As demand has increased, it would appear that greater care is being taken in their production and, as a result, the quality of the top brands is now very good. The price of wine remains low. The two premier names, *Doluca* and *Kavaklıdere*, still sell for about £1 a bottle in supermarkets and wine shops.

Recommended are *Villa Doluca* red (*kırmızı*) or white (*beyaz*), and *Kavaklıdere Çankaya*. Somewhat less expensive are *Buzbağ*, *Dikmen* and *Lal*.

In addition to the supermarkets, the *Tekel* (state monopoly) shops sell a comprehensive range of Turkish wines, spirits and beers. Imported gin, whisky, vodka and cognac are usually available, at highly-inflated prices, in the larger cities.

Soft Drinks and Mineral Water

While water is safe to drink in most places in Turkey, many visitors quickly develop a liking for the pleasant-tasting, locally-produced mineral water (*Maden Suyu*). Children and adults, who do not drink alcohol, may quench their thirst with Coca-Cola, Pepsi-Cola, *Yedigün*, a fizzy, lemon-flavoured drink or any of a number of excellent fruit juices. *Ayran* (see above) is a refreshing drink at mealtime. It goes particularly well with highly-spiced food.

If you are visiting Turkey during the winter months, try *Salep* (see above) or *Boza*, the thick, pleasantly-flavoured drink made from fermented millet. According to the 17C traveller, Evliya Çelebi, Boza was so appreciated by the inhabitants of Bursa that the city had no fewer than 97 Boza-houses!

Menu

As Turkish cooks are ingenious and inventive, they have produced a very wide range of dishes, many of which you will encounter on your travels. Those listed in the Menu below and mentioned in the text above are just a few of the many culinary delights that await the travelling gourmet.

Meze (Hors d'oeuvres)

Arnavut Ciğeri, Spiced liver
Börek, Pastry filled with soft, white cheese and herbs. Sometimes deep-fried
Cacık, Yogurt flavoured with grated cucumber, garlic and olive oil
Fava, Bean paste
Pilaki, White beans and onion with vinegar
Sardalya, Sardines
Taramasalata, A paste red caviar, yogurt, garlic and olive oil
Yaprak Dolması, Stuffed vine leaves

Çorba (Soup)

Domates Çorbası, Tomato soup
Et Suyu, Consommé
Sebse Çorbası, Vegetable soup
Tavuk Suyu, Chicken soup
Yayla Çorbası. Mutton soup with yogurt

Salata (Salad)

Amerikan Salatası, Mixed Russian salad with carrots, peas in mayonnaise
Beyin Salatası, Sheep brain salad on lettuce
Çoban Salatası, Mixed chopped salad of tomatoes, cucumbers, peppers, etc.
Karışık Salata, Mixed salad
Patlican Salatası, Cooked aubergines with yogurt
Yeşil Salata, Green salad

Balık (Fish)

Alabalık, Trout
Barbunya, Red mullet
İstakoz, Lobster
Kalkan, Turbot
Kefal, Grey mullet
Mersin, Sturgeon
Midye, Mussels
Palamud, Tunny

Et (Meat)

Bonfile, Filet steak
Döner Kebab, Slices of lamb roasted on a vertical spit
İzmir Koftesi, Croquettes of lamb in gravy
Pirzola, Lamb chops
Sebzeli Rosbif, Roastbeef served with vegetables
Şis Kebab, Charcoal-grilled chunks of lamb and tomatoes
Şis Köfte, Grilled croquettes of lamb

Sebze (Vegetables)

Bezelye, Peas
Biber, Green sharp peppers
Havuç, Carrots
Kabak, Marrow or pumpkin
Lahana, Cabbage
Taze Fasulye, French beans

Tatlı (Dessert)

Bülbül Yuvası, Pastry with pistachio and walnut purée and ice cream
Dondurma, Ice cream
Kabak Tatlısı, Pumpkin served with nuts and syrup

Mevya (Fruit)

Erik, Plums
İncir, Figs
Kiraz, Cherries
Kavun, Yellow melon
Karpuz, Water melon
Muz, Bananas
Şeftali, Peaches
Üzüm, Grapes

Language

According to a United Nations survey Turkish is one of the world's most widely-used languages. In its various forms it is spoken by c 150 million people in an area that stretches from central Yugoslavia to the province of Sinkiang in China. A member of the Ural-Altaic group, its closest European relatives are Finnish and Hungarian.

Since it was adopted on 4 May 1278 by the Karamanoğlu ruler of Konya, Mehmet Bey, it has been the official language of the Turkish people. One of the SW group of Turkic languages, it was heavily influenced by Persian and Arabic during the period of Ottoman greatness. At that time Persian was the language of courtly literature, particularly of poetry, while Arabic, the language of science and religion, was widely used and known throughout the empire.

In effect, modern Turkish is the language of the Ottoman period purged of the vocabulary and idioms, which it had acquired from Arabic and Persian. This cleansing operation took place in 1932 under the direction of Atatürk, the founder of modern Turkey, a short time after he had organised the changeover from the Arabic to the Roman alphabet.

There are 29 letters in the Turkish alphabet. Atatürk and his reforming committee omitted q, w and x and added six additional letters—ç, ğ, ı, ö, ş and ü. Each letter has a fixed sound, a factor which makes the language easy to read and to pronounce.

Turkish is an agglutinative language—changes are made to the endings of nouns to indicate different meanings e.g. -a or -e = to, -dan or den = from. There are no genders and no articles. To meet the requirements of modern life, its vocabulary has been expanded with borrowings from many European languages e.g *Otogar*, *Kamion*, *Tren*, *İstasyon*, *Gazete*, *Banka*.

With a little application it is possible to acquire a basic knowledge of Turkish in a comparatively short time. Although at first sight the grammar may seem difficult, it is soon mastered. Two books which will aid the student are 'Colloquial Turkish', by Yusuf Mardin, published by Routledge and Kegan Paul and 'Teach Yourself Turkish', by G.L. Lewis, published by Hodder and Stoughton. Travellers with less ambitious aims will find 'Pidgin Turkish' (see below) or the Turkish/English phrasebook published by Berlitz useful aids during their travels. The Berlitz book is accompanied by a very helpful cassette.

Although it is no substitute for a proper knowledge of the language, 'Pidgin Turkish' has a number of attractions. It requires no study and, unlike elaborately-learned phrases, it will not produce lenghty, complicated replies which you may not understand.

Ideal for dealing with recurring situations like booking a room or ordering a meal, 'Pidgin Turkish' is based on the use of a dictionary and three key-words—'*Var*', There is, '*Yok*', There is not, and the interrogative particle '*Mi*'. (A good, inexpensive English/Turkish, Turkish/English dictionary published by the Redhouse Press, İstanbul may be purchased in Turkey.)

To use 'Pidgin Turkish', look up the word for the object or service which you require in the dictionary, e.g. a room, '*Oda*', and say, '*Lütfen, oda var mi*'. If the receptionist replies '*Var*', you have a room. If he replies '*Yok*', you try the next hotel. As you become more proficient and more confident, you can increase the range of your enquiries by the use of words like '*Nerede*', Where, '*Ne*', What, and '*Ne zaman*', When, plus the appropriate noun.

While even a slight smattering of Turkish will greatly increase the pleasure which you obtain from your stay in the country, to communicate with the Turks it is not essential to be able to speak their language. Many adults, who have worked in Germany, Austria or Switzerland, speak fluent German, while practically all young people in Turkey now learn English. They will be delighted to converse with you and to have the opportunity to show off their knowledge of that language.

However, Turks, young and old, will be pleased and flattered, if you take the trouble to master even a few of the Turkish words and phrases, which are in everyday use. '*Merhaba*', Hello, '*Nasılsınız*', How are you?, '*Lütfen*', Please, '*Günaydın*', Good Morning, will evoke beaming smiles from those you encounter on your travels.

Glossary of Turkish words

Ada, Island
Alem, Crescent and star frequently found on top of the dome of a mosque or on a minaret
Bedesten, Domed building in a market or bazaar where luxury goods are sold and stored
Beylik, Domain of a minor ruler of vassal
Bulvar, Boulevard
Cami, Mosque
Caravanserai, Inn; usually on trade route (see also *Han*)

Çarşı, Market

Çeşme, Fountain

Dağ, Mountain

Deniz, Sea

Dere, River

Dershane, Lecture hall, and on occasions study-hall

Divan, Ottoman Council of State and Justice

Eski, Old

Eyvan, Domed or vaulted recess, which is open on one side

Geçid, Mountain pass

Göl, Lake

Hamam, Turkish bath

Han, Inn, usually in a town (see also *Kervansaray*)

Harem, Women's part of the house

Hisar, A fort or castle

Hoca, Teacher

Hüyük, Mound or tell

İlwan, Portal which is higher than the level of the roof

İmam, Islamic cleric who presides over the public prayer in the mosque

İmaret, Soup kitchen which provided food for students and the needy

İrmak, River

İskele, Quay

Kadi, District judge

Kale, A fort or castle

Kapı, Gate or door

Kaplıca, thermal spring with swimming pool

Kaymakam, Governor of a kaza (administrative district)

Kıble, Direction of Mecca

Kilim, Carpet without pile, woven matting

Kilise, Church

Kösk, Pavilion or summerhouse

Köy, Village

Konak, Mansion or official residence

Külliye, Charitable and educational buildings which surrounded a mosque

Kümbet, Mausoleum

Kütüphane, Library

Liman, A harbour

Medrese, College of Islamic theology

Mescit, Small mosque

Meydan, Square

Mihrab, Niche in a mosque which gives the direction of Mecca

Mimar, Architect

Mimber, Pulpit in a mosque

Misafirhane, House for guests

Müezzin, Islamic cleric who gives the call to prayer

Namazgah, Open air mescit or mosque

Nehir, River

Oda, Room

Ova, Plain or meadow

Padişah, Sultan

Pazar, Bazaar or market

Şadırvan, Fountain for ritual ablutions before prayer

Saray, Palace

Sebil, Public fountain

Selamlık, Men's part of the house

Şehir, Town

Sema, Dervishes' dance

Semahane, Hall in dervish convent used for ritual dances

Şerefe, Balcony on a minaret

Sıbyan Mekteb, Koranic school for boys

Sıcakluk, Hot room in a hamam

Soğukluk, Cool room in a hamam

Su, Water

Tabhane, Hospice in a külliye

Tekke, Dervish convent

Tuğra, Official seal of the Sultan

Türbe, Mausoleum or tomb

Yalı, House built near the Bosphorus

Yayla, Summer camping-place or pasture in the mountains

Yeni, New

Yol, Road, street or path

Yurt, Home or native land

Zaviye, A lodging frequently used by dervishes, part of the imaret complex

Customs and Behaviour

Some differences between the customs and behaviour current in N America and Europe and those in Turkey have been touched on already. (See above.) A good deal of the formality, which developed during the Ottoman period, is still retained in Turkish society. For example, when you visit the home of a Turkish friend he will greet you with the expression *'Hoş Geldiniz'* (Welcome), to which the correct reply is *'Hoş Bulduk'* (I am pleased to be here). He will then ask how you are—*'Nasilsiniz'*, to which you reply *'İyiyim, teşekkür ederim'* (I am very well thank you). No matter how often you meet, this formula will be used before a conversation gets under way.

Before entering a Turkish house—particularly in Anatolia—it is customary for visitors to take off their shoes and leave them by the door. As a rule they will be given a pair of slippers by the host. Apart from houses in the larger towns and cities, which are generally furnished in European style, most Turkish houses follow a traditional pattern. The living-room will have a large divan along one or more walls. Sit crossed-legged on this, but be very careful not to show the soles of your feet to anyone present. Similarly do not point your finger at anyone. You will be offered tea and it is polite to drink at least three small glasses. Do not blow your nose in public. If possible leave the room. At least turn your head away and try to carry out the operation as unobtrusively as you can. This is particularly important in places like a restaurant. Displays of affection in public, like kissing and embracing a member of the opposite sex, are regarded as bad manners.

If a lady goes to the toilet in a public place, e.g. a restaurant, it is customary for her escort to accompany her as far as the door, to wait for her there and then to conduct her back to the table.

Be careful to ask permission before taking photographs of people, particularly if the subject is female. If the lady's husband or a male relative is present, make sure that you get his permission also.

If you visit a mosque, leave your shoes at the door. Dress as you would for a visit to a church. Do not wear shorts or jeans or in general give an impression of slovenliness. Do not take photographs using a flash or walk in front of worshippers. Non-Muslims should avoid visiting mosques during the daily prayer periods—which take place in the early morning, midday, mid-afternoon, early evening, night-fall. This is particularly important on Friday, the Muslim Sabbath. During the month of Ramazan, when many Muslims fast during the daylight hours, avoid ostentatious displays of eating, drinking or smoking in public.

You may encounter some behaviour in Turkey which would not be considered acceptable in Europe or N America. A man may be asked his age, whether he is married, how much he earns and other personal questions of this type by casual acquaintances or indeed by perfect strangers. This is not considered impolite and you should not be offended. Be prepared to be stared at a good deal, particularly when you eat in restaurants in the smaller Anatolian towns.

Health

Inoculation. Unless you arrive from an area where diseases like cholera or typhoid are rife, you will not need proof that you have been inoculated to enter Turkey. However, many visitors from Europe and N America, particularly if they are going to spend some time in the country or intend to travel to the remoter areas, have prophylactic inoculations, before departure, against cholera, tetanus, typhoid, polio and hepatitis.

Insurance. Take out a health-insurance policy which will cover you for the duration of your stay in Turkey and the time spent travelling to and from the country. Make sure that the policy covers Asiatic as well as European Turkey.

Malaria. According to the authorities malaria has been eradicated in Turkey, but, unfortunately, the anopheles mosquito ignores international boundaries. If you are going to travel in the S or SE of the country, it is sensible to take all reasonable steps against infection. Some malarial parasites have now become resistant to certain drugs, so consult your doctor or one of the specialist bodies like the London School of Hygiene and Tropical Medicine, Keppel St, London, WC1E 7HT (tel: 01-636 8636), or the Hospital for Tropical Diseases, 3, St. Pancras Way, London, NW1 OPE (tel: 01-387 4411), well in advance of your departure date.

Take one of the recommended anti-mosquito sprays and a mosquito repellent cream with you. Wear clothes that cover your arms and ankles during the evening. Use the spray in your room before going to sleep.

Stomach Problems. For stomach problems take Lomotil or one of the recommended remedies, which may be obtained from your own doctor before departure or purchased, usually without prescription, from a chemist, *Eczane*, in Turkey. Do not overindulge in oily and highly-spiced dishes. Wash and peel fruit before eating it.

Disposable Needles. Increasingly, travellers are taking disposable needles with them, in case they fall ill and need an injection while away from home. These may be purchased from chemists before departure. To avoid problems should your baggage be opened on arrival, have a letter from your doctor which explains clearly why you have the needles in your possession. This should prevent you from falling foul of Turkey's very tough anti-drug legislation.

Chemists (Eczane). Chemists in Turkey fulfil many of the functions performed by doctors in other countries. They provide simple first aid, give injections and are able to advise on the treatment of many of the minor ailments that afflict travellers. They carry a wide range of drugs, some of which are made under licence in Turkey, while others are imported from Germany, Britain and the USA.

Doctors and Hospitals. Apart from the nationals of a few countries, which have reciprocal arrangements with Turkey, all visitors have to pay for drugs, treatment by private doctors and hospital fees. However, the cost of treatment is very low. If you wish to claim against your insurance, when you return home, remember to get receipts for both medicine and treatment. In İstanbul, İzmir and Ankara there are a number of foreign hospitals:

İstanbul
American Hospital, Nişantaşı, Güzelbahçe 20.
French Hospital, Taşkışla Cad. 3. Taksim.
Italian Hospital, Tophane, Defterdar Yokuşu, 37.
German Hospital, Taksim, Sıraselviler Cad., 119.
Austrian Hospital, Bereketzade Medresesi, Sok. 5/7 Karaköy.

İzmir
American Hospital, Alsancak, 9, Eylül Üniversitesi Yanı.

Ankara
American Hospital, Balgat Amerikan Tes.

Rabies. As in many European countries foxes and other wild animals in certain parts of Turkey carry the rabies virus. They are believed to have passed this on from time to time to domestic animals. For this reason it is inadvisable to pat or fondle any animal, which you may meet on your travels. If you are bitten or scratched by a dog or cat, particularly if it is behaving in an uncharacteristic fashion, get immediate medical attention.

Toilets. Outside of the main towns public toilets in places like bus stations are often odorous and not very clean. Usually consisting of a hole in the floor and a place for your feet, they are, theoretically at least, more hygienic than European-style toilets. However, it takes some practice to be able to use them without embarrassment—or worse. Hazards that await the unwary include overbalancing and falling on the floor or having to recover the contents of their pockets from the same insalubrious surface ! For this reason it is advisable to keep valuable possessions like money and passports in a purse, wallet or buttoned pocket.

General Information

Postal Services and Telecommunications
Post. Turkey's postal services are well-organised and efficiently-run. Letters between Turkey and the United Kingdom take about five working days. All post offices bear the distinctive yellow PTT sign. The larger offices are open from 08.00–24.00 from Monday to Saturday and from 09.00–19.00 on Sunday.

If you wish to the use the 'Poste Restante' system, ask to have your letters addressed as follows:
Name
Poste Restante
Merkez Posthanesi
Town/city
Turkey.

To collect mail from the Poste Restante, you will have to produce your passport and pay a small fee. Note that letters are sometimes filed under the addressee's first name and not his or her surname.

Telephone. Most Turkish cities are linked by an efficient direct dialing system. To use the telephone you will need to purchase jetons. These come in two sizes. Small jetons are used for local calls and larger ones, which are more expensive, are required for long-distance calls.

The Turks are enthusiastic users of the telephone and you may have to wait some time, particularly in the evening, to find a vacant booth. Telephone calls made from hotels are usually subject to an additional charge which is retained by the management.

Money

The unit of currency is the Turkish Lira (TL). There are coins of 5, 10, 25, 50 and 100 TL and bank notes of 100, 500, 1000, 5000 and 10000 TL. The current rate of exchange is displayed prominently in the banks and given in the daily papers.

Cheques. Eurocheques and travellers' cheques may be cashed in banks on production of your passport. They are also accepted in payment by some hotels, restaurants and shops.

Credit Transfers. It is possible to transfer money from your home account to a bank in Turkey, but, as this can take time, it is not recommended for those spending a short time in the country.

Credit Cards. Credit cards are accepted by many shops, restaurants and hotels in the larger towns and cities. If you use them to purchase goods, you may be asked to pay an additional amount to cover the commission charged by the card company. This applies particularly to the bazaars or to shops where you have bargained over a purchase.

It is important to note that the display of a credit card symbol does not necessarily mean that establishment concerned is either willing or capable of accepting payment by this method. The author once saw an American Express sticker on the window of a dolmuş in Antalya, where it was being used purely as a decoration. As the fare was only 25 TL, clearly this was a case where payment by a credit card would not do nicely, sir!

The incorrect use of the credit card symbol by shops and, in particular, by restaurants and hotels, which some travellers have encountered in Antalya and in a number of other places in Turkey, is a much more serious matter, as it could cause considerable embarrassment and inconvenience to an innocent traveller. Accordingly, before booking a room or ordering a meal in an establishment, which displays a credit card symbol, it is advisable to check that this method of payment is acceptable to the management.

If you discover any misuse of a credit card symbol, it would be very helpful if you were to report it to the local Tourist Office and to the credit card company concerned, when you return home.

Banks. Banks are usually open between 09.30 and 12.00 and between 13.30–17.00 on weekdays. They are closed on Saturdays and Sundays. When purchasing your travellers cheques, ask which of the many Turkish banks will change them. Unfortunately, not all Turkish banks accept all cheques.

Time

Local time in Turkey is equal to GMT plus 2 hours during the summer months.

Electricity

Electricity has been standarised on 220v all over Turkey. Visitors from Britain should bring an adaptor, as sockets are designed to accept the round two pin European plugs. Adaptors for the American flat pin plugs are available from many of the electrical shops in the cities and large towns.

Newspapers

The chatty 'Turkish Daily News', published in Ankara, is on sale in most large centres. Its staple diet is a mixture of news, mainly about events in Turkey, combined with short articles and brief paragraphs in the 'Ripley Believe It Or Not' style. These are often written in a pawky, semi-humorous journalese. The Daily News is an inexpensive way of keeping up with events.

Foreign papers are available in Turkey the day after publication. Some foreign magazines like *Time, Paris Match* and *Der Spiegel* may be obtained in the cities and resorts on the coast.

Radio

Visitors equipped with a small short-wave radio will be able to pick up the BBC World Service and Voice of America programmes. Details of frequencies and times of broadcasts in English for the E Mediterranean area may be obtained from both organisations.

Turkish Radio and Television Service also has daily broadcasts in English, French and German. These are usually given in the morning and repeated later in the day. Details of the times and frequencies are to be be found in the 'Turkish Daily News'.

Public and Religious Holidays

The following are the official public holidays in Turkey:
January 1, New Year's Day
April 23, National Independence and Childrens' Day
May 19, Atatürk Commemoration and Youth and Sports Day
August 30, Victory Day (War of Independence 1922)
October 29, Republic Day.

Approximately 99 per cent of Turks subscribe to the Muslim faith. The two great feasts of Islam, *Şeker Bayramı*, which celebrates the end of Ramazan and *Kurban Bayramı*, which follows sometime later, are marked by the closing of shops and government offices for three and four days respectively. As these feasts follow the Moslem calendar, they take place at different times each year.

Festivals

Practically every month of the year is marked by a festival or fair somewhere in Turkey. The following are some of the most interesting. A full list may be obtained from any office of the Ministry of Culture and Tourism.
January—Camel-wrestling Festival in Selçuk
April–May—International Childrens' Day, Ankara
May—Efes Festival, Selçuk
May—International Music and Folklore Festival, Silifke
June—Marmaris Festival
June—Bergama Festival
June–July—International Culture and Art Festival, İstanbul
June–July—International İzmir Festival
July—International Culture and Art Festival, Bursa

July—Bursa Fair
August—Troy Festival, Çanakkale
August–September—İzmir International Fair
September—Golden Orange Film and Arts Festival, Antalya
September–October—International Mediterranean Song Contest, Antalya
December—International St. Nicholas' Ceremony, Demre
December—Mevlana Commemoration Ceremony, Konya.

Consulates and Embassies
Visitors staying in Turkey for any length of time are advised to register with their national embassy or nearest consulate.

Embassies
British Embassy, Şehit Ersan Cad. 46A, Çankaya, Ankara (tel: 1274310-15).
American Embassy, Atatürk Bulvarı 110, Çankaya, Ankara (tel: 1265470).
Australian Embassy, Nenehatun Cad. 83, Gaziosmanpaşa, Ankara (tel: 1286715-18).
Canadian Embassy, Nenehatun Cad. 75, Gaziosmanpaşa, Ankara (tel: 1275803-06).

Consulates
British Consulate, Meşrutiyet Cad. 34, Tepebaşı, İstanbul (tel: 1447540).
British Consulate, Mahmut Esad Cad. 49, İzmir (tel: 211795).
American Consulate, Meşrutiyet Cad. 104–108, Tepebaşı, İstanbul (tel: 1513602).
American Consulate, Atatürk Cad. 92, İzmir (tel: 131369).

Summer Opening Times. In the Aegean and Mediterranean areas government offices and some other establishments are closed in the afternoon during the summer months. Check opening hours with the local Tourist Office, as the arrangements may vary from province to province.

Laundry and Dry Cleaning. These services are fast, cheap and efficient in Turkey. Most hotels will arrange for their guests' clothes to be valeted, but visitors who wish to make their own arrangements will find laundry and dry-cleaning establishments in most towns and resorts.

Shops

Shops are usually open between 09.30 and 13.00 and between 14.00 and 19.00. They are normally closed on Sunday. However, during the holiday season shops in the principal resorts tend to stay open for much longer hours. (See also the note on summer opening hours above.)

Turkey is a treasure-house of hand-made products. These range from carpets and kilims, to gold and silver jewellery, ceramics from Kütahya, leather and suede clothing, meerschaum pipes, ornaments fashioned from alabaster, copper pans and vessels. Many happy—and relatively inexpensive—hours may be spent bargaining for these objects in the bazaars of the cities and in the many specialist shops to be found in the coastal resorts.

Resist the temptation to buy antiques. There are many skilfully-produced fakes on sale and the export of genuine antiques is forbidden. Infractions are punished by severe penalties, which may include imprisonment. (See also Antiquities below.)

Museums

Most Turkish museums are open every day from Tuesday to Sunday between 08.30 and 12.30 and between 13.30 and 17.30. Admission charges are very modest, but an additional fee must be paid by those wishing to take photographs or make amateur films or videos. (Professional film-makers require a special permit, which must be obtained in advance from the General Directorate of Antiquities and Museums, Ankara.)

In some Turkish museums not all the objects on display are labelled. In a number they are labelled in Turkish only, in others in Turkish and English or Turkish and German. Although most museums sell postcards and replicas of their best-known exhibits, few publish guide-books. For information about the contents of all the museums in the area covered by the Blue Guide, refer to the main body of the work.

In addition to cards and replicas some museums sell soft drinks, tea, and coffee. These are often served in a pleasant and imaginatively laid-out setting. The pergola-annex to the café in Antalya's Archaeological Museum, where visitors may refresh themselves surrounded by Roman statuary of the 2C AD, is particularly attractive.

Points to Note

Theft and Crime

There is very little petty crime in Turkey. In Anatolia a foreign visitor is still regarded as a *'misafir'*, a guest, and is accorded the traditional protection given to strangers. The safety of his person and property are regarded as being the personal responsibility of his host.

However, it is still advisable to take normal, sensible precautions to protect your property, particularly your money and your passport. Most hotels will keep their guests' valuables for them in the hotel safe.

If you are unlucky enough to lose any property during your stay in Turkey, report the matter as soon as possible to the nearest police-station. Ask for a copy of the statement, which you make to the police, as your insurance company will require you to produce this, if, subsequently, you make a claim.

In shops it is very unlikely that you will be overcharged and even more unlikely that you will be shortchanged. This is also the case in the bazaars in the larger towns and cities, where bargaining is an accepted practice. Once a price has been agreed with the seller, that is all you will have to pay.

Security Areas

Photography is not permitted in certain places e.g. docks, airports, military establishments, and frontier areas. It is also forbidden to photograph military personnel. If you are in doubt about where or when to take pictures, seek the advice of the local Tourist Office.

Drugs

The illegal possession, sale or use of drugs like hashish, heroin, and cocaine is strictly forbidden by Turkish law. Any transgression is likely to result in serious trouble and will, almost certainly, ensure that the offender ends up in prison.

Antiquities

Amateur digging at ancient sites is forbidden in Turkey and visitors should not indulge in this activity. Anyone bringing a metal-detector into the country is likely to encounter some problems.

Visitors to Ephesus, Pamukkale, Perge, Aspendus and some other sites in the Aegean and Mediterranean areas are often approached by persistent small boys or furtive-looking adults, who offer to sell them 'genuine' ancient coins or small antiquities. Usually the vendors claim that the objects were found in a tomb or old building nearby. In most cases the coins and antiquities are modern copies and the only person to suffer is the purchaser, who parts with a large sum for something that has no monetary value.

However, from time to time genuine antiquities, the product of illegal excavation, are offered for sale. Under no circumstances should these be purchased. The sale, purchase and possession of antiquities is strictly controlled by Turkish law and any transgressions are punished severely. For example, the owner of a yacht, who removes or permits any member of his ship's company to remove ancient objects from the seas adjoining the Turkish coast, may have his yacht confiscated and, in addition, he and any other offenders may be sent to prison.

Unfortunately, the illegal digging of ancient sites is all too common in Turkey. This not only robs the country of its patrimony but it also denies archaeologists vital evidence, which would enable them to increase our knowledge of the past. Every illegal purchase encourages the seller to make another illegal dig. Visitors should not allow themselves to become involved in that sordid process.

Sport

Turkey has much to offer visitors, who are interested in watching or taking part in sport. İzmir, Antalya, Adana and many smaller towns have football stadia, where enthusiasts shout themselves hoarse every Sunday afternoon, encouraging their local and national heroes to greater efforts.

Violence at football matches is very rare in Turkey, so it is not uncommon to find a mix of family groups and exuberant teenagers in the stands. Ask the hotel receptionist to get tickets for you.

Look out for the festivals of traditional Turkish sports, which take place in various centres throughout the year, e.g. Turkish wrestling in the great Roman theatre of Aspendus.

Underwater Swimming. Underwater swimming and diving is permitted in Turkey in certain areas. The sport is controlled by the local authorities. Full information may be obtained from the Tourist Office in the resort. (See the note above about illegal diving for antiquities.)

Fishing. Visitors may fish for sport in non-prohibited areas without a licence. Only amateur equipment is permitted. Full information about the regulations covering the sport may be obtained from the Department of Fisheries, Ministry of Agriculture, Forestry and Rural Affairs, Tarım, Orman ve Köyişleri Bakanlığı, Su Ürünleri Daire Başkanlağı, Ankara.

Commercial fishing by foreigners is an offence, which carries severe penalties.

Hunting. Visitors may only take part in hunts organised by those travel agencies, which have been specially authorised by the Ministry of Agriculture, Forestry and Rural Affairs. Full information about the regulations, which apply to hunting in Turkey, may be obtained from the Union of Travel Agencies (TURKSAB), Cumhuriyet Cad. 187, Elmadağ, İstanbul.

Skiing. Skiing has become increasingly popular in Turkey during recent years. The principal resorts in the Marmara, Aegean and Mediterranean areas are located at Bursa—Uludağ and Antalya—Saklıkent. In both cases the season runs from January to April. Further information may be obtained from any office of the Ministry of Culture and Tourism.

Mountaineering. There are interesting climbs to be made in the Beydağları to the W of Antalya. The best starting points are Elmalı and Kemer. Climbing is possible throughout the year. The highest peaks, which give excellent views over the Mediterranean, are Kızlar Sivrisi (3070m) and Tahtalı (2344m).

Advice and assistance may be obtained from the Tourist Office and the representatives of the Turkish Mountaineering Club in Antalya. It is advisable to contact the club before starting out on a climb, so that the authorities are warned and may be able to render assistance, should this be required.

Wild Life

In the national parks and in the more remote parts of Turkey wildlife is varied, abundant, and sometimes potentially dangerous. Bears, wolves, foxes, jackals, wild boar, red and roe deer, water buffalo, lynx, wild goats, snakes, scorpions and spiders of various kinds have been seen by visitors at one time or another. However, this does not mean that any or all of these animals are encountered very frequently. During the course of his extensive travels, which took place over several years, this author's experience of Turkey's more unusual fauna has been limited to the sighting of snakes on two occasions and an interesting encounter with a spectacular jumping-spider.

Camels, singly and in trains, may be seen almost anywhere in Turkey. At the Letoön in Lycia somnolent tortoises sunbathe on the ancient walls, while frogs, the descendants, if legend is to be believed, of the shepherds, who mocked Leto, fill the air with their raucous calls. In spring the fields and hillsides on Turkey's SE and E coasts are home to hosts of brilliantly-coloured butterflies. Along the Aegean and Mediterranean coasts, the butterflies give way in summer to yellow and black striped hornets and other less attractive insects, while the ubiquitous mosquito fills the evening air with its monotonous, menacing whine.

A wide berth should be given to the guard-dogs, which protect the encampments of the *Yürük* (nomad people). These large menacing animals often keep predators away from the flocks of sheep and goats, which feed on the sparse roadside vegetation.

In summer, visitors, who stray from the main paths at Ephesus, Xanthus, Aspendus and other historic sites, or who poke among the stones or crevices in ancient buildings, should keep a look-out for snakes and scorpions. It is unlikely that they will be troubled, as these creatures, sensitive to vibration, usually avoid contact with humans, but it is wise to take reasonable precautions. If bitten or stung seek immediate medical attention.

National Parks

Turkey has a number of large and well-maintained national parks. Those in the area covered by the Blue Guide are:

Uludağ the ancient Mt Olympus, (2554m) near Bursa.

Kuşcenneti in the province of Balıkesir, an ornithological reserve, which is home to more than 200 species of birds.

Sipil Dağ in Manisa province.

Dilek Yarımadası where Samsundağ towers over the sea. This is within easy reach of Kuşadası.

Güllük Dağı at the site of ancient Termessus, near Antalya.

Beydağları W of Antalya.

Karatepe—Aslantaş in Adana province. Hittite and Roman remains in a picturesque setting in the Ceyhan river valley.

Köprülü Kanyon NE of Antalya. Roman bridge and remains of ancient Selge.

Further information on the national parks may be obtained from any office of the Ministry of Culture and Tourism.

Thermal Resorts

For centuries Turkey's thermal resorts, of which there are more than 1000, have offered relief and treatment for a wide range of medical conditions. The principal resorts in the Marmara, Aegean and Mediterranean areas are:

Bursa. Waters contain bicarbonate, sulphate, sodium, calcium and magnesium and are suitable for drinking and bathing. Treatment offered for rheumatism, gynaecological and dermatological problems.

Yalova. Waters contain sulphate, sodium and calcium. Treatment for rheumatism, urinary and nervous complaints.

Oylat. Located in a picturesque, rural setting near İnegöl. Very restful.

Gönen. Province of Balıkesir. Waters contain sulphate, sodium, hydrocarbonate and carbon dioxide. Treatment for dermatological, urinary and nervous complaints.

Çeşme. In the Bay of Ilıca and Şifne to the W of İzmir. Waters contain chloride, sodium, magnesium, fluoride and are suitable for drinking and bathing. Treatment for dermatological and gynaecological and urinary complaints.

Pamukkale and Karahayıt. NW of Denizli. Waters contain hydrocarbonate, sulphate, calcium and carbon dioxide. Suitable for bathing (see p 170)

Key to Route Maps

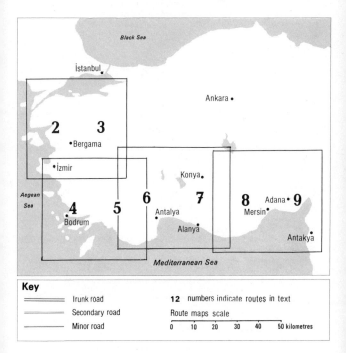

Key

═══════	Trunk road
━━━━━━━	Secondary road
────────	Minor road

12 numbers indicate routes in text

Route maps scale

0   10   20   30   40   50 kilometres

Mediterranean Sea

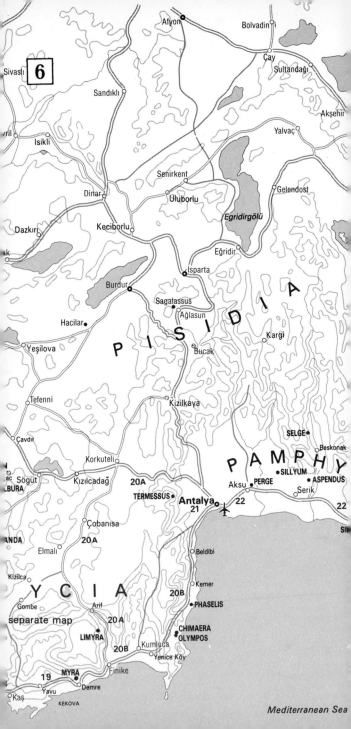

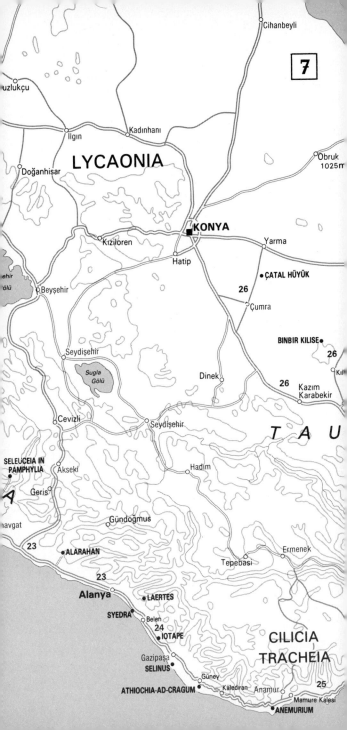

7

Cihanbeyli

uzlukçu

Ilgın   Kadınhanı

LYCAONIA

Doğanhisar

Obruk
1025m

KONYA

Kızılören   Yarma

Hatip

• **ÇATAL HÜYÜK**

26   Çumra

Beyşehir

*ehir
ölü

Seydişehir

BINBIR KILISE •

26

Sugla
Gölü

Dinek   Kıl

Cevizli

26   Kazım
Karabekir

Seydişehir

T   A   U

**SELEUCEIA IN
PAMPHYLIA**

Akseki   Hadim

Geris

navgat

Gündoğmus

Ermenek

23

ALARAHAN

Tepebasi

23

Alanya   • **LAERTES**

SYEDRA•   Belen

24

• **IOTAPE**

Gazipaşa

SELINUS

**CILICIA
TRACHEIA**

Güney

25

ATHIOCHIA-AD-CRAGUM •   Kaledıran   Anamur

Mamure Kalesi

• **ANEMURIUM**

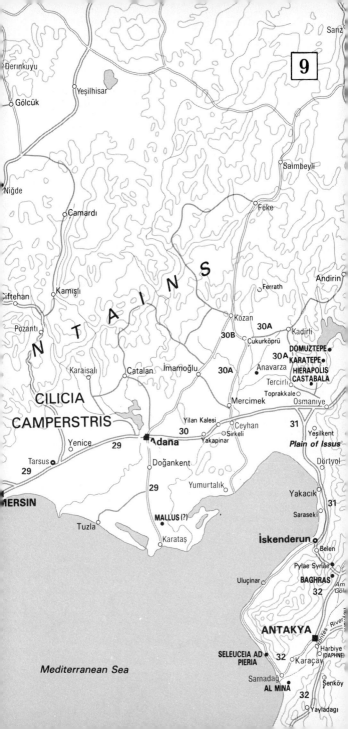

Sarız

Derinkuyu

Gölcük

Yeşilhisar

Niğde

Camardı

Saimbeyli

Feke

Çiftehan

Kamışlı

Ferrath

Andirin

Pozantı

N   T   A   I   N   S

Kozan

30A

Kadirli

DOMUZTEPE

30B

Çukurköprü

30A

KARATEPE

Karaisalı

Catalan

İmamoğlu

30A

Anavarza

HIERAPOLIS

CASTABALA

Tercirli

CILICIA

Mercimek

Toprakkale

Osmaniye

CAMPERSTRIS

Yilan Kalesi

Ceyhan

31

Yeşilkent

Yenice

29

30

Sirkeli

Adana

Yakapınar

Plain of Issus

Tarsus

29

Doğankent

Dörtyol

29

Yumurtalık

Yakacık

31

MERSIN

Saraseki

Tuzla

MALLUS (?)

İskenderun

Belen

Karataş

Pylae Syriae

Uluçınar

BAGHRAS

32

Mediterranean Sea

ANTAKYA

Orontes River

Harbiye

SELEUCEIA AD

32

(DAPHNE)

PIERIA

Karaçay

Samadağ

Şenköy

AL MINA

32

Yayladağı

and drinking. Treatment for heart and circulatory complaints and rheumatism, digestive and kidney diseases.

Balçova. W of İzmir. Water suitable for drinking and bathing. Treatment for sciatica, gynaecological and nervous disorders and urinary and intestinal problems.

Further information about Turkey's thermal resorts may be obtained from any office of the Ministry of Culture and Tourism.

Turkish Bath

No stay in Turkey would be complete without a visit to a Turkish bath, *hamam*. Most towns of any size will have one or more of these establishments. Some are reserved for men, others for ladies. Where there is only one hamam in a town, different days are allocated to each sex.

In keeping with a tradition that dates back to Roman times the Turkish hamam is generally a clean and well-run establishment. It is also very inexpensive. If you have any difficulty in selecting a suitable Turkish bath, your hotel receptionist should be able to advise you and, if a reservation is necessary, make one on your behalf.

1 Bursa to Erdek

Total distance c 112km. **Bursa**—R200 (*Gölyazı*—2km *Apollonia*)—58km *Karacabey*—(c 8km *Hara*)—(3km *Manyas/Kuşcenneti*)—35km *Bandırma*—c 8km *Cyzicus*—19km **Erdek**.

BURSA (614,133 inhab.), the capital of ancient BITHYNIA, has one of the most striking settings of any Turkish city. Built on the verdant slopes of Mysian Olympus and surrounded by gardens and orchards, it is affectionately known to its inhabitants as Yeşil Bursa, Green Bursa. A spa town of note since antiquity, it has become in recent years an important manufacturing centre, in particular of silk and cotton textiles.

Information and Accommodation. The principal *Tourism Information Office* is sited centrally in Atatürk Cad. near Ulu Cami. Detailed information—including current room rates—about Bursa's many hotels and pensions may be obtained there. The Tourism Office can also advise on the best places to eat, give the opening hours of the city's museums, and provide up-to-date information on excursions to places of interest in the surrounding countryside.

Some of the most pleasant, and most expensive, hotels are in the suburb of Çekirge, a 10-minute drive from the city centre. Most of Çekirge's hotels have their own mineral water baths.

Post Office and Banks. The principal post office is in Atatürk Cad. near Ulu Cami. Branches of the main Turkish banks are located nearby.

Transport. Bursa is an important communications centre, linked by good roads with Ankara, İstanbul and İzmir. Frequent long-distance coach services to all of the principal Turkish cities depart from the bus station, which is sited in the lower part of the city near the junction of Ulu Yol Cad. and road 200. There is a ferry-boat service from 55km Yalova to Dolmabaçe in İstanbul. A faster link with İstanbul is provided by coach and hydrofoil via 24km Mudanya. Details of services from Bursa's airport may be obtained from the THY office in Cemal Nadir Cad. No. 8/A or from the Tourist Information Office. Bursa is not on the railway network.

Museums. Bursa is rich in museums: the Archaeological Museum is in the Kültürpark; the Atatürk Museum in Çekirge Cad.; the Museum of Turkish Art near Yeşil Cami and the Murat Evi in Muradiye.

The city is well-known for its production of silk and cotton goods, in particular table-cloths, serviettes, towels and dressing gowns. Interesting antiques may be purchased in the bazaar.

It is famous for its peaches and candied fruits (especially chestnuts), and İskender Kebab and İnegöl Köftesi are among Bursa's other food specialities.

In addition to the private baths in Çekirge's hotels there are several public baths: Yeni Kaplıca and Eski Kaplıca in Çekirge Cad., Kaynarca and KüKürtlü, which is visited for the high sulphur content of the water.

History. Bursa was originally called Prusa after its founder Prusias I (228–185 BC), king of Bithynia. A legendary account states that Hannibal, the great Carthagenian general and enemy of Rome, helped him to choose the site.

According to Herodotus, the Bithynians came originally from Thrace. He describes them as being a cruel and savage race, who fought, clothed in fox skins, with dirk and javelin. The territory which they occupied was bounded by Pergamum and the Sea of Marmara to the W, Pontus to the E, and the Black Sea to the N. Freed from Persian domination by the victories of Alexander, they formed an independent kingdom with its capital at Nicomedia, modern İzmit.

Prusias the grandson of Nicomedes I, the creator of the kingdom of Bithynia, was an ambitious and intelligent man, who enlarged the boundaries of his realm. He incorporated the Greek cities on the Propontis (the Sea of Marmara) and encouraged the development of an overland trade route with Armenia. In founding Prusa and giving it his own name, he was following a fashion popular among the Hellenistic kings.

When Nicomedes IV of Bithynia (94–74 BC), a weak and vicious man, was driven from his kingdom by invading Pontians, he fled to Rome. Restored c 85 BC by the Romans, he ruled as their vassal in all but name until his death. Nicomedes had no legitimate male heir so, following the example of Attalus III

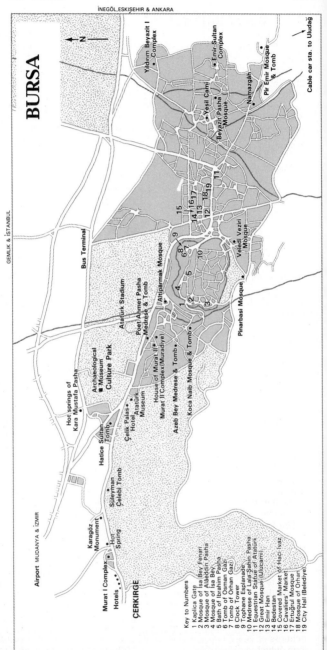

İNEGÖL, ESKİŞEHİR & ANKARA

GEMLIK & İSTANBUL

BURSA

← N →

Airport MUDANYA & İZMIR

Yıldırım Beyazıt I Complex

Emir Sultan Complex

Cable car sta. to Uludağ

Yeşil Cami

Beyazıt Pasha Mosque

Namazgâh

Pir Emir Mosque & Tomb

Veledi Veziri Mosque

Pınarbası Mosque

Bus Terminal

Atatürk Stadium

Poet Ahmet Pasha Medrese & Tomb

Attıpazarı Mosque

Archaeological Museum

Culture Park

Hot springs of Kara Mustafa Pasha

Çelik Palas Hotel

Atatürk Museum

House of Murat II

Murat II Complex (Muradiye)

Azeb Bey Medrese & Tomb

Koca Naib Mosque & Tomb

Hatice Sultan Tomb

Süleyman Çelebi Tomb

Karagöz Monument

Hot Spring

ÇEKIRGE

Murat I Complex

Hotels

Key to Numbers
1 Kaplıca Gate
2 Mosque of Isa Bey Fenari
3 Mosque of Alâeddin Pasha
4 Mosque of Isa Bey
5 Bath of Ibrahim Pasha
6 Tomb of Osman Gazi
7 Tomb of Orhan Gazi
8 Clock Tower
9 Tophane Esplanade
10 Medrese of Lala Şahin Pasha
11 Equestrian Statue of Atatürk
12 Great Mosque (Ulucami)
13 Emir Han
14 Bedestan
15 Covered Market of Hacı İvaz
16 Cavaliers' Market
17 Ertuğrul Mosque
18 Mosque of Orhan
19 City Hall (Belediye)

of Pergamum, he willed his kingdom to Rome. His bequest was accepted and Bithynia came under direct Roman rule in 74 BC.

Prosperous under the Romans and the early Byzantines, Bursa suffered a sharp decline in its fortunes during the period of the Arab raids in the 7C and 8C. Captured by the Selçuk Turks in 1075, it was taken by Christian forces in 1097 during the First Crusade. In the course of the next two centuries it changed hands frequently, sometimes being occupied by the Selçuks sometimes by the Byzantines. Finally, after a protracted siege it was taken in 1326 by the army of Orhan Gazi, who made it the capital of the new Ottoman Empire.

Although the capital was moved later to Edirne and then, after its capture, to Constantinople, Bursa retained much of its prestige. The creator of the Ottoman dynasty, Osman Gazi, and five of his successors were buried there. Bursa was also an important commercial centre on the trade route between İstanbul and the principal cities of the Ottoman Empire. Its mineral springs, known to the Romans and Byzantines, were enjoyed by the Ottomans who ornamented the city with a number of luxurious baths.

For that redoubtable 17C traveller Evliya Çelebi Bursa was an earthly paradise: 'The inhabitants being fair, the air good, the water full of holiness, contribute altogether, to render Brússa one of the most delicious spots on earth'. The city had 9000 shops where everything could be bought. Full of poets, storytellers and entertainers, it was a city of pleasure: 'All coffee-houses, and particularly those near the great mosque, abound with men skilled in a thousand arts [*Hezár-fenn*] dancing and pleasure continue the whole night, and in the morning every body goes to the mosque ... There are also no less than ninety-seven Búza-houses, which are not to be equalled in the world; they are wainscoted with fayence, painted, each capable of accommodating one thousand men. In summer the Búza is cooled with ice, like sherbet; the principal men of the town are not ashamed to enter these Búza houses, although abundance of youths, dancers and singers, girt with Brússa girdles, here entice their lovers to ruin.'

Occupied by Greek troops in 1920, Bursa was recaptured by the Turkish army in 1922. Since then the city has expanded considerably, but fortunately it has managed to retain much of its old-world charm.

The exploration of Bursa is facilitated by the fact that most of its principal monuments are to be found on or near a series of streets that start at Yeşil Cad. in the NE and continue along the lower slopes of Ulu Dağ, through the centre of the city, to Çekirge Cad. in the SW. However, the distance from one end of the city to the other is considerable, so it is advisable to take a bus or dolmuş between the different groups of monuments.

Starting at Cumhuriyet Alanı, popularly known as Heykel (statue) because of its proximity to a statue of Atatürk, go first to Yeşil Cad. In this street are two of the most interesting early Ottoman buildings in Bursa, Yeşil Cami and Yeşil Türbe. Originally they formed part of a complex, which included, in addition to the mosque and tomb, an imaret, a medrese and a hamam.

Yeşil Cami, the Green Mosque, was built during the reign of Mehmet I (1413–21). The son of Yıldırım Beyazit, who died a captive in the hands of Tamerlane, Mehmet did much to restore the fortunes of the Ottomans.

The Green Mosque was never completed, as in accordance with Ottoman custom work ceased at the time of Mehmet's death. However, it remains one of the finest examples of Ottoman architecture. An inscription over the N door makes the proud claim that 'here is a building such as no nation has been presented with since the sky began to turn'. The mosque derived its name from the wonderful green tiles which at one time covered the dome and the tops of the minarets. Evliya Çelebi compared them to emeralds sparkling in the sunlight. The simplicity of its plan—two rectangular chambers in the form of an inverted T surmounted by domes—is balanced by the richness of its interior decoration. Over the entrance is the sultan's loge, which is flanked by screened balconies reserved for members of the imperial family. In the centre of an interior court is a *şadirvan*, which reflects the glowing colours of the windows, tiles and mosaics. Note the fine *mihrab*, which is raised slightly above floor level. The outside of the mosque is clad in pale white Proconessian marble.

Damaged by an earthquake in 1855, the Green Mosque was restored at the command of the Vali, Ahmet Vefik Paşa, by Leon Parvillée.

Nearby is the *medrese* which now houses a collection of Turkish and Islamic Art. This includes examples of fine calligraphy, books and Korans, jewellery, household goods, arms and armaments from the Ottoman period. On the other side of the street at the top of a slight eminence stands **Yeşil Türbe**, the tomb of Mehmet I (died 1421). Its perfect proportions, its position between cypress trees at the top of a short flight of steps, its decoration inside and out combine to make this one of the most beautiful buildings in Turkey.

Tiled sarcophagus of Mehmet I, Yeşil Türbe, Bursa.

A simple octagon, its single chamber, surmounted by a dome, houses the elaborately decorated sarcophagus of the sultan. This is raised above floor level on a tiled dais. Nearby are the tombs of some members of his family and court. The sarcophagi are empty as in accordance with Islamic law Mehmet and the others were buried in the earth in vaults underneath the chamber. An examination of these vaults, which could be entered from the E side of the building, revealed only a few sad bones that had been disturbed by rats. The walls of the tomb, decorated with a revetment of tiles and painted calligraphy, are pierced by small windows filled with richly coloured glass. Note the splendid mihrab and the door and window shutters, with their intricate, interlaced carved patterns.

Like the Green Mosque, Yeşil Türbe was damaged by the earthquake of 1855. Modern tiles from Kütahya were used by the restorers to replace those that had been lost or destroyed. To the left of Yeşil Cami there is a coffee-house, which not only offers refreshment, but also a fine view over the lower part of the city and the surrounding countryside.

A short distance to the right is *Emir Sultan Camii*, which was reconstructed at the beginning of the 19C in a lush, overpowering style popular at that time. Its melancholy cypress-shaded cemetery also offers an excellent view over Bursa and the plain beyond.

The last group of buildings of interest in this part of Bursa is the **Yıldırım Beyazit complex**. Yıldırım (1389–1403), the father of Mehmet I, acquired his name, which means thunderbolt, because of the speed with which he moved his armies. The complex was made up of a mosque, an imaret, two medreses, a hospital, a palace and a türbe. In the past it has suffered much damage and has been restored twice. Today only the mosque, the türbe and one medrese remain.

Built in the familiar inverted T form, the *mosque* is notable for the elaborate niche under the arch, which divides the outer court from the prayer hall. This is the first known use of the so-called Bursa arch. Beyazit's emblem appears frequently in the decoration of the mosque. The *medrese* has been heavily restored; originally the arches in the interior court were not glazed. Note the use of alternate lines of stone and brick in the construction of the building. This was an economy measure borrowed from the example of the Byzantines.

On returning to Heykel walk in a SW direction along Atatürk Cad. **Ulu Cami**, the Great Mosque, is on the right-hand side of the street. Constructed of golden-hued limestone from Mt Olympus, it measures 56m by 68m and was the first congregational mosque erected by the Ottomans.

Before the battle of Nicopolis in 1396, according to a popular tradition, Yıldırım Beyazit promised that, if God gave him victory, he would build 20 mosques. He defeated a mixed force of Crusaders from France, England, Flanders, Savoy, Lombardy, Scotland, and Germany allied with Hungarians under Sigismund, slaughtering more than 10,000 prisoners after the battle. Then, interpreting his promise rather liberally, he used some of the booty he had won to build Ulu Cami, instructing his architect to give it 20 domes. The 20 domes in four groups of five are supported by 12 great pillars. These are decorated with huge inscriptions from the Koran in stylised calligraphy. Under the central dome in the second rank on the N side is the Şadirvan, which takes the form of a pool with a fountain in the centre. The oculus, which lights this area of the mosque, was originally open to the elements. Note the beautiful walnut mimber, which is carved with representations of the heavenly bodies. The entrance on the N is believed to have been built by Tamerlane after he had captured Beyazit and occupied Bursa c 1402.

At first Ulu Cami had one minaret only, erected in the usual position on the NW side. A second minaret was added by Mehmet I, who made it clear that only an imperial mosque could have more than one.

A short distance along Atatürk Cad. is *Orhan Gazi Camii*. Begun in 1339 this is the oldest of Bursa's royal mosques. Much restored, it has a *zaviye*, a hostel for dervishes.

Behind Ulu Cami lies Bursa's *market*. Destroyed by fire in 1955, it has been completely rebuilt. Offering everything from jewellery and the finest silks to essential household goods, on most days it is filled with an animated throng of shoppers bargaining over their purchases. Of the many hans in the market area perhaps the most striking is *Koza Hanı*, the silk cocoon caravanserai, which dates from 1451 and was imaginatively restored recently. In its shops, built around a central couryard, rolls of beautiful silk and brocade cascade

Koza Hanı, Bursa.

temptingly over the counters in a display designed to attract and hold the attention of the casual passer-by.

Gold and silver jewellery and the most expensive products are sold in the *Bedesten*, while the *Sipahilar Çarşısı*, the covered market of the cavalry soldiers, which was built during the reign of Mehmet I, offers goods of every kind. Visitors leaving the market on the E side should look out for Bursa's ornate *Belediye* (town hall).

On returning to Atatürk Cad., continue past Ulu Camii to the point where the roads divide. To visit the *Citadel* take Yiğitler Cad. on the left. This climbs steeply under the *Citadel's walls* constructed during the Hellenistic period but much restored by the Byzantines and the Ottomans.

In the citadel are the *Tombs of Osman Gazi* and *Orhan Gazi*. Osman Gazi (1288–1324), the founder of the Ottoman dynasty was buried here in 1326, two years after the capture of the city by his son Orhan Gazi. His tomb was placed in the baptistery of a church dedicated to the Prophet Elias which had been converted into a mosque. Orhan Gazi (1324–59) was buried nearby in the nave of the former church. The buildings sheltering the tombs were destroyed and reconstructed several times, but a few fragments of mosaic from the church floor may be seen near Orhan's sarcophagus. From the terrace behind the tombs there is an excellent view of the lower part of the city.

In the narrow winding streets of the citadel are some fine examples of old Turkish houses. Many have the typical projecting first floor, which allows the occupants to see what is happening in the street below. At one time these old houses were destroyed in large numbers and replaced by characterless apartment blocks. However, in recent years their historical value has been recognised and they are being carefully restored with the assistance of the authorities.

The **Muradiye complex**, built during the reign of Murat II (1421–51), may be reached by following Kaplica Cad. from the citadel. The complex comprised a mosque, a medrese, an imaret and Murat's türbe. The mosque, elaborately decorated with floral and geometrical mosaics, is designed on the same plan as Orhan Gazi Camii. It also has two zaviyes, dervish hospices; one on each side of the entrance.

The sultan's türbe is in a garden filled with roses and flowering shrubs and shaded by cypresses and plane trees. Although Bursa was no longer the capital of the Ottoman Empire, Murat was brought from Edirne to rest here. A strong and vigorous ruler, according to Gibbon, 'he seldom engaged in war till he was justified by a previous and adequate provocation. In the observance of treaties his word was inviolate and sacred.'

Murat's sarcophagus rests under the open oculus of a dome supported by antique columns. Nearby are the tombs of four of his sons. In other parts of the garden a dozen türbe shelter the remains of members of the imperial family who died in the following century.

Just outside the Muradiye an 18C *Ottoman town house* has been restored and opened as a museum. Sometimes called the Murat House, because it occupies the site of a building which belonged to Murat II, it has a number of rooms furnished in typical Ottoman style.

Descend from the Muradiye by Kaplica Cad. to its junction with Çekirge Cad. On the left-hand side of Çekirge Cad. is the house where Kemal Atatürk stayed during the 13 visits he made to Bursa between 1922 and 1938. Now the *Atatürk Museum* it was first opened to the public in 1973 on the 50th anniversary of the Turkish Republic.

On the right-hand side of the road is Bursa's *Kültürpark*. In addition to a large area of formal gardens, this has an exhibition section, a fun-fair, a boating lake, a small zoo, several restaurants and a number of coffee-houses. Bursa's Archaeological Museum is within its grounds and the city's football stadium is on its E edge. The Kültürpark, a popular meeting place and leisure centre for local people, is usually crowded at weekends and on public holidays.

Bursa's **Archaeological Museum** opened its doors to the public in 1972. Housed in a new building, it has four exhibition halls, a laboratory, and a library, and contains exhibits from the provinces of Bursa, Balıkesir and Bilecik. Many of the items in the museum are labelled in Turkish and English, but provenance and dates are not always given.

Room 1 contains artefacts from the prehistoric period found in and near Bursa. There are also several stone fragments from the Roman period, including a headless *statue of Tyche* and part of a sarcophagus. **Room 2** is devoted to statues, busts and architectural pieces from the Archaic, Hellenistic, Roman and Byzantine periods. These include several representations of *Cybele* and members of the Olympian pantheon, a *reclining Hercules* and a number of Roman portrait busts. In the right-hand corner of the room there are two *columns*, provenance and date not stated, surrounded by coiled, headless snakes. In a linking corridor there are some abstract pattern mosaics and a number of amphorae, which appear to have been recovered from the sea. **Room 3** contains metal, glass and ceramic artefacts from the Hellenistic and Roman periods. These include terracottas, jewellery, ceramics, small bronzes and glass objects. In a case in the centre of the room there is a *bronze statue of a youth*. His inlaid eyes give the face an interestingly animated expression. A small gallery has a display of Roman jewellery and, from the Byzantine period, pottery and metal artefacts, religious objects, including crosses, and ceramics. **Room 4**, to the left of the mosaic corridor, contains a well-displayed *coin collection*. In addition to specimens from Bithynia, including some from Prusa, Nicaea and Nicomedia, there are coins from Mysia, the Troad, Myrina, Phrygia, Lycia, and Pergamum. There is also a representative selection of Roman and Byzantine coins. On the walls are illustrations which explain how coins were made in antiquity and which outline the history of money.

Outside the museum there is an overflow display on the terrace, in the garden, to the side and at the rear of the building. This consists of stelae, architectural fragments, statues and reliefs.

Across the road from the Kültürpark is the oldest, most luxurious and best-known of Bursa's hotels, the *Çelik Palas*.

One of the earliest recorded visitors to Bursa to take the waters was the Byzantine Empress Theodora, who came to the city with a retinue of 4000 courtiers. Since then Bursa has attracted many visitors anxious to improve their health. The curative properties of its mineral springs were known to the Ottomans, who constructed a number of elaborate baths which still exist. Of these the best-known are the *Yeni* and *Eski Kaplıca*. As a spa Bursa reached its apogee in the 19C and early 20C, when minor European royalty and artists and writers like Pierre Loti flocked there to take the cure.

On the right-hand side of the road, a short distance along Çekirge Cad. from the Çelik Palas hotel, are the *Yeni Kaplıca baths*. Built in 1522 by Rüstem Paşa, the Grand Vizier of Süleyman the Magnificent, on the site of a Byzantine baths complex dating from the reign of Justinian, they are reserved for men.

The oldest of Bursa's hamams, the *Eski Kaplıca*, is to be found at the foot of the hill just outside Çekirge. It seems likely that there were baths on this site in Roman and Byzantine times. According to Ibn Battuta, who visited Bursa in 1333, an earlier building provided free accommodation, as custom required, for three days. Evliya Çelebi states that the present structure was constructed during the reign of Murat I (1359–89). The architectural evidence would appear to support this dating.

At the top of the hill are the **Mosque and Türbe of Murat I** (1359–89).

Known as Hüdavendigar, Creator of the Universe, Murat spent most of his reign at war. He captured Edirne and extended the boundaries of the Ottoman Empire into Europe, adding Thrace, Macedonia and Bulgaria to his possessions. He founded the Corps of Janissaries, which was to play such an important part in Turkish history. The Janissaries were chosen from the strongest of the Christian youths, who were taken from their families by the devşirme system and forcibly converted to Islam. For many centuries this highly-disciplined regiment was to form the backbone of the Ottoman army.

At the age of 70 Murat was called to quell a revolt of his Serbian subjects, who with the assistance of the Bosnians, Bulgarians, Albanians and Hungarians sought to regain their independence. He defeated the combined forces, led by King Lazarus of Serbia, at the battle of Kossova on 27 August 1389. However, in the last moments of the battle Murat was fatally wounded by a Serbian noble, Milosch Kobilovitch, who had come to the Turkish camp in the guise of a deserter. Murat lived long enough to order the execution of Milosch and Lazarus.

On the day of Murat's victory and death, his son Beyazit I, who succeeded to the throne, had his brother Yacoub murdered in the presence of the dead body of their father. Yacoub, a brave and honourable soldier, had fought many battles to defend the Ottoman Empire. His murder was considered necessary because it was feared he might contest the succession, and it was justified by a verse from the Koran, which states that 'rebellion is worse than execution'. Beyazit's action initiated a practice that continued for many centuries. On the day of his accession, it became customary for the sultan to have his brothers and all other male relatives executed, so ensuring a trouble-free take over of power.

The mosque, although based on the conventional inverted T plan, has a number of unusual features. These are sometimes explained by the tradition that it was designed by a captured Italian architect. The ground floor combines a mosque with a zaviye. On the first floor there was a medrese.

Across the road on a commanding site on the cliff edge is Murat's türbe. In a chamber $17m^2$ the sultan's sarcophagus is set between the eight columns that support the dome. Damaged by the earthquake of 1855, the türbe was restored on the orders of Abdül Hamit II.

Originally the complex also included an imaret, but this no longer exists. However, a well-appointed toilet is still in use. This consists of a domed chamber with two washrooms, a central fountain and five small cubicles.

EXCURSION TO ULUDAĞ. *Uludağ* (2543m), the ancient Mt Olympus of Mysia, may be reached from Bursa in two ways: by a road which winds up the slope of the mountain for 36km or by a cable-car which takes c 30 minutes. To go by road catch a dolmuş at the bus station; to go by cable-car take a dolmuş from Heykel to Teleferik, the cable-car terminal. The cable-car has two stops, at Kadıyayla and at Sarıalan. *Note* that in bad weather, the cable car may not operate. Current rates for both journeys may be obtained from the Tourism Office.

Visitors with their own transport, who wish to drive to the top, should leave the city centre by Çekirge Cad. and take a turn-off at c 4km marked Uludağ.

At the beginning of the Christian era, according to Strabo, Mt Olympus was the haunt of brigands and vagabonds. During the Byzantine period it became the home of monks and mystics. After the Arab conquest the Christians were replaced by Islamic dervishes, who took over the abandoned monasteries. Today the mountain is one of Turkey's best-known and most popular national parks.

Uludağ National Park occupies an area of c 11,400 hectares. A paradise for naturalists and bird-watchers, its slopes are clothed in bay and olive, chestnut, elm, oak, plane and beach, pine, juniper and aspen. Above 2000m dwarf junipers and alpine flora may be found.

To meet the requirements of summer ramblers and winter-sports enthusiasts a number of hotels have been built on Uludağ. These are relatively expensive. (Current rates may be obtained from the Tourism Office.)

The walk to the summit of the mountain from the hotel area, which takes about two hours, is not difficult. Uludağ is snow-covered to an average depth of 2–3m from December to May. Facilities for skiers are good, if less elaborate than those found in European winter sports resorts. Hotel rooms are in great demand during the winter and reservations should be made as far in advance as possible.

Buses for Erdek, via Bandırma, depart from Bursa's coach station. The journey takes about 2½ hours.

After leaving Bursa, the busy road 200 bisects a featureless plain, whose monotony is relieved only by the gleaming waters of (c 30km) *Uluabat Gölü* on the left. A favourite rendezvous for fishermen and hunters, this shallow lake provides good catches of perch, pike, sturgeon and crayfish and the surrounding countryside supports large numbers of pheasant, heron, crane and woodcock.

The site of the ancient city of APOLLONIA is located near the village of *Gölyazı*. This may be reached by following a left-hand turn from the main road for c 6km. Apart from a number of tombs in the necropolis near the peninsula, which links Gölyazı to the mainland, few traces of Apollonia remain. Today most visitors are attracted by the beauty of the site rather than by its historical associations. There is a regular daily bus service between Bursa and Gölyazı.

Just beyond the W confines of the lake at c 58km is the market-town of *Karacabey*. This was named after a relative of Murat II, who died in 1455. Karaca Bey's elaborate marble *tomb* stands under the five-arched portico of a mosque on the NE side of the town. His wife and daughter are believed to have been buried in the domed building nearby.

A short diversion to the S from Karacabey along road 4 brings the visitor to c 8km *Hara*. Also known as *Karacabey Harası*, this ancient foundation dates back to the time of Orhan Gazi (1324–1359). A royal farm under the Ottomans, it is now a stud (*hara*) and an agricultural station, which specialises in the improvement of livestock and plants. Cattle, horses, fowl, cereals and grasses produced here are sought by farmers from all over Turkey. The station also offers advice and information on how to improve cultivation methods. A small pension and restaurant at Hara offer accommodation and refreshment.

Not surprisingly, the countryside around Karacabey has a reputation for producing excellent vegetables, especially onions.

For *Kuşcenneti National Park* leave road 200 c 12km before Bandırma at the point where it joins road 565 to Balıkesir. After 2km a track to the right leads to the car-park and a small museum. Facilities in the park are limited to an observation tower, toilet, and a supply of drinking water. There is no accommodation or restaurant and picnicking is not allowed.

A Hydrobiological Research Station is maintained at Kuşcenneti by the University of İstanbul. The park's flora and fauna are strictly protected and all visitors are expected to comply with the regulations which have been drawn up the authorities. Each year a large number of scientists, bird-watchers, biologists and nature lovers come to the National Park. This occupies c 52 hectares of woods and marshland on the shores of Lake Kuş, formerly Lake Manyas. As its name, Kuşcenneti, 'Bird Paradise', suggests, it is an important resting and breeding place for migratory and wintering species. Birds which have spent the winter in the S come to Kuşcenneti in the spring to lay their eggs and rear their young. The nestlings, nourished by a rich food supply, are able to grow to maturity in the safe setting of the park's environment.

Between two and three million birds visit Kuşcenneti each year. Among the 239 species that have been recorded are herons, cormorants, pelicans, geese, spoonbills, ibises, ducks and reed warblers. The lake, shaded by willow, alder and ash, swarms with fish. Pike, catfish, carp, grey mullet, and crayfish abound, while the bullrushes resound to the harsh croaking of a myriad frogs.

In the SE corner of Kuş Gölü are the ruins of the garrison city of DASCYLIUM. According to Herodotus and Thucydides Pharnabazus, the Persian satrap ruled Hellespontine Phrygia from here. After Alexander's victory at Granicus, Dascylium was invested by a force under the command of Parmenion.

The scanty remains of the city are likely to be of interest to specialists and students only. A number of reliefs found there and now displayed in the İstanbul Archaeological Museum reveal strong Iranian thematic influences. These depict a bull and a ram being sacrificed in the Persian manner and a stately procession of mounted figures. A recent survey of the site by Turkish archaeologists has resulted in the discovery of a Graeco-Achaemenid funeral stele and of a number of bullae with inscriptions in Aramaic. The stele is in the İstanbul Museum and the bullae are in the Archaeological Institute of Ankara University.

Bandırma is a dusty, undistinguished little town. Linked to İstanbul by car-ferry, it is a convenient disembarkation point for visitors to Erdek and the other small resorts on Kapıdağ peninsula.

A winding road leads across the windswept isthmus that links Kapıdağ, ancient Arctonesus (Bear Island), with the mainland. The monument on the hill to the left commemorates Turks, who died during the Graeco-Turkish War (1919–22).

Conservationists, nature-lovers and the local farmers have been greatly exercised by the industrial growth which has taken place on the isthmus during recent years. In this formerly unspoiled area there are now several chemical installations and a petrol storage depot. As a result sea-bathing is no longer possible.

About 8km from Bandırma are the thinly scattered remains of the city of CYZICUS. These lie to the right of the road to Erdek towards the E side of the isthmus. The site of Cyzicus, which has been excavated by Turkish archaeologists under the direction of Professor Akurgal, is very overgrown and is not easy to visit.

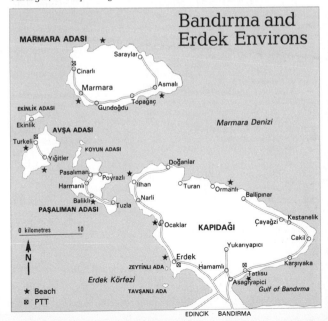

The remains of the city's *amphitheatre* lie in a ravine near the village of Hammamlı. Sections of the aqueducts that brought water from Mt Dindymus, and the hollow in which the theatre was built may still be seen. In the SE corner there is a substantial section of the city walls.

The vaults, which supported the base of the great *Temple of Hadrian*, are known locally as the *bedesten* or *mağarlar*. According to Hasluck, who visited Cyzicus at the beginning of the century, these gloomy structures were shunned by the local people, who believed them to be inhabited by demons.

History. According to a legendary account Jason and the Argonauts were warmly received at Arctonesus by Cyzicus, king of the Doliones. While he was entertaining them, monsters with six arms attacked Argo, but they were defeated and killed by Hercules.

After being provisioned and supplied with instructions for the next stage of their voyage, the Argonauts put to sea. During the night the wind arose and they were obliged to run for cover. They beached the boat in the dark and almost immediately were attacked by unknown men. In the morning they discovered to their horror that the attackers were the Doliones who had thought that their territory was being invaded. Cyzicus was among the slain. Overcome by grief, his wife Clite hanged herself. Jason and his companions mourned their dead friend and joined in the funeral games aranged by the Doliones in honour of Cyzicus.

When they tried to resume their voyage, contrary winds blew the Argonauts back to the shore. They were informed that they had angered Phrygian Cybele, Meter Oreie, the Mother of the Mountains, who under the title Meter Dindymene was worshipped on Mt Dindymus. To obtain forgiveness, Jason and his crew went in procession to her shrine and, imitating the Corybantes, danced around the statue of the goddess while banging their swords on their shields. Cybele, placated by their action, allowed the Argonauts to continue their journey.

Excavations suggest that the city of Cyzicus was a Milesian colony and trading post founded towards the beginning of the 7C BC.

Strabo, writing in the 1C AD, describes Cyzicus as an island linked to the mainland by two bridges. A city of the same name built near the bridges rivalled 'the foremost of the cities of Asia in size, in beauty, and in its excellent administration of affairs both in peace and in war. And its adornment appears to be of a type similar to that of Rhodes and Massalia and ancient Carthage.'

In 334 BC Cyzicus supported Alexander the Great, closing its gates to the armies of the Persian satrap. This action embarrassed the Persians in a number of ways. As they did not mint their own coins they relied on Cyzician currency, one of the most widely-used in antiquity, to pay their hired mercenaries. They were also unable to send their annual tribute to Persepolis.

Under the Romans, Cyzicus was given the status of a free city and awarded a substantial grant of territory in N Mysia because of its resistance to Mithridates in 74 BC. A temple, begun during the reign of Hadrian and dedicated to him, was completed by Marcus Aurelius (AD 167). Regarded as one of the wonders of the ancient world, it was damaged by an earthquake in the 6C AD. However, that inveterate traveller, Cyriac of Ancona, claimed to have seen the whole of the upper section of the building in 1431.

Little remains to be seen at Cyzicus, but objects discovered in the city are to be found in Erdek, İstanbul and Paris. Part of a column decorated with bunches of grapes is displayed in the open-air museum at Erdek. In the İstanbul Archaeological Museum there are artefacts which combine Greek and Oriental elements to produce what may be described as a Propontine style. These include a circular base ornamented in high relief with the representation of a girl dancing between two youths, a kouros, and a relief showing a galloping chariot. There are also a number of fine 5C BC electrum staters in the museum. These depict Poseidon riding a sea-horse, Silenus filling a cantharus and a delicately-executed female head.

A relief in the Louvre, dated to 46 BC, was dedicated to Cybele by one Soterides Gallos. The Great Mother revealed to him in a dream that his friend, Marcus Stlaccius, who had disappeared in battle, had been a prisoner-of-war, but was released at her intercession. The upper portion of the relief shows, under a representation of the enthroned goddess, the preparations for a sacrifice.

The approach to **Erdek** is through an avenue of olive groves, orchards and vineyards. Today a small resort, popular with Turkish visitors, it has a number of simple, comfortable hotels and some good restaurants. Up-to-date information about accommodation, including prices, may be obtained from the Tourism Office. The small open-air museum is in the town centre near the Belediye.

Erdek is a good centre for those who wish to explore Kapıdağ, or to visit Proconnesus, Marmara Island, which was famed for its ancient marble quarries.

A. Bursa to İnegöl and Oylat

Total distance c 58km. **Bursa**—R200 38km **İnegöl**—20km **Oylat**.

If travelling by public transport, allow one day for this excursion. In addition to local services, all long-distance coaches to Ankara departing from Bursa's central garage pass the outskirts of İnegöl. There is a dolmuş service to Oylat, which leaves İnegöl's bus station at irregular intervals, and taxis may be hired in the town.

Most restaurants in İnegöl serve köfte and kebabs. For something more elaborate, try the Şehir Lokantası, which is located near the central square. Oylat has a number of small restaurants, but it is more enjoyable to picnic in the woods that surround the spa.

Several small hotels in İnegöl and Oylat offer basic accommodation to those who wish to stay overnight. Rooms may be difficult to obtain in Oylat during Turkish holidays like Kurban Bayramı. Enquire at Bursa's Tourism Office for information about room availability, prices, etc.

Visitors with their own transport should leave **Bursa** by road 200 in the direction of Ankara. This first crosses a fertile plain dotted with orchards, then climbs steadily passing Bursa Gölü on the left. From the crest the road descends to İnegöl in a series of gentle loops, which offer good views of Ulu Dağ and its foothills on the right. In the hilly country to the left of the road vines are cultivated and in some villages between there and İznik a palatable white wine is produced on a non-commercial basis.

38km **İnegöl** is a pleasant market town famous for its köfte, its fruit and its manufacture of furniture. Throughout Turkey İnegöl köftesi, meat balls made from lamb and served with raw onion rings, are known and enjoyed. However, the town's residents, exhibiting a pardonable campanilismo, claim that the genuine article may be obtained only here. Furniture of good quality, made in a traditional style, is produced in factories on the outskirts of the town. This is sold, not only in Turkey, but in many Middle East countries.

İnegöl is best visited on Thursday, when the weekly market is held. Its crowded streets present an animated spectacle, as villagers from the surrounding countryside sell their produce and make their purchases. Stalls covered with tempting displays of fruit and vegetables fill the market area and overflow on to the lanes nearby.

İnegöl shared a common history with Bursa, İznik, and other towns in NW Bithynia. Fought over by the Byzantines, Arabs, Selçuks and Crusaders, it came under Ottoman control at the beginning of the 14C. Today the only visible relic of its past is the İshak Paşa Complex, which consisted of a mosque, medrese, dershane and tabhanes. This was built in 1482 by İshak Paşa, chief vizier to Mehmet II, who was dismissed and exiled to İnegöl, his home town, by Mehmet's successor, Beyazit II. The principal interest of the complex lies in the positioning of the medrese and the mosque. They face each other across a courtyard, which has a şadirvan in the centre. Only the vaulted bays of the medrese remain. The walls of the mosque, with their mixture of brick and stone, give the building a pleasantly rustic appearance.

İshak Paşa Complex, İnegöl.

Part of İnegöl's population is made up of the descendants of an Islamic minority that came to Turkey in the 19C from Georgia in S Russia. A strikingly handsome people, many of them tall and fair-haired, they have retained a number of their Georgian traditions. They are well-known for their exuberant athletic dancing, which they perform with great zest at weddings, family feasts and folklore festivals.

To get to **Oylat**, c 20km from İnegöl, continue on road 200 in the direction of Ankara for c 10km, then turn right and after 5km right again on to a narrow track that climbs steeply to the crest on which the village is built.

Of the many spas in the vicinity of Bursa, Oylat is probably the least well-known and is certainly the most beautifully sited. Its single small street climbs picturesquely under a beech hanger to the baths.

The baths do not follow the usual hamam design. Apart from having an enclosed trough-like area at one end, Oylat's Yeni Hamam has been built like a conventional swimming pool. Each minute thousands of gallons of naturally hot mineral water pour into the trough and overflow into the pool. There are no masseurs in Oylat's baths, instead great jets of hot water, which cascade over the bathers, provide a rough and stimulating massage.

Admission charges to Oylat's baths are very low. Although towels may be hired, most bathers bring their own. The baths are segregated, separate periods being allocated to men and women.

A few days spent at Oylat provide a healthy and restful break. There is no organised entertainment. Visitors spend hours in bathing, in exploring the beech woods, in playing tavla in the coffee-houses and in enjoying the village's calm and peaceful atmosphere.

B.   Bursa to İznik

Total distance c 76km. **Bursa**—R575 c 28km *Gemlik*—c 48km **İznik**.

Allow one day for this excursion. That will give sufficient time for the journey by public transport, for a visit to the principal monuments, including the museum, and for lunch or a picnic by İznik Gölü.

There are regular bus, and frequent dolmuş services from Bursa's central coach station to İznik. The journey takes c 1 hour.

Visitors who have their own transport should leave **Bursa** by road 575 in the direction of Yalova. Shortly after passing through 28km *Gemlik* (see Rte 1C below), take a signposted right-hand turn on to the minor road that skirts İznik Gölü, the ancient Lake Ascanius.

There are several small restaurants in 48km **İznik**. Some near the lake-shore, which specialise in fish, are open only during the summer season. Near the town there are many places where it is possible to picnic. Accommodation in İznik is limited. There is one small motel. Enquiries to the *Tourism Office*, Kiliçarslan Cad. or to the Tourism Office in Bursa.

History. Founded in 316 BC by Antigonus I Monophthalmos (382–301), it was named Antigonia in his honour. After Lysimachus defeated Antigonus at the battle of Ipsus in 301 BC he renamed the city NICAEA, after his deceased wife, and made it the capital of Bithynia. Nicaea retained this position until 264 BC, when Nicomedes I (279–255 BC) moved the capital to the new city of Nicomedia (İzmit). The last king of Bithynia, the weak and vicious Nicomedes IV Philopator (94–74 BC), willed his kingdom to Rome. Under its new rulers Nicaea prospered, becoming one of the most important cities in the Roman province of Asia.

Nicaea attracted many artists and writers. The 1C BC grammarian and poet, Parthenius of Nicaea, the author of 'Metamorphoses', introduced the Callimachean elegy to the Romans. He edited, from various Greek sources, the book of 'Sorrowful Love-Stories' and is also credited with having taught Greek to Virgil.

Pliny the Younger (born AD 61) was governor of Bithynia from 111 to 113. During his term of office he resided at Nicaea and effected many improvements, including the reconstruction of the the city's theatre and gymnasium.

Concerned about the activities of the Christians in his province, he wrote to the emperor for advice. Trajan replied that they should not be hunted down. Any accused and convicted were to be punished, but those who repented and made sacrifice to the gods should be pardoned.

Destroyed by an earthquake in AD 123, the city was restored by Hadrian. During the Persian invasions in the mid 3C AD, Nicaea was rased to the ground. However, it was rebuilt and later welcomed Diocletian, Constantine and Justinian. After the adoption of Christianity as the official religion of the Roman Empire, it became an important missionary centre. At the First Council of Nicaea in 325 the Arian heresy, which denied the divinity of Christ, was condemned and the Nicaean Creed, which sets out the criteria of Christian orthodoxy, was composed. The first steps were also taken to establish formal co-operation between church and state.

For a short period during the reign of Julian the Apostate (361–363) pagan worship was resumed in Nicaea. In the 6C Justinian (527–565) ornamented the city with many splendid buildings including a basilica and a palace. Nicaea fended off several fierce attacks by the Arabs in the 8C. In 787 the Empress Irene, widow of Leo IV and regent for her son, Constantine VI, summoned the bishops to the Seventh Ecumenical Council which took place in Nicaea's Church of St. Sophia. This settled the controversy about icons. Reverence (Gr. proskynesis), but not adoration (Gr. latreia), could be given to them.

During the centuries that followed, Nicaea was taken and occupied by many armies. Invested at different times by Persians, Mongols and Turks, in 1081 it was captured by the Selçuks, who renamed it İznik and made it the capital of the Sultanate of Rum. Returned to Christian hands in 1097, it was for a short period the principal city of the Byzantine Lascarid dynasty. Finally, in 1331 İznik was taken by Orhan Gazi, the first Ottoman ruler, who made it the capital of his new realm. However, its trials were not yet over. It was captured and sacked by Tamerlane (1335–1405) in 1402.

After the Mongol army had retreated from Anatolia, the city, reoccupied by the Ottomans, entered a period of great artistic development. Large deposits of the raw materials needed for the production of ceramics— kaolin, feldspar and silicon—were found near Bursa and İznik. Sultan Mehmet Çelebi brought skilled craftsmen from Iran and under their tutelage the celebrated İznik ceramic industry was created. In the early 16C there were 300 workshops in the city producing tiles, which were used to decorate the Mosque of Omar at Jerusalem and many of the great palaces and religious buildings of the Ottoman Empire.

Towards the end of the 16C war broke out between Persia and Turkey and the Persian artists in İznik were exiled to Rhodes. Without their skills the quality of the ceramics declined. In c 1605 part of the city was burned down and many of the remaining craftsmen left İznik and settled in Kütahya. According to Evliya Çelebi, who visited İznik towards the end of the 17C, only nine ceramic workshops were in operation.

During the following centuries, İznik continued to decline, until it became little more than a hamlet dwarfed by its ancient city walls. In 1922, when Greece and Turkey were at war, it suffered great damage. Many of its ancient buildings were lost and it became what it is today—the melancholy shadow of a once great city.

The road from Bursa enters İznik by the *Yenişehir Kapısı*. According to an inscription this was built by the Emperor Claudius II Gothicus (268–270) in 268. Repaired and strengthened by the Lascarids in the 13C, the second entrance is set at an angle to the first to facilitate its defence. The scene of fierce attacks by the Selçuks and the Ottomans, it is now in a ruinous condition.

Nicaea was defended by two lines of fortifications separated by a fosse. The older wall, which dates from the 3C, is c 5km in length. The Lascarids restored this and built a second wall, which was protected by more than 100 towers. The city had four gates, three of which remain.

Like many Hellenistic cities Nicaea was laid out in the form of a grid. The modern Atatürk Cad., which links Yenişehir Kapısı in the S with İstanbul Kapısı in the N, follows the line of one of the ancient streets. The E/W axis is marked by Mazharbey Cad., which runs from the Göl Kapısı to Lefke Kapısı.

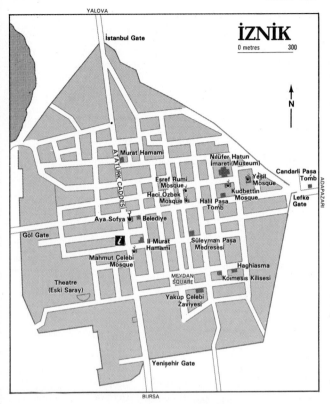

İZNİK

0 metres — 300

N

YALOVA

İstanbul Gate

Murat Hamamı

Nilüfer Hatun İmareti (Museum)

Çandarlı Paşa Tomb

Eşref Rumi Mosque

Yeşil Mosque

Haci Özbek Mosque

Kudbettin Mosque

Halil Paşa Tomb

Lefke Gate

Aya Sofya

Belediye

Göl Gate

İl-Murat Hamamı

Süleyman Paşa Medresesi

Mahmut Çelebi Mosque

Haghiasma

MEYDAN SQUARE

Koimesis Kilisesi

Theatre (Eski Saray)

Yakup Çelebi Zaviyesi

ATATÜRK CADDESİ

ADAPAZARI

Yenişehir Gate

BURSA

A short distance along Atatürk Cad., a turning to the left leads to the ruins of Nicaea's *theatre* (Eski Saray). Built by Pliny the Younger, while he was governor of Bithynia between 111 and 113, it had a seating capacity of c 15,000. Excavations currently under way have revealed that, as in the case of the theatre at Side, the seats were supported by vaults. They have uncovered the scaenium, proscaenium, cavea, vomitorium, diazoma and orchestra. Traces of a 13C three-aisled church and an extensive cemetery have been discovered on top of the cavea. In the scaenium they have found many arithtectural fragments, including a relief with figures of Roman charioteers. Large quantities of Roman, Byzantine, Selçuk and Ottoman pottery have also come to light.

On leaving the theatre, turn left and cross over Atatürk Cad. On the right-hand of the street is the *Zaviye of Yacoub Çelebi*. After fighting bravely at the battle of Kossova (1389), Yacoub was summarily executed by his brother Beyazit I on the battlefield in the presence of their father's corpse. Beyazit, who had just succeeded his father, Murat I, justified his action on the grounds that it would prevent disputes about the succession.

Return to Atatürk Cad. and, after crossing Sığır Meydanı, visit the site of *Koimesis Kilisesi*, the church of the Dormition of the Virgin. Built in the 8C, it was restored several times before being completely destroyed in 1922 during the Greek-Turkish war. Little now remains to be seen except a few pieces of marble sculpture and traces of its mosaic floor. The Lascarid emperor, Theodore I (1204–22), was buried here.

Walk up Istiklal Cad. and take the first turning on the left. On the right-hand side of the road is *Süleyman Paşa medressi*, which was built by the brother of Orhan I on the site of a former monastery in the early part of the 14C. Study-rooms and cells for the students lined the sides of a porticoed courtyard.

Return to Atatürk Cad. and turn right. The ruins of **Haghia Sophia**, the most important Byzantine monument in İznik are to be found at the junction with Mazharbey Cad. Excavations made in 1935 revealed traces of a church constructed on this site by Justinian in the 6C. These include a 7C fresco representing Deësis (prayer) in the nave and parts of the mosaic pavements. Justinian's church was destroyed by an earthquake in 1065 and replaced by a new building on a higher level. This had a narthex and a central nave, which was separated from the choir by a chancel.

After the conquest of Nicaea by Orhan Gazi in 1331 this church was converted into a mosque. A mihrab was placed in the chancel and a minaret added later. During the occupation of İznik by Tamerlane's army in 1402 the mosque was badly damaged and it suffered again from the effects of a fire in the 16C. Süleyman I the Magnificent (1520–66) had it restored by his architect Sinan, but as İznik began to decline in importance, the mosque fell into disrepair and eventually it was no longer used. The destruction of the building was completed in 1922 during the hostilities between Greece and Turkey.

On leaving Haghia Sophia continue along Mazharbey Cad. in the

Nilüfer Hatun İmareti, İznik.

direction of Lefke Kapısı. At the fourth intersection on the left is *Haci Özbek Camii*. Built in 1333, this small building is the earliest Ottoman mosque whose date can be fixed accurately by an inscription. Its walls are constructed of stone blocks separated by a brick on either side and with a layer of three bricks above and below. Originally the mosque had a portico, but this was removed in 1939 to allow the street to be widened.

The third turning on the left, Teke Sok., leads to Yeşil Cami and Nilüfer Hatun İmareti. *Yeşil Cami* was built between 1378 and 1391 by Çandarlı Kara Halil Paşa. The architect, Hacı bin Musa, has produced a pleasingly harmonious design by ensuring that the area of the portico and vestibule equalled the area of the prayer hall. The mosque acquired its name from the fine İznik tiles which covered the minaret. Unfortunately, these were destroyed and have been replaced by poor quality substitutes from Kütahya.

Nilüfer Hatun İmareti was built in 1388 by Murat I (1359–89) and named after his mother, a Greek princess, daughter of the Emperor John VI Catacuzenos. In 1346 Theodora or Nilüfer Hatun, as she became known, married Orhan Gazi, then aged 62, for reasons of state. She was allowed to remain a Christian. A powerful personality, she often acted as regent when Orhan was away on one of his many campaigns. At the imaret, which bears her name, food was provided for students and lodgings for itinerant dervishes.

The imaret, which has been well-restored, is constructed of stone blocks separated by brick. It has an open vaulted colonnade, which leads to a large chamber under a central dome. This is flanked by smaller domed side chambers and it has an exedra at the rear. Now İznik's *Museum*, the imaret houses artefacts found in and near the town and an interesting ethnographical collection.

In the garden are sarcophagi, capitals, stelae, reliefs and inscriptions. There is also a representative arrangement of Islamic gravestones. The central chamber is devoted to objects from the Hellenistic and Roman periods. Note the fine Roman *sarcophagus*, decorated with garlands and representations of Medusa, the collection of Roman glass and the many portrait busts. The exedra has some excellent examples of İznik tiles, plates and bowls. In the ethnographical collection there are flintlock pistols, dishes, censers, Koranic manuscripts, coins, writing instruments and embroidered cloths. The key to the Roman tomb outside the İstanbul Kapısı is kept in the museum.

From the museum return to Mazharbey Cad. and turn left to the *Lefke Kapısı*. This was a double gate, the outer section of which bears an inscription stating that it was dedicated to Hadrian in AD 123 by the proconsul Plancius Varus.

Return to Atatürk Cad. and continue in a N direction to the *İstanbul Kapısı*, the best preserved of all İznik's ancient gates. A double structure, this pierces both the 3C Roman wall and the 13C Lascarid fortification.

From the İstanbul Kapısı it is a pleasant walk along the tree-lined shore of İznik Gölü to the Göl Kapısı and thence to the town centre.

Visitors who have their own transport may wish to return to Bursa by a different route. There are two possibilities: along the N shore of the lake to Orhangazi and from there to Gemlik; or over the soft rolling Bithynian hills to Yenişehir and İnegöl. The second is more picturesque. The road climbs lazily past vineyards and descends into poplar-lined valleys. A fertile land, it is easy to see why so many invaders were attracted to it and decided to make their homes there.

C.   Bursa to Yalova

Total distance 63km. **Bursa**—R575 28km **Gemlik**—35km **Yalova** (66km **İzmit**).

A half-day should be sufficient for this excursion. Gemlik and Yalova are linked with Bursa by many local bus and dolmuş services. In addition, if the long distance coaches going to İstanbul via İzmit have unoccupied seats, they will usually take passengers to both places.

As Gemlik is a popular seaside resort and Yalova is both a spa and the terminal for a ferry service with İstanbul, they are well-supplied with restaurants and hotels.

Visitors who have their own transport should leave **Bursa** by the fast road 575 which has been widened and improved recently. After passing through the city's industrial suburbs, it climbs steadily for c 10km, then descends to the gulf on which 28km **Gemlik** is built.

History. Gemlik was known in antiquity as CIUS. Legend relates that it was named after one of the Argonauts who founded the city after his return from Colchis.

The area also has associations with Hercules. While the Argo was sailing along the coast of the Propontis, Hercules broke his oar and, accompanied by his squire, Hylas, and Polyphemus of Larissa, went ashore to find a replacement. Hylas was sent to the spring of Pegae for a pitcher of water. When he leaned over the spring, a water-nymph, entranced by the beauty of the youth, pulled him down under the surface. Polyphemus hearing Hylas cry out for help, rushed to the boy's aid, but in vain. Later, with Hercules who was distraught with grief, he searched everywhere for the missing youth. In the meantime, a favourable breeze blew up and the crew of the Argo sailed away, leaving Hercules and Polyphemus to their fruitless quest.

Traditionally the spring of Pegae was believed to be located on the strip of marshy ground between Cyzicus and Cius, modern Bandırma and Gemlik. Acccording to Strabo: 'still to this day a kind of festival is celebrated among the Prusians [inhabitants of Cius], a mountain-ranging festival, in which they march in procession and call Hylas, as though making their exodus to the forests in quest of him.'

First colonised by the Milesians, who used it as a staging post on their trading voyages to the Black Sea, Cius fell into the hands of the Antigonids of Macedon. In return for help received during the First Macedonian War, Philip V (221–179) of Macedon gave Cius to Prusias I (228–185) of Bithynia. However, he first sacked the city and enslaved its inhabitants. Cius was later rebuilt by Prusias, who renamed it Prusias-ad-Marem.

Orhan Gazi (1324–59) established a shipbuilding yard there, hence the town's name (in Turkish 'Gemi' is ship).

Gemlik is now a pleasant little seaside resort, which is popular with holiday-makers from İstanbul. Its hotels and pensions are usually full during the season. However, according to recent reports the waters of its beautiful gulf are not always free from pollution. It is advisable to make enquiries before bathing there.

Apart from a 4C BC tomb found near the town, and its shipbuilding industry Gemlik retains few links with its past.

From Gemlik road 575 continues to the village of 10km *Orhangazi*, where a turning to the right leads to İznik. From Orhangazi the road descends on the flanks of the rounded hillsides to the sea.

From the earliest times 35km **Yalova** has been known as a spa, whose waters offered relief from a number of maladies, including rheumatism and skin diseases. Patronised by Roman and Byzantine emperors, it became popular once more in the 19C and early 20C under the later Ottoman rulers.

Like Gemlik the visible signs of its past are few—the outline of a palace erected by Justin II (565–578) and a number of Hellenistic and

Roman stelae in the town centre. Today most visitors go to Yalova in search of a cure or to enjoy its calm and restful atmosphere.

A visitor with time on his hands could extend this excursion to 66km **İzmit**, a modern, heavily-industrialised and utterly charmless town, which occupies the site of ancient NICOMEDIA. Nicomedia, created capital of Bithynia by Nicomedes I (c 279–255 BC), was a city of considerable splendour. Destroyed by the Goths, it was completely restored during the reign of Diocletian (284–305). Under the late Roman and early Byzantine emperors the city continued to flourish, so that at one time it rivalled Alexandria in importance.

However, there are few reminders of the past in İzmit: there is a small museum, and, above the town, the remains of a Byzantine fortress.

2   Erdek to Çanakkale

Total distance 206km. **Erdek**—R200 54km *Gönen*—56km *Biga*
(19km *Karabiga / Priapus*)—56km *Lapseki*—40km **Çanakkale**.

After leaving **Erdek** (see Rte 1) road 200 loops inland through an austere landscape, where rocky outcrops protrude through the thin soil. Slow-moving flocks of sheep search for nourishment in the sparse herbage, while their youthful guardians, leaning impassively on shepherd crooks, gaze incuriously at the passing traffic. 54km *Gönen* is a small market-town and spa. Its mineral baths are patronised by sufferers from dermatological, urinary and nervous complaints. Visitors in search of a cure bathe in and drink the waters which contain chloride, sodium, magnesium and fluoride.

Between Gönen and 56km Biga the road returns briefly to the sea at Denizkent, and then crosses a broad plain watered by the Koca Çayı, the ancient Granicus. Today a pastoral calm reigns over the small villages that dot the plain, each with its threshing floor and decoration of untidy storks' nests. In autumn clouds of pungent smoke from the burning stubble drift across the small river, that 'little trickle of water', as Alexander the Great referred contemptuously to the Granicus, where in 334 BC he inflicted a great defeat on the Persians.

On hearing of Alexander's landing in Asia, the Persians under the command of Arsites, the satrap of Hellespontine Phrygia, left their lakeside fortress of Dascylium (see above) and regrouped their forces, believed to number 35,000 against the Macedonians' 50,000, at the town of Zeleia on the slopes of Mt Ida. Alexander, short of money and supplies, was anxious to engage the enemy in battle as quickly as possible. Ignoring the Greek city of Lampsacus, which closed its doors to him, he marched E to the river Granicus. There, on a late afternoon in May, he found the Persian army drawn up on the opposite bank. According to Arrian and Plutarch, writing in the 1C and 2C AD, Alexander disregarded the advice of the elderly general Parmenion, who suggested that the crossing be made under the cover of darkness. Instead he led the Mounted Scouts and Companions in a dramatic charge across the river and up the steep bank on the other side. This opened the way for the Macedonian infantry to follow.

Diodorus Siculus (fl. 30 BC) gives a different account. He states that Alexander, leaving his camp fires burning to deceive the Persian scouts, quietly marched his army downstream during the night and crossed the river by a ford. The Persians awoke to find the Macedonians, drawn up in battle-order, facing them. All the historians agree that a desperate struggle followed. Alexander, conspicuous in the armour he had taken from the temple of Athena at Ilium, was the target for many attacks. Dazed by a blow that cut through his helmet and opened his scalp, he was saved by the timely intervention of 'Black' Cleitus, his nurse's brother. The king collapsed and the battle raged around him.

The strong thrusting-lances of cornel-wood of the Macedonians broke the Persian infantry line and the Companions and Parmenion's Thessalian cavalry completed the rout. The Greek mercenaries under the command of Memnon, withdrew to a hill and asked for quarters. Alexander, enraged by their action of 'fighting with Orientals against Greeks', refused. Memnon escaped, but of an estimated 20,000 mercenaries only 2000 survived the massacre that followed. They were sent in chains to work as slaves in the Macedonian mines. Casualties amongst the Persians were heavy. Many of their leaders were killed. The Macedonians lost 25 Companions and c 120 cavalry. The battle of Granicus was the first of the many successful military actions that led to the foundation of the greatest empire ever seen in Asia and took Alexander and his army through Syria, Egypt and Afghanistan to the gates of India.

Shortly after leaving *Biga*, with its narrow cobbled streets, a turning to the right leads to 19km *Karabiga*, a small town on the coast. This occupies the site of the ancient city of PRIAPUS, which, according to Strabo, was probably colonised by the Milesians at the time they established their settlements at Abydos and Proconnesus.

As its name suggests, the city was sacred to that lusty Phrygian god of procreation and fertility, Priapus, who, in the words of the poet:

'... came and cried
Why peak and pine, unhappy wight, when thou
mightest bed a bride?' (Theocritus I 81).

The son of Aphrodite and Dionysus or Aphrodite and Hermes, Priapus was abandoned by his mother, because of his grotesque appearance. A popular god, his ithyphallic statues, decked with a garlands, were placed in gardens and vineyards to protect the crops from the evil eye and to encourage growth. Donkeys were sacrificed in his honour, perhaps because of their reputation for unbridled lust or because a donkey awoke the sleeping nymph Lotis before Priapus could surprise her.

Strabo suggests that Priapus was honoured by the inhabitants of that part of Propontis, because his father was Dionysus and, because 'their country is abundantly supplied with the vine'. An alternative version of the Priapus legend states that he was born in Lampsacus, but was exiled by his fellow-citizens because of his grotesque appearance. The gods took pity on him and made him the symbol of fertility and the protector of all growing things.

From Biga road 200 ascends the NE slopes of Dede Dağı before descending to the sea near Şevketiye. It then follows the coastline to 56km *Lapseki*. The ancient city of LAMPSACUS, also associated with the worship of Priapus, was located here (see Karabiga above).

After his fall from power and flight to Persia, Themistocles (c 525–449 BC)) was awarded Lampsacus, Magnesia and Myus by Artaxerxes. Just over 100 years later Alexander, bribed by the philosopher Anaximenes at the behest of the council, by-passed the city on his march to the Granicus. Lampsacus was described by Strabo (c 64 BC–c AD 24) as 'a notable city with a good harbour, and still flourishing, like Abydus'. It was famous for its wines which, its inhabitants claimed, were worthy of the gods.

From Lapseki road 200 follows the coast for some time, then moves inland to pass through a flat and undistinguished stretch of country-side on its way to 40km **Çanakkale**.

Çanakkale, an important communications centre, occupies a stra-tegic position on the Asian side of the Dardanelles, which at this point are a little more than 1km wide. There are frequent services by car-ferry to Eceabat on the European shore.

Because of Çanakkale's proximity to the battlefields of the Gallipoli campaign, and to Troy, its hotels are often full. If possible, reservations should be made well in advance. Information about available accommodation and up-to-date prices may be obtained from the *Tourism Office*, which is located near the ferry terminal. Details of excursions to the battlefields and to Troy are also available there. Good meals are served in the principal hotels and in many of the small restaurants along the sea-front.

Çanakkale has a new and busy bus station c 500m inland from the sea-front. There are frequent services via Bursa and through Thrace to İstanbul and S via Edremit to İzmir. Dolmuş services to Troy also depart from the bus station.

Çanakkale's **Archaeological Museum** is located in a new building c 1.5km from the town centre on the road to Troy. The Askeri Müze, is in the military area S of the ferry-terminal. Details of the current opening hours of both museums may be obtained from the Tourism Office.

History. According to a legend, Helle and her brother Phrixus were obliged to escape from the wrath of their stepmother Ino, who planned to sacrifice them to Zeus Laphystius. Phrixus succeeded in reaching Colchis safely, but Helle fell from the back of the winged ram, which was transporting her, and drowned in the strait that thereafter bore her name.

Because of its strategic situation it is probable that settlers were attracted to the Hellespont from the earliest times. According to Strabo, Abydus, which was a short distance to the N of Çanakkale, was founded by the Milesians, 'by permission of Gyges, king of the Lydians; for this district and the whole of the Troad were under his sway.'

It was from Abydus, according to another legend, that the youth Leander swam each night to visit the priestess Hero, who lived in a high tower in Sestus on the European side of the Hellespont. One stormy night the light, placed by Hero to guide him, was extinguished by the wind and Leander drowned. When Hero saw her lover's dead body she threw herself from the tower and perished.

In 480 BC the Persian Xerxes (?519–465 BC) set out on his expedition to subdue the Greeks. To take his army across the Hellespont, he built a great pontoon bridge that stretched from Abydus to Sestus.

Alexander the Great, after he had sacrificed at the tomb of Protesilaus, the first Greek warrior to land in Asia at the beginning of the Trojan war, crossed from Sestos to Abydus in May 334 BC. As the royal trireme grounded in the shallows, he cast his spear ashore, so making his claim to the Persian Empire. Following the example of Protesilaus, he was the first Macedonian to set foot on Asian soil.

In 1810 Lord Byron, emulating Leander, swam across the Hellespont from the European to the Asian side. In a letter to his friend Henry Drury he wrote: 'Salsette frigate, May 3d 1810 in the Dardanelles off Abydos ... This morning I swam from Sestos to Abydos, the immediate distance is not above a mile but the current renders it hazardous, so much so, that I doubt whether Leander's conjugal powers must not have been exhausted in his passage to Paradise.'

Apart from its museums and one or two Ottoman buildings there is little in Çanakkale to detain the visitor. In the military zone to the S of the quay is the *Sultaniye fortress*, also known as the Çimenlik Kale. This was built by Mehmet II Fatih (1451–81) in 1454 and enlarged during the reign of Abdül Aziz (1861–76). As it is still occupied by the military, visitors are not permitted to go to the top of the walls.

In the compound there is a reconstruction of the Turkish minelayer 'Nusrat', which played an important part in the Gallipoli campaign, also an interesting collection of old French, English and German guns, the relics of many wars. A small museum houses exhibits connected with Atatürk and World War I.

Çanakkale's **Archaeological Museum** is a 20-minute walk from the town centre. Take the main road, which goes S in the direction of Troy. Having passed the market-place and crossed a bridge, you will find the museum on the left-hand side of the road.

The collection, though small, is well displayed. Most of the exhibits are labelled and many bear a description in English. A large mural in the entrance hall shows the location of the principal sites in the Troad. There is no guide-book.

In the garden and on the terrace in front of the building there is a collection of stelae, sarcophagi and funerary urns, from the Troad. Hellenistic and Roman stelae, one with the figures outlined against a

red background, are exhibited in the entrance hall. The main part of
the collection begins with a display of fossils, prehistoric remains, a
kouros from Lampsacus, various finds from Beşiğetepe, and a selection of artefacts dating from the archaic to the classical periods found
at Anafartalar.

Among the exhibits from Troy are a *crystal lion head* and *crystal
amulet* (Troy II); *cycladic-type idols* and a cover in the form of a
female head (Troy III); stemmed goblets and a headless female
statue (Troy VI); terracottas, statuettes, including some from the
Calvert collection (Troy VIII). In addition to a representative collection of Roman, Byzantine and Ottoman coins there is a selection of
electron ornaments and coins from the Troad.

The Dardanos Salon contains artefacts from the Dardanos
Tumulus. Excavated in 1974, the tumulus, which is 11km to the S of
Çanakkale, was used for burials from the 4C to the 1C BC. The
exhibits include bronze utensils, household goods, cinerary urns,
remains of wooden objects, shoes, combs, boxes, terracottas (note the
fine Eros and the figure with a lyre), diadems, gold and ivory
ornaments.

Excavations conducted in 1961 in the necropolis on Bozcaada
(Tenedos) revealed grave goods dating from the 7C to the 1C BC.
Amongst those exhibited are magnificent *gold ornaments*, including
fibulae, a ring with a representation of Artemis, *three seated figures
of Cybele*, and a skyphos with a youth and sphinxes.

3 Çanakkale to Troy

Total distance 32km. R550/E24.

There is a dolmuş service, frequent during the summer, less frequent during the rest of the year, from Çanakkale's bus garage direct to Troy. For the return journey it may be necessary to hire a taxi, as the last dolmuş to Çanakkale sometimes leaves Troy in the mid-afternoon, well before the site closes; the alternative is a 5km walk to the main road, where is it is usually possible to pick up a bus.

During the holiday season there are organised tours from Çanakkale to Troy and other places of interest in the Troad. The time allowed at Troy on these tours, though limited, is usually sufficient for the non-specialist visitor.

From Çanakkale road 550/E24 follows the coastline for c 14km before turning inland. Visitors with their own transport may like to use one of the many reasonably-priced hotels and motels in this area as a base for the exploration of Troy and the N Troad.

A turning to the right leads to the *Dardanus Tumulus*, whose treasures are displayed in Çanakkale's Archaeological Museum (see Rte 2). At present the tumulus is not open to visitors.

The road curves upwards through a pine wood, passing a number of memorials to the Turkish dead of World War I. From the crest, at the village of Intepe, there is a good view of Homer's 'wind-swept' Plain of Ilium.

After crossing the Dümrek Su, the ancient river Simois, a minor road to the right winds over bare, rounded hills to the modern village of *Truva* and the site of **TROY**.

In Truva there are the inevitable souvenir-shops, a few restaurants serving simple meals, and coffee-houses, selling tea and coffee and soft drinks.

The mound of Troy is screened from the road by a clump of trees which provides shade in summer. Entrance is through a small garden, which has a collection of architectural fragments (one near the gate bears the name Alexander) and, incongruously, a modern reconstruction of the wooden horse. To the right are a small museum containing figurines, glass and pottery found at the site, and a wash-room and toilet.

The sudden revelation of the mound beyond the trees is usually sufficient to startle even the most unromantic traveller. Neglected and allowed to decay for centuries, then subjected to a series of violent investigatory explorations, Troy retains a mysterious power over its visitors. In spite of the arguments of archaeologists about its physical remains and the doubts attached by scholars to the historicity of the Trojan War, it remains for many the city of the 'Iliad' and the 'Odyssey', which welcomed Paris and the adulterous Helen and which was finally captured by a stratagem of the wily Odysseus.

According to the 3C AD writer Philostratus Troy was haunted by the ghosts of the great and noble heroes, who had lived, fought and died there. When Julian the Apostate (361–363) visited Troy, he was astonished to find that offerings were being made by Pegasios, the bishop of Ilium Novum, as the city was known in Roman times, at the tomb believed to shelter the bones of Hector, and in the temple of Athena. This association of the site with the Trojan War continued down through the ages and it may have been one of the factors that led Schliemann and the other 19C investigators to it.

Whatever credence one places in the story of the abduction of Helen by Priam's son Paris and of the expedition mounted by her husband, Menelaus, to recover her and avenge the wrong done to him, it is certain that Troy existed at, and indeed long before, the time ascribed to these alleged events.

Excavations at the site have unearthed 46 separate levels of occupation and nine cities or settlements, dating from 3000–2500 BC to AD 400 have been identified.

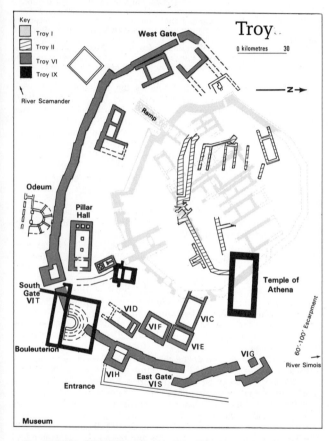

Troy I (3000–2500 BC) was a small fortification, probably occupied by a community that made its living from fishing. There has been considerable change in the geological structure of the area since antiquity and it is almost certain that the sea was much nearer to the site than it is at present. Containers of bronze and of pottery which portray the human face were important finds here. The settlement was protected by walls in which comparatively small stones were laid in a herring-bone pattern. Troy I was destroyed by a conflagration.

Troy II (2500–2200 BC) is one of the first cities in W Asia Minor to show evidence of town-planning. Although the diameter of the area enclosed by its walls was only 110m, it contained a large megaron for the ruler and several smaller megara, which were aligned to make a continuous frontage. As in the case of Troy I, the principal gate was on the S, but there were several other entrances. On the SW there was a large paved ramp, 21m long and 7.5m wide, that slopes inwards as it rises. Schliemann believed that this had been used by the Trojans to bring the wooden horse within the walls. However, the city of the Trojan War, if such a conflict ever took place, is either Troy VI or Troy VIIA and dates from c 1000 years later.

Schliemann was similarly mistaken about the cache of gold and jewellery which he discovered in a section of wall to the left of the ramp and which he described as the 'treasure of Priam'. This also belonged to the period of Troy II. All that remains of this treasure are a gold braclet and gold earrings, which are in the İstanbul Archaeological Museum. The bulk of the find, which Schliemann removed from Turkey without the permission of the government, was displayed in a Berlin museum from where it disappeared during World War II. Its present whereabouts are unknown.

Troy II may have gained some of its wealth and stature from its strategic location. Some authorities believe that for the first time in the city's history its rulers levied taxes on ships passing through the Hellespont and on goods carried overland through Trojan territory to avoid the hazards of that difficult sea passage. Troy II was destroyed by fire, probably as the result of an attack by Indo-European invaders.

Troy III to Troy V (2300–1800 BC) were settlements of minor importance, apparently occupied by the descendants of those who survived the destruction of Troy II. There is no evidence that the invaders, who had taken the city, remained there. The houses were mean and small and, at least during Troy IV, the city was not fortified. The population probably supported itself by farming and fishing.

Troy VI (1800–1275 BC) marks a return to greatness. This city, built by newcomers to the site, was enclosed by well-constructed walls which ran in straight courses turning at an angle where a change of direction was needed. Substantial stretches of these walls remain and there is a good example of one of the city's defensive towers at the NW corner of the mound.

The roof of one of the houses in Troy VI was supported by large square pillars. Note the recesses in the walls which may have served as cupboards or shrines for cult-statues. Most of the pottery found at this level is grey Minyan, but there are also some examples of imported Mycenaean ware and there are many built-in storage pithoi.

Turkish archaeologists believe that this was the city of *Priam*, which for ten years resisted the attempts of the Greeks to take it, and which was finally destroyed by an earthquake. The most recent discoveries tend to support this hypothesis.

Troy VIIA (1275–1240 BC). Troy VIIA is believed by the American archaeologists to be the city of the Trojan War. In support of this hypothesis they cite the following points. After the earthquake the walls were hastily and poorly repaired. There is evidence that many people were crowded into the small area inside the defensive system. Large quantities of food and other supplies were stored in pithoi under the floors of the houses. Trade with Mycenaean Greece ceased and, most tellingly, the city was destroyed by human action. According to Professor Blegen, Troy VIIA 'was ruthlessly laid waste by the hand of man who completed his work of destruction by fire'.

It is worth noting, however, that a number of historians do not accept that there was a war fought at Troy by a combination of Greeks or Mycenaeans against the Trojans and their allies. Among the supporters of this view is Professor Finley, who pointed out 'that the archaeologists had found no trace of war at Troy other than a single bronze arrowhead, and certainly no trace of a coalition, let alone a Mycenaean coalition'. A recent colloquium on the Trojan War reached the same conclusion, stating that 'on present evidence there is neither room nor reason for Mycenaean hostilities against Troy'.

Finley has proposed that the destruction of Troy in the 13C BC may be attributed to the mysterious Sea People, whose activities brought about the downfall of so many civilisations in the E Mediterranean at that time. It appears unlikely that the contentious matter of the Trojan War will ever be resolved.

Sometime after its destruction, the site was reoccupied by new-comers who brought with them a distinctive knobbed ware, prev-iously found in sites in the Balkans. This phase of occupation lasted until c 1100 BC. Profesor Akurgal suggests that Troy may have been colonised by immigrants from the Aegean, who later took part in the destruction of Hattusa c 1180 BC and fought the Assyrian Tiglath-Pileser I c 1165 and Rameses III (1198–76) of Egypt. Perhaps these invaders may be identified with or related to Finley's Sea People.

No remains have been found at Troy from 1100 for a period of c 400 years. The site was occupied by immigrants from Lesbos c 700 BC and the new settlement, Troy VIII, appears to have been a small market town. Captured by the Persians in the 6C, it remained under their control until Alexander's victory in 334 BC. (See above.)

Troy IX (350 BC–AD 400) was the city of the Hellenistic and Roman periods. Before beginning his campaign against the Persians, Alexander made a pilgrimage to the ancient site. He sacrificed at the temple of Athena, leaving his armour as an offering and taking in exchange weapons that were believed to date from the time of the Trojan War. Having made a propitiatory offering to the spirit of Priam, he received gold crowns from Menoetius, his sailing-master and from Chares, a citizen of Sigeium, the place where the Menelaus and his Greek allies had beached their ships. Then, having anointed his body with oil, he ran naked to the place where Achilles was buried. There he honoured the dead hero by placing a wreath on the tomb, while his friend Hephaistion performed the same service at the tomb of Achilles' companion Patroclus.

Alexander accorded a number of privileges to Troy and promised to build a new temple in honour of Athene. This promise was kept by his friend and successor, Lysimachus.

Destroyed c 82 BC during the Mithridatic Wars, Troy was rebuilt after a visit to the city by Julius Caesar in 48 BC. As the birthplace of Aeneas, the mythical founder of Rome, it was accorded special treatment by several Roman emperors. The reconstructed temple of Athena, promised by Caesar, was completed during the reign of Augustus, and later an odeum, a theatre and other elaborately-decorated marble buildings were erected in the city.

Although somewhat overshadowed by the newly-founded Alex-andria Troas in the S Troad, the township of ILIUM NOVUM, as Troy had become known, was an episcopal see in the 4C. Then it appears to have entered a period of gradual decline, perhaps because of the silting up of its harbour. Excavations have shown that it was occupied during the reign of Justinian in the 6C.

Coins and pottery demonstrate that there was still some kind of settlement here as late as the 12C, when the Troad was ruled by the Selçuks. Under the Ottoman Turks the site of the ancient city appears to have been abandoned, but there were several small villages in the surrounding plain.

Abandoned perhaps, but not forgotten, Troy continued to attract visitors during the centuries that followed. In 1444 that indefatigable traveller Cyriac of Ancona visited the area. He was followed almost 20 years later by Mehmet II, who gloried in the fact that he had defeated the descendants of those who had destroyed the city. They had at last, he declared, paid the debt that they owed the people of Asia.

In the early 17C the Scottish traveller William Lithgow cast a sceptical eye over the remains of the ancient city: 'when we landed,' he wrote, 'we saw here and there many relics of old walls and many tombs, which were mighty ruinous. Our Greek [interpreter] pointed us particularly to the tombs of Hector, Ajax, Achilles, Troilus and many other valiant champions—well, I wot I saw infinite old sepulchres, but for their particular names and nomination of them I suspend; neither could I believe my interpreter, sith it is more than three thousand odd years ago that Troy was destroyed!'

In 1781 Lady Mary Wortley Montagu came to a somewhat similar conclusion and Byron, who visited Troy in May 1810, was also appeared unimpressed by what he saw.

'Of Dardan tours let Dilettanti tell,
I leave topography to coxcomb Gell.'

(English Bards and Scottish Reviewers)

In a letter to Henry Drury he wrote: 'The Troad is a fine field for conjecture and Snipe-shooting, and a good sportsman and an ingenious scholar may exercise their feet and faculties upon the spot, or if they prefer riding lose their way (as I did) in a cursed quagmire of the Scamander who wriggles about as if the Dardan virgins still offered their wonted tribute. The only vestige of Troy, or her destroyers, are the barrows supposed to contain the carcases of Achilles, Antilochus, Ajax &c. but Mt Ida is still in high feather, though the Shepherds are nowadays not much like Ganymede.'

Interest in Troy was revived by an English family, the Calverts, that had settled in the Troad at the beginning of the 19C. Frank Calvert had explored many of the ancient sites and he passed on some of his ideas, and his enthusiasm, to Schliemann, the German amateur archaeologist who confounded the experts by his discoveries at Troy and Mycenae.

Heinrich Schliemann (1822–90) was born in Mecklenburg in N Germany, the son of poor parents. Interested from an early age in the Greek myths, his ambition became the discovery of the site of ancient Troy. To this end he taught himself Ancient Greek and several modern languages. He became a successful business man and amassed a considerable fortune. Then at the age of 46 he abandoned his commercial career and, Homer in hand, set out to find the city of Priam.

Schliemann made a number of remarkable discoveries, including the so-called 'Treasure of Priam', at Troy. His work was continued by Wilhelm Dörpfeld and later by Professor Blegen and archaeologists from the University of Cincinnati. Their combined excavations have revealed the nine cities described above, one of which may have been the 'well-walled city with lofty gates' of the 'Iliad' and 'Odyssey'.

Although many visitors from William Lithgow, Lady Wortley Montagu and Lord Byron onwards were disappointed by Troy, the sudden dramatic revelation of the mound beyond the trees seldom fails to produce a frisson of surprise and pleasure. Despite the fact that the site was allowed to decay for centuries and was then ravaged by treasure-hunters and archaeologists, so that today it is 'an overgrown maze of superimposed ruins of many ages, a jumble of gullies and ditches choked with bushes and ruins', there is a sense of having arrived at a place of some importance.

Archaeologists may argue about its physical remains and scholars debate the historicity of the Trojan War, nevertheless for many visitors Troy has a numinous appeal difficult to define. Imagination will help the traveller to see the city of Homer behind the chaotic muddle of stones that make up the site today.

In front of the the excavated area there is a large plan, which shows the location of the remains of the various cities. There are also small descriptive notices in English at various points on the site. Arrows indicate the route to be followed.

The visitor's attention is seized by a substantial section, c 90m long and 6m high, of the *wall* of cities VI and VII. This was reinforced by a tower (VIH on plan). Entrance to the site is by a gate (VIS on plan) on the E side of the mound. To the right there was a *look-out tower* (VIG on plan), which enclosed a large cistern.

Turning towards the centre the route passes on the left the ruins of four large *houses* (VIF, VIE, VIC and VID on plan). Note that one contains a number of storage *pithoi*.

At this point it is worth pausing to admire the excellent view over the Plain of Troy. Two lines of willows mark the present courses of the rivers Simois (to the N) and Scamander (to the SW). These have probably changed course several times. To the N near Cape Sigeum is the *harbour of the Achaeans*, where the Greeks beached their ships. Not far from the harbour are the mounds that, according to tradition, mark the graves of Achilles and Ajax. If the weather is clear, Samothrace, from where Poseidon surveyed the events at Troy, may be glimpsed towering over nearer Imbros. To the SE is Mt Ida, where Zeus sat enthroned during the conflict.

On the right the site of the *Temple of Athena* is marked by a large hole, produced by the activities of various excavators. It was here that Xerxes sacrificed before starting out on his invasion of Greece. According to Herodotus, 'Xerxes had a strong desire to see Troy, the ancient city of Priam. Accordingly he went up into the citadel, and when he had seen what he wanted to see and heard the story of the place from the people there, he sacrificed a thousand oxen to the Trojan Athene, and the Magi made libations of wine to the spirits of the great men of old.' Some fragments of the Doric temple constructed by Lysimachus, which covers part of Troy II's fortifications, may be seen in the excavation, others are kept in Troy's museum.

After passing some of the oldest remains on the site, fortifications and houses from Troy I, the route reaches the *large ramp* (see Troy II above), where Schliemann found the treasure. It then goes outside the fortified area, where there are several remains from the Hellenistic and Roman periods. These include a *baths complex* (note the mosaic pavements), the *odeum* and the *bouleuterion*.

To the left of the bouleuterion the S gate (VIT) provides access to the so-called *pillar-house* (see Troy VI above).

Excavations continue at Troy. The partly-collapsed tower R of Troy I fortifications has been restored and the E part of the trench made by Schliemann cleared.

4 Troy to Assos

Total distance 64km. **Troy**—24km *Ezine* (c 16km *Neandria*) (c 21km **Alexandria Troas**—c 20km *Bozcaada*)—22km *Ayvacık*—18km *Behramkale* (**Assos**) (26km *Apollo Smintheus*).

According to the geographer Strabo, writing in the 1C AD, the Troad, an area of rich farmland and forest, attracted many colonists both Greek and barbarian. Stretching S from Troy, its fields of wheat and maize are punctuated with groves of cypress, tamarisk and valonia oak. Vines and olives are cultivated extensively and the slopes of Mt Ida, which dominates the SE section, are covered with pine forests.

A good bus service links Çanakkale with Ezine and Ayvacık. There are infrequent dolmuş services from Ezine to Odun İskelesi (Alexandria Troas) and from Ayvacık to Behramkale. It may be necessary to take a taxi to both of these places.

Travellers, who do not have their own transport, will need a hire-car or taxi to visit Neandria and Apollo Smintheus. Taxis may be hired for the day at a rate usually fixed by negotiation.

There are a few pensions and restaurants in and near Odun İskelesi and Behramkale has several small hotels, pensions and restaurants in the lower village near the sea. In both places these tend to close outside the holiday season.

To visit NEANDRIA take the road from Ezine to Geyikli and Odun İskelesi. After c 6km, a turning to the left is signposted to the site. Neandria was built on an outcrop of Mt Çığrı sometime in the 7C BC. The city, which occupied an area c 1.5km long by 500m wide, is enclosed by a well-preserved wall. In the centre there are the remains of a small temple of simple construction. Elaborately ornamented Aeolic capitals from seven columns in the centre of the cella, which helped to support the roof of the building, are now in the İstanbul Archaeological Museum. When Alexandria Troas was built towards the end of the 4C BC, the inhabitants of Neandria were moved there by Antigonus I.

On returning to the main road continue for c 5km towards *Odun İskelesi*. The ruins of **ALEXANDRIA TROAS** are scattered over a wide area and consequently are not easy to visit. Indeed, as Eric Newby remarks ruefully in his book, 'On the Shores of the Mediterranean', 'although the city was said to have walls six miles long and itself covered 1,000 acres it was perfectly possible, as we now demonstrated, to walk into it through one of the now enormous gaps in the walls and walk out through a similar gap on the far side, without, apart from tripping over some low-lying remains or else bumping into something shrouded in vegetation which loomed unidentifiable overhead, seeing much of Alexandria Troas at all.'

History. When, after the death of Alexander the Great in 323 BC the empire he created was dismembered by his generals, Antigonus I Monophthalmos acquired Greater Phrygia, Lycia and Pamphylia. About 300 BC he founded a city, which he named Antigonia after himself and to which he brought the inhabitants of Neandria and other settlements in the Troad. In 301 Antigonus, then aged 81, and his son Demetrius were slain at the battle of Ipsus in Phrygia.

The victor Lysimachus, king of Macedonia, took over their territories and renamed Antigonia, Alexandria Troas, in honour of Alexander the Great.

Although the city had only an artificial harbour, it became a major trading centre. Its strategic location enabled it to take over the control, previously exercised by Troy, of the sea and land-traffic between the Aegean and the Propontis (Sea of Marmara).

During both the Hellenistic and Roman periods, Alexandria Troas prospered, acquiring great wealth and status. A city of rich and beautiful buildings, both Julius Caesar and Constantine considered establishing their capitals there.

Alexandria Troas was visited on two occasions by St. Paul. With Timothy he had intended to go into Bithynia, but during the night he had a vision in Alexandria Troas, 'A certain Macedonian stood by him in entreaty, and said, Come over into Macedonia, and help us …. So we put out from Troas, making a straight course for Samothrace, and next day to Neapolis (Kavala).' (Acts 16, 9–12.) On the second occasion Paul continued preaching long after midnight and a young man named Eutychus, overcome by sleep, fell from a third-storey window. 'Paul went down, bent over him, and embraced him; then he said, Do not disturb yourselves; his life is yet in him.' (Acts 20,10.) Later he wrote to Timothy and asked him to bring 'the cloak which I left in Carpus' hands in Troas; the books, too, and above all the rolls of parchment.' (Timothy II, 413.)

As Constantinople increased in importance so Alexandria Troas declined. During the Ottoman period, when the city was known as Eski Stamboul, it was plundered for building material. Stone and marble taken from there were used to construct a number of buildings, including Sultan Ahmet Camii (the Blue Mosque), in İstanbul.

Richard Chandler, who visited the city in the summer of 1764, saw the considerable remains of the city's fortifications, which had square towers at regular intervals. He also found the foundations of a large building, which he believed to have been a temple. He was told that bandits often lay in hiding there, presumably to rob any travellers passing by. However, the only living creatures he saw were large bats, which, disturbed by the approach of his party, eventually returned to settle on the roof. He also found a number of inscriptions and examined the baths, which he wrongly identified as a gymnasium.

Apart from the ruins of the *baths*, which the magnate Herodes Atticus donated to the city c AD 135, very little remains today of Alexandria Troas. The baths, located on the right-hand side of the road at the approach to the site, comprised several large vaulted chambers.

Most of the area formerly occupied by the city is now covered by fields, over whose surface a vast quantity of pottery sherds is scattered. Clumps of valonia oak crown small eminences and outline the boundaries. As Newby noted, unidentifiable architectural fragments, which pierce the thick undergrowth that enfolds them, are encountered from time to time. Down by the harbour there are parts of a few columns, presumably abandoned by those who carried away the stone and marble of Alexandria Troas to decorate the buildings of İstanbul.

Near the harbour and on the road that runs S towards Tavaklı Iskele are several small restaurants. A ferry from *Odun İskelesi* links *Bozcaada* (TENEDOS) with the mainland. It was on this island that Achilles slew Tenes the son of Apollo, and it was to Tenedos that the Greeks withdrew their ships, when they wished to make the Trojans believe that they had abandoned the siege. Occupied by Xerxes for use as a naval base, it later supported Athens during the Peloponnesian War. Reoccupied by the Persians, it was finally liberated by Alexander. Today Bozcaada is best known for its light white wine, which is much appreciated by those who patronise certain restaurants in İstanbul and İzmir.

Visitors, who have their own transport, may wish to go by way of the minor coastal road, via Gülpınar, to *Behramkale*. By making a slight detour at Gülpınar, they will be able to visit the site of the 2C BC *Temple of Apollo Smintheus* at ancient CHRYSE.

Well-signposted, this is reached by following a narrow lane for c 250m from the centre of the village. Partly surrounded by a grove of pomegranate trees, the temple, a pseudo-dipteros of the Ionic order with 8 by 14 columns, is currently being excavated. The stylobate, which measures 24m by 43m, has been exposed and is surrounded with fragments of sculpture, inscriptions and a number of Turkish tombstones. The site was discovered by Spratt in the middle of the 19C.

According to a legend, Teucer, a hero born on Mt Ida in Crete, left the island with his father, Scamander, and a group of followers during a period of famine and came to the Troad. Before their departure they were told by a seer that they should settle at the place where they were attacked by 'the sons of the earth'. On waking one morning they found that their armour and equipment had been partly eaten by mice. Deciding that this must be the place meant by the oracle, they made a settlement there and built a temple in honour of Apollo Smintheus (Apollo lord of the mice). According to Aelian there was the representation of a mouse in the temple of Apollo. Teucer became the first king of Troy and for that reason the Trojans were sometimes called Teucri.

About 100m down the lane there are the remains of some other buildings, which so far have not been excavated.

After returning to the centre of Gülpınar, continue on the road signposted to 26km Behramkale.

From Ezine continue on road 550 to 22km *Ayvacik*. There a minor road winds along the upper edge of a deep valley, then crosses a bare plateau before reaching the village of *Behramkale* (**ASSOS**). A short distance from the village, on the left-hand side of the modern road, the graceful pointed arches of a 14C Turkish *bridge* carry the old road over the Tuzla brook, the ancient Satnioeis. Behramkale is picturesquely sited on the crest of a ridge that drops steeply on the S side to the sea.

Clustered around the harbour at the bottom of the ridge are several pensions, small hotels and restaurants, which are usually open only during the season. Not yet too well known, this is a most attractive and restful place in which to spend a few days. As accommodation is limited, it is advisable to make reservations well in advance.

History. The first settlement in Assos was founded by immigrants from Methymna in Lesbos early in the first millennium BC. In the 6C BC it was ruled by Lydia and later, as part of the province of Phrygia, it came under Persian dominion. The governor of Assos, Ariobarzanes, revolted against Persian rule in 365 BC, but he was defeated by Artaxerxes.

Assos enjoyed its greatest period of glory in the 4C BC, when with the Troad and Lesbos, it was ruled by the eunuch Hermeias. A former student of Plato, Hermeias welcomed a number of philosophers and scientists to the city. Aristotle and Theophrastus stayed there during the years 348–345, a period during which they carried out some important studies in the natural sciences. Aristotle became a close friend of Hermeias and eventually married his niece, Pythia. Later the philosopher moved to Lesbos and then to Pella, where he became tutor to the young Alexander. Hermeias had an unhappy end. He was captured by the Persians and tortured to death.

Cleanthes, the Stoic philosopher, who studied under Zeno, was born in Assos c 331 BC. In Athens he aroused suspicion because he lived without visible means of financial support. When it was discovered that he worked all night drawing water and studied all day, the Areopagus rewarded his diligence by awarding him a small pension. However, Zeno forbade him to take it.

Like Troy, Assos was overshadowed by Alexandria Troas, and declined in importance during the Hellenistic period. From 241–133 BC it was ruled by the kings of Pergamum.

St. Paul, walking overland from Alexandria Troas, came to Assos during his third missionary tour. He met Luke and other companions in the city and together they sailed to Lesbos. During the Byzantine period Assos declined in importance becoming little more than a hamlet, a situation which continued after its conquest by Orhan in 1330.

Interest in Assos was revived in the 19C as a result of research carried out there by an American archaeological team. The site is currently being excavated by Turkish archaeologists.

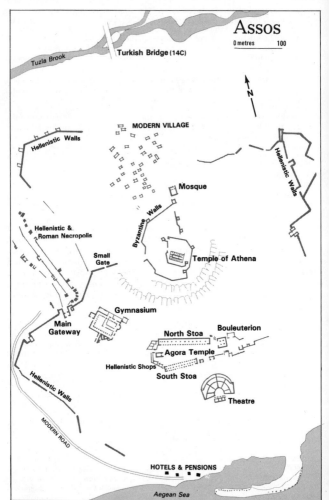

The best way to approach the upper part of the ancient city is through the narrow lanes of the modern village, where children shyly proffer hand-knitted and crocheted garments to visitors. On the left at the top of the hill, having passed the Byzantine fortifications, there is a *mosque*, now secularised, which is believed to date from the reign of Murat I Hüdavendigar (1359–89). Converted from a 6C church, it has two marble columns, each surmounted by a different type of capital, at its entrance. Over the door a marble slab with a cross and Chi-Rho symbol carries an inscription in Greek which states that the church was built by one Cornelius for the forgiveness of his sins. Surmounted by a dome 11m in diameter, the building has traces of mural decoration on its interior walls. Note the interesting lozenge design over the second window from the entrance gate to the enclosure.

There is a fine view over the village and N towards the Turkish bridge from the terrace in front of the mosque.

A short climb leads to a plateau, 238m above sea-level, on which the *Temple of Athena* stood. Like many of the buildings at Assos, this was constructed of andesite, an igneous rock frequently found in volcanic areas. Dating from c 530 BC, it was a mixture of the Doric and Ionic styles, with a decorative frieze on the architrave. A temple in antis with 13 by 6 columns, its stylobate measures 14m by 30m. The temenos, which is currently being excavated by Turkish archaeologists, is covered with scattered columns and Doric capitals. Some of the reliefs from the temple are preserved in the İstanbul Archaeological Museum.

The view from the plateau is one of the most beautiful in W Turkey. To the S, across the calm waters of the Bay of Edremit, Lesbos, homeland of the first settlers in Assos, is clothed in a purple haze. Far below lies the little harbour, from which St. Paul sailed on his missionary journey to spread the new faith, while on terraces cut into the steep slope of the hill the ruins of the ancient city protrude through the maquis.

A goat path leads down from the plateau to the *Agora*, whose buildings of andesite date for the most part from the 3C and 2C BC. At the W end are the barely-distinguishable ruins of the 2C BC *Agora temple*, which appears to have been modified, when it was used for Christian worship. On the N side of the Agora there was a two-storey Doric *colonnade*, which measured 111m by 12.5m; note the holes in the rear wall, which held the timber supports of the upper floor.

On the S this was complemented by a three-storey *stoa* of ingenious construction. The top floor of this structure, which was on the same level as the first floor of the N colonnade, was completely open, so providing a pleasant promenade overlooking both the Agora and the sea. The lower and basement floors, which were closed on the N side, housed 13 shops, a bathing establishment and cisterns. An air gap of 20cm between the middle floor and the rock-wall served to insulate it, ensuring that it was free from humidity and enjoyed an equable temperature throughout the year.

At the E end of the Agora at right angles to the Hellenistic *bouleuterion* stood a *bema*, from which politicians, philosphers and others could address the citizens. The 3C BC Greek-style *theatre* of Assos, of which practically nothing remains, was built on a terrace below the E end of the Agora.

An arched gateway to the W of the Agora temple leads to the site of a 2C BC *gymnasium*, which contained a paved courtyard surrounded by colonnades. During the Byzantine period a church was constructed on the NE side of this courtyard. Today little remains of either structure.

Assos was protected by a magnificent *wall* of carefully-cut and fitted stone blocks, which is one of the most impressive ancient fortifications in Anatolia. Built during the 4C BC, it stretched for more than 3km and was strenghtened by towers, which had slits and openings from which missiles and stones could be projected against attackers. The best preserved section, which reaches a height of 14m, is to the W of the gymnasium. Here was the *principal entrance* to the city. This was flanked by two towers, one of which (on the E side) is almost complete. There were several other gates, all of which differed in style. Note the splendidly-preserved example a short distance to the NE of the main gate.

The necropolis of Assos, which is currently being excavated, was on a hillside to the W of the city. Here is a confusion of Hellenistic and Roman *sarcophagi*, lying in the sad disorder created by ancient tomb-robbers. The sarcophagi of Assos were famous during antiquity and were exported widely. According to Pliny the stone from which they were made contained a caustic substance which consumed the flesh of bodies placed in them within 40 days. This property gave them their name. Sarcophagus means 'flesh-eater'. The stretch of wall to the left of the modern road shows an interesting join between the regular courses laid down by the 4C BC builders and an older polygonal fortification. Note also, on the right-hand side of the road, the remains of a paved street, which descended towards the harbour area.

5 Assos to Pergamum

Total distance c 182km. **Assos**—18km *Ayvacık*—R550/E24 64km Edremit/Akçay—46km *Ayvalık*—30km *Dikili*—24km **Bergama / Pergamum**.

Visitors with their own transport should return to Ayvacık and take road 550/E24 in the direction of Edremit and İzmir. Bus travellers will find that services to İzmir stop at Edremit and intermediately, but some by-pass Ayvalık, dropping passengers on the main road c 5km from the town. A number of long distance services make the detour to Bergama and there are also fairly frequent bus and dolmuş services from Ayvalık.

There are several small hotels in *Edremit/Akçay*. Information about prices, etc. may be obtained from the Tourism Office in Barbaros Meydanı, Edremit.
  Ayvalık is a popular seaside resort and offers a wide range of accommodation, both in the town and at Sarımsaklı Plaj, a pleasant suburb to the S. Apply to the Tourism Office in Yat Limanı Karşısı for up-to-date information.
  While Bergama has a number of small hotels offering basic facilities, many visitors prefer to stay at the comfortable *Tusan Bergama Moteli* which is 8km outside the town at the junction of 550/E24 with the road to Bergama.

From Ayvacık the road climbs in a series of sharp bends over a spur of *Kaz Dağı* (1710m). This was the ancient Mt Ida, where Paris gave the golden apple to Aphrodite, so setting in train the events that ended with the destruction of Troy.

Road 550/E24 then descends through a deep cleft, reaching the sea at Küçükkuyu. There it passes a number of fine sandy beaches, each boasting its complement of holiday villas. The coastline of the Gulf of Edremit, sheltered by Mt Ida, enjoys a warmer, more temperate climate than the Troad. As a result its green and fertile landscape is dotted with tiny villages set in a sea of fruit trees and olive groves.

Edremit and Akçay also have associations with the Trojan War. *Edremit* (64km), which preserves the form of its ancient name, ADRAMYTTIUM, was the home of Achilles' beautiful captive, Chryseis, and it was from Antandros near Akçay that Aeneas, his father Anchises and their Trojan followers set sail for Rome. Today *Akçay* is one of many small, popular seaside resorts in the N Aegean.

After Edremit/Akçay the road turns away from the sea and does not return to it again, until it reaches 46km *Ayvalık*. This pleasant town attracts a large number of Turkish and foreign visitors each year. (For details of hotels in Ayvalık see above.) It has a number of excellent restaurants both in the centre and on Ali Bey Adası, which is linked by a causeway to the mainland. Magnificent sunsets and a panoramic view of Ayvalık's island-studded bay are an agreeable accompaniment to dinner in the restaurant at Şeytan Sofrası (the 'Devil's Dinnertable'), a plateau to the SW of the town.

During the main holiday period (May to September), there is a ferry-boat service on several days each week from Ayvalık to the Greek island of **Lesbos** (*Mytileni*). Out of season this is usually reduced to one boat a week. Details of the current schedule, fares and formalities may be obtained from the Tourism Office in Yat Limanı Karşısı.

From Ayvalık the road traverses a narrow fertile plain as far as 42km Dikili, where it turns inland towards Bergama. *Dikili*, a former fishing village, is now a port-of-call for cruise ships, whose passengers disembark there to visit Pergamum. A pleasant place in its own right, it has a number of small hotels and pensions.

Towards 1100 BC mainland Greeks displaced by the Dorian invasions colonised the W shore of Asia Minor. Those who settled in the area known as Aeolia between the Troad and the River Hermus intermarried with the local people and founded 11 cities. According to Herodotus, although Ionia to the S had a better climate, Aeolia was more fertile. Its people appear to have lived quiet, pastoral lives and little is known about their history. Today the scanty remains of their settlements, which for the most part were scattered along the coastline, are likely to be of interest mainly to the specialist.

About 16km from Dikili a turning to the left is signposted to 8km **Bergama**, the town which occupies the site of ancient **PERGAMUM**. The Tusan Bergama Moteli, mentioned above, is located at this road junction. Dolmuş and bus services to Bergama pass the motel at intervals during the day, and there are taxis for hire.

History. The first settlement at Pergamum was probably by Aeolic Greeks in the 8C BC. However, perhaps because of its distance from the coast, the city appears to have taken little or no part in the affairs of Aeolia.

One of the earliest references to Pergamum is to be found in Xenophon's 'Anabasis'. This work describes the incursion made in 401 BC by the Ten Thousand, a force of Greek mercenaries employed by Cyrus, the younger son of Darius. He wished to wrest the throne of Persia from his brother, Artaxerxes. When Cyrus was killed at the battle of Cunaxa, command of the mercenaries was taken over by Xenophon. In a brilliant defensive march he led the remnants of the band from the plains between the Tigris and Euphrates across Asia Minor to safety. In 399 BC Xenephon and his exhausted companions arrived at the gates of Pergamum, where they demanded food and shelter from Gongylus, the Greek tyrant, who ruled there.

Pergamum came into prominence after the death of Alexander the Great in 323 BC, when it became part of the territory ruled by Lysimachus, one of the Diadochoi. Having amassed great wealth from his new possessions in Asia Minor, he left a substantial part of this, about 9000 talents, in the care of one of his officers, Philetaerus, in the treasury at Pergamum. When Lysimachus, who earlier had murdered his son Agathocles, was slain at the battle of Corupedion in 281 BC by Seleucus I Nicator of Syria, the money and the city were allowed to remain in the control of Philetaerus. He used the treasure to consolidate his position as de facto ruler of Pergamum and to ornament the city with a number of fine public buildings.

Philetaerus was unmarried—it was rumoured that a childhood injury had made him a eunuch—and he adopted his nephew Eumenes as his heir. Though neither man called himself king, Eumenes I (263–241 BC) is usually regarded as the founder of the Pergamene royal dynasty. He soon obtained his independence from Seleucid rule by defeating Antiochus I at the battle of Sardis in 262 BC. His reign was troubled by the incursions of marauding Gauls, a tribe which had come from central Europe c 278 BC and settled in Galatia, the area around Ankara. To keep them at bay Eumenes paid bribes and built fortified cities at Philetaeria in the Troad and at Attalia on the Hermus river to the S. Under his rule agriculture and industry prospered. To facilitate trade he developed the port of Elaea at the mouth of the river Caicus. An inscription records the gratitude of his subjects, who accorded him divine status.

Reconstruction of Pergamum by Dr Wolfgang Radt.

Eumenes was followed by his adopted son, Attalus I (241–197 BC). Perhaps the greatest achievement of his long reign was the defeat of the Gauls, for which he was given the title of Soter (Saviour). Less successful in his encounters with the Seleucids and the Macedonians, he sought the assistance of the Romans. Some accounts suggest that he obtained their help by procuring for them from Pessinus in SW Galatia the bethel, a sacred stone, which was believed to represent Cybele the Magna Mater.

During the reign of his successor, Eumenes II (197–160 BC), Pergamum reached its apogee. Eumenes allied himself with Rome against the Seleucids and their combined armies defeated Antiochus the Great at the battle of Magnesia in 190 BC. Pergamum was given a large part of the lands formerly ruled by the Seleucids. This enlarged its territory, extending it from the Propontis to the Maeander and as far into Anatolia as the modern city of Konya.

From being the ruler of a comparatively small city-state, Eumenes suddenly found himself in control of a population of c 5 million. His kingdom was fertile and well-endowed with industries. Like his predecessors, he used his resources wisely. Agriculture in all its forms was encouraged and, by the extensive

employment of slave-labour, manufactured products like pottery and textiles were made in quantity. One of the most important industrial and cultural developments was the large-scale production of 'pergamena', the writing material made from treated animal skins later known as parchment. This enabled Pergamum to establish and develop a library, which rivalled in scope and size the great library of Alexandria.

Eumenes extended the area of the city and built a new wall to protect it. Terraces were made on the steep hillside and on these magnificent structures like the Great Altar of Zeus and Athena, the theatre, a gymnasium and a new agora were erected. His generosity was not limited to Pergamum. In Athens he had a two-tiered stoa constructed in the Agora. The arts were encouraged and a distinctive Pergamene style—exemplified by works like the frieze depicting the conflict of the Gods and Giants on the Great Altar and the statue of the Dying Gaul—was developed.

During Eumenes' long reign his kingdom was frequently under attack by the Gauls and by predatory and jealous neighbours like Pontus and Bithynia. He died, worn out by illness and labour, in 160 BC.

Eumenes was succeeded by his 60-year-old brother, Attalus II (160–138 BC). Apart from a brief period of coolness, when he suppported his brother-in-law Ariarathes V in his claim to rule the whole of Cappadocia, Attalus was able to maintain good relations with the Romans. He sought their assistance in his struggle with Bithynia and later sent his army to help them in Greece. Anxious to have direct access to the Mediterranean trade, Attalus founded the city of Attaleia, which, as was customary during the Hellenistic period, he named after himself. The site of Attaleia is now occupied by the modern city of Antalya.

Attalus III (138–133), the last king of Pergamum, was very unlike his predecessors. Remote and aloof, he was disliked by his subjects and soon acquired a sinister reputation. A student of medicine and zoology, he was believed to experiment in the production of new poisons, which he tested on criminals. His treatise on agriculture was frequently mentioned by later writers and there is some evidence of military success.

After a short reign, Attalus died in 133 BC, apparently unloved and unlamented. Eccentric to the end, his final act was to bequeath the kingdom of Pergamum to Rome.

Attalus' bequest was contested by Aristonicus, who claimed to be the illegitimate son of Eumenes II. Supported by some sections of the population, it was a number of years before the Romans were able to suppress the revolt and establish their unquestioned rule over the kingdom.

During the last years of the Pergamene monarchy Roman influence in Asia Minor had been increasing steadily. If Attalus had not left his kingdom to them, it appears likely that they would have annexed it under one pretext or another. From the W part—Caria, Lydia, Ionia, Mysia and a section of Phrygia—they constructed the Roman province of Asia. The remainder was attached to various principalities and provinces in Anatolia. Under Roman rule Pergamum was, nominally, a free city.

That the change of rulers was accepted unwillingly is evidenced by the support given to Mithridates, king of Pontus, when in 88 BC he attempted to free the Aegean cities from Roman rule. Pergamum was occupied by him for some time and its inhabitants joined in, enthusiastically, in the slaughter of the Romans and Italians, who were living in the city.

After the defeat of Mithridates, Pergamum entered a more stable phase. Under the Pax Romana, as an important centre of entrepôt trading, it enjoyed a period of commercial expansion. Many new buildings were constructed and its inhabitants became famous for their liberal support of the arts. Among its most celebrated citizens were the rhetorician Apollodorus and the physician Galen. The author of several medical treatises, Galen (129–c 200) practised at Pergamum in the Asclepieum and in Rome, where the Emperors Marcus Aurelius and Lucius Verus were among his patients.

The city began a period of decline towards the end of the 1C and in the early part of the 2C AD. Competition from trading centres further to the E and the damage caused by an earthquake contributed substantially to its decay.

Pergamum is one of the Seven Churches of the Revelation. A reference (Revelation 2.13) to 'the place where Satan has his altar' is believed to relate to the Great Altar of Zeus. After the adoption of Christianity it became an important missionary centre and it was an episcopal see during the Byzantine period.

Subjected to frequent attack by marauding Arabs, the city was sacked by them in 717. During the centuries that followed it passed through many hands. Byzantines, Crusaders, the Lascarid dynasty of Nicaea, the Selçuks—all ruled Pergamum before it fell to Orhan in 1336.

The approach road to Bergama follows the valley of the Caicus, the modern Bakır Çayı, which is devoid of interest for most of the journey. It is not until the outskirts of the town are reached that the theatre and acropolis may be glimpsed, suspended like a painted back-cloth above the roofs of the modern houses.

About 2km from the town a turning to the right leads to a large tumulus known as *Maltepe*. To explore this a lamp is needed. The tumulus has three burial chambers, in which the remains of sarcophagi were found. The names of those buried there are not known, but an examination of the structure suggests that it dates from the 2C or 3C AD.

The ruins of Pergamum are extensive and widely separated. To see them all and to visit the museum would require a minimum of one and a half days. If time permits, it is advisable to make the tour in this order: first the acropolis, then the Kizil Avlu (the Red Hall), next the museums and the Islamic antiquities, followed by the Asclepieum, and finally the ruins in the surrounding countryside. Visitors without their own transport are advised to take a taxi to the acropolis, as the ascent is long and steep.

In the car-park there are kiosks selling postcards, souvenirs and soft drinks at prices appreciably higher than in the town.

The German Archaeological Institute, which has excavated at Pergamum since 1878, has erected a number of useful explanatory notices at various points on the site. These are particularly helpful in drawing attention to the most important and, in some cases, the most recent discoveries.

To the left of the car-park are the ruins of the *heroon* where the kings of Pergamum, particularly Attalus I and Eumenes II were honoured. This had an antechamber and cult-room on the E side of a peristyle court. Originally constructed during the Hellenistic period, the heroon was renewed by the Romans. Across the street are the remains of storerooms or shops, believed to be Hellenistic.

The **Great Altar** dedicated to Zeus and Athena, was erected during the reign of Eumenes II to commemorate Pergamum's victory over the barbarian Gauls by Attalus I. Centered in a square, which was entered from the E, it rested on a 6m-high podium. This was enclosed on three sides by a wall ornamented with a frieze. A second frieze decorated a colonnade, which rested on the wall and in which statues were placed. Access to the altar stone, where sacrifice was offered, was by a magnificent marble stairway c 20m wide on the W side of the structure.

The principal frieze, which depicted the battle between the giants and the gods, was intended to symbolise the triumph of order over chaos. It bore representations of the principal deities of the pagan pantheon, including Leto and her children, Artemis and Apollo, the Fates, Helios, Poseidon, Amphitrite, Zeus and Athena. The colonnade frieze showed the life of the Trojan hero, Telephus, whom the Attalids claimed as an ancestor.

The Altar was carefully aligned with the older temple of Athena, which occupied a terrace c 25m higher up. This ensured that both buildings seen from a distance made a harmonious whole. As all that now remains in Pergamum in situ is the podium, it requires a considerable effort of imagination to visualise the splendour of this structure, considered by many to be the finest example of Hellenistic art.

At some point the Altar was dismantled and the stone blocks, which made up the principal frieze, were incorporated in a wall. Discovered by German archaeologists in the 19C and taken to Germany, they are now exhibited in a reconstruction of the Altar in the Staatliche Museum in East Berlin. There is a small model of the Altar in the museum at Bergama.

Pergamum's *upper agora* was sited immediately to the S of the altar at a slightly lower level. Surrounded by colonnades constructed in the Doric style, it had the usual mixture of shops and storerooms. A small temple, fronted by sacrificial altars, was probably dedicated to Hermes, the god of commerce, wealth and luck. With the exception of the structure in the NW corner, marked by a semicircular recess, which was modified during the Roman period, all of the buildings in the agora are Hellenistic.

From the agora a ramp led upwards to the main entrance to the city. To the left of this is the temenos of the 4C BC *Temple of Athena*.

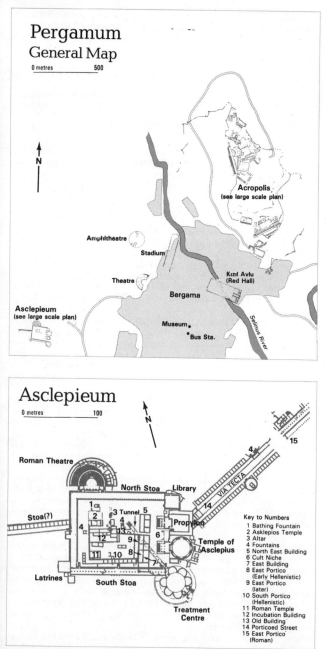

Pergamum
General Map

0 metres 500

Acropolis (see large scale plan)

Amphitheatre

Stadium

Theatre

Kızıl Avlu (Red Hall)

Bergama

Asclepieum (see large scale plan)

Museum

Bus Sta.

Selinus River

Asclepieum

0 metres 100

Roman Theatre

North Stoa

Library

Stoa(?)

VIA TECTA

Tunnel

Propylon

Temple of Asclepius

Latrines

South Stoa

Treatment Centre

Key to Numbers
1 Bathing Fountain
2 Asklepios Temple
3 Altar
4 Fountains
5 North East Building
6 Cult Niche
7 East Building
8 East Portico (Early Hellenistic)
9 East Portico (later)
10 South Portico (Hellenistic)
11 Roman Temple
12 Incubation Building
13 Old Building
14 Porticoed Street
15 East Portico (Roman)

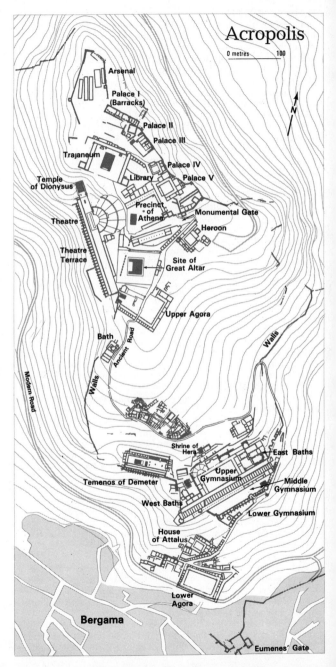

Acropolis

0 metres 100

N

Arsenal

Palace I
(Barracks)

Palace II

Palace III

Trajaneum

Palace IV

Library

Palace V

Temple
of Dionysus

Precinct
of Athena

Monumental Gate

Theatre

Heroon

Theatre
Terrace

Site of
Great Altar

Bath

Upper Agora

Ancient Road

Walls

Walls

Shrine of
Hera

East Baths

Temenos of Demeter

Upper
Gymnasium

Middle
Gymnasium

West Baths

Lower Gymnasium

Modern Road

House
of Attalus

Lower
Agora

Bergama

Eumenes' Gate

The two-storeyed *Propylon*, which provided entrance to the temenos, bears an inscription recording its dedication by 'King Eumenes to Athena the bearer of victories'. It has been reconstructed in the Staatliche Museum in Berlin from fragments recovered on the site. The temple was a peripteros of 6 by 10 columns built of andesite in the Doric style. Of this, the oldest surviving temple in Pergamum, only part of the crepidoma remains.

The kings of Pergamum were passionately addicted to the collection of books and were reputed at one time to have had about 200,000 volumes in their possession. As Athena was the goddess of wisdom and of the intellect, it was not inappropriate for Eumenes II to construct a library, on the N side of the temenos of her temple. Approached through the upper storey of the roofed colonnade, this library was believed to have a capacity of 17,000 volumes, so presumably the remainder of the royal collection was kept elsewhere.

There are substantial remains of the reading room on the E side of the building. Librarians handed books to the readers, who were prevented from reaching the wooden shelves on which the volumes were stored by a low stone bench. This was widened on the N side of the room to support a copy of the statue of Athena by Pheidias which stood in the Parthenon. The Pergamene copy is now in Berlin. An air space between the wall and the shelves helped to preserve the precious volumes from damage by damp.

When the Egyptians, jealous of the growing size of Pergamum's library, prohibited the export of papyrus, the Attalids began to use parchment, an Ionian discovery. This in turn led to the production of paged books, which have many advantages over scrolls.

The library of Pergamum survived into Roman times, when it was given by Antony to Cleopatra. She had it transported to Alexandria, where it remained more or less intact until the 7C AD. Unfortunately it was destroyed at that time on the orders of a religious fanatic, the Caliph Omar, who found its contents irreligious and therefore irrelevant.

The temenos also housed the royal art collection, which included a number of bronze statues commemorating Pergamene victories over the Gauls. A Roman copy in marble of one of these, which depicts a young Gaul about to commit suicide after killing his wife, is preserved in the Museo delle Terme in Rome.

The residences of the Pergamene kings stood on the E edge of the escarpment. The most southerly and the largest, which has been dated to the reign of Eumenes II (197–160 BC), had a private altar and a fine mosaic in one of the rooms on the NW side. Like the other palaces, which are attributed on the basis of material discovered in them and by examination of the structures to Attalus I, Attalus II and Philetaerus, it had a large cistern. All the palaces follow the same simple peristyle design of a colonnaded court surrounded by rooms. The last and the most northerly building was converted at some stage into barracks for the garrison. A considerable section of the ashlar masonry of this building remains standing.

At the highest and safest point of the acropolis a group of buildings served as *storerooms*. Five narrow rectangular structures housed the city's reserve food supplies, weapons, and armour. A quantity of stone 'cannon balls', which were projected by *ballistae*, found near by are now stored in the lower agora.

From this part of the acropolis there is a fine view over the deep valley of the Caicus. To the W the ruins of the Roman amphitheatre are clearly visible and across the town to the SW the Asclepieum may be glimpsed. The remains of the *Roman aqueduct*, which brought water 70km from Soma may also be seen. This supplemented the supply system installed by the Pergamene kings, whose aqueducts linked the source at Madra Dağ, 45km to the N, with the city.

To the S of the storerooms was one of the most magnificent buildings in Pergamum. Constructed during the Roman period, the **Trajaneum** rested on a large terrace, partly cut from the mountain side, partly supported by the arches of huge vaults. The terrace, which measured c 60m by 70m, was surrounded by roofed colonnades on three sides. On the fourth there was a 23m-high supporting wall pierced by a number of windows. Dedicated to Trajan (98–117), and to his distant relative and heir Hadrian (117–138), it was a peripteros of white marble with six by nine columns in the Corinthian style.

Cavea of the Hellenistic theatre, Pergamum.

Currently being restored by German archaeologists, it is to be hoped that the colossal marble heads of the emperors, which were found on the site and are now in Berlin, will be returned to Pergamum, when the work of restoration is completed.

To the SW of the Trajaneum is one of the glories of Pergamum, the **Hellenistic theatre**. As a rule the cavea of a Greek theatre was greater than a semicircle. However, limitations of space at Pergamum made it impossible to respect this convention, so the seating was extended vertically. It has 80 rows of seats, divided by two diazomata, with seven cunei in the lower section and six in the middle and upper sections. With the exception of the marble royal box in the lower section, the seats were constructed of andesite. It had an estimated capacity of 10,000. Entrance was normally from the great terrace that extended from the upper agora to the temple of Dionysus. There was no permanent stage-building. The holes in which posts supporting the scaenae frons and the proscenium were placed are still visible in the pavement. The stone bema, which faces the theatre, dates from the Roman period.

At the N end of the theatre terrace are the ruins of an *Ionic temple*, which, in view of its proximity to the theatre, is believed to have been dedicated to Dionysus. Standing on a high base, the original andesite structure dated from the 2C BC. A sacrificial altar was sited in front of the elaborate stairway that led to the cella. Fragments of an inscription, recording the temple's rededication, after it had been rebuilt in marble, to Caracalla (211–217), 'the new Dionysus', have been found on the site.

From the temple a long *promenade* extended S to the upper agora. This theatre terrace, which measured c 246m, was flanked by Doric stoas of andesite. At the S end there was a twin-arched gateway.

At this point the visit to the upper part of the city finishes. Visitors who have their own transport should take their cars to the lower car-park to avoid the very fatiguing climb back to the upper car-park, and they should read the next descriptive sections in reverse order, beginning with the gate of Eumenes II and the lower agora.

To the W of the path, which descends from the upper agora to a residential area of the city, are the ruins of a *baths complex* constructed during the Roman Imperial period. Part of the tepidarium, marked by a large alcove, is clearly visible.

Recent excavations in the area to the left of the path have revealed the remains of a number of buildings, most of which were erected or restored during the Roman period. The most important of these are a bath-gymnasium, an odeum and a heroon, the so-called 'marble hall'. These interconnected structures formed a multi-discipline complex believed to have been linked with a cult association, where young men could develop their minds and bodies. This was founded in honour of Diodorus Pasparos, who was deified during his lifetime. The portrait head of this Pergamene citizen of the late 1C BC, who was well-known for his generous gifts to the city, is preserved in Bergama museum.

The *Roman bath-gymnasium* had a large courtyard, which doubled as a palaestra, and the usual layout of caldarium, tepidarium, etc. To the W, on the other side of the street, was a latrine, which was connected to the main sewage channel. The *odeum*, which may have been used for meetings as well as performances, adjoined the *heroon*. Copies of 18 reliefs found in the heroon decorate the walls. (The originals are in the Bergama Museum.) These depict the Dioscuri, a fighting cock, armour, weapons etc. Both the odeum and heroon were erected in the 1C BC, but were restored and altered during the Roman period. A relief showing an erect phallus, symbol of good luck and prosperity, found in the complex has been built into the wall of the modern shelter erected by the archaeologists.

To the E of the heroon are the ruins of a small restaurant and of a shop. The *restaurant* had a dining room, which opened on to the street. Cooking was conducted in an area, which was partly excavated from the rock. At the back of the dining room there was another chamber whose walls were covered with paintings. Behind the counter of the *shop* a number of pithoi, used for the storage of wine or oil, were set into the rock surface.

A *hall* measuring 24m by 10m, which appears to have been used for the worship of Dionysus from the 2C to the 4C AD, has been discovered to the NE of these buildings. While sharing a ritual meal, the worshippers lay on a bench or platform 1m high by 2m wide, which ran parallel to the walls. Facing the entrance was an altar and behind it a recess, which probably contained the cult image. Outside the hall there was a fountain and a deep rock-cut pit, which presumably received the blood of sacrificial offerings made during the ceremonies.

The austerity and lack of hope which characterised conventional religion turned an increasing number of people towards mystery cults of oriental origin, which promised a happier after-life to their followers. During the 1C and 2C AD these cults attracted many adherents, particularly from the Roman poor and middle classes. In view of its location and date it is probable that the cult, which used this hall, drew its members from the ordinary people, the merchants and small traders, who lived in that area of the city.

To the right of the road is the last group of buildings on the hillside. The most important of these are the temple of Demeter, a complex of three gymnasia, the temple of Hera, the house of the Consul Attalus and the lower agora.

The temenos of the *Temple of Demeter* occupies a terrace c 100m long by 50m wide. Inscriptions on the altar and temple record the fact that it was erected by Philetaerus (282–263 BC) and his brother Eumenes in memory of their mother, Boa. It was enlarged and extended by his successors and again during the Roman period.

Demeter was the goddess of fertility and rebirth and was particularly associated with corn and the fruits of the earth. It was therefore appropriate that Philetaerus chose to erect her shrine in a rural setting outside the city walls. To the W of the temenos there is a deep stone-lined pit, which received the blood of piglets sacrificed in the goddess's honour. Nearby are the remains of a fountain, where the worshippers were ritually purified.

Access to the temenos was by a *propylon* on the W side, which was donated by Apollonis, the wife of Attalus I (241–197). Two of the unusual columns of this structure have been re-erected. Made of andesite in the Doric style they had Aeolic capitals decorated with a design of palm leaves. Usually found in archaic structures in Aeolia, it has been suggested that the presence of these columns in Pergamum may be attributed to the fact that Apollonis came from Cyzicus.

From the propylon a flight of steps led down into the temenos. This was surrounded on three sides by *stoas*. The stoa on the S, also the gift of Apollonis, was supported by a massive buttressed wall. On the N side the stoa was higher and fronted for half its length by ten rows of seats. Between 800 and 1000 postulants and initiates sat in this theatron to see and participate in the mysteries celebrated in honour of the goddess.

Demeter, in classical mythology the daughter of Cronus and Rhea, was known and worshipped in the ancient world wherever corn was grown. According to the myth, Persephone, her daughter by Zeus, was abducted by Hades, and taken to his gloomy underworld kingdom. Demeter, distraught with grief, wandered over the earth, torch in hand, looking for her lost child. She abandoned her divine duties and, as a result, the earth became barren and mankind was threatened with starvation. To avoid a catastrophe Hades was persuaded to reunite mother and daughter. Unfortunately, while in the underworld Persephone had eaten a pomegranate seed and so was obliged to spend a part of each year there.

Because of the kindness shown to her by King Celeus, when she was looking for her daughter, Demeter entrusted his son, Triptolemus, with a divine mission. He was to travel through the world teaching mankind how to grow and harvest corn.

The legend of Demeter and of her daughter, Persephone, is generally taken to refer to the sowing of corn in the dark earth in autumn, its apparent death during winter and its magical rebirth in the spring. The very ancient cult, which grew up around the myth, promised those who had been initiated into its mysteries a happier afterlife than that offered by official religion. Men and women, freemen and slaves were admitted to the cult. Postulants had to have 'a soul conscious of no evil and have lived well and justly'. Only those, who had sinned grievously and were cursed or defiled, were excluded.

In Greece the principal shrine dedicated to the mysteries of Demeter was at Eleusis near Athens. Ancient authors provide accounts of those parts of the ritual, which took place in public. However, many of the ceremonies were held under cover of darkness and in secret, and little is known about their form or content. Severe punishments were invoked against initiates who broke the oath of secrecy that bound them. For a time Aeschylus went in danger of his life, because he was suspected of giving information about the mysteries in one of his plays, and the brilliant playboy-statesman Alcibiades was condemned to death in absentia for performing a blasphemous version of the ceremonies with his friends. It appears that certain sacred objects, which perhaps included ears of corn, were shown to the initiates and that they went through a ritual purification. In Pergamum, as in Eleusis, it would seem that the ceremonies were held at night. A Roman relief, which was found in one of the stoas of the sanctuary, shows Demeter standing by an altar. In her hand she holds a torch.

Between the principal altar and the temple, which were sited slightly off-centre towards the W end of the temenos, there were several subsidiary altars. The *main altar*, constructed of andesite and adorned with marble volutes, stood in front of the 3C BC *Ionic temple in antis*. This measured c 7m by 13m and was also constructed of andesite. During the Roman period marble columns and a marble pediment were added, changing it into a Corinthian prostyle. At that time the temple was rededicated to Demeter Karpophoros (the fruitful) and her daughter Kore Persephone.

To the W of the temenos of Demeter is the *Shrine of Hera*, the wife of Zeus, and the gymnasia, which made up the largest building complex in Pergamum. The shrine, which comprised a temple and an altar, was built on two levels on the hillside above the gymnasia.

The *temple*, reached by a flight of steps, was a four-columned prostyle in the Doric order. Measuring c 7m by 12m, it was, according to an inscription, constructed during the reign of Attalus II (160–138). Built partly of andesite and partly of marble, it was flanked on the W by an exedra and on the E by a small stoa. The altar of the sanctuary was on a lower terrace. Authorities disagree as to whether the headless marble statue of a male figure, found in the sanctuary,

represented Attalus or Zeus. This is now in the İstanbul Archaeological Museum. No trace of the cult statue of Hera has been found.

The *gymnasia* at Pergamum were designed to deal with all aspects of
the intellectual and physical development of the male youth of the city.
The complex was divided into three separate and distinct parts. The
upper gymnasium was devoted to the young men, the central gymnasium to adolescents and the lower gymnasium to the youngest boys.

The *upper gymnasium* occupied a terrace, which measured c 200m
by 45m. Constructed of andesite during the Hellenistic period, it was
modified extensively by the Romans. Their use of marble and mortar
simplifies the work of distinguishing between the earlier buildings
and the later additions and alterations. The principal feature of the
upper gymnasium was a large court, surrounded by colonnades,
used for training sessions. To the NW of the court was an auditorium
with a capacity of 1000, where the students assembled for lectures
and cultural activities. To the W of this was a small Ionic prostyle
temple dedicated to Asclepius, while on the N a room richly decorated with marble and marked by a double apse was, according to an
inscription, reserved for use by the emperor. Between the emperor's
room and the auditorium was the *ephebeion*, where important
ceremonies concerned with the training and education of the young
men took place. To the S, in the so-called *basement stadium*, athletic
matches were held during the winter and summer. The upper
gymnasium was flanked on the E and W by extensive baths, which
were used by the athletes after matches and training.

The *central gymnasium*, built on the next lower terrace, was
reached by a narrow staircase. Surrounded by walls, it had a long
stoa on the N. One of the rooms on E side of the stoa was dedicated to
the emperor and to Hercules and Hermes, gods associated with
physical fitness. The central area of the gymnasium was used for
exercises and track events. Traces of a small prostyle *Corinthian
temple*, measuring 7m by 12m, have been been found on the E side
of the terrace. On its walls were lists of youths dating from the
Hellenistic to the Roman periods. Note the large Hellenistic fountain
nearby. Its rim is marked by the jugs and pots of those who once
drew water from it.

A well-preserved covered stairs leads to the *young boys' gymnasium*. Constructed during the reign of Eumenes II, a substantial
section of the gymnasium's N wall, which was strengthened by
strong buttresses, remains intact. Niches in this wall contained
inscribed tablets listing the names of prizewinners and statues of the
most outstanding boys. A stele found there listed the ephebes for 147
BC. The towers on the N wall date from the Byzantine period.

One of the most striking and touching reminders of Pergamum's
past is provided by the *ancient street* composed of large andesite
blocks, which leads down from the gymnasia to a group of shops and
houses on the SW. About 5m wide, it shows many signs of wear and
tear: there are deep ruts from chariots and carts and in a number of
places the stones have been polished by the countless pairs of feet
that have passed over them. Note the signs of repair carried out in
antiquity, particularly to the drainage system, which are still clearly
visible.

Where the street turns to the W there are the ruins of a 2C BC
peristyle house, which was modified during the Roman period.
According to an inscription found on the base of a herm the house
belonged to the Consul Attalus. Cheerfully he invited his guests to
join with him in enjoying the good things of life. The lower storey of

the stoa, built around a central court measuring c 20m by 13.5m, was of andesite in the Doric style, the upper storey was of marble in the Ionic. Note the traces of wall paintings and of well-preserved *mosaics*, which are a housed under a protective cover. There were several cisterns, one of which, dating from the Hellenistic period, supplied water to a fountain in the lower agora.

The *lower agora*, which was devoted to commerce, lies to the left of the ancient street. Rectangular in shape it measured c 64m by 34m and has been dated to the reign of Eumenes II (197–160). The paved central courtyard was surrounded by a two-storey Doric stoa, which had shops at the rear. As remarked above, the fountain in the centre received its water supply from a cistern in the house of Attalus. Stone missiles, found near the arsenal on the summit of the acropolis, are stored in the lower agora.

One of the finest existing examples of Hellenistic art, the head of Alexander the Great, now preserved in the İstanbul Archaeological Museum, was discovered in the NW corner of the agora. No trace of the torso has been found. A number of inscriptions which set out the laws governing public works, such as drains, fountains, roads and houses, were displayed in the agora. They are now preserved in Bergama's Museum.

The modern buildings are the headquarters and store of the German archaeologists who are working in Pergamum.

During the reign of Eumenes II the city walls were extended and reached a length of c 4km. Part of these walls may still be seen to the E of the S gateway. All the buildings on the hillside, including the sanctuary of Demeter and the gymnasia, were enclosed and areas vulnerable to attack were protected by the new defences.

The main entrance to Pergamum was by Eumenes' *S gate*, which is sited a short distance below the lower agora. Precautions were taken to prevent hostile forces from using this to get into the city. Travellers, having passed through a fortified entrance on the W side, found themselves in an open courtyard. This measured 20m by 20m and was overlooked by two towers on the S, which were manned by soldiers. The booths of money changers, scribes and small traders sheltered in a colonnade by the E wall of the court.

Entry to the city from the courtyard required a sharp U-turn through a second gate on the W side. This was overlooked by a tower in a corner of the city wall, which also was guarded.

The gateway of Eumenes II is the last monument in the upper area of the ancient city. Visitors should now return to the modern town by the road which descends from the hillside.

Clearly visible from this road is the great bulk of the **Kızıl Avlu**, the Red Hall, so called because of the colour of the brick from which it was built. An examination of this structure, which dates from the first half of the 2C AD, has suggested to archaeologists that it was probably dedicated to the Egyptian gods, Serapis, Isis and Harpocrates. There are, however, dissentient voices. Mortimer Wheeler thought that it could have housed the famous library during the Roman period or even served as the University of Pergamum.

The complex, the largest in the ancient city, was made up of a courtyard measuring c 200m by 100m, the greater part of which is covered by modern houses, a basilica with a nave, two side aisles and a reversed apse, and two circular tower-structures fronted by courts. The river Selinus, the Bergama Çay, is carried through the arched channels of a double tunnel that passes under the courtyard at an angle.

The **basilica**, which measures 60m by 26m, has walls that still stand to a height of 19m. A monumental entrance 7m high and 14m wide admitted to the nave, paved with marble, the W part of which was lit by windows in the side walls. The 10m-tall image of the deity, which rested on a large podium, dominated the tenebrous E section of the basilica. A tunnel under its base allowed the priests to enter the hollow statue, from where they delivered oracular pronouncements, which the faithful believed were made by the god. In front of the podium there was a shallow marble basin containing water. Two staircases near the E wall led to a balcony resting on pillars, which encircled the structure. Some of the coloured marble decoration, which covered the whole surface of the brick walls, is still in position.

Sometime after the adoption of Christianity a church dedicated to St. John the Evangelist was built inside the basilica. Part of the ruined walls of this building and its conventionally oriented apse remain.

The *circular tower buildings*, which flanked the basilica, were approached through courts surrounded by colonnades. Fragments of two of the curiously shaped supports of these colonnades were found near the S tower. They were carved on one side as atlantes and one the other as caryatids. Both types of figure were in the Egyptian style. Hot and cold water was piped to a long, narrow pool in the centre of each of the courts. A warren of rooms underneath the towers may have been used for ritual purposes.

The orientation of the temple complex, which faces W, has suggested to archaeologists that it was dedicated to Serapis, and to Isis and Harpocrates with whom he was often linked. Worship of Serapis, a syncretic deity of the underworld, who was introduced to the Egyptians by Ptolemy I (305–282 BC), spread widely through the Roman world during the first centuries of the Christian era. A temple dedicated to him was found in York and a fine head of the god was discovered in 1954 under the temple of Mithras at Walbrook in the City of London. Characteristic features of Egyptian religion found in the complex like the pools for ritual bathing, the underground river thought to symbolise the Nile and the enormous courtyard eminently suited to processions and assemblies, together with the presence of the Egyptian-style statues, are offered as evidence in support of the archaeologists' theory.

Just inside the modern wall on the W side of the large courtyard there are several architectural fragments, including a number that bear inscriptions in Hebrew and which appear to be late-19C Jewish gravestones.

Between the Kızıl Avlu and the Archaeological Museum there are some Islamic monuments including the *minaret* of a 14C Selçuk mosque and the small, but exquisite *Parmaklı Camii*. Also worth a visit is *Ulu Camii*, which dates from the reign of Beyazit I (1389–1403). This is reached by taking the Kozak road as far as a bridge, Ulu Camii Köprüsü, which crosses the upper waters of the Selinus.

Across the street from the Archaeological Museum is the *Bergama Restaurant*, which serves adequate meals. Nearby are the Post Office and Bus Garage. Branches of the principal banks are to be found in a square 100m to the N. The *Tourism Information Office* is at the S end of the town near the turning, which leads to the Asclepieum.

Bergama's **Archaeological Museum**, which opened in 1936, was the first museum in Turkey to concentrate on exhibiting finds from local excavations. The material, which is well-displayed, is set out in the garden, in a large courtyard surrounded by a colonnade, and in several airy, well-lit rooms. Many of the exhibits are labelled in English.

The garden contains a large number of architectural fragments, including stelae and Islamic tombstones. In the courtyard, immediately inside the entrance, there is a fine sarcophagus decorated with reliefs of garlands, a Medusa head and a horseman. This is flanked by two Hellenistic Aeolic capitals from the sanctuary of Demeter.

In the colonnade there is a large collection of finds from Pergamum and sites in the surrounding countryside. These include part of the sima and dentils from the sanctuary of Athena, a section of the Hellenistic frieze and architrave from the Athena propylon, part of the architrave from the altar of Zeus, a Corinthian and a Composite capital from the Asclepieum, part of the frieze from the Roman temple of Dionysus, a section of a frieze depicting Cerberus, the three-headed dog which guarded the entrance to Hades, a hermaphroditic herm from the valley of the Caicus, and a horse from the altar of Zeus. There are several Hellenistic statues, all headless, a series of Hellenistic stelae, Roman statues, including an Artemis from the Trajaneum, Roman altars and inscriptions, and Hellenistic and Roman inscriptions honouring ephebes from the gymnasia. Note also the small model of the altar of Zeus in the left-hand colonnade and the acroteria from the propylon of the Asclepieum, which are displayed in the centre area.

By the door of the museum there is a fine archaic *kouros* dated to 525 BC from Pitane, modern Çandarlı. A wall-case in the room to the right contains some exquisite terracottas. These include a youth with a goose, Silenus and Dionysus, Venus, and a youth hiding objects in his bunched-up toga. Among the Roman sculptures are a 3C AD head of Caracalla, a colossal *statue of Hadrian* from the Asclepieum, the goddess Fortuna, a head of Vespasian, and a bust of Euripides. Note the Roman Medusa mosaic from the Acropolis.

A glass case by the back wall contains Hellenistic and Roman symbols of fecundity including penes and erotic lamps. There are also several moulds for the production of these objects. Other wall cases contain examples of Roman glass, including tear vases, small bronzes, Hellenistic, Roman and Byzantine coins, pottery and lamps, bronze strigils and tiny models of animals. Of particular interest are the offerings made by patients at the Asclepieum. These include representations of fingers, hands and feet, a bronze snake, and a head of Asclepius. Among the many small statues there are several representations of Cybele, pottery from the archaic and Byzantine periods, jewellery and ornaments of carved ivory and a number of very well-preserved 2C and 1C BC terracottas from Myrina.

The **Asclepieum**, which occupies a large area c 1km to the W of Bergama, may be reached by taking the signposted turning on the right of the Tourism Information Office.

During both the Hellenistic and Roman periods Pergamum was justly famous for its **Asclepieum**, the great medical centre that came to rival, and almost overshadow, Epidaurus in Greece. To judge by ancient accounts, the Asclepieum functioned very much like a fashionable spa in the 18C or 19C. While many came there in search of a cure, others frequented it to take the water, to enjoy the performances in the theatre, to indulge in philosphical discussion or simply to be diverted by watching the more bizarre courses of treatment that were prescribed by the priests and doctors.

Although badly damaged by an earthquake in the 3C AD, the Asclepieum continued to function as a medical centre for some time after the introduction of Christianity. During the Byzantine era a church was constructed on the site of the temple of Asclepius.

According to the legends, Asclepius, the son of Apollo, having been abandoned by his mother was educated by the centaur Chiron, who taught him medicine. Rapidly acquiring great skill, he discovered how to bring the dead to life by using the Gorgon's blood which had been given to him by Athena. Zeus, fearing that this practice would upset the natural order, struck Asclepius dead with a thunderbolt. In compensation he was placed among the stars.

As snakes were believed to have the power to renew themselves, they were sacred to Asclepius. Twined around a post, they formed his symbol. Patients, who had been cured at one of his shrines, offered a cock to the god, a fact that underlines the irony and pathos of Socrates' last words, 'Crito, we owe a cock to Asclepius. Make sure that it is paid'.

Asclepius was not deified until the 5C BC. To Homer he was 'the blameless physician', whose sons, Machaon and Podalirius, served as doctors to the Greek army at Troy. Among his five daughters were Panacea and Hygieia.

The worship of Asclepius was centered initially on Epidaurus and from there it was brought to Pergamum in the 4C BC. Archaeological evidence suggests that there was a shrine honouring a female deity at this site as early as the Bronze Age and that it also may have been connected with healing.

A substantial stretch of the ancient *paved street*, the VIA TECTA, which began at the city theatre and linked Pergamum with the Asclepieum, has been cleared by German archaeologists. The last section of c 150m before the propylon, which provides access to the sanctuary, was flanked by colonnades. On the right-hand side there are the remains of a late fountain and on the left of a large circular tomb, which dates from the first years of the Christian era.

According to an inscription on the pediment of the *propylon*, it was the gift of a Pergamene citizen named Claudius Charax. Like most of the visible remains of the Asclepieum it dates from 2C AD, when, thanks to the generosity of Hadrian, Antoninus Pius and Marcus Aurelius and of local magnates, much rebuilding was done. The propylon was composed of two parts: a square surrounded on three sides by a colonnade in the Corinthian order and, on the W, a temple façade with four Corinthian columns, which fronted a flight of steps leading down into the Asclepieum courtyard. Acroteria from the pediment of the propylon are displayed in Bergama Museum.

The courtyard, which measured 110m by 130m, had buildings on the E and stoas on the other three sides. Immediately to the right of the propylon are the remains of a niche, which may have held a cult statue. The square building in the NE corner was the *library*. This was sometimes called the emperor's room, as the monumental statue of Hadrian, now in the Bergama museum, stood in a recess in the E wall. According to an inscription on the base of the statue, it was the gift of Flavia Melitine. This lady may also have paid for the construction of the library.

While it probably housed a collection of medical texts for use by the doctors, the library almost certainly had copies of the classics and of general works for the amusement and recreation of the patients, who could spend as long as a year at the sanctuary. Light for reading came from windows above the recesses in which the manuscripts were stored on shelves.

There are substantial remains of the *N stoa*, which was originally constructed in the Ionic style. After the devastation caused by the earthquake of AD 175, ten new columns in the Composite style were erected on the E side of the colonnade.

At the W end of the stoa is the much-restored *Roman theatre*. It has a single diazoma and is divided into five cunei. The three rows below the diazoma were reserved for the most distinguished spectators. The stage, which was raised to a height of 1m, was backed by a three-storey stage-building. Dedicated to Asclepius and Athena Hygieia, the theatre had a capacity of 3500.

The Ionic colonnade on the W side has disappeared. It fronted a stoa, behind which there was another building of indeterminate purpose that lay outside the sanctuary courtyard. At the SW corner there were two open-plan *latrines*, built over a channel carrying a constant flow of water. The larger, reserved for men, had 40 marble seats and was ventilated and lit by openings in a ceiling resting on four Corinthian columns. The ladies' room, which had 17 seats, was less lavishly furnished.

Because of the slope, the *S stoa* was constructed over a basement, which supported it. This stoa, too, has disappeared.

Detailed accounts of the methods of treatment given at the Asclepieum are provided by inscriptions found on the site and by the writings of Aelius Aristides, 2C AD orator and hypochondriac, who claimed to have spent 13 years there. Drinking and bathing in the water from the springs in the centre of the court, mud-baths, herbal remedies, massage, dieting, exercise (especially running barefoot in the winter), and colonic-irrigation were among the methods favoured. In addition, patients suffering from psychosomatic illnesses had their dreams analysed by the priests of Asclepius in a way that anticipated the work of Freud.

Medical doctors were also employed at the sanctuary, among them Galen (AD 129–c 200), one of the greatest physicians of antiquity. Born and educated in Pergamum and initially doctor to the city's gladiators, he became a consultant to the emperors.

Treatment was provided in the centre of the court. Immediately to the S of the theatre there was a *Roman fountain*, where patients bathed and drank the water. Towards the centre of the W stoa there was a rock-cut pool, where patients also bathed and coated themselves with mud from the surrounding area. A third source, dated by the archaeologists to the Hellenistic period, was located in the centre of the court, near the exit from the great tunnel that stretches to the large building in the SE corner. Once protected from the elements by a roof, but now open to the sky, this spring still offers its healing water to modern visitors. Aristides claimed that drinking it was an effective specific for asthma, chest infections and foot problems.

To the S of the springs was the *Hellenistic temenos of Asclepius*, which was enclosed on three sides by a colonnade. On the N side of the temenos were the incubation and sleeping rooms, where the patients hoped to be cured by an encounter, in the course of their dreams, with the god. An inscription stated that they had to sacrifice a white sheep decked with olive boughs, had to be dressed in white robes and were forbidden to wear a girdle or rings. Patients not cured by this process had their dreams interpreted by the priests, who with the doctors made a diagnosis and prescribed a course of treatment.

Between the temenos and the theatre were temples dedicated to Apollo Kalliteknos (Apollo the Artist), Hygieia and Asclepius. According to Aristides, Telesphorus, a youthful deity associated with Asclepius, had a shrine in this area. Today only the barest traces of the three temples remain.

From the centre of the court a *Roman tunnel*, 80m long, led to a large circular building, which projected from the SE corner of the complex. A flight of steps provided access to the tunnel, which had openings in the vaulted roof to admit light and air. Sometimes incorrectly described as the temple of Telesphorus, the late Roman circular building had two storeys. Only the lower storey, which is in a good state of preservation, remains. This structure, which had a diameter of 26.5m, was divided into six apsidal sections. Opinions are divided about its purpose, but the presence of recesses for washing and a sun-terrace on the lower floor and its link by the tunnel with the springs in the centre of the court, suggest that it was integrated in some way into the sanctuary's scheme for treating the sick.

To the N of the round building are the ruins of the **Temple of Asclepius**. Modelled on the Pantheon in Rome, this was constructed with the care and skill for which Pergamene craftsmen were famous. Perhaps the most beautiful structure in the Asclepieum, it was the gift of the consul Lucius Rufinus and dates from c AD 150. It consisted of a circular domed building fronted by a colonnaded entrance. A flight of steps led up from the central court into the temple. The dome, which had a circular opening in the centre to admit light and air, measured c 24m in diameter. The wall and floor of the andesite structure were lined with marble mosaics and pierced at intervals with alternate round and rectangular recesses. These held statues of the deities associated with healing. In the central recess, which faced the entrance, there was a giant statue of Asclepius. With the nearby propylon of Charax the temple combined to form a harmonious group of buildings on the E side of the Asclepieum.

At the E end of the Via Tecta, beyond the scanty remains of the *town theatre*, which had a capacity of 30,000, are the ruins of the *Roman amphitheatre* and the site of the stadium. Of the amphitheatre, which was built over a stream, only the damaged remains of a few of the vast arches, which supported the seats, remain. Used for gladiatorial encounters and battles between men and wild animals, amphitheatres provided one of the most popular entertainments during the Roman period.

As the approach to these ruins from the Asclepieum passes near a *restricted area*, access may not possible by this route. The advice of the Tourism Information Office should sought by visitors who wish to see them.

6 Pergamum to İzmir

This route includes a number of diversions to the ancient sites of Pitane, Myrina, Yeni Foça, Yanık, Neanteichos and Larisa.

Total distance c 38km. **Bergama / Pergamum**—(25km Çandarlı / *Pitane*)—(2km *Elaea*)—6km *Gryneum* (5km *Myrina*)—(6km *Cyme*)—(15km *Yeni Foça*—27km *Eski Foça*)—8km *Buruncuk / Larisa* (2km *Yanı Köy*)—c 24km İzmir.

From **Bergama** (see Rte 5) return to the junction with road 550/E24 and continue in the direction of İzmir. This route passes the sites of some of the ancient cities of Aeolia. In most cases only scant traces of these remain and they are often in locations difficult to reach by bus or dolmuş. However, the beauty of their settings and their largely unspoiled nature will commend them to the zealous traveller who has both time to spare and his own transport.

At first the road follows the course of the Bakır Çay. After c 15km a turning to the right leads to 10km Çandarlı, where PITANE, the most northern of the Aeolian cities, was located. Traces of a settlement dating back to the third millennium BC have been found here. A minor member of the Delian League, Pitane at first received help from Pergamum and later was absorbed by its powerful neighbour. This may account for the expression 'a regular Pitane', which was applied sometimes to a person who had suffered excessively from the caprice of fortune.

The city was sited at the end of a finger-shaped peninsula that projects for c 1km into the Aegean. Apart from traces of the ancient *fortifications* and the remains of a *mole* on the W side, little remains to be seen. Stone taken from the city was used to construct the modern village and the *medieval fortress* built by the Venetians, which guarded the landward approaches. An archaic statue of a kouros, now in the Bergama Museum, was found in 1958 near the neck of the peninsula.

Today Pitane is visited mainly for the beauty of its situation. Its pleasant sandy beach makes a good stopping-place for a picnic.

On returning to the main road, continue for c 2km to a point where a turning to the left leads to the site of ELAEA. According to an ancient tradition this was founded at about the time of the Trojan War by settlers from Athens. Never a member of the Aeolian League, it prospered under the Attalids, who developed it as a base for their commercial and naval vessels. Today there is little to see at Elaea. The sea has receded and a part of the ancient *harbour wall* now stretches away into a desolate marsh. Small sections of the *fortifications* remain near the main road.

The next of the Aeolian cities, GRYNEUM, is to be found c 6km to the S of Elaea near the village of Yenişakran. Located on the narrow peninsula of Temaşalık Burnu 1km to the S of the village, this city, a member of the Delian League, was in Persian hands in the early part of the 5C BC. It was captured from them in 335 BC by Parmenion, who enslaved the inhabitants. Later ruled by nearby Myrina, it was, according to Strabo and Pausanias, famous for its oracle of Apollo, who lived in a sacred grove of fruit-bearing and fragrant trees.

Opinions differ about the small *mound* surrounded by broken columns, which lies towards the end of the peninsula. Some authorities believe that this marks the site of the temple of Apollo, but others assert that the remains belong to a later structure, possibly Byzantine. There are no other visible ruins. Pausanias remarked on the profusion of fruit trees and flowering shrubs that surrounded the sanctuary of the god. The trees and shrubs of Gryneum still offer welcome shade to the passing traveller and their blossoms fill the air with a heady scent.

The city of MYRINA is c 5km to the S of Gryneum near the mouth of the Güzelhisar Cayı, the ancient Pythicus. According to Strabo it was named Myrina 'from the Amazon who lies in the Trojan plain [below Batieia] ... which verily men call Batieia, but the immortals the tomb of much-bounding Myrina'.

The city had a chequered history. Destroyed twice by earthquakes, it was rebuilt with assistance from the Emperor Tiberius. To express their gratitude its inhabitants changed Myrina's name to Sebastopolis (the city of the Emperor).

Myrina was built on two hills, now known as Birki Tepe and Öteki Tepe, which are c 2km from the road. Excavations at Birki Tepe have revealed the remains of an early *polygonal wall* and part of a defensive system dating from the Byzantine period. The whole area is heavily overgrown and very difficult to explore.

Towards the end of the 19C c 5000 graves, most of which had not been disturbed by robbers, were discovered in a *necropolis* to the N of Birki Tepe. In these graves were found a large quantity of

Hellenistic terracotta figures and masks, which date from the 2C and 1C BC. Terracottas were frequently buried with the dead as grave-goods for use in the after-life or because they had been favourite possessions of the deceased. Very touching are the articulated figures that had been used as toys, many of which show evidence of wear at the hands of their young owners.

Echoing the style of Tanagra in Greece, the terracottas of Myrina cover a wide range of subjects. Representations of draped female figures, children, animals, Erotes, Victories, sirens, actors and various deities including Aphrodite and Dionysus were made in an expressive lively style. Garments were sometimes reproduced in a series of daring patterns that made little or no attempt to suggest reality. Produced from a fine clay, which ranged in colour from orange to dark red, the pieces usually bear the artist's signature. Examples of terracottas from Myrina may be found in many museums. There are representative collections in İstanbul, London, Paris, Athens and Boston.

Shortly after passing the modern village of *Aliağa*, a turning to the right leads to the site of the ancient city of 6km CYME. Like Myrina named after an Amazon, Cyme was, perhaps, the most important of the Aeolian cities. Under Persian rule at the end of the 5C and the beginning of the 4C BC, it provided naval suppport for Darius and Xerxes in their campaigns against Greece. An indication of its wealth and importance at a later period is provided by the size of its annual payment to the Delian League, which exceeded the amount levied on any other city in Aeolia or Ionia.

Considered slow and stupid by their contemporaries, the people of Cyme appear to have led quiet and comfortable lives. One of their proudest boasts was that the father of Hesiod, perhaps the greatest Greek poet after Homer, was born there. An anecdote told by Strabo sums up the general opinion of the city's inhabitants held by their contemporaries. Ephorus, the city's historian, unable to tell of deeds of his native land in his enumeration of the other achievements in history, and yet unwilling that it should be unmentioned, exclaims as follows: 'At about the same time the Cymaeans were at peace'.

The city was sited partly on a hill and partly in a valley to the S. The remains are scant: on the hilltop a small *temple* in the Ionic style consecrated to Isis; the remains of large building of indeterminate purpose in the valley near the road; and, under water, parts of the ancient *harbour-works*. Much of the site is covered with dense undergrowth, which makes any detailed exploration difficult and uncomfortable.

About 16km to the S of the road junction for Cyme, a turning to the right leads to the small seaside resorts of 15km *Yeni Foça* and 27km *Eski Foça*. Eski Foç, built over the ancient city of PHOCAEA, attracts an increasing number of Turkish holidaymakers each year, while foreigners flock to the Club Mediterranée sited nearby. The town possesses several small, unpretentious hotels, some open all the year round, and a number of good fish restaurants. The best bathing beaches are to the S of the modern harbour.

On the way in from the main road look out for a remarkable 8C BC *rock-tomb*. Popularly known as Taş Kule (the Rock Tower), this is a stone cube 8.5m long by 5.8m wide and 6m high, which is surmounted on the E by a second cube resting on four steps. According to Bean, the top of the structure, which was damaged in antiquity, may have been crowned by a phallus-stone. Entrance to the burial chamber, which contained a rectangular grave in the floor, is through an antechamber on the N side. Akurgal has drawn attention to the number of influences visible in the structure: Lycian—two storeys with a sarcophagus shaped cube on top; Persian—the stepped base under the cube; and Lydian—the decorative pattern near the entrance. It is believed to be the burial chamber of a local princeling or minor king.

Nearer Foça there is another *rock-cut tomb* called Şeytan Hamamı (the Devil's Bath), which has been dated to the 4C BC.

History. Phocaea is believed to have been founded by colonists from the Ionian cities of Erythrae and Teos in the 8C BC. Its name was probably derived from the small hump-backed islands that lie offshore. To the imaginative eyes of Phocaea's early inhabitants these looked like seals—*Phoce* in Greek—animals frequently depicted on the city's coinage.

Because of its excellent harbour Phocaea developed rapidly, becoming an important trading port. Its adventurous citizens ranged widely over the Mediterranean in large ships capable of carrying as many as 500 passengers and substantial quantities of freight. They founded colonies in S France at Massalia (modern Marseilles), in S Spain at Tartessus (near Cadiz), in Corsica at Alalia, and in S Italy at Elea (Velia).

Liberated from Persian rule by Alexander the Great, the Phocaeans sided with the Seleucids against the Romans and, as a consequence, their city was besieged, captured and looted in 190 BC. They were in conflict with Rome again c 133 BC, when they supported the claim of Aristonicus to the throne of Pergamum. (See above.) On this occasion they were saved from Roman wrath by the intercession of their daughter colony, Massalia.

During the Byzantine period Phocaea was an episcopal see. Later, during the Middle Ages, it was occupied by the Genoese, who shipped alum and other products from its port. The city was captured by the Ottomans in 1455.

Pottery sherds and architectural fragments discovered by French archaeologists in the early part of this century established that ancient Phocaea lies under the modern town of Eski Foça. Traces of a temple dated to the middle of the 6C BC, which is believed to have been dedicated to Athena, were found near the site of the modern secondary school. The Genoese occupation is recalled by the *13C fortress*, which crowns a peninsula overlooking the S harbour.

About 8km from the junction for Eski Foça are the villages of *Buruncuk* and *Yanık Köy*. On a hill rising 91m above Buruncuk is the site of a city believed to be that of ancient LARISA.

History. Homer speaks of the 'warlike Pelasgians who dwelt around fertile Larisa', and the site near Buruncuk would fit the city mentioned in the 'Iliad'. Allies of the Trojans, their leader, Hippothous, was slain during the siege. Some time after their arrival from Greece, the Aeolian invaders built a fortress near Larisa, which they named Neonteichos. From this base they conducted sorties against the Pelasgians, until eventually they conquered them. In 546 BC, after Cyrus had overrun Lydia, he moved Egyptians troops, who had assisted Croesus, to Larisa. As a result the city was sometimes referred to from that time onward as 'Egyptian Larisa'. During the Hellenistic period the fortunes of Larisa declined so that by the 1C AD it appears to have been little more than a hamlet.

A section of the ancient *paved road* still leads up to the acropolis. Protected by substantial *walls*, a part of which may be seen on the NE side, this contains the remains of two *temples* and a structure, which has been dubbed 'the palace' by the archaeologists. The city's necropolis was sited on the E slope of the hill and in a valley that lies below it. The remains of a number of tumulus tombs may be seen there.

The site at *Yanık Köy*, which has not been excavated, crowns a hill above the village. Apart from the remains of *defensive walls* on the summit and on the hillside there is little to be seen.

Shortly after Buruncuk road 550/E24 passes through the small town of *Menemen*, whose vineyards produce grapes used in the making of İzmir's wines. To the left of the road the bare, brown sides of Yamanlar Dağı dominate the approach to the city. Soon after the turning on the right at Ciğli, which leads to İzmir's *airport*, the crowded suburbs that clothe the hillsides come into view. Then the road follows the magnificent curve of İzmir Körfezi until it reaches the city centre.

7 İzmir

According to the 1985 census **İZMIR**, the third largest city in Turkey, had a population of 1,489,817, which was increasing by a phenomenal 39 per cent a year. After İstanbul the second busiest port in the country, it is an important road and rail junction and is linked to Turkey's principal cities and many European capitals by frequent direct flights from Çiğli Airport. Each year İzmir is host to an important International Fair, where Turkish and foreign exhibitors display their wares.

The city's splendid setting on the steep hills that surround the blue expanse of İzmir Körfezi, its wide palm-lined boulevards, smart shops, hotels and restaurants, and the bustle of its busy port combine with the mixture of simplicity and exoticism to be found in the old quarter to produce an attractive, elegant amalgam. İzmir enjoys a pleasant climate. In summer the temperature, which can be oppressively hot in the Aegean, is pleasantly modified by the İmbat, a refreshing breeze, which on most days blows in from the sea.

İzmir is an excellent centre for visiting the ancient sites of Pergamum, Sardis, Ephesus, Priene, Miletus and Didyma, all of which are within easy driving distance of the city. For those without their own transport there are frequent bus services to Bergama for Pergamum, to Sartmustafa for Sardis, and to Selçuk and Kuşadası for Ephesus. In addition, there are many special tours bookable through local travel agencies to these sites, and to Priene, Miletus and Didyma. Visits to Teos, Clazomenae, Çeşme, Colophon, Claros and Notium are possible by dolmuş and local buses. However, these services are slow and in some cases relatively infrequent, so the journeys may require careful planning. A representative selection of finds, not only from the city, but from a number of sites in the surrounding area are exhibited in İzmir's modern archaeological museum.

Information and Accommodation. The principal *Tourism Information Office* is at Gaziosmanpaşa Bulv. 10/A near the THY town-terminal and Büyük Efes hotel. This can provide up-to-date information about accommodation, restaurants, travel agencies, museum opening hours and admission fees, and transportation in the city, inter-city and to the surrounding countryside.

There is a wide range of accommodation available in İzmir. This extends from the luxurious, and expensive, Büyük Efes hotel to small pensions providing very basic facilities. Near Basmane railway station there are some good, medium-priced hotels like *Billur* and the new *Hisar*, which has an excellent in-house restaurant.

During the period of the İzmir International Fair (mid August to mid September), and when smaller, specialised exhibitions are being held in the city, it can be very difficult to get accommodation of any kind. Applications for accommodation should be made as far in advance as possible.

Food served in İzmir's premier hotels is of excellent quality. In addition, some of the finest Turkish cuisine may be enjoyed in one of the many restaurants that overlook the sea on Atatürk Cad. (sometimes called Birinci Kordon). A pleasant evening may be spent at Karşıyaka on the N side of the bay, where restaurants line the waterfront. There are frequent ferryboats from Konak. The night-time journey under the stars will appeal to the romantic traveller.

Post Office and Banks. İzmir's principal post office is at Cumhuriyet Meydanı. (See city plan.) Branches of most of the main Turkish banks may be found in various parts of the city.

Consulates. Because of İzmir's importance as a major port more than 20 foreign countries are represented in the city. The British Consulate is at 1442 Sok. 49, Alsancak, the United States Consulate at Atatürk Cad. 386, the French Consulate at Cumhuriyet Bulv. 153, the Italian Consulate at Talatpaşa Bulv. 75/ 3 and the German Consulate at Atatürk Cad. 260.

Transport. Most travellers arrive in İzmir by long-distance bus. From the bus station, which is on the NE outskirts of the city, there is a free courtesy-service by minibus to the centre. However, this operates infrequently and any traveller with luggage is advised to take a taxi. (Taxis are relatively inexpensive.) For budget travellers there are dolmuş taxis, but these are usually full to bursting point and consequently not very comfortable.

Most bus and dolmuş services operating in the city and in the surrounding countryside start from *Konak*. (See city plan.)

Train travellers arrive at Basmane Railway Station. This is in the city-centre near the Kültür Parkı and is a regular stop on many bus and dolmuş routes.

There are frequent buses from İzmir Airport at Çiğli to the THY town-terminal, which is located near the Büyük Efes hotel. The inexpensive journey takes about 30 minutes.

Arrivals by sea disembark at *Yeni Limanı*, the new harbour, in Alsancak. From there it is an easy journey by taxi, bus or dolmuş to the centre.

Visitors arriving by car may have difficulty in finding parking places. They should seek assistance from their hotel reception clerks.

Churches. The cornerstone of the Cathedral of St. John the Evangelist, Şehit Nevres Bulv. 29 was laid in 1862 and the building was completed in 1874. Donations were received from many sources. The Catholics of Lyons in France, which had been converted to Christianity in the 2C by missionaries from Smyrna, were particularly generous in their contributions. So also was Sultan Abdül Aziz (1861–76), who made a gift of 11,000 gold Turkish Lira to help provide this splendid church for his Christian subjects.

The interior of the Cathedral is richly decorated. In the sanctuary, in addition to a fine painting of St. John the Evangelist, by A. von Hammer, there are pictures of St. Augustine, St. Andrew, St. Athanasius, St. John Chrysostom and of Smyrna's own martyr St. Polycarp. This octogenarian bishop of Smyrna refused to deny his faith and was burned to death in the stadium in 156 during the course of a festival and games organised by the proconsul Statius Quadratus (see below). Also commemorated in the Cathedral is St. Vincent de Paul, founder of the Vincentians or Lazarists, the order which has served the Christian community in Smyrna for many centuries.

Since 1965, by permission of the Archbishop of İzmir, both Protestant and Catholic members of the NATO forces and their dependants stationed in İzmir, worship regularly in this church.

The monument of Archbishop Vincent Spaccapierra, Apostolic Delegate to Asia Minor and to the Kingdom of Greece, Archbishop of Smyrna, who dedicated the Cathedral on 14 June 1874, may be found on the N side of Cathedral grounds.

There also the Catholic churches of St. Polycarp at 2354 Sok. 41 and St. Rosaire at 1461 Sok. 8. İzmir's Anglican Church, which has a resident chaplain, is in Alsancak on the corner of Atatürk Cad. and Mahmut Esat Bozkurt Cad.

Museums. As well as İzmir's fine new Archaeological Museum at Konak, there is the Atatürk Museum on Atatürk Bulv. An Ethnographical Museum will be opened shortly in an old Turkish house near the Archaeological Museum.

Shopping. İzmir has an excellent range of shops from the smart boutiques on Atatürk Cad. and in Alsancak to the myriad of small concerns in the Bazaar. All of the usual products—carpets, kilims, jewellery, brassware, clothing—are available. There are also excellent fruit markets, where İzmir's famous fresh figs may be enjoyed in season.

Getting Around. The most enjoyable way to explore İzmir is on foot. However, the distances from the residential quarter of Alsancak in the N to Konak in the S and Kadifekale, the ancient Mt Pagus, in the SE are considerable, and to be enjoyable any such exploration should not be hurried. Travellers, who are not pressed for time, might like to spend several days in the city, making it their headquarters and interspersing expeditions to Pergamum, Ephesus and other sites in the surrounding countryside with visits to the Archaeological Museum, the Bazaar, Kadifekale, the Agora and Old Smyrna. These places represent the irreducible minimum which every visitor to İzmir should attempt to see.

History. Traditionally the birthplace of Homer, who was honoured there in classical times in the Homereium, İzmir, anciently SMYRNA, has a long and distinguished history. The obvious attractions of the site appear to have drawn settlers from the earliest times. The first traces of occupation, which date from the third millennium BC, were discovered at Bayraklı on the N edge of the modern city. This site was excavated first by a team from Ankara University in collaboration with the British School at Athens and latterly by Turkish archaeologists under the direction of Professor Akurgal.

During the second millennium BC the settlement appears to have come under Hittite influence. By some clever detective work George Bean has linked this fact with the legend that the city was founded by the Amazons—on Egyptian monuments Hittite warriors were generally depicted wearing long skirt-like garments, which gives them a somewhat feminine look.

Archaeology has confirmed the story in Herodotus that Smyrna, as the city was known in antiquity, came under the control of Ionian Greeks from Colophon in the 9C BC. Then after a period of considerable prosperity, this early foundation was subjected to sustained attacks by the Lydians, so that eventually it was reduced to a state of impoverishment and decay.

The city was refounded by Alexander the Great as the result of a mystic experience. While resting during a hunt on Mt Pagus, he was told in a dream by the tutelary Nemeseis of the place to establish a new city there. The oracle of Apollo at Claros, having been consulted about the dream, gave the following advice:

'Three and four times happy shall those men be hereafter
Who shall dwell on Pagus beyond the sacred Meles.'

Alexander spurred on by this pronouncement, entrusted the building of the new city to his generals and successors Antigonus and Lysimachus. During the Hellenistic period Smyrna vacillated in its loyalty, sometimes supporting the Seleucids, sometimes the Attalids. Displaying the same diplomatic skill—and inconstancy—in its dealing with Rome, it continued to prosper and, like a number of other cities in the Roman province of Asia, was ornamented with many beautiful buildings. Favoured by several emperors including Hadrian and Caracalla, the city was reconstructed in AD 178 with the help of generous donations from Marcus Aurelius after it had suffered severe damage from an earthquake.

With the adoption of Christianity as the state religion Smyrna played a vital part in the development of the church, becoming an important episcopal see. The words of St. John to the first small group of Christians, 'Only be faithful till death, and I will give you the crown of life,' (Revelation 2.10.11) must have been recalled by those who witnessed the martyrdom of St. Polycarp, Bishop of Smyrna, in 156. Betrayed to the authorities, he was brought to the arena where a pagan festival was taking place. Ordered by the proconsul Statius Quadratus to deny his faith, Polycarp refused saying, 'Eighty and six years I have served Him and He has done me no ill; how then can I blaspheme my King who hath served me?' The enraged crowd in the arena shouted, 'This is the teacher of Asia; this is the destroyer of our gods; this is the father of the Christians,' and placing him on a pyre burned him to death.

Until the Arab raids in the 7C Smyrna continued to be a prosperous and important trading centre. Towards the end of the 11C the Selçuk Turks advanced as far as the Aegean coast for the first time and captured the city. It remained in their hands until 1097, when it was recovered by the Byzantines. From then until the latter part of the 15C, when it was taken by Mehmet I and incorporated in the Ottoman Empire, Byzantines, Crusaders, Genoese and Turks fought each other for its possession.

Members of the Society of Dilettanti made Smyrna their headquarters in the middle of the 18C. Though ravaged by earthquakes at that time, the city continued to maintain its commercial importance. Traders from Britain, the Netherlands and France established offices in there and an Anglican church was built to cater for the growing British community. According to Kinglake it was known as 'Giaour Izmir' (Infidel Smyrna) to the Turks, because of the number of foreigners, who lived and worked there.

In the last days of the war between Greece and Turkey in 1921/22 the city was almost burned to the ground. Many fine old buildings were destroyed and others damaged beyond repair. The İzmir which rose from the ashes of that conflagration is the city visible today.

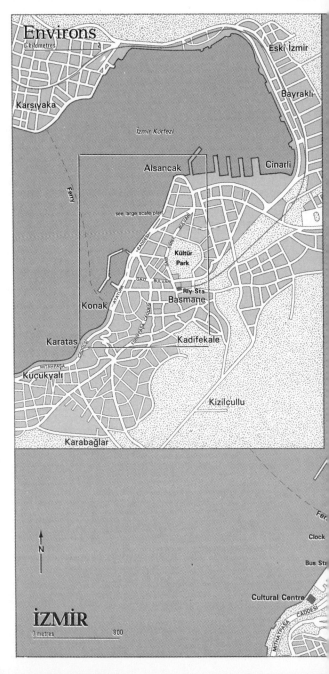

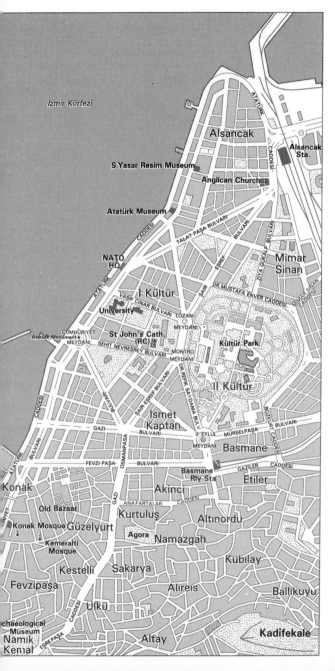

İzmir Körfezi

Alsancak

Alsancak Sta.

S Yaşar Resim Museum

Anglican Church

Atatürk Museum

ATATÜRK CADDESİ

TALAT PAŞA BULVARI

ESREF BULVARI

ZITA GUKAL BULVARI

NATO HQ

Mimar Sinan

MİMAR SİNAN CADDESİ

DR MUSTAFA ENVER CADDESİ

I Kültür

VASIF CINAR BULVARI

University

LOZAN MEYDANI

St John's Cath. (RC)

ŞEHİT NEVRESBEY BULVARI

MONTRO MEYDANI

Kültür Park

CUMHURİYET MEYDANI

Atatürk Monument

ATATÜRK BULVARI

ŞAİR ESREF BULVARI

II Kültür

BOZKURT BULVARI

İsmet Kaptan

DR REFIK SANDAMA BULV.

MURSELPAŞA CADDESİ

9 EYLÜL MEYDANI

Basmane

GAZİ BULVARI

OSMANPAŞA

Basmane Rly Sta

GAZİLER CADDESİ

FEVZİ PAŞA BULVARI

Etiler

Konak

Akıncı

ANAFARTALAR CADDESİ

Old Bazaar

Kurtuluş

Altınordu

Konak Mosque

Güzelyurt

Agora

Kemeraltı Mosque

Namazgah

Kubilay

Kestelli

Sakarya

Fevzipaşa

Alireis

Ballıkuyu

Ülkü

ESREPAŞA CADDESİ

Archaeological Museum

Namık Kemal

Altay

Kadifekale

The *Kültür Parkı*, site of the İzmir International Fair, is a large, pleasant oasis of greenery in the city-centre. The exhibition pavilions line a network of cool, shaded alleyways and are surrounded by gardens. There are several small restaurants and a number of kiosks offering light refreshments in the park.

The waterfront gardens at *Konak* are located in one of the busiest areas of the city. From the late Ottoman *clock-tower*, described by Goodwin as a 'mauresque bibelot', which has become İzmir's unofficial symbol, to the open-air city bus terminal there is a continuous bustle. Indolent strollers savouring the refreshing breeze of the İmbat mingle with impatient passengers waiting for a bus or dolmuş or a ferryboat to Karşıyaka.

A few metres from the sea-front, behind Anafartalar Cad. in a warren of twisting lanes and narrow courts, are the myriad shops that make up İzmir's *bazaar*. There a bewildering range of goods—everything from flowers to antiques—is on offer at bargain prices.

From Konak it is only a few minutes walk to İzmir's **Archaeological Museum**. Cross the main road by the Opera-House and follow the path that climbs the gentle slope of the municipal gardens. A flight of steps leads to the main entrance.

The museum houses an excellent collection of finds from ancient Smyrna and from a number of other sites in the Aegean. Most of the exhibits are labelled in Turkish and English and this information is supplemented at various places in the galleries by panels which give useful background information. There is no guide-book to the collection and none is planned at present.

In the ENTRANCE HALL there is a kiosk where postcards, transparencies and booklets are sold. To the right is a small cloakroom and toilets. Light refreshments are usually available from the museum bar.

The exhibits in the entrance hall are changed from time to time. At present a number of *Roman portrait heads* are exhibited there. These include two female heads from Pergamum, one from the Antonine period (2C AD), the other from 1C AD; a 4C male head also from Pergamum, and an Antiochus-type head from Metropolis (Torbalı).

From the circular opening in the centre of the entrance hall you will get an excellent overhead view of a late *Roman mosaic* found near Kadifekele, which is displayed on the lower floor. By the door that leads to the gallery on the right-hand side of the entrance hall there is a small sculpture of a headless *Dionysus and a satyr*. Dating from the 2C AD this was found at Ephesus.

The BASEMENT GALLERY is devoted mainly to large sculptures and sarcophagi. These include: the head and forearm of a colossal statue of Domitian from the temple dedicated to him at Ephesus; several decorated sarcophagi; the 1C AD head of youthful, Julio-Claudian prince from Stratoniceia (Eskihisar); the lid of a Roman 3C AD sarcophagus showing a reclining couple; a funeral stele with books, another with theatre masks; a reconstructed *Early Bronze Age tomb* (3000–2500 BC) with skeleton from Iasus; two archaic statues of lions, one from İzmir, the other from Bayındır; a 2C AD *sarcophagus* from Laodiceia decorated with portrait heads, erotes, medusa heads and garlands; a late Hellenistic funeral stele from Tralles; three decorated *terracotta sarcophagi*, one from Mordoğan, one from Clazomenae and one from Smyrna, and two 2C AD *portrait statues* from Ephesus, one of a sophist, the other of the magnate Flavius Damianus.

The BASEMENT LONG GALLERY contains Roman *statues* of

Poseidon and *Demeter* from an altar in the Agora of Smyrna; *sculptures* and *reliefs* from the 3C BC Belevi tomb, and 4C and 5C BC *capitals* and *pillars* from Claros and Didyma.

In the LONG GALLERY on the right-hand side of the entrance hall are exhibited statues and reliefs from the Archaic, Classical and Roman periods. These include an archaic *statue of a woman* from Erythrae; a Classical statue of a seated man from Claros; small statues and reliefs of Cybele dating from 30 BC to AD 395 from various sites in W Anatolia; the bust of a priestess of Isis from Mylasa; the Hellenistic statue of a young woman from Magnesia; the late Hellenistic *female 'twins'* from Metropolis; statuettes and heads of various figures—Zeus, Apollo, a satyr, etc.—from W Anatolia dating from 30 BC to AD 395; the 2C AD Roman copy of a late Hellenistic *bronze statue of a runner*, found in the sea off Cyme; a 2C AD Roman copy of a 5C BC *head of Aspasa* from Ephesus; statuettes of Aphrodite 30 BC to AD 395 from W Anatolia; an early Roman male head from Miletus; the Hellenistic bust of a woman from Stratoniceia (Eskihisar); a late Hellenistic funeral stele from İzmir; the archaic head of a young man, and an archaic headless *kore* from Claros.

In the end alcove: a 2C AD chubby, *sleeping Eros* from Ephesus; a Roman head of Hermes from Pergamum; a late Hellenistic head of Athena from Cyme and various female heads from Pergamum and Ephesus.

In the PARALLEL GALLERY there are statuettes of gods and goddesses from W Anatolia 30 BC to AD 395; a headless 2C AD statue of Aphrodite from Claros; a 2C AD *statue of Antinous as Androclus* or, as Akurgal claims, of a hunter from the Vedius Gymnasium, Ephesus; a late Hellenistic head of Hercules from Pergamum; a 2C AD herm of a bearded Hermes from Ephesus; and heads of Dionysus, Pan, etc., from W Anatolia 30 BC to AD 395; a Roman statue of a priest from Halicarnassus; the Roman statue of a sophist from Ephesus, and 2C AD statues of Athena and Tyche from Ephesus.

In the anteroom on the FIRST FLOOR note the Roman mosaic from Smyrna showing a sleeping Aphrodite and Eros. Nearby are two *Roman reliefs* from Ephesus, one depicting Dionysus and nymphs, the other Dionysus visiting the Athenian actor Ikarios. (Compare the latter with a similar relief in the Townley Marbles collection, British Museum.) The RIGHT-HAND GALLERY contains displays of objects found during the excavation of a number of sites in Aeolia and Ionia. From Iasus there are vases and terracottas dating from the Archaic to the Roman periods (700 BC–AD 395). From Miletus Mycenaean, Protogeometric and archaic pottery (1400–300 BC). From Pitane black-figure vases, terracottas, small bronzes, and knucklebones from the Archaic and Orientalising periods (625–480 BC). From Smyrna pottery from the Early Bronze Age to the Archaic period (3000–700 BC), black- and red-figure vases and small heads and statuettes from the Archaic to the Classical period (700–300 BC). From Pitane pottery of the Orientalising period (625–480 BC). From Foça lamps and black-figure vases from the Archaic to the Roman period (700 BC–AD 395). From Iasus pottery from the Bronze Age (3000–2000 BC). From Erythrae Archaic pottery (700–450 BC), terracottas, bronze arrowheads, a bronze decorated penis. Hellenistic terracottas from Myrina dated to 190 BC, including a *head decorated with fruit and flowers* and delicately executed erotes. From Pitane amphorae from the Orientalising period (625–480 BC). From the temple of Athena, Bayraklı, Smyrna a damaged head of a female deity, which is believed to have come from Cyprus, and a decorated capital.

In the LEFT-HAND GALLERY there are Early Bronze Age (3000–2500 BC) pitchers with beaked spouts, Mycenaean pottery (1600–1200 BC) and Classical period (450–300) red-figure pottery all from W Anatolia; Roman pottery (30 BC–AD 395) including a number of inscribed, decorated flasks; terracottas from the Archaic, Classical and Hellenistic periods (700–30 BC), some bearing traces of colour, from various sites in W Anatolia; lamps from the Archaic, Classical, Hellenistic, Roman and Byzantine periods (700 BC–AD 1453), some with erotic scenes.

In the END GALLERY there is a display of *carved seals* with magnified colour illustrations of the designs.

In wall cases there are bronze artefacts from the Archaic to the Byzantine era (700 BC–AD 1453), including lamps, balances, daggers, short swords and spear heads; Roman terracottas from W Anatolia; Byzantine pottery (AD 395–1453); Hellenistic pottery (300–30 BC); Archaic period (700–450 BC) black figure vases from W Anatolia; Early Bronze Age (3000–2500 BC) pottery from W Anatolia; Chalcolitic Age (5500–3000 BC) and Archaic and Orientalising period (700–480 BC) pottery from W Anatolia; two early Hellenistic (300–250 BC) hydrias, black with decoration on rim; Hellenistic and Roman glass (300 BC–AD 395) from W Anatolia.

If the *Museum Treasury* is locked, application for admission should be made to one of the attendants. It contains a rich collection of Roman, Byzantine and Venetian coins. Particularly interesting is a hoard found at Tralles. This includes fine specimens from the reigns of Trajan, Antoninus Pius, Caracalla, Elagabalus, Julia Domna, Geta and Gallienus.

There are several fine small *bronze votive offerings* from various periods, also personal ornaments and jewellery from the 5C BC to the 15C AD. Note the beautiful 4C BC **head of Demeter** found in the sea near Bodrum.

In the garden to the rear of the museum there is a large collection of architectural fragments and sarcophagi from various sites. The exhibits in this area are currently being rearranged.

A new *Ethnographical Museum* will be opened shortly in the old Ottoman house to the right of the main entrance to the Archaeological Museum.

Dolmuş taxis leave at frequent intervals from Konak for *Kadifekale*, the ancient Mt Pagus. The journey takes c 15 minutes. No certain trace has been found there of the Hellenistic and Roman fortifications that once dominated the city. The imposing ruins visible today all date from the Middle Ages.

From Kadifekale there is an excellent view over the harbour towards Karşıyaka. To the W it is possible to discern the shape of the arena where St. Polycarp was martyred and the outline of the Agora at the foot of the hill is clearly visible. Photographers will have plenty of opportunities to exercise their skills, particularly in attempting to capture the spectacular sunsets.

The interior of the fortifications is now used as a playground by children from the neighbourhood. They clamber, shouting, over the walls or play stealthy games of hide and seek in the cavernous vaults. Although present-day visitors are in no danger from cannonballs, on occasions they may be forced to retreat from flying footballs!

Shelter and sustenance may be obtained inside the fortifications from a small café, which serves tea and soft drinks.

To get to the *Agora*, return by dolmuş to Konak and ask to be directed to Anafartalar Cad. From this street it is only a few minutes' walk to the site, which is called *Namazgah* in Turkish. A more interesting and not at all difficult route is through the winding streets of an old quarter of the city. This is an easy downhill stroll from Kadifekale, which should not take more than 20 minutes.

Occupying an area of c 120m by 80m, the Agora was excavated by German and Turkish archaeologists between 1932 and 1941. Surrounded on the W and N by porticoes it had a large altar dedicated to Zeus in the centre. Two statues, one of Poseidon, the other of Demeter, believed to come from this altar, are in now displayed in the basement of İzmir's Archaeological Museum.

The N stoa was on two levels and rested on a substantial basement. The vaults of this structure are still visible. Trials were conducted in an exedra towards the W end of the stoa. A substantial part of the colonnade on the W side of the Agora is still standing. Note the *portrait head of Faustina*, the wife of Marcus Aurelius, on an arch in the colonnade. This may commemorate the handsome contribution made by the emperor towards the reconstruction of Smyrna after the earthquake of AD 178.

Towards the E side of the Agora there are several architectural fragments bearing medieval coats of arms and a stone slab marked out with rectangles which may have been used as a gaming board.

Apart from traces of the *Roman theatre*, which may be found among modern houses near Basmane railway station, the only other remains of Smyrna's past are the *Roman aqueducts* on the road to Ephesus, the so-called 'Baths of Diana', and the site of the first city of Smyrna at Bayraklı.

Strabo states that there was a Homereium, 'a quadrangular portico containing a shrine and wooden statue' of Homer in the city, traditionally thought to be his birthplace. He was associated with the river Meles, which has been identified with the modern Halka Pınar, a small river to the N of Alsancak. This forms a large pool popularly known as the *Baths of Diana*, although no very firm connection has been established between it and the goddess. A statue discovered nearby was taken to represent Artemis. The pool, which covers the foundations of an ancient building and is surrounded by architectural fragments, may be found in the grounds of the İzmir Water Company. Some authorities suggest that this is the place where Homer composed his great epics.

In remote antiquity the area occupied by the modern suburb of *Bornova* was under the sea. It was here that the first settlers in Smyrna built their city on a peninsula that projected into the N part of the bay. Before it was diverted, the river Hermus, during the course of centuries brought down large deposits of soil, which caused the land area to be extended. As a result the site of this early foundation is now some distance inland on a hill in Bayraklı, known as Tepekule.

Tepekule was excavated first by a joint expedition organised by the British School of Archaeology in Athens and Ankara University and later by a Turkish team under the direction of Professor Akurgal. The site, which is rather overgrown and difficult to understand, is likely to appeal mainly to specialists.

The earliest settlement at Tepekule has been dated to the middle of the third millennium BC. Substantial finds of Protogeometric pottery at the site suggest that the first Greek colonists arrived there in the 10C BC.

In about 600 BC King Alyattes of Lydia laid siege to Smyrna and captured it. A large heap of soil discovered at the W side of the site is believed to have been used by the Lydians as an assault ramp. Although it was later reoccupied, the site remained of minor importance and was abandoned completely sometime in the 4C BC.

Among the remains found by the archaeologists at Tepekule are those of houses dating from the 9C to the 7C BC. The most important discovery, however, was of a *temple* dedicated to Athena. This, the oldest E Greek temple or shrine discovered in Asia Minor, was constructed towards the end of the 7C BC. It was altered and enlarged on several occasions, notably after its destruction by the Lydians. Capitals and column bases found there, some of which are exhibited in İzmir's Archaeological Museum, are remarkable for the beauty of their design and delicacy of their execution.

8 Excursions from İzmir

Using **İzmir** (see Rte 7) as a base it is possible to make some interesting excursions not only to Sardis and Ephesus (see Rtes 9 and 10), but to a number of the smaller and less well-known sites in the surrounding area. By private transport these trips are easy to arrange. The distances are comparatively short, so the route depends largely on the number of sites that one wishes to see in a day. Travellers using dolmuş taxis or buses will need to plan carefully. Buses may not always leave or arrive on time and dolmuş taxis depart, when they are full. To avoid being stranded, it is advisable to find out the approximate time of the last bus or dolmuş back to İzmir. Sometimes these leave surprisingly early in the afternoon.

Refreshments of some kind are usually available, even in the smallest villages.

A. The Baths of Agamemnon, Clazomenae, Erythrae and Çeşme

Total distance c 81km. **İzmir**—R300 c 11km *Baths of Agamemnon*—25km *Urla* (c 8km *Clazomenae*)—(35km *Mordoğan*—18km *Karaburun*)—c 37km *Ilica* (c 15km *İldır / Erythrae*)—8km **Çeşme**.

This excursion covers sites and resorts on the N coast of the peninsula that lies to the W of İzmir. Leave the city by road 300 in the direction of Çeşme.This runs for some distance near the sea. After c 10km a turning to the left leads 1km to the *Baths of Agamemnon*. According to a legend Agamemnon was advised by an oracle to bring to this place those soldiers who had been wounded during the campaign against Troy. The baths were known and used in Roman times but there are no visible remains of any great antiquity. When Chandler visited the site in the summer of 1765, he saw a quantity of coagulated sheep blood on the pavement. This, he was told, was often used instead of soap for shaving, an operation frequently carried out in the baths.

A number of springs deliver water, which has an average temperature of 23° C and a high sulphur content. This is believed to be an excellent specific for rheumatism, skin diseases and sciatica. The establishment is still patronised by visitors, some from İzmir but many from more distant parts of Turkey, who come there in search of a cure.

After c 25km a turning to the right at *Urla* leads to the village of *Urla İskelesi*, which is near the peninsula on which the site of ancient CLAZOMENAE is located. Today there is a quarantine station and a hospital for persons suffering from bone disease on the peninsula. To avoid any problems of access to the site, it is advisable to seek the assistance of the Tourism Information Office in İzmir. Its staff should be able to provide information about any permit that may be required.

Very little of the ancient city remains to be seen. Like many of the ancient settlements on the Aegean coast it has been stripped of its stone, which was transported to İstanbul for the construction of new buildings. Clazomenae is another site, which is mainly of interest to specialists.

In antiquity the city was famous for the beautifully decorated terracotta sarcophagi, which were produced there. More than 200 of these dating from the 6C BC were discovered in a small sheltered valley to the SW of Urla Iskelesi. The technique developed by artists to decorate vases was employed to ornament the sarcophagi on the sides and the lid with elaborate scenes of warfare and mythical beasts in heraldic poses. Because of their relative fragility and weight—the lid of a specimen in the British Museum weighs 900kg—they were not transported any great distance from the city.

Unfortunately, a large number of the sarcophagi were destroyed in the fighting that took place in the 1920s towards the end of the Greek-Turkish war. One of the survivors is displayed in the basement gallery of the İzmir Archaeological Museum and there are others in İstanbul and in various European museums.

History. 'Fretted by the incessant gales from the mouth of the gulf,' according to Professor Cook, 'the people of Clazomenae grew up restless and volatile'. Strabo states that the city, one of the 12 members of the Panionium, was founded by Paralus. Archaeologists believe that the first Greek settlers arrived there in the 10C BC. The original site of the city appears to have been on the mainland, but, possibly because of fear of the Persians, the inhabitants moved to an island offshore in the 5C BC. There they remained, relatively secure in their isolation, until the defeat of Darius by Alexander released them from danger. Then, possibly as a result of direct orders from Alexander, the people of Clazomenae constructed a causeway, which linked the island with the mainland. Traces of this structure, which was 700m long by 9m wide, may be seen by the side of its modern counterpart. In the mid 18C Chandler had an exciting ride across the ancient structure, 'we were ten minutes', he writes, 'in passing over it, the waves, which were impelled by a strong inbat, breaking over in a very formidable manner, as high as the bellies of our horses.'

The Clazomenians supported the Romans against Antiochus of Syria, so ensuring their continued prosperity. However, as Smyrna increased in importance, so Clazomenae appears to have declined. At the time of the arrival of the Ottomans on the Aegean coast in the 15C, it was little more than a village.

Clazomenae was the birthplace of two philosophers, Anaxagoras (c 500–428 BC) and Scopelianus (fl. c AD 90). At about the age of twenty Anaxagoras went to Athens. Counting Pericles and Euripides among his friends and pupils, he became a well-known and controversial philosopher. He taught that the universe was composed of an unlimited number of substances. These, under the guidance of an independent intelligence, which he called Nous (Mind), combined to produce all identifiable substances. His teaching was considered heretical and he was saved from prosecution, and possibly death, by the intervention of Pericles. Removing himself from Athens, he went to Lampsacus, where he died in 428 BC.

In the field of astronomy, Anaxogoras was the first to explain the working of solar eclipses. Portions of his treatise, 'On Nature', still exist.

Scopelianus' main claim to fame was his successful plea to Domitian in AD 92 against the harsh provisions of an imperial decree that would have required the destruction of all the vineyards in Ionia. For this he was greatly honoured by the citizens of Smyrna, where he lived and taught.

On the W side of the peninsula a short distance from the causeway is a *cave* containing a sacred well. Also on the W beyond the quarantine station are the remains of an ancient *harbour-wall*. Part of the *city wall* and of a *quay* are on the NW extremity of the peninsula. On the hill nearby the outline of the *theatre*, which is mentioned by Chandler, may be seen and there are traces of a building which is believed to have been a *temple*.

From Urla continue in the direction of Çeşme for c 12km.

A minor road to the right leads to the village of 35km *Mordoğan*, where protogeometric and other pottery and a terracotta sarcophagus of the Clazomenae-type were found. The sarcophagus is exhibited in the basement gallery of the İzmir Archaeological Museum. From Mordoğan the road continues its narrow twisting course for a further 18km to *Karaburun*. To compensate for the difficult driving there are some fine views over the sea.

On returning to the main road continue in the direction of Çeşme. About 15km after Uzunkuyu you reach *Ilica*, a small summer resort much favoured by the citizens of İzmir. Here a turning right leads to the small village of 15km *İldır*, which covers part of the ancient city of ERYTHRAE.

History. According to Pausanias Erythrae derives its name from Erythrus, the 'Red', son of Rhadamanthys, who came here with a band of settlers from Crete. Later, immigrants from Lycia, Caria and Pamphylia and other parts of Ionia were added to this nucleus and the city was ruled by descendants of King Codrus of Athens. Erythrae became a member of the Panionion and, making full use of its excellent harbour, which was sheltered and protected by the islands known as the Hippoi, the horses, it expanded its trade and prospered.

Under Lydian domination c 560 BC, it became subject to the Persians in 545 BC. Later it sometimes supported Athens, sometimes Sparta. Towards the middle of the 4C BC Erythrae was cultivating good relations with Mausolus, the ruler of Caria (377–353 BC). At about the same time it concluded a treaty of mutual assistance with Assos.

Liberated by Alexander, it came under the influence of the Attalids of Pergamum. The Romans gave it the status of a free city attached to the province of Asia. Like Clazomenae it was later overshadowed by its large and powerful neighbour, Smyrna.

Under the Ottomans Erythrae reverted to the state of a village and was largely forgotten. By the time Chandler visited the site in the middle of the 18C, the area had acquired a reputation for banditry. Taking no chances for his safety, he slept there guarded by an armed attendant, while other armed servants protected the periphery of the camp and the enclosure where the horses were hobbled.

Erythrae has also been plundered of its stone, so little remains of its former splendour. There is a large stretch of the late 4C BC *wall*, which guarded the landward approaches to the city. Reinforced by towers and pierced at intervals by gates, this is between 4m and 5m thick and in places still stands to a considerable height. Small sections of the fortifications that protected the acropolis remain, but the principal ruin in this area is that of the *theatre*. Excavated by Turkish archaeologists in 1963, only the stairs remain relatively intact. Most of the seating has disappeared and there is no trace of the stage-building.

Between the theatre and the N wall there is a fine *mosaic floor*. The *aqueduct* to the S of the site dates from the Byzantine era. During earlier periods the city received its water through terracotta pipes, as the stream which flows inside the fortified area is not suitable for drinking. This may be the river Aleon, which, according to Pliny, had the unusual property of encouraging the growth of body-hair.

Erythrae had a famous Sibyl, who was surpassed in importance only by the Sibyl of Cumae. According to Pausanias she was called Herophile and was 'born from a nymph and a shepherd of the district called Theodorus'. Greatly respected in Roman times, over 1000 of her prophetic verses were taken to Rome in 83 BC after the temple of

Captoline Jupiter had been destroyed by fire. Towards the end of the 19C a certain M. Fontrier claimed to have discovered her cave. Unfortunately, the exact location of this has been forgotten and it can no longer be identified.

No trace has been found of the temple of Hercules at Erythrae. According to Pausanias a statue of the god arrived in the city under miraculous circumstances. It had been placed on a raft in Tyre (Phoenicia), and sailed through the Ionian sea to the island of Chios. Both the Erythraians and Chians attempted to capture this mysterious image, but were unable to do so. A blind Erythraian fisherman named Phormion saw in a dream that the image could be brought ashore if the women of his city fashioned their hair into a rope and fastened it to the raft. The Erythraian women refused to sacrifice their hair, but a number of Thracian female slaves gave up their long tresses. The statue was landed and placed in a temple dedicated to Hercules. As a reward only Thracian women were allowed to enter the Herakleion, where the rope made from their hair was preserved. Phormion's sight was restored by the god. The Erythraians were so proud of their statue that they depicted it and the Herakleion on their coinage.

Excavations conducted by Professors Akurgal and Bayburtluoğlu have brought to light the site of the Erythraian temple dedicated to

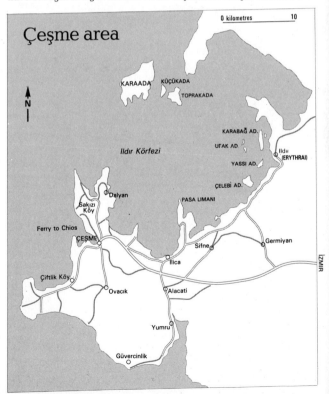

Athena Polias, which is also mentioned by Pausanias. In trenches dug on top of the acropolis, they found a large quantity of pottery and bronze and ivory offerings. An inscription on a bowl stated that the offerings were the property of the temple of Athena. They are now exhibited in a first floor gallery in İzmir's Archaeological Museum.

On returning to road 300 continue to c 8km **Çeşme**. Overlooking a windswept bay, this is a small, rather raffish resort, set in an unexciting landscape. It offers a range of accommodation from the expensive *Altın Yunus* (Golden Dolphin) complex outside the town to small, basic pensions in the centre. There are several reasonably-priced restaurants serving Turkish and 'tourist' dishes. The Tourism Information Office near the harbour in İskele Meydanı can offer information on hotel rates and advise on trips to the Greek island of Chios, including details of the formalities involved, the days and times of sailing.

Near the harbour is a well-preserved 14C *Genoese fortress*. Captured by Beyazit I c 1400, it was enlarged and strengthened by the Ottomans to protect the approaches to İzmir from attack by Christian forces. Nearby are the ruins of a late Ottoman (18C) caravanserai.

The harbour of Çeşme, which now sees little activity apart from the ferry-boat to (10km) *Chios*, was the scene of an attack by the Russian Navy on 5 July 1770, which resulted in the destruction of the Ottoman fleet.

In recent years the town has been developed as a tourist resort and it now attracts a substantial number of Turkish and foreign visitors during the holiday season. There are good beaches around Çeşme, but the sea, even in summer, can be chilly.

B.   Teos, Lebedus, Colophon, Claros and Notium

Total distance to Notium c 95km. **İzmir**—R300 22km *Güzelbahçe*—18km *Seferihisar*—(c 6km *Sığacık / Teos*)—(19km *Doğanbey*—4km *Myonnesus*)—8km *Lebedus*—25km *Bulgurla*—5km *Değirmendere*—1.5km *Colophon*—c 13km *Claros*—2km *Notium*.

Return journey either via 17km **Selçuk** or 20km *Cileme*—5km *Bulgurla*—12km *Cumaovası*.

This is a circular route, which takes the visitor through some interesting countryside to a number of ancient sites and pleasant beaches in the area S of İzmir. Although the roads are of variable quality and require careful and rather slow driving in some parts, it is possible to complete the circuit in one day by using private transport. By bus or dolmuş it is best to divide the route into two parts: İzmir to Teos and İzmir to Claros.

Visitors using Selçuk as a base may find it more convenient to go to Claros, Notium and Colphon by a minor road from there. They should note, however, that this route traverses a marsh and is often waterlogged in bad weather.

Leave **İzmir** by road 300 and continue to 22km Güzelbahçe. A turning to the left just outside the village leads to 18km Seferihisar. From there a road to the right goes to c 6km *Sığacık*, the nearest modern settlement to the site of ancient TEOS.

Sığacık is a pleasant little village nestling in the shadow of a medieval Genoese fortress. The area has been developed in recent years and a short distance away at *Akkum* there are some small hotels and camping places. The clean, sandy beaches near the village offer good bathing.

From Sığacık it is possible to make an interesting excursion by boat to Myonnesus and Lebedus. Visitors continuing by road to Claros will find these sites on or near their route. In the case of Myonnesus a slight diversion, involving a 4km scramble from Doğanbey over a rough track not suitable for vehicles, is required.

History. Teos had an interesting and colourful history. According to Pausanias it was founded at the beginning of the first millennium BC by Minyans from Orchomenus in Boeotia under the leadership of Athamas. Later these settlers were joined by contingents from Ionia and Athens.

From the beginning it would appear that the inhabitants took full advantage of the city's excellent position between two good harbours and developed strong trading interests over a wide area of the E Mediterranean. Early in the 7C BC Teos was of sufficient importance to be proposed by Thales of Miletus as the political centre of the Panionium. After the Persian conquest of Ionia in 546 BC the Teians temporarily abandoned their city and settled at Abdera in Thrace. However, some or all of them returned shortly afterwards, as Teos is recorded as having supplied 17 ships to the Ionian fleet, which was defeated by the Persians at the battle of Lade in 494 BC. The city was liberated from the Persian yoke by Alexander the Great, who considered constructing a canal from Teos to İzmir Körfezi. Later the city came under the control of Antigonus and then of Lysimachus, who moved some of its inhabitants to the new foundation that he had created at Ephesus.

Teos had a large and famous temple dedicated to Dionysus, the god associated, not only with wine, but with the creative and artistic powers of nature. As he was the tutelary genius of drama, it is not surprising that towards the end of the 3C BC Teos was chosen to be the centre in Asia of the Guild of the Artists of Dionysus. These were professional actors and musicians, who performed at the festivals, which were held then in all major centres. At first honoured by their presence, the Teians soon found the artists insufferably arrogant and difficult. After many quarrels between the citizens and members of the guild, the latter were obliged to move to Ephesus. Faring no better there, they were sent to the small settlement of Myonnesus, near Teos, and from there to Lebedus, where they appear to have to have remained.

Teos, which seems to have prospered at first under the Romans, suffered a gradual decline in importance. Like the other Ionian cities it probably could not compete with the growing power and influence of Smyrna. During the Middle Ages and after the Ottoman conquest the remaining population was concentrated in the village of Sığacık.

Richard Chandler, who visited Teos in the middle of the 18C, discovered a wilderness of abandoned ruins. 'We found this city,' he writes, 'almost as desolate as Erythrae and Clazomene. The walls, of which traces were extant, were, as we guessed, about five miles in circuit; the masonry handsome. Without them, by the way, are vaults of sepulchres stripped of their marble, as it were forerunners of more indistinct ruin. Instead of the stately piles, which once impressed ideas of opulence and grandeur, we saw a marsh, a field of barley in ear, buffaloes ploughing heavily by defaced heaps and prostrate edifices, high trees supporting aged vines, and fences of stones and rubbish, with illegible inscriptions, and time-worn fragments. It was with difficulty we discovered the temples of Bacchus; but a theatre in the side of the hill is more conspicuous. The vault only, on which the seats ranged, remains, with two broken pedestals in the area …'.

Anacreon (c 570–485), who has been described as the last great lyric poet of E Greece, was undoubtedly the city's most famous son. With his fellow Teians he moved to Abdera to escape the invading Persians. Later he went to Samos, where he lived as an honoured guest at the court of the tyrant Polycrates. From there he went to Athens at the invitation of Hipparchus.

A bon viveur and a hedonist, he was renowned for his glorification of of the arts, of music and of love. These he celebrated in poems like 'To a Thracian Filly' or in the lines he addressed to his drinking companions:

'Come, let us not think of another Scythian drinking-bout with noise and shouts, but let us drink gently with beautiful songs.'

Anacreon lived a life full of pleasure to the end. At the age of 85 he choked to death on a grape pip.

The site of Teos is c 1km to the S of the village of Sığacık. The city's small acropolis is on a small hill that rises from level ground midway between the N and S harbours. Although heavily overgrown, it is possible to make out the remains of an archaic *polygonal wall* on the W side. A structure to the NE of the acropolis has been identified by an inscription as a *gymnasium*. To the S of the acropolis are the ruins of the *theatre*. The cavea has been largely destroyed, but there are substantial remains of the stage-building. Originally constructed in the 2C BC, the theatre was modified during the Roman period.

The main area of the city lies between the S edge of the acropolis and the S harbour. Enclosed by a 3C BC *Hellenistic defensive wall* is a large rectangular area that has been extended on the E side to include a quay. A short stretch of the W wall remains visible. SE of the theatre are the well-preserved ruins of the *odeum*. Two statue bases found there bear inscriptions honouring Teian citizens of the Roman period.

To the W of the odeum the excavators have laid bare part of an *ancient street* and some *private houses*. To the SW of this area are the substantial ruins of the **Temple of Dionysus**. Dating from c 130 BC, this was an Ionic peripteros with 6 by 11 columns resting on a stylobate which measured 18.5 by 35m. Consisting of an unusually large pronaos, a cella and a small opisthodomos, it was enclosed by a trapezoidal shaped temenos. Believed to be the early work of Hermogenes of Priene, the temple was restored in the Roman period during the reign of Hadrian.

First excavated by members of the Society of Dilettanti in the 18C, further work was done on the temple by French archaeologists in the early 19C and by a Turkish team in the mid 1960s. A certain amount of restoration has been carried out on the structure. Fragments of an acroterion and of a frieze with reliefs from the temple of Dionysus are now kept in İzmir's Archaeological Museum.

Before leaving this part of the site note the small stretch of an *ancient street*, with a central water channel, which lies between the temenos and the W wall of the city.

The area of the small S harbour of Teos has been reduced considerably since ancient times by material brought down by the stream that flows in from the NE. Note the large mooring stones that are partly covered by the sea.

To visit Myonnesus, return to Seferihisar and continue S in the direction of Lebedus. After a very short distance a minor road on the right leads c 19km to *Doğanbey*, and from there it is a c 4km scramble on foot to *Myonnesus*.

A steep rocky islet c 60m high, *Myonnesus*, was joined to the mainland in ancient times by a causeway, which may still be used by hardy souls. Normally the water reaches no higher than the waist. The overhanging cliffs provided ships with shelter from the elements and on at least one celebrated occasion from attack by enemies. However, the islet is too steep and too small to have supported a community of any size. Although no trace of buildings has been found on the mainland—not even of the theatre used by the Artists of Dionysus—the settlement must have been located somewhere on the flat ground near the end of the causeway. On the island there are the remains of an early *cyclopean wall* and the ruins of some buildings and cisterns, which date from more recent times.

Returning to the junction just after Seferihisar and take the minor road to the left, the site of LEBEDUS is c 8km along the coast. The city, which occupied a small peninsula, was one of the poorest in the Ionian League. Surrounded on the landward side by the territory of its neighbours, it had an indifferent harbour and was never able to become a commercial centre of any importance.

According to Strabo Lebedus was founded by Andropompus. Pausanias accords that honour to Andraemon, one of the many sons of Codrus, the last king of

Athens. Andraemon is credited with having driven out the Carians, who were in occupation of the site.

Later, at least part of its population was transferred to Ephesus by Lysimachus. However, the city continued to exist. In 266 BC it was under the rule of the Ptolemies and for a time it was the home of the Artists of Dionysus. Coins were isssued as late as the 2C AD. During the Byzantine era Lebedus was an episcopal see.

Lebedus has not been excavated and the remains of the city are meagre. There are traces of a fortification on the SE wall of the acropolis and on the plain to the E the ruins of some unidentified buildings. On the peninsula there are the substantial remains of a *Hellenistic ashlar wall*, which was strengthened by towers. In the E corner of this protected area are the ruins of a *Byzantine church*. According to Pausanias, 'The baths in the soil of Lebedus are as useful as they are wonderful to mankind'. Chandler visited them in the 18C and describes steam rising from 'a small tepid brook, called Elijah', which was hidden in a deep cleft. The water, as disagreeable as in most spas, tasted, he said, of copperas. One of these baths, sited between Seferihisar and Ürkmez still attracts hopeful visitors in search of a cure for rheumatism and similar complaints.

Visitors who have their own transport can continue to Colophon Claros and Notium by a minor road via c 25km Bulgurla and c 5km Değirmendere, which skirts the edge of Karacadağ.

Colophon, which means summit or culmination (hence the frequent use of the word to describe the tail-piece of a book), was excavated by American archaeologists from Harvard and the American School of Classical Studies in Athens in 1922. The site, which is on the summit of a hill, may be reached by taking a narrow path from the S end of the village of *Değirmendere* (c 1.5km).

History. Legend relates that Colophon, originally occupied by Carians, was taken over by Greek settlers from Pylos, led by the hero Neleus.

The city was renowned for the skill of its cavalry and for using trained dogs to assist its soldiers. In Colophon dogs were singled out for another honour. They were frequently sacrificed to the gods, particularly to Hecate, the mysterious and threatening goddess of the underworld. For her the customary oblation was a black bitch offered under cover of night.

A member of the Ionian League, Colophon was at first vigorous in warfare and active in trade and commerce. Possibly as a result of using trained dogs to they used to capture the city of İzmir its citizens acquired a reputation for guile and cunning. Increased wealth from trading and revenue from the pilgrims, who came to the shrine of Apollo at Claros, produced ostentation, effeminacy and political and military weakness. It is reported that many of the citizens of Colophon were accustomed to go into the agora dressed in costly purple robes and smothered in rare perfumes. As in the case of Sybaris in Magna Graecia, which was destroyed by the Crotonians, the profligate ways of the people of Colphon brought about their downfall. Captured first by Gyges, king of Lydia, the city later fell into the hands of the Persians. Even after its liberation by Alexander the Great Colophon's troubles continued. The city supported Antigonus in his struggle against Lysimachus. The latter was victorious and c 300 BC as a punishment he forced many of the Colophonians to move to Ephesus, to swell the population of his new foundation.

Colophon does not appear to have recovered from this blow. During the Hellenistic and Roman periods it was joined to Notium and became known simply as the Old Town. Overshadowed by nearby Ephesus, Colophon-Notium managed to exist on the dues paid by visitors, who came to consult the oracle at Claros. Its great days of wealth and power ended the city declined gradually into poverty and obscurity.

Apart from sections of a Hellenistic wall there is little to see at the site of ancient Colophon. The archaeologists found parts of a stoa, a baths complex and sections of paved streets. However, the site is now very overgrown and these remains are no longer easy to find. Only the very keen are likely to make the steep climb to the summit.

CLAROS is c 13km to the S of Colophon. Arrows point down a rough path on the left-hand side of the road to the site. The ruins of the sanctuary and oracle of Apollo rest in a depression covered in undergrowth. This was the river valley of the Halys or Halesus, which, according to Pausanias, is the coldest river in Asia Minor. In the mid 18C Chandler identified the site by this factor. Excavated by a French expedition in 1970, flooding in subsequent years has covered much of what the archaeologists discovered. The temple and its associated buildings lie below the level of the water-table and, as at Letoön in Lycia, constant pumping would be required to keep the site clear of water and silt.

History. According to legend Claros was founded by settlers from Crete and Thebes. Among the Thebans was the seer Manto. She married the leader of the Cretans and in due course produced a son, Mopsus, who became an oracle famed for the accuracy of his prophecies.

The first mention of the sanctuary is in the 7C BC Homeric hymn to Apollo. There is no reference to the oracle until the beginning of the Hellenistic period. One of the earliest known prophecies relates to the construction of the new city of Smyrna by Lysimachus in the 4C BC. (See Rte 7.) During the late Hellenistic period the oracle of Claros appears to have been neglected. This may have been due to rivalry and some competition from nearby Didyma and the continuing effect of Colophon's unfortunate support of Antigonus in his struggle with Lysimachus.

The Roman period saw a revival in the fortunes of Claros. In AD 18, Germanicus, adopted son of Tiberius, was told by the oracle that his death was imminent. The prophecy was fulfilled when, within a year, he succumbed in Syria to poison, which many believed was administered, if not at the behest, certainly with the knowledge of the emperor.

Hadrian with his customary generosity contributed handsomely to the reconstruction and rededication of the temple and clients from all over the Roman world flocked to Claros to consult the god. On the steps on the E side of the temple and on the inside walls of the propylon some of their names and homelands are recorded—Pisidia, Pontus, Caria and Phrygia, Corinth, Crete and Thrace. The influence of Clarian Apollo spread wider even than those places. Inscriptions recording the advice of his oracle have been found as far away as Algeria, Dalmatia, Rome and Britain on subjects as diverse as love and the prospects for a good harvest.

Consultations took place at night. On the E side of the temple an underground passageway led by a torturous route to the adyton. Clients were not admitted there. They were obliged to wait in the pronaos. The adyton consisted of two chambers sited directly under the cella, which contained a giant statue of Apollo. In the inner chamber the prophet, who held office for a year, inspired by a draught of sacred water delivered the prophecy to the thespiode, who turned it into verse. The thespiode and the priest, who were appointed for life, waited in the outer chamber. In this room a portion of a large egg-shaped marble stone was found. This was the omphalos, the navel-stone of the world, which, originally associated with the worship of the god at Delphi in Greece, in the course of time came to be regarded as one of his most important symbols.

Entrance to the temenos from the S was by a propylon which rested on a three step crepidoma. On the N side of the columns of the propylon were inscribed the names of some of the clients, who had consulted the oracle. To the right of the propylon there was an exedra and on the left a stoa. The sacred way, which was lined with statues of Roman notables, led to the *Hellenistic temple*. This, a 4C BC Doric peripteros measuring 46m by 26m with 11 by 6 columns, rested on a five step crepidoma. The peripteros was completed during the reign of Hadrian. In the cella there was a giant statue of the god estimated to be c 8m high. Judging by the coins of Claros Apollo was depicted seated, holding a lyre in his left hand and a wreath of bay leaves in his right. He was flanked by the standing figures of his sister and sister and mother, Artemis on the right and Leto on the left. Parts of the statue of the god found during the course of the excavations remain on the site.

A large marble *altar*, measuring 18.5m by 9m, dedicated to Apollo and Dionysus was found c 30m E of the temple. Nearby there was a Hellenistic sundial. To the S of the temple of Apollo was a small temple, believed to date to the 6C BC, dedicated to Clarian Artemis. Coins of the city suggest that the goddess was depicted in a form very similar to that of Artemis of Ephesus.

Some of the finds from Claros, including a splendid archaic statue of a man holding bearing a calf to sacrifice, are preserved in the İzmir Archaeological Museum.

About 2km to the S of Claros is the site of the city of NOTIUM. This occupies an area c 1km long by 500m wide on a hill above the sea. The splendid views S to Samos and SE to Ephesus and Kuşadası from the acropolis provide some compensation for the paucity of visible remains of the ancient city.

Little is known about the history of Notium. According to Herodotus an Aeolian foundation, it was never a member of the Ionian League. In the 5C BC some of its citizens allied themselves with Colophon, which at that time supported the Persians against the Athenians. A wall was raised, which divided the city into two parts and separated the warring factions. However, the Athenians intervened and brought Notium once more under their control.

After Lysimachus removed a substantial part of the population of Colophon to Ephesus (see above), Notium increased in importance and became known as Neocolophon or Colophon-by-Sea. In time, however, as its powerful neighbour Ephesus prospered, its prosperity declined and with Colophon it decreased in size and importance.

Access to the site, which is very overgrown in parts, involves a climb from the main road up a fairly steep slope. The city was enclosed by a *Hellenistic wall* constructed of large, regular stone blocks. This structure, substantial sections of which remain, was c 4km in length. It was strengthened by towers at intervals and had a number of gates. Those on the W and N are still visible. On the W of the site there are the remains of a small Hadrianic *Corinthian temple in antis* dedicated to Athena Polias. On the E side of this there was an altar measuring c 5m by 8m. The temenos was surrounded by a Doric stoa. A flat area further to the E containing a few large blocks of stone marks the site of one of the city's agoras. The structure just beyond the agora was the *bouleuterion*. A small Hellenistic *theatre* with 27 rows of seats, which was modified during Roman times, crowns the summit of the E hill. The *necropolis* was located to NW of the city. Burial was in low walled sepulchres or in tombs cut horizontally into the rock.

After the labour of exploration, an agreeable opportunity to relax is provided by the presence of a sandy beach below the site. The swimming is good and there are plenty of places there for an alfresco meal. Near the beach is a camp site and a number of rather down-at-heel restaurants.

If the weather is good, the return journey from Notium to İzmir may be made by taking the rough track to Selçuk and by then continuing on road 550/E24. A more direct route is by 20km Cileme, 23km Cumaovası and then the 550/E24.

9   İzmir to Sardis via Manisa

Total distance c 99km. **İzmir**—39km **Manisa / Magnesia ad Sipylum**—R250 30km *Turgutlu*—E23/300 30km *Sartmustafa / Sardis*.

As **İzmir** (see Rte 7) is linked to Manisa and Sartmustafa (Sardis) by good, fast roads (565 and E23/300), both places may be reached easily by those who have their own transport. Road 250 from Manisa joins the E23/300 c 5km W of Turgutlu, so making a round trip a feasible proposition. However, as there is a great deal to see in both Manisa and Sardis visitors who are not in a hurry would be advised to make separate journeys to each place.

For these without their own transport there are frequent direct bus services from İzmir bus station to Manisa and to Sartmustafa. In both cases the journey takes c 1 hour. Again the round trip İzmir, Manisa, Sartmustafa, İzmir is possible by public transport, but the service from Manisa to Sartmustafa (direction Salihli) is relatively infrequent so much time could be lost waiting for a connection.

There are also guided tours from İzmir to Sardis and these offer certain advantages. The remains of the ancient city are scattered over a wide area and to visit them all involves a fairly considerable amount of physical effort. However, the time allowed at the site by the tour organisers is usually limited, a fact that may not commend them to those who would like to make a detailed and leisurely examination of the ruins.

The Arab traveller Ibn Battuta, who travelled through Turkey in the early 14C, described Manisa as 'a large and beautiful city built on a mountain slope, in whose territory there are many rivers, springs and fruitful orchards'. Today **Manisa** is a pleasant town (126,319 inhab.) that has been somewhat overshadowed by its large neighbour to the

Valide Külliye, Manisa.

S. Retaining much of its ancient charm, it is a pleasant place in which to spend a day. A visit to its museum, to its fine mosques and to the sites in the surrounding countryside are essential to an understanding of the many civilisations, from the Hittites and Lydians to the Ottomans, that have have left their mark on this part of Turkey.

As Manisa is conveniently close to İzmir, most visitors prefer to stay in the larger city. However, there are several hotels in Manisa and information about them may be obtained from the *Tourism Information Office* in Yarhasanlar Mah. Doğu Cad., 8 Eylül İşhanı No. 14/3. Among the many restaurants in the town centre is the *Turistik Lokanta*, 5 Eylül Cad., which offers meals and refreshments at reasonable prices.

History. A legendary account states that Manisa, the ancient MAGNESIA AD SIPYLUM, was founded by Thessalians returning from Troy c 1190 BC. Captured by Croesus (561–546 BC), the last Lydian king, it fell into the hands of the Persians in 546 BC, when they subjugated Ionia. The city was liberated by Alexander the Great in 334 BC after his victory over the Persian army at the battle of Granicus. To maintain his position in the area he settled a number of Macedonian veterans in the city.

Following the death of Alexander, possession of Magnesia was disputed by the Diadochoi and their successors. The city came under the undisputed control of Pergamum in 190 BC after Antiochus III had been defeated by a combined Roman and Pergamene force.

Magnesia enjoyed a period of quiet prosperity under the rule of the Attalids and this continued during the Roman era. Suffering extensive damage from the earthquake of AD 17, its citizens received substantial financial assistance from Tiberius to enable them to restore their public buildings.

The city remained a centre of some importance under the Byzantines. In the early 13C, when Constantinople was occupied for some years by the Crusaders, the Byzantine king John III took refuge in Magnesia and, constructing a formidable citadel there for his protection, made it his capital.

After the return of the Byzantines to Constantinople in 1261, Magnesia entered a period of decline. For the next half-century the Crusaders and the Selçuk Turks fought bitterly for its possession. Captured by the emir Surhan in 1313, it remained in Turkish hands thereafter.

Ibn Battuta, who came to Manisa in 1333, has left a moving and somewhat macabre account of the obsequies of the son of Surhan. After his arrival in the city, he found its ruler in the burial chamber of the young prince, who had died some months earlier. In the company of the youth's mother, the emir had spent the night of the Feast of the Sacrifice and part of the following day by his son's corpse. The body had been embalmed and placed in a wooden coffin covered with a lid of tinned iron. This had been raised up in the middle of the roofless chamber, so that the unpleasant odours of decay might escape through the opening. Later the roof of the burial chamber was closed by a dome and the coffin, covered with the mourning cerements of the youth, lowered to the ground. It seems likely that this procedure continued an ancient custom of the Turks, who, when they were still nomads, placed the body of a newly-dead member of the clan high in the branches of a tree until it had dried out and become partly mummified.

Surhan and his successors ornamented Manisa with many fine structures. After the capture of the city by Mehmet Çelebi in 1405, a further phase of building was started by its Ottoman rulers. As a result Manisa has an interesting range of Islamic buildings.

For some time in the 18C the city came under the control of the semi-autonomous local dynasty. When Chandler visited it towards the middle of the same century he noted that the town was 'still populous and has a great trade. The mosques are numerous; and the Greeks have a large and handsome church, and also a monastery'. Many of Manisa's fine buildings were damaged during the fighting between the Greek and Turkish armies in the 1920s.

The buildings of greatest interest to the visitor may be found in the centre of the town. The *Muradiye Camii*, which dates from 1586, adjoins the archaeological museum. Note the elaborate mihrab with its fine faience decoration. The painting on the cupola and pendentives is comparatively recent, dating from the early 19C.

Ulu Camii, a short distance away, was built in 1366 during the reign of Işak Bey on the foundations of a Byzantine fortress. Much ancient material was used in its construction. Note the columns of the portico to the prayer hall, which are crowned with Roman and Byzantine capitals. The tomb of Işak is located nearby.

In 1522 the *Valide Complex* with its twin minarets was built by Süleyman the Magnificent in honour of his mother, Hafise Hatun. A number of ancient columns were also in the construction of the portico of the Valide mosque. In the area surrounding the complex, the feast of Mesir Bayrami is celebrated with great enthusiasm on the last Sunday in April. The inhabitants of Manisa flock here to obtain the celebrated sweetmeat made locally since the 16C.

Off Atatürk Bulv. in a public park is the Halk Evı, the House of the People. Here may be seen the walls of an ancient library, where Mehmet II, who later put an end to the Byzantine Empire by capturing Constantinople, pursued his youthful studies.

Manisa's *Archaeological and Ethnographical Museums* were first opened in 1935. The collections were reorganised, when they moved to their present site near Muradiye Camii in 1972.

The archaeological items are housed in a former imaret. In rooms around a central court are artefacts from the Prehistoric, Hellenistic, Roman and Byzantine eras. Of particular interest are the objects found at Sardis, a site which has been excavated by American archaeologists since 1958. The finds are arranged by period and include some excellent mosaics, ceramics, statues, terracottas, bronzes and inscriptions. There are also some objects found in the town and in the surrounding countryside. Note particularly the fine 2C AD statue of a child which was discovered in Manisa.

The ethnographical collection is exhibited in a medrese. The exhibits include weapons, wood carvings, ceramic tiles, embroidered garments, kilims and carpets. One room has been furnished in typical Turkish style.

Around the sides and on the summit of *Sandık Tepesi*, which towers over Ulu Camii, are the remains of various fortifications that date from the foundation of Magnesia to the 13C AD. Modern terracing makes the ascent of the hill somewhat difficult and only the view justifies the considerable effort required. The ruins are rather disappointing. The first two walls are completely Byzantine, the lower dating from the period of occupation by John III (see above) in the 13C. The wall on the summit was built during the middle Byzantine period c 8C on the foundations of a much earlier fortification, believed to date from the first foundation of the city.

In the countryside surrounding Manisa there are a number of interesting sites. On the SW edge of the town to the right of the İzmir–Manisa road there is an natural rock formation that has been identified with a curiosity known since antiquity. This is the so-called *Niobe rock*, which is described by Pausanias. 'I myself have seen Niobe when I was climbing up the mountains to Sipylos. Niobe from close up is a rock and a stream, and nothing like a woman either grieving or otherwise; but if you go further off you seem to see a woman downcast and in tears.' Niobe, the daughter of Tantalus, bore Amphion seven sons and seven daughters. Proud of her achievement she boasted that she was superior to Leto, who had only two children. However, these were the divinities Apollo and Artemis and, to avenge the insult to their mother, they slew all the children of Niobe.

At *Akpınar* c 7km E of Manisa on road 250 there is a very weathered representation of a seated woman. The carving, believed to be Hittite, has been identified as a representation of the Anatolian Mother Goddess, later known as Cybele. She is depicted in full-face, seated in a recess with her arms across her breast. Her feet rest on two footstools. Outside the niche there is an illegible hieroglyphic inscription. The carving, which is sometimes called Taş Suret, the stone figure, is to the right of the main road. It is easily reached by a scramble across the scree and a short climb.

The village of *Sartmustafa* is 60km from Manisa via (30km) Turgutlu. Preserving in its name an echo of its distinguished predecessor, it occupies part of the area of the ancient city of **SARDIS**, but the resemblance goes no further than the name. Described by Spon towards the end of the 17C as '*un pauvre village ou il y a pourtant un grand khan*'; its condition has improved little since then.

Today Sartmustafa, with its two coffee-houses, a school and a scattering of cottages, is bisected by the E23/300. This busy modern road also divides the site, making an unwelcome and ugly intrusion into the tranquillity of the ancient ruins. Fortunately, the hospitality of the people remains unchanged. Unaffected by the large numbers that descend regularly on their village, they are friendly and courteous hosts and willing guides, ever anxious to show visitors the ruins that the past has bequeathed to them.

The ruins of Sardis are extensive and widely spread. Taking into account the time required for the journey from İzmir, at least a day is needed to see them all.

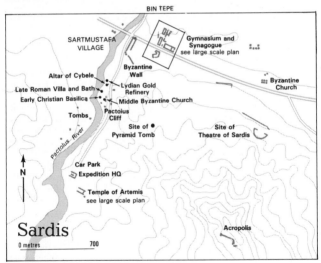

Only tea and soft drinks may be obtained in the village and, as the nearest restaurants are in Salihli c 8km to the E, it is advisable to bring a picnic lunch. This can be enjoyed in a pleasant meadow not far from the temple of Artemis on the banks of the tree-shaded Pactolus.

History. There is a reference in Homer to a people known as the Maeonians, who occupied the area that later became known as Lydia. According to Herodotus the Maeonians changed their name and started to call themselves Lydians. Modern research suggests, however, that the Lydians were invaders, who conquered and dispossessed the Maeonians at some time in the remote past. The Lydian language, which belongs to the Indo-Germanic group displays affinities with Lycian, Phrygian, Etruscan and, some authorities suggest, Hittite. Although the Lydians borrowed the Greek alphabet and were influenced by Greek culture, they were not of Greek origin. They were, however, well known to the Greeks. Homer mentions landmarks in the Lydian landscape like 'eddying' Hermus and 'snowy' Tmolus. Euripides set the birthplace of Dionysus on Tmolus, and Ovid suggested that the gold found in the Pactolus was carried downstream from Phrygia because the legendary Midas had once bathed in its upper reaches.

Sometime in the 8C BC a new line of kings, the Mermnadae, came into being in Lydia. According to Herodotus, Candaules, the last ruler of the Heraclid dynasty, was so besotted by his wife's beauty that he invited a courtier named Gyges to look on her naked body. Despite Candaules' assurance that this could be done without his wife's knowledge, Gyges was seen by the queen. Angered by what had happened, she summoned him to her presence and told him that he must kill the king and take his place or die himself. Gyges murdered Candaules, married the queen and proclaimed himself king. His action was not acceptable to all the Lydians and, to prevent civil strife, he agreed to submit the matter to the judgment of the oracle of Apollo at Delphi. The oracle found in Gyges' favour, but declared that the Heraclids would be revenged in the fifth generation. Gyges and his successors ignored this part of the prophecy, which was fulfilled during the reign of Croesus. Gyges rewarded the oracle hand-somely, sending gifts of gold and silver, including six golden mixing-bowls which weighed nearly 1134kg and which were kept in the Corinthian treasury at Delphi.

Gyges (680–652 BC) and his Mermnadae successors were vigorous rulers who extended the frontiers of their kingdom both towards the coast and inland into Anatolia. They resisted the attacks of the Cimmerians, a barbarous people who, forced by invaders to move from their lands on the N shore of the Black Sea, had conquered Phrygia and advanced into Lydia sacking Sardis. Ardys (651–625) finally destroyed their power and the Cimmerians disappeared and were heard of no more in the accounts of the ancient historians. Ardys then turned his attention to the Greek cities on the coast, capturing Priene. Alyattes (609–560), following his example, took Smyrna.

Croesus (560–546), the last king of the Mermnadae, succeeded in establish-ing control over all the cities on the Aegean except Miletus. He then looked to the E. The Lydians, having overrun Phrygia, had established a common frontier on the river Halys, the modern Kızılırmak, with the powerful Persian Empire. Croesus consulted the oracle of Apollo and was told that if he attacked the Persians he would destroy a great empire. He interpreted this ambiguous piece of advice wrongly and was roundly defeated by the Persian king Cyrus. Croesus did indeed destroy a great empire, but it was his own.

Croesus took refuge in Sardis, which was promptly besieged by the Persians. Herodotus describes how the city, considered to be impregnable, was taken. One of the defenders dropped his helmet accidentally from the fortifications on the S side and clambered down the precipitous slope to recover it. His action was witnessed by a besieging soldier. Next day, with a group from his unit, he followed the same route and led the besiegers into the city.

While his soldiers were sacking Sardis, Cyrus had Croesus bound and placed on a pyre. As the flames began to reach him, Croesus called on Apollo for help. The god responded by sending a great downpour from a clear sky which extinguished the flames. Cyrus, awed by this manifestation of divine interven-tion, had Croesus freed from his bonds and placed the former king on a throne near him. Observing Persian activity in the city, Croesus asked his conqueror what was happening. Cyrus replied that his soldiers were sacking Croesus' city and carrying away his wealth. 'Not mine any longer,' retorted Croesus. 'Nothing there belongs to me now. It is your city they are destroying and your treasure they are taking away.'

The Lydians claimed to have invented games like knucklebones and dice, which they passed on to their Greek neighbours and through them to the whole of the ancient world. Perhaps their greatest contribution to progress was the introduction and popularisation of coined money and the concept of retail trading. They produced the first coins, whose value was guaranteed by the state. These bore no inscription, but a representation of the emblem of Sardis, a lion's head. At first made from electrum, a mixture of gold and silver, pure gold and pure silver coins were introduced during the reign of Croesus. Among the curious customs that distinguished the Lydians from the Greeks Herodotus mentions the practice which permitted their women to chose their own husbands. Also according to him, all working-class girls in Lydia prostituted themselves before marriage, so that they had enough money for their dowries.

The Persians turned Lydia into a satrapy and the province, governed by their nominee, enjoyed a limited degree of freedom. Angered by the revolt of a Lydian named Pactyes, they forced the Lydians to abandon all warlike pursuits and to devote themselves to trade and to the arts. The same measures were taken against the neighbouring Phrygians. One of the results of this policy was the development of the Phrygian and Lydian musical modes. The Phrygian mode was stimulating and exciting, the Lydian calm, reflective and somewhat effeminate in character.

Following its liberation by Alexander the Great from the Persian yoke, control of Lydia was contested by the Diadochoi and their successors. During the reign of Antiochus III Sardis was captured in circumstances reminiscent of those that occurred when the city was invested by Cyrus. Achaeus, a pretender to the throne, took refuge there and the city was besieged by Antiochus. One of the besieging soldiers noticed that vultures and other birds of prey were accustomed to perch for long periods on a section of the city wall above a pit into which refuse including dead animals was thrown by the defenders. Concluding that this section of the fortifications was poorly defended, Antiochus mounted an attack there and captured the city.

After the defeat of Antiochus by a combined Roman and Pergamene force at the battle of Magnesia ad Sipylum (Manisa) in 190 BC, Sardis passed into the hands of Pergamum. Prospering under the Attalids, it came under the control of the Romans in 133 BC, when the last king of Pergamum, the eccentric and cruel Attalus III, willed his kingdom to them. It continued to expand and develop under the Romans, who made it an administrative centre and ornamented it with many beautiful buildings. After the great earthquake in AD 17 Tiberius gave large sums of money for its restoration.

Christianity took root at an early date in Sardis. It was one of the Seven Churches of Asia addressed by St. John in the Book of Revelation. Even though the new faith appears to have made rapid progress there, John was not convinced that all was well. He admonished the Christians of Sardis: 'though you have a name for being alive, you are dead ... For I have not found any work of yours completed in the eyes of my God.' (Revelation 3:1–2.)

Sardis continued to be occupied during the Byzantine era, when it was an important episcopal see. Its later history was marked by decline and decay, which was accelerated by attacks from hostile forces. Captured by the Sassanids in the 7C, it fell into the hands of the Turks in the 11C. In 1401 it was taken by Tamerlane, who rased the city to the ground. Sardis never recovered from this blow and during the centuries of Ottoman rule it was a place of little importance.

The city was rediscovered by travellers from the W like Spon, who came there towards the end of the 17C, and by Chandler, who visited it 100 years later. During the course of centuries the friable rock on the surrounding hills collapsed and the detritus together with silt brought down by the Pactolus covered many of the ruins, causing Chandler to remark that, 'The site of this once noble city was now green and flowery.' The first attempts to explore Sardis scientifically were made at the beginning of this century. Since 1958 a team of American archaeologists from Harvard and Cornell Universities under the direction of Professor M.A. Hanfmann have been unearthing and restoring the remains of the city's ancient buildings.

The principal ruins of Sardis are spread over four large and widely separated areas. The first of these is to the left of the E23 just after the crossroads in the centre of the village. From the large car-park near the entrance to the site a rough path leads to a section of the city's *ancient street*. Paved with marble slabs, this was lined on both sides with colonnades and shops. The S colonnade and associated buildings now lie under the modern road.

The 29 buildings on the N side are Byzantine and have been dated to the 4C AD. They were probably occupied until the city was captured by the Persians in the 7C. Apart from the first structure, which was a public toilet, most were devoted to commerce. Note particularly **W8**, where there is a large basin marked with crosses, which may have been used as a baptismal font. **E2** was a restaurant. Nearby, five columns of the colonnade, some crowned with Ionic some with Corinthian capitals, are still standing. **E7** was Jacob's paint shop. **E10** was a hardware shop. **E13**, the shop of Sabbatios, had a small private toilet. **E14** was the shop of Jacob, an elder of the synagogue.

At the side entrance to the synagogue there is an area of decorated pavement. Note the inscribed slab on the ground nearby. The inscription refers to Germanicus, the nephew of Tiberius, who died under mysterious circumstances in Syria in AD 19. (See above.) The Greek text is believed to date from either AD 17 or AD 43.

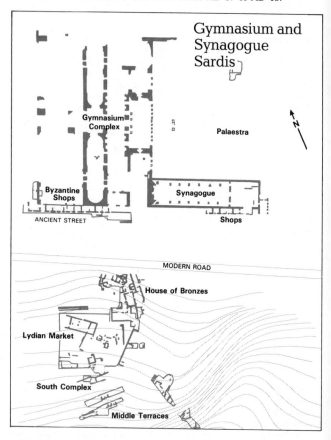

Gymnasium and Synagogue Sardis

Gymnasium Complex

Palaestra

Byzantine Shops

Synagogue

ANCIENT STREET

Shops

MODERN ROAD

House of Bronzes

Lydian Market

South Complex

Middle Terraces

The **Gymnasium complex** to the N of the colonnaded street had two large halls, one on the N and one on S side. After various alterations and changes the S hall was converted for use as a *Synagogue* sometime in the 3C AD. An inscription in Hebrew found there suggests that the building may have been given by the Emperor Lucius Verus (161–169) to the local Jewish community. There is some evidence that Jews had settled in Sardis as early as 547 BC. Some authorities believe that Sardis, *Sfard* in Lydian, may be the city of the Sepharad who are mentioned in Obadiah 20.

The structure, which has been restored extensively, is made up of an atrium, which had a large marble basin surrounded by columns in its centre, and a long narrow hall, which was divided into seven sections. Three doors, of which the centre was the largest, provided access to the main assembly hall from the atrium. Inside these doors are two shrines. It is believed that the S shrine housed the Torah. This unusual arrangement was dictated by the fact that the building had not been designed as a synagogue and the shrines had to be placed there, the Jerusalem-facing part of the hall.

There appears to have been no separate section for women in the synagogue. They either worshipped with the men or were not permitted to enter the hall. There is no trace of any permanent seating for the congregation, who may have sat on the floor or on temporary wooden seats brought in for the services. At the W end of the main hall there was a semicircular apse, which had three rows of marble benches for the elders. In front of the apse stood a large marble table. This had eagles with open wings on the left and right sides and was flanked by double lions that faced backwards and forwards. Much of the floor area was covered by mosaics.

Access to the gymnasium complex was from the colonnades on the N, S and E sides. A substantial part of the W side of this imposing structure, which was completed in its present form in AD 211, has been restored to a height of c 18m. According to an inscription still in position it was dedicated by the citizens of Sardis to Geta and Caracalla, the sons of Septimius Severus, and to their mother, Julia Domna. Beyond the W colonnade there was a large *court* surrounded by walls, which were flanked by a forest of richly decorated soaring columns. This dazzlingly theatrical structure, which was roofed, had floors of patterned marble and walls lined with marble slabs. An arched doorway on the W side, surmounted by a niche, which probably housed a statue of the emperor, led to a large swimming pool.

In the area to the E of the gymnasium are the scanty ruins of a Byzantine church and of Roman and Byzantine baths. On the S side of the main road in the fields near the base of the acropolis a line of vaults marks the site of the city's stadium. Nearby are the remains of the *theatre*, which, restored after the earthquake of 17 AD, had an estimated capacity of 20,000.

Returning towards the village one soon reaches the most recent excavations. A building, which is still being examined by the archaeologists, lies a few metres from the highway. In this area is the so-called *House of the Bronzes*, which has been dated to c AD 550. A number of bronze liturgical objects and a structure which has been identified as an altar were discovered in the basement of this house. Jars containing sulphur and mortars for crushing olives were also found there. It has been suggested that the house was occupied by a Christian ecclesiastical dignitary, perhaps a bishop.

To the S of the house of the bronzes rough walls mark the remains of the *Lydian market place*, which functioned from c 1000 to 550 BC. In the large trench made by the archaeologists quantities of pottery were found.

From the centre of the modern village take the road to the S, which follows the course of the Pactolus river. A short distance along on the right-hand side is the area which has been designated Pactolus North by the archaeologists. By the side of the road are the ruins of an *early Christian basilica* and its associated buildings. This appears to have been abandoned in the 7C, perhaps as a result of the Sassanid invasion. In the 13C during the occupation of Manisa by the Byzantine Lascarids (see above) a smaller *church* with five domes was built on the site of the basilica. A substantial part of this building, including one of the fallen domes, has been uncovered. Beyond the churches are the ruins of a large *Roman villa*, which had its own baths complex. This dates from c AD 350. Some fine mosaics found in the villa are preserved in the museum at Manisa.

The most interesting discoveries lie towards the centre of the site. Here, in a number of small buildings, gold found in the Pactolus was melted down by the cupellation process and then refined in furnaces. This activity was presided over by Cybele, the ancient Anatolian Mother Goddess. Facing E is an *altar*, flanked by crouching lions, which was dedicated to her. All of these structures, which have been partially restored and given protective covers by the excavators, date from the late 7C or mid 6C BC, when Alyattes and his son Croesus ruled in Lydia.

Continuing to the S the road passes over a small stream. At this point a path leads to the so-called *pyramid tomb* which is sited c 400m up on the S slope of the valley. Almost completely buried by landslips, this is not easy to find. Only the base of the structure remains, the burial chamber has disappeared completely. A popular tradition, based on an account in Xenophon, asserts that this structure is the tomb of the Persian Abradates, who was killed in battle. Overcome by grief his wife committed suicide and on the orders of Cyrus was buried with her husband in a magnificent tomb overlooking the Pactolus.

Just before the site of the temple of Artemis, on the left of the road, the house where members of the excavation team are lodged. To the right an open stretch of ground provides ample space for parking and the area by the river, under the shade of the trees, is a favourite place for visitors to rest and enjoy a picnic.

Work on the construction of the **Temple of Artemis** at Sardis was

Temple of Artemis
Sardis

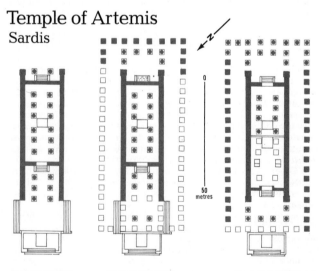

Phase I c.300BC   Phase II 175-50BC   Phase III c.AD150

started c 300 BC, shortly after the city had been liberated from Persian domination by Alexander and at a time when it had begun to be profoundly affected by Greek influence. It is possible that money for the project was provided by the Seleucid kings of Syria. Probably conceived as a dipteros measuring 23m by 67m, only the pronaos, cella and opisthodomus were constructed during this phase. The entrance to the temple was on the W side, an unusual arrangement dictated by the demands of the site. Also on the W side was an antique *altar* dedicated to Artemis, which was considerably older than the temple. The cone of limestone dates from the 6C BC. During the Hellenistic period this was incorporated into the large stepped platform, which is still visible.

Possibly because of the decline of Seleucid influence and patronage in Lydia during the late Hellenistic period, work on the temple appears to have been abandoned for some time and was not resumed until c 175 BC. The plan was then altered and the temple was redesigned as a pseudo-dipteros. Again only part of the project was completed.

Although it seems likely that the temple was damaged by the earthquake in AD 17, the third phase of construction did not commence until c AD 150. During the reign of Antoninus Pius (AD 138–161) Sardis was given neocorate status, which required the city to maintain a temple dedicated to the worship of the emperor and of his family. It was probably at that time that the cella was divided into two parts and an image of Faustina, the wife of Antoninus, was placed in the E section. There is some evidence that Artemis shared her temple with Zeus Polieus during the late Hellenistic period. However, this would not have required the division of the structure. The normal practice would be to place both images side by side in the cella.

The third construction phase left the temple unfinished—the fluting of the columns and the decoration of their bases was not completed. Possibly because of the spread of Christianity the building was finally abandoned sometime during the 4C AD. It was then used as a source of building material for the construction of a new residential quarter that sprang up in the area. Gradually it disappeared under landslips and debris from the steep slopes behind it, so that when the American archaeologists began work the E section of the temple was buried to a depth of more than 9m.

To the NE of the temple there is a small *church*, which is believed to date from the 4C. To the N a pedestal carries a Greek inscription honouring a '*kauein*', the Lydian word for a priestess. On the hillside to the NE there is a statue base, which bears a dedication in Lydian and Greek. According to Bean the Lydian, which is written backwards, may be transliterated, '*Nannas Bakivalis Artimul*'. In Greek this is given as 'Nannas, son of Dionysicles, to Artemis'. Bakivalis appears to be derived from Bacchus, the name by which Dionysus was sometimes known.

The city's *necropolis*, located on the hillsides above the valley of the Pactolus and on the slopes of Mt Tmolus, was in use from the 6C BC to Roman times. Burial was in horizontal stone-lined cists, chamber tombs cut from the rock or elaborate tumuli. Shallow depressions on a hillside W of the Pactolus at a point opposite the temple of Artemis mark the site of a number of graves. Also on the W side of the river c 3km to the S of the temple there are five rock-cut tombs in the cliff face to the right of the road. Although many of the tombs were robbed in antiquity, the archaeologists have recovered

The Temple of Artemis, Sardis.

quantites of grave goods. These include ornaments, figurines, lamps, plates and goblets of metal and pottery. Because of the friable nature of the rock at Sardis many of the tombs examined by the American archaeologists at the beginning of the century are no longer visible. They have been covered by landslides or have been washed away.

The ascent of the *acropolis* at Sardis is probably only for the dedicated. The summit is attained by an exhausting scramble through thorny undergrowth up steep, slippery gradients. Wear stout shoes and allow one hour for the ascent. In the summertime keep a wary watch for snakes, which are reputed to favour the sunnier slopes of the hill.

Only the view over the ruined city and the surrounding country-side justifies the effort involved. The visible ruins are nearly all from the Byzantine period and are not very impressive. On the S side there are the remains of some well-preserved early Byzantine fortifications. A large rock-cut chamber near the summit is believed to have been a chapel. There are some mysterious tunnels, whose function and date have not been established.

Visitors who have their own transport can visit the so-called 'royal cemetery' of Sardis at *Bin Tepe*, c 10km to the N of Sartmustafa. This may be reached by taking the road by the side of the baths complex and continuing in a N direction beyond the railway station.

Some of the tumuli, which are similar to those at Larisa, Hierapolis and İzmir, were probably crowned by phalloi. One of the principal monuments is the so-called *Tumulus of Alyattes*, which has a diameter of 355m, a circumference of more than 1km and a height of 69m. Herodotus states that it was raised by tradesmen, craftsmen and prostitutes working together. He saw the stone inscriptions placed on top of the tumulus, which recorded the amount of work done by each group. According to these the prostitutes' share was the largest! The central burial chamber was examined in 1853 and 1962. More recently the American archaeologists have investigated the tomb of Gyges and several of the larger tumuli in the necropolis. Almost all had suffered from the attention of modern and ancient grave robbers.

To the N of the royal necropolis is *lake Gygaea*, now Marmara Gölü. Chandler found that the lake abounded in fish and that the air above it was full of birds and swarming with gnats. He recalled Strabo's mysterious story (VI.13.5) regarding the temple Diana Coloene, which was built by the lakeside and where on festivals of the goddess baskets danced of their own volition.

10 İzmir to Ephesus (Efes)

Total distance c 79km. **İzmir** (c 5km *Buca*) (c 3km *Belevi*)—c 75km **Selçuk**—c 4km **Ephesus**.

Road 550/E24 to Ephesus leaves **İzmir** (see Rte 7) in a series of wide, lazy bends, which offer a magnificent panoramic view of the city, from the curve of its great bay to the crowded slopes of the surrounding hills. Descending into a gorge, it soon passes an *aque-duct* which brought fresh water to many of the inhabitants during the Roman, Byzantine and Ottoman periods. After c 5km a road to the left leads to *Buca*. This was a residential suburb much favoured by the many foreign merchants who settled in İzmir during the 18C and 19C.

Once clear of the city's straggling suburbs, the road enters a pleasant stretch of fertile countryside, which bears the marks of intensive cultivation. Silver-green olive trees and sombre maritime pines contrast sharply with the vivid hues of the growing crops. The highway, flanked by slender birches, leads eventually to a verdant plain watered by the Küçük Menderes, the ancient river Cayster.

On the N edge of this plain, shortly before the approaches to Belevi, the ruins of a Byzantine castle may be seen high up on a jagged ridge to the right of the road. This is *Keçikalesi* (Goat Castle), which can be reached, with some difficulty, by way of a rough track. However, apart from a splendid view over the plain, there is little to justify the exertion required by the ascent. The castle contains the remains of its fortifications and a number of cisterns and vaulted chambers constructed by the Byzantines, all of which were later refurbished by their Ottoman successors.

A petrol station c 55km from İzmir marks the turning to c 3km *Belevi*. About 2km from the village, in the direction of Tire, a structure may be glimpsed high above the road on the right-hand side. This is a *tumulus*, which has been dated tentatively to the 4C BC. Surrounded by a wall of ashlar masonry, it contains two empty rectangular burial chambers. No sarcophagus has been found. Presumably it was removed by tomb-robbers. The presence of shaped stone blocks on top of the tumulus indicate that it was surmounted originally by a monument of some kind.

The access tunnel, c 18m long, is blocked with the spoil produced by illegal excavations. Although no inscription has been discovered at the tumulus, its size and situation suggest that it was erected for the burial of somebody important, possibly a wealthy local notable.

The **Mausoleum of Belevi** may be found a short distance further on, within a few metres of the right-hand side of the road. It has been described as the most important funeral monument in Asia Minor after the better-known mausoleum at Halicarnassus. Resting on a base c 30m², it consists of a cube-shaped central core c 11m high, which was cut from the solid rock. The surface of the cube was covered with large stone blocks. These were not only decorative, they also concealed the entrance to the burial-chamber, which had been hollowed out of the S side of the rock-cube. The monument had a Doric peristasis, with eight columns on each side of the three-step crepidoma. Now preserved in the Ephesus Museum at Selçuk and the Archaeological Museum, İzmir, are the lion-griffins, which stood on the roof. Ceiling coffers from the mausoleum, which are decorated with representations of funeral games and battles with centaurs, are exhibited in the Archaeological Museum, İzmir.

The sarcophagus from the mausoleum, which is now in the Ephesus Museum, bore a representation of the deceased. He is depicted lying on a couch, resting comfortably on one elbow. The sides of the sarcophagus were decorated with a relief showing finely-carved sirens.

There is much conjecture about who was buried in the mausoleum. Some authorities suggest that it was the feckless Seleucid king, Antiochus II Theos (261–246 BC), who is believed to have been poisoned by his estranged first wife, Laodice while trying to effect a reconciliation with her at Ephesus. Others find Persian influences in the depiction of the lion-griffins, particularly in the presence of a stylised representation of the star of the full and crescent moon on the animals' haunches. A similar carving has been found on lion-griffins in Susa. If the second theory is correct, it would date the burial to the 4C BC, when the Persians occupied Ionia. It would also suggest that, like the nearby tumulus, the mausoleum was constructed for a local worthy. The matter remains, and seems likely to remain, unresolved.

The approach to the small town of (c 75km) **Selçuk** is signalled by the romantic outline of the fortress, which crowns the hill of Ayasuluk to the right of the road. During recent years the number of visitors to nearby Ephesus has increased enormously and as a result Selçuk has experienced an explosion of growth, which has not been entirely beneficial. The town now has too many shops selling cheap souvenirs and not enough good restaurants and hotels.

Information and Accommodation. The Tourism Information Office, which can provide up-to-date details of hotel and restaurant prices, opening times of the site and museum, assistance in finding accommodation, etc., is located in a garden near the Archaeological Museum in the town centre.

There are several small hotels and pensions in and around Selçuk. One, the *Tusan Efes Moteli*, is less than 1km from the site of the ancient city. The modestly-priced *Kale Han Moteli* is located in the centre of the town under the walls of the Byzantine fortress. Visitors who come to Ephesus in the spring and autumn, when the evenings and nights are often chilly, find the large open log-fire in the Kale Han's lounge a very welcome amenity.

Transport. Selçuk is well-served by all forms of transport. Long distance buses, which link İzmir to Kuşadası, Aydın and Denizli, Bodrum, Marmaris and the small resorts in Lycia, call there. There is no bus station in the town. Buses may be joined on the main road near the dolmuş garage. (See below.)

For those, who prefer a slower but more comfortable mode of transport, there are trains to and from Selçuk, which is on the İzmir/Denizli line.

Dolmuş taxis provide frequent connections with the surrounding villages and with nearby towns like Kuşadası. They leave from the dolmuş open-air garage located near the Archaeological Museum. There is no direct dolmuş service to Ephesus. This may be reached by taking a Kuşadası dolmuş as far as the

Tusan Efes Moteli. From there it is an easy 15 minutes' walk to the site.

Taxis are parked near the dolmuş garage. There are fixed tariffs, which are displayed, for the journeys to Kuşadası, Ephesus, Meryemana, etc.

Selçuk's **Ephesus Museum** is one of the best regional museums in Turkey. It houses a large collection of objects found at Ephesus and in the surrounding countryside. Most of these, which are displayed clearly and imaginatively in several rooms and in a large inner courtyard, are labelled in English. There are kiosks in the museum where postcards, slides, and replicas may be purchased and there is a small bar, which offers light refreshments. Allow at least half a day for the visit to the museum, which is an essential complement to a tour of the ancient city.

ROOM 1 contains mosaics, frescoes, statues, and bronzes from Ephesus. Note particularly the fine fresco of Socrates found in one of the private houses on the slopes of Mt Coressus; the beautiful head of Eros, a Roman copy of a work by Lysippus; the small bronze statue of a boy, perhaps Arion or Eros, on a dolphin; the statue of an Egyptian priest, evidence of commercial and cultural links between Ephesus and Egypt; the unashamedly lusty Bes and Priapus; and the mosaics depicting Medusa and Dionysus.

ROOM 2 is devoted to large sculpture and figures from various fountains. Note the Roman 1C head of Zeus, conceived in the Classical style; the statue of a warrior in repose, which fronted a fountain; the Polyphemus group originally from the temple of Augustus, but later placed around the fountain of Pollio; from the fountain of Trajan a particularly fine statue of a youthful Dionysus, and members of the emperor's family; the statues of Triton and nymphs from the fountain of Laecanius Bassus; and a number of idealised portrait heads, including the Roman copy of a 5C BC head of a warrior.

ROOM 3 contains a rich collection of small finds. These include bronze crosses, glazed bowls, panels painted with representations of the Virgin Mary and the saints, a section of a soapstone icon and a number of medallions, all objects dating from the 10C to 12C; coins bearing a representation of Artemis and of a bee, the symbol of Ephesus; a 1C AD glass tray; terracotta drinking cups from the 6C to the 2C BC; lamps and moulds for their production; two statues of Eros; a bust of Marcus Aurelius; terracotta theatre masks; and an ivory frieze from a private house in Ephesus depicting a conflict between Trajan and a barbarian horde.

The COURTYARD contains large sculptures. The most interesting are a fine sarcophagus decorated with representations of the muses; a 1C AD inscription from the reign of Nero dealing with customs duties, which was later incoporated in an ambon found in the basilica of St. John on Ayasuluk; a reconstruction of the pediment from the fountain of Pollio (see above); a 3C AD Roman sun dial; decorated capitals dating from the 7C BC; Hellenistic and Roman grave stelae; and the lion-griffins and the sarcophagus from the Belevi mausoleum (see above).

ROOM 4 is devoted to objects found in tombs in and around Ephesus. These include decorated Mycenaean pottery found in a grave on Ayasuluk; a fine Archaic period terracotta sarcophagus of the Clazomenae-type discovered in the Agora at Ephesus; glassware of the archaic and Hellenistic periods; stelae showing the development of the worship of Cybele from the 5C BC; the 2C BC stele of Olympia, daughter of Diocles; and a variety of small objects found in early Christian graves near the Cave of the Seven Sleepers.

ROOM 5 is devoted to finds concerning the worship of Artemis. The oldest is a small 7C BC gold statuette of the goddess from the Artemision. Other objects include ivory statuettes including one of a Megabyxus (see below); part of a quadriga from the archaic altar of Artemis; the head of a youth from one of the columnae caelatae; various architectural fragments; and, dominating the room, a 1C AD statue, 2.92m tall, of Artemis and another statue of the goddess, 1.74m tall, dated to the 2C AD, both found in the Prytaneion at Ephesus.

Artemis of Ephesus, 2C AD, the Selçuk Museum.

ROOM 6 is the so-called hall of the imperial cults and statues. The most interesting objects here are the frieze from the temple of Hadrian; the 6C AD statue of the Consul Stephanus; part of the altar from the temple of Domitian; and a number of expressive Roman portrait statues from the 2C and 3C AD.

From the centre of the town a street climbs steeply to the buildings on Ayasuluk. Access to the complex is by the so-called *Gate of Persecution*, so named because of a relief, which once decorated it. The relief, which depicted Achilles in combat, was misinterpreted in Byzantine times, when it was believed to show a Christian martyrdom. This misunderstanding probably arose from the original location of the relief. It had ornamented the amphitheatre at Ephesus, where the Romans had organised gladiatorial contests and where some of the early Christians had been killed for their faith. Taken from there and placed over the gate during the Byzantine period, it was later brought to England. Part of the relief is now in Woburn Abbey.

Much reused material was used in the construction of the gate and its flanking towers, which were built in the 7C and 8C during the period of the Arab invasions. At that time the basilica was incorporated in the defensive system of the fortress by new walls. Note the architectural fragments over the central arch and the column sections built into the right-hand tower. When these fortifications were being constructed the size of the interior courtyard was deliberately restricted so that any invaders who succeeded in forcing the gate could be surrounded by the defenders and despatched quickly.

The principal building on Ayasuluk is the *Basilica of St. John*. According to an ancient tradition, the Apostle, accompanied by the Virgin Mary, came to Ephesus c 40. After his death c 100, he was buried in a small church on the hilltop, which was replaced by a wooden-roofed basilica in the 4C. In the 6C the Emperor Justinian (527–565) had this removed when he built the magnificent structure whose remains are being studied and restored at present by American and Turkish archaeologists.

As early as the 2C the tomb of St. John had begun to attract pilgrims and their numbers increased substantially during the centuries that followed. From the saint's name, St. John Theologos, the town began to be called Ayio Theologo, which was modified in the course of time to become Ayasuluk.

Justinian's basilica was a worthy setting for the veneration of St. John, which continued, with some interruptions, until the late Byzantine period. However, after the Turkish conquest, the building was found to be in such a dilapidated state that it required considerable repairs before it could be used as a mosque. The Arab traveller, Ibn Battuta, describes it as being 'built of finely hewn stones each measuring ten or more cubits in length. The cathedral mosque, which was formerly a church greatly venerated by the Greeks, is one of the most beautiful in the world.'

After the construction of the Isa Bey mosque in the 14C, the basilica was neglected and fell into disrepair. Shortly afterwards it was severely damaged by an earthquake and completely abandoned.

The basilica was 110m long and 60m wide. Constructed in the form of a Latin cross, it was surmounted by six domes. The pillars, which supported these domes, may still be seen. Access was from an atrium on the W side, which measured 34m and was 47m and was surrounded by a colonnade. This led by way of an exonarthex and a narthex to the nave, which was flanked by two side aisles covered by galleries. The nave was separated from the aisles by blue-veined marble pillars, which bore on their capitals the monograms of Justinian and of his wife, Theodora. The richly decorated interior of the basilica, whose walls were lined with marble facings, must have been an impressive sight. The *Tomb of St. John*, raised on two steps and covered with mosaics, was sited under the central dome. Its position is now marked by a marble slab. Beyond the transept was a synthronon, where the clergy were seated.

The basilica's *treasury* was attached to the N transept. This was converted into a chapel in the 10C. The baptistery, which antedates the basilica, was on the N side of the nave. It consisted of an octagonal chamber, with a narrow hall on one side. Steps led down into the baptismal pool, which, flanked by a colonnade, was in the centre of the chamber.

From the ramparts of the fortress, erected by the Byzantines, and improved and enlarged by the Turks, which lies to the N of the basilica, there is a fine view across the plain to the sea. Inside the building, part of which is not open to the public, there are a number of cisterns, one of which occupies the site of a Byzantine church, and a ruined mosque.

Below the hill of Ayasuluk, to the SW, is the Selçuk **Mosque of Isa Bey**, which has been restored recently. If the building is locked, enquire at the museum regarding access. An inscription in Arabic above the main entrance records that it was constructed in 1375 by the architect Ali Damescene on the orders of Isa Bey, the son of the emir of Aydın. At that time the area around Selçuk formed part of the territory of the Aydın emirate. During the course of centuries the mosque has suffered many changes of fortune and, unfortunately, the fabric of the building has not escaped damage. The şadırvan has disappeared, the cap of the SW minaret is missing and only the base the NE minaret remains.

Stylistically interesting, it marks an intermediate phase between the Selçuk and Ottoman styles. According to Akurgal it is the oldest known Turkish mosque to possess an entry court and the earliest Anatolian columned mosque with a transept.

It was built on a terrace measuring 51m by 57m, which has been raised artificially on the W. The large court, which was formerly surrounded by a covered colonnade, occupies two thirds of the terrace, the building the remaining third.

Access to the prayer hall is through a triple arcade from the court. The hall is surmounted by two domes, which rest on arches supported by four marble columns taken from a Roman building in Ephesus. As in the case of the basilica, much ancient material was used in its construction. Note the traces of paint and gilding, which remain on the mihrab. The Isa Bey mosque is noted for the quality of its ornamentation, especially the finely-carved stalactite decoration over the main entrance and the beautiful faience mosaic in the S dome.

The last and, perhaps the most historically important, site in Selçuk is that of the great *Temple of Artemis*, one of the seven wonders of the ancient world. Located a short distance outside the town, the site lies a few metres from the right-hand side of the road to Ephesus and Kuşadası. It may also be reached from the Isa Bey mosque by way of a rather rough and dusty path. The scanty remains, which are frequently covered with water, are not impressive. Of the temple only one incomplete column, which has been reconstructed from fragments, and the foundations of the Hellenistic altar survive. It requires a substantial effort of the imagination to picture the building, which so impressed Pliny and other ancient commentators.

There is evidence that from a remote period Cybele, the Anatolian Mother Goddess, was worshipped at Ephesus. Some time after 1000 BC, when Greek colonists first settled in the area, Cybele was assimilated with Artemis. She managed, however, to make the change without losing either her ancient appearance or many of her attributes.

British archaeologists discovered that before the construction of the archaic temple of Artemis in the middle of the 6C BC there were three earlier buildings on the site. The first, an altar, has been dated to c 700 BC, the second and third, which according to Akurgal comprised a naiskos, were built during the following 150 years.

The archaic temple of Artemis, an Ionic dipteros built between 560 and 550 BC, measured 55m by 115m. At the time it was built, it had the double distinction of being the first structure of that size to be constructed entirely of marble and the largest building ever produced by Greek architects. Designed by Chersiphron and his son, Metagenes of Crete, and Theodorus of Samos, it has been postulated that the Cretans were probably familiar with some of the massive buildings erected by the Egyptians and may have been influenced by them, when preparing their plans for the temple.

Pliny, writing about the Hellenistic temple which later occupied the same site, describes the forest of columns, 127 in all, which supported the earlier building. The lower part of 36 of the archaic columns, each of which was 19m high, bore a decorative relief. One of these decorated columns, the so-called 'columnae caelatae', is preserved in the British Museum.

In the long narrow cella, behind the deep pronaos, the statue of the goddess stood in a naiskos. Greek temples as a rule faced E and, although the site did not require it, the archaic temple of Artemis at Ephesus, like the temples of Sardis and Magnesia on the Maeander, faced W. This supports the view that the the deity worshipped there was of Anatolian, and not of Greek, origin.

Further proof is provided by the names of the temple hierarchy, which are quite unlike those found in Greek temples. The Principal Priest was known as the Megabyxus. This is a Persian word, which means 'set free by God'. According to Strabo he was a eunuch and was always selected from non-Greek lands. He was assisted by a group of virgins and by an order of minor priests, known as the Essenes. Other members of the temple staff were the Curetes and the Acrobatae, or walkers on tip-toe!

According to an ancient tradition the archaic temple was destroyed by fire in 356 BC, the year Alexander the Great was born. The fire was started by Herostratus, a madman who believed that he would immortalise his name by this action. When Alexander came to Ephesus in 334 BC, having sacrificed to the goddess in the ruined sanctuary, he offered to rebuild it. According to Strabo, the Ephesians politely rejected his proposal on the grounds that it would be inappropriate for one divinity to erect a temple in honour of another.

The new temple was built on the foundations of the old. Some of the foremost sculptors of the age, including Scopas and Praxiteles, contributed works for its decoration. To prevent the building from flooded, it was raised c 3m above the ground on a 13-stepped crepidoma. The water-level appears to have been a problem also in ancient times. The statue of Artemis, which stood in the same place in the cella, is believed to have resembled the Roman statues of the goddess, which are now exhibited in the Selçuk museum. As in the earlier building, the lower part of some of the columns bore a decorative relief. A part of one of these, which depicts Hermes, Thanatos (Death) and possibly Iphigeneia, is in the British Museum.

The foundations of a horseshoe-shaped altar, which was erected at the same time as the Hellenistic temple, have been uncovered by the Austrian archaeologists, who are currently working on the site.

During the Roman period the temple was stripped of many of its treasures, which were carried off to Italy. It suffered further damage at the hands of the Goths in AD 263 and, with the rise of Christianity, entered a period of neglect and decay. After the suppression of paganism by Theodosius, towards the end of the 4C, it appears to have been abandoned completely. During the Byzantine and Ottoman periods the temple became a convenient source of cut and shaped stone, which was used to construct great churches and mosques. In time the site was covered with silt brought down by the river Cayster and its existence passed from the memory of man.

The story of the rediscovery of the Artemision by John Turtle Wood in the middle of the 19C is one of the great detective stories of archaeology. Undeterred by troubles of many kinds, disease, the collapse of a trench, apalling lodgings, a broken collar-bone, an attempted assassination and murder, he continued his search. An inscription found in the theatre provided the clue that led him to the site. This stated that at the time of a performance certain holy images were brought from the temple along the sacred way through the Magnesian Gate to the theatre. Wood located the sacred way which he found to be very well preserved, and followed it to the temenos of the temple.

Wood's researches, on which he had spent much of his considerable private fortune, were carried on by Hogarth, who discovered a rich foundation treasure in 1904, and more recently by teams of Austrian archaeologists.

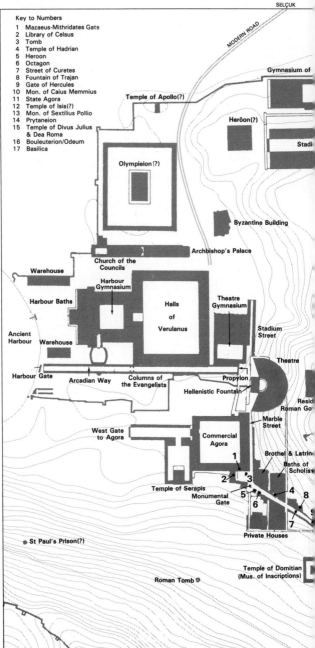

Key to Numbers

1 Mazaeus-Mithridates Gate
2 Library of Celsus
3 Tomb
4 Temple of Hadrian
5 Heroon
6 Octagon
7 Street of Curetes
8 Fountain of Trajan
9 Gate of Hercules
10 Mon. of Caius Memmius
11 State Agora
12 Temple of Isis(?)
13 Mon. of Sextilius Pollio
14 Prytaneion
15 Temple of Divus Julius
   & Dea Roma
16 Bouleuterion/Odeum
17 Basilica

MODERN ROAD

Gymnasium of

Temple of Apollo(?)

Heroön(?)

Stadi

Olympieion(?)

Byzantine Building

Archbishop's Palace

Church of the
Councils

Warehouse

Harbour
Gymnasium

Halls
of
Verulanus

Theatre
Gymnasium

Harbour Baths

Stadium
Street

Ancient
Harbour

Warehouse

Theatre

Harbour Gate

Arcadian Way

Columns of
the Evangelists

Propylon

Hellenistic Fountain

Resid
Roman Go

West Gate
to Agora

Commercial
Agora

Marble
Street

Brothel & Latrin

Baths of
Scholis

Temple of Serapis

Monumental
Gate

1

2

3

5

6

4

8

7

St Paul's Prison(?)

Private Houses

Temple of Domitian
(Mus. of Inscriptions)

Roman Tomb

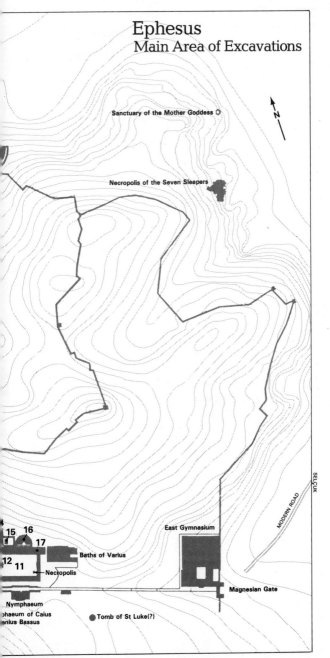

Ephesus
Main Area of Excavations

N

Sanctuary of the Mother Goddess ○

Necropolis of the Seven Sleepers

SELÇUK

MODERN ROAD

East Gymnasium

15 16

17

Baths of Varius

12 11

Necropolis

Magnesian Gate

Nymphaeum
phaeum of Caius
anius Bassus

● Tomb of St Luke(?)

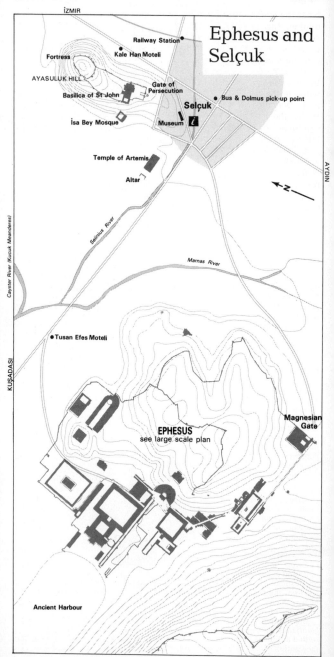

Near the single standing *column* are the foundations of the archaic temple, surmounted by the 3m-high crepidoma of its Hellenistic successor. To the right is the base of the 12th of the outer row of columns. A short distance to the W are the ruins of an ancient sanctuary whose axis was at right-angles to the main temple.

At the W extremity of the site are the remains of the great *altar* of the Artemision. Here animal, and sometimes human, sacrifices were made to the goddess. The altar, which was surrounded by a colonnade, was erected in a paved marble court. It was entered from the W. To the left is a spring, which may have had some ceremonial significance or may have been used for the ritual purification of those taking part in the sacrifice.

At least one day is needed for c 5km **EPHESUS (Efes)**. The ruins are extensive and widely scattered. During the holiday season coaches bring thousands of visitors from İzmir, from the nearby resorts and from the cruise ships which dock at Kuşadası. The crowds tend to restrict access to the more popular parts of the site, so extending the time required to make a complete tour.

Each morning there are frequent dolmuş services on the Selçuk–Kuşadası route, which pass the site. Ask to be set down at the Tusan Efes Moteli. It is an easy walk from Selçuk to Ephesus, but care should be taken, as the road is narrow and very busy and the minimal verges offer little protection from the traffic.

Visitors, who wish to see the most important remains of the ancient city with the minimum exertion and in the maximum comfort, are advised to take a taxi to Ephesus in the early morning. (Details of opening times may be obtained from the Tourism Information Office in Selçuk.) The driver should be told to go by way of the Aydın road to the Magnesian Gate, which is located on the SE of the site. From there an easy walk downhill leads to the principal ruins. Anyone following this route should read the description of the site in reverse order.

In summer the daytime temperatures at Ephesus can be very high and, apart from the area near the theatre, there is little shade.

There is a restaurant at the lower, N entrance near the Vedius Gymnasium. However, during the holiday season it is usually very crowded. It is more satisfactory to bring a picnic lunch. As a rule the authorities raise no objection to visitors taking alfresco meals on the site, providing they do not impede others and leave no litter.

Near the restaurant there are kiosks and boutiques selling souvenirs and cheap bric-à-brac. In this area or on the site itself visitors may be approached by touts offering ancient coins and other antiquities. These are almost certainly modern fakes of no great value. However, if they are genuine, both the purchaser and the vendor are breaking Turkish law and could incur very severe penalties. It is illegal to possess works of art or to purchase them from anyone but a licensed dealer who has obtained the necessary official permit for their sale and possible export.

History. Ephesus would appear to have attracted settlers from the earliest times. It had a sheltered harbour on a river mouth, it was at the end of a traditional trade route that linked the great cities of the Middle East with the the Aegean, and it had long associations with the worship of Cybele, the great Mother Goddess of Anatolia.

According to Pausanias, Strabo and Athenaeus, Ephesus was founded by Androclus, one of the sons of the legendary Codrus, king of Athens. He and his followers had been told by an oracle to settle in a place which would be indicated to them by a fish and a wild boar. On arriving at Ephesus the Greeks found some of the local people roasting fish near the sea-shore. One of the fish fell from the fire and, as it had pieces of burning wood attached to it, set a nearby thicket ablaze. This disturbed a wild boar, which was chased and slain by Androclus.

This sequence of events, which is depicted on a frieze on the temple of Hadrian, was taken to fulfil the prophecy and Androclus and his companions settled at Ephesus. They found Carians and Lydians in the neighbourhood and they intermarried with them, adopted some of their customs and practices and harmonised their religious beliefs, identifying Cybele with the Greek Artemis.

Some authorities suggest that Ephesus was the city which the Hittites called Apasas and which is believed to have existed on the Aegean coast c 1400 BC. The earliest archaeological evidence found in the area comes from a Mycenaean tomb of Ayasuluk. It would appear that the first Greek settlement was made c 1000 BC, at a time when the sea reached much further inland. This was probably sited on the harbour c 1km to the W of the Artemision.

Towards the middle of the 7C Ephesus was taken by the Cimmerians. A century later it came under the rule of the Lydians. Croesus appears to have treated the Ephesians well, donating several of the columnae caelatae to the archaic temple of Artemis. After the defeat of Croesus by Cyrus (see above), Ephesus, with the rest of Ionia, fell into the hands of the Persians. Later it was for a period a member of the Delian League. Then it came under Persian control again and this state of affairs continued until Alexander defeated the Persian army at the battle of Granicus. His visit to the city is described above.

After the death of Alexander Ephesus was ruled by Lysimachus, one of the Diadochoi. Much against the wishes of the inhabitants, he decided to re-site the city in a new location. This is the area occupied by the ruins visible today. He overcame the reluctance of the Ephesians to move by resorting to a stratagem. After a period of torrential rain, he blocked the drains of the old city, with the result that all the houses were flooded. Lysimachus also brought in people from Colophon and Lebedus to swell the numbers of his new foundation. He enclosed his city within a massive defensive wall 10m high and c 9.65km long. Parts of this may still be seen on the summit of Mt Coressus and on the NE side of Mt Pion.

During the wars that followed the death of Lysimachus, Ephesus changed sides frequently. At first it supported the Seleucids, then dallied for a time with the Ptolemies. It passed finally into the hands of the Attalids of Pergamum after the defeat of Antiochus III at the battle of Magnesia ad Sipylum in 190 BC (see above). When Attalus III bequeathed his kingdom to the Romans in 133 BC, Ephesus became one of the most important cities in the new province.

Under Roman rule Ephesus at first displayed traces of its old volatility. It supported the Roman cause against Aristonicus, the pretender to the Pergamene throne, contributing handsomely to his defeat. However, when Mithridates VI, king of Pontus, led a revolt against the Romans in 88 BC, the Ephesians joined him and slaughtered a large number of Romans residing in their city.

Fortunately Ephesus did not suffer because of this act of treachery. It became the seat of the Roman governor and the largest and most important trading centre on the Aegean coast. In early Imperial times its population was estimated to be 250,000. The city was given favourable treatment by several emperors, who allowed centres for imperial worship to be set up there, thus permitting the Ephesians to boast that their city had received the title of Neocorus on no less than four separate occasions. Nero and Hadrian addressed themselves to the problem of the silting up of the harbour and several emperors beautified the city with buildings whose remains may still be seen.

Christianity came early to Ephesus. On his second missionary journey St. Paul, accompanied by Aquila and Priscilla, visited the city, teaching in the synagogue for some time before leaving for Caesarea in Phoenicia and Jerusalem. The celebrated incident produced by the silversmiths of Ephesus took place during the apostle's third journey, when he spent about two years in the city, preaching daily in the synagogue and in a lecture hall. After his caustic remark that gods fashioned by human hands are not gods at all, the sale of images of Ephesian Artemis declined. Demetrius, the leader of the city's silversmiths, fearful for his livelihood, put it about that if Paul were allowed to continue preaching and teaching disaster would overtake the city. Cleverly he appealed to the religious feelings of the people saying: 'the sanctuary of the great goddess Diana (Artemis) will cease to command respect; and then it will not be long before she who is worshipped by all Asia and the civilised world is brought down from her divine pre-eminence' (Acts 19:27). These words produced a riot. The Ephesians rushed through the streets to the theatre where they held a protest meeting, crying loudly: 'Great is Diana of the Ephesians', for several hours. Eventually the mob was dispersed by calming words from the city officials, but Paul found it prudent to leave Ephesus for Macedonia.

Some authorities believe that the apostle was imprisoned in Ephesus, basing their argument on texts like II Corinthians 1:8, 'how serious was the trouble that came upon us in the province of Asia. The burthen of it was far too heavy for us to bear, so heavy that we even despaired of life.' Traditionally a building c 1km to the W of the site, in the harbour area, is known as St. Paul's Prison.

It is believed that St. John came to Ephesus from Patmos and that he took care of the Virgin Mary there during the last years of her life. His tomb was enshrined in the basilica on Ayasuluk. (See above.) The house where Mary lived is at Meryemana, c 8km from Ephesus. (See below.)

Two of the great Councils of the early church were held in Ephesus. In 431 Cyril of Alexandria presided over a gathering of bishops, convoked by Theodosius II and held in the presence of papal legates. At this council a heresy promulgated by Nestorius, patriarch of Constantinople, was condemned. The Nestorians taught that Jesus was two separate persons, one human and one divine and that Mary was the mother of the human person only and, consequently, could not be called the Mother of God.

Theodosius called another council at Ephesus in 449. This was the so-called 'robber council', which deposed Flavian, the Patriarch of Constantinople, and restored the heretical Eutyches as priest and archimandrite.

The silting of the harbour, which proceeded unchecked, the abandonment of the Artemision after the adoption of Christianity as the state religion, and the increasingly ferocious attacks by the Arabs were factors that contributed to the decline of Ephesus. Sometime in the c 6C the remaining inhabitants appear to have moved to the more easily defended acropolis at Ayasuluk. There was a brief revival under the rule of the emirs of Aydın, but after the conquest of the area by the Ottomans, Ephesus became a forgotten backwater.

During the centuries of Ottoman rule travellers from W Europe had a variety of experiences in Ephesus and consequently left varying views about it in their writings. In 1611 Ephesus was visited by William Lithgow. He found the ruined city 'somewhat inhabited with Greeks, Jews and a few Turks, but no way answerable to its former glory and magnificence. Nevertheless it is pleasantly adorned with gardens, fair fields and green woods of olive trees, which on the sea do yield a delectable prospect.' Richard Chandler came to Ayasuluk and Ephesus in 1764–65 and discovered a sad, tumbled collection of ruined buildings, whose melancholy was accentuated by the call of a shrill-owl and of a jackal, which cried mournfully, 'as if foresaken by his companions, on the mountain'. J.T. Wood, who survived cholera, physical injury, apalling weather and criminal workmen, laboured there in the mid-19C and discovered the site of the Artemision. (See above.) In 1936 the ancient city was remote enough for H.G. Morton to describe it as a place with 'no sign of life but a goatherd leaning on a broken sarcophagus or a lonely peasant outlined againt a mournful sunset'. Three years later the road from İzmir was in such a poor condition that the vehicle in which George Bean was travelling ended up in a cornfield.

Today Ephesus is one of the most visited sites in Asia Minor. Its ancient buildings, many of which have been partially restored, are seen by thousands each year. Whether this is an improvement on the situation reported by earlier travellers, is something each visitor must decide for him or herself.

From the Tusan Efes Moteli take the side road signposted to the site. This ascends a gentle slope passing fields that in the summer are full, sometimes of nodding sunflowers, sometimes of the tall rustling golden stalks of maize. Through the trees there are glimpses in the distance of the hill of Ayasuluk with its fortress and ruined basilica.

Just before the road passes through a gap in the Byzantine walls there is a track to the left, which circles Mt Pion and arrives eventually at the SE of the site near the Magnesian Gate. Visitors who are not pressed for time may like to follow this and make a short detour to the *Cave of the Seven Sleepers*. Care should be taken in examining the area around the cave, as many of the vaults and walls are in a dangerous state of disrepair.

An ancient tradition affirms that seven Christian youths, who lived in Ephesus during the reign of Decius (249–251), were unwilling to compromise their beliefs by offering sacrifice in the temple of the emperor and took refuge in a cave on the N slopes of Mt Pion. There they fell into a deep sleep. When they awoke, one of the young men went into the city to purchase bread. His strange appearance, clothes of antique cut and ancient money provoked much comment. On making discreet enquiries, he discovered to his astonishment that he and his companions had been asleep, not for one night but for 200 years, and that Christianity had become the state religion. When the men died eventually they were buried in the cave where they had enjoyed their miraculous sleep, and a church was built over their graves.

The archaeologists have discovered the ruins of a small church above a gallery, which was cut into the rock. This contains a number of sepulchral chambers, on whose walls are written prayers and invocations to the Seven Sleepers. A variety of offerings, including terracotta lamps, has been found in the graves of later Christians, who were buried in the area surrounding the church and gallery. Clearly considered a holy place, the site appears to have been used up to the late Byzantine era, as graffiti dating from the time of the Crusades have been found there.

On returning from the Cave of the Seven Sleepers, continue towards the N entrance to the site. The partially excavated structure on the left of the road is the **Gymnasium of Vedius**. Dedicated to Artemis and Antoninus Pius, it was constructed in AD 150 by Publius Vedius Antoninus, a protégé of the emperor.

The entrance to the gymnasium was at the E side of the structure through a *palaestra*, which had an elaborate propylon in its S wall. To the left of the propylon there was a well-furnished *lavatory*. The long narrow room on the W side of the palaestra was probably used for the worship of the emperor and for various formal ceremonies connected with the gymnasium. The statue, now disappeared, which stood in the alcove in the W wall was, almost certainly, a representation of the emperor. The large room beyond, which extended across the width of the gymnasium, was probably used for indoor athletics and practice sessions during bad weather. To the W was a *swimming pool*. The remainder of the building was taken up with a *baths complex*. Among the statues found in the gymnasium are those of a sophist and a striking representation of Antinous as Androclus. These are now in the İzmir Archaeological Museum.

To the S of the gymnasium of Vedius are the ruins of the *Stadium*, which has been dated by an inscription to the reign of Nero (AD 54–68). It seems likely that this replaced an earlier structure built, when Lysimachus ruled the city. Shaped like a horseshoe, its principal entrance was through a well-preserved monumental gate on its W side. Measuring c 229m by 28m, the stadium was used for athletics, gladiatorial contests, fights with wild beasts and chariot racing. The structure was narrowed in the centre, so that the E section could be turned into an arena for the more gory spectacles. Wild animals were kept in small rooms nearby. On the S side the spectators seats were cut from the side of Mt Pion, while those on the N rested on vaults. During the middle Byzantine period the stadium suffered a great deal of damage, when large quantities of material were taken from it to construct fortifications on Ayasuluk.

Across the road are the remains of a *Byzantine fountain*. Note the three niches, which held statues, and the remains of a trough used for watering animals.

Nearby are the scanty remains of a building whose function has not been determined so far. Some authorities believe it was a heroon, others that it was a macellum (meat market).

A short distance further to the S are the ruins of a large building, which has been described variously as a baths complex and as the private house of a wealthy Ephesian. The structure is Byzantine and has been dated to the 6C AD.

Behind this building are the remains of a *paved street*, which connected the stadium with the theatre. Excavations conducted by Turkish archaeologists have brought to light a number of interesting finds from the ruins of the small shops which once lined it.

The principal entrance to the ancient city lies at the end of a short stretch of road devoted to the commercial exploitation of the modern visitor. The restaurant and shops mentioned above are sited there. Adjoining the large parking area for coaches and private vehicles, there is a taxi station which provides services to Selçuk and Kuşadası.

Immediately inside the entrance to the site there are *toilets* with washing facilities. There is also a tap which provides drinking water. Visitors are advised to stick to bottled mineral water!

A path to the right of the toilets leads to the extensive ruins of the **Church of the Councils**. This curiously elongated building, which measures 260m by 30m, was erected in the early part of 2C AD. It had the typical basilical form of a central nave flanked by two side aisles. There was an exedra at each of the narrow ends, where, according to some authorities, court business was transacted. However, Akurgal is of the opinion that this building was used mainly as a corn exchange. Grain was displayed and sold in the nave, while bankers and brokers conducted their business in the small rooms that lined the side aisles. To support his theory he points to the location of the building, which was conveniently sited near the harbour.

Yet another view is that the structure was a *museion*, a centre devoted to higher education, in particular to medicine and the sciences. Those who favour this theory put forward as evidence an inscription found near the building. This states that the doctors and professors, who staffed the Ephesus museion were to be exempted from taxes.

The building was abandoned sometime in the 3C AD, when the fortunes of the city went into decline. Like other large centres of population, Ephesus suffered from the effects of the great plague which raged through the Roman Empire in the middle of that century. The incursions of the Goths, who raided as far S as Ephesus between 258 and 262, contributed further to the general economic malaise.

A *church* was built in the W part of the basilica at the beginning of the 4C. Entrance to this building was through a large paved atrium and a narthex. The atrium was decorated with marble slabs brought from various buildings in the city, while the narthex had a floor-mosaic of geometric design.

The well-preserved baptistery on the N side of the church had a central pool in which catechumens were baptised. The walls of this cylindrical structure were decorated with crosses and metal rosettes.

Further extensions and alterations, which involved the construction of one and possibly two other churches and a chapel, were made to the original design. These included a small domed building erected in the 6C during the reign of Justinian. The Austrian archaeologists who are currently working on this part of the site have provided a plan which helps to explain the various complicated phases of the development of the structure.

Appropriately, it was here, in the first church to be dedicated to Mary the mother of Jesus, that the Councils of Ephesus were held (see above). When Pope Paul VI visited Ephesus in 1967, he commemorated these events by praying with a large congregation in this building which had witnessed so many important developments in the early church.

A short distance to the right are the ruins of the largest structure in Ephesus. This complex, made up of the *halls of Verulanus*, the *harbour gymnasium* and the *harbour baths*, was completed during the reign of Domitian (AD 81–96). Only a part of the extensive area covered by these structures, which measure c 356m by 240m, has been excavated. At present exploration of the ruins is hampered by the thick undergrowth and the marshy nature of the ground.

An entrance from the Arcadian Way led to the halls of Verulanus, which surrounded a tiled court, used as a palaestra, measuring 200m by 240m. The walls of the court were lined with marble slabs of 13 different colours, the gift of Claudius Verulanus, chief priest of the Roman Province of Asia during the reign of Hadrian (AD 117–138). To the W lay a smaller palaestra and beyond that the baths. The hall to the N of the small palaestra was devoted to the worship of the emperor, while a similar room on the S was used for lectures and discussions.

During the 1896 season of excavations the Austrian archaeologists recovered from the lecture room a fine *bronze statue*, 1.92m high, of a youth cleaning his body with a strigil. This Roman copy of a 4C BC Greek original was reconstructed from 234 separate fragments. They also discovered a 2C BC Hellenistic bronze candlelabrum, 50cm high, which depicts Hercules battling with a centaur, and a delightful group, 62cm high, of a child playing with a goose. This is a 2C AD Roman copy of a 3C BC original. All are now exhibited in the Ephesus Museum in Vienna.

To the E of the halls of Verulanus lie the remains of the 2C AD *theatre gymnasium*. This consisted of a palaestra, which measured 30m by 70m, surrounded on three sides by colonnades. On the N there were rows of seats for spectators. This allowed the gymnasium to be used as a miniature stadium. So far, only the palaestra has been uncovered. The baths, which completed the complex, await excavation.

Few visitors to Ephesus can fail to be impressed by the **Arcadian Way**, the great marble street that stretches from the theatre to the middle harbour gate. This was constructed during the reign of the Emperor Arcadius (AD 395–408), the unintelligent and ineffective elder son of Theodosius the Great who ruled the E Roman Empire.

The Arcadian Way was a colonnaded street 11m wide and 600m long. On each side it had 5m-wide covered footpaths, which were paved with mosaics and lined with shops. These walk-ways, protected from the excessive heat of summer and the cold rains of winter, must have been a favourite meeting place for the Ephesians. Refreshed by cool breezes from the harbour, they could learn the latest news from abroad, as they strolled among the crews of the ships that had brought cargoes from Alexandria, from Rome and from all the ports of the Mediterranean to Ephesus.

The mid-point of the Arcadian Way was marked with statues of the evangelists on four Corinthian columns. These were erected during the reign of Justinian (AD 527–565). Today only the shafts of the columns remain.

The harbour street was lit at night. An inscription found in the city claimed that 'Arcadiane contains in its two stoas, as far as the wild boar, fifty lamps'. (The wild boar must be a statue of the animal, which is mentioned in the account of the foundation of the settlement by the mythical Androclus and his followers. See above.) Ephesus was one of the three cities in the Roman Empire to have street-lighting. The other two were Rome and Antioch.

The ends of the Arcadian Way were marked with elaborately decorated propyla. The propylon at the harbour end probably ante-dated the street. It is believed to have been constructed during the early Roman period.

At the E end of the Arcadian Way is the great Graeco-Roman **Theatre of Ephesus**, where St. Paul fulminated against false gods and particularly against Artemis. This has been restored substantially in recent years—an action which has not pleased everyone and has provoked some controversy.

Constructed during the Hellenistic period, the theatre was enlarged and enriched with lavish decoration during the reigns of Claudius and Trajan. The skene, started in the time of Nero, was completed towards the middle of the 2C AD. Thus the building visible today is almost completely Roman. A few traces of the Hellenistic structure of Lysimachus may be seen in the Roman skene.

The theatre is 145m wide and 30m high and had an estimated capacity of 24,000. There are two diazomata, 12 stairs, 11 cunei below the second diazoma and 22 above, and two paradoi. A colonnade at the top helped to improve the acoustics. Part of the cavea was covered with an awning, which gave the spectators some protection from the weather.

In the Hellenistic theatre the actors performed without scenery. The first two storeys of the elaborately ornamented skene were erected c AD 54. A third was added towards the middle of the 2C, giving a total height of 18m. The ground floor of the skene had a long corridor with eight rooms opening off it. This part of the structure is in a good state of preservation.

It is worth making the stiff climb to the top of the theatre for the sake of the fine view over the harbour area of the city. Note how the slope of the building increases as one ascends. This constructional device helped the spectators in the upper rows to have a clear view of the stage.

Behind the theatre on the slopes of Mt Pion are the substantial ruins of a Roman building, which has not been identified with certainty. Some authorities believe it may have been the residence of the governor of the city. There are also the remains of a street that ran from the theatre to the baths of Scholasticia and the street of the Curetes.

Before leaving the theatre note the fine *Hellenistic fountain* set between two slender Ionic columns, which has been built into the terrace wall. Water was delivered from three marble lion heads into the bowl. This structure has been dated to the late 3C or early 2C BC.

From the theatre it is but a short walk along along the *marble street* to the library of Celsus. This thoroughfare, one of the most pleasant in Ephesus, was paved with large marble slabs in the 5C AD, the gift to the city of a man named Eutropius. One of the main arteries of Ephesus, it formed part of the Sacred Way which, encircling Mt Pion, linked the Artemision with the principal buildings in the city.

Deep ruts in street's surface testify to the frequent passage of wheeled vehicles. Pedestrians were able traverse its length by means of a *Doric colonnade* on the W side, which was erected in the time of Nero (AD 54–68). There were steps at each end of the colonnade, which was raised c 1.70m above the level of the street.

It was lined with a series of reliefs depicting gladiatorial combats.

Manholes placed at intervals in the centre provided access to one of the city's main drains. Note the graffiti showing the head of a woman, a heart and a foot, the result, perhaps, of its proximity to the brothel that lay behind the baths of Scholasticia.

The Library of Celsus, Ephesus.

Undoubtedly the best-known monument in Ephesus is the **Library of Celsus**, which has been extensively restored after years of labour by the Austrian archaeologists. Through its widespread reproduction on posters promoting tourism and in books, magazine and pamphlets, it has become a symbol, not only of Ephesus, but of Turkey's archaeological heritage. While some purists may regret the changes that restoration have produced in the appearance of the library, few will claim that in its present form it is less accessible or understandable to the non-specialist visitor.

An inscription in Latin and Greek on the side of the front steps of the building states that the library was erected by the Consul Gaius Julius Aquila in AD 110 as a memorial to his father, Gaius Julius Celsus Polemaeanus, governor of the Roman province of Asia c AD 105–107. He was buried in a marble sarcophagus decorated with erotes, garlands, rosettes and representations of Nike, which was placed in a vault under the W apsidal wall of the building. In 1904 the archaeologists discovered the undisturbed tomb during the course of their restoration work. The body had been laid in an inner lead coffin, which was then enclosed in the sarcophagus. It has been replaced in the vault, where it was found.

The library contained 12,000 scrolls, which were kept in rows of niches in the walls of the inner chamber. This measured c 11m by 16.70m. Galleries, rather like those found in modern libraries, provided access to the niches on the upper levels. Between the inner and outer walls there was an air-gap of 1m which helped to prevent the scrolls being damaged by humidity or sudden variations in temperature. As at Pergamum, a librarian handed the scrolls to the readers. A sum of 25,000 denarii was left by Gaius Julia Aquila for the maintenance of the library and the purchase of new works.

A number of architectural devices were used to give the library, which was constructed between existing buildings, a greater impression of width. The façade was placed on a convex podium reached by nine steps and the columns and capitals on the sides were made smaller than those in the centre.

On the lower of the two storeys of the façade, pairs of Corinthian columns flank the three entrances to the inner chamber. Niches in the outer wall contain reproductions of statues representing the four virtues: Sophia (Wisdom), Arete (Valour), Ennoia (Thought) and Episteme (Knowledge). The originals are in the Ephesus Museum in Vienna.

In the middle of the 3C AD the library was badly damaged during attacks on the city by the Goths. A century later it was partly restored and a fountain was placed in front of the façade. This was surrounded with reliefs of the Parthian wars of the mid 2C AD, which probably came from a monument that had been erected in honour of Marcus Aurelius and Lucius Verus. These reliefs are now preserved in the Ephesus Museum in Vienna. Sometime in the 10C the building suffered further grave damage from an earthquake and it remained in a ruinous condition, until restored by Austrian archaeologists. A number of plaques erected by them provide information in Turkish and German about the methods used to construct the library and to restore it.

Note the remains of a circular Hellenistic building in the area in front of the library near the street. The 2C AD sarcophagus lying nearby was discovered in 1968. It belonged to Tiberius Claudius Flavianus Dionysius and had been robbed in antiquity.

To the right of the library is the commercial agora of Ephesus. This may be reached by the *Gate of Mazaeus and Mithridates*, which is being restored (at time of writing) by the archaeologists. Mazaeus and Mithridates were wealthy freedmen, who had this three-arched gateway built in the 3C BC in honour of Augustus and of his son-in-law Agrippa. Only the sockets for the gold-plated bronze letters of the inscription, which was in Latin and Greek, remain.

Note the unusual graffito on the left side wall and the admonitory scribble in a niche on the opposite side. The latter promises that, 'Whoever relieves himself here shall suffer the wrath of Hecate'. Inside the gate is a 3C AD inscription, which states that a 14oz loaf of fine bread cost four obols and a 10oz loaf of inferior bread two obols.

The first commercial agora on this site was constructed during the Hellenistic era. It was altered extensively during the Roman period, particularly during the reigns of Augustus, Nero and Caracalla. In the 4C AD, when further restoration work was undertaken to repair earthquake damage, columns of different architectural styles were used.

Surrounded by stoas, the agora measures 110m by 110m. The two-storeyed Doric colonnade on the E side, the upper part of which lined the marble street (see above), dates from the reign of Nero. In addition to the gate of Mazeus and Mithridates there were entrances on the W and N sides. In the centre of the agora there was a ὡρολόγιον horologion, a combined sundial and clepsydra (water-clock). Only the foundations of this remain. Inscriptions on the large number of extant bases show that the agora was ornamented with statues of philosophers, rhetoricians, heroes, athletes and public officials. The shops in the colonnades sold not only food but all kinds of manufactured goods. In view of the agora's proximity to the harbour it is probable that much of the produce on offer was imported.

A flight of steps in the SW corner of the agora leads to the ruins of a massive building dating from the 2C AD, which archaeologists believe was devoted to the cult of Serapis. This conclusion results from the discovery there of fragments of an Egyptian granite statue and of a number of inscriptions concerning the cult of that deity.

Egypt was the granary of the Roman world and it is not unlikely that there were strong commercial links between Ephesus, the principal city of the Province of Asia and Alexandria. There is some evidence which suggests that there was a colony of Egyptian traders in the city. They could be expected to promote the worship of one of their best-known deities. A number of objects of Egyptian provenance, including the fine statue of a priest which is now in the Selçuk museum (see above), have been found in various places in Ephesus. Serapis was a popular god in Imperial Rome and temples dedicated to him, sometimes in association with Isis, have been found in the capital and in many parts of the empire, especially in the cities of Asia Minor.

Originally the *Temple of Serapis* was reached by way of a stoa 160m long and 24m wide, which extended from the W gate of the Agora. A flight of steps led to the temple forecourt, which was surrounded by colonnades on three sides. On the fourth side a wide staircase led to the porch of the sanctuary where eight massive Corinthian columns supported an architrave, frieze and pediment. The monolithic columns, which were 14m high and had a lower diameter of 1.5m, weighed c 57 tons. Note the traces of the red colour with which they and other parts of the temple were painted. Heavy doors, studded with iron, moved on wheels to admit to the 30m-wide cella, which was covered by a stone vault. The grooves in which the doors moved may still be seen.

After the adoption of Christianity, the temple of Serapis was converted into a church. Traces of the baptistery, which was added then, may be seen in the E part of the building.

Clearly visible from the temple of Serapis are the well-preserved Hellenistic walls on Mt Coressus with which Lysimachus enclosed his new city. Visitors, who are not pressed for time, may like to explore these. Allow a full day for the expedition. Wear boots and thorn-proof clothes. Take refreshments and be prepared for a fairly stiff climb. (The summit of Coressus is c 358m above sea-level.) The reward: a splendid view over the city and the surrounding countryside and an opportunity to examine a part of Ephesus that is rarely visited.

The so-called *Prison of St. Paul* (see above) may also be seen from the temple. This lies on the SW slope of Coressus above the marshy area, which marks the site of the ancient harbour.

Where the marble street joins the street of the Curetes, note the ruins on the right-hand side of a *monumental arch*. Archaeologists are of the opinion that this resembled the arch of Hadrian in Athens and so have dated it to the 2C AD. There are plans in hand for an anastylosis.

Across the street from the arch is a group of buildings comprising a *brothel* and *public latrine*, both dated to the 1C AD, and the early 5C AD *Baths of Scholasticia*. The downstairs rooms of the brothel, which had entrances in both streets, were built around a small atrium. The floor of the main reception room was covered with a mosaic depicting the four seasons. The figures of winter, whose head is covered, and of autumn, who is garlanded with flowers, are well-preserved. There is a stone bed in one of the rooms. Other cubicles used by the girls to entertain their clients were on the first floor. The grotesque Priapus figurine, displayed in the Selçuk museum, was found in the well on the side of the brothel near the street of the Curetes. This well is still in use.

The latrine was constructed over a channel, which had an uninterrupted flow of water. The area occupied by the toilet seats, which were ranged around the walls, was roofed. The remainder of the large room, which had an impluvium in the centre, was open to the sky. As in the case of most public buildings, the floor was covered with mosaics.

At the beginning of the 5C AD the whole complex was renovated by a wealthy lady named Scholasticia. The 1C AD buildings were enlarged and improved with material taken from other structures. Some of the columns in the entrance hall were brought from the temple of Hestia Boulaea. (See below.) They bear lists of the members of the Curetes, an order of priests, which served in the temple of Artemis. (See above.)

The baths of Scholasticia had a large hall, which patrons could use as a club-room and meeting place. There they conducted business and exchanged gossip. The remainder of the building was taken up with the usual arrangement of hot and cold rooms found in a Roman bath house. A *headless statue*, believed to be of Scholasticia, has been re-erected near the entrance to the baths.

On the right-hand side of the street are the remains of *three tombs*. The largest, known as the octagon because of its shape, was surrounded by Corinthian columns and had a pyramid-shaped roof. It was ornamented with a design of palm, lotus and acanthus leaves. Entrance to the burial chamber is by way of a passageway under the house at the rear. Archaeologists found the skeleton of a girl aged between 18 and 20 in an andesite sarcophagus. The tomb has been dated to the end of the 1C BC.

A *Byzantine fountain* has been erected on the site of a heroon dating from the reign of Augustus. Nearby are a number of imperial decrees relating to the reconstruction of the city after the earthquake in the 4C AD.

Ephesus was proud of the fact that it was four times a Neocorus and there was a temple dedicated to the worship of Hadrian somewhere in the city. So far, this has not been discovered.

The small temple in the street of the Curetes, which is generally known as the *Temple of Hadrian*, was, in fact, dedicated c AD 118 by one Publius Quintilius to Hadrian, Artemis and the people of Ephesus. After the library of Celsus probably the best-known monument in Ephesus, this simple structure consists of a pronaos and a cella. The pronaos has two pillars and two columns in the Corinthian style. They supported a pediment (now disappeared) and an architrave and decorated frieze, which curve into an arch. In the centre of the arch is a representation of the *head of Tyche*.

In the pronaos there are copies of reliefs (the originals are in the museum in Selçuk), most of which were taken from a 3C building and placed in the temple at the time of its reconstruction in the 4C. These borrowed reliefs depict: Androclus slaying the boar; the fight between Hercules and Theseus; and Amazons with various divinities. The fourth section, which was made at the time of the 4C reconstruction of the building, is the most interesting. It shows the Emperor Theodosius I, that implacable enemy of paganism, with his family in the company of a group of gods, which include Athena and Artemis of Ephesus. This is an interesting illustration of the power which pagan deities, and particularly Artemis, continued to exercise in Ephesus after the triumph of Christianity.

Depicted in the arched *tympanum* over the entrance to the cella is the semi-nude figure of a girl surrounded with a decoration of acanthus leaves. On the podium at the end wall stood the cult statue of Hadrian.

In front of the temple there are bases on which rested statues of four Roman Emperors: Galerius, Maximian, Diocletian and Constantius Chlorus.

Across the street from the temple of Hadrian there are are ten small shops fronted by a 1C AD colonnade, which is paved with a delightful geometric mosaic. This mosaic, which dates from the 5C AD, was commissioned by a man named Alytarchos. Two of the shops had staircases which led to small first-floor rooms, which were probably occupied by the owners or the sales staff. Behind the shops on the slopes of Mt Coressus are the well-preserved remains of a number of luxurious private houses. These have been excavated by the Austrian archaeologists during the last few years.

Two of the **private houses**, which were occupied from the 1C to the 7C AD, have now been opened to the public. In line with current practice, objects found by the archaeologists during the course of the excavations have not been taken away to museums, they have been left in the area where they were found.

The decor and furnishings of the houses have provided some interesting information about the life of the wealthy middle-class in Ephesus during the Roman and early Byzantine periods. Inevitably, they have been compared with similar buildings found in other parts of the Roman Empire, particularly with the 1C villas of Pompeii and Herculaneum. The consensus of the experts appears to be that the life-style of the Ephesians has nothing to fear from any such comparison.

The houses may be reached from the street of the Curetes by a flight of steep steps. Room A1 of the first house is paved with a fine black and white mosaic. In the centre of the marble floor of A2, the atrium, there are the remains of a fountain. The walls of A10 and A11, which lie behind the fountain, are decorated with frescoes.

Undoubtedly, the most interesting room in the house is A3. This, the so-called 'theatre room', may offer a clue to the profession of one of its owners. It was given its name by the archaeologists because of the frescoes of theatrical subjects with which it is decorated. On the right-hand wall there is a scene from Menander's comedy, 'Perikeiromene' or The Girl Who Gets her Hair Cut, and on the left from the 'Orestes' of Euripides. There is also a fine representation of a mythological subject, the battle between Hercules and the river god, Achelous, for the hand of Deianeira. Achelous, who had the ability to transform himself into any shape he wished, assumed the form of a dragon and of a bull during the conflict. Only when Hercules tore off one of his horns did he accept defeat.

The second house, which is larger, was built in the 1C AD, altered and extended on a number of occasions and finally abandoned sometime in the 6C. Many of its rooms are decorated with mosaics and frescoes. Note particularly the frescoes of the muses in B9 and B10. It has two atria, the larger of which has a number of fine

Corinthian columns. These border a passageway ornamented with a beautiful floor mosaic of a triton and a sea-nymph.

However, the great treasure of the second house is the delicate and unusual 5C **glass mosaic**, which is to be found on the vault of a niche in the atrium. In this niche, which is flanked by a decorative fresco of erotes supporting a garland, the heads of Dionysus and Ariadne, refulgent against a background of luxuriant foliage are surrounded by a glittering array of animals and birds. As the light in the atrium changes, the glass tesserae sparkle and glow, so that the figures in the mosaic appear to move, as though momentarily endowed with life.

The houses appear to have fallen into a gradual decay. After they had been abandoned for some time a number became filled with soil from landslips. This helped to preserve them and their contents.

Further up the street of the Curetes on the left are the remains of the *Fountain of Trajan*. According to an inscription this was erected c AD 114 by Tiberius Claudius Aristion in honour of Trajan (AD 98–117).

A colossal statue of the emperor towered over a rectangular pool, which was surrounded on three sides by a two-storey colonnade. The columns in the upper storey were Corinthian, those in the lower storey Composite. Statues, now in the Selçuk Museum, stood in the niches between the columns. These included representations of Aphrodite, Dionysus, a reclining satyr and members of the imperial family.

A partial anastylosis of the fountain has been made. Only the feet of the statue of Trajan and a large globe, on which it stood, remain.

The top boundary of the street of the Curetes is marked by the so-called *Gate of Hercules*, which is believed to date from the beginning of the 4C AD. This two-storey structure had a large arched central opening. The pillars of the gate bore representations of Hercules, clothed in the skin of the Nemean Lion, and there were winged victories on the upper corners of the archway.

In the street of the Curetes there are the bases of several monuments erected by the Ephesians in honour of local worthies. These include the plinth which supported the statue of the consul Stephanus, which is now in the Selçuk Museum. (See above.)

The large structure with four columns beyond the gate of Hercules is the *hydreion*. When this rectangular fountain was reconstructed in the 3C AD, statues of Diocletian, Maximian, Constantius Chlorus and Galerian, emperors also honoured at the temple of Hadrian, were placed in front. (See above.)

Nearby is the *Monument of Caius Memmius*. This structure, which rested on a square base, had pillars decorated with dancing female figures. The pillars flanked arched niches, above which there were reliefs depicting Memmius, his father, and his grandfather, the dictator Sulla. It dates from the 1C AD. This is a somewhat surprising monument, as Sulla can hardly have been a popular figure in Ephesus. He sacked the city in 84 BC as a punishment for its support of Mithridates and for the murder there of many Romans citizens during the revolt. (See above.)

The circular *monument* nearby was brought from another place in the city and erected here in the 4C. The relief of the winged victory came from the gate of Hercules. (See above.)

After the Ephesians had constructed the temple of Domitian towards the end of the 1C AD, the city was given the title of Neocorus or Temple-Warden for the first time. Few traces of the building,

Gate of Hercules, 4C AD, Ephesus. Hercules clothed in the skin of the Nemean lion.

which was sited on a terrace measuring c 100m by 50m, remain. It was a small prostyle of 8 by 13 columns with 4 columns in front. The stylobate, which rested on an eight-stepped crepidoma, measured c 24m by 34m. The cella containing the cult-statue was 9m by 17m. The head and forearm of the huge statue of the emperor are preserved in the İzmir Archaeological Museum.

In the last years of his reign Domitian, the self-proclaimed *Dominus et Deus*, was tormented by doubts and suspicions. He set in motion a campaign of terror against members of the senate and prominent Romans, whom he accused of plotting against him. Eventually, frightened by his excesses, his wife, Domitia, induced the praetorian guard to assasinate him. When the news of the death of Domitian reached Ephesus, an exultant mob demolished the statue of the hated tyrant.

Underneath the terrace, on which the temple of Domitian rested, there were shops and storerooms. These rooms, which are well-preserved, are now devoted to a display of some of the most important inscriptions found in the city.

Unfortunately, the *Museum of Inscriptions* keeps irregular opening hours. To ensure admission, it is advisable to apply in advance to the museum directorate in Selçuk.

Amongst the inscriptions, the earliest of which has been dated to the 7C BC, are some relating to property and to the criminal law (a request for the the death penalty for a number of persons who had mistreated ambassadors and stolen temple gifts), a commendation for a good tutor from Attalus II of Pergamum and a tablet erected to commemorate the visit of Hadrian to Ephesus in 128.

Facing the square of Domitian was a two-storey *terrace*, part of which has been restored. The lower storey was an unfussy structure in the Doric style. The upper storey was more flamboyant. The pillars, which supported it, bore representations of the more exotic eastern gods.

Backing on to the state agora are the ruins of a *monument* erected by Caius Ofillus Proculus c AD 8 in honour of Caius Sextilius Pollio, who constructed the Marnas aqueduct. A statue of this benefactor of Ephesus stood in the central arched niche of the monument.

The structure was later embellished with ornamental sculpture, the so-called Polyphemus group now in the Selçuk Museum, which was brought from another building (the Temple of Isis) in the city. It was also joined to the Domitian fountain sometime after AD 93.

The *Nymphaeum of Caius Laecanius Bassus*, erected c AD 80, was functional as well as decorative. It supplied water to buildings in the neighbourhood.

An elaborate façade, whose pediment reached a height of c 9m, was ornamented with statues of some of the minor deities, nereids, river-gods, and tritons, which were associated with water. From delicately-chased conch shells and bowls, disposed about the structure, water flowed into a large central basin.

Between the temple of Domitian and the state agora there are two statue bases or pillars from a gate, now demolished. (The authorities are divided about the function of these remains.) One has a relief of a naked, youthful Hermes, who can be identified by his caduceus, leading a ram. The other shows a youth, who is gripping a goat. Both animals may on their way to the sacrificial altar. Note also the depiction of an omphalos and a tripod.

The *prytaneion* was one of the most important civic structures in Ephesus. Dedicated to the goddess Hestia (Vesta), it contained the sacred flame of the city which was never allowed to go out. Hestia, the sister of Zeus and Hera, had charge of the hearth, the centre of domestic worship, and so was honoured not only in the temples but in every home.

The prytaneion was also the place where official guests were received by the religious and civil dignitaries of the city. Although a building must have existed on the site from the time of the refoundation of Ephesus by Lysimachus in the 3C BC, the structure, whose remains are visible today, dates from the reign of Augustus (27 BC–AD 14).

It consisted of a Doric courtyard surrounded on three sides by a colonnade, which fronted a large temple-like hall. The courtyard was decorated with a mosaic, on which were depicted the shields of Amazons against an ornamental background. In the hall there are the remains of a basalt altar. Note the names of the Curetes (see above) on two of the pillars, which have been re-erected. It was from the prytaneion that Scholastica took columns and other material for the refurbishment of the baths at the bottom of the street of the Curetes.

Archaeologists found the two beautiful statues of Artemis, now in the museum at Selçuk, in the prytaneion. The larger statue, which dates from the end of the 1C AD, was found in the hall. The other, which was made about half a century later, had been placed carefully in the ground in a small room in the sanctuary.

Next to the prytaneion was the site of the double *Temple of Divus Julius and Dea Roma*, erected on the instructions of Octavian in AD 29 in honour of Julius Caesar and of Rome.

The *odeum*, was built c AD 150 by Publius Vedius Antoninus. It had a single diazoma and two paradoi covered with a wooden roof. The odeum had a seating capacity of 1400 and was probably used for lectures and musical performances as well as for the transaction of the city's business. (It was not uncommon for an odeum to function also as a bouleuterion, i.e. council chamber. The proximity of the building to the state agora suggests this was the case in Ephesus.)

The state *agora* occupied an area c 56m by 160m with colonnades on the N and S sides. It covered part of the city's ancient necropolis. On the W side on a raised platform there are the foundations of a small *temple*. Archaeologists have found a number of objects on the site which indicate that this building was dedicated to Isis. The head of a colossal statue, which some authorities have identified as a representation of Mark Antony, was found nearby. In view of his connections with Egypt it has been suggested that Antony may have been responsible for the construction of the temple.

The Ionic colonnade on the N side, which dates from the early part of the 1C AD, was divided by two rows of columns into a central nave and two side aisles. Additional Corinthian columns were added later. Referred to in an inscription as the basilica, this structure was probably used as the city's law courts and for the transaction of official business. Part of the colonnade has been excavated. Note the bulls' heads which adorn some of the Ionic capitals. Traces of a Hellenistic stoa have been found underneath the Roman structure.

The well-preserved remains to the E of the odeum mark the site of the so-called *Baths of Varius*. Erected towards the end of the 2C AD by Flavius Damianus they comprised a bathhouse and palaestra. Flavius Damianus, a sophist, lived in Ephesus c AD 200. His statue is preserved in the İzmir Archaeological Museum.

To the S of the the state agora there was a large *nymphaeum*, which received water from the Marnas river and distributed it to various parts of the city. It received its supplies by means of a conduit erected by Caius Sextilius Pollio. (See above.) The aqueduct, which may be seen c 5km E of Ephesus on the Aydın road, formed part of this system.

The last major building in this part of the city is the *East gymnasium*. The discovery here of a statue of the sophist Flavius Damianus (see above) suggests that this building was also constructed by him c AD 200.

The ruins of the small *circular building* to the right of the road, which at some point was turned into a church, is believed by some to mark the site of the tomb of St. Luke. However, there is no substantial evidence to support this belief.

An insignificant jumble of stones is all that remains of the *Magnesian gate*. So called because it marked the beginning of the road to Magnesia on the Maeander, it was erected during the reign of Vespasian (AD 69–79).

A modern road leads from the Magnesian gate to the site of 5km **Meryemana** (or Panaya Kapulu). According to an ancient tradition this was the house occupied by the Virgin Mary during the last years of her life. Confided by Christ to the care of St. John, it is believed that he brought her to Ephesus sometime between AD 37–48.

Catherine Emmerich, a 19C German mystic, who had never visited Ephesus, described the house and its situation, which she had seen in a vision, in great detail. Towards the end of the 19C the Lazarist fathers from İzmir instigated a search and discovered a building which fitted the description provided by the mystic. This had long been a place of pilgrimage for Orthodox Christians from the surrounding countryside. They went there in great numbers each year on 15 August, the Feast of the Assumption of Mary.

Archaeologists, who have examined the small T-shaped building, believe that it dates from the 6C or 7C, but that the foundations are much older— probably from the 1C. The room on the right was the bedroom, that on the left was the kitchen. Still in the care of the Lazarist fathers, the little church attracts a large number of pilgrims from many countries each year. It is claimed that a number of unexplained cures have taken place there.

Inevitably there has been some commercial development at Meryemana. A small restaurant has been constructed to cater for the pilgrims and there are shops selling souvenirs. However, the site has not been spoiled, and, irrespective of one's religious beliefs, the excursion to Meryemana is likely to prove interesting and enjoyable.

11 Ephesus to Kuşadası, Priene, Miletus and Didyma

Total distance c 104km. **Ephesus**—17km **Kuşadası**–(20km **Panionium**)—R525 37km **Priene** / *Prien*—16km **Miletus** / *Milet*— 20km **Didyma** / *Didim*—14km Altınkum.

The road from **Ephesus** (see Rte 10) to 17km Kuşadası, though narrow in parts, is well-surfaced. Carrying a good deal of traffic for most of the year, it is particularly busy during the holiday season, when large numbers of coaches take visitors from the resort to Ephesus, Selçuk and İzmir.

Once across the delta of the Cayster, the Küçük Menderes, the road skirts the W edge of the Durmuş Dağı. Then it descends to Kuşadası through a series of wide bends which give some fine views over the sea.

During recent years **Kuşadası** has become increasingly popular with holidaymakers from W Europe and its attractions are set out at length in the tour-operators' brochures. Its rapid growth has resulted in a proliferation of smart boutiques and specialist shops which cater almost exclusively for the tourists. Fortunately, these are concentrated in the centre and this small Aegean town has not lost all of its charm. In the morning sunlight the sight of its gleaming white houses, which cling to the bare brown hills around the harbour, can still touch even the most hardened traveller.

Information and Accommodation. Up-to-date information about hotel and pension prices, restaurants, transport, and excursions (including boat-trips to Samos) may be obtained from the Tourism Information Office, İskele Meydanı.

Kuşadası offers a wide range of accommodation. Among its hotels and pensions, which include the comfortable and inexpensive *Akman Hotel*, there should be something to satisfy every taste and meet every price-range. During the holiday season many hotels take block bookings from foreign tour-operators and visitors who have not made a reservation may find it difficult to get a room.

The town has a number of excellent restaurants. Those near the harbour offer a range of Turkish dishes in an agreeable setting at very reasonable prices. Not surprisingly the fish in Kuşadası is particularly good.

Transport. There are frequent bus services to İzmir, Aydın, Denizli, Muğla, Fethiye and other towns in SW Turkey. Buses may be joined at the the companies' offices, at the Otogar or at convenient points along the route. It is advisable to purchase travel tickets in advance, particularly during the holiday months.

Dolmuş taxis, which serve the surrounding countryside, leave from a station in the town-centre. There are frequent services in the morning to Selçuk, which pass near Ephesus.

A number of travel agencies in the town organise visits by coach during the holiday season to sites like Ephesus, Pamukkale, Aphrodisias, Priene, Miletus, and Didyma, and by boat to Samos and the Samsandağı National Park.

Marina. Kuşadası has an excellent marina which offers a variety of services to boat-owners. These include a small restaurant and a shop.

Recreations. There are facilities for fishing, sailing, horse riding, windsurfing and swimming in Kuşadası. The best and cleanest beaches are located some distance outside the town. Nature lovers and bird watchers will find much to interest them in the Samsandağı (or Dilek Yarımadası) National Park. Open from April to December, it is one of the finest in Turkey. It may be reached by road (28km from Kuşadası) or by boat.

Occupying an area of c 10,985 hectares, the park has a variety of wild life, which includes leopards, foxes, wild boar, lynxes, badgers, bears, jackals, striped hyenas, hares, martens and porcupines. The vegetation ranges from Mediterranean maquis on the N to red and Austrian pine on the S slopes. The average height is 600m and the highest point in the park, Dilek Tepesi, 1237m.

There are facilities for picnics and barbecues, but the park has no restaurants or accommodation. Bathing is from clean, sandy or pebble beaches.

As in all Turkish National Parks visitors are required to respect the laws concerning the flora and fauna, which are protected, and to observe all safety precautions, particularly in regard to fires. Contraventions of the regualtions may result in severe penalties.

Kuşadası is believed to occupy the site of an ancient city named Neapolis. However, no trace of this has been found so far. During the Byzantine era the town was known as *Ania*. Later, when the Genoese and Venetians were trading on this part of the Turkish coast, they renamed the small port *Scala Nuova*.

A short distance to the N of Kuşadası near the beach at *Pamucak* there are Byzantine remains which have been dated to the 13C. Some authorities believe that these were built over the remains of the ancient city of Pygela, which Strabo located in that area.

Kuşadası is an excellent centre for visiting the many historical sites in this part of Turkey, all of which may be reached without difficulty.

An interesting EXCURSION from Kuşadası is to the site of the (20km) **Panionium**, the religious and cultural organisation, in which the 12 principal Ionian cities were loosely united.

An ancient tradition states that the league was founded c 800, when a number of the cities in the area combined to bring the people of a small settlement called Melia to heel. They took over the sanctuary of the Melians and, dedicating it to Poseidon Heliconius, made it the cult-centre of the new organisation.

In addition to meetings of the league, a festival, the Panionia, was held there at regular intervals. On a medallion issued by Colophon during the reign of

Gallus (AD 251–253) there is a representation of the kind of sacrifice made by the delegates from the member cities. Thirteen figures, their right hands raised in blessing or intercession, stand around an altar, at which a bull is about to be offered.

The members of the league were: Miletus, Myus, Priene, Samos, Ephesus, Colophon, Lebedus, Teos, Erythrae, Chios, Clazomenae and Phocaea. Some accounts state that after dissidents from Colophon had seized Smyrna, an Aeolian foundation, that city also applied for membership and was eventually admitted to the league. However, Strabo asserts that Smyrna was 'induced by the Ephesians to join the Ionian League; for the Ephesians were fellow-inhabitants of the Smyrnaeans in ancient times, when Ephesus was also called Smyrna'.

Members of the Panionium retained complete freedom of action and all attempts to turn the league into a political organisation failed. About 600 BC Thales of Miletus suggested that the Ionian cities form an assembly in Teos, so that they could work out a common foreign and domestic policy. That advice, like the proposal made by the Prienian philosopher Bias after the Persian conquest of Ionia that members of the Panionium abandon their cities and found new settlements in Sardinia, was ignored. After a period of inactivity during the Persian occupation, the league was revived by Alexander and his successors and the Panionia continued to be celebrated, albeit in a reduced fashion, into Roman times.

As the sanctuary was located in Prienian territory, the priest was usually chosen from that city. To facilitate communication there was a road over Mt Mycale, which joined Priene with the shrine. When Freya Stark visited Ionia in 1952, she glimpsed a track high up on the side of the mountain, which, she conjectured, could be a relic of that ancient highway. The broken pavement, which Chandler and his companions followed in the spring of 1765 on their journey over the shoulder of Mycale from the site of the Panionium to the cities in the S, may also have formed part of the same route.

Through its dedication to Poseidon Heliconius, the Panionium was linked to the Greek city of Helice, one of the principal centres of the worship of Poseidon. Helice was named after the wife of Ion, the legendary ancestor of the Ionians. An interesting reference to the Panionia occurs in a letter dated to c 303 BC from Antigonus to the people of Teos regarding a proposal to unite that city with Lebedus in a synoecism. The letter ordains that whoever attends the Panionia should carry out the 'common rites for the same period of time, that he should pitch tent, take part in the festival together with (your envoys) and be called a Tean'.

The remains of the Panionium, all of which are overgrown and difficult to explore, lie on the N slopes of Mt Mycale (Samsun Dağı) near the village of Güzelçamlı. The site may be reached by taking a secondary road from Kuşadası first to Davutlar and then to Güzelçamlı.

On top of a small hill, formerly named after St. Elias and now known as Otomatik Tepe, there are the ruins of the *temenos wall*. Excavations carried out there by German archaeologists have revealed, in the centre of the temenos, traces of an ancient stone *altar* measuring c 17.5m by 4.25m. At the foot of the hill are the ruins of a structure which is believed to have been the *meeting-place* of the league. This had 11 rows of seats facing a levelled area which presumably served as a bema for delegates addressing the assembly.

A pleasant day's EXCURSION from Kuşadası to the sites of ancient Priene, Miletus and Didyma may be followed by a late afternoon bathe at the beach of *Altınkum*. This involves a round trip of c 176km through a varied and interesting landscape. Visitors who do not have their own transport are advised to take a coach tour. It would be very difficult, if not impossible, to see all three sites in one day by any combination of the public transport services.

While some refreshments may be obtained at or near all three sites, it is more enjoyable and less time-wasting to take a picnic lunch.

Leave Kuşadası by the Söke road. This passes through a wooded valley which provides shelter for a number of small, neat villages. At 24km *Söke* take road 525 in the direction of Milas. After c 5km a turning to the right leads to 8km *Güllübahçe*, the nearest village to the site of Priene.

A rough track climbs steeply from the car-park to the ancient city. As it ascends, this offers fine views over the lower reaches of the Maeander, the Büyük Menderes. The ruins of Priene's neighbour, Miletus, are sometimes visible through the haze. They lie across the river, far away to the S. Entry to **PRIENE** is through a breach in the ancient walls. The city occupied a series of terraces on the side of Mt Mycale, Samsun Dağı.

History. Legend would have us believe that Priene was founded by a group of adventurers led by Aepytus, grandson of Codrus, king of Athens and that they were joined sometime later by a band of Thebans under the command of an adventurer named Philotas. It would appear that there was some truth behind the myth, as the inhabitants of Priene always felt that special ties linked them with Athens.

Apart from a single coin, no trace of the first settlement at Priene has been found. It seems likely that it lies buried under the silt brought down by the Maeander. The action of the river has been pushing the sea back for thousands of years. Visible proof of this is provided by the position of the former island of Lade, where in 494 BC the Ionian rebel cities were defeated by the Persians in a naval battle. This is now marked by a small hill to the W of the theatre of Miletus and about 6km distance from the present coastline. Strabo, who wrote his Geography towards the beginning of the 1C AD, placed Priene c 6.5km from the sea.

Priene was a leading member of the Panionium which was sited in its territory to the W of Mt Mycale (see above). The Prienians had the right to appoint the official who presided over the meetings of the organisation. It was customary also for one of their number to hold the office of priest at its sanctuary which was dedicated to Poseidon Heliconius.

In 334 BC, when Alexander the Great came to Priene, the inhabitants were building their new city on the side of Mt Mycale. It is believed that they chose this site because it was near their harbour at Naulochus, which had served the first settlement also. Alexander offered to defray the costs of the new temple dedicated to Athena, part of which had been constructed. The people of Priene, less proud than the Ephesians (see above), accepted his offer. An inscription, which commemorates Alexander's generosity, is now preserved in the architectural gallery in the basement of the British Museum.

After the death of Alexander Priene came under the rule of the Attalids of Pergamum and from them it passed to Rome. Unlike Ephesus and some of its other neighbours, Priene received few gifts from its new masters. Apart from some relatively minor alterations to the theatre and some of the other public buildings, the Hellenistic city was left untouched by the Romans. Perhaps because of the silting of its new harbour, which appears to have become unusable, hardship produced by the Mithridatic wars and the exactions of greedy Roman tax collectors, Priene entered a period of decline. During the Byzantine era a bishop's see, it sank into obscurity under the Ottomans and was largely forgotten.

In 1765 Richard Chandler celebrated Easter in a village near Priene with Greek Orthodox Christians who gave him presents of coloured eggs and cakes. He has left a record of an interesting natural phenomenon which he witnessed before one of his visits to the ancient city. 'We were sitting on the floor early one morning at breakfast, with the door, which was toward the mountain, open; when we discovered a small rainbow just above the brow. The sun was then peeping only over the opposite mountain, and, as it got higher, the arc widened and descended towards us; the cattle, feeding on the slope, being seen through it, tinged with its various colours as it passed down, and seeming in the bow.' Undeterred by this portent of a visitation from Iris on behalf of Jupiter Pluvius, or, perhaps encouraged by it, Chandler went on to make a precarious descent from the upper slopes of Mt Mycale to the site of Priene's temple.

After the publication of the site by the Society of Dilettanti, excavations were carried out by the German archaeologists Carl Humann and Theodore Wiegand towards the end of the 19C. As was customary at the time, most of important finds were taken to Germany.

The city was surrounded by a *wall*, which dates from the middle of the 4C BC. Constructed of a local marble, this reached an average height of c 6m. At intervals sections of the wall projected in a sawtooth pattern which allowed the defenders to engage enemy attackers on the flank. The principal city gate was on the NE side. There were other gates on the E and W.

Priene was constructed in accordance with the grid-iron plan popularised by Hippodamos of Miletus (fl. c 450 BC), which was much favoured during the late Classical and early Hellenistic periods. Philosopher, town-planner, and political scientist, Hippodamos was the friend and confidant of Pericles. Notable use of his town-planning theories was made at Rhodes, Miletus, Ephesus and Piraeus.

In Priene, the main streets, which ran E–W, were intersected at right-angles by lanes or alleyways, many of which had flights of steps to accommodate the sloping conditions of the site. As a rule there were four private houses in each insula formed by the grid-iron, while public and religious buildings occupied one or more insulae.

The *Temenos of the Egyptian gods* was in the fourth insula to the SW of the city's main gate. It contained an altar 7.30m by 14.60m by 1.70m and was entered by a propylon on the NW side. An inscribed altar stone found there was dedicated to Serapis, Isis and Anubis, other inscriptions set out in detail the rituals to be followed by the worshippers and prescribed penalties for any contravention of the rules.

Two insulae to the W of the temenos of the Egyptian gods is the partly-excavated *Upper Gymnasium* which dates from the middle of the 4C BC. This consisted of a peristyle and courtyard. During the Roman Imperial period a bath and small temple dedicated to the worship of the emperor were added to the complex.

In the next insula to the W there are the partly-uncovered remains of a *Byzantine basilica*. The pulpit and the foundations of the altar are still visible.

The whole of the insula to the N of the basilica is occupied by the *theatre*, which in its earliest form is believed to date from the second half of the 4C BC. The presence of a clepsydra at the SW end of the passage behind the prohedria (see below), which could have been used to regulate the length of speeches, suggests that public meetings as well as theatrical performances were held in the building.

Constructed in the Greek style, the cavea is greater than a semicircle. It was supported at each end by retaining walls and had an estimated capacity of 5000. Spectators entered the theatre through two unroofed paradoi and ascended to their seats by six narrow stairs. Only part of the seating has been uncovered.

The orchestra was separated from the cavea by a 4C BC *prohedria*, which took the form of a semicircular bench with a high back. The prohedria incorporated five marble chairs, which have been tentatively dated to the beginning of the 2C BC. Reserved for the principal religious and civil dignitaries, they were presented to the city, according to an inscription, by one Nysios. In the centre of the prohedria there was a 2C BC altar dedicated to Dionysus, where sacrifices were offered before the performances. The space behind the prohedria had a double function: it provided access to the cavea and also allowed rain-water to drain away.

A substantial part of the proskenion and skene, which have been dated to the beginning of the 2C BC, remains. The proskenion is a narrow building 21m long and 2.75m wide, through which the performers passed into the orchestra. A stairs on the L provided access to the roof. When, towards the middle of the 2C BC, performances were moved from the orchestra to the roof of the proskenion,

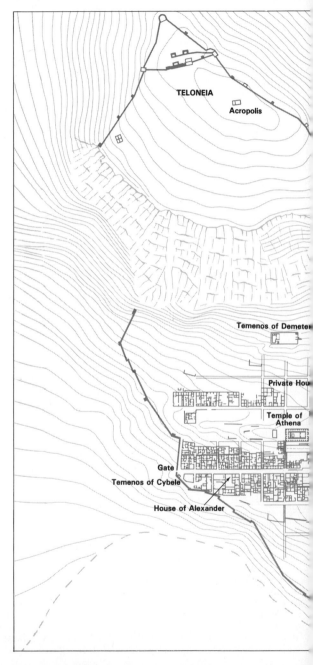

TELONEIA

Acropolis

Temenos of Demeter

Private Hou

Temple of
Athena

Gate

Temenos of Cybele

House of Alexander

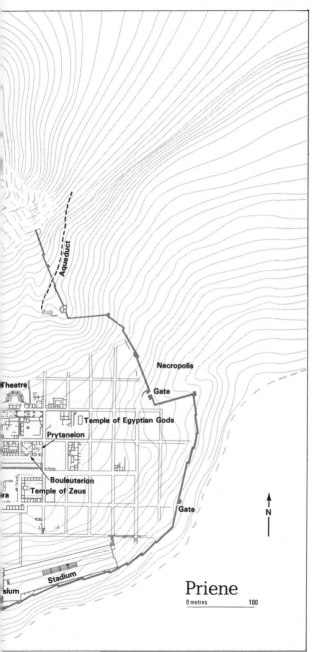

Priene

0 metres   100

a new prohedria was built in the centre of the cavea in the fifth row of seats.

The original skene was a two-storey construction 18.5m by c 6m. Only the lower storey remains. It was modified considerably in the 2C AD during the period of Roman rule to give the actors more room. The existing structure on the upper storey was removed and was replaced by a new construction, which, resting on arches, was placed 2m farther back. This increased the width of the area over the proskenion from 2.75m to 4.75m.

Some of the most important buildings in Priene lay to the S of the upper gymnasium. One insula was occupied by the bouleuterion and the prytaneion. These buildings were flanked by the sacred stoa, while across the principal street were the agora and the temple of Zeus.

The *bouleuterion*, which is in an excellent state of preservation, measured 20m by 21m. It is believed to date from the middle of the 2C BC. Rows of seats on three sides enclosed a small area which contained a marble altar decorated with bulls heads, garlands and representations of the gods. On the S side there was a large recess where speakers stood to address the elected councillors who composed the boule. The structure had a wooden roof which was supported at first by pillars resting on the upper rows of the seats. Later, further pillars were added to provide additional strength. It is estimated that the bouleuterion could seat abut 640 persons.

The *prytaneion*, the administrative headquarters of the city, was sited next door to the bouleuterion. Part of this building contained the sacred fire of the city. The remainder was used by the prutaneis, the presidents of the boule. It contained their dining room which was maintained out of official funds.

To the N of the agora lay the *sacred stoa*. This 116m-long structure is believed to date from the second half of the 2C BC. It was a gift to the city from Ariarathes VI of Cappadocia. Six steps led up from the street to a 6.5m-wide promenade. Like the Arcadian Way in Ephesus this must have been a popular meeting place for the Prienians. There they could enjoy the cool breeze from the sea, exchange gossip and conduct business. Behind the promenade lay the stoa, its façade decorated with 49 Doric columns. The interior was divided into two equal sections by 24 Ionic columns, which supported the roof. The structure was completed by 15 rooms at the back, which were reserved for the use of the principal officials of the city. During the Roman period the room towards the centre, which contains a seat, was devoted to the imperial cult. The walls of the stoa were covered with inscriptions which provided information about Priene.

The *agora*, which measured 75m by 35m, occupied two insulae. Dating from the 3C BC, it was surrounded on three sides by Doric porticoes. Because of the slope the S portico was supported by a basement. There were shops in the W portico and on the W and E sides of the S portico. The centre of the S portico, which was protected by a wall from the cold N winds, formed another promenade. This offered excellent views over the lower gymnasium, the stadium and, in the distance, the harbour.

An altar dedicated to Hermes occupied a central position. To the E of the altar there was a double dais covered by an awning. This was probably reserved for the dignitaries, civil and religious, who presided over the many functions held there. Only the bases and foundations of the many statues which once ornamented the agora still remain.

The insula to the E of the agora contained the 3C BC *Temple of Zeus Olympios*. This, an Ionic prostyle, which rested on a stylobate 13.5m by 8.5m, opened to the E. Only the foundations of the temple and of the altar, which faced the entrance, now remain on the site. A number of finds by the German archaeologists were taken to Berlin. The temenos of the temple, which could be reached from the agora through the E portico, was bounded on the N by a colonnade. During the Byzantine period a castle was erected over the E part of the temenos.

In the insula to the W of the agora there was a *market* for foodstuffs, clothing and household goods.

Four insulae to the W of the market is the *House of Alexander*, so called as some authorities believe that it may have been occupied by Alexander the Great, when in 334 BC he spent some time in Priene during the siege of Miletus.

An inscription on the door-post states that only the pure, clothed in white garments, were permitted to enter the sanctuary. In a room to the N of the interior courtyard the archaeologists found a number of terracotta and marble figurines on a stone bench. In front of the bench a marble altar-table had been placed over a natural fissure in the floor. The discovery in the house of the head and upper part of the torso of a small marble statue which bears a strong resemblance to Alexander, has led to the belief that this was the Alexandrium mentioned in an inscription found in the city. An alternative view, supported by the presence of the altar over the fissure, is that it was a sanctuary dedicated to the gods of the underworld. The inscription and the statuettes are now preserved in Berlin.

W of the house of Alexander and close to the city wall is the *Temenos of Cybele*. Cybele, the ancient Mother Goddess of Anatolia, had shrines in Ephesus and in many of the other Ionian cities. She is frequently associated with Attis and the hermaphrodite Agdistis. Attis was a handsome youth who is portrayed sometimes as the son, sometimes as the lover of Cybele. When during a fit of jealous rage she struck Attis with madness he castrated himself. He then became the beloved of Agdistis. This part of the myth has been used to explain the orgiastic rites which accompanied the worship of Cybele.

The goddess is usually depicted wearing a crown of towers and seated on a throne between two lions. Her priests were known as Galli. Despite the disapproval of the more conservative elements, the cult of Cybele spread widely throughout the Roman Empire, attracting many followers. It became extinct only after the adoption of Christianity as the state religion.

Today there is nothing to see in the temenos except the *sacrificial pit*. A small headless statue of Cybele found in the temenos is now in the İstanbul Archaeological Museum.

Four insulae to the E of the temenos of Cybele a stairway leads up to the **Temple of Athena Polias**. This, the most ancient and most prominent ruin in Priene, is sited c 100m above sea-level. A partial anastylosis was made in 1964.

The temple, which was entered from the E side, was an Ionic peripteros of 11 by 6 columns. It was erected between the 4C and 2C BC. Constructed of marble from Mt Mycale, it consisted of a large pronaos, a cella and an opisthodomus which rested on a stylobate 37m by 19.5m. The entrance to the pronaos was flanked by two columns. The cult statue of Athena stood on a pedestal at the E end of the cella. There is some evidence that there was a grill or enclosure between the side-walls and the two columns in front of the opisthodomus, which suggests that the temple's treasure was kept there. Traces of red and blue paint have been found on the ornamented parts of the building.

The Carian architect, Pytheos (fl. 353–334), who built the Mausoleum at Halicarnassus, designed the temple of Athena Polias at Priene. In ancient times it was generally accepted that this building represented the definitive form of the Ionic order. Pytheos wrote a treatise about the temple which dealt not only with its construction and the merits of its design but also touched on the training of architects. According to Vitruvius this was still used as an instruction manual two centuries later.

The temple benefited from the generosity of a number of royal patrons. Alexander's contribution (see above), is recorded in an inscription now in the British Museum which states, 'King Alexander presented this temple to Athena Polias'. The cult statue of Athena, which is believed to have been a copy of the famous statue by Pheidias in the Parthenon in Athens, was the gift of a Cappadocian prince, Orophernes, who appears to have spent part of his youth in the city. Some fragments of a small Nike held by Athena were recovered by British archaeologists during their excavations in 1868–69.

The *altar*, which stood to the E of the temple, was a small-scale version of the great altar of Zeus of Pergamum. Only the foundation of this structure remains on the site. Reliefs, depicting a gigantomachy, which decorated its base, are preserved in the İstanbul Archaeological Museum.

During the 2C BC a *stoa* was constructed to the S of the temple. This was 78.5m long and had a single row of Doric columns. Like the sacred stoa and the portico to the S of the agora, it provided another pleasant rendezvous for the citizens of Priene. Still visible are the steps and part of the wall of an elaborate propylon which was erected at the E end of the temenos of the temple of Athena Polias during the 1C AD. At this time also the temple was rededicated. Athena was obliged to share her sanctuary with Augustus. Part of the inscription on the architrave, which recorded this event, lies at present on the stylobate.

The *private houses* of Priene have provided a great deal of information about life in the city. Although many are very overgrown, their rooms filled with pine saplings and scrub, they merit an examination. These 3C and 4C BC houses have been compared frequently with the 1C AD houses discovered at Pompeii and Herculaneum. They have many features in common. Both the Hellenistic and Roman builders used a design which has proved itself effective all over the Mediterranean. Their houses were built in such a way as to protect the occupants from the fierce heat of the summer sun and from the cold of winter.

The entrance, which was not always on the main street, led through a vestibule to a large courtyard, which admitted light and air. To the N of the courtyard was an open-fronted antechamber which provided access to the dining and living rooms. The remains of stairs in some of the houses shows that a number had an upper floor. As in Athens during the Classical period, this may have been reserved for the women of the household. To ensure that they were cool and airy during the summer the ground floor rooms had high walls. Windows were placed near the top to ensure privacy. As in many village houses in Turkey today the rooms were heated with portable stoves. Decoration was simple and usually restricted to geometric patterns, though some of the walls had stucco which imitated marble.

A variety of stone, bronze and terracotta objects have been found in the private houses. These include coins, mostly from the 3C BC, lamps, cooking utensils, bedsteads, statuettes and figurines. Surprisingly, only one small bathroom has been found. This measured 1.8m by 1m and contained a basin in which the occupant could place his feet. A few of the houses had toilets. Again this is surprising as there appear to have been no public latrines in the city.

One of the largest of the private houses is located in the fourth insula to the W of the theatre. This had 26 rooms, including separate women's quarters, an indication that it belonged to someone of wealth and importance. Many objects of value and an altar dedicated to Zeus Olympios were found there.

A short scramble up the slope leads to the *Temenos of Demeter and Kore*. The temenos, which dates from the 4C BC, measures 45m by 17.75m. In front of the entrance, which was on the E side of the sacred enclosure, are pedestals on which statues of two of the priestesses, Timonassa and Nikeso, stood. The marble statue of Nikeso is now in Berlin. To the S of the temenos were the modest quarters occupied by the priestesses.

Demeter was the goddess of growth and fruitfulness, particularly of life-sustaining corn. This belief was acknowledged by the early coins of Priene which bore a representation of a corn sheaf.

According to the legend, Demeter's daughter, Persephone or Kore (the maiden), was abducted by Hades and taken by him to the underworld. Demeter wandered through the land grieving for her lost child. Nothing grew and mankind was in danger of starvation. In desperation, Zeus persuaded Hades to allow Kore to return to her mother. Hades agreed, but tricked the maiden into eating a pomegranate, so ensuring that she would spend three months of every year with him in his gloomy kingdom.

The goddesses were credited with bringing the gift of corn to mankind. When Demeter was looking for Kore, she was befriended by the king of Eleusis. Later, to thank him for his kindness, she gave some sheaves of corn to his son, Triptolemus. He was charged by her with the task of spreading knowledge of its use and benefits throughout the world.

This myth of Demeter and Kore is usually taken to symbolise the sowing of the seed-corn, its stay in the soil for part of the year and then its growth and harvest for the benefit of mankind. It was a subject much favoured by artists in antiquity. A well-known example is the 5C BC relief found at Eleusis near Athens, which is now kept in the Athens National Museum. Triptolemus is shown as a nude youth receiving a sheaf of corn from Demeter under the benevolent gaze of Kore.

Both goddesses were honoured by the celebration of mysteries, the most famous of which took place at Eleusis. According to Burkert these mystery cults were linked with reports of strange and perverse sexual practices, which included the coupling of Demeter with Poseidon, who came to her in the form of a stallion.

Just inside the temenos, on the right side, are the remains of a Roman altar. Between the entrance and the temple there is a large open space which presumably accommodated the participants at the mysteries. There is, however, no trace of the seating which was generally provided. (See the entry on Pergamum above.) The *temple*, which occupies the W end of the temenos is of a most unusual design. A slender passageway separated it from the N, W and S walls of the temenos. Entrance was through a narrow doorway which had three Doric columns in the side walls. Beyond this pronaos was the cella which had a N–S orientation. On the W side of the cella there was a high shelf or podium where votive offerings were placed.

Outside, on the S side of the temple there was a *sacrificial pit* where sows were offered to the goddesses. It is believed that this square, stone-lined structure was covered with boards through which the blood of the sacrificial animals was allowed to flow.

Visitors who are not too pressed for time, who do not suffer from vertigo and who are sure-footed, may like to visit Priene's *acropolis* on the summit of Mt Mycale. Allow at least 90 minutes for the ascent and examination of the site which was known in antiquity as TELONEIA.

Take a path at the back of the theatre which climbs diagonally across the slope towards the E fortifications. At the point where the aqueduct entered the city there are three Hellenistic *cisterns* which were repaired by the Byzantines. Water was distributed from these through terracotta pipes to various parts of Priene.

Paint marks on the rocks indicate the path to be followed. Note the small Hellenistic *shrine* with some reliefs and niches for statues cut into the cliff-face. Little remains of the *fortifications* which date from the 4C BC. There is, however, a splendid view of the city and of the green valley of the Maeander, with Miletus and the sea in the far distance. Chandler was impressed by this 'most abrupt and formidable precipice, from which we looked down with wonder on the diminutive objects beneath us. The massive heap of a temple below appeared to the naked eye but as chippings of marble.' Then descend by the path which Chandler described in such dramatic terms: it 'soon became difficult and dangerous', he writes, and ' ... frequently [was] not wider than the body, and so steep as scarcely to allow footing. Avoiding as much as possible the frightful view of the abyss beneath us, and shrinking from the brink ... we were astonished at what we had done.'

The visit to Priene ends with an examination of the stadium and lower gymnasium. They are located near the S wall, c 60m below the city centre. They may be reached by a stairway which descends from the insula to the SW of the agora.

The *gymnasium*, the gift of a local magnate named Moschion, has been dated by an inscription found in the city to c 130 BC. Entered from the W through a Doric propylon, it consisted of a central palaestra, which served as an exercise area, surrounded by four Doric stoas. Rooms for study and lecture lay behind the N and W stoas.

In the centre of the N stoa there was an ephebeion where the young men of the city aged between 18 and 20 studied. Like students everywhere they have left a record of their presence in the form of graffiti. The walls of the ephebeion are covered with inscriptions, which consist of the word for place (ὁ τόπος) followed by the name of the student, and sometimes of his father, in the genitive case. Examples quoted by Bean are: 'Phileas, son of Metrodorus, his place', and 'Epicurus son of Pausanias, his place'.

The other rooms in the ephebeion were used by the athletes to prepare themselves for exercise or for the games. In one the boxers pounded a punchbag; in another the wrestlers covered themselves with fine sand to provide a firm grip; while in a third contestants lubricated their bodies with olive oil. Olive oil was used to reduce the incidence of minor skin injury caused by falls or scrapes and to keep the pores free from dirt. Its importance for athletes may be judged by the fact that the early names for a trainer were *athletes* (oiler) and *paidotribes* (boy rubber). The oil was very expensive and it was the duty of the gymnasiarch, the elected or wealthy voluntary official who superintended activities in the palaestrae, to pay for it out of his own pocket. Such large quantities were used that this involved a considerable expenditure of private funds.

After exercise or a contest the athletes used a strigil to scrape the film of oil and dirt from their bodies. In the upper gymnasium during the Roman period there was a heated bath house with the usual complement of hot room, sweat room and cold plunge available for their use. Contestants in the lower gymnasium followed a simpler and more spartan regime. They used cold water. The wash basins, from whose lion-head spouts a constant stream of water poured, are still there. So, also, are the stone foot-baths.

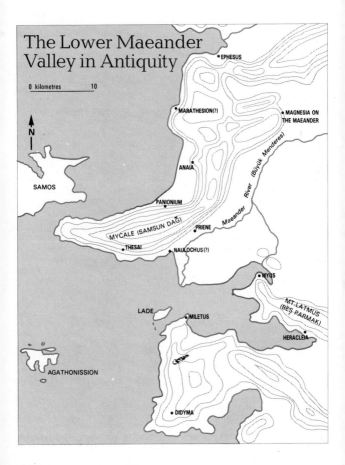

To the right of the gymnasium was the *stadium* which measured 190m by 18m. Dating from the 2C BC, it replaced an earlier structure. On the N side there was a raised open *terrace*, where citizens could take the air and watch the contests as they took place below. Behind the terrace there was a Doric stoa where instruction was given to the athletes and training took place during bad weather. Below the terrace there were rows of seats for the spectators. Only the centre seats were made of stone, the remainder were of wood.

Races in the stadium were run from W to E. Two sets of *starting blocks* may be seen on the W side of stadium. The eight square stones in front, which have holes in them, date from the Hellenistic period. The ten stones behind are Roman. Various theories have been advanced to explain how the starting blocks were used. It has been suggested that in Roman times some kind of mechanism was employed to ensure that all runners started at the same time. A number of literary references indicate that mechanical means were

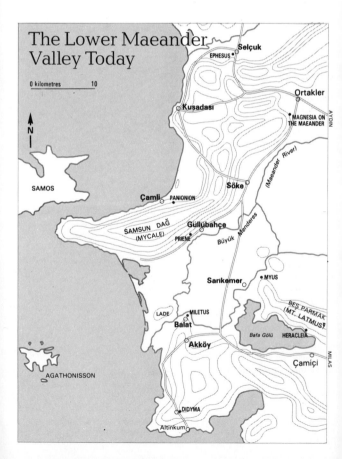

The Lower Maeander Valley Today

not used during the Classical and Hellenistic periods.

In addition to foot-races, other contests held in the stadium would have included boxing, wrestling, the pentathlon and the pancration. The pentathlon included running, wrestling, jumping, throwing the discus and the javelin. The pancration, which means 'complete victory', was like all-in wrestling without the rules. Only biting and gouging were prohibited. Kicking, boxing, wrestling and the application of pressure-locks and strangleholds were all sanctioned. In this contest, designed to determine the ability of one individual to establish physical mastery over another, there was no set number of rounds. Victory was declared when one of the participants was no longer able or willing to continue the fight.

In order to avoid the long, steep climb back to the agora, visitors, who are not unduly pressed for time, are advised to follow the line of the walls round to the either the SE or the W gates. This will give them an opportunity to examine the fortifications in detail and, in particular, to appreciate how the Prienians used natural features to strengthen the defences of their city.

From Priene return to the village of Güllübahçe and continue across the Maeander valley to 16km **MILETUS** (*Milet*). Until the new road and the bridge across the river were constructed, a visit to the site of this ancient city was something of an adventure which involved a certain amount of hardship.

Miletus is not one of the most attractive sites in SW Turkey. During late autumn, winter, and early spring much of the area occupied by the ruins is an unpleasant morass. In summer this becomes a drab brown wilderness covered with low thorny scrub. A sense of profound melancholy broods over the ancient city, a feeling of abandonment and decay that is accentuated by the monotony of a landscape little relieved by the occasional tall clump of reeds or jagged stump of a ruined building.

To picture the city as it was in ancient times requires a considerable effort of imagination. Then it stood on a promontory at the head of the gulf of Latmus. Now the sea is far away, thanks to the unceasing labour of the Maeander, the Büyük Menderes, that river so aptly described by Herodotus as 'the worker'. The position of the island of Lade, where the Ionian fleet was defeated by the Persians in 494 BC, is now marked by a low hill by the side of the road. The Classical and Hellenistic cities of Miletus disappeared a long time ago, and the Roman city that replaced them has neither the majesty of the setting of Pergamum nor the splendour of the ruins of Ephesus. Indeed, after Priene on its strikingly dramatic mountain site, many visitors find Miletus a considerable anti-climax.

Near the large parking place in front of the theatre there are kiosks which offer light refreshments (there are several restaurants at Didyma). As the ruins are scattered over a wide area, allow at least two hours for the visit to Miletus. Three hours are necessary if you also wish to see the interesting collection of finds in the museum.

History. Excavations by German archaeologists on the acropolis, located on Kalabak Tepe to the SW of the site, have shown that there was a Mycenaean colony there as early as 1500 BC. They found traces of fortifications and some houses as well as Minoan pottery. Miletus is mentioned by Homer who says that the city was occupied by barbarous Carians who fought on the side of the Trojans.

It seems likely that the first Greek colonists arrived at Miletus as early as 10C BC. Perhaps because it had poor land communications and was farther away than Priene and Myus from the great inland trade route that terminated at Ephesus, Miletus concentrated on sea-borne commerce. The Milesians are credited with the creation of no fewer than 90 colonies in places as far apart as Naucratis in Egypt, Cyzicus on the Sea of Marmara and Sinope on the shores of the Black Sea.

According to Strabo, Miletus was founded by Neleus, son of Codrus, king of Athens. He joined forces with some Messenians who had been dispossessed by the Heraclids. The newcomers ousted the native Carians, taking their land and all their possessions. Herodotus tells a curious story about the Ionian colonists who settled in Miletus. Soon after their arrival they killed all the male Carians and took their women to wife. He then relates the piquant result of this slaughter. 'The fact that these women were forced into marriage after the murder of their fathers, husbands, and sons was the origin of the law, established by oath and passed down to their female descendants, forbidding them to sit at table with their husbands or to address them by name.' Herodotus does not say how long this law was observed.

As a result of its extensive trading activities and of commerce generated by its proximity to the oracle of Apollo at Didyma, Miletus soon became one of the wealthiest cities in the Aegean. In the 7C and 6C BC this prosperity produced a climate that favoured remarkable developments in philosophy and science. Miletus was the home of Thales (636–546 BC), of Anaximander (610–c 546 BC) and Anaximenes (fl. c 544 BC), Hippodamus (fl. c 450 BC) and Hecataeus (fl. 500 BC).

Thales, who is counted as one of the Seven Sages, was, perhaps, the first man to postulate a common basis for all physical phenomena. This he suggested was water. Among his many experiments was one in which he calculated the height of the pyramids by measuring their shadows at the time of day when a man's shadow equalled his height. He predicted an eclipse of the sun that took place during a battle between Alyattes of Lydia and Cyaxares the Mede in 585 BC. He formulated 'Thales Theorem', which describes the inscription of a right-angled triangle in a circle. In the field of philosophy he proposed the dictum: 'Know thyself'. The Greeks considered this to be of sufficient importance to inscribe it on a herm in the temple of Apollo at Delphi. The natural philosophers, Anaximander and Anaximenes, also propounded theories on the nature of the universe, while the architect, Hippodamus, is credited with promoting a grid-iron plan (see below) for towns. This was used in his native Miletus, in Priene and in many other cities of the ancient world. Hecataeus was a traveller and geographer whose work was greatly esteemed by his contemporaries and successors in those fields.

Women in the Greek city states of the Classical period had a low standing. It was accepted that their principal function in life was to perpetuate the race. This attitude is exemplified by Thales' statement that he was glad to be a human being rather than an animal, a man rather than a woman, a Greek rather than a barbarian.

However, in spite of this unfortunate state of affairs, women of wit and intelligence could still make their mark on society. One of the best known and most successful was the *heitairea* or courtesan, Aspasia (fl. 440 BC), who was born in Miletus. She became the friend of Pericles and, according to Socrates, taught him oratory. In no way inhibited by the fact that she kept a brothel, the philosopher frequently brought his pupils to hear her speak.

Perhaps the greatest Milesian contribution to Greek civilisation was the Ionian alphabet, which, adopted by decree for legal documents in Athens in 403/2 BC, eventually superseded the other versions, and has continued to be used ever since. The Greeks are believed to have learned the alphabet from the Phoenicians—they called letters, 'phoinikeia', Phoenician things—possibly as the result of trading contacts between Miletus or Al Mina (see below) and Phoenicia.

In the 6C BC all the Greek cities on the Aegean, except Miletus, came under the rule of Lydia. The Milesians, led by the tyrant Thrasybulus, successfully repulsed the attacks of Gyges, Alyattes and Croesus. After the defeat of Croesus and the capture of Sardis by Cyrus in 546 BC (see above), the Persians went on to take the Ionian cities one by one. The Panionium, of which Miletus was a leading member, proved quite unable to organise a united resistance. However, the Milesians were successful in securing special terms from the Persians who allowed them a considerable measure of freedom.

With the assistance of Athens, then a growing power, Miletus took part in the abortive revolt by the Ionian cities against Persian rule in the period between 500 BC and 494 BC. The city sent 80 ships to fight at the battle of Lade in 494 BC. After the revolt was crushed by the Persians, Miletus was occupied for the first time in its history. Most of the men were killed. Those who were spared were sent as prisoners to Susa. The women and children were enslaved. The temple and oracle of Apollo at Didyma were plundered and burned. Persians expropriated property in the city and the surrounding countryside.

In Athens the news of these events was received with consternation. When a dramatist named Phrynichus put on a play called 'The Capture of Miletus', Herodotus describes what happened: 'the audience in the theatre burst into tears, and the author was fined a thousand drachmae for reminding them of a disaster which touched them so closely. A law was subsequently passed forbidding anybody to put the play on the stage again.'

After the defeat of Darius by the Athenians and their allies at Marathon (490 BC) and the failure of Xerxes at Salamis and Platea ten years later, the Ionian cities regained their freedom. An organisation, the Delian League, was formed to unite the Greeks under the leadership of Athens so that they could resist any further expansionist moves by the Persians. Miletus was rebuilt and quickly regained much of its former status and prosperity. Its recovery may be judged by the fact that in the mid 5C BC the Milesian annual contribution to the Delian League was assessed at five talents, almost as much as that levied on Ephesus.

In 404 BC the Peloponnesian War ended with the defeat of Athens and the Delian League came under the leadership of the Spartans. Unfortunately, they lacked the necessary organisational and diplomatic skills to run the League successfully and the Persians had litle difficulty in re-establishing control over the Ionian cities. However, even after their rule was formally acknowledged by the King's Peace of 386 BC, undercurrents of revolt against them continued in Ionia. These are evidenced by the close relations which Miletus appears to have established with neighbouring Caria. Milesian coins were issued bearing the names of Hecatomnos, the Carian ruler, and of his better-known son, Mausolus.

However, the Persians were in control of Miletus once more when Alexander came to Ionia in 334 BC. The commander of the city's garrison, Hegisistratus, refused to surrender to him. Alexander occupied the outer suburbs, but the Persians retreated to the citadel and, closing the gates, prepared for a siege. Alexander anchored his fleet of 160 ships at the island of Lade and landed a contingent of troops to secure his position there. Then, undeterred by the presence of a much larger Persian fleet of 400 ships crewed by experienced Cypriots and Phoenicians which had anchored near Mt Mycale, he brought up siege engines and stormed the citadel.

After the death of Alexander in 323 BC his kingdom was divided among the Diadochoi. Miletus, with the other Ionian cities, was ruled first by Antigonus, then by Lysimachus. For a time it was under the control of the Seleucids of Syria, then under the Ptolemies until it finally passed into the hands of the Attalids. When Attalus III, the last king of Pergamum, bequeathed his kingdom to Rome in 133 BC, Miletus became one of the most important cities of the new Roman province of Asia.

Classed as a free city, it continued to flourish and its citizens to prosper. It received many benefits and favours from its new rulers, as the ruins visible today testify. During the reigns of Claudius, Trajan and Hadrian local magnates vied with their imperial masters and with one another in their efforts to adorn the city with fine buildings.

Miletus had early connections with Christianity. St. Paul paid a brief visit there c AD 57 at the end of his third missionary journey. Though hurrying to Jerusalem to celebrate Pentecost with the brethren, he wished to address the bishops and elders of the church in Ephesus before leaving Asia. To save time he summoned them to meet him in Miletus. Having reminded them of their duties to guard the infant church, which had been placed in their care, he told the assembled Ephesians that he would see them no more. Then, having knelt and prayed with the apostle, the bishops, weeping profusely, accompanied him to the ship. This took Paul, by way of Cos and Rhodes, to Tyre in Syria and thence to Jerusalem.

During the late Roman period it became more and more difficult to use the harbour of Miletus because of the increasing quantities of silt brought down by the Maeander. By the 4C AD the area around the promontory had become a swampy marsh and the island of Lade had been abandoned by the sea. The inevitable decline in trade which resulted brought about a reduction of the

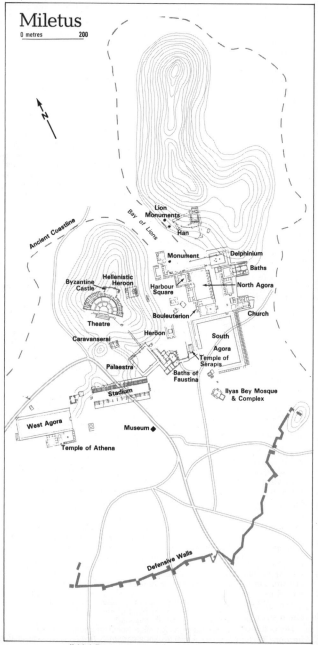

Miletus

0 metres   200

Ancient Coastline

Bay of Lions

Lion Monuments

Han

Monument

Delphinium

Baths

Byzantine Castle

Hellenistic Heroon

Harbour Square

North Agora

Theatre

Bouleuterion

Church

Caravanserai

Heröon

South Agora

Palaestra

Temple of Serapis

Baths of Faustina

Ilyas Bey Mosque & Complex

Stadium

West Agora

Museum

Temple of Athena

Defensive Walls

Kalabak Tepe

city's wealth and in time of its population. For the few families left in the city life was miserable. The marshes were a breeding ground for mosquitoes which spread fever and other diseases among them. In time the impoverished settlement changed its name and became known as Balat. This is a corruption of Palatia, the fortress, which the Byzantines built on the hill that towers over the ruins of the theatre.

During the Ottoman period the site of ancient Miletus became 'the very mean place', which Chandler visited between September and October 1764. A little more than a century later the first excavations were carried out there by German archaeologists and their work, interrupted only by two world wars, has continued ever since.

Archaeologists have established that, after its destruction by the Persians in 494 BC, the city of Miletus was rebuilt in accordance with the grid-iron plan promoted by the Milesian architect, Hippodamus. Although he did not originate this system of town-planning, older cities in Mesopotamia like Babylon had streets that crossed each other at right-angles, Hippodamus popularised it in the W Mediterranean. Traces of the plan may still be detected in the ruins.

On the level ground in front of the theatre are the ruins of a 15C *caravanserai*, erected when the area was ruled by a Turcoman clan, the Menteşe. This measures 30m by 24m, had two storeys and a central courtyard 10.5m by 16m. The ground floor was taken up by stabling and the upper floor had rooms for the merchants and travellers who stayed there.

Perhaps the most striking ruin in Miletus is that of the *Graeco-Roman theatre*. The first building on this site was constructed in the 4C BC. It had an estimated capacity of just over 5000. During the Roman period the Hellenistic theatre was reconstructed and increased in size, its capacity becoming 15,000. Alterations were also made to the division between the cavea and orchestra to allow the building to be used for gladiatorial shows and wild animal fights. This is the structure visible today.

In accordance with the usual Roman design the cavea, which has a diameter of 140m, is semicircular. Constructed on the S side of a small hill, the theatre faced one of the city's ancient harbours. The seating up to the first diazoma is well-preserved and there are substantial remains of the stage-building which resembles that of the great theatre of Ephesus. Some of the reliefs which decorated it may be seen on the SW side. In the centre of the front row of seats there are two of the four pillars which once supported the baldacchino that stretched over the imperial loge. The vaulted passages of the vomitoria are in an excellent state of repair.

On the wall towards the W of the upper diazoma there is an unusual inscription recording a dispute between workers and management during the construction of the theatre which was settled by the oracle of Didyma.

On the hill behind the theatre there is a section of a *defensive wall* and the ruins of a *castle*, both of which date from the Byzantine period. The outline of the promontory occupied by the ancient city is clearly visible from this position. Partly buried in the marsh to the NE are the apotropaic lion statues, dating from the Hellenistic period, which marked the approach to the principal harbour and gave it its name. In times of danger the harbour of the lions could be closed by a chain stretched across its entrance.

Descending the SE slope of the hill we pass the remains of a *heroon*. This Hellenistic structure was made up of a courtyard with a circular tomb in its centre and rooms on its E and W sides. Nearby are traces of private houses and of a *synagogue* constructed on a basilical plan. Apart from this building, evidence for the existence of an important Jewish community in Miletus is provided by an inscription in the theatre which marks the 'place of the Jews also called the God-fearing'.

By the harbour of the lions are the remains of a Roman *monument*, which commemorated the victory of Octavian and Agrippa over Antony and Cleopatra at the battle of Actium on 2 September in 31 BC. On a stepped base a plinth supported a structure which was ornamented with reliefs of tritons and shaped at each end like the prow of a trireme. Above this there was a decorated slab bearing an inscription. The monument was surmounted by a cauldron 7.5m high, which rested on the backs of lions. A partial restoration has been made by the archaeologists.

Nearby was a smaller *monument* which is believed to date from the reign of Vespasian (69–79). According to an inscription it was erected at the behest of a Roman citizen named Grattius. On the NE side of the harbour are the extensive remains of Roman *baths* which were constructed towards the end of the 1C AD. The complex consisted of a *palaestra* surrounded by a stoa on the S and, on the N, a large vestibule and the usual complement of apodyterium, frigidarium, tepidarium and caldarium.

The harbour was surrounded on three sides by a *quay* paved with marble which was constructed during the Roman period. On the S side there was a row of shops which were conveniently sited both to serve the needs of travellers and to supply the Milesians with freshly imported products. The shops were fronted by a Doric stoa 160m long which dated from the Hellenistic period. No doubt this sheltered many departing voyagers while they bade farewell to their friends. St. Paul may have taken his leave of the Ephesian bishops and elders here. (See above.)

To the E of the stoa was sited the *Delphinion*, the oldest shrine in Miletus dedicated to Apollo. This very ancient personification of the god, as Apollo Delphinius, was explained by a legend, which connected the divinity with dolphins (Greek, delphis: a dolphin). The delphinion consisted of a temenos, measuring 60m by 50m, surrounded by a Doric stoa (changed to Corinthian by the Romans). The archaeologists have found three separate levels of construction, the earliest dating from the 6C BC. The remains extant are of the original Hellenistic structure with its Roman modifications. In the central courtyard there were a Hellenistic heroon, an altar and two exedrae. According to Bean a large number of inscriptions, which provided interesting information on the history of Miletus, were found in the delphinion.

A *monumental gateway*, dated to the 1C AD, provided access to the city centre. This marked the N boundary of a magnificent Roman street, the so-called *processional way*, which measured 100m by 28m and had pavements 5.75m wide. This was bounded on the E side by an Ionic *portico* which was constructed during the middle of the 1C AD. This is currently being restored.

The portico provided access to the enormous *Capito baths*. According to an inscription found there, the baths were built by Cornelius Vergilius Capito, procurator of the Roman province of Asia towards the middle of 1C AD. They consisted of a large palaestra which led through a vestibile to the customary arrangement of changing room, cold room etc.

To the S of the Capito baths are the scant remains of a Hellenistic *gymnasium* dating from the 2C BC. A propylon led into a palaestra surrounded by stoas. Behind the N stoa there was an ephebeion flanked by study and practice rooms in an arrangement reminiscent of the lower gymnasium at Priene.

To the W of the processional way was the *N agora*. A peristyle surrounded by shops, it was constructed during the late 5C and early 4C BC and was altered during the Hellenistic and Roman eras. To the NW was a small market-place which had a similar history of reconstruction and alteration.

A short distance to the W of the N agora are the remains of the *Church of St. Michael*. This 6C AD Byzantine basilica was constructed over a temple dedicated to Dionysus. An atrium provided access to the nave and side aisles. At the E end there was an apse where the base of the altar may still be seen. Otherwise little more than the outline of various parts of the structure is visible today. Adjoining the church was an *Episcopal Palace*. Part of the mosaic floor of this building remains. This has been roofed over to preserve it from the elements.

Nearby are the ruins of the *Mosque of Forty Steps*. This dates from 14C and derives its name from the stairs in the NE angle of the building which served as a minaret.

To the S of the N agora are the ruins of two structures which have been tentatively identified as *temples* dedicated to Asclepius and to the cult of the emperors. They adjoin the well-preserved ruins of the *bouleuterion*. This structure was built during the reign of the Seleucid king Antiochus IV Epiphanes (175–164 BC) by Timarchus and Herakleides. A Corinthian propylon with three arched entrances provided access to a courtyard measuring c 25.5m by 23.75m. This was surrounded on three sides by Doric porticoes. In the centre of the courtyard there are the remains of a Roman tomb. The hall where the boule of Miletus met was on the W side of the courtyard. Four doors led into the chamber which could seat 1500 persons. Some rows of seats remain. The wooden roof of the bouleuterion rested on the walls and on four Ionic columns.

Facing the bouleuterion was the magnificent Roman **Nymphaeum** constructed during the 2C AD. Water brought by aqueducts from a source 6km to the SE filled two reservoirs at the back. From there part of the supply went to a large central decorative basin, while the remainder was distributed through a network of pipes and channels throughout the city. The basin was backed by an elaborate three-storey façade which was flanked on each side by a double-storey colonnade. The façade was ornamented with vaulted niches, columns and statues of deities and nymphs. A number of the statues from the nymphaeum are in the İstanbul Archaeological Museum, while others are exhibited in the Staatliche Museum in Berlin. The three lower niches, which have lost their marble covering, and a number of architectural fragments are all that remain of this splendid structure.

To the SE of the nymphaeum are the ruins of a large 6C *church*. Not easy to explore, this Byzantine building consisted of a central nave, two side aisles and an apse on the E side. Entrance from the street was through an atrium. The building to the N of the atrium was probably a baptistery while the circular structure to the S of the apse was a martyrion. The four-columned propylon which admitted to the church was taken from 3C AD building in another part of the city.

A monumental 2C AD propylon to the SE of the bouleuterion provided access to the enormous *Hellenistic S agora*. German archaeologists recovered the substantial remains of this gateway in 1908. It has been re-erected in the Staatlichen Museen zu Berlin. Only a part of the S agora, which measured 164m by 194m, has been excavated. The remainder is covered with rough pasture. However, enough has been laid bare to establish the general plan of the structure. Rows of shops and storerooms stood behind the Doric stoas which surrounded all four sides of the agora. To the W there was a storage building c 163.5m by 13.5m, which dated from the Hellenistic period.

Adjoining the S part of the store are the ruins of the *Temple of Serapis*. This basilical structure dates from 3C AD. A tetrastyle propylon in the Corinthian manner, resting on a platform approached by six steps, provided access to the central nave and two aisles of the temple. The roof of the propylon was ornamented with reliefs of the Egyptian gods while the pediment, still extant, bears a splendid representation of Serapis Helios. Most of the structure is concealed in the dense undergrowth.

A short distance to the NW of the temple of Serapis are the scant remains of a Roman *heroon*. Constructed in the form of a temple in antis, only traces of the building are visible.

A substantial section of the *fortifications* constructed during the reign of Justinian (527–565) lie between the temple of Serapis and the *Baths of Faustina*. This baths complex, which is in an excellent state of preservation, is named after the wife of Marcus Aurelius (161–180). It is interesting to note that it does not fit in with the grid-iron pattern established by Hippodamus.

On the W side of the complex there is a palaestra, which measured c 77.5m by 79.5m and which was surrounded by Corinthian colonnades. Bathers entered the apodyterium from the E side of the palaestra. This was a long narrow room which had cubicles for undressing along the sides. The discovery of statues of Apollo and of the muses at the N end of the apodyterium suggests that it may have been used for lecture purposes. In the frigidarium there was a large pool in the central hall. Fountains in the form of a lion and of a reclining river god, the Maeander, have been left in their original positions. From the frigidarium the bathers went to the caldarium in the SE part of the complex. From there they passed to the tepidarium on the W side and then back to the apodyterium where they resumed their clothes.

The statues of Apollo, Telesphorus, Asclepius, Aphrodite and other deities and the muses found in this richly-ornamented structure have been removed to the İstanbul Archaeological Museum and to the Staatliche Museum in Berlin.

A survey and partial excavation has established some facts about the stadium of Miletus which was sited to the W of the baths of Faustina. This Hellenistic structure was built c 150 BC and enlarged by the Romans during the 3C AD. With a capacity of 15,000, it measured 191m by 29.5m. As the stadium was constructed on level ground, the spectators' seats on each of the long sides were supported on vaults. At the W end of the stadium there was a Hellenistic gateway. During the late Roman period this was matched at the E end by an elaborate propylon which had seven arched entrances flanked by eight pairs of Corinthian columns.

To the NW of the stadium there are traces of the city's Roman W baths. The *Hellenistic W agora* was located between this structure and the city wall. Soundings by the archaeologists have established that the agora measured c 191 by 79m. The area is now covered by an Ottoman cemetery.

A stone podium to the S of the W agora marks the site of the 5C BC *Temple of Athena*. This measured 18m by 30m. Finds suggest that the temple had a peristasis of 6 by 10 Ionic columns and that the cella took the form of a temple in antis.

The discovery, near the temple of Athena, of houses containing Minoan and Mycenaean pottery dating from 1500 BC to 1100 BC demonstrates that this part of the city was occupied from the earliest times. Protogeometric and geometric pottery from 900 BC to 700 BC, which has also been found there, suggests that the first Hellenic settlements in Miletus were located in this area.

Before leaving the site for Didyma, visitors not pressed for time may like to visit a well-preserved 15C *mosque*. Hidden and almost forgotten amongst clumps of reeds, this exquisite little building lies a short distance to the left of the main road. Built c 1404 by İlyas Bey, emir of the Menteşe, the mosque, which is 18.3m², is surmounted by a dome. It has lost its minaret.

Much of the material used in the construction was taken from the ancient city. This includes the marble panels which cover the walls and form the pavement of the courtyard. Although the medrese and imaret, which were once located in the courtyard, have disappeared, the fine şadirvan remains. Note in particular the doorway which is surmounted by an arch ornamented with carved stalactites, and inside the building the beautifully decorated mihrab.

The small *Museum* of Miletus, which contains finds from both the ancient city and the surrounding countryside, is located to the right of the main road a short distance to the S of the mosque. First opened to the public in 1973, its two halls, courtyard and terraces contain a rich collection which is well-displayed.

In the first hall small objects from the Mycenaean, Archaic, Classical, Hellenistic and Roman periods are arranged in chronological order. These include statues, amphorae, architectural fragments, protogeometric, geometric, black, and red figure vases, terracotta figures and coins. In the large hall there are mosaics, statues and stelae. Outside are larger sculptures, inscribed slabs and architectural details from Myus as well as from Miletus. These date from the earliest period to the Byzantine era. Note especially the lion statues and the reliefs from the temple of Serapis.

After leaving the museum look out for the site of *sacred gate* which marked the exit from Miletus of the Sacred Way. This paved road linked the Delphinion (see above) with the temple of Apollo at Didyma. The gate, which dates from c 5C BC and which was restored during the reign of Trajan (98–117), was flanked by fortified towers. Its position today is marked by a depression in the ground which is waterlogged during the winter months and covered with dense vegetation for the rest of the year.

The road from Miletus to 20km **DIDYMA** pursues its leisurely course through a pleasant but rather nondescript landscape which has a strangely deserted appearance. Only the occasional sighting of a coach full of tourists serves as a reminder that ahead lie the ruins of one of the great monuments of antiquity. Away to the right

of the modern road the distant gleam of the sea marks the site of the
port of Panormus, where during the Classical, Hellenistic and
Roman periods nobles and commoners, rich and poor disembarked from the ships that had brought them to the shrine of
Apollo.

They were joined at the temple by those clients of the god who had
travelled over the Sacred Way which linked Miletus with Didyma. The end of their journey was signalled by the stiff, imposing
statues of priests and priestesses which lined the approach to
the temple until Newton carried them away to the British Museum
a century ago. The modern traveller receives no such warning.
Suddenly, dramatically, the temple appears at the top of a
gentle rise, the columns of its ruined façade outlined against
the skyline.

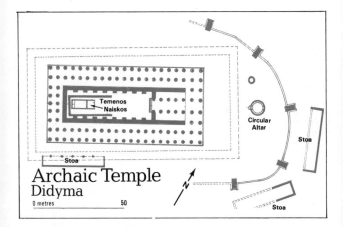

Archaic Temple
Didyma
0 metres   50

Temenos
Naiskos
Circular
Altar
Stoa
Stoa
Stoa

Many travellers arrive at Didyma full of memories of the splen-
dours of Ephesus and Priene. Nothing, they feel, can surpass those
places. Then, confronted by the ruins of the great **Temple of Apollo**,
they realise that this majestic structure overshadows all that they
have seen before.

The early evening is one of the best times to visit Didyma. By then
most of the coaches have departed and only a few silent figures
linger among the giant columns of the ancient structure. The walls
glimmering in a ghostly afterglow provide a safe haven for the flocks
of rooks which nest in the shrine.

The temple merits a leisurely visit, as it is important not only
to examine its impressive remains, but also to savour its atmosphere.

There are several restaurants in Didyma where a good, but inexpensive, dinner
may be obtained. An overnight stay is possible at one of the hotels or camp-sites

at 4km *Altınkum*. Note, however, that during the holiday season rooms at this small resort are difficult to obtain and it is advisable to make reservations as far in advance as possible. (Enquiries to the Tourism Information Offices in Kuşadası or Aydın.) Apart from being conveniently close to Didyma, Altınkum has another attraction: its clean sandy beach offers excellent bathing.

History. According to Pausanias, 'The sanctuary of Apollo at Didymoi and the oracle there are more ancient than the Ionian settlement.' All the available evidence supports this view. It would seem that the Greeks, when they arrived in Ionia, found an oracular shrine linked to a spring and a sacred grove already established at Didyma and that, as in Ephesus and in other places in Asia Minor, they absorbed this into their own religious beliefs and practices. A counter view, which proposes a Greek source for the cult, draws attention to the resemblance between 'Didyma' and the Greek word for twins ('didymi' δίδυμοί), pointing out that Artemis, the twin sister of Apollo, was also worshipped there. However, this theory is now generally rejected and it is agreed that the name of the shrine is not derived from the Greek but, like Sidyma and Idyma, is Anatolian in origin.

Didyma was not a town in its own right. It formed part of the territory of Miletus. Only the priests and the servants of the temple lived in the village settlement within the temenos described by Strabo. The geographer also mentions the sacred grove, which continued to play a part in the ceremonies.

During the early period the priests were called Branchidae, as they claimed descent from Branchus, the son of Smicrus a native of Delphi, who had settled in Miletus. Branchus, a handsome youth, was a shepherd. One day, while guarding his father's flocks in the mountain pastures, he was seen by Apollo, who became infatuated with him. Branchus in gratitude for the god's affection dedicated an altar to Apollo the Friendly and received from him the gift of divination. According to the legend, he then established the first oracular shrine at Didyma.

The earliest structures at Didyma appear to have been erected towards the end of the 8C BC. German archaeologists have found traces of a temenos wall, a well and altar from that period. A century later the fame of the oracle had spread as far as Egypt. Herodotus relates that after Necho, the Egyptian king, (609–593 BC) had defeated the Syrians at Magdolus, he made a gift of the armour he was wearing at the moment of victory to Apollo at Branchidae (Didyma). The most ancient statue of the god, the work of Canachos of Sicyon, has been dated to 500 BC. This portrayed Apollo Philesis, Apollo the Affectionate, in the form of a nude youth holding a bow in his right hand and grasping a stag by his left.

It is believed that the archaic Didymaion, the first temple at Didyma, was completed c 560 BC. Herodotus mentions a gift which was given to the shrine about that time by Croesus, king of Lydia. He sent bowls and sprinklers of gold and silver and other costly offerings to the oracles of Apollo at Didyma and Delphi. (See above.)

The archaic temple was an Ionic dipteros which measured c 85m by 38.5m. The peristasis had a total of 104 columns. The walls of the cella, which was unroofed, were c 18m high. This contained the sacred spring and laurel tree and the ancient temenos, within which there was a small naiskos to house the statue of Apollo Philesis. The temple was built of tufa, but the capitals and columns were of marble and much of the visible structure was covered in marble slabs. Eight columns supported the roof of the pronaos. The lower sections of these columns bore reliefs similar to those which decorated the temple of Artemis at Ephesus.

In front of the temple there was a circular altar. Water from the sacred well to the right of altar was probably used by clients to purify themselves before they presented their questions to the priests. The E side of the temenos was enclosed by a wall 3.5m high. Five sets of steps led up to a terrace on which there were two stoas and a number of statues.

After the defeat of the Ionian cities by the Persians at the battle of Lade in 494 BC, the archaic Didymaion was destroyed and its treasures, including the statue of Apollo, were carried away. Either at that time or after the battle of Plataea in 479 BC, the ancient historians disagree in their accounts of the events, the Branchidae behaved in a cowardly fashion, handing over the property of the temple to their conquerors. Then, fearing the wrath of the Milesians, they begged the Persian king to take them with him. He did so and settled them in a colony in Sogdiana.

The descendants of the traitorous priests were discovered by Alexander during his victorious march through the Persian Empire a century and a half later. Having taken advice from his Milesian allies, he razed the settlement to the ground. The statue of Apollo finally came home to Didyma towards the end of the 4C. One of the Diadochoi, Seleucus Nicator, founder of the Seleucid Syrian dynasty, found it in Ecbatana and returned it to the shrine.

Following its destruction by the Persians, the oracle of Didyma appears to have gone into a period of decline. This lasted for almost 150 years, until Alexander arrived in Ionia, an event marked by supernatural portents at the sanctuary. The sacred spring in the cella, which had long been dry, began to gush forth water once more and the oracle predicted Alexander's victory at the battle of Gaugamela.

Alexander ordered the construction of a new temple at Didyma, and Seleucus, who had returned the cult statue to the sanctuary, commissioned the architects Paionios and Daphnis to design the building. This is the structure visible today. Despite being plundered by marauding Gauls in 278 BC and raided by pirates in the 1C BC, work on the great building continued for almost 500 years.

When Ionia became part of the Roman province of Asia, Didyma benefited from the generosity of its new masters. Several emperors interested themselves in the temple. Caesar extended its limit of sanctuary by 3km and c AD 100 Trajan paid for the paving of the Sacred Way from Miletus. Until the middle of 3C AD, when the shrine came under attack once again, this time from the Goths, the oracle continued to function and to attract enquirers.

However, a new and more formidable enemy had appeared on the horizon. Christianity was bitterly opposed to oracles, which, as works of the devil, were forbidden to the faithful. The new religion attracted more and more converts and the authority and power of Didyma declined. During the reign of Julian the Apostate (AD 361–363) this trend was reversed for a short time. On his orders a number of shrines dedicated to the Christian martys were removed from the vicinity of the sanctuary. However, the end came in AD 385 with the edict of Theodosius. This administered the *coup de grâce* to Didyma. It prohibited haruspicy and the consultation of oracles and provided severe penalties for those, who disobeyed its provisions.

The temple, which after nearly 500 years of work remained incomplete, fell into disrepair and eventually a Christian church was erected in the cella. Little is known about the history of Didyma during the Byzantine and Ottoman periods. It appears to have continued to decline in parallel with its parent city, Miletus.

The visit of Richard Chandler in 1764 and the plates published by the Society of Dilettanti did much to revive interest in Didyma and other sites in Ionia. Chandler was captivated by what he found there. In 'Travels in Asia Minor', he writes: 'The memory of the pleasure which this spot afforded me will not be soon or easily erased. The columns yet entire are so exquisitely fine, the marble mass so vast and noble, that it is impossible perhaps to conceive greater beauty and majesty in ruin. At evening, a flock of goats, returning to the fold, their bells tinkling, spread over the heap, climbing to browse on the shrubs and trees growing between the huge stones. The whole mass was illuminated by the declining sun with a variety of rich tints, and cast a very strong shade. The sea, at a distance was smooth and shining, bordered by a mountainous coast, with a rocky island. The picture was as delicious as striking.'

Excavations conducted by the German Archaeological Institute during recent years have revealed much useful information about the temple and the buildings surrounding it. The remains of the Hellenistic Didymaion are sufficient to ensure a substantial restoration of the structure sometime in the future.

The **Hellenistic Didymaion** was built around the site of the archaic temple. Substantially larger than its predecessor, the stylobate of the new temple measured c 109m by 51m. An Ionic dipteros, it had 108 columns in the double peristasis; 21 on the longer and 10 on the shorter sides. There were a further 12 columns in the pronaos. Apart from those at the corners, which had representation of bulls' heads and of Zeus, Apollo, Artemis and Leto, the columns in the peristasis

Hellenistic Temple
Didyma

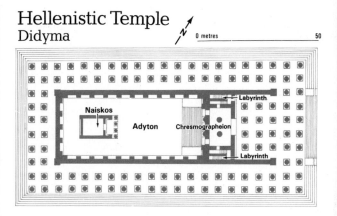

were in the Ionic style. Two from the inner row, complete with capitals and architrave, have been re-erected on the N side of the temple. Note the decorated bases of eight of the columns on the E section of the outer peristasis. These are believed to date from c AD 37.

The majesty of the structure was increased by the 3.5m-high crepidoma on which it stood. This was divided into seven levels, but, as these were much too steep to be used as steps, there was a monumental stairs with 14 steps in the centre of the E side of the crepidoma. This led to the pronaos where those who had come to consult the oracle presented their questions. Behind the pronaos, and c 1.5m higher, was the 3C BC chresmographeion. This was the room where the oracular statements were written out and delivered by the priest. Two Corinthian half-columns flanked the entrance to the chresmographeion and there were two more full columns inside. (See also below.)

As in the archaic temple the adyton or cella of the Hellenistic Didymaion, which measured c 53.5m by 21.5m, was open to the sky. This could be reached from the chresmographeion by a broad flight of steps or by way of two vaulted passages which still exist. These passages, whose floors are worn smooth and slippery, were probably used in ceremonies connected with the cult. Inside the adyton note the fragments of the 2C BC frieze composed of griffins, scrolls and lyres, symbols associated with Apollo which decked the top of the wall.

Today only the foundations of the *naiskos*, which sheltered the cult statue of Apollo and the sacred spring, are visible. Resting on a three-stepped crepidoma, this took the form of a small Ionic prostyle with four columns across the front which measured c 14.25m by 8.25m. According to Akurgal it was the first Hellenistic structure in Asia Minor to show the influence of the Attic style.

To the E of the temple is the lustral *well* and the circular *altar* on which sacrifces were offered by those who had come to consult the oracle. The giant *medusa head* lying on the ground nearby came from the 2C AD frieze which ornamented the architrave over the outer row of columns. Akurgal suggests that this frieze and the

decorated capitals are probably the work of sculptors from Aphrodisias. A staircase led from the temenos to a terrace which marked
the end of the Sacred Way linking Didyma with Miletus.

Clients who wished to consult the oracle began by purifying themselves with
water from the well sited in front of the E face of the temple. Then they offered
sacrifice (the victim was usually a goat), to establish if the god were present.
From the altar they went to the pronaos where they gave their query to the
priest.
    Predictions at Didyma were made by a prophetess who had fasted and
purified herself. According to a late account (4C AD) she placed her feet in or
inhaled vapour rising from the sacred spring which was located in the naiskos.
Her words, uttered in a state of delirium, were noted by the priest and turned
into hexameter verse by him or by his assistant. The priest of Apollo was a high-
ranking Milesian official who lived during his year of office at Didyma.
    Prophecies given were recorded and kept in the chresmographeion. Most
authorities now agree that this was the room behind the pronaos. (See above.)
However, a number have suggested that it was located somewhere else in the
temenos and attest as evidence for their belief the discovery of a number of
stone slabs scattered around the temple which bear the names of prophets.
    The earliest prophecies of which records remain date from the 6C BC. While
many are on personal matters, e.g. should the enquirer get married, start a
business venture, make a journey or embark on piracy; some are concerned
with affairs of state. The oracle foretold Alexander's victory at Gaugamela and
warned Seleucus I Nicator (321–280 BC) against crossing to Europe. Seleucus
disregarded the advice and was assassinated by Ptolemy Ceraunus, the son of
his old friend and ally.
    Sometimes the replies given by oracles were ambiguous. Croesus was told by
the oracle of Delphi that, if he attacked Persia, he would destroy a great empire,
but it was not made clear that it was Croesus' own empire that would fall.
    Visitors came to Didyma not only to consult the oracle about the future, but
also to attend the festival of the Great Didymeia. Celebrated every fourth year,
this included competitions involving the arts—music, oratory and drama—as
well as athletic events. The drama festival was held in the temenos of the
temple and the athletic events in the *stadium* which lies to the S. The steps of
the sanctuary were used as seating and many still bear the names of the
spectators who sat there.

Beyond the terrace on the E side of the temple a section of the **Sacred
Way**, which ran from Didyma to Miletus, has been uncovered.
Nearby are the ruins of a Roman *baths complex* which has a number
of black and white floor mosaics. The Sacred Way passes through a
small depression which some authorities believe may mark the site of
the sacred grove mentioned by Strabo. (See above.)

12 Kuşadası to Bodrum

Total distance c 161km. **Kuşadası**—24km *Ortaklar*—4km **Magnesia on the Maeander**—(7km *Myus*)—(8km **Heracleia under Latmus**)—60km *Euromus*—(19km **Iasus**)—(c 13km **Labraynda**)—18km **Milas**—(c 5km *Peçin Kale*)—R330 (c 18km *Güllük*)—(c 40km *Ören / Ceramus*)—55km **Bodrum**.

Some of the places on this route, in particular Myus, Heracleia and Iasus, are difficult to visit without the use of private transport or taxis. They may be reached by a combination of dolmuş taxis, buses and walking, but only at the cost of much time and of considerable expenditure of energy. In the case of Myus there is so little to see at the site that it is likely to be of interest to specialists only. Finally, as refreshment facilities are very limited before Lake Bafa, it is advisable to take a picnic.

Visitors, who have returned to **Kuşadası** (see Rte 11) from Didyma, should take the secondary road for c 12km to the junction with E24 and continue in the direction of Aydın for a further 12km to Ortaklar and there turn right on to road 525 towards Milas. The site of **MAGNESIA ON THE MAEANDER** is c 4km after the junction of road 525 with E24. (Those who have stayed at Altınkum should return to Akköy and there turn right, continuing for 7km to the junction with road 525. They should then turn left and proceed through Söke to c 43km Magnesia.)

Apart from the ruins of the temple of Artemis, there are few visible remains of Magnesia on the Maeander which, during the Roman period, proudly described itself on its coinage as the seventh most important city in the Province of Asia. Buildings revealed between 1891–93 by the excavations of the German archaeologist, Carl Humann, have disappeared once more under silt deposited by the river Lethaeus or are covered by an almost impenetrable tangle of vegetation. As a result, this ancient city is now little visited. Only those interested in Magnesia's chequered past spare it more than a glance as they hasten to more spectacular ruins. However, it is well worth the hour, which is all that is needed to see the principal remains.

History. The first settlers are believed to have been Aeolians, whose original home had been in Magnesia in N Greece. Preserving its links with Aeolia, Magnesia on the Maeander never became a member of the Ionian League. Originally the city was located at the point where the Lethaeus and Maeander met. It was moved c 400 BC to its present position.

In the 7C BC, when Magnesia was occupied by the Lydians, it received particularly harsh treatment from Gyges because of its rough handling of of the poet, Magnes, one of the Lydian king's favourites. Magnes had abused the hospitality of the Magnesians by seducing the wives of some of the city's prominent citizens.

According to Strabo, Magnesia was rased to the ground by the Treres, a Cimmerian tribe, and later occupied by its Ionian neighbours from Miletus. Despite the lack of militancy suggested by these reverses, Magnesia was not without success in warfare. On more than one occasion it conducted skilful campaigns against the Ephesians. The Magnesian cavalry earned itself a considerable reputation and, like Colophon, its army used specially-trained dogs as part of a formidable battle-force.

About 530 BC Magnesia came under Persian rule. In 464 BC Themistocles, who had defeated the Persians at Salamis, came to live in the city. Exiled by the Athenians, he sought refuge with his former enemies and was warmly received by them. Artaxerxes, the king of Persia, awarded him the revenues of three cities: Lampsacus was to provide him with wine, Myus with (ὄψον) roast meat or fish to eat with his bread, and Magnesia with his daily bread.

Themistocles appears to have enjoyed some at least of his brief period of exile in Magnesia. At a temple, which he dedicated to the Phrygian Mother Goddess, Cybele Dindymene, his daughter Mnesiptolema or perhaps his wife, as Strabo suggests, served as priestess. When c 462 he was ordered by the king's messenger to take the field against Greece, he decided to end his life. Plutarch describes what happened: 'Having, therefore, sacrificed to the gods, assembled his friends, and taken his last leave, he drank bull's blood or, as some relate it, he took a quick poison, and ended his days at Magnesia, having lived sixty-five years, most of which he spent in civil or military employment.' Themistocles was not forgotten in death. The Magnesians erected a fine funerary monument in the agora in his honour.

During the 5C BC the city was moved to its present site, probably to escape the seasonal flooding by the rivers which had plagued it. The Spartans, who controlled Magnesia at that time, may also have felt that its proximity to the shrine of Artemis Leucophryene (the white-browed) might afford it some protection from Persian attack. Unfortunately, this did not prove to be the case and the city was re-occupied by the Persians and it remained under their rule until the coming of Alexander the Great to Ionia.

According to Arrian, representatives of Magnesia and Tralles (Aydın) came to Ephesus to offer their submission to Alexander in 334 BC. He received them well and sent a force of cavalry and foot-soldiers under Parmenion to secure both cities. Magnesia played no great part in the struggles of Alexander's successors. Its citizens appear to have accepted the rule of the Seleucids and the Attalids without protest and to have spent their time quietly increasing their wealth.

Magnesia lay in a fertile area which produced an abundance of agricultural produce. It was famous in antiquity for the quality of its figs and olives, which with wheatmeal and soft cheese formed the standard diet of its athletes. The city lay at the crossroads between the routes from the Gulf of Latmus E to Cilicia and N to Byzantium. From the traders who passed through it the Magnesians took their share of profit.

The city was also a meeting place of many cultures and, according to Strabo, suffered as a consequence. With some indignation he lists the cultural lapses of a number of Magnesians. 'Hegesias the orator ... initiated the Asiatic style ... whereby he corrupted the established Attic custom. Simus the melic poet ... corrupted the style handed down by the earlier melic poets and introduced the Simoedia [an obscene kind of song] ... just as that style was corrupted still more ... by Cleomachus the pugilist, who, having fallen in love with a certain cinaedus [degenerate] and with a young female slave who was kept as a prostitute by the cinaedus, imitated the style of dialects and mannerisms that was in vogue among the cinaedi.'

When Attalus III of Pergamum bequeathed his kingdom to Rome in 133 BC, Magnesia was incorporated in the new Province of Asia. It supported the Romans against Mithridates VI, king of Pontus, in 88 BC and was rewarded handsomely for its loyalty. Declared a free city, it became an important administrative and judicial centre.

Under Roman rule Magnesia continued to produce its quota of interesting characters. Anaxenor the Citharoede (one who accompanied himself on the Cithara, a kind of lyre), a protégé of Mark Antony, was one of the bright young men who decorated the triumvir's E court. Strabo has a juicy piece of gossip to retail about Anaxenor's rise to fame and its unwelcome consequences for the city of his birth: 'Antony exalted him all he possibly could, since he even appointed him exactor of tribute from four cities, giving him a body-guard of soldiers. Further, his native land greatly increased his honours, having clad him in purple as consecrated to Zeus Sosipolis, as is plainly indicated in his painted image in the market-place. And there is also a bronze statue of him in the theatre, with the inscription, "Surely this is a beautiful thing, to listen to a singer such as this man is, like unto the gods in voice."

Unfortunately, Strabo continues, the Magnesians' gesture misfired, earning them not fame, but a reputation for being ignorant and ill-read. The sculptor, because of insufficient space on the statue base, left out the last letter (iota) of the last word in the second verse of the quotation from the Odyssey and so changed a dative into a nominative. As a result, the Magnesians became the laughing-stock of their neighbours.

There is an interesting modern sequel to Strabo's story. Towards the end of the 19C German archaeologists found this statue base in the theatre. According to Bean they reported that there was just sufficient space at the edge of the stone for the insertion of a narrow letter. There was a mark in that space on the base, but whether it was a badly formed iota, scratched in by a Magnesian tired of jokes about his city or the result of damage and abrasion is impossible to say.

The stone is now in Berlin.

After the adoption of Christianity, Magnesia became the seat of an important bishopric. During the Byzantine era it continued to be a relatively prosperous trading and market centre for the surrounding countryside. However, in the troubled 11C it began to decline and this trend continued, until it was finally abandoned.

Magnesia was visited by Richard Chandler in 1765. He found some architectural fragments in the Corinthian and Ionic styles on the site, but was unable to discover a place which Pausanias called the tunnels. There, according to that ancient traveller, there was a grotto dedicated to Apollo, 'not very marvellous for size, but the statue of Apollo is extremely ancient and gives you physical powers of every kind; men consecrated to this statue leap from precipitous cliffs and high rocks, they pull up giant trees by the roots, and travel with loads on the narrowest footpaths'. Modern archaeologists have been equally unlucky in their search for the place where this shamanistic cult was practised.

Road 525 cuts through the Byzantine defences—the ancient city was unwalled, relying for protection on the temple of Artemis—and divides the site into two unequal parts. The large structure to the E of the road is believed to have been a Roman bath.

The temenos of the *Temple of Artemis* lay to the W of the modern road. The temple, which was designed by the architect Hermogenes, dates from c 130 BC. It replaced an earlier structure which may have been dedicated to the Phrygian mother goddess.

Hermogenes (fl. c 130 BC), was a native of Priene. In addition to the temple of Artemis Leucophryene at Magnesia, he also designed the temple of Dionysus on Teos. Both structures exemplify his strong preference for the Ionic style, which he praised in his teaching and writings.

The temple was an Ionic pseudo-dipteros with 15 by 8 columns, which rested on a stylobate measuring 41m by 67m. Facing W, it stood on a nine-stepped crepidoma. Entering through the large pronaos, one passes into the cella where the base of the cult statue may still be seen. Behind the cella there was a spacious opisthodomus. The wall separating the two sections of the structure has disappeared. The spacious pronaos overlooked an altar which was modelled on the altar of Zeus at Pergamum. During the Roman period the temenos was surrounded by a Doric stoa. Sculptures from the temple's frieze are kept in the museums of İstanbul and Paris.

According to Strabo the temple of Artemis at Magnesia 'in the size of its shrine and in the number of its votive offerings is inferior to the temple of Ephesus, but in the harmony and skill shown in the structure of the sacred enclosure is far superior to it. And in size it surpasses all the sacred enclosures in Asia except two, that at Ephesus and that at Didymi.'

The use of the pseudodipteral style produced a pleasing contrast between the brightly lit and shaded parts of the temple and greatly enhanced its appearance, while the space freed by the employment of a single row of columns formed a pleasant promenade sheltered from the elements. The success of this design, which was taken up by the Augustan architect Vitruvius, had a profound effect on architecture and has been copied in countless buildings from the Renaissance to the present day.

A massive propylon on the W side of the temenos opened on to the agora, in the centre of which stood the temple of Zeus Sosipolis (Saviour of the City). This temple, a small Ionic prostyle dating from the middle of the 2C BC, and all the other structures in this area have been covered by alluvial deposits.

Nearby are the remains of a small *theatre*, which had an estimated capacity of 3000. Only one row of seats and parts of the stage-building are visible. A tunnel which connected the stage-building with the centre of the orchestra was probably used by actors to make spectacular entrances, perhaps as underworld deities. When Bean saw it in 1939, the tunnel had lost its roof and was a deep, masonry-lined trench choked with brambles. Since then it has been filled in, presumably to prevent accidents. To the S of the theatre there was an *odeum* and beyond that a *stadium* and a *gymnasium*. All date from the Roman period. However, the dense undergrowth which covers most of the site of Magnesia makes any detailed exploration of these structures very difficult.

On leaving Magnesia continue S on road 525 across the plain of the Maeander for c 25km to the turning on the left which leads c 7km to Myus. This area has long been famous for the production of liquorice from the roots of *Glycyrrhiza glabra*, a hardy shrub which grows wild in the Maeander valley and on the slopes of the surrounding hills. The approach of Lake Bafa is signalled by the dramatic outline of *Mt Latmus* which, because of the rocky peaks that crown it, is known to the Turks as Beş Parmak (Five Fingers).

A reasonable side road leads from road 525 to Sarıkemer from where there is a rough track to the hamlet of Avşar. The sparse ruins of MYUS may be found on a hillside to the NW, near the river. Today the site of this ancient settlement, one of the least successful in Ionia, has a desolate, forgotten air in keeping with its history.

History. According to Strabo, Myus was founded by Cydrelus, bastard son of Codrus, king of Athens. It was sited on a promontory c 15km to the NE of Miletus. As the silt brought down by the Maeander pushed the shoreline farther and farther to the S, the fortunes of the city declined. In 499 BC 200 warships, under the command of the Persian Megabates, anchored there. Five years later Myus was able to contribute only three vessels to the Ionian squadron at the battle of Lade. Not only was the economy of the city weakened by a loss of trade caused by the disappearance of its harbour but the health of its citizens was undermined by the mosquitoes which bred in increasing numbers in the new marshlands.

In 464 BC Myus was one three cities—the others were Magnesia and Lampsacus—presented by the Persian king, Artaxerxes to Themistocles, who had abandoned the Greek cause. Magnesia was to supply him with bread, Lampsacus with wine, and Myus with (ὄψον), delicacies like roast meat and fish to eat with his bread. (See above.) About 250 years later Myus suffered the humiliation of being given away again. Philip V of Macedon awarded the city to the Magnesians who had supplied his hungry troops with a quantity of figs.

Impoverished by their declining trade, harrassed by their Milesian neighbours, who claimed a part of their territory, weakened by malaria-carrying mosquitoes and demoralised by being awarded as a prize by foreign tyrants, the people of Myus eventually admitted defeat. Pausanias (fl. c AD 150) describes how, taking all their movable goods and the statues of their gods, they left their city and moved to Miletus. The abandoned buildings proved a useful quarry for the Milesians, who carried away any reusable stone or marble. When Pausanias visited the city he found 'nothing there but a white marble temple of Dionysus'. The work carried out by German archaeologists at Miletus has verified this ancient account. They have discovered architectural fragments bearing inscriptions which refer to Myus in the temple of Athena and in the theatre of Miletus.

Chandler visited the Maeander valley in 1764, but confused Heracleia with Myus. The site was excavated for the first time by Wiegand in 1908. A number of architectural fragments and some reliefs depicting chariot-races were sent by him to Berlin. Further excavations, made by a German team between 1964–66, have established the identity of the few ruins of Myus that have survived centuries of spoliation and neglect.

The most prominent building visible on the site is *Avşar Kale*, the Byzantine castle that crowns a small rise near the river. The city occupied the area to the SE of this hill where a number of cisterns, rock-cut tombs and houses have been found.

Below the hill are two terraces on which buildings stood. On the upper terrace were found the remains of an archaic Ionic temple which is believed to have been dedicated to Apollo Terebintheus. The lower terrace had a 6C BC Ionic peripteros with 6 by 10 columns, which rested on a stylobate measuring c 17.25m by 29.75m. The reliefs of the chariot-races found by Wiegand came from a frieze which is believed to have decorated the cella of this building. The discovery of the base of a single marble column has suggested to some authorities that this may have been the temple of Dionysus, described by Pausanias. However, Akurgal argues convincingly that as it opened on to the W it may have been dedicated to an Anatolian deity who in time became identified with a member of the Greek pantheon, perhaps Artemis. (See also the entries on Sardis, Ephesus and Magnesia on the Maeander.)

Leaving the remains of unsuccessful Myus behind we return to road 525 and, continuing S in the direction of Milas, soon reach *Lake Bafa* (Bafa Gölü). The stretch of road which runs parallel to the lake for c 20km is without a doubt one of the most beautiful in Turkey.

On the left the blue waters of Bafa whose surface is dotted with tiny islands, mirror the barren, arid peaks of Mt Latmus. Overhead, flocks of waterfowl, disturbed by passing cars, protest noisily as they wheel and circle before returning to the lake to resume their feeding. By the roadside herds of goats snatch greedily at every edible scrap of vegetation while patient yürük children try to guide the straggling column of animals towards their encampment, pausing only to round up the strays that have wandered on to the road.

The S shore of Lake Bafa is an agreeable setting for a picnic or for a meal in one of the small roadside restaurants. Their fish dishes, especially the grey mullet, are excellent. Near the restaurants there is a camp-site, which offers rather basic facilities.

Visitors who are not in a hurry may like to cross the lake by boat to the village of *Kapıkırı* which occupies the site of **HERACLEIA UNDER LATMUS**. A less romantic and certainly less comfortable route is by a c 8km-long rough, dusty and rather potholed track from the village of

Byzantine ruins at Heracleia under Latmus.

Çamiçi at the E side of the lake. This passes through a strange
landscape of tortured, convoluted granite boulders—ancient rockfalls from the mountain.

At the entrance to Kapıkırı the road divides. The lower branch
goes to a number of small lakeside restaurants which are open
during the holiday season, while the upper branch leads to the
modern village and the principal ruins.

Heracleia under Latmus was never a place of much importance.
Miletus at the entrance to the gulf captured most the seaborne trade
and the settlement was too far to the S of the inland trade route to
derive much profit from the caravans that passed through Magnesia
on their way to and from Ephesus. Although geographically in Ionia,
Heracleia was a Carian city in character and its history was shaped
by events in Caria. One of the earliest references to the area is
somewhat unflattering. Among the supporters of the Trojan cause
Homer ('Iliad' 2. 868) counts those 'who dwell around Miletus and
Phtheiron' (the mountain of lice). Strabo states that the Milesian sage
and geographer Hecataeus (c 550–490 BC) opined that Phtheiron
could be identified with Mt Latmus.

History. The first inhabitants in the area lived in a settlement called Latmus
located to the E of the modern village. They were of Anatolian origin. Although
certainly influenced by their Aeolian and Ionian neighbours, the process of their
Hellenisation was probably not completed until the end of 4C BC, when
Alexander the Great removed the Persian presence from Asia Minor.

In the 5C BC, when the annual contribution from Miletus and Ephesus to the
Delian League was assessed at between six or seven talents, Heracleia
contributed only one talent. In the 4C BC Mausolus of Halicarnassus used a
stratagem to capture Latmus which he then fortified. Shortly afterwards the
inhabitants moved to the new settlement of Heracleia on the W. This was later
surrounded by a massive defensive wall.

Although it acquired many fine buildings during the Hellenistic and Roman
periods, from about the end of the 1C BC the prosperity of Heracleia, like that of
its more powerful neighbour Miletus, began to decline. The change in fortune
was due to the loss of trade caused by the closing of Heracleia's link with the
sea. Accumulated silt brought down by the Maeander gradually turned the inlet
of the Gulf of Latmus, on which Heracleia was sited, into the large freshwater
lake that exists today.

Many ancient writers link Heracleia with the legend of Endymion: the
handsome shepherd who was seduced by Selene the moon goddess. Loved also
by Zeus and, perhaps by Hera, the youth escaped from death and old-age by
begging Zeus to let him sleep for ever in a cave on Mt Latmus. There he was
seen by Selene who was so moved by his beauty that she laid with him at night.
Endymion, without waking once from his magic slumbers, gave her 50 daughters.

In Christian times the story was given a more decorous twist. Endymion, it
was said, was a mystic who, after years of studying the moon, learned the secret
name of God. Once a year the priests opened his tomb and, in an attempt to pass
on his secret to men, his bones emitted a strange humming noise.

The story of Endymion has captured the imagination of artists and poets from
many ages and cultures. One of the best-known of the ancient representations
of the legend is a relief in the Capitoline Museum in Rome. The sleeping youth
is depicted half-reclining on a marble bench, while his abandoned dog bays at
the moon.

In the 'Merchant of Venice', Act 5, Shakespeare reminds us that,

' … the moon sleeps with Endymion,
And would not be awaked !',

while Keats avows,

' … tis with full happiness that I
Will trace the story of Endymion.'

Sometime in the 7C AD anchorites and monks who had fled from Arabia began
to settle in caves on Mt Latmus, in small communities around Lake Bafa and on
its islands. Surviving repeated attacks by the Saracens, they produced saints

like Arsenius, Acacius and Paul Junior, whose fame spread through Christendom and attracted pilgrims from as far away as Rome.

St. Paul Junior, whose wish was to be a stylite, settled eventually for life in a cave in one of the most inaccesible parts of the mountain. Despite the inconvenience of frequent earthquakes he stayed there for many years, living frugally on a diet of acorns. Eventually his reputation for holiness made him so popular that he fled to Samos in search of solitude.

In the middle of the 11C the monks were obliged to leave the area around Mt Latmus because of attacks by the advancing Turks. They returned once more after the Crusaders' victory at Dorylaeum on 29 June 1097 and remained at Heracleia until the beginning of the 14C, when W Anatolia came under Turkish rule.

Heracleia was visited by Chandler in 1765. He described the site, which unfortunately he confused with Myus, as being 'as romantic as its fortune was extraordinary'. He located the theatre, which even at that time had lost its marble seats, the agora and the temple of Athena. He was impressed by the city walls and noted their similarity with the Lysimachean fortifications at Ephesus. He found the necropolis down by the lake and a funerary inscription commemorating the untimely death of a youth named Seleucus.

Chandler was taken by some of the villagers up the mountainside to examine an anchorite's shelter and chapel. 'We came', he writes, 'in about an hour to a large rock, which was scooped out, and had the inside painted with the history of Christ in compartments, and with heads of bishops and saints. It is in one of the most wild and retired recesses imaginable. Before the picture of the crucifixion was a heap of stones piled as an altar, and scraps of charcoal, which had been used in burning incense'.

Commenting that Latmus had become 'a holy retreat, when monkery, spreading from Egypt, toward the end of the fourth century, overran the Greek and Latin empires', he concluded that the presence of a lake abounding in large fine fish, which 'afforded an article of diet not unimportant under a ritual which enjoined frequent abstinence from flesh,' must have been an important factor in influencing the choice of the holy men.

Heracleia's attraction springs more from its situation than from the quality or variety of its ancient remains. Apart from the Hellenistic fortifications, which are a spectacular engineering achievement, the ruins are unimpressive. The city was constructed on the grid-plan popularised by Hippodamus of Miletus, but it is difficult to see evidence of this now. An hour should be sufficient for an examination of the principal sites. However, if you intend to explore the fortifications on the mountain your visit should be extended by a further two to three hours.

There is a pleasant beach where good swimming may be enjoyed, providing those stretches covered with reeds or weed are avoided.

The anchorites' cells and chapels on the mountainside, one of which was visited by Chandler (see above), are difficult to locate. It is not advisable to attempt to find them without the help of a local guide.

The schoolhouse and its playground in the centre of the modern village occupy the site of the *Hellenistic agora*. At the S end there are the well-preserved remains of a market building which was divided into separate shops. Across the street, at the rear of some modern houses, are the scanty remains of the 2C *bouleuterion*. This was similar in construction to the council chamber in Priene. Only a few rows of seats and part of the supporting wall are extant.

A short distance to the E, picturesquely situated in an olive grove, are the scanty ruins of the *Roman theatre*. Traces of the seating and stage-building remain. To the left are the remains of a *nymphaeum* and of a structure identified as a *temple*.

Behind the city, the *Hellenistic city walls*, which extend for 6.5km and rise to a height of c 488m, are in a remarkable state of preservation. It appears likely that they were built by Lysimachus

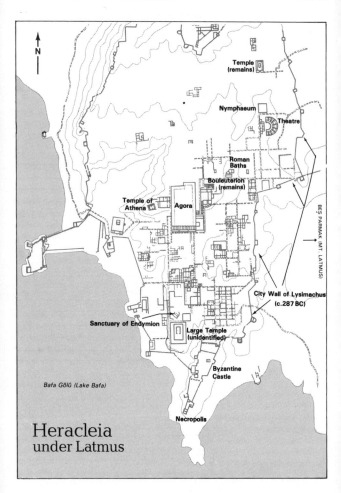

Heracleia
under Latmus

c 287 BC. 'Grey like the mountain', writes Freya Stark, 'they climb
through the chaos of boulders high up the mountain shoulder; they
lose themselves and reappear among rocks like a swimmer in
waves.' There are towers, stairs, gates and sally-ports in plenty to
explore. In places, where the wall has disappeared, the niches, which
held the missing stones, look like giant hand-holds. A stout pair of
shoes and a walking stick are essential equipment for anyone who
wishes to walk on Mt Latmus.

Prominently sited on a spur below the agora is the Hellenistic
Temple of Athena. This building, identified by an inscription, was a
temple in antis made up of a pronaos and cella which were approximately the same size.

The small island across from the landing stage was fortified during the Byzantine period. It was formerly joined to the mainland by a wall which has been submerged by the rising waters of the lake.

The lower track out of the village passes the ruins of one of the most unusual buildings in Heracleia. This is believed to have been a *sanctuary dedicated to Endymion*. It took the form of a prostyle with a small pronaos and a cella. The pronaos has a structural oddity which can scarcely have facilitated access. It was fronted by an uneven number of columns—five—with pilasters at each end. The semicircular cella incorporated sections of unworked natural rock. These were joined by a wall of shaped stone which originally extended above them. The sanctuary faced W, as is customary in buildings erected in honour of heroes or demi-gods.

A short distance to the E on a promontory overlooking the lake are the remains of a Byzantine castle. An ancient *necropolis* was sited below this building. The tombs, which are all of the Carian type, were cut out of the rock and covered with shaped stone lids. Some now lie under water. All were disturbed and robbed of their grave-goods in antiquity.

About 1km to the E of the promontory is the site of the original foundation of Latmus. This lies 500m to the N of the track leading back to Çamiçi. Surrounded by a wall, constructed by Mausolus, the site was occupied from c 6C BC. The buildings inside the walls, both public and private, have provided useful information about pre-Greek settlements in Caria. The site was abandoned in the 4C BC, when the inhabitants moved further W to the new settlement of Heracleia. Rather touchingly, however, they continued to bury their dead in Latmus. The site was reoccupied during the late Byzantine period, possibly because it was more easily defended. Evidence of this occupation is provided by the ruins of two churches and of a number of private houses.

The road from Çamiçi climbs steadily, passing through a pleasantly-wooded landscape which gives way gradually to a chequered pattern of cultivated fields and pastures grazed by flocks of black-haired goats. About 4km beyond the village of Selimiye is the site of the ancient city of EUROMUS. Here, half-hidden in a grove of olive trees, are the remains of one of the best-preserved temples in Turkey.

The city began to be called Euromus sometime towards the end of the 4C BC, when Caria came under strong Hellenistic influence promoted by Mausolus and other members of the Hecatmnid dynasty. A century earlier it was known as Kyromus or Hyromus, both names of non-Greek origin. A settlement of some size and prosperity, it ranked next in importance to Mylasa, with which it was joined uneasily for some time in a sympolity. Euromus appears to have prospered during the Hellenistic and Roman periods, issuing its own coinage from the 2C BC to the 2C AD.

From the left side of the main road a short, bumpy track leads to the site. By the side of the track, half-hidden by the dense vegetation, are some interesting examples of typical *Carian tombs*. Partly cut from the living rock, partly excavated, they were covered with huge stone lids. Unfortunately, all were opened and robbed of their grave-goods a long time ago.

The best-preserved monument of Euromus is the **Temple of Zeus**. During the course of a survey and partial excavation of this building and of the temenos begun in 1969 by Turkish archaeologists some

Temple of Zeus, 2C AD, Euromus.

interesting discoveries were made. The archaeologists found a number of archaic terracotta slabs, ornamented with chariots, birds and floral motifs, which suggests that a shrine existed at the site as early as the 6C BC. An inscription from the Hellenistic period mentions Zeus Lepsynus to whom the sanctuary was dedicated at that time. Lepsynus is a non-Greek word which would suggest that some kind of synthesis had taken place between a native Carian deity and Zeus.

The building extant is a peripteros in the Corinthian style with 6 by 11 columns, which rests on a stylobate measuring c 14.5m by 26.8m. It is believed to date from the reign of Hadrian (AD 117–138). The fact that some of the columns are unfluted suggests that the temple was never completed.

Inscriptions on a number of the columns record the fact that they were the gift of prominent citizens of Euromus. Menecrates, a state physician and magistrate donated five, while Leo Quintus, a magistrate, paid for seven.

Entrance to the temple was on the E side through a double row of columns. Steps led from the pronaos to the cella, where the cult-statue rested in a niche inside a naiskos. There was a small opisthodomos with two columns in antis. To the E of the temple are the remains of a marble altar, dating from the Hellenistic period.

Chandler came to Euromus in 1764. An examination of the remains led him to believe mistakenly that he had found Labraynda. He was horrified to discover a number of furnaces near the temple of Zeus. In these the peasants burned marble to produce lime which they used as fertiliser and to decorate their houses. How much of the ancient building was lost by this infamous practice will never be known.

Today 16 of the temple's columns are still standing. They support a part of the architrave. Note the *decorative lion head* on the S cornice, which served to carry rain water away from the roof.

The temple was built outside the confines of the city which lay a short distance to the N. This area has not been excavated and is very overgrown. Euromus was enclosed by substantial fortifications, which date from the early Hellenistic period. A *defensive tower* and part of the *city wall* crown a slight eminence to the N of the temple. Buildings identified in the city include the *theatre*, of which some seats and a part of the stage-building remain, a Roman baths complex and the agora which was surrounded by colonnades.

Euromus and its temple attract few visitors. Apart from the track, which has been made to provide access to the temple from the main road, the site remains much as it was when Chandler visited it in the middle of the 18C century. This graceful building, set among silver-green olive trees, is still a place where the traveller may rest quietly for an hour savouring the atmosphere of the past.

About 4km from Euromus a turning to the right by an isolated coffee-house is signposted to 19km **IASUS**. This minor road is narrow, but has a reasonably good surface. Passing through pine woods it emerges eventually on the crest of a hill overlooking a stretch of marshy ground to the SE, in the vicinity of Güllük. Shortly after descending into the plain it divides. Take the left-hand turning for Iasus.

The modern village of *Kuren*, which covers part of the site, is built around a S-facing harbour. At the water's edge there are several small restaurants which serve simple, inexpensive and very palatable meals. In continuation of an ancient tradition the fish-dishes of Iasus are particularly good.

Like Euromus, Iasus does not attract many visitors. During the holiday season a certain number cross over by boat from the small resort of Güllük. However, for much of the year only the village people and the archaeologists are to be seen among the ruins of this ancient city. The site has been surveyed and excavated by an Italian team under the direction of Professor Doro Levi since 1960. The most important finds are displayed in the İzmir Archaeological Museum. A number of objects may also be seen in the small museum which is housed in the Roman mausoleum at the entrance to the village.

History. Iasus is a very ancient foundation. The excellence of its harbours, the richness of its fishing-grounds, and the presence of quarries producing a fine red-tinted marble must have been among the factors which attracted colonists to the site. Legendary accounts state that it was founded by Greeks from Argos who were assisted in their enterprise by the inhabitants of nearby Miletus. The first Greek settlers are believed to have arrived sometime in the 9C BC. However, the archaeologists have found evidence which shows that the site was occupied long before the arrival of the Greeks: it would appear that it was inhabited from the beginning of the second millennium BC. Minoan pottery (dating from c 2000–1550 BC) and the remains of Minoan houses point to a strong link between Iasus and Crete, while quantities of Mycenanean pottery, discovered at higher levels, indicate contact with the Greek mainland at a very early period.

In the 5C BC Iasus was a member of the Delian League and was assessed for an annual payment of one talent, the same amount as Mylasa contributed. A supporter of Athens, Iasus was sacked by the Spartans, who were allied with the Persians, in 412 BC. There is some evidence to suggest that it invested again eight years later by a Spartan army under the command of Lysander. On that occasion the male inhabitants were slaughtered and the women and children sold into captivity.

Shortly after Sparta's influence in the Aegean was destroyed by Conon's victory off Cnidus in 394 BC, Iasus joined a league of Aegean states which wished to rid the area of all foreign influence. The league, which included powerful cities like Ephesus, Rhodes and Byzantium, was not very successful. After the settlement known as the King's Peace in 386 BC, which recognised the suzerainty of the Persians over the Greek cities in Asia, Iasus came once more under foreign domination.

Apart from a brief period, when that enlightened despot Mausolus of Halicarnassus endeavoured to establish an independent state in Caria, Iasus and its neighbours continued to be ruled by Persia until the arrival of Alexander the Great in 334 BC. After the confusion and disorder following his death had been resolved, Iasus came under the rule first of the Ptolemies of Egypt, then of the Seleucids. Following the intervention of the Romans, Iasus passed under the control of the Rhodians c 190 BC. The city supported Mithridates VI, king of Pontus, in 88 BC in his revolt against the Rome and, after his defeat, suffered for their bad judgment. Freebooters, allies of Rome, were permitted to sack the city.

During the Imperial period Iasus prospered. It was ornamented with a number of fine buildings, the gifts of Hadrian, Commodus and some prosperous local magnates. As the surrounding countryside is not very fertile, most of the city's wealth must have come from its fishing fleet. Strabo tells a story about a visiting musician who held an Iasian audience enthralled until the bell that announced the opening of the fish market was rung. Then, apart from one man who was somewhat deaf, the audience rose and departed. Surprised and displeased, the musician approached this man and, not knowing that he was deaf, complemented him on his good manners and good taste in staying to hear the music after the bell had been rung. On hearing that the fish market was open the man hastily excused himself wished the musician good day and rushed after his fellow citizens.

Another story about Iasus involved a boy and a dolphin. After his daily exercise in the gymnasium this boy was accustomed to swim in the sea near the city. There he was befriended by a dolphin who would wait for him every day and carry him out to sea, later returning him safely back to shore. When Alexander the Great heard about this unusual occurrence, he sent for the boy and appointed him priest of Poseidon. The people of Iasus, proud of this strange event, commemorated it on the city's coinage which showed the boy swimming near the dolphin while resting one arm on its back.

Iasus continued to issue its own coins down to the 3C AD. The discovery of the ruins of several churches and of extensive fortifications testify to the city's importance during the Byzantine era. It was the seat of a bishop who was subject to the Metropolitan of Aphrodisias. During the Middle Ages a castle was built on the summit of the small hill in the centre of the peninsula by the Knights of Rhodes.

Little is known of the history of Iasus after the Turkish conquest. It appears to have declined in importance and the bulk of its inhabitants probably moved away. Like Alexandria Troas and a number of other ancient sites on the Aegean, it was plundered of its cut and shaped stone. This was used for building purposes in İstanbul.

When Chandler came to Iasus in the autumn of 1764, he found the ruins of the ancient city almost deserted. Pinks and jonquils grew among the mastic bushes and there were large numbers of partridges feeding on the berries. He received a mixed reception from the few people, many of them Greeks, who lived among the ruins. Initially, he was refused entrance to the site by a Greek who lived in a sepulchre near the isthmus. Only when he returned armed with a permit from the ağa of Melasso, in whose jurisdiction Iasus lay, was he able to complete his examination of the site.

A rude and ignorant Greek priest tried to prevent him from copying an inscription which mentioned the theatre, the prytaneum and some other public buildings. He identified the theatre and discovered the substantial remains of the fortifications. Among the inscriptions which he found was one recording the victory of a Iasian at Olympia and at the Capitoline games in Rome. He and his companions stayed in the sepulchre for some time, sharing the limited floor-space with the Greek and his family. In his journal he recorded that they were guarded by two fierce dogs which 'were continually in motion round about, barking furiously at the jackals and then looking in on us with an attention as remarkable as friendly and agreeable'.

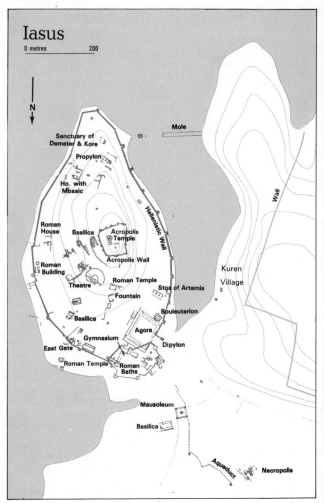

Iasus

0 metres　　　　　　200

N

Sanctuary of Demeter & Kore

Propylon

Ho. with Mosaic

Roman House

Basilica

Acropolis Temple

Acropolis Wall

Hellenistic Wall

Roman Building

Theatre

Roman Temple

Fountain

Stoa of Artemis

Mole

Wall

Kuren Village

Basilica

Bouleuterion

Gymnasium

Agora

Dipylon

East Gate

Roman Temple

Roman Baths

Mausoleum

Basilica

Aqueduct

Necropolis

The *necropolis* of Iasus was sited outside the city. Tombs dating from the third millennium BC to the Roman period may be seen on the right-hand side of the road at the approach to the modern village. Some of these are of the Carian type with a recess for the body cut from a horizontal slab of rock which was closed by a stone slab.

The most striking is a magnificent *mausoleum*, dated to the Roman period, which is located near the remains of the aqueduct. Originally this was thought to be the fish-market mentioned in Strabo's story (see above) or a gymnasium. It takes the form of a temple-tomb in the Syrian style. The burial chamber is surmounted by a beautiful little *Corinthian temple in antis* which rested on a ten-stepped crepidoma. Several skeletons were discovered in the burial chamber, but there was no inscription to indicate either the names or rank of those interred there. The mausoleum was surrounded by stoas which now house some of the finds, in particular fragments of sculpture, inscriptions and pottery from the Mycenaean to the Byzantine eras discovered by the Italian archaeologists at Iasus.

To the right of the road, behind the village of Kuren, are the extensive remains of a *defensive wall* which has been dated to the 4C BC. It surrounded a large area, roughly rectangular in shape, which some authorities believe to have been occupied by the garrison defending the city. The area may also have provided a place of refuge for the inhabitants during times of danger. The limited excavations which have been made so far have revealed a number of buildings, some of which have been dated to c 400 BC. Dense brushwood make any detailed exploration or excavation of this area very difficult.

A muddy path leads across the isthmus which links the village of Kuren with the site of Iasus. The principal remains lie to the N of a little hill clothed in olive trees. Traces of the fortifications which permitted the Iasians to close the S harbour by means of a chain may still be seen. These, and the wall around the peninsula, were repaired during the Byzantine period.

A dipylon led to the *agora* which has been partly excavated. The remains to the left of the entrance belong to a Byzantine fort which still awaits exploration. A number of proto-geometric and geometric *graves* found in the agora suggest that this area was used as a cemetery at a time when the inhabitants occupied the fortified area (see above) on the mainland. The stylobate and part of the Roman colonnade, which surrounded the agora, have been revealed and partly restored by the archaeologists.

To the S of the agora are the well-preserved remains of the *bouleuterion* which dates from the Imperial period. Four stairs divide the rows of seats, behind which there is a covered corridor. On either side steps lead to the interior through vaulted entrances.

On the E side of the agora are the ruins of a rectangular hall which measured 13m by 17m. This has been identified as a *Caesareum*. Artemis Astias, Zeus Megistos (the supreme) and Apollo were the most important deities worshipped at Iasus. The remains of the *stoa of Artemis Astias* lay to the S of the agora. According to an inscription this was erected during the reign of Commodus (AD 180–192). It would appear that the cult statue of the goddess stood in an unroofed cella.

The scanty ruins of the *theatre* may be found on the E slope of the hill. Only the retaining walls of the cavea and a part of the Roman stage-building remain. There is a 2C BC inscription on the N wall which recalls the dedication of a section of the cavea and the stage to Dionysus and the people of Iasus.

Near the fortifications, which overlook the E harbour, there are the ruins of an *early Christian basilica*. This is believed to cover the site of the temple of Zeus Megistos, the temenos of which extended to the NE gate. Visitors with time to spare may like to follow the line of the city wall to its most S point. This route will take them near the extensive remains of a Roman *villa* which has a number of fine mosaics and traces of wall-paintings. (The mosaics are covered with sand to protect them from the elements.) At the S end of peninsula there are the ruins of a shrine dedicated to Demeter and Kore. This was approached from the sea by a magnificent stepped propylon.

An easy ascent leads to the summit of the small hill which dominates the penisula. Traces of occupation dating to the end of the third millennium BC were found here. Inside the walls of the medieval fortress are the remains of a small temple of unknown dedication. The modern building at the NE end houses the Italian archaeologists. There is a good view over the site and the surrounding countryside.

On returning to road 525, continue in the direction of Milas. Some distance before the town a minor road to the left is signposted 13km **LABRAYNDA**, one of the most interesting ancient sites in Caria. Unfortunately, it is difficult to visit, as the rough track from the main road demands both a four-wheel drive vehicle and iron nerves. Because of the risk of damage to their vehicles, local taxi-drivers are usually unwilling to go to Labraynda. This situation may change in the future, as there are plans to improve the access road.

Visitors who make the difficult journey to the site are rewarded with fine views over the plain of Milas. In the spring the banks by the road and the clearings amid the trees are covered with wild flowers. These, together with the blossoms of the many shrubs that grow on the mountainside, provide a rich harvest for the bees of the local villagers whose blue hives are to be seen in almost every sunlit glade.

History. Excavations conducted at Labraynda by Swedish archaeologists since 1948 have not revealed any finds earlier than the end of the 7C BC. In initiating the excavations Professor Axel Persson of Uppsala University had hoped to discover material at the site which would have assisted him in his work on Minoan and Mycenaean scripts. A few fragmentary Carian inscriptions were turned up, but the majority of the finds dated from the Greek and Roman periods.

Labraynda was never a city. It was an important religious centre linked with Mylasa by a Sacred Way. It was also a place of safety in times of danger and a pleasant refuge from the heat of the plains during the summer months. The settlement, which is c 600m above sea-level, was built on a series of terraces cut from the steep hillside. Herodotus (484–420 BC), who was born in nearby Halicarnassus (Bodrum), presumably knew the area well. He does not mention a temple, but says that there was a grove of sacred plane-trees, known as the precinct of Zeus Stratius (the Warlike), at the site. However, Strabo, writing c 400 years later, refers to an ancient shrine and a statue of Zeus Stratius in his Geography.

During the 4C BC the Hecatomnid dynasty of Mylasa (Milas) encouraged the worship of Zeus Stratius or Zeus Labrayndus, as the deity was sometimes known. On their coinage he is shown carrying a spear in his left hand and resting a labrys (double axe) on his right shoulder. The ancient cult statue, which is pictured on some coins, had a curious androgynous character. Bound in a tightly-fitting garment, the god was crowned with a polos and looked not unlike Artemis of Ephesus. This suggests that at some time in the remote past Zeus took over the shrine from a female deity whose attributes and, to some extent, appearance he adopted.

After the death of Alexander, possession of Caria was contested by the Seleucids and the Ptolemies. It was also controlled for a period by the Chrysaoric League which was based at Stratoniceia. The priests of the shrine at Labraynda had a certain amount of autonomy which they guarded jealously, frequently disputing the hegemony of neighbouring Milas. Apart from the fact that they erected two baths and an andron there, little is known of the effect of Roman rule on Labraynda. The site continued to be occupied into the Byzantine era. Evidence of this is provided by a large church which was built from materials salvaged from other buildings. Labraynda was finally abandoned in the 11C when the Selçuk Turks occupied W Turkey.

As Labraynda occupied a series of artificial terraces on a steep mountain slope, exploring the site involves a certain amount of scrambling and climbing. The Sacred Way, which stretched for a distance of c 13km from Mylasa, terminated at the *S and E propylaeae*. It seems likely that one of these imposing entrances to the temenos was a replacement for a gateway destroyed or damaged by

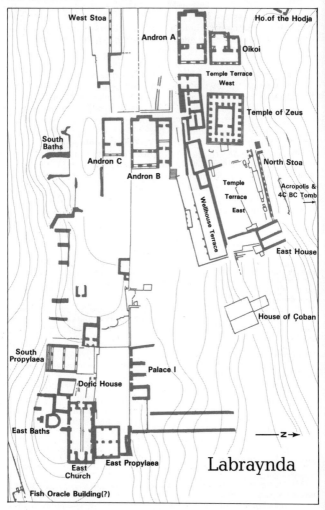

an earthquake. To the E of the S propylaea are the remains of the *Doric house*, so called because it was fronted by four Doric columns. During the Roman period part of this building was incorporated in a *baths complex*, the ruins of which lie to the right. At the extreme E of the terrace are the remains of a Byzantine *church*. A short distance to the SE is a building which the Swedish archaeologists describe as an *ablutions chamber*. Another theory is that this structure housed the fish decorated with gold jewellery which are mentioned by a number of ancient writers. (Perhaps the fish functioned as an oracle like those at Sura.)

A magnificent *staircase*, c 12m wide, leads from the area near the S propylaea to the level that contains the remains of a *stoa* and of *andron C*, which dates from the Roman period. The andron, one of three at Labraynda, was used for sacred banquets given in connection with ceremonies at the shrine. Nearby is the more solidly constructed *andron B*, which was built by Mausolus (fl. 377 BC). Larger and better-preserved is *andron A*, which is located to the SW of the temple of Zeus. Dedicated by Idrieus, the brother of Mausolus, andron A is a large rectangular structure which only lacks its roof. It was well lit by a number of large deep windows which were fitted with shutters for protection against the elements. Both androns A and B had rectangular recesses at the W end which may have contained statues.

A *sanctuary* dedicated to Zeus was built sometime in the 5C BC. This was incorporated in the structure dedicated by Idrieus a century later. The earlier building, a temple in antis, consisted of a rectangular cella and a pronaos. The pronaos had two columns between the antae. Idrieus added a small opisthodomus on the W side and surrounded the the new building with an Ionic colonnade. To the W of the temple are some rooms, preceded by a small porch and four Doric columns. These are the so-called *oikoi*. An inscription describes them as houses dedicated by Idrieus to Zeus Lambrayndus. Some authorities are of the opinion that they were used to store the temple's records, others that they served as a residence for the priests.

A path leads up to the *acropolis* which is now in ruins. This may have been the fortress called Petra which is mentioned in a number of inscriptions. The view from the summit is worth the effort demanded by the climb. A short distance from the path is a fine *tomb* which has been dated to the 4C BC. This consists of a large forecourt and two burial chambers, one behind the other. The outer chamber contains fragments of two sarcophagi. In the inner chamber there are three well-preserved sarcophagi. Overhead there is a roofed chamber which has a window-like opening on to the forecourt.

The sanctuary of Labraynda is surrounded by Carian tombs, particularly along the Sacred Way, but this, the largest and most splendid of them all, clearly belonged to someone of importance. Perhaps, as some assert, Idrieus is buried there.

Milas, c 18km from Euromus on road 525, is a pleasant market town which has served as commercial and administrative centre for this part of Caria for many centuries. Today its narrow, winding streets often contain a striking mixture of the ancient and modern. Large diesel buses and farm tractors compete with horse-drawn carts, which differ little in design from those on ancient reliefs, for the limited space available. The plaintive cries of a flock of sheep or goats being brought to market add their sad contribution to the mildly anarchical, but not unattractive uproar, which is seems to be a permanent feature of the town-centre.

Down by the canal the sagging façades of dilapidated Ottoman mansions are a melancholy reminder of the town's past glories. It may have been these houses that Chandler had in mind when he wrote, rather unflatteringly, about his visit to Milas in the autumn of 1764. The town's buildings, largely constructed of plaster, were, he affirmed, infested with scorpions which entered through the doors and windows and lingered in the rooms. Fortunately for modern travellers this state of affairs no longer appears to be true.

History. It seems likely that MYLASA, the predecessor of Milas, was sited originally on the more easily defensible Peçin Kale (see below), which is located

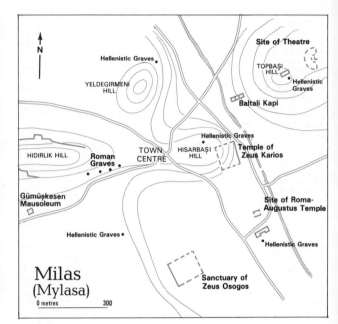

Milas
(Mylasa)

0 metres   300

c 5km outside the town on the road to Muğla. The ancient city was probably moved in the 4C BC during the rule of the Hecatomnids to the site occupied by the modern town.

The earliest known reference to the city comes from the 7C BC, when Arselis of Mylasa assisted Gyges in his struggle to seize the kingdom of Lydia. The people of Caria were well-known for their interest in soldiering and appear to have served frequently as mercenaries. As a consequence the epithet 'Carian' was applied to military equipment like helmet crests, shield-holders and shield-emblems. Strabo quotes Anacreon, who wrote: 'Come, put thine arm through the shield-holder, work of the Carians', and Alcaeus, who spoke of 'shaking the Carian crest'.

By the mid 6C BC nominees of the Persians had replaced the Lydians as rulers of Mylasa and the other Carian cities. When, in 500 BC, the Carians and Ionians revolted against Persian rule, Mylasa joined in the struggle for freedom. Unfortunately, this was unsuccessful. The Persians defeated the allied forces at Miletus in 494 BC and then moved S into Caria where they re-established their control.

Following the Greek victories at Salamis and Plataea in 480/479 BC, Mylasa joined the Delian league which was controlled by Athens. The city was assessed for an annual contribution of one talent. The Delian league was disbanded after the defeat of Athens by Sparta in 404 BC and under the terms of the King's Peace in 387 BC the cities of Asia Minor came once more under Persian control.

The enormous Persian Empire was ruled by satraps who enjoyed a considerable degree of autonomy. Caria was placed under the control of a citizen of Mylasa named Hyssaldomus. He was succeeded by his son Hecatomnos who gave his name to the dynasty which continued in power for the next half century. Perhaps the best-known of the Hecatomnids was Mausolus who was satrap 377–c 353 BC. A wise and capable ruler, he did much to consolidate his own position and the authority of his family. He managed to increase his independence, while remaining on good terms with the Great King. An admirer of all things Greek, he undertook a systematic campaign to Hellenise his subjects. It is probable that the capital of Caria was moved during the rule of

Mausolus from Peçin Kale to Milas. Later, recognising the superiority of the site at Halicarnassus (modern Bodrum), he made that his principal city.

After his untimely death, Mausolus was succeeded by his wife and sister Artemisia. She, grief-stricken for her husband and brother, constructed the splendid monument which was named after him and which became one of the seven wonders of the ancient world. After her death, her older brother Idrieus married his younger sister Ada and became dynast. After the death of Idrieus, Ada was exiled to Alinda by another brother Pixodarus. There she remained until Alexander the Great restored her possessions to her in 334 BC.

Mylasa appears to have suffered little from the move of the administration to Halicarnassus. Fortunate in being sited near a quarry, which produced a marble of excellent quality, it was soon ornamented with splendid civic and religious buildings. A popular story of the time was told about the celebrated musician and wit, Stratonicus, who instead of the usual prefatory words ('Akoúete, Laoí) 'Hear, O people', introduced his performance in Mylasa with ('Akoúete, Naoí) 'Hear, O temples'.

Because of its proximity to Labraynda, the great Carian religious centre which was linked by a Sacred Way c 13km long to the city, Mylasa continued to exercise a strong influence in the region during the Hellenistic period. Following the death of Alexander, it shared the fate of the rest of Caria. Its possession was disputed by the Diadochoi and their successors. However, despite the protests and intrigues of the priests of Zeus Labrayndus, it managed to retain control of the shrine at Labraynda and had its protective status confirmed by both its Seleucid and Macedonian rulers.

During the reign of Ptolemy II Philadelphus (282–246 BC) Mylasa was dominated to some extent by the Chrysaoric League, a grouping of Carian cities based at neighbouring Stratoniceia. Later it was given a limited degree of freedom by the Syrian, Seleucus II Callinicus (246–226 BC). After the defeat of Antiochus III (223–187 BC) by a combined Roman and Pergamene force, Caria, including Mylasa, came for a time under the control of Rhodes. This situation was bitterly resented by the Mylasians and they were able to free themselves eventually from the rule of the hated Rhodians. Later, Mylasa endeavoured to consolidate and improve its position in Caria by forcing a number of its smaller neighbours to join with it in a sympolity. These included Euromus and Labrayanda.

Mylasa was a conventus, a judicial centre, and an administrative city in the Roman province of Asia. According to Strabo (64 BC–AD 25), Mylasa, Alabanda and Stratoniceia were the three most important cities of inland Caria. About 40 BC the city was invested by the rebel Labienus at the head of a Parthian army and suffered considerable damage, which was not quickly repaired. However, calm was restored during the Imperial period and, despite a number of financial difficulties, the city enjoyed a moderate degree of prosperity, continuing to issue its own coinage until the 3C AD.

Apart from the fact that it was an episcopal see, whose bishop was subject to the Metropolitan of Aphrodisias, little is known about the history of Milas during the Byzantine period. The city enjoyed a renaissance in the 14C when the Menteşe, a Turcoman tribe which preceded the Ottomans in SW Turkey, made it their capital. During the rule of the Menteşe a number of fine mosques and other buildings were erected in Milas and on Peçin Kale (see below). Their domination was ended by Murat II in 1425 when the city was absorbed in the Ottoman Empire.

The most important of the surviving remains in Milas is *Gümüşkesen* (the silver purse). This is a tomb, which, for lack of evidence, has not been dated precisely. It is believed to have been built sometime between the 1C and 2C BC. Because of its shape and the proximity of Milas to Bodrum, a number of authorities believe that its design was influenced by the great mausoleum of Halicarnassus.

Located on the lower slopes of Hıdırlık hill to the W of the town, it consists of a burial chamber of cut and shaped stone, which rests on a substantial base. Above the burial chamber is a platform surmounted by a shallow pyramid which has suffered some damage. The platform, which is supported by four pillars in the burial chamber, is enclosed by a Corinthian-style colonnade. This has square pilasters in each corner with two columns in between. The roof of the upper storey, which bears traces of colour, is decorated with an elaborate

Gümüşkesen, 1C or 2C BC, Milas.

pattern of foliage, squares, circles and lozenges. A hole in the floor
permitted mourners to pour libations of wine and honey into the
burial chamber below. There is no inscription and no remains were
found in the tomb which was desecrated and robbed of its grave-
goods many centuries ago. Chandler states that the interior was
painted blue and some traces of paint remain on the stonework.

After centuries of neglect and misuse—when Freely visited it, the
tomb was being used as a cow-shed—the inside of the burial
chamber has been cleaned and the surrounding area cleared of
rubbish. A small garden has been planted and a guardian appointed
to look after the monument. A ladder has been provided for the
rather precarious ascent to the upper storey which any detailed
examination of the delicate carving on the roof and of the colonnade
requires.

Near the post office in the town centre on the side of Hisarbaşı hill are the scant remains of a *temple* which has been dated to the middle of the 1C BC. The one slender Corinthian column that remains standing now supports an untidy stork's nest. The temple, which rested on a podium 3.5m high, was enclosed by a temenos wall of fine masonry. Part of this, on the E side, is still standing. The site is surrounded by houses, which makes any detailed examination difficult. It is believed that the temple was dedicated to Zeus Carius or Zeus Stratius.

A short distance away, across the canal, is *Baltalı Kapı*, the gate of the axe. Dated to the 2C AD, it gets its name from the carving of a labrys or double axe on the keystone on the N side of the gate. A water colour by William Pars, who was commissioned in 1764 by the Society of Dilettanti to accompany Richard Chandler's expedition, shows the considerable remains of ancient structures at the side of the gate. These have largely disappeared.

The site of the *Temple of Zeus Osogos*, a Carian deity with marine associations who with Zeus Stratius played a tutelary role in Mylasa, lies to the SW of the town. Only part of the polygonal temenos wall survives. The shape of Mylasa's *theatre* may be discerned on the slope of Topbaşı hill to the E of the town. There are the remains of a protective wall which encircled the acropolis on Hıdırlık hill. The site of the *temple* dedicated to Rome and Augustus has been identified near the Orta Okul, which is located to the left of the road from Milas to Bodrum. Scattered around Mylasa and in the surrounding countryside are a number of Hellenistic and Roman *tombs*. Perhaps the most interesting of these is the rock-tomb known as Berber Yatağı, which is c 3km from Milas on the road to Güllük.

The Menteşe period of Milas's history is commemorated by a number of fine mosques. Of particular interest is *Firuz Bey Camii* which was built in 1394 with material taken a number of Hellenistic and Roman structures. Also noteworthy are *Ulu Cami* (1398) and *Salaheddin Camii*, which was built by Orhan Bey in 1330.

About 5km from Milas on the Muğla road there is a remarkable flat-topped hill which dominates the surrounding countryside. This is Peçin Kale (height 213m), which was fortified by the Menteşe Turks in the 14C. Visitors who have not eaten in Milas may enjoy a pleasant picnic here under the trees. A brief stop at Peçin Kale also provides a welcome rest for the driver who will need to gather his forces before tackling the torturous, winding road to Bodrum.

The site, which is little visited, is approached by a paved Turkish road on the W side of the hill. This leads to the ruins which are scattered through a series of wooded glades watered by rivulets and streams. The beauty of its setting and the atmosphere of tranquillity and calm at Peçin Kale make it one of the most attractive sites in this part of Turkey.

Some authorities believe that the first city of Mylasa was located on the hill (see above). Certainly the site was occupied from very early times. Bean witnessed the discovery there of an obsidian blade-core, which has been dated to the Early Bronze Age, c 2000 BC, and sherds from the 7C BC to the beginning of the 4C BC, including protogeometric and geometric Carian pottery, have also been found on the site. The absence of remains from the Hellenistic and Roman periods tends to support the theory that the city was moved from the hill to the site now occupied by Milas by one of Hecatomnids, probably Mausolus, in the 4C BC.

The early remains on Peçin Kale are meagre. On the slope under

the Turkish castle there is a short section from a shaped stone wall
and inside the fortress on the right-hand side are six marble steps
which are believed to come from a temple dedicated to Zeus Carius.
It has not been possible to date either of the remains with any degree
of precision.

In addition to the castle, there are the ruins of a two-storey
medrese. This is flanked by a *eyvan* which also served as a *türbe*. In
the eyvan are four barrel-vaulted cells and the *tomb of Ahmet Bey*
which has become the subject of Sufi mysticism. Also on the site are
the ruins of a *hamam*, a *mescit* and a *han* of unusual design, which
had two floors.

From Peçin Kale return to road 330 and continue in the direction of
c 75km **Bodrum**. The small domed structures visible at intervals in
the fields or by the roadside are cisterns used to store rainwater for
irrigation purposes.

There are several small sites in this part of Caria which do not attract
the crowds, but whose beauty and isolation are more than adequate
reward for the effort required to locate and to reach them. Accommodation in Milas is limited and, on the whole, not much used by
foreign travellers. However, visitors with their own transport will find
the small seaside village of (c 18km) *Güllük*, which is just beginning
to attract the attention of tour operators, a good centre from which to
make expeditions to the surrounding countryside.

To reach Güllük, continue c 12km along road 330 and take the
right-hand turning for c 6km. From Güllük it is possible to make
boat-trips to Iasus (see above) and BARGYLIA, a site which may also
be approached, though with some difficulty, from road 330. There are
no refreshments available at Bargylia, but many suitable places for a
picnic.

History. Legend relates that Bargylia was named after Bargylus, the friend of
Bellerophon, who was killed by an accidental blow from the hoof of the winged-
horse Pegasus. However, there is no record of Greek colonisation and the name
is almost certainly of Anatolian origin. Bargylia appears to have come into
prominence under the Hecatomnids. Because of its location and the safety
offered by its harbour it became, with Iasus, an important trading centre.

After the death of Alexander, Bargylia shared the history of its neighbours,
being occupied by the Seleucids, Macedonians and Rhodians amongst others. It
is recorded as declaring itself against Aristonicus, the rebel who contested the
bequest by Pergamene Attalus III of his kingdom to Rome. The city's principal
deity was Artemis Cindyas, whom it appropriated from neighbouring Cindya.
Representations of the goddess on Bargylian coins, which were issued from the
beginning of the 2C BC to early in the 3C AD, suggest that she was of Carian
origin.

Remains found on the site show that Bargylia continued to be occupied
during the Byzantine era. It was probably abandoned sometime after the
conquest of Caria by the Menteşe Turks.

Today the site of the ancient city is surrounded by windswept
marshes and disused salt-pans. The most prominent monuments are
Byzantine: a castle, a church and part of a defensive wall. Among the
many architectural fragments scattered through the area is a shattered *altar* which bears representations of Artemis Cindyas and
Apollo and of a cloaked figure who may be Bargylus. The ruined
theatre, almost hidden in an olive grove, stands on a hill-slope above
the landlocked bay. The outline of the diazoma and part of the stage-
building may still be seen. The city also had an *odeum* of which little
remains. Part of the Roman *aqueduct* which supplied Bargylia with
water is visible on the hillside to the NW of the Byzantine castle.

In spring the site is carpeted with wild flowers and throughout the year the bay and salt flats provide a home for innumerable marsh birds. However, interest in Bargylia is not limited to nature-lovers. It will also attract those travellers who derive pleasure from the melancholy contemplation of ruins long abandoned.

Another interesting EXCURSION from Güllük is to the city of CERAMUS. This necessitates a return to Peçin Kale from where a secondary road of reasonable standard leads to c 40km Ören, the nearest village to the site. There are no refreshment facilities in Ören so bring a picnic.

Very little is known about the history of Ceramus. Its name means pottery or tile in Greek and statuary, dated to the 6C BC, found there show some evidence of Greek influence. Ceramus was a member of the Delian League and Chrysaoric leagues. Later it was joined, uncomfortably, for a time in a sympolity with a neighbouring city, which may have been Stratoniceia, and it also had an uneasy relationship with Rhodes. The city issued its own coinage from the 2C BC to the 3C AD.

According to Bean, the ruins of Ceramus have suffered badly at the hands of ignorant vandals and, as a result, many of the remains recorded by earlier visitors have disappeared. There are the ruins of an early Hellenistic *polygonal wall* on the mountainside. In the *necropolis*, which lies outside the wall, are several sarcophagi and a number of Carian tombs. There are the badly damaged remains of two *temples*, one of which was probably dedicated to Zeus Chrysaoreus. The head of an archaic kouros found in this temple is now preserved in the İzmir Archaeological Museum. The walls of the second temple bore a number of *decorative shields* which carried inscriptions commemorating, in rather flowery terms, its priests and their families.

From Güllük return to road 330 and continue c 38km to **BODRUM**. The road, which follows the coastline for much of the way, offers tantalising glimpses of secluded bays, each fringed with a line of clean white sand. It descends finally to Bodrum through a landscape lightly forested with pines interspersed with the clumps of maquis which during the summer months fills the air with its heady perfume.

Bodrum, which means subterranean vault or dungeon in Turkish, probably derives its name from the remains of the ancient buildings of Halicarnassus. During the last few years this small town has become one of the most popular resorts in SW Turkey. Fortunately, most of the hotel development has taken place on the outskirts of the town. This has permitted the narrow, winding streets of the old quarter to retain much of their original charm. (Unfortunately, during the holiday season this charm is diminished considerably by the traffic jams which block the centre, when motorists, resident and visiting, search frantically for a place to park.)

Visitors interested in the past will find much to examine and explore in Bodrum. In addition to the site of the Mausoleum, one of the Seven Wonders of the Ancient World, there is the Crusader castle of St. Peter which now houses one of the finest regional museums in Turkey. In September the town holds its annual Arts and Culture Festival. This includes special displays and exhibitions, fashion shows and concerts. Accommodation is usually very difficult to obtain during the period of the Festival.

Information and Accommodation. Bodrum has a wide variety of hotels, apartments and pensions. The town's range of accommodation is matched by its excellent selection of restaurants which serve splendid meals at reasonable prices. The fish-dishes are particularly good. Details of accommodation in and around Bodrum, including room-prices, may be obtained from the *Tourism and Information Office* at 12 Eylül Meyd. Because of Bodrum's popularity, it is advisable to make reservations well in advance during the period from May to September, when most of the hotels take block bookings from foreign tour operators and when many visitors come for the Festival.

Bodrum has a good climate. This ranges from c 30°C in July and August to c 7°C in February. Even in the warmest months the high temperatures are modified to some extent by a cooling breeze from the sea. During January, February and part of March there is a good deal of rain, but it is seldom cold. Spring and autumn, when there are fewer visitors and prices are lower, are the best seasons to visit Bodrum. In spring the countryside is carpeted with wild flowers and in the autumn citrus fruit is in season. Bodrum's tangerines are justly famous.

During the summer months Bodrum has a lively night-life, when its many bars, tavernas and discos which offer everything from pop and jazz to folk music are crammed with visitors and townspeople.

Transport. Visitors who do not have their own transport should have little difficulty in getting to Bodrum. Despite the fact that it is sited at the end of a peninsula, it has good transport connections. The nearest airports are at İzmir and at Dalaman. They are linked to Bodrum by bus services which take five and three hours respectively. For those who prefer a more leisurely and more comfortable method of travel, there are the regular sailings from İstanbul operated by Turkish Maritime Lines.

Sports. The town has recently constructed a yacht marina to the NW of the castle. Providing a comprehensive range of facilities, this has begun to attract an international clientele and is much used by visiting sailors and by yachtsmen who make Bodrum their permanent headquarters.

There are excellent facilities for aquatic sports in and around Bodrum. These include sailing, fishing and water-skiing. The clear waters of this part of the Aegean will be irresistible to those who enjoy exploring the depths of the sea. One of best places for underwater swimming is Adaboğazı, where, in the area around the island, the bottom is visible to a depth of 30m.

In the past Bodrum was an important boat-building centre and the characteristically-shaped craft produced in its yards were a familiar sight in most of the ports of the Aegean. Today they are still made, but as pleasure craft rather than cargo vessels. In the boatyards, which are sited to the W of the harbour, visitors are welcome, providing they behave sensibly and do not interrupt the work.

Bodrum is a good centre for EXCURSIONS. During the season there is a daily service to the Greek island of **Cos**. The journey, for which passports are required, takes two hours in each direction. Boats also leave the W harbour at regular intervals for the excellent beaches at *Bardakçi, Gümbet* and *Karaincir*. (Because of pollution it is not advisable to bathe near the town where, in any case, the beaches are small, stony and weed-filled.) Full information about the service to Cos and boat-trips and excursions in and around Bodrum may be obtained from travel agencies like Karya Tour, Karantina Cad. 13 (near the castle), where reservations may also be made.

History. According to Herodotus and Strabo, HALICARNASSUS was founded by Dorians from Troezen in the E Peloponnese c 1000 BC. To judge by the names found on inscriptions in the city, the newcomers appear to have established themselves without much difficulty, intermarrying with the native Carians and producing a mixed population. After some time the settlement came under the influence of its N Ionian neighbours to such an extent that it was expelled from the Dorian Hexapolis. This was a grouping of six cities—Cos, Lindus, Camirus and Ialysus on Rhodes, Cnidus and Halicarnassus—which met from time to time during the festival of Triopian Apollo near Cnidus.

After the Persians had conquered Lydia and overrun the Greek cities on the Aegean, Halicarnassus was governed on their behalf by Carian dynasts. Artemisia the Elder was, perhaps, the best-known of these rulers. In 480 BC she fought on the side of Persia commanding a ship at the battle of Salamis where the vigour of her attack attracted the attention and won the approval of Xerxes. Following the defeat of the Persians, Halicarnassus became a member of the Delian league, contributing the modest sum of 1²/₃ talents annually to its funds.

After the promulgation in 386 BC of the settlement known as the King's Peace, Caria came once more under the rule of the Persians. It was governed for

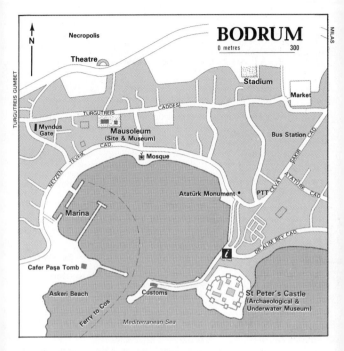

them by a satrap named Hyssaldomus. His son, Hecatomnos, was the founder of the dynasty bearing his name that remained in power for more than 50 years. Perhaps the most able of the Hecatomnids was Mausolus, who managed to increase his personal authority and that of his family without losing the friendship of the Great King. An admirer of Greek civilisation, he embarked on an ambitious scheme to Hellenise his subjects. Having improved the defences of Caria, he turned his attention to its cities which he decorated with fine buildings. In his new capital Halicarnassus, which was protected by an elaborate defensive system c 5.5km long, he built himself a luxurious palace whose walls were sheathed in Proconnesian marble. Determined that his reign should be commemorated properly, he began the construction of an elaborate funerary monument. This structure, which was to perpetuate his name, was completed after his death by his sister Artemisia the Younger, who was also his wife, and by other members of his family. The extent of Artemesia's affection for her brother-husband may be judged by the fact that every day until her death she drank her wine mixed with some of Mausolus's ashes.

Like Artemisia the Elder, she also distinguished herself in warfare, inflicting a resounding defeat on the Rhodians, who made the mistake of thinking that a mere woman could not defend her territory. She captured their city and, to their shame and mortification, had a monument erected there to commemorate her victory. As custom prevented the Rhodians from removing this monument, they erected a building around it to conceal it from public view.

Artemisia was succeeded by other members of her family, power passing finally to her younger brother Pixodarus, who, until his death, ruled jointly with the Persian satrap, Orontobates. When Alexander the Great attempted to take the city in 334 BC, he was resisted by the Persian who was aided by the Rhodian mercenary, Memnon. After the city's capture by the Macedonians, Alexander restored power to the former Queen Ada, an elder sister of Pixodarus, who had been exiled by her brother to Alinda.

During the confused period that followed the death of Alexander, Halicarnassus shared the fate of the other cities in Caria. At various times it was ruled by the Ptolemies, the Seleucids, the Macedonians and the Rhodians. After the establishment of Roman rule, it became an important city in the new province of Asia. Impoverished by the extortions of the the infamous Verres, it suffered also from the unwelcome attentions of the tyrannicdes Brutus and Cassius. The city's fortunes were restored under the empire, a period marked by the erection of several temples, including one dedicated to Mars.

During the Byzantine era Halicarnassus was an episcopal see under the jurisdiction of the Metropolitan of Aphrodisias. The city came under Turkish rule in the 11C, but it was recaptured by the Christians, to whom it was known as Mesy, during the First Crusade (1096–99). In the middle of the 13C it was taken by the Menteşe Turks (see above), but, after the defeat of Beyazit I at the battle of Ankara in 1402, the city was occupied once more by a Christian army. Using material from the Mausoleum, which appears to have collapsed during an earthquake, they built the Castle of St. Peter on the promontory which dominates the harbour. The architect of the new structure was a German, Henry Schlegelholt. The Christians continued to occupy Bodrum until 1523. Then, after the fall of Rhodes to Süleyman the Magnificent, they abandoned the town and castle and withdrew their forces to Malta. Bodrum and its fortress became part of the Ottoman Empire.

In the centuries that followed Bodrum's history was equally stormy. In 1770 it was bombarded by ships of the Russian fleet sent by Catherine the Great to support a Greek rebellion against Ottoman rule. During the first World War the French attempted, unsuccessfully, to land an expeditionary force there. In 1919 the town was occupied briefly by the Italians. After they had been compelled to withdraw by nationalist forces revitalised by Atatürk's leadership, Bodrum was restored to Turkish control.

Halicarnassus was the birthplace of two historians—Herodotus, the 'father of history' (484–420 BC) and Dionysius (died 8 BC). Writing in the Ionic dialect, with admixtures of Dorian and Attic, Herodotus chronicled the epic struggle between Greece and Persia, its antecedents and aftermath. A great traveller, he visited many countries including Egypt, Babylonia, and Scythia. His history is full of entertaining stories and contains a wealth of general information about the places and the personages which form its subject. Dionysius is remembered principally for his history of Rome from the city's mythological foundation to the middle of the 3C BC. Part of this work has been preserved.

Halicarnassus was also the home of the elegiac poet Heraclitus (fl. early 3C BC). Callimachus of Alexandria mourned the death of his 'Halicarnassian friend' in a celebrated poem:

'Someone spoke of your death, Herakelitos. It brought me
Tears, and I remembered how often together
We ran the sun down with talk . . .'

Of the work of Heraclitus only one epigram remains. This was written in memory of Aretemias of Cnidus, who died in childbirth and who speaks from beyond the grave:

'I left one twin to guide my husband's old age,
and took the other to remind me of him . . .'

About 18km to the W of Bodrum is the village of Turgut Reis which is named after a celebrated corsair who, according to popular tradition, was born there. Reis, also known as Dragut, was the scourge of European commercial shipping in the Mediterranean during the mid 16C. Promised the governership of Tripoli by Süleyman the Magnificent, if he could take it from the Knights of St. John of Malta he laid siege to the city and captured it. Turgut Reis then led his forces against Malta where, during an unsuccessful assault on the citadel, he was killed in 1565. His bones lie in Tripoli, but his native village, in addition to bearing his name, has erected a statue in memory of its buccaneering son.

On a windy hill behind the village of Gümbet 2.5km to the W of Bodrum is the resting place of one of Turkey's most interesting modern writers, Cevat Şakir Kabaağaçlı. Better known as the Fisherman of Halicarnassus, he wrote a number of captivatingly simple books about the lives of the fishermen and sponge-divers of Bodrum. In these he set out his understanding of the monuments of the past which surrounded him and of the philosophy that inspired them. Unfortunately, his books are available only in Turkish at present.

Interior of the Castle of St. Peter ('Antiquities of Ionia', 1769–97), Bodrum.

Undoubtedly the most striking monument in Bodrum is the **Castle of St. Peter**. Sited on a rocky promontory to the E of the main harbour, it occupies an area of c 180m by 185m. Access to the inner keep is by seven massive gates. A short ramp behind the police station in the harbour square leads to the first gate. This bears an inscription in Greek placed there on the orders of Jacques Gatineau (Captain of the Castle, 1512), which warns spies that they will be punished.

The castle's occupation by Christian armies is marked by almost 250 coats of arms. These are to be found in various parts of the building. Inside the first gate there are several examples including the arms of Guy de Blanchefort, Grandmaster of the Order of St. John and, in the centre of the group, those of Jacques Gatineau. To the left of the ramp is the N moat which serves as an arena for displays and theatrical performances during the Bodrum Festival. The building to the right is now used as an art gallery. Under the trees to the left are a number of antiquities including altars and sarcophagi from Halicarnassus and the surrounding countryside. The gate at the top of a flight of steps bears the arms of Cardinal Pierre d'Aubusson, Grandmaster from 1476–1503. He came from Rhodes on several occasions to visit the front line garrison of St. Peter. To the right are the arms of an English nobleman, Thomas Dowcra, warden of the castle from 1498–99. He was a Turcopolier, a cavalry soldier who had adopted the arms and strategy of his Turkish opponents. The third gate, which is in a good state of preservation, bears the arms of Grandmaster Philibert de Naillac (1396–1421). After penetrating two more gates, also with coats of arms, you reach a short corridor decorated with representations of the Virgin and Child, St. Peter, St. Catherine and St. Mary Magdalene. This leads to the sixth gate which bears an inscription in Latin invoking God's protection on the garrison: 'O Lord, protect us in our sleep, save us when we wake. Without your protection, nobody can keep us from harm.' Beyond lies a vaulted entrance, built above one of the 14 cisterns which ensured an adequate supply of water to the garrison. This finally admits to the lower courtyard of the castle.

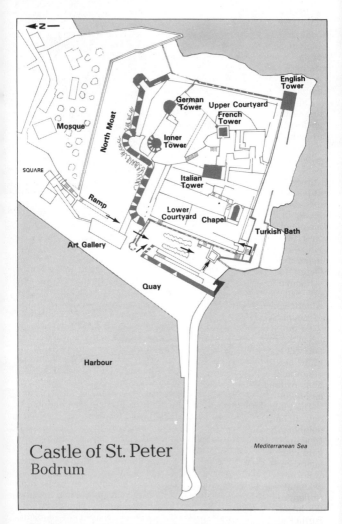

Castle of St. Peter
Bodrum

The museum authorities have taken full advantage of the castle's magnificent setting and of its fine buildings to present the antiquities from Bodrum's Hellenistic, Roman, Byzantine, Medieval and Turkish past in the most interesting way possible. It is one of the most romantic and imaginative displays in Turkey.

Within the castle's walls there is a representative collection of the

trees and plants which are found in the Bodrum peninsula. Underneath its ancient battlements, peacocks strut and display among the
laurels, oleanders, olives, myrtles and plane trees. In summer the still
air between the towers is heavy with the scent of roses. A pile of
shell-encrusted amphorae, lately rescued from the bed of the sea, lies
in the purple shade of a clump of carnations, beneath a crumbling
wall. Overhead, clouds of white doves wheel and glide between the
towers of the castle and, coming to rest in the groves of pine,
pomegranate and mulberry, fill the air with their soothing calls. In
sheltered corners the violet flowers and orange fruits of the man-
drake hide. This mildly poisonous plant, which was believed to
shriek when pulled from the ground, was used during the Middle
Ages in philtres by the love-sick, and, more practically, was
employed by doctors as a pain-killer.

On the right-hand side of the entrance is the castle's *chapel*. This
fine Gothic-style building, constructed between 1402 and 1437 from
ancient materials, including some of the characteristic green stone
from the Mausoleum, was restored by Spanish knights in 1519. After
the occupation of the castle by the Ottomans in 1523, a minaret was
added and the chapel was turned into a mosque. The building was
badly damaged when the French shelled the castle in 1915.

The chapel now houses finds from the Bronze Age. These include
pithoi which date from c 2500 BC; a number of Mycenaean objects,
including amphorae, cups, incense burners and perfume bottles
found in a necropolis in Ortakent; and a quantity of artefacts,
including weights, ingots, tools and amphorae, discovered in the
wreck of two boats. The first, which was lost off Cape Gelidonya near
Finike c 1200 BC, was a Syrian trader bringing a cargo of copper
ingots from Cyprus. The second, which was discovered at Şeytan
Deresi near Çatalburun in Gökova bay, was lost in the 16C BC. This
contained pithoi, amphorae and craters of local manufacture. The
objects from these ships, which were recovered by a joint Turkish-
American team of archaeologists, form the nucleus of Bodrum's
Museum of Underwater Archaeology.

To the S of the chapel is a 19C *hamam*, which was constructed
when the castle was used as a prison. This is currently being restored
and will house an ethnographic collection in due course. By the side
of the chapel a path lined with 2C and 1C BC *cinerary urns*, which
are ornamented with erotes, bulls' heads, garlands and representations of the head of Medusa, leads up to an open air display of
amphorae.

The building to the right is also devoted to underwater archaeology. It houses two ships which foundered near *Yassiada* in the
neighbourhood of Turgut Reis. One lost c AD 350 had more than
1000 amphorae aboard, the other, which sank c AD 641, contained
gold coins bearing the head of the Emperor Heraclius (610–641),
lamps, carpenter's tools, cooking pots and a fine bronze steelyard. A
scale model explains the methods used by the archaeologists to
examine wrecks and recover objects from them. To the N is the
serpent's tower, named from the relief carved on the wall to the left of
the lower entrance. This also contains a collection of amphorae.
Further to the E is the *German tower* built between 1437–1440. In
due course this will house an exhibition of objects connected with the
Knights of St. John. Adjoining the tower is a collection of stone
anchors recovered from the sea. Some of these have had their
wooden shafts restored.

The *Italian tower* completed in 1436, which lies to the S at a higher

The 15C English tower, Bodrum.

level, contains three exhibition rooms. The lowest is devoted to a display of coins and jewellery. Note in particular the coins issued by the Hecatomnid dynasty, including a rare example from the period of Hecatomnus, the father of Mausolus. The middle floor contains objects from the Classical period. These include a fine 4C BC statute of Hecate; bronze and terracotta representations of deities; statuettes of women water-carriers and priests from Theangela; and a number of red figure vases. There is also a fine 4C BC female head from Cnidus which bears traces of the paint with which it was covered originally. On the top floor there are objects from the Hellenistic period. The most important are the bronze statues of a negro boy and of the goddess Isis, the protectress of sailors, which were found in a wreck lying on the sea-bed at a depth of 84m off the NW coast of the Bodrum peninsula. The distended stomach of the negro, who has typical facial features, shows that he suffered from malaria. Also noteworthy is a Roman copy of the famous statue from Cnidus of Aphrodite Euploia (of fair voyages) by Praxiteles which was the subject of an ancient scandal. (See below.)

To the E of the Italian tower is the *French tower*, the lower floor of which contains a number of finds from the medieval period. The most interesting are the objects from the wreck of an early 11C Byzantine or Fatimite vessel discovered near Bozukkale, c 40km from Marmaris. These include amphorae, examples of Islamic glass and pottery, a steelyard ornamented with pigs' heads, daggers, spear-heads, chess and backgammon pieces, gold coins of El-Hakim and Byzantine copper coins bearing the head of Basil II Bulgaroctonus (the Bulgar Slayer). On the upper floor are preserved objects dating from the 11C to the 6C BC. The most interesting are: a 9C BC terracotta sarcophagus, which contained two skeletons, discovered by Professor Akurgal at Göçebel, a kantharos bearing a snake design from Dirmil, archaic kouroi, and a protogeometric crater with a rare representation of a ship.

The *English tower*, sometimes called the lion tower because of an archaic sculpture of a lion on the W wall, is located in the SE corner of the castle. Today its dungeons are used as storerooms, the middle floor serves as a workshop for the preservation of glass artefacts, and the top floor, the banqueting hall of the knights, has been restored in the medieval style.

Over the entrance to the banqueting hall are the arms of Henry IV (1399–1413) during whose reign the tower was built. Inside the hall, the banners of the Grand Masters and of their Turkish opponents, including the standard of the corsair Dragut, sway gently in the candle-lit gloom. Today, while the muted strains of lutes fill the incense-laden air, youths in medieval costume offer goblets of wine to visitors. While drinking, they might spare a thought for those English soldiers who made the long journey from their native land to this remote castle in S Turkey more than five centuries ago. Some were filled with a fervent desire to serve their Order, while others had baser aims—the pursuit of fame or the acquisition of riches. The names of some of these English knights, which were carved on the window ledges of this tower in moments of idleness, constitute the sole memorial to their faith or to their greed.

Outside the castle is a two-storey *han* built by Hacı Molla in 1769. Now a restaurant, the upper floor served as a hotel until comparatively recently. Note the inscription carved above the entrance.

To the W of the harbour was the area known in antiquity as SALMACIS. A suburb of Halicarnassus, which enjoyed a certain measure of independence, Salmacis had a rather unenviable reputation. It possessed a fountain whose waters had an unusual property. They were reputed to make men effeminate. Strabo indignantly questions the veracity of this story. According to him effeminacy is caused by riches and wanton living! Modern visitors to Bodrum need not worry about the fountain of Salmacis. Because of erosion and changes in ground-level it is now under the sea. Careful observation may locate its waters which bubble up near the light that guards the entrance to the harbour.

Not far away are the ruins of the *Myndus gate* which, according to Arrian, was the scene of a foolish sortie by members of the Persian garrison during Alexander's siege of the city. From this point it is possible to trace much of the ancient city wall which ran, first to the N, then E over Göktepe, the hill behind the theatre. On the summit of Göktepe is a levelled space which may mark the position of the temple of Ares which was mentioned by the Augustan architect, Vitruvius.

The remains of the *Mausoleum of Halicarnassus* lies to the NW of the Castle. To reach it, take the street that runs N from the harbour mosque to the T-junction. The entrance to the site is a short distance to the left.

As in the case of the temple of Artemis at Ephesus, it requires a considerable effort of the imagination to picture the Mausoleum of Halicarnassus as it once was. Indeed, many visitors leave the site with feelings of disappointment. Of this structure, one of the Seven Wonders of the Ancient World, which is believed to have covered an area 38m by 32m by c 55m tall, only its foundations and a few architectural fragments remain.

Years of painstaking research and inspired detective-work by a team of Danish archaeologists have made it possible to reconstruct the general appearance of the monument. The mausoleum designed by Pytheos, who was responsible for the temple of Athena at Priene, was surrounded by a huge peribolos measuring c 242m by 105.5m. It consisted of a solid base on which rested a four-sided colonnade of 9 by 11 columns surrounding a rectangular chamber. This was surmounted by a 24-step pyramid on which—according to some authorities—rested a quadriga bearing giant statues of Mausolus and of his sister/wife Artemisia. The sides of the structure were covered with friezes and statues by Bryaxis, Scopas, Leochares and Timotheus, the best sculptors of the time. The friezes depicted a chariot race, and battles between Amazons and Greeks, Lapiths and Centaurs.

Work on the construction of the funerary monument, which eventually was named after him, was begun by Mausolus c 355 BC. It was continued after his death by Artemisia and other members of the Hecatomnid dynasty.

An object of admiration and wonder in antiquity, the mausoleum is known to have existed in an undamaged state as late as the 12C when it was described by Bishop Eustathius. However, in 1402 the Knights of St. John found it in ruins, destroyed, perhaps by an earthquake. They removed most of the cut stone and burned the marble to make lime, using these materials to construct the Castle of St. Peter. The distinctive green granite of the mausoleum may still be seen in various places in that fortress. In 1522, requiring more stone to strengthen the walls of the castle, the knights returned once again to the mausoleum. Burrowing into the base they discovered the burial chamber. A contemporary account by a knight named De La Tournet relates that as they were about to open the tomb the evening curfew was sounded. When the knights came back next morning, they found that thieves had entered the chamber during the night and removed some of its precious contents.

In 1846 Sir Stratford Canning, British Ambassador to the Porte, obtained permission to send to England 13 slabs of a frieze from the mausoleum, which were discovered in the Castle. Eleven years later Charles Newton searched for and found the site of the mausoleum. There he uncovered a number of treasures, including the statues of Mausolus and Artemisia, and the head and forepart of one of the horses from the quadriga. Having received the Sultan's firman, he sent these statues and a number of other sculptures to the British Museum where, with the frieze despatched by Canning, they are now displayed. Only one panel of the frieze, which shows a Greek warrior attacking an Amazon, and a number of architectural fragments remain in Bodrum. During his search for the mausoleum, Newton uncovered some fine Roman mosaics in the ruins of a 4C AD villa. These are also preserved in the British Museum.

The modern study of the Mausoleum commenced with the Danish archaeological mission which, under the direction of Professor Christian Jeppesen, has been working in Bodrum since 1966.

It is advisable to begin the visit by examining the plans and models which have been prepared by the Danish archaeologists. These are displayed in a small antiquarium on the E side of the site. The explanatory texts are in Turkish and English. In the adjoining area there are a number of fragments of the frieze which were found in the castle, and some architectural remains recovered during the course of the excavations. Part of the wall, which enclosed the temenos, may also be seen here. The frieze is a copy of the original kept in the British Museum.

Descending into the great depression, which marks the position of the Mausoleum, one sees on the S side a staircase which belonged to an earlier funerary monument. A door to the right of the stairs leads to a tomb which has been dated to the 6C BC. Note the niches in the walls where offerings to the dead were placed. The channels in the floor were used to drain away any water that gathered in the substructure. The funeral chamber was located at the foot of the main stairs. In this area the Danes found the bones of animals which, presumably, had been sacrificed to the spirits of the dead.

The *theatre* is most easily reached by following the main road above the town. Constructed during the rule of Mausolus, it was modified during the Roman period. Although only the section below the diazoma has been preserved, it has been possible to estimate the capacity of the building at 13,000. Some of the seats in the lower section, which was divided by 12 stairs, bear the names of regular patrons. A rectangular altar in the orchestra, which was larger than a semicircle, was dedicated to Dionysus. Between the cavea, which was supported by retaining walls, and the stage-building there were two parodoi. When the theatre was modified in the 3C AD for wild-beast shows and gladiatorial exhibitions, barriers were erected for the protection of the audience. During the Byzantine period the stage-building, most of which has disappeared, was converted into a residence.

Behind the theatre, near the summit of Göktepe, there are many Hellenistic and Roman rock-cut tombs. The dense undergrowth and rough terrain make these difficult to reach. In some there are traces of frescoes, but most have suffered from being used as shelters by shepherds. Their walls have been blackened by fires and the façades damaged by vandalism and neglect.

Among the many EXCURSIONS that may be made by boat from Bodrum, two are of particular interest. It is a long but pleasant journey E along the coast to the village of Ören which is near the site of ancient CERAMUS. (See above.)

A shorter voyage may be made to *Karaada* (Black Island), the ancient ARCONESSUS, which lies to the SE of Bodrum. On the summit, which may be reached by a brisk climb from the landing-place, there are the remains of a small temple. The views towards Cos and the mainland are particularly fine.

It is a somewhat difficult journey by land to the ancient sites of SYANGELA-THEANGELA which are c 12km to the E of Bodrum near the villages of Alazeytin and Etrim. Of interest mainly to specialists, they contain a number of Lelegian remains.

At the W end of the Bodrum peninsula, near the village of *Gümüslük*, are the scanty remains of the city of MYNDUS. Host to rebel Aristonicus, c 131 BC, its harbour sheltered the ships of the tyrannicide Cassius after the murder of Julius Casesar in 44 BC. The city, which was under-populated during the Hecatomnid period, issued its own coinage during the Hellenistic and Imperial eras. It was reputed to produce very poor quality wine which when mixed with brine, as was customary in antiquity, caused a bad hangover and pronounced flatulence, but was considered to be good for the stomach.

The city of PEDASA is located at a place called *Gökçeler* c 8km to the N of Bodrum. It takes an hour to walk there but the effort is justified as the site has a number of interesting ruins including chamber graves. Because of its successful resistance to the Persians, Pedasa acquired a reputation for producing tough fighting men. It was also quite prosperous at one time: its contribution to the Delian League was assessed at 2 talents, when that of Halicarnassus was only 1$\frac{2}{3}$.

13   Bodrum to Aydın

Total distance c 166km. **Bodrum**—R330 c 60km *Peçin Kale*—32km *Eskihisar / Stratoniceia*—10km *Yatağan*—(c 18km *Lagina*)—(c 6km *Gerga*)—c 29km *Çine* (c 8km **Alabanda**)—(c 25km **Alinda**)—(c 20km *Amyzon*)—c 35km **Aydın**.

Leave **Bodrum** (see Rte 12) on road 330 and return to c 60km *Peçin Kale* on the outskirts of Milas (see Rte 12). There take the right-hand turning in the direction of Yatağan and Muğla. Shortly after the junction the road begins a steady climb along the N flank of the Akdağ. Below, the ground falls steeply away to deep valleys which shelter a few lonely steadings. Above, pine woods clothe the slopes that lead to the highest peaks of the range. By the roadside and in clearings between the trees the local people place rows of the traditional blue-painted beehives. This is one of the areas which produce çambalı, pine honey, a delicacy which is much appreciated in Turkey.

After the long drive from Bodrum, a pleasant stop may be made at a strategically-located rest place set among the pine trees a short distance before the village of *Eskihisar*. As the culinary resources of Yatağan are decidedly limited, travellers may prefer to lunch here at the small restaurant or enjoy an alfresco meal in the adjoining picnic-area.

The site of the ancient city of **STRATONICEIA**, which was located near the village of Eskihisar, is perilously close to a large and rapidly expanding quarry. As a consequence, it has been necessary to rehouse the villagers and to undertake a good deal of rescue archaeology. How much longer the ruins of Stratoniceia will remain inaccessible to visitors is difficult to forecast.

History. The city named Stratoniceia came into existence in the early 3C BC, when the Seleucid kings of Syria began to extend their rule over large areas of Asia Minor. It appears to have replaced an earlier Carian foundation which, with the country around it, was called Chrysaoris or Idrias.

At the age of 60, Seleucus I Nicator (321–280 BC), king of Syria, remarried. His new bride, chosen largely for reasons of state, was Stratonice the daughter of Demetrius the Besieger, ruler of Cyprus and of a number of Aegean and Phoenician cities. Sometime after the wedding, his son Antiochus conceived a violent passion for his stepmother and, feeling that his situation was hopeless, went into a decline. When Seleucus learned the cause of the young man's illness, although Stratonice had already borne him a child, he decided to give her to his son. From that time onward Antiochus ruled jointly with his father. It is not recorded whether Stratonice's second marriage was a happy one, but she gave Antiochus three children. The new Carian settlement, which was orna-mented with many fine buildings by its royal founders, was named after her.

In c 201 BC it appears to have been occupied for a time by Philip V of Macedon, but it was later returned to the control of Rhodes, into whose hands it had passed from the Seleucids. Stratoniceia supported Rome against Mithri-dates VI of Pontus in 88 BC and, after its capture by him, paid dearly for its fidelity. Later it was compensated for its suffering and losses by the Romans. In 40 BC Labienus, an associate of the tyrannicides Brutus and Cassius, led an army of barbarian Parthians into Asia Minor. They caused much destruction in Caria. Having failed to take Stratoniceia, Labienus attacked the shrines of Lagina and Panamara which were located in Stratoniceian territory. He failed to capture Panamara—his army was repulsed through the intervention of Zeus Panamaros—but he sacked the temple of Hecate at Lagina.

During the Imperial period Stratoniceia prospered. Augustus provided finan-cial assistance for the restoration of the temple of Hecate at Lagina and Hadrian ornamented the city with a number of fine buildings. Stratoniceia continued to be occupied during the Byzantine era. Its bishop was subject to the Metro-politan of Aphrodosias.

The site of Stratoniceia was visited by Richard Chandler in the autumn of 1764. Well received by the inhabitants of Eskihisar, he found the remains of the theatre and a number of altars and tombs and he recorded several inscriptions.

The principal deity of Stratoniceia was Zeus Chrysaoreus (of the golden sword), an epithet which Homer and Pindar applied also to Apollo and a number of other gods. It was at this temple that delegates from the cities in the Chrysaoric League met at regular intervals for their deliberations and to offer sacrifice. Membership of the league, which was first mentioned in 267 BC, was open to all Carians. The site of the temple of Zeus Chrysaoreus is believed to lie c 4km to the E of Eskihisar village near the main road from Muğla to Aydın.

The large building of white stone in the centre of the village was probably the city's *bouleuterion*. Access to the interior of this rectangular structure, which has been dated to the Roman period, was provided by two staircases, one on each side. The orchestra, greater than a half-circle, was surrounded by rows of seats arranged in a hemicycle. However, some authorities are of the opinion that the building was a Serapeum and not a bouleuterion. An inscription found on the N wall would appear to support this hypothesis. It offered thanks to Helios Zeus Serapis for preservation from the dangers of war and the perils of the sea. Another inscription in the same place recorded a reassuring answer received from the oracle of Zeus Panamaros concerning the possibility of an invasion by barbarian tribes, probably the Goths, in the 3C AD. The temple was surrounded by a wall c 90m by 90m. Only the gate on the W side of this wall remained standing into modern times.

The position of the city's *agora*, which lay to the W of the bouleuterion or Serapeum, was marked by a line of marble blocks. To the NW of the agora there was an elaborately ornamented structure which has been identified as the city's *gymnasium*. Sections of the wall, which protected Stratoniceia, and of the main gate on the N side were also visible. Just inside the gate there was a single unfluted Corinthian column. A rectangular fortress, constructed of massive stone blocks, overlooked a ravine on the NE side of the city. This was repaired and extended during the Byzantine era.

Stratoniceia's *theatre*, which could seat 10,000 spectators, lay to the S of the city at the foot of the acropolis-hill. Access to the seats in the cavea was provided by ten stairs. There was a single diazoma. Unfortunately, only the foundations of the stage-building were preserved. In a level space on the slope of the acropolis above the theatre the ruins of a small Ionic temple, dedicated to the imperial cult, were discovered by the archaeologists.

Objects found at Stratoniceia and in the surrounding countryside are preserved in a small *antiquarium* in the village. The most important of these, a Mycenaean cup decorated with parallel red stripes, suggests that the site was occupied as early as the 12C BC. There are also a number of tombstones and inscriptions, most of which date from the Roman period.

At Eskihisar the pine woods come to an end and the road to 10km Yatağan enters an uninteresting upland plateau which is covered in thorny scrub and scarred by the great, ugly pit of the quarry. Yatağan is a dusty, unattractive town which matches the desolate and uninviting landscape. Few travellers will be tempted to linger there. Whatever importance the town possesses, it owes to its position at the junction of the Aydın/Muğla road (550) with the route to Milas, Selçuk and İzmir and its proximity to a number of industrial establishments.

A short distance before Yatağan a turning on the left leads to c 18km LAGINA, which is located near the modern village of *Turgut*. The site may also be reached from the Aydın road.

The shrine at Lagina was dedicated to Hecate, one of the strangest and most sinister of the non-Olympian deities. Perhaps of Carian origin, this goddess could grant success in business, victory in battle or eloquence in debate. She could also withhold these gifts. In time Hecate came to be regarded as the ruler of the dead and custodian of the key to the gate of Hades. She became, too, a deity associated with witchcraft and sorcery.

The temple at Lagina is one of the few shrines dedicated to Hecate. A moon goddess, she was usually worshipped under the cover of darkness at crossroads or road junctions. This may account for the location of her shrine at Lagina, as the ancient roads probably followed the same routes as their modern counterparts. Cake, cheese, fish and, sometimes, dogs were sacrificed in her honour.

Statues of Hecate frequently took the form of three conjoined female figures (as in the museum at Bodrum) or as a female body with three heads.

The earliest known inscription referring to Hecate of Lagina dates from about the middle of the 2C BC, but it is likely that the goddess was worshipped there long before that time. After the defeat of Mithridates (see above), the Senate issued a decree which guaranteed the shrine from profanation, and a new festival entitled Hecatesia-Romaea was instituted at Lagina. Evidence of Rome's continued interest in the cult is provided by the handsome contribution which Augustus made to the repair of the temple after its sack by Labienus and his Parthians in 40 BC. It would appear that the cult of Hecate continued to be practised at Lagina as late as the 3C AD. Presumably it ceased sometime after the issue of the edicts of Theodosius in AD 381 and 385 which largely put an end to pagan practices in the Roman Empire.

Traces of the ancient paved way c 9.5km long, which stretched from Stratoniceia to Lagina, may still be seen. As the site at Lagina is now very overgrown, it is advisable to take a guide from Turgut. Village children, anxious to practise their English, are often willing to provide this service. Though they rarely request it, it is appropriate to offer them a small payment.

The temenos of the temple of Hecate measured c 150m by 134m. This was enclosed on three sides by a Doric stoa. On the S side of the temenos there were steps, which may have been used as seats by those, who had come to see and take part in the mysteries. On the E side of the steps there was a massive *propylon*. The jambs and lintel of this structure are still standing. The *Temple of Hecate*, which was built towards the centre of the temenos, was a Corinthian pseudodipteros of 8 by 11 columns. On the E side a large pronaos with two columns in antis provided access to the cella. There was no opisthodomus. A partial investigation of the site at the end of the 19C yielded substantial sections of a frieze showing Hecate at the birth of Zeus, Greeks and Amazons, a gigantomachy and a number of other subjects. These are now in the İstanbul Archaeological Museum. All that remains at Lagina of the temple is a confused mass of broken columns and architectural fragments.

A short distance to the E of temple are the remains of a structure which has been tentatively identified as an *altar*. Perhaps a full excavation of the site would reveal traces of the buildings occupied by the priests, their assistants and the temple servants who lived inside the temenos.

The second sanctuary of Stratoniceia, that of ZEUS PANAMAROS, lies c 11km to the SE of Eskihisar, near the village of *Bağyaka*. Apart from the remains of the sanctuary's peribolos on a hilltop and a long stretch of the paved road that joined Panamara and Stratoniceia, little remains on the site. The temple of Zeus Panamaros has not been found. Panamara is likely to of interest mainly to specialist visitors.

On leaving Yatağan continue N on road 550 in the direction of Aydın. After a few kilometres the landscape changes dramatically. The road, entering a gorge, follows the course of the Çine Çayı, the ancient river Marsyas, for some distance.

This beautiful stretch of wild, savage countryside was the setting for a legendary contest between the satyr Marsyas and Apollo. Marsyas, the son of Hyagnis and Olympus, was a follower of Cybele, the Great Mother. One day, while wandering by the river that later bore his name, he found a flute which Athena had made from the bones of a deer. This had been discarded by the goddess who was angered by the ugly way her cheeks puffed out when she played it. Marsyas, ignoring a prohibition placed by Athena on the flute, played it and was delighted by the music which it made. Then, filled with a foolish pride, he had the temerity to challenge Apollo, the god of music, to a contest. Apollo accepted the challenge on condition that the winner could select the punishment to be suffered by the loser. The first contest ended in a draw. Then Apollo suggested that they play the instruments upside down. Marsyas lost and the god punished him savagely. He tied Marsyas to a pine or to plane tree—the accounts differ—and flayed him alive. The legend of Apollo and Marsyas was a subject much favoured by Classical and Renaissance artists.

At a point where the arches of an ancient *bridge* rise from the tumbling waters and boulder-filled bed of the river Marsyas (c 10km to the N of Yatağan), adventurous travellers may like to make a DETOUR to GERGA, one of the more interesting of the smaller and remote sites in Caria. As this requires a walk through fairly rough country, it is advisable to wear stout shoes and to carry a stick. It would also be helpful to take a guide from Eskiçine or Çine.

Having crossed the river by the bridge, proceed in an E direction for c 6km. The first signs of the settlement are provided by a number of inscribed slabs bearing the word 'Gergas' or 'Gergakome' (village of Gerga) in Greek letters. The letters of the inscriptions vary in height from c 0.5m to c 1m.

Few traces of Greek influence have been found in Gerga. Archaeologists, having examined the ruins, are of the opinion that this was mainly, if not purely, a Carian settlement. Despite the archaic appearance of some of the statues and the rough workmanship of the stone structures, nothing is believed to date from before the Roman Imperial period.

The most important remains of the settlement, which occupied a number of levelled spaces on the hillside, include a number of dwelling houses, a temple or temple-tomb, two monumental stelae, a number of statues, and several open-fronted structures. The *temple*, which is an excellent state of preservation, still retains its roof. Gergas is inscribed in Greek letters on a massive slab over the entrance. The stelae, which are c 3.35m high and pyramidal in shape, also have the word Gergas on them. Note the colossal headless *statue* lying on the ground to the SW of the temple.

Some archaeologists are of the opinion that the settlement was a sanctuary dedicated to a Carian deity named Gergas, and that the open-fronted structures were tombs containing the bones of the priests and of local dignitaries. Bean disagrees. He suggests that the open-fronted structures were fountain-houses or cisterns which the almost waterless state of the site rendered necessary. Perhaps a further examination of Gerga sometime in the future will solve the mystery and also provide an explanation for the presence on the site of the many slabs, which are inscribed with the name of the settlement.

A short distance after the bridge over the Marsyas river (c 10km N of Yatağan) road 550 climbs to a height of c 400m at the Gökbel Pass before descending into a broad upland plain. This has two important centres, Eskiçine and Çine. Until the beginning of the century the area was governed from Eskiçine. Today the kaymakam has his seat at *Çine*, which is c 9km to the N.

A passable road leads W from the centre of Çine to site of the ancient city of 8km **ALABANDA**. This is partly occupied by the modern village of *Araphisar*.

History. According to Strabo, the city of Alabanda was located at the foot of adjoining hills which bore the appearance of an ass laden with panniers. He quotes the ancient wit, Apollonius Malacus, who described it as 'an ass laden with panniers of scorpions', as the area was reputed to swarm with these unwelcome creatures.

An ancient tradition states that the city was called Alabanda after a mythical hero whose name was derived from a combination of two Carian words, 'ala', horse and 'banda', victory. The youth Alabandus was given his name by his royal father to celebrate a great victory gained by the Alabandian cavalry.

Towards the end of the 3C BC Alabanda was renamed Antiocheia of the Chrysaorians as a gesture of gratitude to the Seleucid king, Antiochus III, who, it was claimed, had preserved the democracy and peace of the city. Besieged and captured by the Macedonian, Philip V c 201 BC, it reverted to its old name after the Seleucid domination in Asia Minor was smashed at the Battle of Magnesia in 190 BC. With the rest of Caria it then came under the rule of Rhodes. However, it would seem that Alabanda managed to enjoy a considerable degree of freedom of action under the Rhodians whose control appears to have been largely nominal.

In about 40 BC Alabanda was occupied by Labienus (see above), who placed a garrison in the city. When the inhabitants rebelled against his rule and put his soldiers to the sword, he punished them severely. They were fined and the temples were robbed of their treasures. The city's fortunes improved under the empire. Alabanda became a 'conventus', a centre for the administration of justice, and it gained a reputation for luxurious living. According to Strabo, writing in a censorious vein, it was a city of debauchery 'containing many girls who play the harp'.

Alabanda had few claims to fame. It was the home of two orators, the brothers Menecles and Hierocles, who were admired by Cicero. In the area around the city gemstones, resembling garnets, and an unusual red-brown marble were found.

Little is known about the city's later history. It continued to issue its own coinage until c AD 250. During the Byzantine era, like many of its neighbours, Alabanda was an episcopal see under the metropolitan of Aphrodisias.

There are few visible traces of Alabanda's greatness and none of the debauchery mentioned by Strabo. The most striking building on the site may be found at the N end just inside the line of the city walls. This has been identified as the *bouleuterion*. The S wall of this structure, which stands to a height of c 9m, was pierced by four doors. Traces of the semicircular seating may be found in the interior. In all four walls there is a horizontal row of square holes whose exact purpose is not known. They appear to be a late addition to the building.

A large level area to the S of the boulerion, which measures c 110 by 73m, has been identified as the *agora*. Of the colonnade, which once surrounded it, no trace remains.

The site of the *Temple of Apollo Isotimus*, one of the principal deities of Alabanda, has been located a short distance to the SE of the agora. The title, which means 'equal in honour', presumably refers to the god's standing in relation to Zeus Chrysaoreus. There is some speculation that Apollo Isotimus may have been a Carian deity who was at some time Hellenised. Little remains of the temple. When it was excavated at the beginning of the century, sections of a decorative frieze showing a battle between the Greeks and Amazons were discovered. An Ionic pseudo-dipteros with 13 by 8 columns, it is believed to date from c 200 BC.

A confused mound of stones to the W of the temple, which awaits exploration, is believed to mark the position of a *baths complex*. The site of a second temple, dated to c 200 BC, was discovered on the slopes of the hill to the S of the city. Resting on a man-made terrace, this Doric structure of 11 by 6 columns had a deep pronaos, a cella and no opisthodomus. As the entrance was on the W side, it is believed to been dedicated, like the similarly oriented structure at Magnesia on the Maeander, to Artemis.

The ruins of the *theatre* are to be found at the base of Alabanda's other hill. Apart from a section of the retaining walls of the cavea, very little remains of this structure. The passages, which provided access to the interior, have been closed with stones in modern times. There are a few traces of the stage-building and of the proscenium. The cavea is greater than a semicircle which suggests that the original building probably dates from the Hellenistic period.

To the W, on the outskirts of the city, there is a large *necropolis*. The stone sarcophagi, simple in design, are closed with massive granite lids. Unusually, each states the occupation of the deceased. Among the doctors, architects and schoolmasters in the equality of death lie also a lamplighter and a seller of pheasants.

About 6km to the N of Çine, a turning on the left leads to the village of 25km *Karpuzlu* (the place of watermelons). There the ruins of an ancient city, which has beeen identified as **ALINDA**, are located.

History. Alinda made a dramatic appearance in the history of Caria towards the end of the 4C BC. When Ada, the sister of Mausolus of Halicarnassus (see above) was deposed by her younger brother Pixodarus c 340 BC, she left Halicarnassus and took up residence in Alinda. In the safety of this mountain-fortress she awaited an opportunity to recover her lost kingdom. When, in 334 BC, Alexander the Great, campaigning to remove the Persian threat from Greece and from the Greek cities in Asia Minor, marched into Caria at the head of his victorious army, this finally arrived. Ada left her fortress-city and went to meet the youthful conqueror. Offering to surrender Alinda to Alexander, she told him the story of the wrongs which she had suffered from her kinsmen, and promised to help him to conquer Caria.

A firm friendship was quickly established between Alexander and Ada. She, having offered to adopt him as her son, with motherly concern first sent choice food to tempt his appetite and then skilled cooks to prepare special meals. Alexander, touched by the recital of Ada's misfortunes and the regal manner with which she had sustained them, returned Alinda to her control. He also allowed himself to be called her son. The food and the cooks were gracefully refused. His preparation for breakfast was, he said, a night march and for lunch a frugal breakfast.

After Alexander had taken Halicarnassus and put the Persians and their allies to flight, he restored Ada to her throne and confirmed her rule over Caria. There is a theory that, as an expression of gratitude to her adopted son, Ada renamed Alinda, Alexandria-by-Latmus. If this is correct, it would appear that the city resumed its original name sometime in the following century.

During the years that followed Ada's reign there seems to have been a marked increase in Greek influence in the area. This is evidenced by the reported presence in a shrine dedicated to Adonis in Alexandria-by-Latmus of a statue of Aphrodite by the celebrated sculptor Praxiteles. There is also a reference in an inscription, which may refer to the city, of an administrative section of the citizenry named after Erechtheus, a legendary king of Athens.

Very little is known about the history of Alinda before and after the celebrated incident involving Alexander and Ada. It was probably one of the places which were fortified by Mausolus when he was consolidating his rule over Caria. (See above.) Alinda issued its own coins from about the beginning of the 2C BC to the 3C AD. It was a member of the Chrysaoric league during the period, when Caria was under the control of the Ptolemies and the Seleucids. Antiochus III, recognising the city's strategic importance, established a garrison there. After the adoption of Christianity Alinda had its own bishop who came under the jurisdiction of the Metropolitan of Aphrodisias.

One of the first travellers from W Europe to visit Alinda was Richard Chandler. He investigated the ruins of the ancient city in the spring of 1765. Making his way there from Heraclea under Latmus, he camped ovenight by a stream where he was 'serenaded in a disagreeable manner; frogs croaking, as it were in chorus; owls hooting; jackals in troops howling; and the village dogs barking'. Perhaps his disturbed slumbers account for the lacklustre description of Alinda in his journal. Mistaking the site for that of Alabanda, he lists, almost without comment, the principal ruins: aqueduct, market building, theatre, tower, cisterns, necropolis and city walls. In later years the site was visited by Charles Fellows, who identified it correctly on the basis of coins discovered there. Curiously, there is a complete absence of inscriptions in Alinda. Perhaps a number still await discovery and will be revealed, when, hopefully, the site is given the systematic examination which it undoubtedly deserves.

Certainly the most striking of Alinda's ruins is the **Hellenistic market building** which may be reached by a short but fairly stiff climb from the modern village. This well-preserved structure c 99m long had three storeys. Access to the bottom storey was provided by 12 large doors which open from a narrow terrace, part natural, part artificial. The interior was divided laterally into two sections. In the front there was a line of shops of varying sizes and behind them a series of dimly-lit storerooms. The middle storey, which was divided by a line of columns in the middle, may also have been used as storage space for the shops on the bottom and third storeys. Apart from some architectural fragments, very little remains of the third storey which led directly to the agora.

Alinda's *agora*, which measured c 30m by 30m, was surounded by a colonnade of which only a few traces remain. Olive trees have rooted themselves among the fragments of shattered columns and they mark the line of the wall which separated the agora from the buildings on the terrace above.

A short distance to the E are the ruins of a substantial building which has not been identified. In view of its location it was almost certainly connected in some way with the administration of the city.

On the hillside are the ruins of the *theatre*. This Graeco-Roman building, of which a substantial part remains standing, had a diameter of 65m. The original structure is believed to date from the beginning of the 2C BC. The Roman modifications probably took place during the reign of Augustus. Two arched entrances led to the single diazoma which divided the 35 rows of seats. Note the fine Hellenistic masonry of the supporting walls of the cavea. The ruined stage-building is almost completely buried. There is a fine view over the surrounding countryside from the vaulted gallery at the top of the cavea.

Continuing up the hill, one soon reaches the well-preserved remains of a two-storey *Hellenistic tower* constructed of ashlar masonry. Near the tower is the entrance to a tunnel. This, according to a popular local myth, provided a link with the theatre where its supposed exit is pointed out to visitors by the villagers. On the summit of the hill there are traces of a large *semicircular structure* which some authorities believe was a nymphaeum. A more likely explanation is that it was an exedra where the citizens of Alinda sat while enjoying the evening air.

To the NW in a second *acropolis* surrounded by stout ashlar walls, the remains of many private house have been found. The presence of six large cisterns suggests that the area may also have been used as a place of refuge in times of danger.

In the valley below the acropolis there is a substantial stretch of the city's *aqueduct*. Four arches and a section of wall, pierced by an opening which permitted the passage of traffic, support the covered water-channel.

Alinda was surrounded by an extensive *necropolis*. Although there are several undecorated sarcophagi, most of the burials were in graves of a type found all over Caria. These were cut from horizontal rock-surfaces and covered with a closely-fitting stone lid. Unlike the inhabitants of nearby Alabanda who even recorded the professions of the deceased, the tombs of Alinda bear no inscriptions.

Visitors imbued with a sense of adventure may like to continue their tour to 20km *Gafarlar*, the nearest modern settlement to the site of the ancient city of AMYZON. According to Bean the road from Karpuzlu to Gafarlar was one of the worst he ever encountered. It has improved but little in recent years and should only be attempted by four-wheel drive vehicles.

Amyzon may also be reached from the N. Take the road to 10km Koçarlı, which leaves the E24 on the left c 8km to the W of Aydın, and continue to Gafarlar which lies c 12km to the S. This route also needs careful driving. Because of the difficulty of the terrain and the remoteness of the site, it is advisable to obtain the services of a guide at Koçarlı or Gafarlar. Allow at least a half-day for the excursion and take a picnic lunch.

Very little is known about the history of Amyzon and its ruins are not particularly striking. The attraction of the city springs mainly from the wild beauty of its remote mountain location. Little visited and relatively unknown, it will appeal principally to those travellers who enjoy the contemplation of ancient ruins undisturbed by coach parties or souvenir-vendors.

Strabo makes a throwaway reference to Amyzon when he includes it in a group of Carian places which he esteems to be of minor importance. According to inscriptions found at the site, the city supported the Ptolemies and the Seleucids in turn. In 203 BC, while under Syrian control, Antiochus III confirmed the right of asylum claimed by a temple in Amyzon dedicated to Artemis and Apollo. During the troubled period that marked the end of the Roman Empire and the beginning of its Byzantine successors the city's temple-terrace was transformed into a fortified area. After the arrival of Christianity in Caria Amyzon became an episcopal see.

The sparse remains of the 4C *Temple of Artemis and Apollo*, constructed in the Doric style, rest on a terrace which was approached by a ceremonial stairs. Within the temenos there was accommodation for the priests and temple servants. Bean reports the discovery of an inscription which at some time had been been placed in an upside down position in the wall of the building. This listed the names of the officials of the temple.

Almost hidden by dense vegetation at the extreme end of the terrace are the ruins of another structure which may have been a small theatre or an odeum. On the S of the site just within the 4C BC *city walls*, stretches of which stand to a height of c 6m, are several large *underground rooms.* These were probably used for the storage of cereals. It is not known how Amyzon received its supplies of water. So far no trace of an aqueduct or cisterns has been found.

From Çine to c 35km Aydın road 550 runs for some time parallel to the Marsyas, the Çine Çayı, until finally that river turns away to the NW and adds its waters to the Büyük Menderes, the ancient Maeander. About 31km further on the road crosses the torpid, sluggish Menderes and soon after it enters the leafy suburbs of **Aydın**.

14 Aydın to Pamukkale

Total distance 153km. **Aydın**—E24 35km *Sultanhisar*—(2km *Nysa*) (38km *Geyre* / **Aphrodisias**)—98km **Denizli**—(20km *Colossae*)—(c 3km *Laodiceia ad Lycum*)—20km **Pammukale / Hierapolis**.

AYDIN (59,000 inhab.), the administrative centre of the province of the same name, is a pleasant, bustling town whose wide tree-lined boulevards climb steeply from the busy E24. Sited at an important road junction, it is also on the railway line, which links İzmir with Denizli.

While there are no hotels in Aydın which are registered with the Tourism Ministry, those who wish to stay overnight will find a number of simple establishments which offer rather basic accommodation. However, most visitors find that one day gives sufficient time to see the Islamic monuments and the objects preserved in the museum. One of the best of Aydın's many restaurants is to be found at the railway station.

History. Aydın occupies the site of the ancient city of TRALLES which, according to Strabo, was founded by Argive colonists and Trallians, a barbarian tribe from Thrace, after whom it was named. The city was built on a trapezium-shaped plateau which had good natural defences. After the Peloponnesian War, when Sparta was endeavouring to fill the place formerly occupied by Athens in Asia Minor, a Spartan army tried, without success, to take Tralles from the Persians. In 334 BC after Alexander's arrival at the head of his victorious army in Ephesus, delegations from Magnesia on the Maeander and Tralles came to offer the submission of their cities. Later Antigonus, one of the Diadochi, held Tralles from 313 to 301, when it came under the rule of the Seleucids. After their defeat at the battle of Magnesia ad Sipylum in 190 BC, Tralles came under Pergamene rule. The elaborate palace of brick, which Attalus II (160–138 BC) built there, was later occupied by the priest of Zeus. Between 133 BC and 129 BC the city supported the Pergamene pretender, Aristonicus, against the Romans and, after his defeat, its citizens paid for their bad judgment by having the right to mint their own coinage taken away from them.

Tralles was a *conventus* for some time under the republic, but eventually that honour was transferred to Ephesus. During the Mithridatic war the sons of Cratippus, according to Strabo, ruled in Tralles. Tyrants, they were responsible for ordering the murder of many Roman residents. When Tralles was badly damaged by an earthquake in 27 BC Augustus provided generous aid for its reconstruction. In gratitude its citizens called it Caesarea, a name it retained for some time.

Strabo described Tralles as a wealthy city, adding that some of its citizens held 'the chief places in the province [of Asia], being called Asiarchs'. A cultural centre of some importance, it was the home of a number of famous orators and teachers. Among those singled out for mention by Strabo are Pythodorus, who moved there from Nysa because of Tralles' greater fame, and the orators Dionysocles and Damasus. The latter had the curious sobriquet of Scombrus (tunny-fish). Tralles was also the birthplace of Anthemius, the 6C architect and author of a number of mathematical treatises. With Isidorus of Miletus he designed the great church of Haghia Sophia in Constantinople. The stele of Seikilos, which dates from c 100 BC was found at Tralles. This is an interesting example of the Greek system of musical notation which used letters to indicate the notes.

The principal deity of Tralles was Zeus Larisaeus, who was worshipped at a shrine c 5km to the N of the city on the slopes of Mt Messogis. The office of chief priest was not always entirely free from risk. In Strabo's time Menodorus, who held that position, was dispossessed through the machinations of a rival and murdered.

During the Roman Imperial period, with the permission of the emperor, games based on the great contests of Classical Greece were held in various cities of the Province of Asia. Those at Tralles were named after the famous athletic festivals of Delphi and Olympia.

Sometime after the conversion of Constantine, the inhabitants of Caria adopted Christianity and, in due course, Tralles became an episcopal see. After the defeat of the Byzantine army at the battle of Manzikert in 1071, the Selçuk Turks swept across Anatolia. By the end of the 12C they had captured most of the cities in Caria, including Tralles. For a number of years the city formed part of the sultanate of Konya. Retaken by Manuel I Comnenus (1143–80), it remained in Byzantine hands until 1282, when it was successfully invested by the Menteşe Turks. It was at that time that it was renamed Aydın, which means light, clear, or enlightened. Finally, in 1403, it was captured by Mehmet I and became part of the Ottoman Empire.

Today there are few visible traces of Aydın's past. The site of Tralles is part of a military zone and it is necessary to obtain a permit to visit it. Applications should be addressed to the Vilayet. Excavations carried out there by Turkish archaeologists at the beginning of the century revealed the remains of a stadium, a theatre, an agora and a gymnasium. An interesting feature of the theatre was a tunnel c 2.5m deep under the orchestra. This permitted actors playing the parts of demons and underworld deities to make dramatic entrances and exits.

Only a few *column stumps* and a section of the *wall* and three tall *arches*, the so-called Üç Göz, of the 3C AD gymnasium are visible on the site today. The arches, which may be seen clearly from the E24 on the W approaches to the town, were constructed of a mixture of brick and stone covered with stucco.

Many of the objects found at the site of Tralles were taken to İstanbul, where they are now displayed in the Archaeological Museum. Perhaps the finest of these is the so-called *Ephebe of Tralles*. This, a marble statue 1.48m tall of a youth wrapped in a thick mantle, is believed to date from the late 1C BC or early 1C AD. The sculptor has chosen to portray the boy in the period immediately after exercise or after a contest. In an attitude of exhaustion and dejection, with downcast gaze, he leans gracefully against a pillar. His swollen ears and battered nose suggest that he was either a boxer or a wrestler. This powerful and moving work of the early Roman Imperial period has too much humanity and immediacy to be anything but the representation of a real person.

Incorporated in the gateway of Aydın's prison are two *towers*, which formed part of a Byzantine fortress. In the town there are two Islamic monuments of particular interest. The *Ramazan Paşa Camii* and the *Bey Camii* were both constructed in the 16C. The latter contains a good deal of material taken from the buildings of ancient Tralles.

In Aydın's *Museum*, located a short distance to the W of the town centre, there is a fine collection of objects from Tralles and the surrounding countryside. These are contained in a building which was first opened in 1973. In a pleasant garden, half-hidden by flowering shrubs, are architectural fragments, sarcophagi, stelae and statues, most of which date from the Roman period. Inside the building, the exhibits, which are arranged in chronological order, include prehistoric bowls and platters, flint and obsidian tools, primitive cult statues, stone axe heads and arrows. The Hittite culture is represented by a number of gold crowns and diadems, jewellery and ceramics. From the Greek, Byzantine and Roman eras there are statues, reliefs, busts, coins, terracotta, bronze and marble figurines, lamps, glass objects and vases. Note in particular a fine statue of Nike, and busts of Athena and of the Emperor Marcus Aurelius.

In the ethnographical section most of the objects date from the 19C and the beginning of the 20C. Collected in the Aydın area, they include elaborately embroidered garments, napkins, bed covers, silver jewellery, carpets and kilims.

The busy E24 on its way E from Aydın to Denizli follows the upper reaches of the Maeander river. On the left-hand side the foothills of the Aydın Dağları, the ancient Mt Messogis which have been tortured into strange shapes by thousands of years of erosion, are riven by the deep beds of torrents. These precipitous mountain streams, whose channels overflow during the winter, are arid, brown and dry, the nesting-place of scorpions, during the scorching days of summer. The road follows the line of an ancient trade route, which brought the products of E Anatolia and Mesopotamia to the Aegean ports from where they were shipped to Greece and Rome. It passes through a rich and fertile area that is justly famed for the quality of its fruit. Today the grapes, peaches, oranges, lemons, and figs from the farms and orchards of the Maeander valley find a ready sale in the market places of Turkey.

Reaching 35km *Sultanhisar* there is a good road to the remains of the ancient city of 2km NYSA AD MAEANDRUM. At present there are no refreshment facilities at the site. Visitors who wish to explore the ravine and tunnel, will find a pocket torch useful. Two hours should be sufficent for a leisurely examination of the remains of the city and for a pleasant picnic in the shade of one of the many olive trees scattered among the ruins.

According to Strabo (63 BC–AD 25), who studied rhetoric and grammar there under Aristodemus, and who consequently should have been well-informed about its history, Nysa was an amalgamation of three cities. These had been established by the brothers, Athymbrus, Athymbradus, and Hydrelus, who came to Caria from Sparta. The united city was known as Athymbra. This account is supported by inscriptions, which show that as late as the 3C BC the inhabitants were referred to as Athymbrians, a name which is also used in letters to the city from the Seleucid monarch, Antiochus I Soter. A late chronicle states that the city was renamed Nysa in honour of the wife of Antiochus I. However, this version of events has not met with general acceptance. Modern historians agree only that it began to be called Nysa sometime towards the beginning of the 2C BC.

Nysa's fame as an educational centre drew pupils from all over Asia Minor. Aristodemus, a follower of the Stoic philosopher Panaetius, was one of the many teachers, who opened a school there. (See above.) The city also had in its territory the Plutonium, a shrine dedicated to Pluto, the god of the underworld, and to Kore, his consort. Near the Plutonium was the Charonium, a famous centre of healing. This attracted large numbers of the sick, who flocked to Nysa in the hope of obtaining a miraculous cure. (See below.)

To judge by the visible remains of the city, Nysa appears to have flourished under the empire. It issued its own coinage from the beginning of the 1C AD to the middle of the 3C AD. After the adoption of Christianity, it became an episcopal see. The bishops of Nysa are recorded as having attended the Councils of Ephesus and Constantinople. Later, somewhat overshadowed by its neighbour Tralles, and increasingly menaced by Arab raids and the advancing Turks, it was abandoned. The inhabitants moved down from the mountain and occupied the site covered by the modern town of Sultanhisar. During the late Byzantine period Nysa had the same general history and shared the same fate as the other cities of Caria.

One of the first visitors to Nysa in modern times was Richard Chandler who came there in the late summer of 1765. He found the theatre, which at that time had most of its seats intact, and he explored the ravine located below the amphitheatre. Later Nysa was visited by Leake, Fellows and Hamilton. The first scientific examination of the site was carried out by German archaeologists at the beginning of this century.

In recent years further work on the ruins of the city has been done through local initiative aided by financial help from the Turkish government. At the moment Nysa is little known and little visited. As a rule it is by-passsed by the tourist buses on their way to the better-known sites of Aphrodisias and Hierapolis (Pamukkale). In an attempt to change this situation, the authorities plan to hold a festival there each year during the month of May.

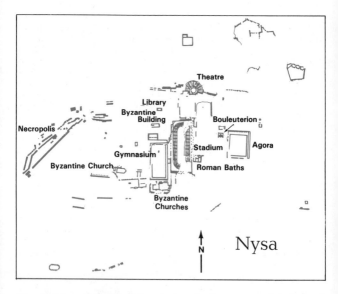

The road from Sultanhisar terminates at a large car-park in front of the theatre. In ancient times this area, a square or piazza supported by vaults, was used for ceremonial purposes.

The well-preserved cavea of the **Roman theatre** is slightly larger than a semicircle. There are 23 rows of seats below and 26 above the single diazoma. The spectators, who entered the theatre through vomitoria at each side, gained access to their seats by way of stairs, nine below the diazoma and 17 above. The orchestra had a diameter of 27m. Recent clearance of the stage-building has disclosed some fine reliefs of Dionysiac revels. Apart from the gentle rustling of the olive trees which have invaded the cavea and whose roots twine and snake between the seats, little now disturbs the silence of Nysa's theatre.

Strabo has left an interesting description of the city, as it was in his time. By the use of a little imagination it is possible to gauge the accuracy of his observation by taking a seat at the topmost level of the theatre. According to the geographer, a deep ravine with a stream at its base lay to the S. This divided the city into two parts. At one point the ravine was spanned by a bridge, at another covered by an amphitheatre. On the W side of the ravine was the gymnasium of the ephebes and on the E side the city's agora and the bouleuterion. Away to the S he could glimpse the plain of the Maeander with its farms and orchards and busy trade-route.

From the E side of the theatre a path descends steeply into the ravine. There during the dry season it is possible to walk through a Roman *tunnel* which carried the waters of the mountain stream away from the city centre. The tunnel, c 150m long, was covered by barrel vaulting, which supported the piazza in front of the theatre. To the S of the tunnel are the sparse ruins of the *bridge* joining the two parts of the city, which is mentioned by Strabo. Of the *amphitheatre* even less than the bridge has remained standing. This huge structure, c 44m by 192m, which had 30 rows of seats, rested on vaulted supports over the stream. To permit the staging of naval battles, a diversion much favoured by the Romans, it was possible to draw water up from the stream and use this to flood the arena.

On the W side of the ravine a large rectangle, 70m by 165m, marks the site of a later version of the *gymnasium* described by Strabo. When this structure was enlarged in the 3C AD it was surrounded by a stoa, all traces of which disappeared a long time ago. A short distance to the N of the gymnasium are the substantial remains of the *library*. This building, which dates from the 2C AD, had two or possibly three storeys and a reading room measuring c 13.5 by 15m. To prevent the manuscripts and scrolls from being affected by damp, there was an air space between the niches in which they were stored and the outer walls of the building. It is to be hoped that one day this library, the most important in Asia Minor after the library of Celsus at Ephesus, will be be restored to something approaching its former glory. To the S and W of the gymnasium there are the ruins of two *Byzantine churches* which are believed to occupy the sites of Roman temples. In the *necropolis* of Nysa, which was located at the W edge of the city, the dead were placed in barrel-vaulted chambers. These were arranged in tiers to make a continuous structure. A number of sarcophagi have been discovered in the chambers. The *Sacred Way*, which joined Nysa to the Plutonium and the Charonium at Acharaca, ran in a W direction from the necropolis. As the bridges, which carried the ancient road across the ravines, are no longer in existence it is not now possible to follow this route. Today the site may be reached from the E24. (See below.)

The ruins of Nysa's well-preserved *bouleuterion* lie to the E of the ravine. This building, which has been dated to the 2C AD, is a Roman version of the Gerontikon or house of the elders described by Strabo. Inside the rectangular structure 12 rows of limestone seats, divided by five stairs, and arranged in a semicircle, face the speaker's rostrum. The walls of rough masonry were concealed beneath a covering of decorative marble slabs. A short distance to the S of the bouleuterion, enclosed by the remains of a portico, are some *mosaics* and an *ornamental basin*. To the NE a scattering of olive trees and a few architectural fragments mark the site of the city's *agora*. In its final form the agora, which was enlarged during the Roman Imperial period, measured 105m by 89m. It was surrounded by a colonnade, Doric on the N and W, Ionic on the S and E.

Before leaving the site energetic visitors may like to climb to the top of the hill behind the theatre. Apart from obtaining a fine view over the site and the valley of the Maeander beyond, they will be able to examine the large square *cistern* from which Nysa obtained its water-supply.

To visit *Acharaca*, the site of the Plutonium and the Charonium (see above), it is necessary to retrace one's steps. Take the E24 from Sultanhisar in the direction of Aydın to the village of 5km Çiftekahveler and continue from there to the hamlet of Salavatlı.

According to Strabo the Plutonium, the shrine dedicated to Pluto and Kore was enclosed in a richly-ornamented sacred precinct. The healing-centre known as the Charonium was located in a natural cave a little way above the shrine. The sick, who lodged in the nearby village, were sometimes placed by the priests inside the cave where they remained 'in quiet, like animals in their lurking-holes, without food for many days'. Patients were cured by following the treatment prescribed by the gods. They, or on occasions the priests acting on their behalf, were informed of this in the course of a dream. Only the priests and the sick were allowed to enter the Charonium. For all others it was a dangerous and forbidden place.

At about noon on the day of the annual festival held in honour of the gods, a strange sacrifice was made at the Charonium. Boys and young men from Nysa, nude and anointed with oil, hastened to the cave carrying a bull. On being released the animal entered the sacred precinct, advanced a short distance, and then, abruptly keeling over, died. Presumably it was asphyxiated by noxious vapours.

The site of the *Plutonium* lies to the E of the depression which carries in its depths the waters of the Sarısu, the Yellow Stream. From the few architectural fragments which remain, the archaeologists have prepared the following very tentative reconstruction of the temple. It would appear that this unusual structure, which opened on the N side, was surrounded by a colonnade of 6 by 12 columns. The arrangement of the interior was also uncommon. For reasons that are not clear it seems to have been divided by parallel walls into long narrow corridor-like sections.

Of the *Charonium* no certain trace has been found. Bean suggests that the natural cave, mentioned in Strabo's account, may have been located in the ravine above the source of the Sarısu. This could have collapsed during the course of the intervening centuries. His theory is supported to some extent by the high concentration of sulphur in the Sarısu, over whose waters the nauseous smell of that substance sometimes hangs. Sulphur was almost certainly the principal curative agent employed in the Charonium.

From Sultanhisar continue E along the E24 in the direction of Denizli. On the right-hand side the sluggish waters of the Maeander pursue their winding course westwards to the sea. Here the river flows at a leisurely pace through the lush, green landscape, which it has created, its reed-clothed banks sometimes approaching sometimes drawing away from the road. A short distance to the N, on the left side, rise the eroded peaks of the Aydın Dağları. Their shapes, which become increasingly strange and bizarre, contrast with the harmony and pastoral calm of the river valley.

Travellers without their own transport may find it a little difficult to reach Aphrodisias. If they are unable to get a dolmuş from 13km Nazilli direct to 55km Geyre, the nearest village to the site, they should travel to 45km Karacasu and from there take a bus, dolmuş or taxi to 10km Geyre.

There are organised tours from İzmir and Kuşadası to Aphrodisias during the holiday season, but they suffer from a number of disadvantages viz. a very early start, a long coach-ride and a comparatively short stay at the site. As a rule these tours do not pick up passengers en route.

Motorists should leave the E24 by a turning on the right-hand side of the road c 14km to the E of Nazilli. This is signposted to Karacasu, Geyre and Aphrodisias. To the left of the road, just after it crosses the Maeander, a low hill marks the site of ANTIOCHEIA AD MAEANDRUM, which has never been excavated.

In recent years the site of the ancient city of **APHRODISIAS**, which was located in a valley watered by a tributary of the Maeander, has excited worldwide interest because of the spectacular discoveries made there by an international team of archaeologists working under the direction of Professor Kenan Erim of New York University. They have brought to light the substantial remains of a theatre, an odeum, temples, baths, streets and public squares, a building that may have been a bishop's palace, several churches, and most recently a Sebasteion in which a propylon, porticoes and a processional way lead to a temple dedicated to Aphrodite with Tiberius and Livia and probably also to Augustus. In addition, they have recovered from these structures a large number of statues of outstanding beauty, the work of local sculptors. They have also published two substantial corpora of inscriptions which throw an interesting light on the history of the city and on the life of its citizens. While the principal finds are exhibited in a well-arranged museum at the site, not all the buildings and sculptures described in the following paragraphs are accessible at present to visitors.

Until the archaeologists began their work much of Aphrodisias was hidden under the houses and fields of Geyre, a village which preserves in its name a memory of the ancient province of Caria. In 1956 Geyre suffered some damage from an earthquake which devastated the area to the SE of the ancient city. Following this, and with a view also to excavation, it was decided to rehouse the villagers at a new site c 2km to the W.

Between Karacasu and modern Geyre there are several small restaurants which provide simple meals. However, as these establishments are usually full to the point of suffocation with coach parties during the holiday season, it is advisable to bring materials for a picnic meal. During the summer months drinks may be obtained from a café on the site.

Fortunately, Aphrodisias has been preserved from the excesses of commercialism that detract so much from the pleasure of exploring places like Ephesus, Pergamum and Side. Visitors to this site are unlikely to be harassed by vendors of postcards and souvenirs and peddlers of fake antiquities.

There is ample parking-space near the museum which is located at the entrance to the site. Allow at least three hours for a leisurely tour of the ruins which are spread over quite a wide area, and one hour for the museum which should be visited last.

History. Excavation of the höyüks, artificial mounds in the centre of the city, have revealed traces of occupation that have been dated back to c 5800 BC. Finds from that area include a number of small violin-shaped idols of marble and stone which have been dated to the Bronze Age (c 2900–1200 BC). It would seem that from very early times there was a fertility cult at Aphrodisias which probably sprang from the desire of the early farmers, who occupied this river valley, to placate the Megale Meter, the Great Mother, and so ensure rich harvests and fecund animals.

According to Stephanus, writing in the 6C AD, the settlement was at first called Ninoe after Ninus, the legendary founder of the Assyrian Empire. He was credited with having conquered most of W Anatolia. There is archaeological evidence to show that this foundation-legend was current earlier. Figures on a relief from the end of the 3C AD found in the city are captioned as Ninus and his consort, Semiramis. An interesting connection has been suggested between Ninus and Nin, the Akkadian goddess of love and war, who was better known by the Semitic name of Ishtar. It is not impossible that the Assyrians established a shrine dedicated to Ishtar at Aphrodisias and that in time she adopted further characteristics and took on the duties of the Great Mother who had long been worshipped there. Later Ishtar became Aphrodite. 'Behind the figure of

Aphrodite there clearly stands the ancient Semitic goddess of love, Ishtar-Astarte, divine consort of the king, queen of heaven, and hetaera in one.' (Burkert 'Greek Religion'.)

The development of Aphrodisias was probably assisted by its location on the borders of Caria, Lydia and Phrygia and its proximity to the great E–W and N–S trade routes. However, for many centuries it appears to have been no more than a shrine, albeit an important one, dedicated to the goddess of love and war, Ishtar-Aphrodite. No doubt the settlement around the shrine housed the priests, their attendants and the servants of the goddess. By the 2C BC it was certainly known as Aphrodisias, but no description of it as a city has come to light before the second half of the century and then it was coupled with its neighbour Plarasa, with which it was joined in a sympolity. (Plarasa is identified with the unexcavated s.te of Bingeç S of Karacasu.)

There was a dramatic change in the fortunes of Aphrodisias under Roman rule. During the horrors of the war against Mithridates VI (120–63 BC), king of Pontus, when more than 80,000 Romans were slaughtered in the province of Asia, Aphrodisias gave unstinted support to the Roman cause. Its citizens, declaring that life without the shield of Roman power would be impossible, voted to muster an army to assist the Romans in Caria. Such loyalty did not go unrewarded.

In 85 BC, after he had defeated Mithridates, the dictator Sulla sent gifts to Aphrodite. These included a double axe, a traditional symbol of power in Caria, and a gold crown. Later Julius Caesar, whose family claimed Venus (Aphrodite) as an ancestress, had a gold statue of Eros dedicated at her shrine in Aphrodisias. He also granted the temple certain rights of asylum. Sacked by Labienus and his Parthians in 40 BC, the city was assisted in its recovery by Octavian who arranged that Aphrodisias became an ally of Rome and received the status of a free city. This meant in effect that it was removed from the control of the governor of the Roman province of Asia. When, as Augustus, Octavian had assumed the supreme power, he continued to display a warm interest in the welfare of Aphrodisias and of its citizens and this benevolent attitude was continued by many of his imperial successors.

Under the empire Aphrodisias was an important intellectual and cultural centre. Its schools attracted students not only from Asia Minor but from other parts of the Roman dominions. Towards the end of the 1C AD Xenocrates, the author of several treatises on medicine, taught there. At about the same time Chariton, the author of the oldest Greek novel, 'Chaereas and Callirhoe', was writing his romantic story of star-crossed lovers. There is an amusing trace of campanilismo in the opening sentence, which manages to include a reference to his native city. 'I, Chariton of Aphrodisias, clerk to the rhetor Athenagoras will relate the love affair which occurred in Syracuse ... '.

Aphrodisias was close to a quarry producing fine pale white marble which was capable of taking a high polish. This fact assisted the growth and development of a school of sculpture which acquired widespread fame in antiquity. The work of sculptors from Aphrodisias reached Rome and other great centres of the empire. Fine examples have been found in far-away Lepcis Magna in N Africa on an arch which was erected in honour of Septimius Severus and in a basilica erected by him at the beginning of the 3C AD. Two centaurs from Hadrian's Villa at Tivoli have also been identified as the creation of craftsmen from Aphrodisias, while a handsome relief of Antinous, that emperor's Bithynian favourite, discovered at Lanuvium near Rome, was signed by Antonianus of Aphrodisias.

Christianity made some progress in the city before the edict of Milan in AD 313 put an end to persecution, for two Aphrodisian martyrs are recorded, either under Decius or Diocletian. It is recorded that a bishop from Aphrodisias attended the Council of Nicaea in AD 325. However, pagan influence continued to be strong in the city for a very long time. In AD 391 Theodosius I banned the practice of paganism throughout the Roman Empire. This ban was repeated and extended by several of his successors, but there is evidence that in Aphrodisias sacrifice to the gods continued to be offered for at least another century. Even in the 6C missionaries were still converting pagans in the area, but the prosperity of the Christians by this time is indicated by the dramatically ambitious conversion of the temple of Aphrodite to a Christian church.

The Church's problems were not limited to conflicts with the pagans. Heterodox Christian beliefs flourished in Aphrodisias and at the beginning of the 6C its bishop was deprived of his see for his stubborn adherence to the Monophysite heresy. At the end of that century or the beginning of the next in an attempt to break away from the pagan associations of its old name

Aphrodisias was christened Stavropolis, the City of the Cross. Later it was simply known as Caria, a name recalled by its corrupt form Geyre, which is still in use.

Apparently in the middle of the 4C a wall was constructed for the first time around the city. About AD 350 Aphrodisias was badly damaged by an earthquake which devastated much of Caria and the neighbouring provinces. The 7C was marked by further calamities—Persian incursions into Anatolia and another disastrous earthquake. This time the city was too impoverished to repair the damage and many buildings were left in ruins. A citadel was constructed around the höyük behind the theatre to provide the inhabitants with a place of refuge in times of peril.

At the end of the 12C the city was captured by the Selçuk Turks. Changing hands several times during the following century, its inhabitants were dispersed by its Turkish rulers c 1279 and the site was abandoned. Some time later peasant farmers returned to the area and established a small village, Geyre, among the ruins of the shattered buildings.

One of the first travellers from W Europe to visit Aphrodisias in modern times was the British botanist William Sherard who explored the site in 1705. His main interest was the inscriptions. A later visitor was W.R. Hamilton who came to Aphrodisias in 1803. He was followed nine years later by members of the Society of Dilettanti under the leadership of William Gell. Their discoveries were published in 'Ionian Antiquities' between 1821–1915. Charles Texier, who examined the ruins in 1835, wrote of his visit in 'Description de l'Asie Mineure', published in 1849. The first excavations of the city were conducted by a French engineer Paul Gaudin in 1904. In 1937 an Italian team discovered a beautifully carved frieze from the Ionic portico dedicated to Tiberius in the Agora. This is now preserved in the garden of the new Archaeological Museum at İzmir.

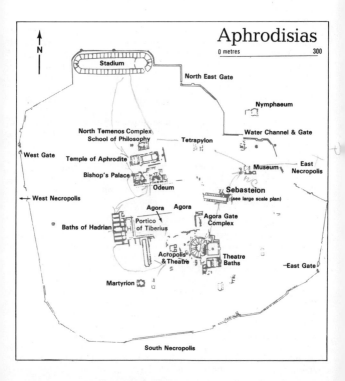

Professor Erim, who started his work at the site in 1961, has continued to add to our knowledge of the city each year since then.

The approach to Aphrodisias from Karacasu is marked by the remains of tombs in the extensive cemeteries in the fields on the right of the road and by the striking sectors of the city wall built of white marble blocks. A number of sarcophagi found here are displayed in the Museum.

Entrance to the site is from the large car-park on the E side of the wall which surrounded the ancient city. Aphrodisias appears to have relied for protection on the sacred character of its shrine until about the middle of the 4C AD. At that time work on a *fortification wall*, roughly circular in shape and extending for c 3.5km around the main area of the city, was begun. This was reinforced by towers and had four main gates, one at each point of the compass. Evidently litter-louts were not unknown in Aphrodisias, as built into the NE side of the wall is a re-used stone which carried the following inscription: 'Whoever throws rubbish here shall incur the curse of the 318 fathers', i.e the bishops, who took part in the Council of Nicaea (AD 325).

At the beginning of the 5C this fortification may have been strengthened with building-material taken from earlier structures which had probably been damaged by earthquakes. This patchwork is particularly noticeable on the N side where inscribed bases from statues and carved stone blocks have been built into the wall. The walls seem to have been maintained until the late 6C after which there was a withdrawal to the Acropolis.

One of the most recent and most exciting of the discoveries at Aphrodisias has been made in an area a short distance to the SW of the museum. Here are the ruins of the **Sebasteion**. This complex, which has been dated to the first half of the 1C AD, was dedicated to Aphrodite, with, no doubt, Augustus and certainly to Tiberius and Livia. Gaius, Claudius, and Nero and other members of the Julio-Claudian family were also honoured there subsequently. Throughout the Roman provinces, to regard the emperor as a divinity to be worshipped was a step which placed him in an understandable and acceptable context. In Aphrodisias the Sebasteion served this purpose.

The Sebasteion was the gift of two families. Menander and his brother Eusebes together with Eusebes' wife donated the N portico and the propylon. Tiberius Claudius Diogenes dedicated the S portico and the temple, which had been promised by his father Diogenes and his uncle Attalus and his uncle's wife Attalis Aphion.

The Sebasteion consisted of twin parallel porticoes 80m long, which flanked a paved area 14m wide. At the E end a flight of steps led up to a large Corinthian-style temple. The W end was closed by a propylon which was built at an oblique angle to the porticoes. The propylon was ornamented with a statue of Aphrodite as first mother of the imperial family together with statues of other members of that family and of their legendary ancestors. The aim of the architect and his patrons was to lead worshippers along a processional avenue, whose decorative sculpture glorified Augustus and his Julio-Claudian successors especially for their military successes, to the temple where sacrifices were offered to them and to Aphrodite.

The porticoes, 12m high, were divided horizontally into three sections and within each section vertically by half-columns, Doric at the bottom, Ionic in the middle and Corinthian at the top. The spaces

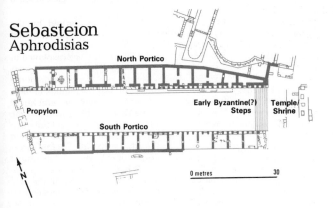

Sebasteion
Aphrodisias

North Portico

Propylon

Early Byzantine(?) Steps

Temple/ Shrine

South Portico

N

0 metres 30

between the columns in the middle and top sections were filled with deeply-carved reliefs. On the S portico these were representations of mythological scenes and of members of the imperial family in heroic poses. Some of the most striking pieces of sculpture found there showed the Three Graces, Bellerophon and Pegasus, Leda and the Swan, Achilles and Penthesilea, Nero conquering Armenia (this relief was later defaced), a victorious Claudius about to despatch a prostrate Britannia, and a nude, youthful Augustus holding a cornucopia and an oar, symbols of his dominion over land and sea.

There are fewer reliefs extant from the N portico as this was greatly damaged by the earthquake at the beginning of the 7C and material from it was used to fortify the theatre area. (See above.) A number of the captions for the sculpture here survive, however, and show that it represented the peoples conquered by Augustus—Egyptians, Dacians, several Thracian and Gallic tribes—together with other scenes from which we have a fine representation of the youthful Nero being crowned by his mother in the guise of Tyche. Even after many centuries the lively and vivacious sculptures, which decorated the monument, provide a vivid and lasting demonstration of the skill of the Aphrodisian artists who created them so long ago.

During the 4C the rooms on the ground floor of the porticoes were probably used for a short period as shops. At about the same time the statues and reliefs of the more obvious pagan deities were mutilated to avoid offending Christian susceptibilities.

The dedication of the porticoes and their associated buildings to Aphrodite with the imperial family placed the Julio-Claudians firmly in the context of traditional Greek religious beliefs and accepted Greek culture.

To the S of the Sebasteion lie the substantial remains of a large structure which has been identified as a 2C *propylon*. Originally it was believed that this led to the agora, which was located a short distance to the W, and as a consequence it was described at one time as the agora gate on plans of the site.

Recent surveys of the area and an examination of statuary and architectural fragments found there have produced a revised view. Archaeologists are now of the opinion that the monumental gate may have provided access from the agora to another building or complex, also dating from the 2C AD, whose remains lie in the unexcavated area to the E.

Sometime in the 5C the propylon was converted into a nymphaeum, probably in an attempt to contain the flood waters which, after the earthquakes of the mid-4C, caused many problems in this part of the city. Among the sculptures recovered from the structure are a massive, headless Antoninus Pius and the togaed statue of a pensive youth. There are also a number of friezes portraying mythological subjects e.g. centaurs at a banquet and a gigantomachy, which were taken from another building to decorate the nymphaeum. (This is very similar to what happened to the Library of Celsus at. See above.)

Immediately to the S is the höyük or tell which Gaudin and the early archaeologists believed to be the city's acropolis. On the E side of the höyük there is a large rectangular open space, the so-called *tetrastoon* which has been dated by finds to the reign of Julian (360–363). As its name suggests, this consisted of a paved area surrounded on all four sides by stoas. There was a circular fountain in the centre. The tetrastoon fulfilled a number of purposes. It provided an additional meeting-place for the citizens of Aphrodisias; it facilitated access to the theatre; and small shops in it would, no doubt, provide a useful commercial centre in this part of the city. Among the sculptures discovered in the tetrastoon are a sensitive representation of a sad-faced adolescent, reworked as a 4C prince from an earlier 1C statue, and the striking statue of grim, tight-lipped Flavius Palmatus, a late 5C governor of Caria and acting vicar of the larger area of Asiana.

The well-preserved **Theatre** of Aphrodisias had an estimated seating capacity of c 8000. Its horse-shoe shaped cavea had two, possibly three, diazomata. Of its seats, which were divided into 11 cunei, 27 rows remain. According to an inscription, the stage-building was constructed at the expense of a late 1C BC notable, Iulius Zoilos. A former slave, he played an active part in the affairs of the city at that time. Various factors have permitted the date of the construction to be narrowed down to the period between 39 BC and 27 BC. There were six vaulted chambers behind the stage. Names on the doorframes suggest that these were the dressing rooms used by some of the more important performers.

Originally constructed in the late Hellenistic period, the theatre was modified considerably during the second half of the 2C AD. By removing some of the lower rows of seats, dropping the level of the orchestra and erecting protective barriers and a parapet, it became possible to use it for gladiatorial contests and wild-beast shows. At the same time proedriai and a loge were added. Because of these alterations it was necessary to raise and widen the stage as had been done in the theatre at Priene (see above). Wild beasts were kept in a number of secure cells underneath the stage before being released into the arena for the savage animal fights which were so much in favour with audiences at that time.

In the N parodos the wall of the stage-building and the adjoining analemma are covered with inscriptions, letters and decrees which date from the period of the late Republic through to the middle of the 3C AD. Recently published, they provide a unique record of the relationship between a loyal provincial centre and Rome. There is the text of a decree setting out the rights and privileges conferred on Aphrodisias by the Senate together with letters to the city from a number of emperors including Trajan, Hadrian, and Septimius Severus.

Among the mass of statuary discovered in or near the stage-building there are two pieces of particular interest: a 1C AD relief bust of Aphrodite and a more than lifesize statue of a youth. The goddess, who gazes serenely at her worshippers, is portrayed wearing a polos. Suspended from an elaborate pectoral a crescent moon rests between her swelling breasts. According to an inscription on the base the youth is a personification of the Demos, the people of Aphrodisias.

During the Byzantine period small chapel-like rooms were constructed at each end of the stage-corridor. In one of these a fragmentary 6C fresco depicting the Archangel Michael was found.

It would appear that the theatre was so badly damaged by the earthquake at the beginning of the 7C that the reduced population of the city was unable or unwilling to repair it. Because of the unsettled nature of the times the inhabitants turned their energies instead to making a fortress on the 'acropolis'. This they did by constructing a wall, complete with watch-towers, around the lower slopes. No attempt was made to rescue the stage-building from the debris, but a number of rough shelters were improvised among the tumbled masonry of the remainder of the structure.

The summit of the hill behind the theatre is easily reached from the top row of seats. Like the tells of Mesopotamia this is a höyük, an artificial structure composed of the remains of many successive levels of occupation. One of the oldest human settlements in Anatolia, the earliest finds have been dated to c 5800 BC. It has been established that as early as the fifth millennium BC the people who lived here were receiving goods from many distant sources. For instance they used obsidian tools which originated in the islands of the Aegean. Excavations on the hill have produced substantial finds of pottery, gold and silver jewellery, tools, weapons, and primitive idols.

To the S of the tetrastoon was a long *hall* which formed part of the *theatre baths complex*. This was unroofed except at the N end, where there was a small chamber which may have contained the statue of an emperor. The chamber had a simple pavement of black and white marble. Two pilasters, which flanked the entrance to the chamber, were carved in typical Aphrodisian style with an elaborate pattern of erotes, birds, and animals placed against an intricate background of foliage. The central paved area was flanked by colonnades, their blue-grey marble Corinthian columns separating it from the offices and shops which lined its sides. In the 4C an opening was made in the wall of the chamber. This provided access to the hall from the S stoa of the tetrastoon.

Behind the hall lie the ruins of a large structure, the *theatre baths*. Note especially the enormous caldarium whose walls were 10m high. In the substantial remains of this chamber, now minus its roof, there are four arched niches, two of which lead to other parts of the complex. A large circular room contained two adjoining bathing pools.

Leaving the theatre baths we continue towards the site of the agora which lies to the NW of the acropolis. To the S are the remains of a large *basilica* which is believed to date from the second half of the 1C AD. This structure, which was c 100m long, had the typical form of a civil basilica, i.e. two aisles flanking a central nave. In the 3C the building appears to have assumed a new importance. This may have resulted from the establishment of the united province of Caria-Phrygia which had been created apparently in the reign of

Decius (249–251). At about that time a number of reliefs portraying various mythological subjects were placed in the spaces between the columns on the E side. One of these shows Ninus, the legendary founder of Aphrodisias, and his wife, Semiramis. (See above.)

Another striking discovery in this area was the text of two decrees issued by Diocletian in AD 301. One revalued the silver currency, the other set out the maximum prices for a variety of goods and services including most foods, wood, metals, wooden and metal goods, cloth, shoes, drugs and transport.

Behind the palaestra and peristyle court, which were partially cleared by Gaudin at the beginning of the century, lie the substantial ruins of the *Baths of Hadrian*. This complex, dated by a dedicatory inscription, contained a large central hall, the caldarium, which was flanked on each side by parallel rectangular chambers. The ruins of a tepidarium and of a sudatorium were discovered among the chambers on the N side, the only ones excavated so far. A nice touch is provided by an inscription found by Gaudin, which warns bathers against leaving valuables with their clothes. The baths stayed in use well into the Christian period. An inscription by a Christian cloakroom attendant has also been found.

Among the debris of the baths the archaeologists found three fine marble heads. One, which has been dated to the 2C, is believed to portray a priestess of Aphrodite. She wears an elaborate diadem, which is decorated with a pattern of six-pointed stars. (A similar star appears on the relief of the goddess, which was discovered in the theatre. See above.) The other two heads were representations of Apollo and Aphrodite.

A line of standing columns to the N and E of the baths marks the position of the great *double agora* of Aphrodisias. The N section, which was surrounded by a Doric portico, measured 205m by 120m. The S section, the *Portico of Tiberius*, which was in the Ionic style, measured 212m by 70m. This contained a number of small rooms suitable for offices, shops and workshops, together with latrines. The enormous statue of a female deity and the damaged figure of a galloping horse were recovered here.

To the N, beyond a screen of poplar trees, are the extensive ruins of a building, which, after the mid-3C AD, is believed to have housed an official of some importance, perhaps the governor of the province of Caria-Phrygia and later of Caria or of the late Roman province. Subsequently it may have served as the palace of the bishop of Aphrodisias and Caria. The principal feature of this structure was an 'audience chamber' which had three large apses, a common characteristic of the residences of important officials. Similar rooms have been found in the houses of officers of state in other parts of the Roman Empire.

A number of the attractive blue-grey marble columns unearthed in the peristyle court, which provided access to the audience chamber, have been re-erected. Note the presence of a small bathroom and latrine on the S side of the S apse, which is proof that this was not purely a public building. On the N of the peristyle court, at a slight-higher level, there was a long narrow hall with an apse at its E end.

The discovery of a lead seal in the ruins, which mentions the 'Metropolitan Bishop of Caria', and the proximity of the building to the principal church in the city (the former temple of Aphrodite) suggest that it became an episcopal palace during the Byzantine era. In addition parts of two frescoes, one portraying Nike, the other the

Three Graces, found there had been covered over with a rough coating of plaster. Presumably they were considered unsuitable for the residence of a cleric.

One of the most beautiful and best-preserved buildings in Aphrodisias lies to the E of the bishop's palace. This is the **Odeum**, where concerts, theatrical productions requiring small casts, lectures, discussions, political gatherings and meetings of the city council could be held. Built towards the end of 1C AD or the beginning of the 2C AD, it had, in its original state, a capacity of c 1700. Badly damaged by the earthquakes of the 4C, the odeum became subject to flooding because of the disturbance of the water-table. It also appears to have lost its roof about then, so leaving the spectators unprotected from the elements.

Today the cavea retains nine rows of seats. These are divided into five cunei. Some of the seats carry rough inscriptions probably reserving them for particular groups, eg. young men, Jews, partisans of the Blue Faction. Note the carved lion-heads at the end of some of the rows. The orchestra floor was covered with a fine opus sectile design whose pattern was made up of segments of blue and white marble and red slate. The stage of the odeum was decorated with statues placed in naiskoi. Some of those discovered by the archaeologists portray seated writers or philosophers, others have been identified as representations of local prominenti. There are a number of amusing graffiti on the walls of a passage at the back of the stage. One, perhaps the work of a bored performer awaiting his turn, is the spirited depiction of a horseman. The stage was separated from the agora by a portico with a double row of columns, Ionic on the outside, Corinthian on the inside.

It would appear that the odeum replaced an earlier building which may have been a gymnasium. Near the remains of this structure was a 1C heroon. A simple sarcophagus decorated with garlands rested on a circular dais supported by three steps. Nearby was a round altar, ornamented with wreaths of flowers intertwined with bunches of fruit and the finely-carved figures of gay, carefree erotes. The tomb was robbed in antiquity. As burial within the city was a very high honour, it can be assumed that the deceased must have performed some outstanding service.

The discovery of a large quantity of marble chippings in this area led the archaeologists to the site of one of the many workshops which produced the sculpture that had made Aphrodisias famous in many parts of the Roman Empire. Among the discarded and unfinished works found there were an exquisite statue of a young Hercules, which conveys admirably the gaucherie and uncertainty of adolescence, a blue and white marble representation of the rape of Europa and a particularly fine head of a bearded philosopher.

A short distance to the N are the ruins of the *Temple of Aphrodite*. We owe much of our understanding of this building to the skill and patience of Professor Erim and his colleagues, who had the not inconsiderable task of tracing its structural history through the disturbance of the site caused by earlier archaeologists and the extensive alterations made by the Byzantine architects, when they converted it into a church.

The temple, a pseudo-dipteros in the Ionic style with 8 by 13 columns, was begun in the 1C BC and continued in the 1C AD. Some of the columns bear inscriptions (still *in situ*) recording the fact that they were the gifts of individual citizens to the goddess and to the Demos of Aphrodisias. Of the 40 columns which decorated the structure only 14 are still standing today. The temple had a pronaos and cella. There was no opisthodomus.

It is clear that Aphrodite and the fertility deity, who preceded her, were worshipped in this place long before the construction of the temple. (See above.) Excavations have revealed traces of much older structures, possibly treasuries, some of which date from the 7C BC. Fragments of terracotta statues of the goddess, dated to the 6C BC, have also been found on the site. When the pronaos of the temple was being constructed, the builders cut through a roughly-executed black and white Hellenistic mosaic depicting animals within a border. This is believed to belong to one of the earlier buildings.

During the reign of Hadrian (AD 117–138) the temple was enclosed on all four sides within elaborate porticoes, consisting of colonnades of Corinthian columns in front of walls decorated by niches.

When towards the middle of the 5C the temple was converted into a Christian basilica, probably dedicated to one or more of the archangels, the cult statue of the goddess and all traces of her worship were removed. A striking reminder of this dramatic change in the religious beliefs of the Aphrodisians was provided by the discovery in the area to the S of the temenos of parts of a huge *marble statue of Aphrodite*. After the head and arms of the goddess had been crudely hacked off, the battered torso was built into a Byzantine wall. However, despite this deliberate act of vandalism, enough remains to demonstrate the majesty and numinous quality which this work of art possessed in its undamaged state.

The reconstruction of the temple involved not only the destruction of the pronaos and cella, which contained the cult statue, but also the removal of the columns from the E and W ends. These were added to the existing columns on the long sides of the building. An apse was constructed at the E end and material from the Hadrianic peribolos was used to erect a narthex and an exonarthex. To complete the transformation of the temple into a church, an atrium and baptistery were added to the W end.

The alterations inside the basilica included the construction of an iconostatis in front of the sanctuary and of a synthronon. On the walls of a covered corridor behind the synthronon the archaeologists discovered the remains of 10C and 11C frescoes. These depicted Christ in glory, the Virgin Mary and a number of the saints. Christian worship in the Temple/Church, which was repaired after the earthquake in the 7C and again in the 11C, ceased finally in the late 12C, when it fell into the hands of the Turcoman and Selçuk tribesmen, who swept into W Anatolia at that time.

A short distance to the N of the peribolos of the temple of Aphrodite are the remains of the so-called *school of philosophy*. Access to this 3C structure was by way of a marble-paved courtyard on the E side. This was surrounded by columns of the local blue-grey marble and had a square pool in the centre. On the W side of the building there was another large courtyard which had an apse built into one wall. A third courtyard to the S and a number of rooms completed the structure.

Aphrodisias was the home of a number of noted philosophers, including Alexander and Asklepiodotos, and this fact coupled with the appearance and lay-out of the rooms in this complex, which are similar to those found in a number of schools of philosophy in various parts of the Greek world, suggested its name and use to the archaeologists. The building appears to have been occupied to a late date.

From the school of philosphy a path leads N to the *stadium* of Aphrodisias, which was located c 350m from the temple. Although this has been surveyed and soundings have been taken in various parts of the structure, no further work has been undertaken in it. One of the best-preserved Graeco-Roman stadia in Asia Minor, it was constructed during the 1C or 2C AD. Rounded at its E and W ends, it measures 262m by 59m. Its 30 rows of seats had an estimated capacity of 30,000. Special arrangements were made for the comfort of the spectators. The lines of seats on the long sides bulge slightly in the centre to ensure that everyone had an uninterrupted view and it would appear that there were loges for the more important officials and distinguished visitors in the centre of each side. Inscriptions on some of the seats indicate that they were reserved for particular groups, e.g. ephebes and certain craftsmen.

With the permission and approval of the emperor many cities in the Roman province of Asia promoted games and competitions based on those held at the great Greek festivals. At Aphrodisias they were modelled on Delphi's Pythian Games. In addition to the athletic events, which included foot-races, boxing, pancration and wrestling, there were music and drama competitions, exhibitions of oratory and competitive productions of tragedies and comedies. Prizes were modest, often no more than a wreath of laurel leaves, but as a rule the victor was adequately rewarded in other ways by his jubilant patrons and followers.

An alteration of some importance took place in the stadium. A wall was built across the E end and a number of other changes were made in that part of the structure in the 7C. It is likely that the adapted area was used for circus performances.

Later, when the city was menaced by threats of invasion and attack, the stadium was incorporated into its defensive system. The long N section became part of the fortifications and the access tunnels under the W end were closed off by walls.

On leaving the stadium turn in a SE direction and walk towards the entrance to the site. A short distance to the E of the temple of Aphrodite are the remaining columns of a magnificent **Tetrapylon**. This structure of four rows of four columns appears to have marked the junction of a NS street with, perhaps, a processional way to the temenos and the temple. Note the variation in the decoration of the column shafts of the tetrapylon. Those on the W are smooth, while some of the others have spiral markings. Fragments of the pediment reliefs recovered from the ruins of the tetrapylon portray chubby erotes hunting wild animals and figures of Nike emerging from a tangle of acanthus leaves.

Apart from those works left *in situ* and those being restored in the workshops, most of the statues and architectural remains discovered by Professor Erim and his team are displayed in a well-arranged *museum* at the site. Financed jointly by the Turkish government and the National Geographic Society of America, this building was opened formally in July 1979. An hour spent in the examination of its exhibits provides a fitting conclusion to the visit to Aphrodisias, one of the most beautiful and most stimulating archaeological sites in Turkey.

Travellers, who have their own transport, may, if they wish, continue to Denizli by way of 35km *Tavas*. This picturesque route is somewhat shorter, 69km as against 104km, than that via Karacasu and the E24. There are also bus and dolmuş services via Tavas, but they are relatively infrequent and may involve a number of changes.

A dazzling white scar on the monotonous brown slope of a mountain to the NE of Denizli marks the position of the great travertine basins of Pamukkale. Clearly visible from the E24 on the W outskirts of the town, they have become a major tourist attraction in recent years.

Denizli, the principal town and seat of the governor of the province of the same name, has a population of 171,360. An important market centre for the surrounding area, it is linked by train to İzmir and İstanbul and is well-served by a number of inter-city bus services. The Tourism Information Office is located at the railway station on the W side of the town.

When Charles Texier came to Denizli in the mid 19C, it was a quiet provincial backwater. Then the town was surrounded by beautiful gardens, to which its inhabitants repaired during the summer. Abandoning their houses for months at a time, they rested at their ease in leafy bowers, enjoying the excellent fruit and garden produce, for which the region was famous. According to Texier visitors arriving in Denizli found it quite deserted, so that even the fortified area, *'la Cassaba, n'est plus habitée que par les chiens errants'.* ('Asie Mineure', Paris, 1862.)

Today few travellers stop in Denizli for any length of time. It is no longer a staging post on the tourist-circuit that takes in Ephesus, Aphrodisias and Pamukkale. Although there are a number of 2- and 1-star hotels in the town (details from the Tourism Information Office), most visitors make their overnight stop in the more comfortable—and more expensive—establishments of Pamukkale.

Frequent bus and dolmuş services leave Denizli's otogar during the daytime for 20km Pamukkale. Visitors, without their own transport, arriving in Denzili in the evening or at night, who wish to go on to Pamukkale, will have to take a taxi.

As well as Hierapolis (Pamukkale) there are two sites of particular interest to Christian travellers in the neighbourhood of Denizli: Colossae and Laodiceia ad Lycum. The remains of COLOSSAE are located c 20km to the E of Denizli. Take the E24 in the direction of Dinar for 8km to the point where it passes the ruins of the 13C Selçuk Ak Han caravanserai on the left. There take the turning on the right-hand side, which leads to the village of *Honaz*: the ruins of Colossae are c 5km N of Honaz.

History. The double -ss in its name, relic of a pre-Greek language, suggests that Colossae was a settlement of considerable antiquity. The earliest known reference to the city is found in accounts of Xerxes' invasion of Anatolia in 480 BC. When Xenophon embarked on the ill-fated expedition of the Ten Thousand in 401 BC, Colossae was a large and prosperous place. Like neighbouring Laodiceia, it was a producer of fine wool which, according to Pliny the Elder, was dyed a purple 'colossinus'. As Laodiceia increased her share of the trade, so the fortunes of Colossae began to decline. By the time of Augustus it had become a place of minor importance.

Christianity was brought to Colossae by Epaphras, the friend and companion of St. Paul who was imprisoned with the apostle either in Caesarea or in Rome. Although it is unlikely that the apostle ever visited the city, it is clear that he took a deep interest in the growth and development of the Christian community there. In his letter to the Colossians he warns its members of the dangers posed by paganism. In particular they are advised to beware of the activities of those who 'try to enter into some vision of their own.' (Colossians 2:18.) This has been taken to refer to the adherents of the many mystery religions, which flourished in the cities of the Roman Empire at that time.

Damaged by earthquakes, its trade taken away by Laodiceia, the ruin of Colossae was completed by the incursions of first the Arabs and then the Turks. At about the beginning of the 9C the city was abandoned, the remaining inhabitants removing themselves and their possessions to nearby Chonae (Honaz).

Colossae was built on the S bank of the river Lycus at the head of a gorge. Today very little remains of its ancient buildings. At the top of the low acropolis there are the scanty ruins of a *defensive wall*. Near the W edge is a large deep *stone-lined pit*, whose purpose is not known. The outline of Colossae's small *theatre* may be traced on the E side of the acropolis. In the city's necropolis, located on the N bank of the Lycus, the tombs, covered with flat slabs, were let into the ground. A church dedicated to St. Michael, one of the most important Christian shrines in Asia, was probably located in this area.

The *Ak Han caravanserai* (see above), which dates from the 13C, consists of a large square courtyard partially surrounded by arches and a covered hall. According to an inscription over the door of the hall, it was completed in 1253 by Karasungar during the reign of Sultan Kaykavus, the remainder of the structure being finished a year later.

LAODICEIA AD LYCUM is nearer to Denizli than Colossae. A turning on the left c 3km from the town on the road to Pamukkale leads to the site. Little visited today except by those interested in its Christian connections—it is one of the Seven Cities of Asia mentioned in the Book of Revelation—Laodiceia has suffered from a combination of neglect and spoliation. Much of its worked stone has been removed for building purposes and, unfortunately, little is being done to preserve its remaining structures from further damage.

History. Laodiceia was a Hellenistic foundation, which may have replaced an earlier settlement called Diospolis. According to one tradition the city was established by the Syrian king, Antiochus I Soter (280–261 BC) in honour of his sister Laodice. However, it seems more likely that it was the foundation of his successor Antiochus II Theos (261–246 BC), who named it after his wife. If that theory is correct, it would fix the date of Laodiceia's establishment between 261 and 253, the year in which Antiochus II divorced Laodice.

Clearly the location of the city had been carefully chosen. It was at the junction of two very important trade routes, one running N–S between Lydia and Pamphylia and another EW between the Euphrates and the Aegean. It was c 1.5km from the Lycus, a substantial river which eventually flows into the Maeander, and it had an assured water-supply from two nearby streams, the Asopus and the Caprus.

Little is known of the early history of Laodiceia. In 188 BC it came under the rule of the kings of Pergamum and from them it passed to Rome becoming in 129 BC part of province of Asia. When Mithridates VI, king of Pontus, invaded Asia in 88–85 BC it provided a refuge for a Roman general, but under the stress of siege surrendered him. It is not known to have suffered serious penalties as a result. In 50 BC Cicero, in his capacity as governor of Cilicia, spent some months in Laodiceia administering justice and attempting to redress some of the wrongs perpetrated by his predecessor in office, Appius Claudius.

It suffered in the civil war that followed the death of Julius Caesar and again when Labienus invaded Asia Minor in 40 BC, but during the imperial period Laodiceia became a very wealthy city. After the earthquake of AD 60 it was able to repair the damage sustained by its public buildings without assistance from the imperial treasury. It is probable that much of the city's wealth came from wool and from the cloth produced from it. Laodicean wool was very soft, of a fine texture and deep black. According to Vitruvius it owed its distinctive colour to the presence of certain minerals in the sheep's drinking water.

Galen stated that Laodiceia was for a time the sole source of an important medicine called *nard*. Strabo mentions another connection of the city with healing. There was, he said, a temple in the neighbourhood of Laodiceia dedicated to the youthful Anatolian moon-god Men, who was usually associated with death and rebirth. He continues: 'In my own time a great ... school of medecine has been established [there]. A market was also held there under the protection of the god.'

However, the principal deity worshipped in the city was Laodicean Zeus or Zeus Aseis. It has been suggested that the latter name may have some relation to the Arabic, *'aziz'* (powerful). This may indicate a Syrian influence, as among Laodiceia's cosmopolitan population there were many citizens of Syrian origin. There was also a large and prosperous Jewish community whose members were guaranteed freedom of worship.

Christianity was introduced into Laodiceia by Epaphras of Colossae (see above). It seems likely that the rapid spread of the new faith in the city was assisted by the presence of the many Jews, who lived there. However, there were also some who hesitated. John's forthright comment in Revelation 3. 15–17 is evidence of that. 'I know all your ways; you are neither hot nor cold. But because you are lukewarm, neither hot nor cold, I will spit you out of my mouth.' During the Byzantine period Laodiceia was an episcopal see and in the 4C an important Ecumenical Council was held there.

Badly damaged by an earthquake towards the end of the 5C, Laodiceia never recovered its former importance. It was ruled by the Byzantines until the Selçuk and Turcoman invaders swept them away and put an end to their rule towards the end of the 12C. For some time afterwards the city, known as *Ludik* by its new rulers, continued to be inhabited, but eventually the site was abandoned and the remnants of its population moved to Denizli.

Laodiceia occupied the slopes and level ground on a low hill located between the rivers Asopus and Caprus. On the SW approaches to the city there are traces of the *aqueduct* which brought water 8km from a spring in Denizli. Fed into a large tank outside the city walls, it was delivered under pressure to a *water-tower* on the S slope of the hill. The remains of this structure are still visible.

Near the water-tower are the ruins of the *stadium* which was erected in honour of Vespasian in AD 79. This was 347m long and, like the stadium at Aphrodisias, had rounded ends. According to an inscription it was used for athletics and gladiatorial contests. Only a few rows of seats remain.

To the E of the stadium are the substantial ruins of a building that has been identified variously as a *gymnasium* and a *baths complex*. This was dedicated to Hadrian and his wife Sabina. Because of its unusual shape and its proximity to the water-tower, the view put forward by Bean that it was a bath is now generally accepted.

About 100m to the N are the insignificant remains of an *odeum*. Only a few rows of seats remain. As was often the case, it is probable that this building was also used as a bouleuterion.

Almost in the centre of the plateau are the ruins of a structure, which was built as a *nymphaeum* probably during the reign of Caracalla (211–217), but which was changed substantially several times. In its original form it consisted of a large square basin surrounded by a colonnade on two sides, with two semicircular fountains to the S and E. The nymphaeum was ornamented with statues, including a life-size figure of Isis, and decorative friezes. Note the inscribed base of a statue of the consul Anicius Asper, one of the city's benefactors.

During one of the many alterations the square basin was removed and a small chamber built in its place. The structure was then used by the Christian community of Laodiceia for some purpose, which so far has not been determined. The nymphaeum was excavated by French Canadian archaeologists between 1961–1963 when the statue of Isis was discovered.

To the N of the nymphaeum a few stones mark the site of an *Ionic temple*. Beyond, at the crest of the N slope of the hill, are the remains of Laodiceia's two theatres. The *larger theatre* on the right, which faces towards the NE, is reasonably well preserved. Some of the seats and a part of the stage-building are still visible. The *smaller theatre*, which looks towards the NW, retains part of its cavea only.

Laodiceia's fortifications were pierced by gates on the E, N and NW sides of the city. The E gate, the so-called *Syrian gate*, is the best preserved. Note the remains of a *Roman bridge* over the river Asopus below the (NW) Ephesus gate.

As was the custom, burials took place outside the city. Sarcophagi have been found by the sides of the ancient roads which passed through the Syrian and Ephesian gates. According to Bean it was outside the Syrian gate that the sophist Polemo was buried while in the last stages of mortal illness. It is reputed that the dying man cried out as the tomb was being closed, 'Make fast, make fast, let the sun never see me reduced to silence.'

After completing the visit to Laodiceia return to the main road and continue to c 17km Pamukkale.

After passing a small village which nestles at the base of the cliff, the road from Denizli begins to climb steadily to **Pamukkale**. Neither the exaggerated prose which travel companies have employed all too often to describe this magnificent natural phenomenon nor its repeated appearance on posters promoting tourism are able to diminish its appeal. Fortunately, too, the scale and grandeur of this unique geological formation save it from being completely spoiled by the misguided commercial exploitation which it has been exposed to in recent years. Pamukkale rarely fails to impress its visitors.

For countless millennia a spring located somewhere on the plateau, probably in the neighbourhood of the theatre of ancient HIERAPOLIS, has been pouring out streams of hot, mineral-saturated water. These have plunged over the mountain-side creating in the process enormous circular basins which are fringed with stalactites and surrounded by a huge area of smooth, dazzlingly-white calcareous rock—hence the name Pamukkale, Cotton Castle.

The description of Richard Chandler, who visited Pamukkale in the late summer of 1765, has seldom been bettered. 'Our tent stood on a green dry spot beneath the cliff. The view before us was so marvellous, that the description of it, to bear even faint resemblance, ought to appear romantic. The vast slope, which at a distance we had taken for chalk, was now beheld with wonder, it seeming an immense frozen cascade, the surface wavy, as of water at once fixed, or in its headlong course suddenly petrified. Round about us were many high, bare, stony ridges; and close by our tent one with a wide basis, and a slender rill of water, clear, soft and warm, running in a small channel on the top. A woman was washing linen in it, with a child at her back; and beyond were cabins of the Turcomans, standing distinct, much neater than any we had seen; each with poultry feeding, and a fence of reeds in front.'

Even as recently as 1939 little had changed. George Bean, who came to Pamukkale in that year, describes how 'the white cliffs, the ancient buildings, and the tombs stood deserted, and the sacred pool lay inviting the occasional visitor to a free and solitary bathe'.

Today the sacred pool is enclosed in the grounds of a motel! A modern resort, highly artificial in character, has been developed in Pamukkale. This is made up of a number of motels, a museum, a post-office and a clutter of mean shops peddling tawdry souvenirs. The motels concentrate almost entirely on catering for the coach parties, which fill most of their rooms during the holiday season. These groups spend an average of one night in Pamukkale before passing on to the next stage of their tour.

Perhaps because most visitors stay for such a short time at Pamukkale, some of its motels fail to reach the standard of comparable establishments in other Turkish resorts. In return for high prices travellers are offered poor service and badly-cooked meals by surly, ill-trained staff. Unless this situation changes soon, tourism in Pamukkale runs the risk of being damaged beyond recovery.

Some of the best accommodation in Pamukkale is to be found in the village at the base of the cliff where there are a number of modest, inexpensive pensions. The proprietors of these establishments still offer their guests that warm welcome which Turks traditionally extend to visitors. Unfortunately, the number of rooms available in the village is limited and demand almost always exceeds supply. Anyone wishing to stay there should make an early reservation.

According to an ancient tradition a number of maladies may be treated by bathing in or drinking the mineral waters of Pamukkale. They are supposed to be particularly effective against diseases of the kidneys and heart, and ailments of the digestive system. Be that as it may, it is undoubtedly very pleasant to lie submerged for hours in one of the many pools, especially in the autumn or spring, when there is a gentle nip in the air. As the water emerging from the underground sources is at a temperature only slightly less than that of blood heat, during those seasons a small cloud of steam marks the position of each pool. A leisurely and extended bathe produces a delightful feeling of relaxation and well-being. It is an excellent restorative after a strenuous day spent visiting the extensive and scattered remains of Hierapolis. Unfortunately, it also leaves a whitish crust or deposit on the hair and skin, which is difficult to remove.

Visitors may try the different pools by purchasing day-passes for a small sum from the motels which have enclosed them. Undoubtedly the most impressive is the so-called sacred pool in the *Turizm Moteli*, where one may bathe among submerged Roman columns. There is also a public swimming bath filled with hot mineral water from the underground springs. This establishment is clean and cheap, but during the holiday season it is usually very crowded. Its facilities and surroundings also have a distinctly municipal public-utility character.

History. It is almost certain that the unique appearance and curative properties of Pamukkale's springs attracted settlers from very early times. Herodotus (c 484–420 BC) writes about a city called Cydrara in this area and later there are references to a settlement named Hydrela (ὑδρηλή, watery). Hierapolis, which is first mentioned in 183 BC in connection with Apollonis, the mother of the Pergamene king Eumenes II Soter (197–160 BC), is believed to derive its name from Hiera, the wife of Telephus. When the Greeks made their first expedition against Troy, she led the women of Mysia against them and was killed by Nireus. The Pergamene dynasty claimed her as one of their ancestors. However, it is not certain that the city was founded by Eumenes or by one of his predecssors. A number of inscriptions from the 2C and 3C AD contain names like Antiochidos, Seleucidos and Attalidos, which suggests that it may have been a Seleucid foundation which was taken over by the Attalids. This may have occurred after the defeat of the Seleucid Antiochus III at the battle of Magnesia ad Sipylum in 190 BC.

With its neighbours Hierapolis became part of the Roman province of Asia in 129 BC. Apart from the fact that it was devastated by serious earthquakes in AD

17 and AD 60, very litle is known about the city's subsequent history. Certainly it was a prosperous trading centre producing a number of manufactured products. Inscriptions found there mention coppersmiths and nail-makers and, like neighbouring Laodiceia, Hierapolis had a flourishing wool industry. It also supplied a special kind of marble, whose unique colouring was believed to have been produced by the seepage of mineral water from the hot springs.

Among the city's distinguished sons was Antipater, a philosopher and rhetorician who became tutor to Caracalla and Geta. As in Aphrodisias there were contests and festivals in Hierapolis during the imperial period. In addition to games based on their Pythian and Olympic models, there was a special local celebration, the 'games of the Chrysorrhoas' (the golden stream). According to Bean this has been identified with a fast-flowing rivulet to the N of the city not far from the necropolis.

Hierapolis seems to have enjoyed a considerable degree of imperial favour. It received help from Nero to repair damage caused by the great earthquake in AD 60. Further signs of interest are provided by the visits by Hadrian in AD 129, by Caracalla in AD 215 and by Valens in AD 370. Coins of the Claudian era show a temple dedicated to the imperial race, 'genei Sebaston'. In AD 221 Hierapolis was granted the coveted title of Neocorus by the invert and degenerate Elagabalus (218–222). This was a valuable status symbol. It permitted the city to erect a temple in honour of the emperor and to celebrate imperial festivals at regular intervals. Elagabalus appears on the city's coins of this period offering sacrifice.

As well as the Roman emperors the Olympic gods, frequently merged with their Anatolian equivalents, were worshipped in Hierapolis. Thus, Apollo, the city's principal deity, was associated with a local sun-god Lairbenus and Leto, his mother, with Cybele the Megale Meter. In view of the many earthquakes suffered by Hierapolis, Poseidon the earth-shaker was feared and placated by its citizens. Offerings were made also to Pluto, the god of the underworld, in a dangerous and sinister cavern located near the temple of Apollo. (See below.) In view of this evidence of religiosity it is not surprising that on some occasions the city's associations with the legendary Hiera were ignored and its name Hierapolis (ἱερα πόλις) was simply taken to mean 'the holy city'. Interestingly, it was also called Hieropolis, 'city of temples', on its coinage as late as the end of the 1C BC.

Like Laodiceia and Colossae, Hierapolis adopted Christianity at an early date. The presence of a sizeable Jewish community may have assisted the spread of the new faith. Hierapolis is mentioned in Paul's epistle to the Colossians. 'Your own fellow-countryman Epaphras sends you his greeting, a servant of Jesus Christ who ever remembers you anxiously in his prayers, hoping that you will stand firm in the perfect achievement of all that is God's will for you; I can vouch for him as one who is greatly concerned over you, and those others at Laodiceia and Hierapolis.' (Colossians: 4, 12 and 13.)

A contemporary of Epaphras was Epictetus. Born a slave in Hierapolis Epictetus became a Stoic philosopher. Perhaps influenced by the early Christians he wrote about the perfect missionary whose bed is the ground, whose covering is the sky, and who must love those who do him injury.

The apostle Philip is believed to have lived in Hierapolis and to have been martyred there. According to an ancient tradition he was nailed upside down to a tree and stoned to death in AD 80. The remains of a martyrion erected in his honour are on the side of a hill to the N of the city. (See below.) Another resident of Hierapolis was a disciple of St. John named Papias. He was the author of a work, now lost, called 'The Sayings of Jesus'.

Justinian (527–565), who appointed the celebrated Bishop John of Ephesus in 542 to stamp out paganism, gave Hierapolis the status of a metropolitan see. John's authority extended over the provinces of Caria, Asia, Phrygia and Lydia, so it is unlikely that he ignored Hierapolis. This city so full of reminders of the old gods almost certainly engaged his attention. With his assistant priests and deacons John laboured mightily for several years destroying temples and shrines, demolishing pagan altars and cutting down sacred groves. Then, having made 80,000 converts to Christianity, he erected 98 churches and 12 monasteries to serve their needs. (John of Ephesus, Vitae Sanctorum Orientalium, XL, XLIII, XLVII. Vide A.H.M. Jones 'The Later Roman Empire', vol. 2.)

Little is known about the history of Hierapolis during the middle and late Byzantine period. No doubt, like its neighbours, it suffered from the incursions first of the Arabs, then of the Turcoman and Selçuk raiders. Towards the end of the 12C the city passed permanently into Turkish hands. Shortly after that time, when the people of nearby Laodiceia moved to Denizli, it, too, was probably abandoned. The 18C traveller Richard Chandler (see above), one of the earliest

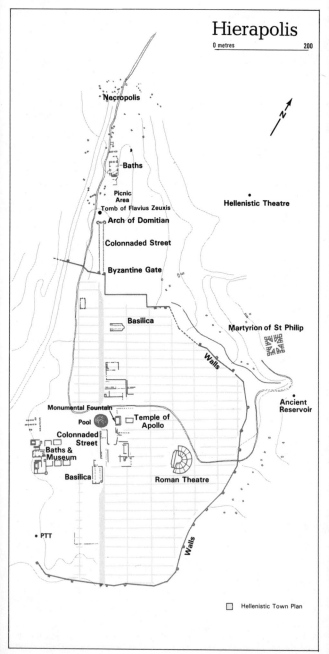

Hierapolis

0 metres   200

N

Necropolis

Baths

Picnic
Area
Tomb of Flavius Zeuxis
Arch of Domitian

Hellenistic Theatre

Colonnaded Street

Byzantine Gate

Basilica

Martyrion of St Philip

Walls

Monumental Fountain

Pool

Temple of
Apollo

Ancient
Reservoir

Colonnaded
Street

Baths &
Museum

Basilica

Roman Theatre

PTT

Walls

☐ Hellenistic Town Plan

visitors from W Europe, found only a small Turcoman village at the foot of the cliff. The first scientific examination of the site was made by a German team at the end of the 19C. Italian archaeologists, who began to work in Hierapolis in 1957, continue with their labours.

As the distances between the remains of some of the ancient structures is fairly considerable and a certain amount of gentle climbing is necessary, it is advisable to allow about four hours for the visit to Hierapolis. Take a picnic lunch, which may be enjoyed on the hillside above the city or in the small picnic area located in the copse near the remains of the *N baths*. All the ruins now visible are of buildings constructed during the Roman and Byzantine periods. Nothing from the Hellenistic era appears to have survived the earthquakes.

Behind the museum, which may be left to the end of the visit, are the not inconsiderable remains of a 6C *basilica*. This was probably the cathedral of Hierapolis and it may have been erected to mark the elevation of the see to metropolitan status. The vaulted structure has a large central nave, which ends in a semicircular apse and is flanked by two side aisles. There is a small chapel or baptistery at one end. To the E of the basilica is a section of the colonnaded *street*, which ran through the centre of the city roughly in a N–S direction. To the W of the basilica is the so-called *sacred pool*. Enclosed in the grounds of the Turizim Moteli, this has a Roman foundation and a number of submerged columns. According to Bean it is believed to have been called, appropriately, Thermodon.

On the right of the road leading to the theatre are the remains of the restored 4C AD *nymphaeum*. A large basin, enclosed by walls on three sides, was approached by steps from the street. Five niches, three on the back wall, one on each of the side walls, surmount the same number of semicircular recesses. Water was supplied to the basin from the central niche. The whole structure was elaborately ornamented.

The ruins of the SW facing *Temple of Apollo* lie slightly to the right of the nymphaeum. The Italian archaeologists who excavated this building are of the opinion that while the foundations were laid during the late Hellenistic period the existing remains of the upper structure are more recent. They believe them to date from the 3C AD. The building, which measures c 18m by 13.5m, rests on a shelf of natural rock at the rear. The front, which was supported by an artificial platform c 2m high, was approached by a broad staircase. Behind the pronaos, which was preceded by a row on unfluted columns, lay the cella. There was no opisthodomus.

During the excavation of the temple the work of the archaeologists was impeded considerably by quantities of noxious gas which seeped through from the foundations. It was found that this gas originated in the Plutonium which lies to the right of the temple and is joined to it by a section of pavement. It appears that the gas was also a problem in ancient times, as the builders of the temple have placed a number of vents in the substructure to allow it to escape. These are clearly visible on the left side of the platform.

According to Strabo a narrow entrance in the hillside provided access to the *Plutonium*, a sanctuary dedicated to Pluto, the god of the underworld. In front of the cleft was a paved area c 4.5 sq m, which was enclosed by a handrail. The poisonous vapour, believed to be carbon dioxide, was visible as a thick mist on the floor of the enclosure. Capable of killing animals as large and powerful as a bull, only the Galli, the priests of Cybele who voluntarily castrated

themselves in honour of the goddess, appeared to be unaffected by it.
Strabo is not sure whether their invulnerability was shared by 'all
who are maimed in this way' or whether it resulted from divine
intervention or some special physical attributes.

By the 2C AD the Plutonium appears to have become something of
a tourist attraction. When the historian Dio Cassius (fl. AD 180–229)
visited it, he discovered that an auditorium had been built over the
courtyard, which was filled with the deadly vapour. Having tested its
lethal properties on birds, he remarked also on the apparent immu-
nity enjoyed by eunuchs. In the 5C AD a doctor, Asclepiodotus, was
able to penetrate some distance into the chamber. Winding his cloak
over his face to conserve a supply of fresh air, he continued to the
point where his way was barred by a channel of deep water.

Today three shallow steps lead down into a small dark, paved
chamber c 2.75m². Waves of noxious vapour rise from a fast-running
stream half-hidden in a deep natural cutting c 1m wide at the back of
the chamber. The vapour acts like tear-gas, making the eyes water
and producing a state of temporary incapacity. For the protection of
visitors the entrance to the Plutonium is now closed by an iron grill
and the authorities have placed a notice there warning of the danger.
Fortunately, the disgusting practice mentioned by Bean, of testing
the gas' lethal properties on birds and small animals appears to have
ceased.

Behind the temple and slightly higher up the hillside are the well-
preserved remains of a late *theatre*. Though slightly larger than a
semicircle, it is not Greek, but dates from the 2C AD. In the reign of
Septimius Severus (193–211) it was restored. An inscription on the
stage-building records its dedication and there is a decorative frieze
showing the emperor, surrounded by his family, in procession with
the gods. Two vomitoria provided access to the cavea, which has a
diameter of 91m. There was a single diazoma. Note the loge for
distinguished spectators in the centre of the cavea.

The elaborately ornamented stage-building was c 3.70m high. A
number of the reliefs used to decorate it have been left in position by
the archaeologists, others are displayed in the museum. The frieze
from the hyposcaenium was recovered almost intact. This shows the
birth of Dionysus, the god of drama and of wine, his triumphal
progress through Asia in a car drawn by leopards, which is surrounded by capering ithyphallic satyrs, sileni, bacchantes, a lusty
Pan and a well-endowed Priapus. There are also portrayals of a
procession and sacrifice at the temple of Artemis and of the terrible
punishment inflicted on boastful Niobe and her children by Apollo
and his sister, Artemis.

A further inscription records that in the middle of the 4C the stage-
building was discovered to be in urgent need of repair. The necessary work was put in hand on the orders of Constantius (337–361)
who was resident in Hierapolis on 4 July 343. Alterations were also
made to the orchestra and the surrounding area at that time, so that it
could be filled with water for the staging of aquatic displays. No
doubt the re-enactment of naval battles, that popular spectacle of the
4C and 5C, took place there frequently.

After visiting the theatre, return to the road and continue up the
hill for c 250m. An unmarked turning on the left leads, by way of a
rough track across the mountainside, first to a large *water-storage*
tank and then to the *Martyrion of the Apostle Philip*. The martyrion,
which has been excavated and restored by the Italian archaeologists,
dates from the beginning of the 5C. Approached from the SE by a

broad flight of steps, it is a square building with nine small rooms on each outer face. These in turn enclose a central area made up of six rectangular rooms, formed by two crosses placed at an angle to each other, outside a large octagonal chamber. Openings in the centre of the four sides of the building lead directly to the octagon which contained a synthronon. As no trace of an altar or of a tomb has been found in the martyrion, it is believed to have been used for processions and the preaching of panegyrics on the saint's day. The hole in the floor of the synthronon probably marks the position of a lectern. Note the crosses over the arches in the octagon. The small rooms on the outside of the building may have been used to house pilgrims.

From the martyrion an easy scramble along the hillside in a NW direction for c 150m will take you to the site of a *theatre* which is believed to date from the Hellenistic period. This route passes a number of tombs and sarcophagi, all of which have been robbed. Only the outline of the cavea and a few rows of seats remain to mark the position of the theatre. From the upper level of the cavea there is a splendid view over the whole site. The buildings on the plain immediately below the theatre date from the Byzantine period.

Descending from the theatre, a short walk brings you to the grove where the *picnic area* is sited. This has rustic tables, seats and barbecue pits. The enormous arches on the right-hand side of the road belong to the *NW baths* which were erected towards the end of the 2C or the beginning of the 3C. This complex was converted into a church in the 5C.

Roman tomb at Hierapolis.

During the Hellenistic and Roman periods burials were not usually permitted within the city boundaries. At Hierapolis a number of graves have been found outside the Byzantine walls on the SE side, but the city's *main necropolis* was located a short distance beyond the NW baths. Perhaps the largest cemetery in Asia Minor, it contains tombs dating from the Hellenistic era to the early Christian period. For a distance of c 2km they stretch on both sides of the road—sarcophagi, in groups or singly, each resting on a low base; house and temple-tombs elaborately ornamented; and circular tumuli surmounted by phallic symbols. The tumuli are not unlike those found in some cemeteries in Etruria.

Many of the tombs bear inscriptions and more than 300 of these have been transcribed and published. In addition to information about the deceased, some of the epitaphs prescribe measures to be taken against overcrowding in the cemetery and the protection of graves from desecration or damage. Most content themselves by setting out the fines to be paid by a transgressor, but one quoted by Bean invoked a comprehensive curse against the offender. Having expressed the wish that his life should be without joy or children, it continues 'may he find no land to tread nor sea to sail, but childless and destitute, crippled by every form of affliction let him perish, and after death may he meet the wrath and vengeance of the gods below. And the same curses on those who fail to prosecute him'.

At Hierapolis the tombs were surrounded by gardens which were maintained by guilds or trusts established specifically for this purpose. These organisations were also charged with the duty of placing wreaths on the tombs on those days each year which had been nominated by the deceased or his family.

A number of the larger monuments incorporated exedrae. These permitted the citizens of Hierapolis to enjoy the melancholy pleasure of meditating on the transient nature of human life and earthly happiness and to contemplate the imminent approach of their own inevitable dissolution, while seated in beautiful surroundings and in close proximity to the bones of their ancestors.

A *triple arch* marks the N end of the great colonnaded street which bisected the centre of Hierapolis. Constructed of the local travertine and flanked by two round towers, this was dedicated, c AD 83, to Domitian (81–96) by Julius Frontius, proconsul of Asia. Like the better-preserved Hadrianic arch at Antalya, it had an upper storey, now lost. A short distance to the right of the Domitian arch is the fine *tomb* of a merchant of Hierapolis, Flavius Zeuxis. This building, which has been restored by the archaeologists, had a marble door carved to resemble wood, a Doric frieze ornamented with rosettes and pilasters at the corners. According to an inscription Flavius Zeuxis was a traveller of some note. He claimed to have made 72 journeys by sea to Italy.

The *colonnaded street*, once the commercial centre of the city, has long been abandoned to colonies of torpid, sun-worshipping lizards. On warm days they form decorative patterns on the confused mass of stone blocks and architectural fragments, which mark its position. The street is also the lair of youthful shepherds and village boys who, equipped with quantities of fake antiquities and fake coins, lie there in wait for gullible visitors.

From the arch of Domitian return by the modern road to the centre of Pamukkale. The *agora* of Hierapolis is believed to lie somewhere in this area, but, largely because of the difficulty in penetrating the thick layer of calcareous matter laid down by the springs, it has not been discovered.

Most of the objects found by the archaeologists in Hierapolis have been placed on display in the *museum*, which is housed in a 2C AD *bath* located to the right of the car-park. The complex, which has been extensively restored, had a large palaestra in addition to the usual caldarium, tepidarium, frigidarium, etc. There were also rooms reserved for the worship of the emperor and other religious and civic ceremonies.

The exhibits, which are well-arranged and clearly labelled, fill several of the large vaulted rooms in the baths complex. They include a number of fine funerary stelae, a terracotta coffin, a statue of Isis, heads and torsos of Marsyas and Eros, Asclepius, Dionysus and Tyche; sarcophagi, a wide variety of architectural fragments; and pins, lamps, medical instruments, jewellery, and coins from the Hellenistic, Roman and Byzantine periods.

From Pamukkale return to Yatağan via Denizli and Aydın and continue by Rte 15 to Muğla and Marmaris.

15 Yatağan to Marmaris

Total distance 75km. *Yatağan*—R400 27km **Muğla**—18km *Gökova İskele*—30km **Marmaris**—(17km Hisarönü)—(7km *Amos*)—(c 41km *Bozburun*).

From Yatağan road 400 continues in a SE direction through a rather dull and uninteresting stretch of countryside to 27km **Muğla** (31,364 inhab.). Travellers who wish to go direct to Marmaris or Fethiye may bypass Muğla by taking the right-hand fork immediately before the town.

Muğla, as well as being the provincial capital, is the most important marketing and trading centre in the region. It has several hotels two of which are licensed by the Ministry of Culture and Tourism. Full information about accommodation, including room prices, as well as restaurants and excursions to places of interest in the province may be obtained from the helpful staff of the *Tourism Information Office* in Er Beyazıt Mah., Marmaris Bulv., 24.

Muğla occupies the site of ancient MOBOLLA, which for some time during the 2C BC was under Rhodian domination. There are the sketchy remains of a number of buildings from this period on a hill behind the town. To the SW were the cities of PISYE (modern *Pisiköy*) and THERA. At Pisiköy there are traces of the acropolis and a few scattered stones from the ancient city. The remains of Thera are equally insignificant. In 333 BC it was occupied briefly by the Persian Orontobates, who succeeded the Hecatomnids as ruler of Caria.

After the first Turkish invaders had consolidated their hold on Caria in the 14C, Muğla was much favoured by the Menteşe emirs. A reminder of their presence in the town is provided by *Ulu Camii*, which was built by Ibrahim Bey in 1344. From the Ottoman period there are a number of interesting houses in the old quarter.

Once it has passed the farms and orchards that mark the S outskirts of the town, the road begins a steady climb through low hills covered with thorny scrub. This rather uninspiring landscape does little to prepare the traveller for the splendid sight which is presented to him without warning from the crest of the picturesquely named Çiçeklibeli Pass. Almost 800m below the 'flower-decked pass' is the fertile plain that lies at the head of Gökova Körfezi, the ancient Gulf of Ceramus. As the road descends in a series of spectacular curves there are tantalising glimpses of the glittering waters of the gulf with its many islands and sheltered bays. To the S an avenue of

eucalyptus trees marks the turning for Marmaris, while away to the E
is the great expanse of the lake at Köyceğiz. A new restaurant-café,
which has been built on a levelled terrace a little below the crest of
the hill, provides a safe viewpoint from which to admire this magnificent panorama.

From a very early period the cities of Rhodes possessed territory—the Rhodian
Peraea—in this part of Caria. After the formation of a unified Rhodian state in
408 BC it was ruled from the island and its people were granted Rhodian
citizenship. Confined at first to the Loryma peninsula to the SW of Marmaris, in
the course of time the Rhodian Peraea extended as far N as Stratoniceia and as
far E as Caunus. Later the Peraea was reduced considerably in size, but the
influence of Rhodes continued to be felt in SW Caria as late as the 2C AD.

The remains scattered along the hillside belong to ancient IDYMA.
One of the earliest references to this city dates from the beginning of
the 5C BC, when it was listed as a member of the Delian League. It
came under the rule of Rhodes sometime before 200 BC.
    Clearly visible from the road is a substantial section of the wall of
Idyma's acropolis. In the centre of the fortified area are the remains of
a building which contained several rooms. Lower down the hill are the
ruins of a medieval fortress and a number of rock-cut tombs. Two
of these, constructed in the form of Ionic temples, are believed to date
from the 4C BC.
    A turning to the right at the foot of the hill leads to the small village
of Gökova İskele, a pleasant stopping-place for a picnic or a meal in
one of the unpretentious restaurants that look out over the gulf.
    A short distance across the gulf from Gökova İskele is Şehir Ada,
where there are the ruins of CEDREAE, a city which derives its name
from the Greek word for cedar. Although a Carian foundation,
Cedreae was also a member of the Delian League. During the
Peloponnesian War this city paid dearly for its support of Athens.
Besieged and captured in 405 BC by the Spartans under Lysander, its
unfortunate inhabitants were sold as slaves. Later Cedreae came
under the domination of Rhodes.
    The island may be reached by boat from Gökova İskele or from the
villages of Gelibolu or Taşbükü on the opposite side of the gulf. In
addition to the remains of a substantial fortification, complete with
towers, there are traces of a Doric temple dedicated to Apollo and the
considerable ruins of a medium-size theatre. All are buried in dense
vegetation. According to inscriptions no less than three athletic
festivals were held in Cedreae. The city's necropolis, which was
located on the mainland, contains a number of sarcophagi and
vaulted tombs.
    At the bottom of the hill road 400 divides. One branch goes E along
the plain to Köyceğiz, Dalaman and Fethiye, the other S to Marmaris.
The road to 30km Marmaris starts as a splendid straight avenue, 2km
long, of tall, umbrageous eucalyptus trees. It then passes into the
pine woods, where the famous çam balı (pine honey) of Marmaris is
produced. Following a winding, convoluted course through shaded
gorges, it rises gradually to the Cetibeli pass, from where it begins its
long, slow descent from a height of 550m to sea-level at Marmaris.
    The pine-clad hills, which encircle **Marmaris** and its long fiord-like
harbour, make a refreshing change from the brown scrub-covered
surroundings of other resorts in the SE Mediterranean. Popular with
N Europeans, its streets are filled during the summer months with
throngs of holidaymakers.

In recent years the development of a flourishing yacht-marina has attracted the rich and famous, both Turkish and foreign, to Marmaris. Unfortunately, this popularity is reflected in the prices charged by many of Marmaris's hotels, restaurants and shops. Another regrettable development, also attributed to the town's over-exposure to tourism in recent years, is the uncouth behaviour of some of its young people. If unchecked, this could damage the reputation of a very attractive resort.

There is a wide range of accommodation, from luxurious hotels to simple pensions, in Marmaris. However, this is taxed to the limit during the holiday season, when the town's normal population of 8000 is trebled or quadrupled by visitors. During the period from May to September it is advisable to make a reservation. Full information about accommodation, including room-prices, may be obtained from the *Tourism Information Office* at İskele Meyd. 39.

Most of the large hotels, which cater almost exclusively for foreign visitors, are situated some distance from the centre of Marmaris. Some provide a free minibus service to and from the town, but in many cases it is necessary to use taxis. As parking is not permitted on the Kordon, a visitor staying in the town centre may have to leave his/her car some distance from the hotel. To avoid problems, it is advisable to enquire at the Tourism Information Office about transport and parking arrangements before making a hotel reservation. The office can also provide information about parking facilities—and parking restrictions—in the town.

The Tourism Office can also advise about dining out in Marmaris and about the entertainment available. It can put visitors in touch with firms offering yacht cruises and yacht-charters and with companies arranging day trips to *Datça, Cnidus* and the beaches on the *Loryma peninsula* and on the islands.

Tickets for the c 3 hour boat-journey to **Rhodes** (passport required) may be purchased from many of the travel agents in the town. As this service is quite popular, it is advisable to reserve places well in advance.

There are frequent bus services to İzmir (c 6 hours) and Fethiye (c 3 hours), and dolmuş services to *Muğla* and *Bodrum*. There are also *dolmuş services* to *Köyceğiz* and *Datça*.

Passengers arriving at Dalaman airport may be able to make the c 100km journey to Marmaris by one of the special minibuses which meet the charter flights. Otherwise they should travel by regular bus or dolmuş from Dalaman village.

History. Marmaris occupies the site of ancient PHYSCUS, a deme that was attached to the city of Lindus. Although information about the early history of Physcus is sparse, it is certain that it was under Rhodian rule by the latter part of the 4C BC.

In 1522 the forces of Süleyman the Magnificent were assembled in Marmaris for the successful assault which the sultan mounted against Rhodes. According to a contemporary account a Turkish fleet of 700 ships, manned by 40,000 sailors and carrying 20,000 auxiliaries, sailed from İstanbul to Marmaris. There it was joined by an army of 140,000, which, with Süleyman at its head, had marched overland from the capital. Further reinforcements of ships and men were provided by the buccaneer-adventurer Cortoğlu. The great harbour of Marmaris was able to accommodate this vast force without difficulty, as it was able later to shelter the fleet of Nelson. In 1798 the British ships sailed from here to Egypt, where at the battle of Aboukir they defeated the French, earning for their commander the title of Baron Nelson of the Nile.

The scanty remains of Physcus, first recorded by C.T. Newton in the mid 19C, may be seen on Asar Tepe, a hill c 1.5km to the N of Marmaris. Only the ruins of some *Classical* and *Hellenistic fortifications* are now visible. There are a few pieces of sculpture and some inscriptions in the playground of the high school in the town centre. These include a *relief of a youth with a horse*, a headless *marble lion* and a marble *female head* from the Roman period. The picturesque *castle* near the yacht-marina dates from c 1522, during the reign of Süleyman.

There are a number of archaeological sites on the *Loryma peninsula* to the S of Marmaris. Because of their attractive locations these sites, although of only minor importance, attract large numbers of visitors. Many may be reached by roads of variable quality. However, it is more pleasant and a good deal less tiring to visit them during the course of a leisurely boat-trip along the coast of the peninsula. Allow at least a day for this journey, so that there is time for a bathe and a picnic meal at one of the many fine beaches en route. Arrangements for boat-trips around Marmaris, which are very reasonably priced, may be made either through one of the many travel agencies in the town or directly with the boatmen concerned.

Near the mouth of the great harbour of Marmaris, about one hour's boat-journey from the town or 7km by road is the site AMOS. Here there are the remains of a *Hellenistic wall*, which is 3.5m high in places. Note the towers and gate on the N side. There are the foundations of a small *temple in antis* and of a moderately-well preserved *theatre*. Sections of the seating and parts of the supporting walls of the cavea remain standing. There are also traces of the stage-building. The principal deity of Amos was Apollo Samnaios.

The ancient city of LORYMA, which is located at the tip of the peninsula, may only be reached by boat. On a slender promontory, which dominates the sheltered harbour of Bozukkale, there are the ruins of an impressive elongated *fort*. An ashlar wall 2.5m wide, which was strengthened by nine towers on the long side walls and one at each of the narrow ends, enclosed an area measuring c 320m by 27.5m. Zeus Atabyrius, a Rhodian deity, was worshipped in Loryma.

The harbour of Loryma provided a sheltered base for the Athenian fleet during the Peloponnesian War. Conon, the Athenian commander, spent some time there before the sea-battle near Cnidus in 394 BC (see below), which effectively ended Spartan influence in this part of Caria. Almost a century later, when the Diadochi disputed control of Alexander's empire, Loryma was used by Demetrius, the son of Antigonus the One-eyed, to assemble part of the force, which he employed against Rhodes, the ally of Ptolemy. Despite the use of 40,000 soldiers, 200 warships, 170 transports, 30,000 labourers and an array of catapults and siege-engines, Demetrius was unable to capture the city. After a year's siege he was forced reluctantly to agree terms with the Rhodians and withdraw his army.

After passing the strait between the Greek island of *Syme* and the mainland, continue to *Bozburun*, which is sited at the head of a deep, sheltered inlet. There is also a rough track to c 41km Bozburun, via Amos, from Marmaris. Here near the village of *Saranda* (ancient deme of Thyssanus) a number of inscriptions referring to rites connected with the worship of Zeus and Hera have been found.

Further to the N at the end of the Hisarönü Körfezi, near the village of *Hisarönü*, is the site of BYBASSUS. This may also be reached by a track which diverts to the left from the Marmaris to Datça road c 17km from Marmaris. Apart from traces of Hellenistic walls on the side of the acropolis, little remains of the ancient settlement. The fort on the top dates from the Middle Ages.

Bean reports the discovery of a shrine on the ridge of Evren Dağı,

274m above the plain to the S of Hisarönü, dedicated to a minor goddess called Hemithea. Traces of 4C BC Ionic temple with Doric accretions have been found there. Surrounded by a colonnade of 11 by 6 columns, this had a pronaos and cella only. Hemithea was a goddess of healing, frequently invoked in difficult cases of childbirth. For about two centuries a festival called the Castabeia was held at this site in her honour.

16 Marmaris to Cnidus

Total distance c 108km. **Marmaris**—c 70km *Datça*—(c 4.5km *Datça İskele*)—c 38km **Cnidus**.

A daily service by dolmuş and minibus links **Marmaris** to 70km Datça. As this is intended primarily for local people, is much used by them and has limited capacity, it is advisable to book seats in advance. Visitors who wish to continue to Cnidus may hire a taxi in the village or, if they arrive early enough, take one of the boats which operate during the holiday season from Datça İskele. Before going on to Cnidus those who are not staying overnight in Datça are advised to check on the departure time of the last service back to Marmaris, as this sometimes leaves in the early afternoon.

Car-drivers are advised that the journey from Marmaris to Datça requires both a clear head and a steady hand on the wheel. The road is narrow and has many curves. There are unfenced, vertiginous drops at frequent intervals which need to be negotiated with care. It is recommended that those unfamiliar with this route should not use it in darkness. After Datça the road deteriorates dramatically; the rough track to Cnidus is suitable for four-wheel-drive vehicles only.

Shortly after leaving Marmaris (see Rte 15) the road enters the Reşadiye peninsula at its narrowest point near the little village of *Bencik*. Only c 800m wide, and no more than 15m high, the peninsula is known in Turkish as Balıkaşıran, 'the place where the fish jump over'. Historians believe that it was here the inhabitants of Cnidus, faced with the threat of a Persian invasion in the middle of the 6C BC, tried to separate the peninsula from the mainland by cutting a channel through the isthmus. (See below.)

From Bencik the road follows a tortuous course through pine woods, now clinging to the high, steep sides of the peninsula's mountainous backbone, now descending without warning to the sea. Before reaching Datça it passes through a number of isolated forest-clearings where stacks of timber and the neat houses of the foresters are the only proof of the presence of man in this wild and beautiful stretch of country.

During recent years the picturesque village of **Datça** has begun to attract an increasing number of visitors, drawn by its quiet, relaxed atmosphere, the product of an isolated situation. This is in pleasant contrast to the frenetic activity that characterises Marmaris and Bodrum, particularly during the holiday months. *Datça İskele* (c 4.5km to the S), the village's harbour, is also becoming a popular port-of-call for yachts cruising in the waters of SW Turkey.

The village has three hotels and a holiday complex licensed by the Ministry of Culture and Tourism. In addition, rooms may sometimes be obtained in private houses. However, there is a great demand for accommodation in Datça during the holiday season. To avoid disappointment reservations should be made as far in advance as possible. There is no accommodation at Cnidus.

Undoubtedly the most pleasant way to visit Datça and Cnidus is to take one of the boats which operate each day from Marmaris during the summer months. Apart from the enjoyment offered by a leisurely cruise along the very beautiful coastline of the Reşadiye peninsula, these mini-voyages avoid a difficult road-journey, give more time to examine the site at Cnidus and offer the possibility of a stop for a swim and picnic at one of the many excellent beaches, which are passed en route. Reservations may be made through a travel agency in Marmaris or with one of the many boat-operators on the Kordon.

During the season there is also a boat-service between Bodrum and Cnidus. The voyage can take between three and five hours—it depends on the weather and the size of the boat. If the meltem, the NW wind, is blowing, this sea-crossing may prove too uncomfortable for all but the most hardened sailors.

Visitors who have not brought a picnic may lunch well at one of several restaurants in Datça or at the site of ancient Cnidus. In both places the fish dishes are particularly good.

History. According to one ancient account **CNIDUS** was founded by Dorians from the Peloponnese in the early part of the first millennium BC, shortly after the end of the Trojan War. However, another chronicler states that a group of colonists from Argos led by Triopas, a hero of uncertain lineage, formed the nucleus of the first settlement. Triopas is commemorated in the name of a shrine dedicated to Apollo, which historians believe was sited in Cnidian territory near Palamut Bükü, a bay between Datça and the promontory of Deveboynu. Most authorities now accept that the original site of Cnidus was in the neighbourhood of the modern village of Datça. (See below.)

Largely because the rough terrain of the peninsula made communication with the mainland difficult, Cnidian expansion was by sea. By the mid 6C BC the city had set up a number of colonies—first on the N coast of Sicily then on the nearby island of Lipari. It was also an active participant in the affairs of the Greek trading post which had been established in Egypt in the 7C BC. This was located at Naucratis near the mouth of the Nile. The success of the colonisation and commercial enterprises undertaken by Cnidus may be gauged by the splendid offerings which the city was able to deposit in its treasury at Delphi.

Following their victory over the Lydians in 546 BC the Persians attacked and occupied, one by one, the Greek cities on the Aegean mainland. In a desperate attempt to keep the invaders from their doors, the Cnidians tried to isolate their peninsula from the mainland by cutting a deep channel at its narrowest point. This was near the village of Bencik. (See above.) Unfortunately, many of those engaged in this desperate project were seriously injured on the face or in the eyes by flying splinters of rock. Dismayed by these unlucky portents the Cnidians sought the advice of the oracle of Delphi. The reply they received can hardly have been very welcome. The god told them to abandon their plan, adding that if Zeus had wanted to make their land an island, he would have done so. The Cnidians accepted the advice and surrendered their city to the Persian general Harpagus.

After the invasions of Greece by Darius and Xerxes had been defeated at the battles of Marathon, Salamis and Plataea, Athens created the Delian League c 478 BC to prevent the Persians from re-establishing their hold on the Aegean coast. Most of the Greek cities and towns on the Asian mainland were enrolled in the League and were obliged to make an annual contribution to its funds. Cnidus was assessed for a sum which varied between two and five talents. The Athenian admiral Cimon based his fleet of 200 ships at Cnidus in 468 BC. From here his forces went on to effect a decisive defeat on the Persians at the battle of Eurymedon c 467. (See below.) In 412 BC the city transferred its allegiance briefly to Sparta. However, after the victory of the Athenian Conon at a naval battle near Cnidus in 394 BC put an end to Spartan influence in the area, the city returned to the Athenian fold. Following the signing of the King's Peace in 386 BC, Cnidus came once more under Persian rule. Liberated by Alexander the Great in 334 BC, like its neighbours its possession was disputed by the Diadochi after his death.

About 360 BC the Cnidians moved their city from near Datça to Tekir at the tip of the peninsula. This apparently inexplicable change of location from a relatively fertile stretch of land to the barren and almost waterless area at Cape Crio, the modern Deveboynu, was made for sound commercial reasons. When the meltem, the strong NW wind, blows, ships sailing from the S are unable to round the cape. Obliged to shelter for days at a time in the fine new harbour, which the Cnidians constructed at the cape, the ships and their crews contributed substantially to the city's revenues.

By the end of the 4C BC Cnidus, like its neighbour Cos, had established a famous medical school. This produced a number of well-known practicioners, whose care was not limited to their fellow citizens. They travelled widely. Ctesias (fl. early 4C), one of a family of Cnidian doctors, earned the gratitude of Artaxerxes II, when he cured the Great King of a severe battle-wound. While at the royal court he collected information for the 'Persika', his entertaining, if somewhat inaccurate, 23-volume history of Persia.

Eudoxus of Cnidus (408–335 BC) was a philosopher, astronomer and mathematician. Some of his work on the doubling of the cube, the volume of spheres, and conic sections was incorporated in Euclid's 'Elements'. Credited with the discovery of the star Canopus, Eudoxus formulated a number of theories to explain the movement of the stars and the planets.

About 279 BC Sostratus of Cnidus designed and constructed the Pharos, the great lighthouse of Alexandria. One of the Seven Wonders of the Ancient World, the Pharos was commissioned by Ptolemy I Soter and completed during the reign of his son Ptolemy II Philadelphus (282–246 BC).

When Lieutenant Spratt visited Datça in the middle of the 19C, he commented on the many fine olive groves and fruit orchards in the fertile area around the village. To some extent these trees represented a continuing tradition, as in ancient times Cnidus was well-known as the source of a number of gourmet products. Its vinegar was comparable to the best produced in Egypt and it was renowned for a type of cabbage known as 'briny'. Best of all was Cnidian wine, which was believed to improve the blood and ease the movement of the bowels. Even when drunk in immoderate quantities it produced no ill effects. On the contrary it soothed an upset digestion.

Down to the middle of the 2C BC, while Cnidus was under the rule of Rhodes, its affairs continued to prosper. Thereafter the city's fortunes entered a downward spiral, though it managed to retain some of its importance. During the imperial period Cnidus was declared a 'free' city and after the adoption of Christianity it became an episcopal see.

Not much is known about the last days of Cnidus. Its exposed position must have made it very vulnerable to attacks from the sea. At first the raiders were common pirates in search of booty. Later came the Arab corsairs, who terrorised the coastal cities of the E Mediterranean from the 7C onwards and caused many to be abandoned. Sometime in the late Byzantine era the last inhabitants of Cnidus moved away and the city was abandoned to the creatures of the wild, its existence largely forgotten.

One of the first travellers from W Europe to visit Cnidus was James Caulfeild, fourth Viscount Charlemont. To remove him for a time from the perils and pleasures of mid-18C Dublin's dissolute society, this rich and handsome youth was despatched by his mother on a grand tour of Greece and Turkey. On Sunday 9 November 1749 Charlemont's ship, like many before it, was delayed by contrary winds near Cape Crio. Remembering that here lay the 'favoured seat of that universally adored divinity',

> Quae Cnidon
> Fulgentesque tenet Cycladas et Paphon
> Junctis visit oloribus.

('Who holds Cnidos and the gleaming Cyclades, and visits Paphos with yoked swans.' Horace. Odes. 3,18, 13-15)', Charlemont had himself rowed ashore to the site of ancient Cnidus.

The young man was greatly impressed by the ruins of the city, particularly by the fine theatre of white marble. He noted in his diary that the seats were 'hollowed in, or shaped into a concave form, for the greater convenience of sitting'. Higher up the hill, at the ruins of a magnificent temple of Parian marble, he speculated that this might be the building which had housed Praxitele's masterpiece, the famous nude statue of Venus. (See below.)

Not only was the city favourably placed for trade, but Charlemont thought its position must 'have greatly contributed to the delight, as it certainly did to the wealth of the inhabitants, who in their parties of pleasure could every day vary their visits to innumerable great and polished nations'. Venus, he concluded, could 'not have chosen any habitation more worthy of Loves and Graces'.

The next visitor to Cnidus, a little more than a half-century later, was also an Irishman, Captain Beaufort, later Admiral Sir Francis Beaufort best known for his invention of the Beaufort Scale. While conducting a survey of the S Turkish coast for the Admiralty during the years 1811 and 1812, Beaufort landed briefly on Cape Crio. In 'Karamania' he provides an interesting description of Cnidus as it was at that time. 'On each side of the isthmus, there is an artificial harbour; the small one has a narrow entrance between high piers, and was evidently the closed basin for triremes, which he [Strabo] mentions. The southern and largest port is formed by two transverse moles; these noble works were carried into the sea at the depth of nearly a hundred feet; one of them is almost perfect, the other, which is more exposed to the southwest swell, can only be seen under water.

Few places bear more incontestable proofs of former magnificence, and still fewer of the ruffian industry of their destroyers. The whole area of the city is one promiscuous mass of ruins; among which may be traced streets and gateways, porticoes and theatres; but the shortness of our stay left no time to examine them in detail, being chiefly employed in making a sketch of the two harbours and the adjacent coast.'

One of Beaufort's sketch plans of Cnidus shows the location of the city's two theatres and of the moles in the S harbour. The remains of both moles now lie under the clear waters of the bay, where they constitute a dangerous obstacle which must be negotiated carefully by modern vessels.

William Gell visited Cnidus on behalf of the Society of Dilettanti in 1812. An account of his travels and discoveries is contained in 'Ionian Antiquities' (Vol. I 1821, Vol. II 1840). In 1857 Charles T. Newton conducted some excavations at Cnidus. The fine statue of Demeter and the colossal marble lion, which he discovered in the city, are now displayed in the British Museum. The exploration of Cnidus has been continued in this century by American archaeologists from Long Island University under the direction of Miss Iris Love. They began a systematic examination of the site in 1967.

It is clear that the old city of Cnidus near Datça was not abandoned when the bulk of the population moved to the new settlement at the tip of Cape Crio. However, apart from the ruins of its fortifications, little remains of the earlier foundation. The city's *acropolis* was sited on a promontory c 1.5km from Datça İskele. No buildings remain standing inside the walls, but evidence of occupation over a long period is provided by the large quantity of pottery sherds recovered by the archaeologists. These date from the 7–2C BC. It would seem that at some point the old city of Cnidus was renamed Stadia. This usage continued during the Byzantine period and is echoed in the name of the modern village of Datça.

A road linked Stadia to Triopium where the members of the Dorian Hexapolis (see above) held a festival in honour of Apollo. In addition to the usual athletic and musical competitions horse-races also formed part of the celebrations. After Agasicles, a competitor from Halicarnassus, broke with tradition by keeping his prize, a bronze tripod, instead of dedicating it to Apollo and leaving it in the sanctuary of the god, his city was expelled from the league. That left Cnidus as the only mainland member of the renamed Dorian Pentapolis. The site of Triopium is believed to be near the village of Kumyer, which lies behind behind Palamut Bay.

New Cnidus fell into two well-defined sections, one on the mainland, the other on the island to the S. Most of the public buildings were located on the mainland, while private houses occupied the greater part of the terraces on the island. Cnidus was laid out on the gridiron plan, popularised by Hippodamus of Miletus. This had streets crossing at right-angles. In many places the gradient was so steep that, as in Priene, flights of steps had to be used. The Cnidians constructed an artificial causeway, pierced by a channel, between the island and the mainland. This was flanked by the naval harbour, Strabo's 'harbour of the triremes' on the N, and by the larger commercial harbour on the S. It was in the S harbour that vessels waited for the fair wind which would allow them to continue their voyages northwards.

During the course of centuries the channel in the causeway became filled with silt, so creating the narrow isthmus, which now joins the former island firmly to the mainland. At present parts of the area to the S of the isthmus are closed to members of the public for security reasons.

To the W of the city wall, not far from the modern lighthouse, there is a fine *Roman tomb*. Entrance to the burial chamber is through a vestibule. Note the fine black and white mosaic on the floor. In the chamber, which has an apse at the rear and niches in the side walls, archaeologists found the remains of three sarcophagi.

There are the ruins of a number of private houses on the island terraces which faced the commercial harbour and the mainland. Near the S mole are the remains of an ancient *lighthouse*.

Visible on the isthmus are traces of the ancient *bridge abutment*. The agora of Cnidus was located at the the foot of the hill to the N of the harbour of the triremes. During the Byzantine period two large churches were built here.

It is a stiff climb up the steep hillside to the N of the harbour of the triremes to the site of the 4C BC *Temple of Aphrodite Euploia*, Aphrodite of the fair voyages. This was identified partly from the descriptions in ancient writers and partly from the discovery of a large quantity of erotic and pornographic pottery in the area around the ruins. A circular structure surrounded by 18 Doric columns, which supported a cupola, it rested on a stepped base. The altar, on which sacrifices were made to the goddess, faced the temple's main entrance, which was located, in the customary position, on the E side of the building.

The temple contained a famous statue of Aphrodite by the Athenian sculptor Praxiteles (active c 370–330 BC). It is known that c 360 BC his studio contained two versions of the goddess. One, which was clothed, was purchased by the Coans, the other, which portrayed Aphrodite in naturalibus, was chosen by the citizens of Cnidus to be the principal ornament of their new city. Believed to be the first monumental free-standing statue of a woman, the Aphrodite of Cnidus became the standard against which all subsequent representations of feminine beauty were measured. Subjected to profound critical appreciation and prurient voyeurism in equal measure, it was, according to Pliny, one of the great tourist attractions of the ancient world. Many travelled to Cnidus from afar to see it. Some of these visitors, having seen it, wished to possess it. One, Nicomedes, king of Bithynia wanted the statue so badly that, in exchange, he offered to to pay all the city's outstanding debts.

The best surviving description of the temple and of the statue of Aphrodite Euploia is contained in a dialogue known as the Erotes or Love Affairs. Sometimes ascribed to the 2C AD satirist and philosopher, Lucian of Samosata (c AD 117–180), it was probably written by a later admirer and imitator of that author. The Pseudo-Lucian, as many contemporary and earlier aesthetes had done, came by ship to Cnidus to see Praxiteles' masterpiece. Before going to the temple he played the part of the diligent tourist. Accompanied by two friends, who were according to him skilled in the art of love, he visited the the principal sights of the city. Having sauntered through the portico of Sostratus, he examined the goods offered for sale and found 'no little amusement in the wanton products of the potters, for I remembered I was in Aphrodite's city'.

There follows an interesting account of how some worshippers paid their respects to Aphrodite. Approaching the temple from the E, they entered a garden, whose shaded alleys were lined with bay trees, planes, cypresses and sweet-smelling myrtle, a plant beloved of the goddess. They passed the entrances to secluded bowers closed by screens of ivy, that symbol of true love, and vines heavy with bunches of grapes. 'For Aphrodite is more delightful when accompanied by Dionysus and the gifts of each are sweeter if blended together.' Then, after they had offered sacrifice and admired the famous statue, they made their way to one of the quiet alcoves scattered throughout the garden there to ἀφροδισιαζω, i.e. to celebrate the rites of love.

According to Pliny the statue of Aphrodite was so placed that it could be examined from all sides. This is confirmed by the Pseudo-Lucian. Having inspected it with great care, he concluded that the back view was as beautiful as the front. Noticing a small dark patch on the inside of one thigh, he asked the temple guardian if this were not due to some flaw in the marble. It was, she told him, the result of an ancient scandalous occurrence. A young man became so infatuated with this representation of Aphrodite that he spent every day in the temple contemplating its beauty. Carried away by the strength of his unnatural love, he contrived one evening to secrete himself in the sanctuary and to spend the night there alone with the statue of the goddess. Next morning the result of his illicit passion was all too clearly visible. The youth, perhaps overcome by remorse for his sacrilegious act, jumped from a high cliff into the sea, but the stain remained as a permanent reminder of his sin.

The American archaeologists have discovered a plinth, which they believe supported the statue of Aphrodite Euploia. An imperfectly preserved inscription found nearby bears the letters PRAX ... and others, which have been teased out to spell out the name of the goddess. Of the statue itself no certain trace has been found. The cult of Aphrodite incurred the wrath of early Christian moralists like Clement of Alexandria, who railed against the licentiousness which surrounded it. As a result the temples of this goddess, born from the foam that sprang from the 'lecherous members' of Ouranos, as Clement described them, suffered greatly. It is unlikely that her shrine at Cnidus, with its garden of love and famous statue by Praxiteles, escaped the general orgy of destruction which followed the adoption of Christianity by the Roman Empire.

However, some idea of the power and beauty of the Aphrodite of Cnidus may be gained from the city's coins. In addition, a few copies or variants of Praxiteles' masterpiece, produced for the delectation of wealthy admirers, have survived. They may be found in Munich in the Glyptothek (the so-called Venus Pudica), in New York's Metropolitan Museum and in Rome in the Museo Vaticano and the Museo Capitolino.

To the E and S of the temple of Aphrodite are the substantial remains of a *monumental building*. So far it has not been possible to establish the purpose for which this was constructed. On a lower terrace a confused heap of architectural fragments marks the position of a small marble Hadrianic *temple*, which was recorded by members of the Society of Dilettanti. Seven steps on the E side of this Corinthian-style building led up to to the pronaos. Entrance was through a façade ornamented with four columns. The sides had six engaged half-columns, while a section of the pediment was decorated with a handsome relief of shields.

To the W are the foundations of a *temple*, which, according to an inscription, was dedicated to Apollo Karneios, a manifestation of that deity much honoured by the Spartans. Pausanias suggests that the punning epithet Karneios was derived from κράνειαι, the wild cherry trees sacred to Apollo which grew on Mt Ida near Troy and which were cut down to make the Wooden Horse. A festival, the Karneia, was established to propitiate the angry god. In this part of the city the archaeologists discovered an unusual *sun-dial*, which showed both the seasons as well as the hours.

To the S of the temple are the ruins of a massive *Doric stoa*, which was c 113m long and c 16m wide. Some authorities identify this with the so-called Pensilis Ambulatio, the famous hanging walk which Sostratus, who constructed the Pharos of Alexandria (see above), built for his native city.

Just to the N of the commercial harbour are the substantial remains of the *lower theatre* of Cnidus. Constructed during the Hellenistic period, it was modified later. The stage-building, including an elaborate scaenae frons, dates from the Roman era. The theatre, which had 35 rows of seats separated by two diazomata, had an estimated seating-capacity of 8000. Many of the seats are in good condition though the orchestra is largely covered with coarse herbage. Of the *odeum/bouleuterion* of Cnidus, which was located a short distance to the E of the theatre, little is visible today.

Visitors who have sufficient time and energy may like to climb the steep slope that rises from the bouleuterion to the *Shrine of Demeter and Kore*. There, under the lowering crags of the acropolis, volcanic action has created a smooth cliff, c 18m high and 98m long, in which three niches for statues or offerings were carved. Below the cliff is an artificial terrace 76m long and 46m wide supported on three sides by polygonal walls. The shrine, constructed c 330 BC through the generosity of a pious benefactor, was a comparatively small structure. It contained the cult statues of Demeter, Kore and a number of other deities associated with the growth and cultivation of corn.

The massive Demeter of Cnidus, now displayed in the British Museum, was found in the sanctuary towards the middle of the 19C by C.T. Newton and taken back to England by him. The head and body of this impressive work of art were carved from separate blocks of Parian marble. It is the product of an unknown Athenian sculptor who was active in the middle of the 4C BC.

A short distance to the E are the scant remains of a large *theatre*. In the early part of the 19C this was almost completely denuded of its stone which was sent to Egypt. There it was used to construct a residence for the upstart Albanian militia officer Mehmet Ali (1769–1849), who ruled that country from 1805 to 1848.

The best-preserved section of the *fortifications* of Cnidus is to be found on the E side of the acropolis. The city walls, which enclosed two-thirds of the island and an area c 1.6km by 800m on the mainland, were constructed of regular ashlar. Strengthened at intervals by towers, they had three gates, two on the N and one on the E side of the city.

About 5km to the S of the city on a cliff high above the sea was sited the so-called *lion monument* of Cnidus. Dated to the 2C or 3C BC, the monument was composed of a sandstone base 12m square, which was covered with marble and ornamented with Doric half-columns. This was surmounted by a stepped pyramid crowned with the marble statue of a recumbent lion. In the base was a circular chamber c 5m in diameter which was surrounded by 12 alcoves. In view of its size—it was 19m high—and prominent location, it is believed that the monument was a communal tomb erected to honour the dead of an important naval victory. The statue of the lion was found at the site by C.T. Newton and brought to England by him aboard HMS *Supply* in 1858. It is now exhibited in the British Museum, near the Demeter of Cnidus.

Some distance to the E of the city is the extensive *necropolis* of Cnidus. It contains a large number of tombs of many different kinds, some arranged singly, others in family groups.

17 Marmaris to Fethiye

Total distance 146km. **Marmaris**—62km *Köyceğiz*—14km *Akçakavak* (7km *Dalyan / Caunus*)—24km *Dalaman*—46km **Fethiye**.

There are frequent bus and dolmuş services from Marmaris to 62km *Köyceğiz*, a picturesque village located a short distance to the S of road 400. The buses to Fethiye and most of the local dolmuş services stop at the garage which is located in the village centre.

Travellers using their own transport should take road 400 N to the plain of Gökova. At the end of the avenue of eucalyptus trees, which leads to the road-junction, they should turn right and continue in an E direction towards Fethiye.

On the left are the craggy slopes of Boğa Dağ (Bull Mountain), which give way to the even more bleak and forbidding peaks of Ali Dağ at the approaches to Köyceğiz.

The turning on the right, which leads to the village, offers no hint of the splendour that lies at the end of the main street. There, just beyond a small, well-maintained public park stretches the great expanse of *Köyceğiz Gölü*. This enormous freshwater lake is particularly entrancing in the soft light of early evening.

Köyceğiz village, as yet relatively unknown, will be appreciated most by those travellers who subscribe to the philosophy of *dolce far niente*. The best time to visit is in late spring or early autumn. In those seasons a candle-lit dinner on the terrace of the well-run *Özay Oteli*, a few metres from the edge of the lake, is an experience to be savoured at the time, and remembered later with pleasure.

Full information about accommodation in Köyceğiz and nearby Dalyan may be obtained from the *Tourism Office* on the Kordon, Göl Park No. 1. There are two hotels in Köyceğiz, which are registered with the Ministry of Culture and Tourism. At present there are a few simple pensions at Dalyan, but there are plans to open a modern hotel there in the near future.

Although official campaigns have reduced the numbers of mosquitoes in the Köyceğiz area, they have not been eliminated completely. Visitors, sensitive to the bites of these and other insect pests, are advised to use one of the modern repellent creams. The hotels will supply, without charge, sprays and other devices which keep bedrooms free of mosquitoes and other insects during the night.

An interesting whole-day EXCURSION may be made from Köyceğiz to the site of ancient **CAUNUS**. Take a taxi or dolmuş to Dalyan, where you can lunch near the river, and continue by boat to Caunus. This excursion can be extended down the river to the sea.

During the holiday season there are boat-trips to both Dalyan and Caunus from Köyceğiz. Details of the cost and frequency of this service may be obtained from the Tourism Information Office.

Until such time as the new road to Dalyan has been completed, visitors using their own transport should take road 400 in the direction of Fethiye to a point just beyond the village of 14km *Akçakavak* (White Poplars). There, a signpost on the right marks the turning to 7km Dalyan. This minor road has a good surface, but is narrow and has many sharp bends. It carries a considerable amount of farm traffic and drivers should be prepared for frequent encounters with tractors and farm-machines as well as straying livestock.

Sleepy *Dalyan*, its name means 'Fish Trap', achieved a degree of international fame, when Turkish and foreign conservationists expressed anxiety about proposals which would have disturbed its unique environment and might have had an adverse effect on the breeding-ground of a species of Mediterranean turtle. The Turkish Government accepted the arguments of the naturalists and decided to permit limited development of the area only. Its ecosystem will not be disturbed.

Behind the village's somnolent main street the Dalyan river flows deep and fast between its reed-lined banks. Here the boats leave for their trips downstream to Caunus and beyond. Here, too, is an excellent small restaurant, the *Denizatı*, which offers good food and wine, coupled with friendly service, at very reasonable prices.

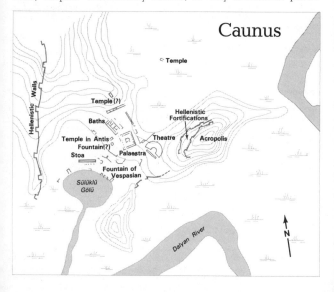

Fish-lovers will wish to sample the fresh bass or mullet, which are served grilled or fried.

A group of Carian temple-tombs across the river is clearly visible from the tables on the restaurant's outdoor terrace.

During the season boats take parties of up to 25 persons to Caunus at intervals during the day. The tariff for the trip is fixed by an association to which all the boat-operators belong. Out of season visitors may have to agree a price with the boatman of their choice. If a visit to the rock-tombs is included, allow at least three to four hours for the excursion, and a further two hours for journeys that continue as far as the sea.

History. Sherds found at Caunus suggest that a settlement of some kind existed there as early as the 9C BC. In a work of the 4C BC, the 'Periplus' (i.e. Account of a Sailing Voyage) attributed to the Pseudo-Scylax, it is stated that Caunus was a Carian foundation. There is no evidence that the Greeks ever established a settlement there. When the Carian cities were Hellenised, it became fashion-able for them to trace their establishment to a deity, demi-god or hero. Possibly to keep up with this trend and to explain the very un-Greek name of their city, which may be of Hittite or Lelegian origin, the Caunians 'discovered' an eponymous founder.

Caunus, according to Theocritus, Ovid and a number of other writers, was the son of Miletus and, consequently, the grandson of Apollo. One account states that he fled to Caria to escape from the incestuous advances of his twin sister Byblis. Another version suggests that Caunus was the guilty party and that he went into voluntary exile, as he was unable to control his unlawful desires. These stories may account for the expression 'a Caunian love', which was frequently used in antiquity to describe an unhappy romance.

Worship of Caunus was not limited to his own city. A trilingual inscription found at Xanthus in Lycia refers to the establishment there of a cult in honour of the 'King' (Basileus), a deified version of Caunus. There is some evidence that this deity continued to be honoured into Roman times.

As, according to the legendary accounts, Miletus had been expelled from Crete by Minos, the Caunians believed that their ancestors too had come from that island. This version of the city's early history is not accepted by Herodotus, who held that the Caunians were of Anatolian origin. However, both their customs and language marked them as being different from their nearest neighbours, the Carians. As Bean discovered, they adapted the Carian script, by the addition of a number of special characters, to meet the requirements of their own language. Neither Carian nor its Caunian variant has yet yielded its secrets to the translators.

When c 540 BC the Persian Harpagus marched into Caria and Lycia, Caunus and Xanthus were among the few cities to offer any resistance to the invaders. According to Herodotus, they shared a close relationship, a factor which may explain the presence in Xanthus of a shrine dedicated to the mythical founder of Caunus. (See above.)

Perhaps because of fear of Persian reprisals the Caunians did not at first join the revolt of the Ionian cities, which took place in 500 BC. After the defeat of the allies at the battle of Lade in 494 BC and later near the river Marsyas, Persian rule was re-established over the city. It did not last long. The expeditions of Darius and Xerxes against Athens and her allies came to grief at Marathon (490 BC), Salamis (480 BC) and Plataea (479 BC), and the Athenians formed a defensive organisation, the Delian League, in 478–477 BC to crush any further attempts at expansionism by the Persians. Caunus became a member of the League, its contribution being fixed at half a talent. This was later raised to ten talents. However, it is not certain that either sum was ever paid.

The victory of the Athenian admiral-general Cimon at the battle of the Eurymedon river near Aspendus c 467 BC provided a further check to the Persians. As a result a number of the cities of Pamphylia and Cilicia were persuaded to enrol in the Delian League. However, after the defeat of Athens in 404 BC at the end of the Peloponnesian War, the victors, the Spartans, proved to be inept rulers. Very quickly they lost control of the League and its members, so that soon Persian rule was re-established in the Ionian cities, a fact formally acknowledged by the King's Peace in 386 BC.

Caunus became part of the satrapy of Caria, which was governed by Hecatomnos and his successors. The Hecatomnid dynasty rapidly developed a considerable degree of independence from Persia, particularly under Mausolus, the son of Hecatomnos. He was a great admirer of Greek civilisation and culture and began an active campaign to Hellenise the territory under his control.

Evidence of his interest in Caunus is provided by the discovery of statue-bases bearing his and his father's name in the city. The long walls surrounding Caunus suggest that he had grandiose plans for its development.

The decisive victories of Alexander the Great over the Persians at the battles of Granicus in 334 BC and Issus in the following year heralded a period of comparative freedom for Caunus. As in the case of Caria, the city probably came under the rule of Ada, the last of Hecatomnids. This situation lasted until 323 BC, when Alexander's successors, the Diadochi, began a prolonged and unseemly struggle for possession of his empire. Caunus, like its neighbours, was caught up in the imbroglio. Antigonus, Ptolemy, Lysimachus and their descendants all ruled the city at different times.

Towards the beginning of the 2C BC Caunus was purchased from the Ptolemies by Rhodes for 200 talents. However, in 167 BC the Caunians succeeded in conjunction with their neighbours in throwing off the Rhodian yoke. Despite protests from Rhodes, Rome gave the city its freedom. This it retained until 129 BC, when it was incorporated in the newly-formed Roman province of Asia.

In 88 BC Caunus made a fateful choice. It supported Mithridates against Rome. As in Ephesus and a number of other cities in the province, there was a ruthless and bloody massacre of Roman citizens in Caunus. After the defeat of Mithridates, the Romans punished Caunus in 85 BC by returning it to Rhodian rule. With some interruptions this state of affairs continued well into the 1C AD.

Although Caunus appears to have been a wealthy city—it was famous for its exports of salt and slaves—it had few claims to fame and produced few citizens of note. Probably because it was reputed to be an unhealthy place, not many foreigners chose to live there. In addition, the dour, unattractive character attributed to its people by many of the ancient commentators can hardly have helped immigration.

In ancient times the unhealthy appearance of the Caunians was attributed in part to their addiction to fruit, which was believed by many physicians, including Galen, to be a dangerous food. However, there seems little doubt that malaria was the real cause of the city's health problems. The marshes, which extended around Caunus then, as now, provided an ideal breeding-ground for mosquitoes.

Among the many unkind jokes made about the health of Caunus and of its citizens, perhaps the best-known and most amusing is attributed to the 4C BC citharist and wit, Stratonicus. Noting the greenish cast of their complexions, he remarked that in Caunus he understood for the first time in his life Homer's statement: 'as are the leaves of the trees, so are the generations of men'. When the Caunians protested at his gibe, he replied tartly, 'How could I possibly call your city unhealthy, when every day dead men may be seen walking its streets!'

Though the site of Caunus was known from the middle of the 19C, it attracted few scholars until George Bean made a series of exploratory visits there between 1946 and 1952. Since 1967 Turkish archaeologists, under the direction of Professor Baki Öğün and Associate Professor Ümit Serdaroğlu, have conducted surveys and excavations of the site. During the same period the rock-tombs at Dalyan have been studied by Paavo Roos of the University of Lund.

The rock-tombs at Dalyan are not always included in the excursion to Caunus. Travellers wishing to see them should check with the boatman before embarking. An additional payment may have to be made. Allow c 30 minutes for the visit, which requires a crossing of the swift waters of the Dalyan river, followed by a scramble up the slippery mud-bank and rocky slope that lie below the cliff-face.

There are two kinds of rock-tombs at Dalyan—simple chambers hollowed from the cliff in the lower row and more elaborate temple-tombs higher up. Most are believed to have been constructed towards the middle of the 4C BC, a time when the Hecatomnid dynasty was conducting a vigorous campaign to Hellenise the satrapy of Caria. Some authorities see the use of Greek architectural forms in the service of the ancient, indigenous tradition of rock-burial as an interesting example of this tendency.

Most of the tombs have two or more Ionic columns *in antis*. Some are surrounded by a passageway, others have an empty space above the roof, which may be flat or barrel-vaulted. Inside there are usually three benches on which the bodies of the deceased were laid. Finds in the tombs have shown that they were used and reused down to the Roman period. All those excavated had suffered at some time from the hands of tomb-robbers. Many have been damaged by earthquakes or weathering. Others have been destroyed deliberately by human action e.g. to make lime. A number have been partially demolished by ignorant treasure-hunters, who believed, mistakenly, that they contained hidden riches. Today some of the tombs are used to shelter animals by the local farmers.

Note the large *unfinished tomb* in the upper row. The roof, pediment and frieze were completed, as were the tops of four capitals. Below the rock-surface was smoothed, but no further work was undertaken.

A short distance to the W of the principal group of rock-tombs are a number of Carian-style burials: the graves are cavities cut from the rock and covered with stone lids. Nearby are niches in which the mourners left offerings for the deceased.

From Dalyan the river swings around in a wide arc to the S before it turns again towards the site of Caunus. The boat, having passed through the modern fish-trap, which has replaced an older installation located near the village, enters a narrow channel. This is fringed by swaying banks of tall golden reeds, which reflect, distort and magnify the sound of the engine, turning it into a rhythmic, hypnotic beat.

From the landing-stage at Caunus a wooden causeway stretches across an area of marsh to firm ground. From there it is a short walk to the site. Today the city lies c 5km from the sea, separated from it by a vast expanse of fen, the result of centuries of activity by the Dalyan river.

The *acropolis* of Caunus was located to the SE of the city on a steep hill, which was once surrounded on three sides by the sea. The great harbour to the NE is now a marshy plain, while Sülüklü Gölü, the Lake of the Leeches, is believed to mark the site of the W harbour. According to Strabo, this could be closed in times of danger by a chain. The 152m-high acropolis-hill is crowned by the ruins of a *Hellenistic fortified area*, which is surrounded by a fine ashlar wall measuring 39m by 20m. The *lower fortifications* are medieval or later.

To the NW and N of the city is one of the best preserved *defensive walls* in Anatolia. Around 8m high and strengthened with towers, it resembles the defences of Iasus and Heracleia-under-Latmus. Enclosing a vast area, which never appears to have been used productively, it ends abruptly at a cliff overlooking the village of Dalyan. The N stretch is believed to have been constructed by Mausolus. The NW section is later, probably dating from the Hellenistic era.

Near Sülüklü Gölü are the remains of a 1C AD Roman *nymphaeum*. Sometimes called the 'fountain of Vespasian' because an inscribed slab bearing that emperor's name was found in the street nearby, the nymphaeum has been restored by Turkish archaeologists. On its S wall there is the text of an interesting decree on customs dues. To encourage foreign traders to make greater use of the port of Caunus a number of citizens donated 60,000 denarii to the city's treasury. Certain remissions of duty were offered, e.g. slaves, for which Caunus was famous, might be exported without the payment of tax.

To the N of the nymphaeum there was a two-storey, *Hellenistic stoa*, 94m long and 6.30m wide, which faced the harbour. This was ornamented with a large number of statues and furnished with exedrae. Among the statue-bases discovered there are two inscribed with the names of Mausolus and Hecatomnos.

On a raised terrace to the NE are the ruins of a mysterious *building*, which some authorities believe to have been a fountain, others a bathing pool. Dated to the late Hellenistic period, it was encircled—except on the E—by a colonnade of flat-fluted columns, which rested on a narrow stylobate. Entrance was on the E side by way of a three-stepped, semicircular exedra. Slots in the columns suggest that the space between them was closed by a grill. Inside the building a low plastered wall, surmounted by unfluted columns, surrounded a shallow pool, in the centre of which lay a circular, flat purple stone. The exact purpose of this structure continues to be the subject of speculation and discussion.

Behind the circular building are the remains of a small late Hellenistic *Doric-style temple in antis*. Traces of stucco were found by the Turkish archaeologists on the sandstone triglyphs and metopes of this building.

Higher up the slope are the substantial remains of a *Roman bath* with a large *palaestra* to the E. After the adoption of Christianity by the Caunians an imposing *church* with three aisles and an apse was erected in the centre of the palaestra. There are plans to restore the baths complex and use it to display finds from the site and house the archeaologists during the excavation season.

To the N are the ruins of a late *structure*. Sometimes described as a temple, Bean suggests that it may have been a library. The ridge near this building overlooks a large stretch of the Dalyan river and the marshy ground which today marks the site of the NE harbour.

Perhaps the most imposing ruin in Caunus is that of the **theatre**. Constructed in the Greek style, the cavea is substantially greater than a semicircle. It has a diameter of c 76m. Supported on the N side by substantial walls, on the S it rests against the hillside. The single diazoma, with 18 rows of seats below and 16 above, is divided by steps into nine cunei. Note the two arched entrances on the N side of the structure which, with two parodoi, provided access to the cavea. The stage-building measured c 38m by 8.5m. From the top row of seats there is a fine view W over the city towards Sülüklü Gölü.

Energetic visitors may like to take the steep and difficult path which leads upwards from the rear of the theatre to the acropolis. Apart from the medieval and Hellenistic fortifications, no traces of human occupation remain on the hill. However, the magnificent view from its 152m-high summit over the site of Caunus, the Dalyan river and the surrounding countryside is ample reward for the effort required by the climb.

From Caunus and Dalyan return to road 400 and continue in an E direction towards Fethiye. Just after *Ortaca* the road crosses the broad, gravel-strewn bed of the Dalaman Çayı, the ancient Indus. According to Pliny this river, which rises c 100km away in the hills of NW Lycia not far from the site of Cibyra, had more than 60 tributaries and was fed by many torrents.

A short distance from *Dalaman village* is the busy new airport, which has done much to open up SW Turkey to holidaymakers. During the season there are frequent direct services to Dalaman from Gatwick and from a number of European cities. As a result, resorts like Bodrum, Marmaris and Fethiye, as well as a number of the smaller centres on the Lycian coast, now attract visitors who were previously deterred by the long overland transfers required by flights which terminated at İstanbul or İzmir.

About 5km to the S of Dalaman, on the coast, are the remains of a medieval settlement identified by George Bean as PREPIA, a city mentioned in an Italian *portolano*. (This may have occupied the site of an earlier foundation named Pisilis.) In addition to the substantial ruins of a church, a reservoir and the extensive medieval fortifications there are traces of occupation from the Hellenistic and Roman periods, possibly from Pisilis. Nearby, on the island of *Baba Adası* is a pyramidal structure which is believed to have been a lighthouse or a beacon.

Between Dalaman and Fethiye there are a number of sites of minor interest. About 4km beyond the village on the right-hand side of the road are traces of a settlement which has been identified as that of ancient CALYNDA, at one time a place of some importance. A ship and crew from Calynda fought on the side of Xerxes at the battle of Salamis (480 BC). This had the ill-luck to be sunk with the loss of all hands by another vessel from the Persian fleet which was commanded by Artemisia, the ruler of Halicarnassus. Today, apart from the remains of some Hellenistic fortifications, there is little to be seen at the site.

Road 400 climbs steeply from the plain of Dalaman through the pine-clad hills that signal the approach of Rugged Lycia. From the heights of the Göçek pass the road descends in a series of sharp curves which provide occasional, tantalising glimpses of the island-studded Gulf of Fethiye. On the left, high above the road, there is a cluster of square tombs cut into the steep hillside. Not unlike those at Pinara (see Rte 18), they belonged to the ancient city of DAEDALA. A fortified acropolis, the broken walls of private houses, a number of rock-tombs some Lycian in style, and a number of sarcophagi may be reached with some difficulty and a considerable expenditure of energy. With the pigeon-hole tombs they are the only surviving traces of a settlement, which at one time formed part of the Rhodian Peraea and which, according to Strabo, marked the frontier between Caria and Lycia.

At Göçek, half-hidden in the pine woods, are a number of attractive camp-sites. They make an ideal base for excursions to the islands on the W side of the Gulf of Fethiye. On the largest island, *Tersane Adasi* (i.e. Dockyard Island), there are the ruins of an ancient look-out post and of an elaborately-decorated tomb.

On the mainland nearby a small fortified acropolis, a cistern, and some temple tombs are belived to belong to the city of CRYA, which was mentioned by Pliny and was shown on a 1C BC pilot's guide to the Mediterranean. Further to the S, near the tip of the peninsula, was LYDAE. According to Bean the ruins of this settlement, all of which date from the Roman and Byzantine periods, include two moderately-well preserved mausolea, a fort, and a quantity of architectural fragments.

From Göçek, road 400 follows the curve of the bay, the Glaucus Sinus of the ancients, to the pleasant holiday resort of **Fethiye**. This is the gateway to Lycia, land of a fiercely independent people and of a strikingly different civilisation.

18 Fethiye to Kaş

Total distance 109km. **Fethiye**—R30 (c 15km *Olü Deniz*)—(c 40km *Kaya*)—c 22km *Kemer*—(c 35km *Oenoanda*)—(c 4km *Termessus Minor*)—(c17km *Balbura*)—(c 8km *Bubon*)—(c 25km *Toriaeum*)—(c 12km *Cibyra*)—(c 7km **Tlos**)—(c 7km **Pinara**)—(c 10km **Sidyma**)—c 41km *Kınık*—(c 4km **Letoön**)—(c 0.5km **Xanthus**)—(c 6km **Patara**)—c 16km **Kalkan**—c 27km **Kaş.**

Fethiye is a pleasant town built around a large sheltered bay. In 1957 it was almost completely destroyed by an earthquake which devastated SW Turkey. Most of the buildings visible today have been erected since that date. Part of the reconstruction is a promenade along the sea front. This is flanked by gardens, where one can find a number of small restaurants and tea houses. Fethiye is a popular tourist resort and a good centre for visiting the many sites in W Lycia.

There is a wide range of accommodation available in and near the town and at (15km) Ölü Deniz. Full information about hotel and pension prices, restaurants, boat hire and excursions may be obtained from the *Tourist Office* in İskele Meyd., near the yacht harbour and the Dedeoğlu hotel.

Fethiye is blessed with a pleasant climate. It is seldom too warm in summer and its winters are mild and relatively dry. Like most places in this part of Turkey the heaviest rainfall occurs in January and February. There are good bathing beaches at *Çalışburnu*, *Belçelğiz* and at *Ölü Deniz*, where a small fee is sometimes charged.

There are frequent bus and dolmuş services from the *bus station* (Otogar) on eastern outskirts of Fethiye.

History. The early history of TELMESSUS, the ancient city which occupied the site of present-day Fethiye, is somewhat obscure. The presence of the double 's' in its name suggests that it was a pre-Greek foundation.

Legend states that Lycia was colonised by Sarpedon after his expulsion by his brother, Minos, from Crete, but it is likely that the earliest inhabitants were Anatolians, who later intermarried with Greek and Cretan colonists. The legend of its Cretan foundation is supported to some extent by the fact that in antiquity the bay of Fethiye was known as the bay of Glaucus (Glaucus Sinu) after the companion and friend of Sarpedon. Originally Telmessus was not considered to be part of Lycia. In a record dating from the 5C BC, which lists the cities paying tribute to the Delian League, Telmessus is shown separately from those in Lycia, and in the 4C BC Pericles of Limyra at the head of the forces of the Lycian League conducted a campaign against Telmessus and captured it. In 334 BC Alexander was well received by the Telmessians, although subsequently Nearchus the Cretan, who ruled on behalf of Alexander, was obliged to resort to a stratagem to recapture the city. He asked if he could leave some captured women singers and boys in Telmessus. The inhabitants agreed, unaware that the boys carried weapons, concealed in flute cases. Once inside the city these weapons were produced and the city was seized by their escort. After some time in the hands of the Ptolemies, Telmessus passed to the kings of Pergamum. Later it became part of the Roman province of Asia. In AD 451 Telmessus was represented at the Council of Chalcedon. During the following centuries it was pillaged by marauding Arabs and its importance decreased considerably. Under Byzantine rule it changed its name briefly to *Anastasiopolis* in honour of Anastasius II. In the 9C it became known as *Makri* and this name persisted until the 20C, when it acquired its present name, Fethiye.

Apart from its famous rock-tombs, little remains today of the ancient city. An 18C traveller mentions the existence of a large Roman theatre, and in the early part of the 19C Fellows and Spratt confirmed that this could still be seen on the W side of the town near the sea shore. By 1881 most of this building had been destroyed. Its stones were used for the construction of barracks in İstanbul. There appears to have been a smaller theatre on the W side of the acropolis.

Access to the *acropolis* is by a steep road which rises from the harbour area, near the yacht marina. This leads to a pleasant path

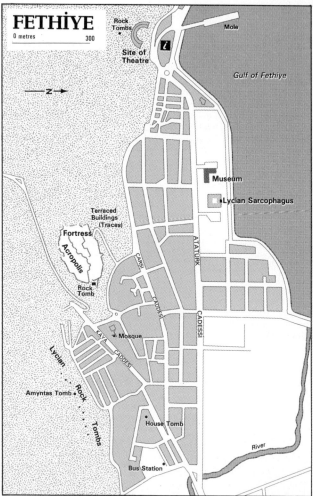

KEMER, KALKAN, KAŞ & KÖYCEĞİZ

which gives a splendid view of the city and bay. To get to the base of
the acropolis it is necessary to pass through the dusty streets of a
small village. From there it is a scramble by a rough track to the top.
The acropolis is crowned with the remains of a *medieval castle*,
believed to have been founded by the Knights of St. John at the
beginning of the 15C. On the E side of the acropolis there are two
small rock-tombs.

The most important remains of Telmessus are the rock-tombs sited
to the E of the town. The finest of these, the **Tomb of Amyntas** which
dates from the 4C BC, can be seen from most parts of Fethiye.
Forming part of a group of tombs cut into the rock-face above the
road to Kemer, it may be reached by an easy 20 minutes' walk from

Atatürk Cad., crossing over Çarşı Cad. and Kaya Cad. The tomb of Amyntas is one of three constructed in the form of an Ionic temple in antis. It has two Ionic columns framed by projecting pilasters or antae. Each pilaster is decorated with three rosettes. The pediment has three acroteria, two of which have been damaged. Below the pediment there is a dentil frieze. The left pilaster bears the inscription, 'Amyntou tou Ermagiou', Amyntas son of Hermagios. (Nothing is known about Amynthas.) Four steps lead up to the entrance to the chamber. Over the door Charles Texier, the 19C traveller who did so much to inform western Europe about the antiquities of Asia Minor, has left a record of his visit. Entrance to the tomb was effected originally by a sliding stone slab on the bottom right-hand side. This was broken by tomb robbers some time in antiquity. The chamber has three stone seats or benches, on which the dead were laid. To the left of the tomb of Amyntas there are more rock-tombs. Some of these have two or three storeys, others are just pigeon holes like those at Pinara. (See below.)

Fethiye has also some interesting examples of *Lycian sarcophagus tombs*. The finest of these is to be found near the sub-prefecture in Atatürk Cad. Sarcophagus tombs of this type were designed to reflect Lycian domestic architecture. Houses were generally constructed of wood, so the stone tombs have imitation morticed joints and beams, and are covered by pointed arches. This gives them the appearance of upturned boats with their ridged keels uppermost. The example near the sub-prefecture is elaborately decorated with reliefs of warriors.

Fethiye's *Museum*, off Atatürk Cad., which was closed for a number of years for rearrangement, opened again in April 1987. It contains stelae, capitals, vases and statuettes from the Lycian, Roman and Byzantine periods.

There are fairly frequent services from the dolmuş garage near Atatürk Cad. to (15km) *Ölü Deniz*. Taxis are available from several points in the town or may be hired through your hotel reception. Ölü Deniz, the 'Dead Sea' is a sheltered lagoon of great beauty. It has a fine beach for bathing and facilities for sailing, windsurfing, fishing, etc. Meals may be obtained from one of several simple restaurants. There is a motel and a number of camping sites not far from the beach. In recent years it has become a popular tourist destination.

On the nearby island of *Gemile* are the ruins of an ancient city and necropolis. A visit to the c 20km ghost town of *Kaya* may be made by taxi or hired car. Kaya had a Greek population of about 3000 until 1923, when there was a general exchange of Turks and Greeks and the town was virtually abandoned. Today the presence of the few Turkish families, who cultivate their gardens and graze their cattle there, tends only to emphasise the pervading atmosphere of melancholy.

NE of Fethiye there are four interesting sites—Oenoanda, Balbura, Bubon, and Cibyra—which are not often visited. They may be reached from Fethiye by taking road 400 to (c 22km) *Kemer* and by then turning N on the old road to *Korkuteli*. It is advisable to use private transport as minibus and dolmuş services to the villages near the sites tend to operate at irregular intervals and at inconvenient times.

From Kemer continue for c 35km to the village of *İncealiler*. From there a track leads to the site of OENOANDA. The city has not been excavated, but during recent years it has been surveyed by British archaeologists.

History. Very little is known about the history of Oenoanda. A long inscription dated to the 2C BC, summarising the Epicurean philosophy, has been found there. This covers a wide range of subjects—chance, the nature of dreams, the creation of the world. It was the gift of a citizen, named Diogenes, who, in his old age, presented this wayside pulpit to the city 'for the salvation of men, present and future'. Of the complete text, estimated to have been 100m long, only a part has been found so far. The search for the remainder is unlikely to be easy, as in later times the inscription was broken up and parts were used to strengthen the city walls. Remains of other Hellenistic structures have been found in Oenoanda and it is known to have been a member of a tetrapolis, headed by its neighbour, Cibyra, in the 2C BC. It was probably influenced by the Lycian cities to the S and even by faraway Termessus, which founded a colony nearby. The city flourished under the Romans, reaching its period of greatest affluence during the 2C and 3C, when its architecture showed signs of being affected by the style of Aphrodisias. Towards the end of the 3C it suffered a temporary decline, but its fortunes revived again under the Byzantines.

Sited on a hill, which slopes to the S, the principal buildings were enclosed by walls. These include a number of unidentified structures and the agora. To the N, on the highest point, is the *theatre*. This had a diameter of c 30.5m, no diazoma and an unusually large orchestra. Portions of the proscenium, which was described by Lieutenant Spratt as being 'very perfect', may still be seen under the debris. The S part of the city wall is Hellenistic. This still stands to a height of c 10m. Two towers and two postern gates, one of which is ruined, remain. The section on the NW is, apart from a short stretch which may be Hellenistic, of reused material and dates from much later. A small building N of the walls has been identified as a *temple*. On the NE of the city outside the line of the existing walls, a large flat area may have been the site of Diogenes' inscription. Blocks from this have been found here, inside, outside and built into the wall.

W of the site there are several *tombs* of the Carian type. In these the sarcophagus was cut from in the rock and covered with a separate lid. There are also a number of free-standing sarcophagi, surmounted by the carving of a lion, and the ruins of a particularly fine 2C marble tomb on the S slope of the hill to the W of the aqueduct. This carries a long inscription which traces the genealogy of a local family back to the legendary founder of Cibyra, the Spartan, Cleander.

N of Oenoanda, just after the point where the road crosses the Eşen Çayı, the ancient river Xanthus, is the site of TERMESSUS MINOR. The settlement, which is divided by the modern road, was built on two low mounds. A colony of Termessus, which lies c 80km to the E, it was founded in the 3C BC on a site that could not have been defended. It must, therefore, have depended heavily on the good-will of Oenoanda and, indeed, it came under the control of that city in Roman times.

About 12km N of Termessus Minor the road divides. To get to Balbura, Bubon and Cibyra take the left-hand fork in the direction of Gölhisar. About 5km after the junction, a side road to the right leads to the site of BALBURA. Apart from the fact that it belonged to the tetrapolis, nothing is known about the history of this city. No excavations have been made there.

Set in a valley watered by a tributary of the Eşen Çayı, the ruins are dominated by an *acropolis* built on a fortified hill, whose summit is c 1500m above sea level. Below the acropolis, on the SW slope, there is an unusual small *theatre*, most of whose cavea is taken up with a large mass of unworked rock. About 500m to the S, on the opposite hillside, there is a 48m long, narrow platform resting on arches. A few rudimentary seats on one side suggest that it may have been used not for theatrical performances but for public meetings. In the city only the agora, the principal street and a temple dedicated to Nemesis have been identified with certainty.

On returning to the main road continue for c 8km to the village of *Altınyayla*, where the ruins of BUBON are to be found. A member of the tetrapolis, Bubon, under its leader Moagetes, is known to have invaded the territory of its S neighbour, Araxa, in the 2C BC. Araxa appealed to Cibyra and managed to obtain a satisfactory settlement. However, sometime later Bubon, under its leader Moagetes, raided Araxa again and this time the Araxians appealed to the Lycian League for help. Although neither city belonged to the league, they appear to have accepted its arbitration. Diodorus Siculus mentions a ruler of Bubon c 145 BC named Molkestes. He was murdered by his brother, who replaced him as tyrant. Some authorities are of the opinion that Molkestes may be the Moagetes, who was involved in the quarrel with Araxa.

An inscription found by Bean at Bubon shows that the fortunes of the city had improved considerably by the 2C AD. At that time it was a member of the Lycian League. The inscription, a copy of a letter from the Emperor Commodus (180–192), commended the Bubonians for their work in rooting out brigands from the area. It also confirmed a decision of the league to raise the number of the city's votes from two to three, the maximum permitted. This placed Bubon on the same level as Xanthus, Pinara, Patara, Tlos, Myra and Olympus.

Spratt described the ruins at Bubon—a small theatre, some terraces strewn with scattered fragments, and a walled acropolis—as disappointing. A century later Bean found that a lot of unofficial digging by the villagers in search of buried treasure on the site had removed all trace of the ruins.

A track leads NE from Bubon and Balbura to c 25km TORIAEUM, near the modern village of *Kozağaçı*. Not far from the village there are many rock-carvings which date from the Hellenistic period. These consist of representations of human figures cut, in relief, into the cliffs and rocky projections. Higher up, in a little valley, there is a small sanctuary dedicated to Mases, a local equestrian deity. Kozağaçı may also be reached by a left-hand turn on the road S from Çavdır.

The site of CIBYRA is c 12km to the N of Bubon, near the modern town of *Gölhisar*.

History. According to Strabo, the first settlers in Cibyra came from Lydia. Later they were displaced by Pisidians, who transferred the city to a more easily defended position. Towards the end of the 2C BC the Roman consul, Manlius Vulso, came to N Lycia in pursuit of the Galatians, who had supported Antiochus III. However, he also took the opportunity to raise money from the cities he visited. Arriving at Cibyra, he managed to extract 100 talents and 10,000 bushels of grain from its unwilling ruler. Later Cibyra, with Bubon, Balbura and Oenoanda formed a tetrapolis. Cibyra, as head, had two votes, the others one each. The city grew in importance and wealth and developed a formidable army. According to Strabo (13.4.17) it could put 30,000 foot soldiers and 2000 horses in the field.

The tetrapolis continued to function until 82 BC, when it was abolished by the Romans. Bubon and Balbura were transferred to Lycia, Cibyra remained in the Roman province of Asia. It continued to prosper, becoming the seat of the provincial governor. Strabo states that the city was famous for the skill of its ironworkers. Perhaps because of its geographical situation, it became a place where many different races met. Pisidian and Solymian, as well as Greek and Lydian were spoken there. In AD 23, Cibyra was destroyed by an

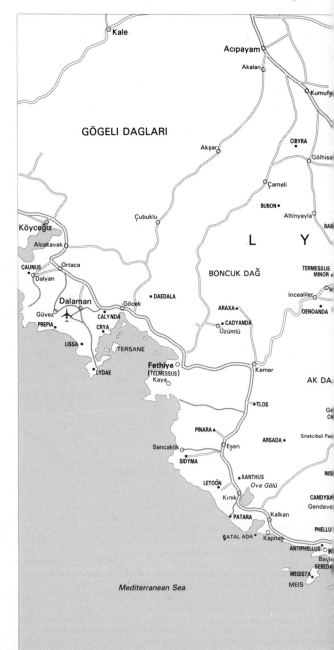

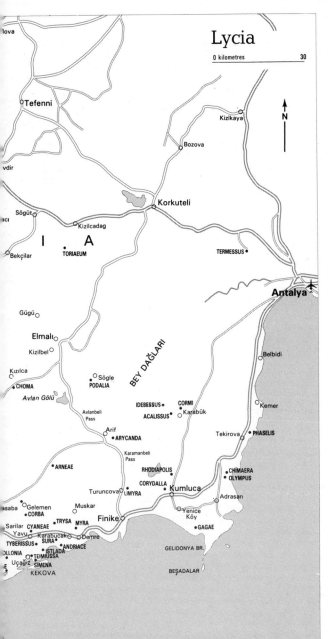

Lycia

0 kilometres — 30

N

lova

○Tefenni

Kizikaya ○

Bozova ●

vdir

Söğüt ○

Korkuteli

acı

○ Kizilcadag

Bekçilar ○

I · A

TERMESSUS ●

● TORIAEUM

Antalya

Gügü ○

Elmalı ○

Belbidi ●

Kizilbel ●

Kızılca ○

BEY DAĞLARI

● CHOMA

○ Sögle
PODALIA

Avlan Gölü

Kemer ○

Avlanbeli
Pass

IDEBESSUS ● ● CORMI

ACALISSUS ● ○ Karabük

Arif ●
ARYCANDA

Tekirova ● PHASELIS

Karamanbeli
Pass

● ARNEAE

RHODIAPOLIS ●

CHIMAERA ●
OLYMPUS ●

CORYDALLA ●

Turuncova ○ LIMYRA ● Kumluca

asaba ○ Gelemen
● CORBA

Muskar ○

Adrasan ●

Finike ○

Yenice
Köy ○

Sarilar ● CYANEAE ● TRYSA ● MYRA

Yavu ● Karabucak ○

● GAGAE

TYBERISSUS ● SURA ●

Demre ○

OLLONIA ●

● ANDRIACE

GELIDONYA BR.

E Uçağız ● TEIMIUSSA ● ISTLADA

● SIMENA

KEKOVA

BEŞADALAR

earthquake, but rebuilt soon afterwards with aid received from the Emperor Tiberius.

The site of Cibyra has not been excavated or treated to a detailed survey, so it is not possible to identify all the buildings which remain. The approach from the E is by way of a street lined with tombs. To the left of a ruined arch, there are the extensive remains of the *stadium*. This had a triple-arched entrance on the N, seats on the E and W sides and was rounded on the S. The centre of the city is occupied by a group of buildings which remain unidentified. Behind them, to the W, are the theatre and a small odeum. The *theatre* had one diazoma and c 50 rows of seats of which some are still visible. Access to the *odeum*, which is S of the theatre, was through five arched and two rectangular doors. Some of the seats remain.

Visitors who are not pressed for time may consider returning by a picturesque route, which passes Çavdır, Korkuteli, Elmalı and Kaş. (See also Rte 20A.)

Leaving Fethiye on road 400, after c 22km we reach *Kemer*. About 10km from Kemer there is a signpost on the left for (7km) **TLOS**, which is sited near the modern village of *Asar Kale*. The road is rough, with many bends and steep ascents.

The *acropolis*, the most prominent feature of Tlos, dominating as it does the N end of the Xanthus valley, can be seen from a considerable distance. Most of the visible remains on the top date from the Ottoman period; the residence and barracks of a local 19C brigand, Kanlı Ali Ağa, occupying the highest ground.

History. The discovery of a bronze hatchet, dating from the second millennium BC, is proof that the site of Tlos was occupied from a very early date. In Lycian it was known as *Tlawa* or *Tlave*, and references in Hittite records from the 14C BC to Dalawa are taken to refer to Tlos. However, very little is known about the history of the city. Its oldest monuments date from the 5C BC. Coins from the 4C BC bearing the name of Tlos in Lycian have been found. In the 2C BC Tlos, as the possessor of three votes, was one of the six most important cities in the Lycian League. In the 2C AD it was the recipient of a grant of 60,000 denarii from the magnate Opramoas of Rhodiapolis. This was mainly used for the construction of the theatre (see below). Tlos was represented at the Chalcedon in 415 and in Byzantine times was the seat of a bishopric.

William James Müller (1812–45), the English artist who visited Lycia in 1843 (see also Xanthus below), spent ten days sketching at Tlos. Of all the places that he visited in Turkey, this relatively remote site appears to have made the greatest impression on him. In a letter to a friend he rhapsodises about the magnificent scenery to be found in this part of Lycia: 'such mountains and valleys, such a distance, melting away and uniting with the sky!'

On the E side of the acropolis there are the remains of a Lycian wall, a substantial part of a later Roman wall and two important groups of Lycian tombs on the E and N sides.

Adjoining the open space, which marks the site of the *agora* (see also below) between the bottom of the acropolis and the village of *Kale Asar*, there are the ruins of several buildings. Near the base of the hill are the scanty traces of the *stadium*, whose seats are partly supported and protected by the Roman wall. The double line of stones in the centre was probably the *spina*, around which chariots were raced. The long building on the E side has been described variously as a basilica or a market house. Beyond this is the *palaestra* and beyond the palaestra, the *baths*. One of the rooms of the baths, known as 'Yedi Kapı', the seven doors, offers a splendid view over the Xanthus valley. To get to the theatre it is necessary to return to the modern rough track. This passes on the right the remains of a

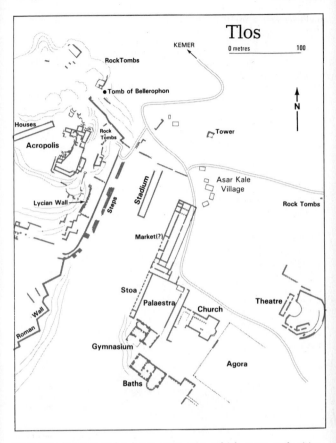

Byzantine basilica and a large open area, which some authorities believe may be the site of the agora of Tlos.

The *theatre*, very overgrown and difficult to examine, was built in the middle of the 2C AD with a large donation from Opramoas of Rhodiapolis and smaller sums from the priest of Dionysus and from private citizens. This had one diazoma. Many of the highly decorated stone blocks from the stage-building remain.

To the N of the village of Kale Asar there is a well-preserved Roman tower and several sarcophagi. Crossing a small stream, we pass by the stadium to the steep N face of the acropolis hill. Following a narrow goat-path high above the river valley we reach a group of rock-tombs. The most important of these is the so-called *Tomb of Bellerophon*. This is a temple-type tomb with pilasters between the antae. There are three carved doors. Note the elaborate decoration on the centre door. The side doors, which provided entrance to the tomb, are raised above the ground on stone blocks, each of which is carved with the figure of a horse. The carving, which gives the tomb its name and which is believed to represent Bellerophon mounted on Pegasus, is on the left wall of the porch. When

Fellows visited the tomb in the early 19C, there were still traces of paint on the saddle-cloth. Above the left door is the figure of a lion or leopard. The funeral chamber on the left-hand side has a niche for offerings and four stone slabs on which the dead were placed. One slab, presumably intended for the most important corpse, has a stone pillow. The chamber on the right-hand side is smaller and has places for three bodies only. There is no inscription, so it is not known for whom the tomb was built. From the tomb of Bellerophon we descend by the goat-path to the valley and, crossing the stream, reach the track which leads back to the main road.

From this point to the signposted turn-off for *Minare* the road passes through pine woods whose glades are carpeted with anemonies and other wild flowers each spring.

To reach the ancient city of **PINARA** take the very rough track on the left—just before the village of Minare—which climbs sharply from the road. Continue c 2km to the large grassy space which is used as a car-park and picnic area. From here it is necessary to proceed on foot.

History. Like many of the Lycian cities not much is known about the early history of Pinara. One account from the 4C BC states that because of overpopulation the people of Xanthus founded a new city on a peak that curves out from Mt Cragus. They called it Pinara, after the Lycian word for round. There is a reference in Homer to a Lycian archer called Pandarus, who may be the same Pandarus honoured in later times in Pinara (Strabo, Geography, 14.3.5). The city enters history properly in 334 BC, when it surrendered to Alexander the Great. However, there is no doubt about Pinara's importance. It had three votes in the Lycian League. When, after his death, the empire of Alexander was divided among his generals, Pinara became part of the kingdom of Pergamum. After Attalus III bequeathed his kingdom to Rome in 133 BC Pinara became a Roman city. In the 2C AD, like Tlos and some other Lycian cities, it received a substantial gift of money from Opramoas of Rhodiapolis. In Roman times it

Drawing of Pinara by Sir George Scharf (1820–95).

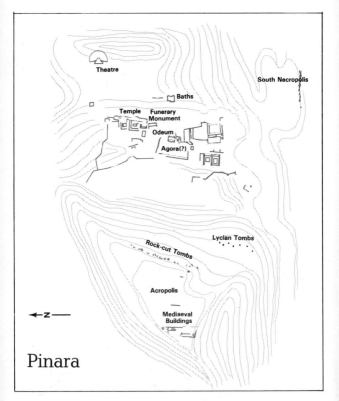

Pinara

enjoyed a considerable degree of prosperity and, although badly damaged by earthquakes in AD 141 and AD 240, it continued to be occupied until the 9C.

In November 1843 William James Müller (1812–45), the English artist (see Xanthus), spent nine days exploring and sketching the ruins of Pinara. Eventually, the exceptionally bad weather—wind, rain and violent thunderstorms— forced him to return to his base at Xanthus.

A sight which never fails to impress is the great red cliff which, rising to a height of about 500m, dominates Pinara. The summit of this cliff may be reached, with some difficulty, by a path that starts from the S side. Presumably to protect its inhabitants, the earliest settlement at Pinara was located on the top, but little of that remains to be seen today. The buildings in the SW area are thought to date from the Middle Ages, when the inhabitants retreated again to the acropolis for safety. Their most astounding creation, the hundreds of caves in the cliff's E face, can only be reached by an experienced climber using elaborate equipment. While most scholars are of the opinion that these were rock-tombs, some have suggested that they could have been used for food storage. Whatever their purpose, they remain as a striking testimony to the skill and daring of their creators.

In more settled times the city was moved to a smaller hill to the E of the cliff. This is very overgrown and difficult to explore. There is a small theatre or odeum on the NW side and on the NE and S a number of interesting rock-tombs. One of these, the so-called *Royal Tomb* has relief carvings on the lintel and inside the porch. Those on the lintel show horses and people, while inside there are representations of four fortified Lycian cities, possibly Xanthus and Telmessus. Note in particular the depiction of the typical Lycian ogival tombs. Because of its rich decoration and the fact that it has a single burial-shelf, this tomb is thought to have been the last resting place of a prince or king. To the N of the Royal Tomb there is another rock-tomb decorated with a pointed arch surmounted by ox-horns. Both tombs have been damaged by shepherds who have used them as shelters. The walls have been blackened by their fires and some of the lower architectural features chipped and broken.

Pinara's *agora* is believed to have been to the N of the smaller hill, but little remains to be seen. Between the presumed site of the agora and the theatre there are the remains of a large *temple*. The *theatre* which was cleared in recent years, was constructed in the Greek form: it was larger than a semicircle. It had no diazoma and its 27 rows of seats were divided into nine cunei. A substantial part of the stage-building still remains.

To reach **SIDYMA**, perhaps the least known of the Lycian cities, due largely to the fact that it is not easy to reach, return to road 400. Passing Eşen and (3km) the village of Gölbent, turn right along the valley for 1km until the road divides. There take the left fork for 6km to Doduga/Sidyma following a succession of rough tracks which cling to the side of the mountain and skirt deep ravines. As the road is composed of loose gravel, is very narrow in parts and has many unfenced drops, it will not appeal to the timid driver. The ancient site of Sidyma (nearly 600m above sea level) can be found in the upper part of the village of Doduga.

History. The name 'Sidyma' suggests that the city was of considerable antiquity. However, its early history is shrouded in mystery. A coin of the Lycian League from the 2C BC, bearing the inscription 'Lukion Si', is believed to refer to Sidyma, but it is not until the 1C BC that the city begins to appear in written records. Under the Romans and Byzantines Sidyma enjoyed a considerable degree of prosperity. It is possible that its fame in later years came from its connection with the E Emperor Marcian (AD 450–457). While taking part, as an ordinary soldier, in a campaign against the Persians, Marcian fell ill and stayed for some time in Sidyma where he was nursed by two brothers. One day after his health had been restored he went hunting with the two young men. While resting from the noon-day heat the youths were astonished to see that their former patient was being shaded from the sun's rays by a huge eagle. Assuming that this was a portent of greatness to come, they asked him later what he would do for them if he became emperor. Marcian promised that he would make them fathers of their city. When, unexpectedly, he succeeded Theodosius II as E emperor, he remembered his promise and gave the young men important positions in Lycia.

The village of *Dodurga* now occupies the centre of the ancient city. Unfortunately, this has resulted in some damage to the ruins, which fall into two distinct groups: those on the acropolis which is to the N of the village and those at its base around the village. The extant wall and towers on the acropolis are Byzantine. The theatre, of which only a few very damaged rows exist, is also a late building. Near a public toilet in the centre of Dodurga there are a few columns of a stoa built in the time of the Emperor Claudius (AD 41–54). There are also scant remains of a small temple dedicated to the Roman emperors. The village mosque has been built with material taken from Sidyma. Note the inscription on the rear wall which lists some of the principal pagan gods: Athena, Apollo, Artemis and Zeus.

Sidyma's necropolis lies to the E of the village. Many of the tombs, nearly all of which date from the Roman period, are in gardens or in fields near the modern houses. One of the most interesting, built in the form of a temple, has a roof decorated with well-preserved carvings of human heads and rosettes. Nearby are the remains of a large structure which was constructed mainly with material taken from other buildings. Note the door on the N side, with its ornamentation of rosettes and lions' heads. Not far away is a fine double tomb, which was occupied by two members of the same family, both named Aristodemus.

For the **LETOÖN** (4km) take a right-hand turn from road 400 1km before *Kınık*. Apart from the signpost on the main road, there are few directions to the site, which is near the modern village of *Bozoluk*.

History. One of the most evocative descriptions of the Letoön from antiquity is provided by Ovid in Book VI of the Metamorphoses. There he writes of 'an ancient altar ... black with the fires of many sacrifices, surrounded with shivering reeds'. This was the shrine dedicated to Leto and to her children, Apollo and Artemis, the principal deities of Lycia. Several legends exist to explain their connection with the Letoön. According to one, Leto, pregnant by Zeus, was harried by his jealous wife, Hera, who did not want the children to be born. Eventually, Leto gave birth on the island of Delos and then brought her children to Lycia, as she wished to wash them in the river Xanthus. Some boorish shepherds tried to stop her from doing so, but wolves came to her assistance and drove them away. As a punishment Leto turned the shepherds into frogs. She also changed the name of the country from Termilis to Lycia, after the Greek word for wolf, λύκος. It has been suggested that the name Leto is derived from the Lycian word *lada*, woman. This would indicate a non-Greek origin for the cult and there is some evidence that a spring at the site was linked with the worship of the Mother Goddess and the Nymphs before the 7C BC. A stele inscribed in Greek, Lycian, and Aramaic has been found near one of the temples at the Letoön. This records the institution by the satrap, Pixodaros, the brother of Mausolus of Halicarnassus, of a cult devoted to the worship of two gods. These were the Carian deities Basileus Kaunios and Arkesimas; the latter a deity about whom nothing is known. Those who offended against the provisions of the decree were threatened with the wrath of Leto, Apollo, Artemis and the Nymphs. This confirms the association of Leto with the Nymphs as early as the 4C BC and shows that even then the Letoön was a place where important religious texts were displayed. Later it also assumed political importance when it became the place of assembly of the Lycian League. Representatives of foreign countries came to the shrine and Lycian national festivals were celebrated there. Some scholars believe that it was at the Letoön that Alexander the Great received the famous prophecy concerning the destruction of the Persian Empire which is recounted by Plutarch: 'In Lycia, near the city of Xanthus, there is a spring which it is said, gushed from the ground without apparent cause and, overflowing, threw up from its depths a tablet of bronze covered in archaic characters. There it was read that the Persian Empire would end, destroyed by the Greeks. Encouraged by this prophecy, Alexander proceeded to clear the coastline of Persians as far as Cilicia and Phoenicia.' A divine intervention of another kind took place at the Letoön at a later date. In 88 BC Mithridates, the king of Pontus, besieged Patara. To make siege-engines for his assault he began to cut down trees in a grove sacred to Leto. Warned in a dream of his sacrilege, he was obliged to desist. The site of the Letoön continued to be occupied well into the Christian era when a church was erected there. It would appear that the last temple was not demolished until the 7C, when the site was finally abandoned at the time of the Arab raids on Lycia.

Interest in the Letoön was revived in the 19C by the accounts published by Fellows, Spratt and Forbes of their travels in Lycia. However, for many years it was little visited because of malaria and the generally unhealthy conditions in the area. Professor George Bean examined the site in 1946 and French archaeologists began to excavate there in 1962. They have uncovered three temples, a nymphaeum and two porticoes. In 1984 a number of interesting inscriptions were discovered. One laid down the conditions to be observed by anyone entering the sanctuary. According to M. Christian Le Roy visitors to the shrine were required to dress simply in tunics and plain shoes. The wearing of rich jewellery, especially brooches and rings, was forbidden. So also were elaborate hairstyles and headwear like the πέτασος (a broad-brimmed felt hat). They had to be unarmed. Those not offering a sacrifice were not permitted to spend the night in the portico of the shrine. These ordinances were previously unknown among religious laws and are of great interest to historians of the sanctuary. The work of the French archaeologists continues.

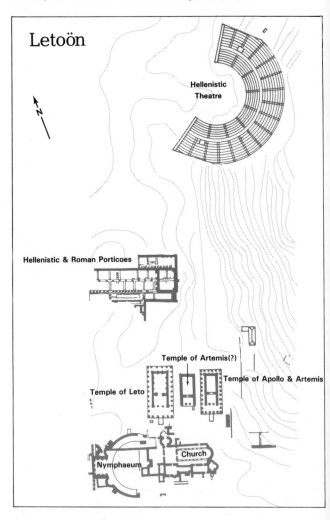

The site of the Letoön is compact and it is possible to make a reasonably full visit in 1½ hours. There are no refreshment facilities so bring a picnic lunch. Entering from the car-park, you make your way to the ruins of *three temples*. Little of these exists above ground level. According to an inscription found in the cella, the first and largest (30.25m by 15.75m) was dedicated to Leto. Built in the Ionic style, it was a peripteros of 11 columns by 6. It had a deep pronaos and engaged half columns on the cella walls and it has been dated to the 3C BC. The temple in the centre, the smallest (18.20m by 8.70m) and the oldest (4C BC), was also in the Ionic style, but without a colonnade. The cella of this temple had a mysterious rocky structure, partly composed of rough stone blocks and partly of a natural rocky outcrop at its N end. The third temple (27.90m by 15.07m), which dates from the Hellenistic period, was constructed in the Doric order. This was built over an earlier Lycian structure. It was also a peripteros of 11 by 6 columns and it had engaged half-columns on the cella walls. The fine mosaic on the floor depicting a lyre, a bow and quiver suggests that it was dedicated to Apollo and Artemis. (Ask the guardian of the site to brush away the protective covering of sand.) It was near this temple that the stele with the trilingual inscription concerning the cult of Basileus Kaunios and Arkesimas (see above) was found. All three temples opened towards the S.

SW of the temples lies the *nymphaeum*. This structure, which replaced an earlier Hellenistic building, is composed of two parts, from different periods. On the E there is a rectangular basin lined with marble between retaining walls c 16m apart. This leads to a semicircular construction 27m in diameter with a depth of 4m. Some of this part of the nymphaeum may date from the Hellenistic period. Beyond the semicircular basin, and linked to it, is a room, flanked by two exedrae which had several niches for statues. The principal niche on the W side bears a dedication to Hadrian, which has been dated to about AD 130. Later a church (c 4C) was built over part of the E section of the nymphaeum. This was destroyed during the Arab invasions of the 7C.

Turning to the N we come to the partially-excavated porticoes. A *Doric portico* (Hellenistic period) enclosed the N and W sides of the temple area. This was altered considerably in Roman times, when, during the Claudian era, a second portico in the Ionic style was built inside the Doric construction. It had columns of brick resting on stone bases. On the N the new double portico was enclosed by a wall and there the archaeologists made an exciting discovery. They found 15,000 fragments from ten broken and burnt marble statues. Five of the statues, which date from the 2C BC, have been painstakingly reconstructed and are now displayed in the Antalya Museum. Beneath the porticoes are the remains of earlier shrines. These have been dated to the 4C, 5C, and 6C BC. Fragments of archaic pottery from the 6C BC have also been found there, clear evidence that the site was occupied at an early date.

Much of the Letoön is below the level of the water-table and as a result for most of the year part of the area occupied by the porticoes and the nymphaeum is flooded. While this adds considerably to the problems encountered by the archaeologists, it provides an agreeable environment for the many tortoises and frogs that live there. The latter keep up a noisy chorus, so reminding us of the comment Ovid made about the metamorphosed shepherds: 'Even now, as of old … [they] exercise their foul tongues in quarrel, and all shameless, though they may be under the water … try to utter maledictions.'

The Hellenistic *theatre* is about 100m NE of the porticoes. Partly cut out of the hillside and greater than a semicircle, it has one diazoma. Apart from the loss of its stage-buildings, it is in good condition. Access to the cavea is by two vaulted passages. On the outer face of the

passage on the NE side there is an interesting collection of masks.
Amongst others these depict Silenus, Dionysus, a satyr and a girl.

Before leaving the Letoön area it is possible to make a brief
excursion to the site of ancient PYDNAE. Instead of turning right to
return to Kınık, take the left fork and continue on a good road for
about 10km. Just before the beach you will see Pydnae on the
hillside. This is one of the best-preserved Hellenistic fortresses of the
region. A ring-wall with several towers encloses the ruins of a
Byzantine church. Near the beach there are a number of simple
restaurants.

Return to road 400 and continue for c 2km to Kınık. At the entrance to
the village a modern bridge carries the road over the Xanthus river,
the Eşen Çayı. There are a number of simple restaurants in Kınık, but
a picnic on the site—c 0.5km from the village centre—is likely to be
more enjoyable. There are no refreshments available at Xanthus.

Xanthus river

Allow at least 3–4 hours for a reasonably detailed examination of
Xanthus. Wear stout shoes and thornproof clothing, especially if you
intend to explore the more overgrown areas, e.g. the Hellenistic and
Roman residential quarter and the upper acropolis.

XANTHUS is probably the most interesting of all the Lycian cities.
Its magnificent situation on the great cliff, which rises steeply from

the Xanthus river, ensures that its ruins are visible from a consider-able distance. The ancient site, which is clearly signposted, may be reached from the centre of *Kınık*. A leisurely 20-minute walk takes one to the ridge, which separates the Lycian from the, higher, Roman acropolis.

History. The earliest written reference to Xanthus, which was always consid-ered to be the greatest of the Lycian cities, it is in the 'Iliad'. Sarpedon, one of the heroes who fought on the side of the Trojans, speaks of their good fortune to Glaukus, his friend: 'Cousin, why do the Lycians pay us semi-divine hours? Why do we get the most honourable seats at banquets, the finest cuts of meat, the fullest goblets, and the great estates of orchard and wheatland beside the River Xanthus?'

Xanthus was twice razed to the ground and its inhabitants slaughtered. Around 540 BC the Persians under their general, Harpagus, attempted to conquer the W part of Asia Minor. Advancing along the river valley, they besieged the city. Seeing that resistance was useless, the inhabitants put their wives, children, slaves and property in the acropolis and set fire to it. Herodotus describes what happened next. 'Then the warriors of Xanthus made their final attack on the Persians, their voices raised in oaths of war, until every last man from Xanthus was killed.' The city was later re-established by a number of Xanthian families (c 80 according to Herodotus), who happened to be away at the time of the siege. Evidence that it soon regained its former status is provided by the fine monuments erected in the 5C. In 334 BC Xanthus, with Pinara, Patara and about 30 smaller Lycian cities surrendered to Alexander the Great.

After Alexander's death the city was for some time under the rule of the Ptolemies who captured it from Antigonus. In 197 BC it acquired the status of a free city under the nominal control of Antiochus III of Syria. However, Lycia was awarded to the Rhodians after the defeat of Antiochus at the battle of Magnesia ad Sipylum in 190 BC and for a number of years its inhabitants fought bitterly for their freedom. In 167 BC the Roman Senate abolished the rule of Rhodes and Lycia became free once more. Early in the 2C BC an attempt was made to set up a tyranny in Xanthus. This was suppressed by the Lycian League. The city's second great ordeal took place in 42 BC. Brutus the tyrannicide came to Lycia to raise money for his struggle against Antony and Octavian. The member cities of the Lycian League refused to contribute, they were engaged by the Roman forces and defeated. Xanthus was besieged by the Romans. A furious battle ensued. The Xanthians showed great bravery, but finally the city fell to the Romans. The Xanthians then slaughtered their families, put their belongings on pyres and threw themselves on the flames. Only about 150 were captured by the Romans. However, Xanthus rose once again from its ashes. As a city of the Roman province of Asia it prospered, was ornamented with many fine buildings and continued to enjoy its place as the premier city of Lycia. Under Byzantine rule the city walls were repaired and a monastery was built on the upper acropolis. It was the seat of a bishop under the Metropolitan of Myra.

In the 19C interest in Xanthus was revived in W Europe by the exploration and writings of Sir Charles Fellows and by the works of art which were transported back to England by the Royal Navy. When these were displayed for the first time in the British Museum they caused a sensation. Visitors flocked to admire the magnificent Nereid Tomb, the tomb of Payava and the reliefs from the Harpy tomb. The latter still stands in the Lycian acropolis, but, sadly, the reliefs on it are plaster casts of the originals supplied by the British Museum!

William James Müller (1812–45), the Bristol born painter, visited Turkey at the invitation of Sir Charles Fellows in 1843. After an agreeable stay in Smyrna (İzmir), where he was captivated by that city's exoticism, its picturesque inhabitants, and the entrancing sight of 'long strings of camels laden with fruits and other merchandise,' he made his way S to Lycia.

Camping at Xanthus, Müller spent his days sketching the ruins of the ancient city, returning only at sunset for a simple meal and the escape provided by his tent against the 'malarious miasma' which pervaded the river valley. During the course of his stay he also produced dozens of sketches illustrating the lives of the villagers and of the nomad Yürük people. His Turkish neighbours were friendly and hospitable, though somewhat suspicious, perhaps because of their religious beliefs, of his artistic skills. Dramatic evidence of their attitude was provided by an incident which he recounted in a letter. Hoping to break down their prejudices and interest them in portraiture, he made a sketch of a local

A Xanthian boy with a bow. Drawing by William James Müller, 1843/4.

youth and gave it to them as a present. His mortification may be imagined when they stoned the drawing before his face. However, Müller was not deterred by this unfortunate incident and continued to make sketches of the local people. These were exhibited with considerable success at the Graphic Gallery in London in 1844 and a number, together with his larger oil paintings, are preserved in the Tate Gallery and in the art galleries of Bristol and Birmingham.

On the left, about half-way up the dirt track which leads from Kınık to Xanthus, are the remains of a *Hellenistic gateway* which bears an inscription commemorating the consecration of the city in 197 BC by Antiochus III to the gods of Lycia. (See above.) Just beyond is the well-preserved 1C AD *Arch of Vespasian* and traces of the ancient roadway that linked Xanthus with Patara and the Letoön. On the high bank on the right are the few sad remains of the **Nereid Monument** (5C BC). Only the base and a few architectural fragments remain: the friezes and statues were taken to London in 1841/42 by Charles Fellows (they are now in Room 7 of the British Museum). The Nereid tomb is of particular interest, as it was the only major tomb in Xanthus in a Greek architectural style. Constructed in the form of an Ionic temple on a high podium, it gets its name from the statues of the female figures placed between the columns. These have been identified variously as the Aurai (Breezes) or the Nereids, the daughters of Nereus, a sea god associated with the Aegean. The tomb was richly decorated with friezes showing battles between Greeks and barbarians, the siege of a city and hunting scenes. A seated male and female figure on the E pediment probably represent the personages for whom the tomb was built.

Continuing to the top of the hill we pass on the left the *Lycian acropolis*, the *Roman theatre*, and the *Roman agora*. The wall which encircles the Lycian acropolis was built at different periods. The section on the E side, constructed from polygonal masonry, dates from the 4C BC, while that on the SW is Hellenistic. Note the massive free-standing house-tomb between the agora and the road.

The NE corner of the agora is dominated by the so-called **Inscribed Pillar**. This is in fact a normal pillar tomb erected for a Xanthian dignitary towards the end of the 5C BC and derives its name from the inscription in Greek and Lycian which covers its four sides. This appears to recount the life and exploits of a prince called Kerei. As Lycian is little understood most of our information about him comes from the 12 lines of verse in Greek on the N side. Kerei, son of Harpagus (not to be confused with the Persian general of the same name), was a great wrestler in his youth, the conqueror of many cities, a champion who killed seven Arcadian foot soldiers in a day. The reliefs depicting his exploits, which are believed to have taken place during the Peloponnesian War, are now in the İstanbul Archaeological Museum. The Lycian inscription runs to 250 lines, the longest known so far. It is particularly interesting, as the text on the W and part of the N side is written in a form of the language that is found in only one other place, on a tomb in ancient Antiphellus (Kaş; see below).

Prominently set on the W side of the agora are two other tombs, a *Lycian sarcophagus* set on upright slabs, and the so-called Harpy Tomb. The first poses a puzzle for archaeologists, as the burial found in its base can be dated by accompanying pottery to the Hellenistic period (3C BC). However, it also contained an archaic slab depicting wrestlers, now in the İstanbul Archaeological Museum, which dates from the 6C BC. Presumably the sarcophagus on the top must also be Hellenistic unless this was also brought from another location and re-used. The marble slabs which once decorated the top of the so-called **Harpy Tomb** (early 5C BC), which stands 7.6m high, were taken to London by Fellows and are now exhibited in Room 5 of the British Museum. They have been replaced by the Turkish authorities with plaster casts of the originals. The winged figures at the N and S sides were originally identified as the harpies who stole the daughters of King Pandareus to make them slaves of the Furies. However, it is now believed that they represent the Sirens who carried the souls of the dead to Hades. The seated figures receiving offerings may be members of the deceased's family or alternatively deities—Artemis has been suggested for the E side, Aphrodite and Hera for the W. In Byzantine times there was a small church near the Harpy Tomb and there is some evidence that the tomb was occupied for a period by a Christian hermit.

To the S of the forum is the *Roman theatre* (mid 2C AD). This was built with the help of a donation of 30,000 denarii from Opramoas of Rhodiapolis. The theatre, which has two parodoi, was so constructed that it did not obscure the Harpy Tomb or the pillar tomb. Part of the stage-building remains. At some time several rows of seats were removed from the lower part to turn it into an amphitheatre, while others from the top were later incorporated into the Byzantine wall which lies behind. Note the terracotta pipes at the top levels on the W

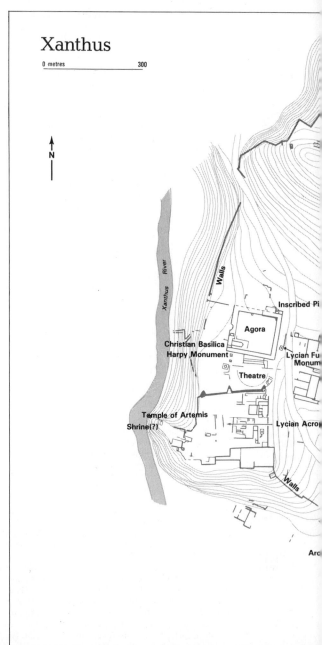

Xanthus

0 metres — 300

N

Xanthus River

Walls

Inscribed Pi

Agora

Christian Basilica
Harpy Monument

Lycian Fu
Monum

Theatre

Lycian Acro

Temple of Artemis
Shrine(?)

Walls

Arc

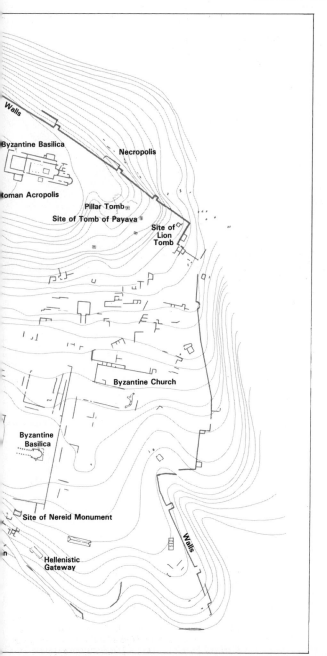

Walls

Byzantine Basilica

Necropolis

Roman Acropolis

Pillar Tomb

Site of Tomb of Payava

Site of
Lion
Tomb

Byzantine Church

Byzantine
Basilica

Site of Nereid Monument

Walls

Hellenistic
Gateway

The Harpy Tomb, by Sir George Scharf (1820–95).

side. These were used to convey water to the houses on the acropolis.
On the E side of the theatre, near the road, are the remains of a
Lycian pillar tomb which dates from the 4C BC. Presumably this was
moved and placed in its present position when the theatre was built.

The *Lycian acropolis* is sited on a flat-topped hill behind the
theatre, high above the Xanthus river. Geometric pottery found here
dates the earliest occupation of Xanthus to the 8C BC, the time of
Homer. As the acropolis contains the remains of a number of
buildings from widely differing periods, and is very overgrown, it is
not easy to understand.

In the NE corner there was a Byzantine church and monastery. The
SE houses the foundations of a building, which it is believed was the
palace of the earliest rulers of Xanthus. This was destroyed when the
city was captured by the Persian, Harpagus, in 540 BC. To the W are
traces of a temple dedicated to Artemis, while on the cliff above the river
there was another house or shrine richly decorated with friezes.
Sculptures from this and from two other buildings on the acropolis were
later incorporated in a Byzantine wall which was added to the back of
the theatre to form a new defence. These were removed by Fellows and
brought to England (now in Room 5 of the British Museum). The friezes,
an interesting blend of Greek and Persian subject-matter and style,
depict satyrs stalking wild animals, fighting cocks with attendant hens,
a procession of warriors and a banqueting scene. In the same room are
the ogival gables from two Lycian tombs, each of which shows a pair of
facing sphinxes guarding the false door of the tomb.

Retracing our steps, we cross the dirt road to the car-park and
continue on a rough track for about 200m to the *Hellenistic agora*.
This was also the residential area of the Hellenistic and Roman cities.
Now densely covered with undergrowth it is difficult to explore. The

only building of importance, which has been uncovered so far is a large *Byzantine basilica*. Excavation of this structure, begun by French archaeologists in 1970, still continues. According to Professor Henri Metzger the basilica was abandoned towards the end of the early Christian period, but was redecorated and brought into use again in the middle Byzantine period. It had three naves separated by a stylobate made of reused material. A section of the mosaic floors may be seen in the W section of the building. At the E end there was a semicircular apse with raised synthronon. Three doors provided access to the central nave and one to each of the side aisles from the narthex. In size and decoration the building bears comparison with churches in the large Byzantine cities. A smaller Byzantine church, largely hidden by the undergrowth, has not yet been excavated. Apart from the vestiges of the retaining walls and a striking view of the Dumanlı mountains to the E there is little to see in this part of the site. The level space of the agora still fulfills a useful purpose, however. It is much used by the youth of Kınık as a football pitch!

Walking diagonally across the hillside towards the N we soon reach the site of the *Tomb of Payava*. All that remains is the base as the tomb was taken to London by Fellows and is now exhibited in Room 10 of the British Museum. It is a typical Lycian tomb decorated with reliefs in the Greek style. These show the various warlike exploits and peacetime occupations of the deceased. There is an inscription in Lycian which is believed to mean 'Payava built this monument'. At the eastern side of the Hellenistic and Roman acropolis there is a striking group of rock-tombs dominated by a pillar tomb. One of the rock-tombs, constructed in the Greek style, has an inscription in Lycian. The climb to the top of the *Roman acropolis* is not difficult but, apart from enabling the visitor to enjoy a fine view of the whole site and to examine the ruins of a well-preserved early Byzantine monastery, there is little to justify the effort. Some care is necessary, as the whole area is covered with tangled undergrowth and there are many loose blocks of stone. Descending from the acropolis, we reach the Hellenistic walls. In an angle are the remains of the *lion tomb*, so called from a sculpture which shows a lion attacking a bull. The reliefs from this tomb are now in the British Museum. Crossing over the Hellenistic walls we reach the *necropolis* of Xanthus. Here there are many rock-tombs and sarcophagi scattered over a wide area. On leaving the necropolis we turn left on the dirt road. This brings us under the Roman acropolis and, passing the theatre and the Lycian acropolis on the right we return to Kınık.

Take road 400 from Kınık in the direction of Kalkan and Kaş. Towards the end of the plain, c 8km beyond the village of Kınık, a sign on the right-hand side of the road indicates the dirt track which leads to c 6km **PATARA**. This track, though narrow and curving, has a reasonably good surface.

History. Among the many legends about the foundation of Patara one, related by Strabo, states that it was named after Patarus, the son of Apollo and a nymph named Lycia, the daughter of Xanthus. This tradition may have arisen from the fact that in antiquity Patara had a famous oracle of Apollo. It was believed that the god spent the winter in that city, and summer on the island of Delos. Although little is now known with certainty about the prophecies made in Patara, its oracle had an importance that rivalled that of Delphi. While fish were used for divination purposes by another oracle of Apollo at nearby Sura, there is no precise information about the methods employed at Patara. There is a suggestion in Herodotus (1.182) that predictions were based on the dreams experienced by the priestess of the god. After a period of silence in the 1C AD, the oracle was revived during the reign of Antoninus Pius (138–161), when Opramoas of Rhodiapolis made a generous donation to the shrine. Nothing is known about its later history. Presumably it was suppressed, when effect was given to Theodosius' law of AD 385 against oracles. So far neither the temple of Apollo nor the shrine of his oracle has been found.

Pottery found at Patara has been dated to the 5C BC. However attractive the rather fanciful legends recounted by Strabo and other ancient historians and geographers may seem, the truth appears to be that the city was a Lycian foundation. Its Lycian name, *Pttara*, has been found on coins and insciptions. It is probable that it owed its development to two factors, the presence of an oracle—at first of a Lycian god and later of Apollo—and the fact that it had one of the best harbours on that part of the Lycian coast.

Patara enters written history in 333 BC, when, with Xanthus and other Lycian cities, it surrendered to Alexander the Great. In the wars of succession that followed the death of Alexander its importance as a port attracted the attention of two of the contestants, Antigonus and Demetrius, and it was occupied by each in turn. Under the control of the Ptolemies during the 3C BC, it took on the name Arsinoe briefly in honour of the formidable wife of Ptolemy II. In 196 BC Patara, Xanthus and several other Lycian cities were captured by Antiochus III of Syria. After some years of rule by the Seleucids, Lycia passed into the control of Rhodes, the ally of Rome in the war against Syria. It was not until 167 BC that it was finally granted its freedom by the Romans.

During the following century little is known about Patara. A period of peace and development, it was marked by the revival of the Lycian League. Proof of the importance of Patara at that time is provided by the fact that, with Xanthus, Pinara and Tlos, it was entitled to three votes in the League's Assembly, the maximum permitted. In 88 BC war came once more to Lycia and Patara was besieged by Mithridates, king of Pontus. He cut some of the trees in the sacred grove at the Letoön to provide wood for battering rams and ballistae. (See above.) In 42 BC the city was again invested, this time by Brutus and Cassius who had come to Lycia in search of funds for their struggle against Antony and Octavian. After resisting the Romans for some time, Patara surrendered and consequently was treated more leniently than Xanthus had been. There was no massacre or enslavement, Brutus was content with the confiscation of the city's public and private wealth. Eighty years later when Lycia was attached to Pamphylia and annexed by the Romans (AD 43), Patara's importance increased rather than diminished. The Lycian League continued to be active, at least in internal affairs, and its official documents were deposited in Patara. Finally, the Romans' estimation of the city may be judged by the fact that the governor of the joint province of Lycia-Pamphylia had his seat there.

Patara also figured in early Christian history. When St. Paul and St. Luke went from Miletus to Jerusalem, during their third missionary journey, they stopped at Patara and changed ships there. 'When ... at last (we) put out to sea, we made a straight course, sailing to Cos, and next day to Rhodes, and thence to Patara. There, finding a ship crossing to Phoenice, we went on board and set sail.' (Acts 21:1–2).) It seems likely that the Christian Church was established in Patara in apostolic times or very soon afterwards. St. Nicholas of Myra was born at Patara (c 300) and spent his youth there. Bishop Eudemus of Patara attended the Council of Nicea in AD 325.

Patara continued to be of some importance until the Middle Ages—pilgrims to the Holy Land used it as port of call. However, as the harbour gradually silted up, it began to decline until finally it was abandoned completely and virtually forgotten.

Interest in Patara was revived in the 19C, when Fellows and his companions explored the Xanthus valley and the surrounding countryside. From there in 1842 the treasures of the city of Xanthus—the Nereid Monument, the tomb of Payava, the friezes from the Harpy Tomb—were loaded on to HMS *Beacon* by Lieutenant Spratt and his men and taken to England. However, before Fellows and Spratt came to Patara, Francis Beaufort, captain of HMS *Frederikssteen*, had surveyed the southern coast of Turkey for the Admiralty in 1811/12. He has the distinction of rediscovering that ancient city. His description of 19C Patara in his book 'Karamania' shows that little has changed in the last 177 years. 'This place, once a celebrated oracle of Apollo, still preserves its former name, and many traces of its former grandeur ... It is evident, from both Strabo and Livy, that Patara had formerly a harbour; the situation is still apparent, but at present it is a swamp, choked up with sand and bushes, and all communication with the sea cut off by a straight beach, through which there is no opening ... The sand has not only filled up the harbour, but has accumulated to a considerable height between the ruins and the river Xanthus ... Patara is now uninhabited; but a few solitary peasants were found tending the cattle that wandered about the plain.'

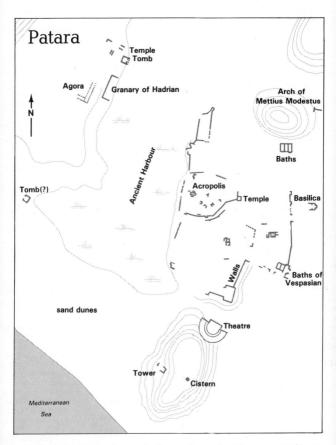

Appropriately, the entrance to Patara is marked by a magnificent *Roman triumphal arch* (c AD 100) which is in a fine state of preservation. This was erected by Mettius Modestus, a governor of Lycia and Pamphylia. The three gateways of the arch were decorated on either side with busts of the donor and of his family. The consoles on which the busts stood still carry the original inscriptions. These have enabled the monument to be dated accurately. Near the arch are many well-preserved sarcophagi from the Roman period. Some archaeologists believe that the small hill to the SW of the arch may be the site of the temple of Apollo, which so far has not been discovered. A giant head of the god found there lends some support to this theory.

The ruins S of the hill mark the position of a *baths complex*, whose plan has not been determined. To the S and E of these baths are the scanty remains of a *basilica*. On the W side of the site a small acropolis overlooks the ancient harbour. This is surrounded by walls that were constructed during the Hellenistic and Byzantine periods. At the base of these walls, on the E side, there is a small, richly-decorated *temple in antis apteros* (without a row of columns) built in the Corinthian style. This dates from the 2C AD. Although sometimes called the temple of Apollo, it is generally accepted that this is much too small to be the building mentioned by the ancient writers. (See above.) Access to the temple, the interior of which is filled with undergrowth, is difficult in wet weather as the surrounding terrain is marshy.

Beyond the temple, to the S, are the extensive remains (105 by 48m) of *Roman baths* which, according to an inscription found there, were built by Vespasian (AD 69–79). The usual five chambers had an elaborate decoration of marble or bronze plaques on its walls. The holes used to fix them are still visible.

The *theatre* of Patara is located SW of the baths of Vespasian, at the foot of a small hill. It has a single diazoma. Entry to the cavea, which was divided into eight cunei, is by way of vaulted passage-ways. Now largely covered with sand, it exudes an air of romantic melancholy. When Beaufort visited Patara in 1811 the greater part of the structure was visible. He describes it as: 'somewhat more than a semi-circle, whose external diameter is about two hundred feet; it contains thirty-four rows of marble seats, few of which have been disturbed; but the superior preservation of the proscenium distinguishes it from most ancient theatres which are extant, and would render it well worthy of more minute architectural detail. At the eastern entrance there is a long and very perfect inscription, recording the building of the theatre, by Q. Velius Titianus: and its dedication by his daughter Velia Procla, in the fourth consulate of the Emperor Antoninus Pius.' In fact, the inscription refers to certain

The theatre at Patara, from a drawing by Charles Texier, mid 19C.

alterations and additions to the proscenium, stage and auditorium made in AD 147. The theatre is much older than the 2C AD, as another inscription concerning repairs made to the structure during the reign of Tiberius (AD 14–37) makes clear.

From the rear of the theatre it is an easy climb to the top of the hill. Those who make the effort are rewarded by a striking view of the ancient city and its surroundings. To the N lie the theatre, the baths of Vespasian, the Corinthian-style temple, the Byzantine acropolis, the ancient harbour, the granary of Hadrian, the arch of Mettius Modestus and the ruined sarcophagi of the necropolis. To the S and W a fine beach stretches away into the distance. This is bordered by high sand dunes, the barrier which cut Patara off from the open sea and brought about its decline and eventual abandonment. On top of the hill there are remains of two structures, the stylobate of the *Temple of Athena* and a curious construction which has aroused much interest and controversy. This is a *circular pit* about 10m in diameter and the same in depth, partly cut from the natural rock, partly constructed from masonry. In the centre there is a stone pillar which rises about 2m above ground. A staircase cut into the rock provides precarious access to the bottom of the pit. Many theories have been put forward to explain its purpose. Although not positioned on the very summit of the hill, some are certain that it was a lighthouse, while others have decided that it marks the site of the oracle of Apollo: Beaufort appears to have originated the latter theory. However, most authorities now accept the view that the structure was a cistern for water storage and that it dates from the time before aqueducts were constructed in Patara.

For the adventurous, a visit to the granary of Hadrian and the necropolis, which lies near it, should not present too many problems. It is necessary to descend the W side of the theatre hill and, traversing the sand dunes, skirt the edge of the fen that marks the site of the ancient harbour. As there is no fixed path, care should be taken to avoid straying on to the marshy ground. In places the undergrowth is dense and difficult to penetrate.

During one of his visits to Patara, Bean found the base of a *large building* projecting from the sand at the W edge of the ancient harbour where one turns N towards the granary. This, he concluded, was the lighthouse of Patara which had been built, probably on a mole, at the entrance to the harbour. The *granary*, which, according to an inscription in Latin on the façade, was erected during the reign of Hadrian (117–138), is similar in size and construction to that at Andriace. It measures c 65m by 32m and was divided into eight single-storey rectangular rooms. Apart from being roofless, it is in a very good state of preservation. The façade of the building had two storeys and was ornamented with busts, which were placed on pedestals above the doors. The interior, which is very overgrown, appears to have had a single storey. A short distance N of the granary are the remains of an elaborate free-standing pseudo-peripteral temple-tomb, built in the Corinthian style. The presence of this and other tombs and sarcophagi nearby suggests that one of the necropolises of the city was located here.

In Roman times Patara obtained its water supplies from two aqueducts. The remains of these may be seen near the Letoön and in the hills above the modern village of Kalkan.

Patara has one of the finest beaches on the Lycian coast. It is necessary to go as far east as Andriace or as far west as Ölü Deniz to find anything comparable. The beaches at Kalkan and Kaş are much smaller, pebbly, and too near the town to be entirely free from pollution. At Patara the swimming is excellent and the conditions are usually good for surfing and windsurfing. The beach is composed of fine sand and is sufficiently large to be uncrowded on most days. During the holiday season light refreshments may be obtained from a small café on the shore. For those who, seduced by the numinous character of the place, would like to absorb its atmosphere at leisure by wandering among the holm oaks and ruined buildings or by lazing on the beach, there is a small pension which offers simple accommodation.

Spring is one of the best seasons to visit Patara. Then the site is carpeted with wild flowers: *anemone coronaria*, asphodel, the flower of the Elysian Fields, and many more.

On reaching road 400 turn right and continue in the direction of c 10km Kalkan. The road passes a large marsh, the *Ova Gölü*, on the left. A century ago leeches were collected in this fen and shipped from Kaş to Europe for medicinal purposes. The road, shaded by pines, now climbs steeply through a series of sharp bends. The plain of Xanthus lies far below. On the other side of the ridge the descent is equally steep. Flanked by olive groves, the road cuts a red scar across a mountain side pockmarked with scattered clumps of maquis. After c 2km a sign indicates an almost right-hand turn to the pretty village of **Kalkan.**

Like Kaş, its close neighbour, Kalkan is built at the foot of a steep mountain. Its white houses sit at the N end of a fiord-like bay, whose mouth is protected by Çatal Ada. Kalkan is one of several places on the Lycian coast which has adapted itself with a considerable degree of success to meet the needs of tourism. In spite of its plethora of boutiques and pensions it has managed to retain much of the character of a small Turkish fishing village. Among its smart shops, there are many others—bakers, butchers, general stores, tailors, drapers, and handicrafts—that cater as much for the needs of the villagers as for the tourists.

From Kalkan there are frequent bus and dolmuş services to Fethiye and Antalya and to the towns and villages in between.

Most of the accommodation available is in reasonably priced, good, clean, family pensions, some of which have rudimentary cooking facilities. Many have roof terraces which give a view over the harbour. Kalkan has a few small, inexpensive restaurants. In summer these are full of visitors from the pensions and from the boats in the new yacht marina. There are few good swimming places near the village. The beach on the W, beyond the quarry, is by tradition reserved for ladies, foreign and local. To the E the foreshore is pebbly, subject to frequent rockfalls, and too near the village to be entirely free from pollution. For the best swimming take a boat to one of the more distant beaches, or a dolmuş to the small beach at *Kapıtaş* 6km along the road to Kaş (see below).

Kalkan attracts not only those visitors who prefer to stay in small resorts, but also those who want a base from which to explore the ancient sites of Lycia, particularly Xanthus, the Letoön and Patara. It is also a good centre for walking. On the E side there are a number of attractive 'hidden' valleys, which can be reached easily on foot. Spring, autumn and early winter are the best times to visit Kalkan. In summer the heat is overpowering, accommodation is strained to its limits and prices are at their highest. Spring comes early in Kalkan. By the end of February the winter rains are ending, wild flowers transform the surrounding countryside, there are few tourists, and pensions offer rooms at bargain rates.

The road from Kalkan to Kaş (27km) follows the coastline. Although narrow and curving it is well surfaced. However, care should be taken, especially on corners, as sheep and goats, which graze the verges, frequently stray on to the road. At c 6km *Kapıtaş* there is a bridge over a small gorge. Steep steps by the side lead down to a pleasant pebble and sandy beach. A marble tablet on the nearby cliff wall commemorates four workmen who were killed during the construction of this new road.

The approach to Kaş is announced by a peninsula which stretches like a long finger S towards the Greek island of **Meis** (Kastellorizo). This separates the town from the NW harbour (Bucak Limanı), formerly known as Vathy.

Kaş, which means 'eyebrow' or 'something curved' in Turkish, straggles decoratively along the seafront at the base of the great cliff that towers 500m over the town. During recent years it has become increasingly popular with Turks and foreign visitors, who are attracted by the charm of its situation, excellent climate and restful atmosphere.

Although a number of hotels and pensions have been erected in the last few years, strict planning laws protect Kaş from over-development, and it has been saved from the high-rise constructions and sprawling holiday complexes that have ruined so many Mediterranean resorts.

Up-to-date information about hotel and pension prices, restaurants, monuments, sites and excursions may be obtained from the *Tourist Office* on the E side of the main square. Rooms in private houses are also available. These are generally inexpensive and have the added advantage of introducing the visitor to Turkish family life. Ask at the Tourist Office or bus station for details. The square is the centre of the town's social life. Here visitors and locals meet in the cafés for an evening aperitif, to play backgammon, or to plan the next day's programme. The restaurants in the square and along the sea-front are slightly more expensive than those in other parts of the town. One, housed in a barrel-vaulted room which it is believed once formed part of a church, has an excellent range of Turkish dishes. On the W side of the square there is a small street covered with awnings. There you will find restaurants which offer meals at very reasonable prices. The covered street leads to a large open area that serves as a market place. Continue along the road, which runs up-hill beside the market square, to reach the *bus and dolmuş terminal* on the left above the crossroads.

The town's *post office* and *bank* are to be found in a street on the right of the square.

Down by the harbour, just beyond the shops, there is a comfortably furnished journalists' club which serves drinks and light refreshments. This is also open to non-journalists, but members of the profession get a discount on production of their business cards. Its pleasant club-room has a large open fire, a welcome amenity during the cool spring and autumn evenings.

EXCURSIONS BY BOAT. During the season it is possible to make the 40-minute crossing to the Greek island of **Meis**. Boats may be hired at the harbour for this purpose. As Meis is not an official entry point to Greece, admission may not always be granted. When visitors are allowed to land, their stay is usually limited to a few hours. Passports are required for the trip. The charter-boat skipper will obtain the necessary customs and emigration clearances from the Turkish authorities. He will also negotiate entry to Meis with the Greek port officials.

Another popular excursion is to the *Mavi Mağara* (Blue Grotto) between Kalkan and Kaş. It is possible to combine this with a visit to the beach at Kapıtaş.

There are also daily excursions to the island of *Kekova*, famous for its submerged harbour, and to the sites of *Aperlae*, *Simena* and *Teimiussa* (see below). The best beaches are some distance from the town and are most easily reached by boat. Bathing in the immediate neighbourhood of Kaş is not recommended. The beaches are small, stony and not always very clean, while the sea near the rocks on the E and W sides of the town and on the peninsula is deep, rough and often heavily polluted.

History. In antiquity Kaş was known as ANTIPHELLUS in Greek, *Habesos* in Lycian. It was the port of the city of *Phellus*, which according to most authorities was sited in the mountainous area behind the modern town. Originally Phellus, which means stony land, was the more important foundation. The site of Antiphellus suffered from several disadvantages: it was vulnerable to attack and the lack of level ground inhibited expansion. Excavations have revealed that in the 4C BC it consisted of a few buildings near the harbour and some rock-tombs. A century later the situation had changed. Antiphellus had become a busy port, probably for the export of timber from the hinterland, while the star of Phellus had begun to wane. In Roman times Antiphellus was one of the major trading cities of Lycia. According to Pliny it was famous for the quality of its sponges.

Lion tomb at Antiphellus (Kaş), by Sir George Scharf (1820–95).

Today there are few visible reminders of the past in Kaş: a Hellenistic theatre, some fragments of wall and a number of tombs. It would seem that much was lost comparatively recently. In the 19C Charles Texier, the celebrated French traveller, found several buildings including a basilica and a circular Byzantine church near the theatre. These have vanished completely. In 1842 Lieutenant Spratt noted that there were more than a hundred sarcophagi in Kaş. Most of these have disappeared, broken up for the sake of the stone slabs that could be fashioned from their sides and bottoms. Only the rounded covers, useless for building purposes, remain.

To reach the *Hellenistic theatre* take Hastane Cad., which starts near the Ali Baba Hotel. A little way along on the left-hand side there are the remains of a small *temple* which dates from the 1C BC. It is not known to whom it was dedicated. Just before the theatre, again on the left, part of the Hellenistic sea wall may be seen. The theatre, surrounded by ancient olive trees, is to the right of the road. Greater than a semicircle, it has 26 rows of seats, no paradoi, no diazoma. It would seem that there was no permanent stage-building; the low curved wall is a modern construction. The retaining wall of the cavea is constructed from huge stone blocks which vary considerably in size and shape. These are best seen on the W side of the theatre. Continue up the slope to the level of the top row and you will be rewarded with a splendid view of the sea and of the distant island of Meis. It is particularly beautiful in the early evening, when daylight begins to fade and the lights of the little island's port glow like jewels against the velvet of the growing dark.

About 100m behind the theatre, on the top of the hill, there is a very fine rock-cut tomb. This, the so-called *Doric Tomb*, dates from the 4C BC. It consists of a single chamber (5m by 5m). Traces of decoration remain on the outside. The tomb was closed by a sliding door. At the back the couch on which the body was placed is decorated with a striking frieze. This shows a number of tiny female figures performing a ritual dance: holding hands, they move in a stately measure which causes their skirts to billow outwards in graceful folds. Sadly, the tomb is now being used as a shelter for animals. It is fouled and odorous and its walls and floor are black from the smoke of fire.

By continuing across the hill we soon reach the Bucak Limanı. From there it is but a few minutes' walk back to the town centre. On the great cliff that dominates Kaş there are a number of Lycian rock-tombs. Access to these is by a narrow path which makes its sinuous way through some private gardens and then climbs the hillside at an angle. It would seem that one of the tombs was used twice, as it carries two inscriptions made at different periods, one in Lycian and another in Latin. Of greater interest is the so-called **Lion Tomb**. This can be found in a small street that leads off the NE corner of the square. The top part of the monument is one of the finest examples extant of a Lycian ogival sarcophagus. The lifting bosses on the cover are carved in the form of lions' heads resting on their forepaws, hence its name. On the top part of the gable-end two figures are carved in shallow relief. The sarcophagus rests on a stone base and beneath this there is another burial chamber. Both burial chambers were broken into and robbed in antiquity. On the side of the lower chamber there is a long inscription in an unusual form of the Lycian language similar to that found on the Inscribed Pillar in the agora at Xanthus. Although it has not been deciphered, it is presumed to be an epitaph, perhaps written in a poetical form. On the harbour mole there is another ogival Lycian sarcophagus and there are several examples E of the town.

Excursion to Aperlae, Kekova, Kale (Simena), and Hacımusala (Teimiussa)

One of the most popular day excursions from Kaş is a boat trip to Kekova and to the sites of the ancient cities of Aperlae, Teimiussa and Simena.

During the season boats leave from the harbour mole at about 9.00, returning in the evening at 18.00. Having passed the island of Meis on the right you enter a narrow bay, at whose head stands the ruins of the city of **APERLAE**, a Lycian foundation. During the Roman period the leader of a sympolity, which included Apollonia, Isinda and Simena, Aperlae was never a place of great importance. No trace of a temple or theatre has been found there. As the boat approaches the shore it passes over the remains of the ancient harbour buildings. On the W side there was a quay, capable of berthing a number of ships.

The fortifications of Aperlae date from two distinct periods. Stretching down from the acropolis are the walls of the later city, which appear to have been erected to protect the harbour area. Note the gate on the E side, which is now partly submerged. Between the inner and outer walls there are several ogival-type sarcophagi. The inner wall of the city was constructed of ashlar. This has been repaired in several places. On the W side there are three well-preserved gates. The main entrance to the city, which had defensive towers on each side, was on the S wall. The acropolis of Aperlae, which is enclosed by the inner wall, is covered with undergrowth and as a consequence is not easy to explore.

From Aperlae the boat usually goes next to the island of **Kekova**. During the Hellenistic period there was a considerable increase in maritime trade between the cities of Lycia and other parts of the Greek world. Unfortunately, this growth in commerce was paralleled by a marked increase in piracy. As a result islands like Kekova were fortified and became both refuges in times of danger and advance warning posts for the cities on the mainland. Centuries later, during a period of Arab raids, they served the same purpose.

As it skirts the shoreline of the island your boat glides over the remains of buildings, stairs and pavements, which are clearly visible under the sea. Usually there is time for a swim and a picnic at a small beach on the N side of the island. Prominent here are the remains of an apsidal construction, which some authorities believe to be part of a Byzantine church, while others are of the opinion that it was a small boatyard. Its local name, 'Tersane', would appear to support the second hypothesis. Care should be taken in swimming near the underwater ruins as they, and the surrounding rocks, are covered with spiny sea urchins. Note that skin-diving is forbidden near the

Kale, near Demre.

submerged buildings. There are severe penalties for transgressing this rule and for removing any antiquities found in the sea or on land. There are the remains of a number of buildings on the island, but these are almost hidden by the dense and thorny undergrowth and can only be explored with difficulty.

Near Kekova there are several islets whose shaved and sculptured outlines betray the fact that they were used as quarries by ancient builders. It is a short journey to the mainland and to the village of *Kale* (Castle), the site of the city of SIMENA. Kale has a few pensions which provide basic accommodation, and there are a number of small restaurants down by the harbour which offer simple meals. On the left of the landing-stage there are some partly submerged ruins, while the remains of a Roman *baths complex* (c AD 79) may be found on the sea-shore nearby. An inscription states that this structure was dedicated by the city of Aperlae to the Emperor Titus. The ascent to the medieval *castle*, which dominates Kale, is by a steep path. This winds between the houses and through the gardens of the village. It passes two sarcophagi, one dedicated to Mentor, the son of Idagrus; the other has a small exedra. The last stage of the climb is over a section of very slippery rock which should be negotiated with care. On the left below the ramparts there is a small rock-cut *theatre*. This could accommodate about 300 spectators in its seven rows of seats. The view from the theatre across the bay to the island of Kekova and down to the village of Kale is magnificent. Equally striking is the vista from the ramparts of the castle northwards to *Üçağiz* and the site of Teimiussa. On the way down to the landing-stage, a path to the left leads to the *necropolis* of Simena. This has several ogival sarcophagi and some rock-cut tombs, one of which bears an inscription in Lycian.

Üçağiz like the earlier Greek name Tristomo means 'the three mouths'. This refers to the channel which leads to the village and the two openings E and W of Kekova island. The village has a number of small restaurants and some pensions offering accommodation.

While most visitors to Üçağiz prefer to go there by boat, it can also be reached by road. A right-hand turn c 20km from Kaş on road 400 to Demre leads to a dirt road. This is passable as far as the village of *Siçak* (c 9km), by most vehicles, but it deteriorates rapidly there-after.

Siçak is the site of the ancient settlement of APOLLONIA, a place not mentioned by the ancient writers; the site has been identified by inscriptions found on the spot. Some of these relate to dedications made by the 'People of Apollonia' to Augustus and Tiberius. However, the settlement existed long before Roman times. Proof of this is provided by the presence of several Lycian pillar tombs and a Lycian rock-tomb with an inscription in Greek. Apollonia was built on a hill about 90m above the modern village of Siçak. In addition to the tombs there are the remains of the city walls, traces of the theatre and some cisterns.

The site of TEIMIUSSA is a short distance to the E of the village of Üçağiz. Like Apollonia it has been identified from an inscription. It was a small settlement, without walls or public buildings. The remains extant are almost all tombs. Many of these lie in a marshy area half hidden by clumps of reeds. Near the shore there are two rock-cut tombs. The tomb on the right, bears a relief showing a nude youth and has the Lycian name 'Kluwanimi', by the side of the decorated entrance. Beyond this tomb there is a jumbled mass of ogival sarcophagi from the Hellenistic and Roman periods. Many bear inscriptions in Greek, stating that their occupants were citizens of Cyaneae or Myra, proof of Teimiussa's dependence on one or both of these cities. E of the site there is a small rock-cut landing-stage, surrounded by desecrated tombs. One, which is placed about 2m above ground level, may be approached through a natural cleft in the rock.

Excursion to Gömbe, Comba and Choma

Take road 400 E from Kaş towards **Demre** (see Rte 19). After c 11km branch left for (c 95km) Elmalı via (c 12km) Kasaba. This picturesque road, which crosses the Kohu Dağ by two passes, Karaovabeli Geç (1080m) and Sinekçibeli Geç (1545m), should not be attempted during bad weather.

In its name, the village of (c 25km) *Gömbe*, situated near the S end of the Elmalı plain, commemorates the ancient city of COMBA. The site of Comba is on a hilltop to the SW of the village. The few pathetic remains of the city do not justify the exertion of the climb.

Apart from being an episcopal see and possessing a Council and an Assembly little is known about Comba. Its main claim to fame is that it was the cult centre of the Twelve Gods of Lycia. More than 20 carvings commemorating these hunting deities have been found in various places, including about eight in the neighbourhood of Gömbe. One is displayed in the Antalya Museum. The stelae, which are remarkably similar, are 3C AD. In the upper section of the carvings the 12 gods are shown dressed in tunics, with another figure, generally male, in the centre. On the lower register the donor is portrayed flanked by 12 animals, which appear to be dogs. In general, the inscription is limited to the name of the donor and a statement to the effect that the carving was dedicated to the Twelve Gods at his command. Although the portrayal of the figures is crude, the stelae have an attractive, artless simplicity that disarms criticism.

About 8km from Gömbe, near the village of *Hacımusalar*, on a hüyük is the site of the city of CHOMA. This has been identified by inscriptions dated to the period of the Roman Empire. There are few visible remains. About 5km NW of Choma, near *Kızılca* there are two Lycian rock-cut tombs. One bears an inscription in the Lycian language, which mentions Pericles, the dynast of Limyra.

After c 5km road 635 from Finike on the S coast of Lycia is reached. From the junction it is a further 6km to *Elmalı* (see Rte 20).

19 Kaş to Demre (Myra)

Total distance c 37km. **Kaş**—R400 c 23km *Yavu* (c 3km *Cyaneae*)—(c 2.5km *Tyherissus*)—(c 4km Istlada)—(c 12km *Trysa*)—(c 0.5km *Sura*)—c 14km **Demre / Myra**.

Road 400 climbs in a series of spectacular bends to the plateau above Kaş. From the summit there are magnificent views over the bay to the Greek island of Meis and westwards towards Kalkan. After c 11km a turning to the left leads to Antalya by an inland route via Elmalı and *Korkuteli* while at c 20km a very rough track on the right goes to Apollonia and Üçağiz (see Rte 18). At this point the road enters a wild, picturesque and inhospitable stretch of countryside whose rocky skeleton protrudes through a thin covering of soil and where only the tough, thorny maquis can survive. In antiquity, there were many small cities and settlements between Kaş and Demre. Now long abandoned and forgotten, except by archaeologists, their ruined fortifications, silent theatres and desecrated tombs bear silent witness to their past glories. Lycian, Hellenistic and Roman ruins abound, while only a few tiny cultivated fields and scattered olive groves and an occasional shepherd brooding over his flock testify to the continuing presence of man in this past of Lycia.

The village of (c 23km) *Yavu*, sited between a bluff which towers to more than 200m and a plain which slopes gently towards the sea at distant Kekova, is the starting point for visits to the ancient city of **CYANEAE**. From the centre of the village a rough track is signposted (3km) to the site. However, a more interesting, if somewhat more difficult, route starts from behind the village. This ascends at an angle until it reaches the base of the bluff towards its E end. Allow about one hour for the climb. It is advisable to take a guide, as the path to the summit is overgrown in parts and difficult to follow. Also there are a number of partially concealed cisterns inside the acropolis which should be approached with care.

Cyaneae has been identified by inscriptions found on the spot. How it obtained its name, which means 'dark blue', is not known. (The English words 'cyanic' and 'cyanide' are derived from the same Greek root, Κυάνεος.) It may be that it is based on the city's, unknown Lycian name. Although mentioned by Pliny and other ancient writers, little is known about the history of Cyaneae. During the reign of Antoninus Pius (AD 138–161) the Lyciarch, Jason of Cyaneae, was involved in a dispute concerning certain honours that had been voted to him. The dispute was submitted to the emperor who found in his favour. Jason, like his contemporary Opramoas of Rhodiapolis, was famous for his benefactions. Several Lycian cities profited from his generosity. The territory of Cyaneae extended as far S as Kekova and is mentioned in a number of inscriptions found at other sites. Originally a Lycian foundation, most of the extant remains date from the Roman period. In Byzantine times, although an episcopal see and still a city of some importance, its fortunes began to decline. This process of decay continued and Cyaneae was finally abandoned in the 10C.

Near the base of the bluff there are the vestiges of an ancient pathway which has steps cut into the rock at intervals. This passes an interesting group of early tombs. One of these appears at first sight to be a typical ogival sarcophagus with decorated lifting bosses in the form of lions' heads. However, the lid and body are made from a single piece of stone and it was necessary to make an opening on the W side for the admission of the body.

The acropolis of Cyaneae is enclosed by walls on three sides, the fourth (S side) is protected by the precipice. It contains the remains of a number of constructions which have been identified as a baths complex, a library and cisterns. However, it is not easy to find these buildings as the whole area is now covered with thick, tangled undergrowth which makes exploration almost impossible. Cyaneae is reputed to have more sarcophagi than any other Lycian city. (A fine example stands outside the entrance gate of Antalya's Archaeological Museum.) Apart from those on the S slope, the greatest concentration is to be found to the W of the acropolis where an avenue lined on both sides with tombs, most of which date from the

Lycian tomb at Cyaneae,

Roman period, stretches almost to the site of the theatre. Many of the sarcophagi are decorated with reliefs and bear inscriptions. Apart from the almost complete disappearance of the stage-building and some damage to the retaining wall of the cavea the theatre is in a good state of preservation. It has a single diazoma with five cunei below and nine above the division. Most of the original seats remain. Some of the rows have holes for wooden posts, which were probably used to support the Velum. This was used to support an awning, which protected the spectators from the elements.

On the way down to the village of Yavu the path passes underneath an interesting rock-tomb which has several unusual features. Built in the form of an Ionic temple, it has a single pillar in the centre of the entrance to the principal chamber and a sarcophagus has been placed on top of the pediment in a deep recess cut into the rock. According to an inscription above the lintel, Perpenenis, for whom the tomb was built, is buried with his wife in the sarcophagus, while other members of the family were placed in the upper and lower chambers.

Cyaneae, which is little visited, has an atmosphere of brooding melancholy derived in part from its isolated position and neglected state. The effort required to climb to the top is more than repaid by the view at sunset along the street of tombs or by the sight of the windswept theatre, empty except for a few agile goats that pluck daintily at the bushes which sprout among the broken seats.

S of Yavu there are two settlements of minor importance—TYBERISSUS and ISTLADA. The former is sited on a hilltop about 400m above sea-level. It has a number of tombs which date from the Hellenistic and Roman periods and a small church built over a Doric temple dedicated to Apollo. The latter has the remains of some stone houses and a number of sarcophagi. Both have been identified by inscriptions.

A turning on the left-hand side c 6km from Yavu leads to c 12km TRYSA, another site which has been identified by inscriptions. Nothing is known of its history, but it may have been the fortified stronghold of a local chieftain. Trysa is situated on a small hill near the modern village of *Gölbaşı*. Its remains are some of the oldest to have been found in Lycia, a number dating back to the 5C BC. Most are in a very poor state of preservation. Apart from fragments of a pillar tomb and a small ruined temple there is the usual complement of ogival sarcophagi one of which is ornamented with reliefs and decorative bosses. However, Trysa's most remarkable feature is the heroon (4C BC) located towards the NE of the acropolis. A wall 3m high surrounds the square enclosure containing the sarcophagus of the deified hero and his family. This wall was covered with a frieze in two bands representing various mythological subjects: the life of Theseus; incidents in the 'Iliad' and the 'Odyssey'; the battles of the Centaurs and Lapiths and the siege of a town. Unfortunately, the frieze is no longer in Trysa or indeed in Turkey. It has been removed to Vienna where it is preserved in the Kunsthistorisches Museum.

The main road continues through another tract of wild countryside, first clinging to the side of the mountain, then turning through a series of lazy bends to descend at last to the fertile plain of Demre. From the top of the hill this is a startling sight. A mosaic of plastic and glass-covered greenhouses, relieved by the vivid green tesserae of orange and lemon groves, covers a huge area from the foot of the mountain to the sea. On a curve towards the bottom of the hill an isolated cluster of houses, near a dewpond, marks the nearest point on the main road to Sura. There are no sign posts to the site, which is about 20 minutes' walk due W over the fields. Visitors are advised to take a guide from the village, as there is no clearly defined path. A guide would also help to repel the agressive sheepdogs, which guard the farms and flocks near the site.

SURA, like Patara, probably owed its importance to the presence of an oracle of Apollo. However, unlike Patara the settlement never developed a political dimension, remaining a centre of religion and divination and a dependency of Demre. This is reflected both in its size and in the type of buildings found there.

History. Little is known about its history. Most of the references to Sura by the ancient writers are to the unusual method of divination used by the oracle.

These excited a considerable amount of interest. Pliny stated that fish, summoned 'three times on the pipe' to give augury, were thrown pieces of meat. If they took the meat, that was a good sign, if they pushed it away with their tails, a bad sign. A more detailed description is provided by the author of 'Lycia', the Hellenistic writer Polycharmus. 'When they come to the sea, where is the grove of Apollo by the shore, on which is the whirlpool on the sand, the clients present themselves holding two wooden spits, on each of which are ten pieces of roast meat. The priest takes his seat in silence by the grove, while the client throws the spits into the whirlpool and watches what happens. After the spits are thrown in, the pool fills with sea-water, and a multitude of fish appear as if by magic, and of a size to cause alarm. The prophet announces the species of the fish and the client accordingly receives his answer from the priest. Among smaller fish there appear sometimes whales and sawfish and many strange and unknown kinds.' Finally, the geographer Artemidorus of Ephesus (fl. c 100 BC) stated that large fish appeared in a whirlpool of freshwater and that those who came to consult the oracle threw pieces of meat, barley and wheat cakes to them. The three accounts, which may refer to practices employed at different times, disagree on one point only—whether the predictions were based on the type of fish in the pool or on the way they reacted to the offerings.

No information is available about the later history of the oracle of Sura. We do not know, if, like Patara, it suffered a period of decline and revival in the 1C and 2C AD. There is no record of when the last prophetic utterance was made. It is possible that the influence of St. Nicholas of Myra and of the Christian community of that city had some effect on the oracle by the middle of the 4C, a time when Christian shrines began to appear in the great temple of Apollo at Didyma. It is probable that the edict of Theodosius in 385 abolishing all oracles gave the oracle at Sura the *coup de grâce*. This stated that 'no mortal man shall have the effrontery to encourage vain hopes by the inspection of entrails, or attempt to learn the future by the detestable consultation of oracles. The severest penalties await those who disobey.' Perhaps it was at this time that the triumph of Christianity over paganism at Sura was confirmed by the erection of a small church near the site of the temple of Apollo.

The scanty remains of ancient Sura are in two parts. At the W end of the plain there are the ruins of the tiny acropolis, the so-called house

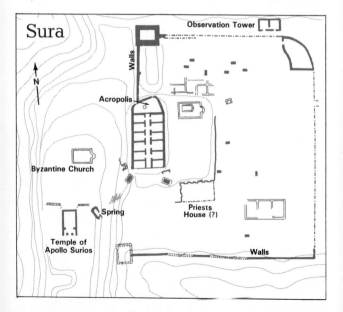

of the priests, two watch-towers, part of the walls and a number of tombs. Down by the ancient harbour, now silted up and overgrown, are the ruins of the temple of Apollo, the sacred spring and the walls of a small church.

Approaching the site from the main road the first building encountered is a *watch-tower*. This structure, which is in a good state of preservation, lies just outside the line of the ancient walls to the NE of the acropolis. The agora and residential area, which date from a late period of occupation, are between this tower and the acropolis. Sura's acropolis is built on a rocky spur c 10m high, near the extreme W edge of the plain at the point where it slopes steeply towards the harbour. It contains a fortress (some parts 5C BC) divided into 12 small cell-like chambers, six on each side of a narrow passage. The junction of the W and N walls of the fortified area is marked by a square watch-tower. At the S end of the acropolis there is an interesting group of funeral monuments. Below and to the left of a typical Lycian rock-tomb a large burial chamber has been constructed by the side of the hill. Resting on the flat roof of this structure is a tall *pillar tomb* with an ogival lid. Apparently this monument, dated to the 4C BC, was intended for family burial, the owner being placed in the pillar tomb and members of his family in the chamber underneath.

The site of the so-called *House of the Priests*, which some authorities believe formed part of a larger sacred area, lies to the SW of this group of tombs. All that remains is a terrace c 15m by c 9m which has been cut from the rock. Sockets for roof beams on the N wall 8m above the ground suggest that the structure had a wooden roof. On the N and W walls decorative tablets, carved in relief, list the names of the priests of Apollo Surius.

In ancient times access to the harbour area was by way of a rock-cut stairway, which descended from the plateau at a point about 50m W of the house of the priests. Traces of this stairway still remain. Today the lower part of the site is a marsh, passable only in summer, through which the stream that rises in the sacred spring meanders lazily for c 1.5km to the sea. The temple of Apollo is a small building, c 14m by c 7m, constructed in the Doric style. A temple in antis, built during the late Hellenistic period, it stood on or near the ancient harbour. The sacred spring is a few metres from the temple, near the bottom of the stairway. The small Byzantine church is a short distance to the N.

Some visitors are tempted to walk the few kilometres that separate Sura from Andriace. However, the route through the marsh and along the shoreline is difficult, uncomfortable and, in certain circumstances, may be dangerous. A more pleasant walk is to the *Roman tomb* at the road junction with Andriace and then through the citrus groves to 5km Demre.

On returning from Sura to the main road, continue E towards Demre. After c 2.5km the road divides at the bottom of the hill. The left fork goes to Demre, the right to Andriace. At this crossroads there are the remains of a Roman *temple tomb*. Apart from extensive damage to the W side, it is in a good state of preservation. Neither the exact date of its construction nor the name of its owner is known. Built entirely of closely fitting masonry, it stands to a height of c 13m. Access to the interior is from the N side by an elaborate, tall doorway, flanked on the left by a Corinthian pilaster. The matching pilaster on the right has disappeared. Entrances on the S side, closed by stone slabs, led to two underground burial chambers. On the E and W walls there are stone benches, which may have been used for the support of additional sarcophagi. Note the large false arches on the E and S walls and the carved lion heads on the sima.

From the Roman tomb, a road flanked by citrus groves and greenhouses leads c 2.5km to **Demre**, an undistinguished country town, important only as a marketing centre for fruit and vegetables and of interest to the visitor because of its proximity to the site of ancient Myra.

Accommodation in Demre is limited and of poor quality. However, Finike and Kaş, both just an hour's travelling time away, have several small hotels and pensions offering inexpensive accommodation. There are frequent bus and dolmuş services to and from Finike, Kumluca and Antalya to the E, and Kaş, Kalkan and Fethiye to the W. As there is no bus station in Demre, services provided by the two principal companies serving this part of Lycia stop in the town centre at their respective offices. Tickets may be purchased and full details of the services obtained there. In the centre of Demre one or two unpretentious restaurants provide simple meals. The post office is 150m to the E of the main square.

About 1.5km S of the town is a long beach of mixed gravel and sand. However, the best bathing is at Andriace c 2.5km SW (see below). Andriace has one small restaurant, but no hotel or pension. During the summer there are daily excursions by boat from Andriace to Kekova.

The ruins of the ancient city of **MYRA** are 1.5km N of Demre.

History. Although the earliest written references date from the 1C BC, evidence from Lycian inscriptions and monuments suggest that there was a settlement here at least as early as the 5C BC. During the 3C BC an elaborate system of watch-towers, stretching from Sura in the W to the E edge of the Demre plain, was constructed. In the 2C BC Myra was one of the six most important cities in the Lycian League: it issued federal coins, and was entitled to three votes, the maximum permitted in the League's Assembly. An ancient tradition stated that the city's name was derived from the Greek word for myrrh. That this belief persisted into Byzantine times is evidenced by the description of Constantine VII (Porphyrogenitus; 913–959) of 'thrice blessed, myrrh-breathing city of the Lycians, where the mighty Nicolaus, servant of God, spouts forth myrrh in accordance with the city's name'. There is no evidence that myrrh was ever produced in Myra and modern scholarship leans towards a more prosaic explanation. As in the case of Patara, 'Myra' is almost certainly a variant of the original, unknown Lycian name of the city.

Despite an unpropitious beginning, Myra had reasonably good relations with Rome. In 42 BC, after he had captured Xanthus, Brutus sent an officer, Lentulus Spinther, to obtain money from the city. The Myrans were unwilling to pay and Spinther had to force his way through the chain that closed the entrance to the harbour at Andriace. The city then reluctantly agreed to Spinther's demands. A year before his tragic death near Antioch in AD 19 Germanicus, the adopted son of the Emperor Tiberius, accompanied by his wife Agrippina, paid a visit to Myra. This event was commemorated by the erection of statues at Andriace in their honour.

According to the Acts of the Apostles, when St. Paul was being taken as a prisoner to Rome in AD 60, his ship called at Myra: 'Then, setting sail, we coasted under the lee of Cyprus, to avoid contrary winds, but made a straight course over the open sea that lies off Cilicia and Pamphylia, and so reached Lystra (Myra) in Lycia. There the centurion found a boat from Alexandria which was sailing for Italy, and put us on board.' This was the voyage, which dogged by gales and contrary winds, ended in shipwreck off the coast of Malta.

In the 2C AD Myra benefited considerably from the gifts of large sums of money from Opramoas of Rhodiapolis and Jason of Cyaneae. (At about the same time it acquired the status of a metropolis.) The gifts were used for the renovation and decoration of public buildings. With the spread of Christianity throughout the Roman Empire, Myra abandoned its pagan past. In the 4C it acquired new and widespread fame because of the miracles performed by its bishop, St. Nicholas. The city reached its apogee in the reign of Theodosius II

(408–450) when he made it the provincial capital of Lycia. Myra began to decline in the 7C when, in common with neighbouring cities, it suffered greatly from Arab raids. In AD 809 it was occupied for some time by Haroun al Rashid and in 1034 it was attacked once again from the sea by the Arabs. Finally, exhausted by warfare, constantly threatened by earthquakes and impoverished by the silting of the river Myrus, most of its inhabitants moved away.

The accounts of Fellows and Texier of their travels in Lycia revived interest in Myra in the 19C. When Beaufort came to Andriace in 1811 he describes Myra as being a small village situated on a plain well-stocked with cattle. This plain was 'partly cultivated; it also displayed some symptoms of commerce, in the heaps of billet wood and deal plank, which lay on the beach ready for embarkation'. Cockerell, who visited Myra a year later, sketched the ruins of the city and of the theatre, which were better preserved than at present. He was churlishly treated by the local inhabitants whom he described as being more than ordinarily jealous and ferocious. In the middle of the 19C S Lycia was still a dangerous area to visit. Newton describes how not far from Myra pirates attacked a boat which was proceeding from Rhodes to Finike. Luckily, the 400 passengers only had their money taken from them. The previous day the same pirates boarded and sank a small boat from Symi and murdered all the crew.

A century later, when Freya Stark came to Myra, difficulty of access and a degree of physical discomfort had replaced the earlier dangers. Travel to and from Antalya was usually done by sea. The excellent coast road, which today links Myra with that city, was something the inhabitants talked and dreamed about.

The antiquities of Myra fall naturally into three distinct zones. The first, on the SW of the site, includes the theatre, the so-called sea necropolis and the area occupied by the agora. The second, on the N, covers the acropolis, the buildings on it and the surrounding walls. The third, on the SE, encompasses the river necropolis and the channel which supplied Myra with water.

The **Theatre** of Myra, destroyed by the earthquake that devastated the city in AD 141, was restored shortly afterwards through the generosity of Opramoas of Rhodiapolis. Some time later it was modified so that it could be used as an arena for gladiatorial games. There are six rows of seats above and 29 below the single diazoma. Holes indicate the places where a velum was erected to shelter spectators from the elements. The cavea, whose centre rests against the rock face, is supported at the sides by vaulted passages. These contain the stairs by which the spectators entered the auditorium. The two-storey passage on the W is flanked by a number of small rooms. An inscription in one of these states that it was used by a trader called Gelasius, probably for the sale of refreshments. The wide diazoma is backed by a 2m-high wall in whose centre, near the stairs leading to the upper rows, there is a representation of Tyche, goddess of fortune, and an inscription which reads: 'Fortune of the city, be ever victorious, with good luck'. Note the graffiti on the diazoma—these may indicate the reserved seats of regular patrons.

A substantial part of the stage-building remains. The façade facing the cavea was richly ornamented with theatrical masks and representations of mythological scenes and personages. These included Zeus' rape of Ganymede, and Medea and her children.

The so-called **Sea Necropolis** is on the cliff face behind and to the NW and NE of the theatre. It contains a remarkable collection of rock-tombs, several with richly-decorated façades. Most are of the familiar 'house' type, believed to copy the dwellings of the early inhabitants of the area. Some have stylised representations of the wooden beams used as roof-supports in Lycian houses. A few have reliefs that still bear traces of colour. Inscriptions, where they exist, are usually in Lycian.

*Rock-tombs at Myra (Demre), by Sir George Scharf
(1820–95).*

At the base of the cliff an interesting tomb at ground level has a
sculpture on the pediment which depicts a critical moment in the
conflict between two warriors. The figure on the left appears to be
fleeing, but he is being restrained by the warrior on the right, who
has placed his hand on the other's shield.

A narrow goat path leads to a group of three tombs c 10m above
ground level. One of these is decorated with an elaborate relief,
which dates from the middle of the 4C BC. In the centre panel a male
figure, perhaps the deceased, is shown reclining on a couch, flanked
on the right by a seated female figure and on the left by a musician
and by a young slave carrying a bowl. On the extreme left there are
three male figures. One in armour is receiving his helmet from a
page. The other two are nude, well-muscled youths, who gaze
tranquilly into the distance.

The *agora* of Myra was probably to the E of the theatre. So far this
part of the city has not been excavated. On the left of the road
leading from Myra to Demre there are the remains of a *brick
building*, which dates from the late Roman period. This has been
described variously as a basilica or a baths complex. Several interesting inscriptions have been found in this area. One sets out the
regulations which deal with a ferry service operated during the
Roman period between Andriace, the port of Myra, and Limyra.
Unauthorised operators were obliged to pay a heavy fine to the city.
The other inscription details the payments to be made to the Lycian
League from import duties collected by Myra.

Coins issued by Myra show that the city's main deity was Artemis Eleutheria, a
form of Cybele the ancient mother goddess of Anatolia. Like the fecund

Ephesian Artemis, her representations were usually decorated with a profusion of fertility objects, which have been variously described as breasts, eggs, or bull's testes. After the earthquake of 141, her temple was restored magnificently by Opramoas of Rhodiapolis. Probably sited in the neighbourhood of the theatre and the agora, it has not yet been discovered.

The *acropolis* may be reached from the plain by an ancient path. The outer walls of the fortification were constructed during the Byzantine period. The inner Lycian walls are of polygonal masonry and date from the 5C BC. The central area contained a watch-tower and cisterns for water storage. Near the S gate there is the base of a small Roman temple. Apart from the view, largely spoiled by the plastic greenhouses, there is little to justify the exertion of the climb.

The **river necropolis**, visited less often than the ruins on the W side of the site, contains several fine tombs including one, the Painted Tomb, which is of outstanding interest. The necropolis can be reached by a rough path that runs parallel to the cliff-face in a E direction. This passes a group of tombs, on the SW side of the bluff, which can only be reached with difficulty. Just beyond the point where the acropolis projects into the plain, a track leads from the road across some fields to the cliff base. The tombs of the river necropolis should be seen early in the day, when the architectural details are illuminated by the morning sun.

The **Painted Tomb** is one of the most remarkable in Lycia. When visited by Charles Fellows in the 19C, its reliefs still bore traces of yellow, red, blue and purple paint. Today—apart from some red and blue in the background to a reclining male figure—these have disappeared. Access to the tomb is by rather precarious stone steps, which lead to a narrow platform. The painted tomb is furnished with stone benches on which sarcophagi could be placed. Around the outside and in the entrance porch there are a number of life-sized figures carved in relief. Inside the porch on the left a reclining man holds a wine-cup and on the right a seated woman is flanked by two children, one of whom is nude. On the left, outside the porch, where the rock has been smoothed, there is a magisterial male figure dressed in outdoor clothes and holding a staff. This is balanced on the right by the figure of a woman accompanied by a female child, who is holding her hand. The reliefs are believed to relate to the indoor and outdoor lives of those for whom the tomb was constructed. However, an element of mystery is introduced by the presence of three other figures, separated by an angle in the rock-face from the main group. These are a veiled woman carrying a box in her hands which she extends towards a youth facing her; he stands in a casual pose with legs crossed, resting on a staff, and offers her a flower; behind him is a child who grips the youth's cloak timidly. How these figures relate to those in the main group, if at all, is not known.

Bean mentions another tomb higher up on the cliff-face. This had a pediment decorated with a relief showing a lion attacking a bull. On the entrance porch there was a frieze with figures, which he believed to be dancers, flanking a lion's head. Freya Stark, however, suggests that the figures represented Artemis of Thera, 'who stands on her double fish-tail between lion heads, and holds her long locks with upraised arms under a high crown'. Unfortunately this tomb has been damaged, apparently by a rock fall, and now scarcely merits the effort needed to reach it.

Myra received its water supply from a source high up in the plateau c 20km inland. It reached the city through an open channel, part of which may be seen to the N of the river necropolis.

The **Church of St. Nicholas** is on the W side of Demre, about 150m from the main square. On the left of the entrance in a small garden, the saint is depicted, rather incongruously, as Santa Claus carrying a sack of presents and surrounded by children.

Apart from the fact that he was born in Patara c 300 and later became bishop of Myra, little is known with certainty about the life of St. Nicholas. The son of wealthy parents it is said that he travelled to Palestine and Egypt in his youth. To judge by the stories that have grown up around him, he appears to have exercised considerable influence on the early and medieval church. In the 6C a basilica was erected in his honour in Constantinople and by the late Middle Ages 400 churches were dedicated to him in England alone. He became the patron saint of Greece, Russia, children, prisoners, sailors and travellers. Many legends are told about his life and works. His elevation to bishop was accomplished by divine intervention. The electors and elders assembled at Myra were advised by heaven to select the first man to enter the church next day. That was Nicholas. An early biographer recounts his suffering during the persecutions of Diocletian: 'As he was chief priest of the Christians of this town [Myra] and preached the truths of faith with a holy liberty, the divine Nicholas was seized by the magistrates, tortured, then chained and thrown into prison with many other Christians. But when the great and religious Constantine, chosen by God, assumed the imperial diadem of the Romans, the prisoners were released from their bonds and with them the illustrious Nicholas, who when he was set at liberty returned to Myra.' There is a tradition that he took part in the Council of Nicaea in 325 where, infuriated by the obstinacy of the heretic Arius, he slapped the face of that turbulent priest with such vigour that his bones rattled.

It was said that Nicholas appeared in a dream to Constantine and ordered the emperor to release some prisoners, who had been unjustly condemned to death. It is also recorded that he escaped unscathed from a church that fell down around him. It became a tradition in E Mediterranean countries for mariners to wish each other a safe voyage with the expression: 'May St. Nicholas hold the tiller'. Nicholas destroyed the temple of Artemis Eleutheria by supernatural means and demons fled before his approach. Once, he saved Myra from starvation by commandeering a quantity of grain from ships that had called at Andriace on their way from Egypt to Byzantium. Miraculously, the cargo was found to be undiminished when the ships arrived at their final destination.

Two stories suggest why Nicholas came to be regarded as the patron saint of children. In a time of famine a butcher lured three youths to his house. While they slept he killed them, cut up their bodies and placed the pieces in a barrel of salt, intending to sell them for food. The saint, told by an angel of this dreadful occurrence, hastened to the butcher's house and restored the boys to life. On another occasion Nicholas heard that the three daughters of a merchant, who had fallen on hard times, were about to take up a life of prostitution as they had no marriage dowries. The saint saved them from sin by throwing three bags of gold into the merchant's garden during the night, so enabling the girls to get married. This legend is sometimes used to explain the custom of giving presents to children at Christmas.

Although an unsuccessful attempt was made to destroy his tomb in the 9C during the occupation of Myra by the Arabs, the body of St. Nicholas rested, undisturbed, for more than 700 years in a sarcophagus in the church. In 1087 a group of Italian merchants, ignoring the protests of the monks, broke open the tomb. Inside they found the saint's bones covered in myrrh. They transported them to Bari and placed them in a shrine in the cathedral. This was a time when European cities competed vigorously with each other for the possession of sacred relics. So it is not surprising that shortly afterwards the Venetians also claimed to have the body of the saint, stating that they had removed it from Myra at the time of the First Crusade. Today the only relics of St. Nicholas in his native land are a few sad bones—and these are of doubtful authenticity—which are believed to come from the church at Myra. They are now displayed in a casket in the Antalya Museum.

While it is possible that a church existed on the site from the 3C or 4C, the building visible today has suffered many alterations and extensions. It was probably damaged by the earthquake of 529 and subsequently repaired at the same time as Myra's other buildings with help received from the Emperor Justinian. It is unlikely that it remained unscathed during the period of the Arab invasions.

Certainly, after the occupation of Myra in the 11C, it was restored by Constantine IX in 1043. A walled monastery was founded nearby at about the same time.

By the middle of the 19C the church was in a very dilapidated condition. The roof had fallen in and the building was almost completely covered with soil and debris. Two attempts by Russian interests to restore it were only partially successful. While it is difficult to distinguish in the present building between alterations and repairs made at different periods, the bell tower and upper storey are clearly relatively modern constructions. Now mainly visited by tourists, the church is used for religious purposes on one day every year: on 6 December, the feast day of St. Nicholas, the Orthodox Metropolitan of Myra celebrates the Sacred Liturgy there.

Access to the building is by a ramp which descends steeply by the side of the garden to a level c 5m below the road. Constructed in the form of a basilica, the church has three side aisles, two of which are on the S side. They have chapels at the E end. The central nave is covered by a groined vault and it has a synthronon with a covered passage in the apse. The stone altar is surrounded by four broken pillars. From one of the rooms beyond the N aisle stairs lead to the upper storey. On the N side the well-preserved cloisters are frequently waterlogged. Note the customary narthex and exonarthex at the W end of the church. There are fine marble pavements throughout.

The sarcophagus honoured as that of St. Nicholas is in the S aisle, between two pillars and behind a broken marble screen. It is surmounted by a damaged lid, which presumably came from another tomb as it has the effigies of a husband and wife on it. The position of the tomb does not agree with the account of the merchants of Bari, who said that they found the body of the saint under the marble floor. However, a record of the 9C suggests that the sarcophagus was in an accessible place, as myrrh could be collected from it by pilgrims.

To get to (c 2.5km) **ANDRIACE** return to the Roman tomb on the W side of Demre and take the left fork at the crossroads. The road, straight with a good surface, is flanked on the N by the ancient Androkos which enters the sea at Andriace. Across the stream there are many sarcophagi, the ruins of a water mill and of several large buildings dating from the Roman period. The remains of the aqueduct, which brought water from Demre, also lies N of the road. The modern harbour, which has become silted up and is shallow for a considerable distance from the shore, is used only by local fishermen and for a ferry-boat service to Kale and excursions to Kekova during the summer months. The beach, a mixture of sand and mud, is clean with the best bathing on the W side. At the point where the Androkos flows into the sea, there is a restaurant that serves simple meals. There are no hotels or pensions in Andriace. It is a small, unpretentious place popular both with Turks and foreign visitors.

History. There is some doubt as to whether Andriace was an independent Lycian city from the time of its foundation or just the port of Demre. Certainly, archaeological evidence shows that from Hellenistic times (4C BC) it formed an important part of Demre's defensive system, which stretched from Sura on the W to Andriace on the S, and E to the edge of the Demre plain. The earliest written reference to Andriace is found in accounts of the campaign of Antiochus III of Syria in 197 BC, when he attempted to capture the Aegean cities from the Ptolemies. In 42 BC Lentulus Sphinter broke the chains at the entrance to the harbour and, proceeding to Myra, extracted money from the unwilling citizens for Brutus' struggle against Octavian and Antony. In AD 18 statues were erected in Andriace to commemorate the visit of Germanicus and Agrippina, while a century later Trajan, on his way to make war on the Parthians, surveyed the port facilities. Evidence of Andriace's later importance is provided by an inscription on the granary wall which records the preparation of weights and measures, based on standards sent from Byzantium, for Myra and Arneae.

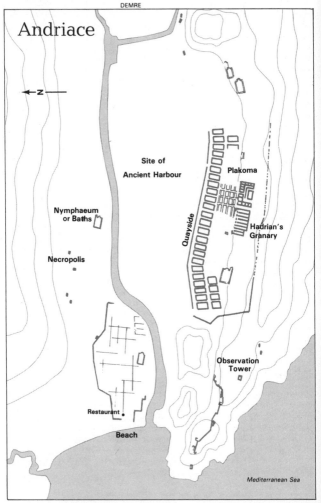

The most important existing monument in Andriace is the *Granary of Hadrian*. This is reached by turning left c 200m before the beach into a small clearing. The granary is a further 250m to the SE. To avoid the worst of the undergrowth and an area which is often marshy in spring and late autumn, walk to the base of the hill and then turn E.

This granary, like the building at Patara and others in the E Roman Empire, played an important part in the economy. It was used to store grain that had been grown locally or imported from other countries in the E Mediterranean, before it was sent to Rome, allocated to the army or otherwise distributed by the administration. Constructed during the reign of Hadrian (117–138), the granary measures 65m by 32m and has eight rooms. Six are of equal size while two, on the W, are smaller. The rooms, entered by doors on the N side of the granary, have dividing walls and a back wall constructed of polygonal masonry. Internal communicating doors are set near the entrances. The façade, constructed of large, closely fitting square blocks, is flanked by two rooms for the supervisors. On the W side, part of the pediment remains. When Beaufort visited Andriace in 1811, the inscription was still complete: HORREA IMP. CAESARIS DIVI TRAIANI PARTHICI F. DIVI, NERVAE NEPOTIS TRAIANI HADRIANI AUGUSTI COS. III. Over the main door there are two busts. The male figure is Hadrian. The identity of the female figure is disputed. It may be Hadrian's wife Sabina or, as some scholars believe, Faustina the Elder, the wife of Antoninus Pius. There is a small relief on the front wall near the second door from the W. This depicts two deities, Serapis standing and Isis reclining on a couch with a griffin between them. According to the inscription, this was erected by an official of the granary called Herakleon, in obedience to instructions received in a dream.

Beaufort reports having seen the ruins of a small temple, constructed from very white marble, on the hill to the S of the port. This may be the building which modern scholars believe was a watchtower. Across the river Androkos, at a point level with the granary, there are the substantial remains of a construction which is sometimes described as a *nymphaeum*. However, as Andriace is known to have had mineral springs it is more likely to have been a baths complex where the inhabitants took the cure. To the W of the granary, a building with an apse may have been a temple or a civil basilica. The so-called *Plakoma* (or market area), which was surrounded by a colonnade, lies to the E of the granary. In the centre there is a large cistern enclosed by a double vault. Between the Plakoma and the harbour lay the residential quarter where remains of houses 8–10m long and streets 3m wide may still be seen. Further to the N is the quay which was once lined with warehouses. Beyond the quay, the site of the ancient harbour of Andriace is now a reedy fen that has been abandoned to the frogs and the marsh birds.

A visit to the site of ARNEAE is a challenging experience as, although only c 24km NW of Demre, poor communications make it one of the most isolated sites in Lycia. According to Bean a road goes as far as the village of Muskar. From there the route to the site is by way of the hamlet of Çağman.

All the information available about Arneae has been gleaned from an examination of its ruins. Evidence of the city's antiquity is provided by an inscription in Lycian and it is known that it headed a sympolity of towns, one of which was called Coroae. In Byzantine times the bishop of Arneae was subject to the metropolitan of Myra. An inscription on the Granary of Hadrian at Andriace states that Arneae and Myra were to adopt weights and measures in line with standards despatched from Byzantium.

Arneae's situation provides a good natural defence and this was reinforced by a strong circular wall. Inside the wall there are the remains of two churches and some houses. In addition to a number of Lycian rock-tombs there are several sarcophagi. Built into the wall there are many inscriptions from the Roman period, one of which records the conversion of a gymnasium to a public guesthouse during the reign of Trajan. Bean mentions the favourable impression made on visitors by the beauty of Arneae's situation and the profusion of its vegetation.

20 Demre to Antalya

A. Via Limyra, Elmalı and Termessus

Total distance c 209km. **Demre**—R400 c 27km **Finike**—R635 c 6km *Turunçova*—(c 4km **Limyra**)—c 20km *Arif*—(c 1km *Arycanda*)—c 32km **Elmalı**—c 54km *Korkuteli*—(c 9km **Termessus**)—(c 1km *Evder Hanı*)—c 70km **Antalya**.

Road 400 from Demre to Finike, which follows the coastline, has many curves. It passes a number of small, clean, tempting beaches, but few have adequate parking spaces for motorists. On the E edge of the Demre plain a large lake, well stocked with fish, is home to flocks of sea birds. Apart from a narrow channel, which is usually closed by fishermen's nets, this lake is separated from the open sea by an enormous sand-bar.

Finike, a small sea port which is beginning to turn to tourism, has a number of modest hotels and pensions. Near the harbour there are several good fish restaurants. It is a useful base for visiting Demre and ancient Limyra or for making lazy boat trips along the Lycian coast.

To reach **LIMYRA** take road 635 from Finike for c 6km, as far as the village of *Turunçova*, and then turn E and continue for c 4km to the site. Visitors without their own transport may take a bus from Finike to Turunçova and walk or take a taxi from there to Limyra, which is located at the end of a sprawling, untidy hamlet. There is a parking place near the theatre.

History. There is evidence that Limyra existed as early as the 5C BC. Known in Lycian as *Zemu(ri)*, the city reached its apogee in the 4C BC, when its ruler, the dynast Pericles, made it the capital of Lycia. Pericles had successfully resisted the attempts of the Persian satrap Mausolus to conquer Lycia and at the Battle of Issus in 333 BC Alexander the Great finally lifted the shadow of Persia from Asia Minor. Following the death of Alexander in 323 BC, Limyra and the rest of Lycia came under the domination of his squabbling generals and their descendants. Ruled at various times by the Macedonians, the Ptolemies and the Seleucid kings of Syria and for a brief and stormy period by the Rhodians, it was made a free territory by the Roman Senate in 167 BC.

In AD 4 the young Gaius Caesar, grandson and adopted heir of Augustus, died in Limyra on his way home from Armenia. He was commemorated there by a magnificent funeral monument, decorated with reliefs showing his achievements. When in AD 43 Lycia was joined with Pamphylia to form a new Roman province in Asia Minor, Limyra, like many neighbouring cities, entered on a period of prosperity. Partially destroyed by the earthquake of 141, the city's public buildings, including the theatre, were restored with the aid of generous donations from Opramoas of Rhodiapolis. Like Sura, Limyra had a fish oracle. According to Pliny, if the fish took the food offered to them, it was a good omen. If they refused it, a bad omen. The city's principal deity was Zeus, whose thunderbolt appeared on the coinage.

During the early Byzantine period Limyra's importance was little diminished. It became the seat of a bishop. However, from the 7C to the 9C it suffered grievously from raids by Arab pirates and finally, like Demre, most of its inhabitants moved away and the city was largely abandoned.

The first European visitors to Limyra in the 19C were from Britain. Cockerell and Beaufort came in 1811 and they were followed in 1030 by Fellows, who copied some of the inscriptions in the necropolis. Spratt and Forbes came later

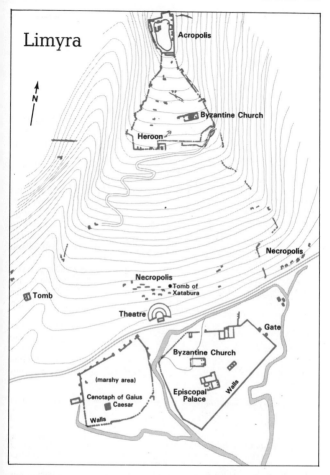

and explored the acropolis. In recent years German archaeologists under the direction of Dr Jürgen Borckhardt have been excavating the site.

On the left of the road from Turunçova there is a fine two-storey tomb in a citrus grove. Another nearby, dated to the 5C BC, bears an interesting relief around the door. These, with some rock-tombs, form the W necropolis of the city. On the right of the road are the remains of the Roman and Byzantine walls which, unfortunately, are being raided continually to provide dressed building stone. Beyond the walls, to the S, the marshy ground makes it very difficult to examine the ruined cenotaph of Gaius Caesar and the remains further to the E of an *episcopal palace*, and of a richly ornamented *Byzantine church* which may have been Limyra's cathedral.

The *theatre* has a single diazoma, backed by a wall c 1.6m high. This has a number of openings into a covered passageway. During intemperate weather the audience was protected by a velum.

Sockets for the poles which supported this may be seen in the upper rows of seats. The unusually large orchestra is flanked by two vaulted entrances. Of the stage-building only a few blocks of stone remain. A gift of about 20,000 denarii from Opramoas helped to repair the earthquake damage it suffered c 141. Behind the theatre there is a group of *rock-tombs*, many of which are elaborately decorated. To the E of these there is a remarkable free-standing ogival *sarcophagus* on a tall base which dates from the 4C BC. An inscription in Lycian states that it was the tomb of Xatabura, who may have been related to Pericles, the founder of the Lycian League. It bears a number of fine reliefs. On the N there is a chariot with an armed warrior; on the S a funeral feast and sacrifice and on W the

Tomb of Xatabura, 4C BC, Limyra.

judgment of Xatabura after death. He is depicted as a nude youth, standing between his seated, elderly judges. He holds his clothes in his left hand, and his gaze is fixed unwaveringly on the land of the dead.

A visit to the heroon and acropolis on the top of *Tocak Dağ*, which towers to the N of the site, offers many rewards, not the least of which is a magnificent view over the plain of Limyra to the sea. The ascent, if made in the early morning, by the path from the back of the village, should take c 40 minutes and is not over-taxing. The earliest evidence of occupation found in the acropolis dates from the 4C BC. Today, little more than traces of the defensive wall remain. Below the acropolis, to the SE, are the ruins of a Byzantine church. The *heroon* or mausoleum, which was probably constructed for Pericles, is S of the crest on an artificial terrace measuring 19m by 18m. Careful examination of its remains suggest that, structurally, it resembled the Nereid tomb at Xanthus. A lower burial chamber supported a small temple. This had four caryatids in the front and four in the back. The Limyra caryatids, heavier and less graceful than those in the Erectheum at Athens, wear bracelets crowned with lion heads, a type often found in Persian art, and carry funerary libation vessels in their hands. The sides of the upper chamber were decorated with a long frieze depicting the hero in a chariot, leading a motley band of soldiers who wear Persian, Greek or Lycian clothing. A further Persian motif may be found in the acroterion which decorated the middle of the pediment. Now in the Antalya Museum, this shows Perseus, from whom the Persians claimed descent, hurrying away in triumph with the severed head of Medusa. Apart from its magnificently commanding position on Tocak Dağ, the interest and importance of the Limyra heroon comes from its intriguing blend of Persian and Greek elements and for the light it throws on Lycia's central position between these two great cultural influences.

From Finike road 635 to Elmalı at first runs parallel with the Yaşgöz Çayı, the ancient Arycandus. Though narrow in parts, this road has a good surface and is usually very busy, mainly with lorries carrying timber from the forests in the interior.

At (6km) Turunçova there is a right-hand turn for (c 4km) Limyra (see above). The road then begins to climb steadily through a magnificent pine-clothed gorge, until it reaches a height of 1290m at the pass of Karamanbeyli Geçidi. This is the territory of the Tahtacılar (the woodcutters), a taciturn race sometimes shunned because they were believed to indulge in unorthodox religious practices.

For a visit to **ARYCANDA** follow road 635 as far as the village of (c 20km) *Arif*. A signpost on the right points to the site, which is c 30 minutes' walk from the main road. The setting of Arycanda is one of the most beautiful in S Turkey and has been compared, not unfavourably, with Delphi. (Take refreshments.)

History. The '-anda' in Arycanda suggests that the city was of considerable antiquity (many pre-Greek settlements have '-ss' or '-anda' in their names). However, nothing is known of its history before the 5C BC. Coins found at Arycanda bear the name of Pericles of Limyra. It is probable that, like much of Lycia, it was under Persian domination until the arrival of Alexander the Great in 334 BC. Subsequently, the city was ruled at different times by the Ptolemies and the Seleucid kings of Syria. The Arycandans, sybaritic and profligate by temperament, lived well beyond their means. As a result in 197 BC they sided with Antiochus III against the Ptolemies in the hope of paying off their debts. During the 2C BC Arycanda became part of the Lycian League and issued its own coins. In c 188 BC it was briefly under the control of Rhodes and finally, in AD 43, it became part of the Roman province of Lycia-Pamphylia.

From Byzantine sources it is known that Arycanda had its own bishop and that it changed its name to *Acalanda*. During this period the city was moved to a new site, which continued to be occupied until the 11C.

The *acropolis* of Arycanda is on a small hill to the right of a track which leads from the main road. Steps lead up to the gateway. Inside the defensive wall are the remains of a small building. A short distance to the N there are the substantial remains of a large *basilica*. This has a well-preserved synthronon and some fine floor mosaics. To the right of the river there are several temple tombs which form part of the E *necropolis*. Near these is a small temple or temple tomb—there is some dispute on this point—constructed in the Corinthian order. This building appears to have been adapted for Christian worship. On the S wall of the pronaos there is a cross and the inscription 'Jesus Christ is victorious'. Below the tombs is a huge *baths complex* with walls standing to a height of 10m. The circular E section is reminiscent of the baths of Tlos. NW of the baths an area has been identified as a *palaestra*.

Continuing to the N, the *agora*, which had a colonnade on three sides, is to the left of the path. In the centre a tree, surrounded by a ruined wall, is believed to mark the site of a small temple. As only a few shops were found in that part of the city, it is assumed that the agora was used mainly for meetings and debates and that the city's commercial quarter was situated elsewhere.

The N colonnade of the agora, which is 75m long and 8m wide, has five archways, three of which provide access to a small *odeum*. The centre arch was decorated with a sculpture of Hadrian, those on either side with representations of deities. Above the odeum, to the NE, there is a fine *theatre* which has been excavated recently. Dated to the 2C AD, it is constructed in the Greek manner, i.e. larger than a semicircle. There is no diazoma; the 20 rows of seats are divided into seven cunei. The stage-building is well preserved.

Access to the *stadium*, which is at the highest level of the site, is by a stairway behind the theatre. Supported by a massive retaining wall, it is c 100m long and has seating on the N side only. Arycanda's *bouleuterion*, sited to the W of the stadium, is approached by a long stoa. Although it has not yet been excavated, certain features, like the seats cut from the rock, are clearly visible. Below the retaining wall there is a large cistern.

On returning to Arif continue N on road 635. Having crossed over the Bey Dağları, the road descends from the Avlanbeli Geçidi (1090m) by pleasant mountain pastures to the rather featureless Elmalı plain. This lunar landscape, which has been produced by the draining of a number of large lakes, finally gives way to the clusters of orchards that mark the approaches to the 'apple town'.

Surrounded as it is by gardens full of fruit trees it is appropriate that **Elmalı** (10,000 inhab.) should derive its name from 'Elma', the Turkish for apple. The town's wide main street climbs towards Elmalı Dağ, the mountain which dominates the landscape.

Serving the surrounding area as a marketing and shopping centre, Elmalı has a number of small, unpretentious restaurants and one or two hotels. From the bus station, in the SE of the town, there are regular services to Finike and to Antalya and, by dolmuş, to nearby villages.

Apart from a fine 15C mosque, *Ömerpaşa Camii*, in the centre of the town, Elmalı has few buildings of interest. However, it has become well-known during recent years because a group of American archaeologists, under the direction of Professor Machteld Mellink, have made several exciting discoveries in the surrounding countryside. At *Karataş-Semayük* they have found nearly 500 tombs and a fortified house, which date from the Early Bronze Age (c 3000–2000 BC). Most of the burials were in pithoi, large pottery jars, placed with their openings to the E. An examination of the skeletons has shown that inhabitants of the site were well-built and well-nourished, but there was some evidence of arthritis and malaria and in a few cases of leprosy. Some of the pithoi and grave-goods—ear-studs, brush handles, bronze pins and spearheads—together with an imaginative reconstruction of a pithos-burial, may be seen in the Antalya Archaeological Museum.

The American archaeologists also found two painted tomb-chambers in tumuli, one at *Kızılbel*, c 4km SW, near the lake of Elmalı, the other at *Karaburun*, 7km NE, on the Korkuteli road. Because of the blend of Greek, Lycian, and Persian influences which they display, these tombs are of great importance. Both were robbed in antiquity.

The painting in the Kızılbel tomb, which dates from c 525 BC, shows the departure of a warrior, a banquet, and a number of mythological subjects including Gorgons and the birth of Pegasus. Executed in the E Greek style, the painting is in shades of black, white and red on a light background. There was also a quantity of furniture, including a table and a kline made of stone, in the tomb. The skeletal remains suggest that its occupant was a well-built, active man aged about 50.

The tomb at Karaburun, which dates from c 475 BC, was decorated in a Graeco-Persian style. The paintings show the owner reclining on a couch. Elaborately dressed in a green himation and wearing a diadem, he beckons imperiously at two servants clad in Persian-style garments. Behind him stands his wife holding an alabastron and a fillet. There is also the depiction of a battle, of a funeral-procession with a wheeled throne, and of a funeral-cart and attendants. An examination of the bones indicated that the occupant of the tomb was a little older than 50 at the time of death, tall and of strong physical build.

Because of the fragility of the paintings, it is necessary to preserve an even temperature in the tombs. As a consequence, they are not open to visitors.

The route to (c 54km) Korkuteli, on road 635, traverses the N end of the Elmalı plain. Like its S counterpart, it is featureless and bare, lacking appeal and interest. At *Korkuteli*, a small town of no great importance, road 635 joins with road 350. This soon begins to descend towards Antalya, and, as it does so, the landscape changes dramatically. Wooded mountain slopes replace the arid, lunar plateau and on the lush roadside verges youthful shepherds and goatherds graze their flocks.

About 20km from Korkuteli road 350 is crossed by an ancient ashlar wall. Too far away to be part of the defences of Termessus, it may have been a control point where the inhabitants of that city exacted a toll from passing travellers. The presence of a gateway on the old route supports this hypothesis. 5km further on, a road to the right, signposted (9km) **TERMESSUS**, leads to the ancient city.

A short distance from the entrance, admission tickets to the site, which forms part of the Termessus National Park, may be purchased at a small group of buildings on the right. One of the buildings has an interesting display on the flora and fauna of the National Park, which are strictly protected. No refreshments are available, but there is a spacious, well-maintained picnic area. Visitors to the ruins of the city are advised to wear strong shoes, the terrain is rough and very overgrown.

From the entrance, a bumpy track, passable by cars in good weather, climbs for 9km to a parking area. From there the city, which is 500m further on and 200m higher up, may be reached by a very rough footpath. Like Olympus and Phaselis, the site of ancient Termessus is covered in a tangled mass of undergrowth. As a result, it is often difficult to locate and examine some of the ruins. Like those cities, too, much of the charm of Termessus is derived from its setting high on a mountain side, more than 1000m above the Pamphylian plain. Without doubt it is one of the most striking of Turkey's ancient sites.

History. The people of Termessus were neither Greeks nor Lycians. They came from Pisidia, the mountainous area N of Pamphylia. According to Strabo they called themselves the Solymi, after Mt Solymus, the modern Güllük Dağ, which towers over the site. Confusingly, the word Termessus, by which their city came to be known, is linked with Termilae, a name sometimes used for the Lycians.

From the beginning the Termessians had a reputation for being warlike and aggressive, and records show that they were frequently in conflict with their neighbours. On one occasion they were brave or foolhardy enough to take on all 30 cities of the Lycian League. Because of the remote and inhospitable location of Termessus, where olives were the only food-crop, it is probable that they were driven to banditry from time to time to supplement the meagre return from their lands. Certainly, their strategic position enabled them to control—and interfere with—trade between the coast and the interior and it seems likely that in later times they levied a tax on passing travellers (see above). They were not intimidated by the formidable army of Alexander the Great and he was obliged to raise the siege on their city in 333 BC. Even under the Romans they enjoyed a considerable degree of freedom. However, they cannot have been entirely without diplomatic skills and the capacity to make friends, as they founded a colony, Termessus Minor, c 80km to the W, in the shadow of Oenoanda. The site of Termessus Minor could not have been defended successfully, therefore the Termessians of both cities must have been on very good terms with the Oenoandans.

Although the date of the foundation of Termessus is not known the Solymi are mentioned in Book VI of the 'Iliad', so the city probably existed as early as the 8C BC. Homer tells the story of the hero, Bellerophon, who was falsely accused of seduction by the wife of the Argive king, Proetus. The young man was sent by Proetus to his father-in-law, Iobates, king of Lycia with a request that he be put to death. Iobates was unwilling to do the deed himself, so he set Bellerophon a series of tasks, which he believed to be impossible. First he ordered the youth to destroy the Chimaera. Having successfully disposed of that terrible monster, Bellerophon was then told to subdue the warlike Solymi. Pegasus carried him over the heads of this savage tribe, far above the reach of their arrows, and he rained down rocks on them until they and their allies, the Amazons, retreated in disorder. Then he returned to Iobates who, growing tired of the game, gave Bellerophon his daughter in marriage and accepted him as his heir.

Termessus is next mentioned in connection with an incident in the campaign which Alexander the Great conducted in Lycia and Pamphylia in 333 BC. Having conquered the cities of Perge and Aspendus, Alexander decided to march N to Phrygia. His chosen route, which took him near Termessus, is described by Arrian in the following terms: 'the town stands on a lofty and precipitous height, and the road which leads past it is an inconvenient one, because a ridge runs right down to it from the town above, breaking off short with the road at the bottom, while opposite to it, on the other side, the ground rises again in an equally steep ascent. The two cliffs make a sort of natural gateway on the road, so that quite a small force can, by holding the high ground, prevent an enemy from getting through. And this is precisely what the Telmessians [sic] did.'

This event probably took place in the valley, later closed by a wall, which is described above. Alexander did not attempt to force his way through immediately. He made camp and waited for night-fall. When most of the Termessians had returned to their homes, he attacked the small force remaining and overcame it easily. He then took up his position under the city walls. There he was joined by representatives from the Pisidian city of Selge. Those enemies of the Termessians were unable to persuade him to continue with the siege. In any case, it is more than likely that he was discouraged by the formidable nature of the city's natural and artificial defences. He raised the siege, returned to Perge and marched N, by way of Sagalassus, to Phrygia. Termessus thus shares with Sillyum the distinction of having successfully stood out against Alexander and his army.

After the death of Alexander, his generals fought among themselves about the division of his empire. Termessus supported Alcetas, an opponent of Antigonus Monophthalmos, who was trying to bring Asia under his rule. When Alcetas was defeated in battle in 319 BC, he sought refuge in Termessus. Antigonus came to the city and demanded that his enemy be handed over to him. The Termessian elders were inclined to accede to this request, but they were fiercely opposed by the young men of the city. According to the historian, Diodorus, to resolve the matter to their satisfaction the elders suggested the following stratagem to Antigonus. He should withdraw his forces and, while the young men were harrying his rearguard, they would hand Alcetas over to him. However, Alcetas learned of the plot and, not wishing to fall into the hands of Antigonus, he killed himself. Then the elders delivered his corpse to Antigonus, who subjected it to many indignities and, when it was beginning to decay, marched away, leaving it unburied. The young men, full of rage at the deception that had been practised on them, decided at first to raze Termessus to the ground and take to a life of brigandage in the mountains. However, they limited themselves finally to attacking the lands occupied by Antigonus and to recovering the body of their friend. This they buried in a splendid tomb, which archaeologists believe they have identified on the NW side of the city.

According to an inscription, the bellicose Termessians were at war with the Lycian League c 200 BC and just 11 years later with the neighbouring city of Isinda. When Attalus II of Pergamum attempted to subdue Selge c 158 BC, it is very likely that he was supported by their ancient enemies, the Termessians. Attalus was unsuccessful in his war and, anxious to consolidate his position in Pamphylia, founded the new city-port of Attaleia (the modern Antalya). He also caused a magnificent portico, which bore his name, to be erected in Termessus, perhaps as a thanks offering.

As a reward for its support during the Mithridatic War, Termessus was accorded a considerable degree of freedom by the Romans. This state of affairs continued during Imperial times, when the city issued coins which did not bear an effigy of the current emperor, but which carried the word, 'Autonomous' on them. During the early Byzantine period, Termessus retained some of its importance, becoming the seat of a bishop. However, the city appears to have been abandoned in the 5C, possibly because of the remoteness of its situation.

The numbered, descriptive signs provided by the authorities to direct visitors to the principal ruins in Termessus are not quoted in this guide as visitors have often found that these useful indicators have been defaced, destroyed, or reversed by vandals.

The ascent to the car-park is marked by a series of ruins: first a look-out tower, then traces of the so-called 2C AD King Street, and finally the base of a great gateway which provided a ceremonial entrance to the area around the city. To the right of the car-park the handsome *Propylon of Hadrian* leads to a ruined Ionic peripteros, which has a cella 8m wide. The portal, with a finely carved lintel, is surrounded by a mass of architectural fragments, which, hopefully, will be used one day to reconstruct this building. A path to the left leads to the *N necropolis*, containing a number of decorated tombs, including one with a fine relief of lions.

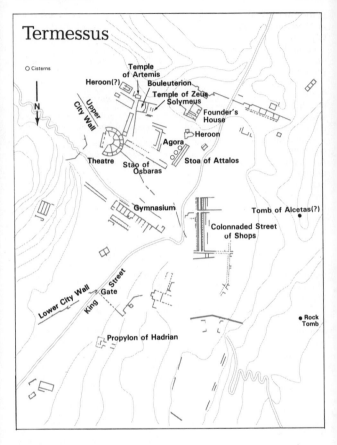

On returning to the car-park, take a path, centre-left, which ascends steeply to the site of the ancient city. For part of the way this route follows King Street, the 2C paved road that led to the city centre. Across the valley, to the right, there are several rock-tombs. These may be reached by a rough track that descends from the agora area to the valley.

After climbing for some time, you reach the *outer wall* of the city which is marked by a fine *look-out tower* above and to the right of the path. The inner side of the *gateway* bore an interesting *dice-oracle*. This consisted of a series of set answers, each of which was linked to a specified throw of the dice. The following is an example quoted by Bean:

44466 24 Cronos the Child-Eater
Three fours and two sixes. This is the god's advice:
Stay at home and go not elsewhere,
Lest the destructive Beast and avenging Fury come upon you,
For I see that the business is neither safe nor secure.

In the later Roman Empire, when superstition and credulity were rife, methods of divination like the dice-oracle and the tomb-oracle of Olympus, however imprecise, enjoyed wide popularity.

From the gateway, it is possible to see, high on the mountain-side on the left, the ruins of an *aqueduct* which supplied the city with some its water.

A series of steps leads to the *inner fortification wall*. On the left there are the extensive remains of a large *gymnasium* which is smothered in vegetation. Just beyond is the site of the *agora*, all of whose buildings have been laid low by earthquakes and further damaged by the unchecked growth of the luxuriant vegetation. This was bounded on the NW by a two-storey *stoa* composed of Doric columns. According to an inscription, this stoa was dedicated by Attalus II, king of Pergamum (160–139 BC) (see above). On the NE, there was a matching *stoa*, constructed during the Roman period by a rich citizen named Osbaras. Underneath the paved surface of the agora, on the NW side, there are five large *cisterns*. These were used to store rain water, so supplementing supplies from other sources within the walls and brought in by the aqueduct. Now open and unprotected, they have an average depth of 8m, and should be approached with caution.

In the SW corner of the agora a large natural rock-outcrop was converted into a monumental tomb for some local dignitary. His name and the date of the construction of the *heroon* are not known. The inscriptions carved in large letters on the back wall are believed to relate to two people who wished to be buried in or near the tomb of the hero. A stairway leads to a platform 6 sq m. The tomb, which was covered by a slab, was in the rear wall. On the W side of the rock-outcrop there are three niches, where, perhaps, offerings to the dead man may have been placed.

Perhaps the most striking monument in Termessus is the well-preserved **Hellenistic theatre**. Facing the twin peaks of Mt Solymus, it occupies a position of incomparable beauty to the SE of the agora. Constructed in the Greek style, the theatre has a single diazoma with eight rows of seats above and 16 below, and a cavea which could seat more than 4000 spectators. Until alterations during the Roman period extended the cavea on the right-hand side as far as the stage-building, so providing extra seating, it had two parodoi. The right-hand parodos was then replaced by a covered passage. Entrance to the cavea below the diazoma was by a stairway which led from a large door in the back wall. Access to the seats above the diazoma must have been by doors in the retaining wall, which have now disappeared. The stage-building, which dates from c 2C AD, was backed by a long, narrow room. It had five doors and was faced by free-standing columns whose pedestals remain. Below the stage level five smaller openings, c 1m high, were used to admit animals into the orchestra area, when the theatre was used for wild-beast shows.

To the S of the theatre, steps lead down to a small *temple*. This was erected on a podium, which rested on a terrace cut into the hillside. Usually, temples erected in honour of deities were entered from the E, and as access to this building was by a flight of steps on the W side, it was probably dedicated to a hero or deified mortal. The site is very overgrown and difficult to investigate.

W of this temple there are the substantial remains of a building, dated to the 1C BC. This may have been the *bouleuterion* of Termessus or, as some authorities believe, an *odeum*, where musical recitals and poetry performances were given. The upper part of the outer walls, which stand to a height of 10m, are decorated with narrow Doric pilasters. The presence of windows on the S and E sides suggest that is was roofed. In the interior, which is filled with broken masonry and vegetation, there are the remains of several rows of seats and traces of polychrome marble which was probably used to decorate the walls. Inscriptions cut into the N wall between the pilasters record the names of victors in various sporting events — wrestling, foot-races, horse-races. These probably took place in the city's small, *gymnasium*, which was sited to the SE of the agora.

S of the odeum there are the foundations of an Ionic *temple*. Reliefs of the sacrifice of Iphigenia and a dedication found there show that this was dedicated to Artemis.

To the N there is a smaller temple, also dedicated to Artemis, which has been dated to the beginning of the 3C AD. An inscription records that this building and the cult-statue were donated by Aurelia Armasta and her husband. NW of the odeum there are the substantial remains of a small *temple* dedicated to Zeus Solymeus. Only the walls, which stand to a height of 5m and, a bench on which statues were placed, remain. The principal temple of Zeus Solymeus has not yet been discovered. Fragments of reliefs showing Zeus and other deities, found by Austrian archaeologists towards the end of the 19C, suggest that it was located somewhere to W of this small shrine.

Due W of this temple there are the ruins of the so-called *founder's house*. This derives its name from a rough inscription on the door, which describes a man called Besas as a 'founder' of the city. The term probably means, as in the case of the founders of Perge, someone who contributed substantially to the city, perhaps by the construction of public buildings. The house, which appears to follow the usual Roman pattern, was entered through an atrium. It is now in a very dilapidated condition and is choked with vegetation.

W of the agora the path divides. The left-hand fork leads to a group of rock-tombs on the W cliff-face. On the left of this path there is a spring of fresh water, as refreshing and welcome to the modern visitor as it must have been to the Termessians. E of the path, covered in undergrowth, the inscribed bases of a number of statues mark the site of a street of shops.

A scramble of about 150m through the thicket leads to a *rock-tomb*, at the base of the cliff. Dated to the end of the 4C BC, some archaeologists believe that Alcetas (see above) was buried here. On the left-hand wall, framed by a rough arch, there is a splendid life-like relief of a mounted soldier. He has been portrayed at the moment, when, with cloak billowing out behind, he reins in his mount. His horse, balanced on its hind legs with front legs raised, is still pulling against the bit. Clad in a corselet, right hand lifted to throw a spear, he rides without a saddle, gripping the horses's flanks with his knees. It is a pose reminiscent of some of the heroic representations of Alexander the Great, e.g the bronze in the Museo Archaeologico, Naples. Unfortunately, the relief has suffered some damage, partly from natural causes, partly from the destructive activity of treasure hunters. The rider's head, which was probably helmeted, has been defaced and the hindquarters of the horse are missing. Below the relief there is the carving of a crested helmet, a pair of greaves, a round shield and a sword.

On the right-hand side of the tomb there is a badly damaged sarcophagus in the form of a kline. This has legs ornamented with

Rock-tombs at Termessus,

palmettes. To the left of the sarcophagus there is an ostothek. This had a false door carved on the front. To the right of the sarcophagus, offerings to the deceased spirit were placed in three containers, two of which bear carvings. A low table in front was used for the same purpose. On the wall behind the sarcophagus, a trellis set between columns is carved in low-relief. This is surmounted by an an eagle in flight carrying a snake in its claws.

The car-park may be reached by a very rough path, which descends in a NE direction from the tomb of Alcetas. This passes several other rock-tombs of lesser interest. However, hardy spirits will prefer to return to the agora and take the path from behind the theatre, which climbs to the *upper necropolis*. This contains a large number of tombs, dating from the 1C to the 3C AD. Most are sarcophagi, but some were constructed in the form of small funerary temples. Elaborately decorated with portraits of the deceased, with garlands or with the motif of crossed spears surmounted by a shield, which occurs so often in Termessus, they are scattered through the undergrowth in macabre, apocalyptic confusion. Gaping open, resting at strange angles they resemble a Last Judgment scene inspired by the imagination of Bosch or Breughel. Their inscriptions, in addition to giving the names of the owners, frequently carry a curse for tomb-violators and specify the penalty for such desecration. This was usually a substantial fine payable to the temple of Zeus Solymeus.

A short walk leads upwards from this necropolis to a *view-point*, which is crowned with a small hut used by the forest fire-watchers. From here there is a magnificent view over the Termessus National Park, the site of the ancient city and part of the plain of Pamphylia. The walk may also provide an opportunity to see some of the shy mountain goats which live in the upper section of the park.

On leaving the National Park turn right (road 350) in the direction of Antalya. After c 5km a narrow road on the left leads to *Evdir Hanı*, a well-preserved Selçuk caravanserai. This was built by Sultan Alaettin Keykavus between 1214 and 1218, one of a chain that linked his capital, Konya, with the sea. Note the fine decoration on the beautifully proportioned doorway, which is flanked by two niches.

Between the road and the caravanserai there are the scattered ruins of a more ancient settlement. When the site was visited by Lieutenant Spratt in 1842, he saw several hundred sarcophagi. Unfortunately, only a few have survived. Not far from the road there are the remains of a small, richly-ornamented temple, where George Bean found two architectural fragments decorated with representations of strange demonic creatures.

The name of this site is not known with certainty. Bean suggests that in the 5C it was called Eudocias, after Eudoxia, wife of the Emperor Theodosius II and that it came under the control of Termessus. He further proposes that in earlier times it may have been called Anydrus, which means waterless, an attractive hypothesis in view of the fact that the site is crossed by a number of channels which bring water from some distance to irrigate it.

On returning to road 350, continue for c 7km to the junction with road 650 from Burdur and turn right for (c 11km) **Antalya**. The road descends to the plain in a series of gentle curves and enters the city on the N side by a wide boulevard. Note the whitewashed water cisterns in the central reservation. These date from the Ottoman period.

B.   Via Olympus and Phaselis

Total distance 119km. **Finike**—R400 c 21km *Kumluca*—(c 2km *Corydalla*) (c 3km *Rhodiapolis*)—(c 10km *Idebessus*)—(c 4km *Gagae*)—(c 9km **Olympus**)—c 45km *Tekirova*—(c 2km **Phaselis**)—c 8km *Kemer*—45km **Antalya**.

Return to Finike take road 400 to 21km *Kumluca*. The site of CORYDALLA is c 2km W of the town, near the village of *Hacıveliler*.

Today, apart from a few blocks of stone dispersed over the site and the shape of the theatre on a hill to the S, there are no visible remains of the ancient city. In the mid 19C Spratt reported the existence of extensive ruins, including an aqueduct and theatre. Unfortunately, the site has been illegally and systematically stripped during recent years of all usable building material. On one of his visits George Bean saw a constant stream of lorries carrying material away from the city. Many of the houses in Kumluca and the neighbouring villages contain inscribed stones brought from Corydalla. Indeed one house in Kumluca has a bilingual text in Greek and Lycian built into it.

The spoliation of Corydalla did not rest with the removal of the stones. A valuable Byzantine treasure of Church plate discovered there some years ago was broken up. Part of this remains in Turkey and may be seen in the Antalya Archaeological Museum. The remainder, after a series of obscure adventures, has turned up in the United States of America, where it is now on display.

Kumluca itself is a small, dusty town totally lacking in charm. Its only interest is to the visitor-sleuth, who may enjoy looking for traces of ancient Corydalla in its modern buildings.

RHODIAPOLIS, 3km N of Kumluca, may be reached from the villages of Haciveliler or Seyköy. The road to the site is rough and it is advisable to use a four-wheel drive vehicle. Take a guide from one of the villages.

History. Although the name Rhodiapolis means 'city of the Rhodians' and E of Kumluca the ancient settlements are much less Lycian in character, it has been suggested that this city was named after Rhode, daughter of the legendary Mopsus. Whatever its origins, however, Rhodiapolis was certainly accepted as a full member of the Lycian League. This is proved conclusively by its coins.

The city's main claim to fame is that it was the home in the 2C AD of Opramoas. An important official in the Lycian League, who lived during the reign of Antoninus Pius (138–161), his generous benefactions to the cities of Lycia made him famous, not only in his own province but throughout the Roman Empire.

The ruins of Rhodiapolis are scattered through a pine forest and have suffered from much illegal excavation. In the middle of the city there is a well-preserved small *theatre*. Greater than a semi-circle, it has two unenclosed paradoi and no diazoma. Part of the stage-building still exists. S of the theatre are the remains of the *Tomb of Opramoas*. This building, c 8m by 7m, was ornamented with copies of letters from the emperor and provincial governors, which recorded the honours received by Opramoas and his many gifts to Rhodiapolis and to other Lycian cities. Unfortunately, it has been badly damaged and the inscriptions lie on the ground in a state of disorder and neglect. W of the theatre are the ruins of a *Byzantine church*. On top of the hill there is a *Hellenistic tower* which was altered at a later period. There are several cisterns and traces of an aqueduct. Lycian sarcophagi are to be found scattered on the hillside below the city and there are several interesting rock-tombs.

IDEBESSUS is c 10km N of Kumluca. It can also be reached from *Haciveliler*, with a four-wheel drive vehicle. Go first to the dam at Alăgir and then to the village of Yenikişla.

The city is about 900m above sea-level, on a ridge which forms part of the Bey Dağları. With Acalissus and Cormi it formed a sympolity which belonged to the Lycian League. Although Idebessus and

Acalissus have the pre-Greek '-ss' in their names no Lycian rock-tombs or inscriptions have been found at either of them. Acalissus, the head of the sympolity, received a donation from Opramoas and issued coins during the reign of the ill-fated Gordian III (238–244) who was assassinated by Philip the Arab.

Idebessus has a small, badly-damaged theatre which could hold an audience of c 600. There are the ruins of baths and of a Byzantine basilica. The city does not appear to have had a necropolis, but there is a profusion of late *ogival tombs* scattered among the civic buildings. Many are decorated with reliefs which show cupids carrying garlands, or playing with animals. There are also representations of wild-beast fights.

According to Bean the ruins of nearby ACALISSUS and CORMI are fewer and less interesting than those of Idebessus, but almost equally difficult to reach. A number of inscriptions found at Cormi include one relating to the first Mithridatic War (88–84 BC) and another apparently to the defeat of the pirate Zencites in 78 BC by Servilius Vatia, Roman governor of Cilicia.

Return to Kumluca and take road 400 in the direction of Antalya. At a point c 16km from Kumluca a pleasant diversion can be made by following a track on the right to the village of *Yenice*, which leads to the site of (c 4km) GAGAE. This is located on a hilltop c 200m high, not far from the sea-shore.

First mentioned in the 4C BC, Gagae was probably a Rhodian foundation. Legend relates that a ship from Rhodes, having survived a severe storm, made a landfall there and the crew, overwhelmed with joy and relief at their escape, cried out 'ga, ga', the Doric form of 'ge', earth or land. In antiquity, Gagae was famous for a mineral, *lapis gagates* or jet. No trace of this is found there today.

Spratt reported seeing considerable ruins at Gagae in the 19C and in 1960 Bean found the remains of a small *theatre*, built into the NW side of the hill. This has now disappeared. Apart from some scattered blocks of stone and the remains of a wall and tower on top of the hill, nothing survives of the ancient city. The ruins of Gagae, like those at Corydalla, have been plundered to provide building material for modern houses.

Road 400 begins its ascent of the mountain spur that terminates in Cape Chelidonia, the ancient *Promontorium Sacrum* which was believed to mark the boundary between the Phoenician and Greek seas.

Here in a deep cleft in one of the *Beş Adalar* (the Five Islands), HMS *Frederikssteen* sheltered in 1811. Beaufort describes how 'its perpendicular sides screened the people while eating their dinners from the scorching sun; no trifling luxury this, after the fatiguing operations of six hours, with the thermometer at 90° in the shade', an observation likely to raise sympathetic feelings in anyone who has visited this part of S Turkey in mid-summer. Having reached the summit, the road enters the *Beydağları Sahil Milli Parkı*, the Bey Mountains Coastal National Park, the home of the *tahtacılar* or wood-cutters who have a reputation for being taciturn recluses addicted to strange religious practices.

About 23km from Kumluca a sign to the right points to (9km) **OLYMPUS**. For 5km the road is reasonably good, after that it degenerates into a track suitable for four-wheel drive vehicles only. The 4km walk to the site is pleasant and not too strenuous.

Ancient Olympus is very overgrown, there is no accommodation and basic refreshments only are available. Because of the marshes,

mosquitoes abound. However, it has a good beach and the tranquillity and beauty of its setting will more than reward the determined traveller who is not put off by a little minor discomfort.

History. Olympus is believed to be a pre-Greek word for mountain. In the
ancient world more than 20 peaks bore that name and in many cases gave it to
an adjacent town or city. Mt Olympus, the modern Tahtalı Dağ, is 16km N of the
site.

Originally, neither Olympus nor its larger neighbour, Phaselis, formed part of
Lycia. No Lycian tombs or inscriptions in the Lycian language have been found
in either city. Olympus may have been founded during the Hellenistic period,
but it is first mentioned in the 2C BC, as a member of the Lycian League.
Towards the beginning of the 1C BC, when Phaselis had withdrawn from the
League, Olympus represented E Lycia and had the maximum number of three
votes in the League's Assembly. Shortly afterwards, the city and much of the
neighbouring coastline came under the control of Cilician pirates. According to
Plutarch the pirates introduced the worship of Mithras to this area, practising
strange, rites in secret on Mt Olympus. Mithras, a deity of Indo-Persian origin,
was a god of light and creation. Restricted to men, his cult was popular with
soldiers who helped to spread it far and wide through the Roman Empire.
Sharing some of the same rites and beliefs (e.g. the Taurobolium has been
compared to baptism) it was to become a strong rival of Christianity in later
centuries.

Until defeated in 78 BC by Servilius Vatia, the Roman governor of Cilicia, the
pirate chief, Zenicetes, made Olympus his headquarters. Servilius declared
Olympus and nearby Phaselis to be public property which could be sold or let to
anyone interested and this situation probably continued until Imperial times. A
further outbreak of piracy was ended by Pompey the Great, when he defeated
the Cilician corsairs at the battle of Coracesium, now Alanya, in 67 BC.

When Lycia was joined with Pamphylia and brought into the Roman Empire
in AD 43 the fortunes of Olympus revived. It became once again an important
member of the Lycian League. Opramoas of Rhodiapolis made a generous gift,
which was used for the restoration of many of the city's public buildings. There
are records of solemn celebrations for the god Hephaestus, the principal deity of
Olympus. An inscription in honour of Hadrian suggests that he may have visited
the city c 130. In time Christianity came to Olympus, and during the reign of
Diocletian (284–305), Methodius, the city's bishop was martyred. Also in the 3C,
renewed attacks by pirates started a decline which was never completely
arrested. In the 5C the successors of Methodius attended the councils of
Ephesus and Constantinople. During the later Byzantine Empire Olympus lost
much of its importance. There was a brief revival in the 11C and 12C, when it
was used as a trading centre by the Venetians and Genoese, but it appears to
have been abandoned finally sometime in the 15C, when the Ottoman navy
established its domination over the E Mediterranean.

Because of the dense vegetation Olympus is not easy to visit. Its
attraction springs as much from the beauty of its situation as from the
importance of its remains. These lie on both sides of a river which
dries to a trickle in the summer. On the right there is an extensive
necropolis. The tombs, of a kind not common in Lycia, consist of
vaulted chambers cut into the rock which are closed with a vertical
slab. In the W section, two of them bear, in addition to the usual
epitaph, some curious inscriptions, which, according to Bean, were
letter-oracles. There are 24 lines of advice, each of which is preceded
by a different letter of the alphabet; a device which enabled the
enquirer to consult his ancestors. To the E of the necropolis, on the
side of the hill, lie the remains of the *theatre* which dates from the
Roman period. The seats have vanished and, like most of the
buildings on the site, it is covered with tangled growth. One fine
entrance arch remains. NE of the theatre the ruins of a *Byzantine
basilica* and of several unidentified buildings, believed to be Roman,
protrude from a spinney. The S bank of the river is marked by a fine
stretch of polygonal wall which has been dated to early Hellenistic
times. While some authorities believe that this was constructed to
canalise the river, the more widely accepted opinion is that it formed

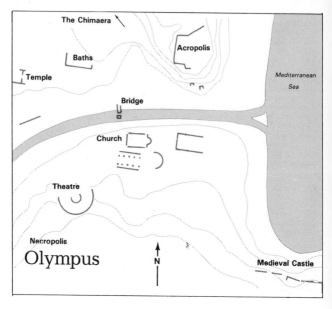

part of the harbour. The quay, 5m wide, is backed by a 3m-high wall, which terminates in a crudely constructed building which may have been a warehouse. The entrance to the river is now closed by a sand-bank.

The stream can be crossed easily at a point level with the basilica where there are the remains of an ancient bridge. The site of the acropolis is on the N side of the river on a steep hill to the right, near the river-mouth. A splendid view of the whole area from the summit justifies the climb. The main part of the city lay to the NW of the acropolis. Today, apart from a *Roman baths complex* which has some fine geometric mosaics and the decorated portal of a substantial building, little remains to be seen. The portal which is within a few metres of a marsh, once an ancient lake, is probably the most remarkable monument in Olympus. Approximately 5m high, it is believed to be the entrance to an *Ionic-style temple in antis*, dating from the 2C AD. The lintel and uprights, which are decorated on one side only, are flanked by a fine ashlar wall, while nearby is the base of a statue dedicated c 172 to the Emperor Marcus Aurelius. Several large column-drums and parts of the architrave lie on the ground. As there is no room between the existing ruins and the lake for a building of this size, the decoration of the portal and the statue-base appear, curiously, to be on the inside of the structure.

The Turkish name for Olympus is *Yanar*, which means flame or fire. This refers to a natural phenomenon, known in antiquity as the **Chimaera**, which may be seen at a place c 90 minutes' walk N of the city. Visitors wishing to see the Chimaera are advised to take a guide, as the path, which follows part of the ancient route, is not now easy to find. On a mountain slope c 250m above sea-level, a perpetual flame burns in a small opening c 1m². Probably produced by methane gas, this cannot be put out with water, but if covered with soil, it can be extinguished temporarily. At night the flame is clearly visible from the sea. It takes its name from the fire-breathing Chimaera which terrorised ancient Lycia. This was a composite creature which had a lion's head and front, a goat's middle and a snake at the rear. The hero, Bellerophon, was set the task of killing this fearsome beast by Iobates, king of Lycia. He did so by dropping lead into its mouth, which melted and choked it. Originally, the legend of the Chimaera was attached to an area of W Lycia, near Mt Cragus, but was transferred to Olympus at some time, probably because of the mysterious flame. Hephaestus, the god of fire and the divine blacksmith, was worshipped at Olympus and the ruins of his shrine may be seen near the flame. There are also the remains of a Byzantine basilica whose walls bear some traces of fresco.

Speculation in recent years that there might be petrol at the site of the Chimaera caused some investigations to be made, but these do not seem to have produced any positive results.

On the beach, there is a pierced rock (*Deliktaş* in Turkish), which has a tunnel wide enough for a man to pass through. This was used as late as the 19C as a passageway along the shore.

On returning to road 400 continue in the direction of Antalya. This is one of the most beautiful routes in S Turkey, passing as it does through the wild, dramatic scenery of the National Park. After c 21km a sign to the right indicates the turning for (2km) **PHASELIS**.

A well-surfaced track leads to a clearing where there are toilets, a small museum and parking for coaches and where light refreshments and admission tickets to the site are sold. In fine weather private cars may drive 1km further to a parking place near the sea. Phaselis has been recently excavated, and a baths complex in the city centre has been partially restored.

History. Legend states that Phaselis was founded by a group of colonists from Rhodes c 690 BC. According to this story the ground on which the city was built was owned by a shepherd named Cylabras. As money did not exist in the 7C BC, Lacius, the leader of the colonists, offered to purchase the site for a quantity of corn or some dried fish. Cylabras took the latter, a choice commemorated in later days by the practice in Phaselis of using dried salted fish as a sacrificial offering. This gave rise to the expression 'a Phaselitan sacrifice', meaning an inexpensive offering.

An extensive survey, begun in 1968 by German archaeologists, which has revealed no trace of pre-Greek occupation tends to support this legend. The deserted state of the site and the fact that, apart from Olympus, it has the only good harbour on this part of the coast could have attracted the Rhodian colonists to Phaselis. In addition, its hinterland supplied timber, an eagerly sought export commodity, in vast quantities and the city was well placed for trading with most ports in the E Levant. The business acumen of the Phaselitans was demonstrated as early as the 6C BC, when the city combined with eight other Greek cities in Asia Minor to found the trading colony of Naucratis in the Nile Delta. However, in the 4C BC this same acumen was denounced by Demosthenes, who categorised the Phaselitans as dishonest. Their pride in their commercial activities is evidenced by coins issued in the 5C BC which show the prow of a ship on one side and the stern on the reverse. By that time Phaselis was under Persian domination. Clearly, they did not find the yoke a heavy one, as, when the Athenian, Cimon, came to liberate the Lycian cities, the Phaselitans threw in their lot with the Persians. The city was besieged and they suffered grievously. Eventually, through the good offices of their friends, the Chians, they came to terms with Cimon. Plutarch relates that the Chians 'shot leaflets, attached to arrows, over the walls to tell the inhabitants what was happening. Finally, they brought the parties to terms, the Phaselitans agreeing to pay ten talents and accompany Cimon on his campaign against the barbarians.'

Following the defeat of the Persians by the Athenians c 467 BC at the battle of the Eurymedon river, Phaselis, with other Lycian cities was enrolled in the Delian League. The city's wealth and importance at this time may be judged by the fact that, while the annual contribution from Ephesus to the league was assessed at six talents, the levy on Phaselis varied between three and six talents. This sum was paid regularly.

At the beginning of the 4C BC the rule of Persia was restored and Lycia and Phaselis were placed under the control of Mausolus, satrap of Caria. The

Lycians, led by the dynast Pericles of Limyra, raised the standard of revolt. However, the Phaselitans, who did not always agree with their Lycian neighbours, sided with Mausolus. Their independent status at this time is proved by the existence of a treaty between them and Mausolus, which both parties signed as equals.

The arrival of Alexander the Great in 333 BC was welcomed by the Phaselitans. They offered him the customary gold crown and opened the city's gates to him. In return Alexander helped them in a campaign against the Pisidians, who had been ravaging Phaselitan territory. After the death of Alexander, Phaselis sided with Antigonus Monophthalmos, but with the rest of Lycia soon became a Ptolemaic possession. In 197 BC Lycia, and presumably Phaselis, was occupied by Antiochus III of Syria. Following his defeat by the Romans in 190 BC it was given to their allies, the Rhodians. However, Rhodian rule was bitterly resisted and, finally, in 167 BC Rome gave Lycia her freedom.

The Lycian League was revived. Phaselis became a full member and issued

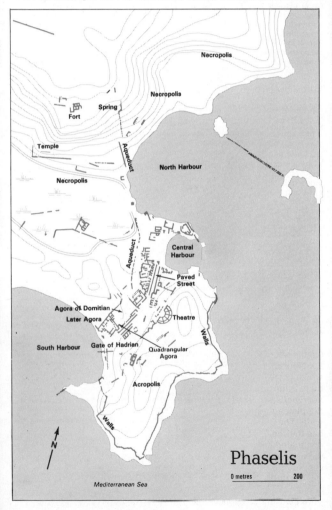

federal coins. At the beginning of the 1C BC the city and its neighbour, Olympus, were occupied and plundered by Cilician pirates. After the campaigns of Servilius Vatia in 78 BC and Pompey in 67 BC had eliminated the pirate threat, Phaselis began to recover. However, progress was so slow that in 48 BC the Roman poet, Lucan, could call the city 'little Phaselis'.

In AD 43 Claudius created the new province of Lycia-Pamphylia and incorporated it in the Roman Empire. Like most cities in the empire Phaselis appears to have enjoyed a prosperous, relatively uneventful existence. It was visited by Hadrian in 129, an event commemorated by the erection of many statues of the emperor and a ceremonial gateway. Because of his generous benefactions, Opramoas of Rhodiapolis became a citizen of Phaselis. This was a somewhat doubtful privilege, as the Phaselitans were alleged to have sold their citizenship to anyone prepared to pay 100 drachmae for it. The city was also notorious for a hairstyle called 'sisoe' which Christians found particularly offensive, probably because it was forbidden in the bible. 'Ye shall not make a 'sisoe' of the hair of your heads.' (Leviticus, 19,27.) Knox translates this as 'There must be no tonsuring of heads.' Phaselis acquired a reputation for being unhealthy. Livy describes a fever, which may have been malaria, produced among Rhodian sailors. This he attributes to the unpleasant smells found there. These may have come from the swamp near the N fortress, which today harbours many mosquitoes. Aelian, writing c 200, says that the city had to be abandoned, presumably temporarily, because of a plague of wasps.

In Byzantine times Phaselis was an episcopal see; its bishop attended the Council of Chalcedon in 451. Having suffered greatly from Arab raids in the 7C AD, the city's prosperity revived in the 8C, when its fortifications were renewed and many new buildings were erected. In 1158 it was captured from the Byzantines by the Selçuk Turks and, with the growth in importance of the ports of Antalya and Alanya, it declined gradually as a trading centre until it was finally abandoned sometime in the early 13C.

Phaselis was visited in 1811 by Beaufort, when he surveyed the S coast of Turkey for the Admiralty. Most of the ruins that he saw are still visible today. His party found one sarcophagus, which had escaped the tomb robbers. This had been concealed 'by a thick covering of earth, which the surf had lately removed, and exposed one end to view. Elated with the discovery, we eagerly proceeded to explore its contents: while the necessary implements were collecting, our imagination was on the stretch; and urns, or coins, or ancient weapons were, at least, expected to reward our labour. At length the tools arrived; the ponderous lid was removed; and the bones of a single skeleton were discovered, and nothing more. These were strong and firm, and did not undergo any immediate change from exposure to the air; the skeleton was of the middle size, and was placed with the face up, and the head to the northward.' Having listed the principal ruins and transcribed a number of inscriptions, Beaufort affirms that everything was replaced where it was found or placed in a position calculated to aid its preservation. 'A practice,' he adds, 'which we constantly adopted, for the benefit of future travellers.'

Visitors to Phaselis are moved by the beauty of its situation between the mountains and the sea. The sight of fragments of ancient buildings protruding from the lush undergrowth produces a mood of gentle melancholy. For Bean Phaselis had 'a charm beyond most others. The sleepy summer heat, the sea and the superb mountains, the contrast of the utter solitude with the busy life of the ancient city, combine to leave a memory not easily effaced.'

On the left of the track, which connects the site with the main road, is the N fortified area of Phaselis. This is enclosed by a Hellenistic wall which is well preserved at its SW corner. At this point, on the slope, there is the foundation of a *temple* or *monumental tomb*. A part of the *necropolis* is to be found below the W side of the hill. On the E side of the plateau a ramp leads to a fortified area 150m long and 25–50m wide. The 3C BC N wall of this fortification, which is now 3m high, has the remains of a tower and three arrow slits. The fortified area dominated the city and protected a spring, now dry, which was near the base of the ramp. Water was carried from here in a clay conduit supported first by a solid wall and then by arches. This skirts the W side of the N harbour and ends near the rear of the quadrangular agora.

To the right of the track there is an extensive swampy area, which

according to Strabo was once a lake. The swamp is now separated
from the N harbour by an area of sand dunes and scrub c 150m wide.
The N harbour, which appears to have been used mainly as a
roadstead, is protected from the NE by a line of rocks which extends
for 300m into the sea. An artificial breakwater 4m wide was constructed on top of this natural feature. The largest section of the city's
necropolis lies around the shore of the N harbour. There are a
number of interesting sarcophagi and other tombs which date from
the Roman and Byzantine periods.

The central harbour of Phaselis, which was used for small and
medium-sized ships, is c 100m to the SE. Facing E, it was protected
on the N and NE by a wall which extended outwards over a
breakwater and terminated in a tower. The 18m-wide harbour
entrance between this and another tower on the S could be closed in
time of danger. In the SW corner of the harbour one of the bollards,
which projected horizontally from the ashlar facing of the quay wall,
may still be seen. Behind the quay there were a number of warehouses on the hillside.

Archaic pottery sherds found on the *acropolis*, which lies to the S of
the central harbour, suggest that the earliest occupation of Phaselis
took place there. Fortified on the seaward side, it is covered with
undergrowth through which the ruins of several buildings, tentatively identified as houses and a church, may be seen. Because of its
cool sea breezes and its distance from the noisome smells of the
marsh the SW tip of the acropolis peninsula was one of the favoured
areas of the city. It is known that public buildings and later, in
Byzantine times, churches and private houses were constructed there
on a series of terraces. No trace of the temple of Athena Polias where,
according to Pausanias, the spear of Achilles was kept, has been
found in Phaselis. Some authorities believe that it was on the
acropolis, and the discovery of a stone, dated to the 5C BC, bearing
the name of the goddess, which had been built into the wall of the
stage-building of the theatre in late Roman or Byzantine times,
appears to support this theory. However, until the dense vegetation
has been cleared from the acropolis and the area has been investigated properly, the exact location of the temple must remain a matter
of speculation.

A broad, *paved street* c 22m wide, flanked by steps and sidewalks,
passed through the city centre and linked the S and central harbours.
It was made up of two sections which met at an obtuse angle in front
of the theatre. At the NE end of this street, near the central harbour,
there was a long, narrow two-storey building, probably used for
business purposes. Behind this, an elaborate *baths complex* still
retains traces of its mosaic pavements. To the SW, a wall of ashlar
masonry marks the site of the quadrangular *agora*, which was
probably the administrative centre of the city. This can be dated to
131 by a dedicatory inscription to Hadrian on the door lintel. Statue
bases on either side of the entrance bear inscriptions commemorating some of the city's benefactors. One so honoured was Opramoas of
Rhodiapolis. In Byzantine times a small, three-aisled basilica was
constructed in the NW part of this agora.

Further to the SW lies the agora of Domitian. Dated to c 93, this is
an open area, c 60m by 40m, with rooms on the SW and SE sides only.
Beyond is a late agora, opening on to the S harbour, constructed of
materials salvaged from other buildings. This has been dated to late
Imperial or Byzantine times.

The *theatre* of Phaselis, which dates, probably, from the 2C AD, faces the quadrangular agora from the opposite side of the street. Its cavea has been excavated from the acropolis hillside. Though much overgrown, several rows of seats and substantial parts of the stage-building remain. Three monumental doors provided access to the stage area. This was c 2.5m above ground level and was probably constructed of wood. Below the stage four small doors, which opened on to the orchestra, were used to admit animals when the theatre was used for wild-beast fights. The pits in the orchestra floor have been made by illegal treasure-hunters. It is probable that this building replaced an earlier Hellenistic theatre. At some point, perhaps during the Byzantine period, the wall of the stage-building was incorporated in the acropolis fortifications.

The S end of the main street is marked by the remains of a ceremonial *marble gateway*, rected to commemorate the visit of Hadrian to Phaselis in 129. The S harbour, the largest of the three, lies outside the fortifications. This was where the larger ships were loaded and unloaded by lighters or at the quayside. The harbour was protected from the weather on the SE by a breakwater, which extended for c 100m from the acropolis promontary. It is not known with certainty when this breakwater and the other harbour structures at Phaselis were made. They probably date from the middle of the 2C AD, when Antoninus Pius and Hadrian promoted the construction and improvement of harbours in Asia Minor.

Of the W part of the ancient city little remains to be seen. It is covered under sand dunes and the luxurious vegetation. NW of the marsh, to the left of the track which leads back to the main highway there is a stretch of c 300m of the ancient road that linked Olympus, Phaselis and Attaleia (Antalya). This is flanked by a number of tombs.

Road 400 from Phaselis to c 45km **Antalya** follows the coastline closely, passing a series of attractive beaches on the way. Here the pine-clad mountain ridges sweep down to the road and project into the sea great jagged promontories. River beds, dry in summer, punctuate the valleys. After c 8km a turning right leads to *Kemer*, where there are a number of hotels, a marina and a large holiday camp. Here the landscape is gentler, filled with orange and lemon groves. At *Beldibi*, c 20km beyond Kemer, there is a pebbly beach, a number of holiday villages and a camping-place. The outskirts of Antalya are signalled by the commercial harbour on the right. Beyond the harbour the huge *Konyaaltı beach* stretches away in a great curve towards the city.

Visitors driving along road 400, the link between the coastal towns and villages of E Lycia and Antalya, may be unaware that this was not completed until comparatively recently. The rugged terrain which lies between Finike and Antalya raised constructional problems of a kind that could only be solved by the skills and machinery available to modern civil engineers. Before the construction of this excellent road many travellers made the journey to and from the regional capital by sea. For individuals the problems which this caused were considerable. For groups they were almost insuperable.

The absence, until recently, of a passable route through E Lycia serves to remind us of an interesting historical puzzle. When, in 333 BC, Alexander the Great decided to march from Phaselis to the cities on the Pamphylian plain, he was faced with the problem of getting his army through a wild and trackless stretch of country. Arrian claims that he overcame the difficulty with the help of the gods. Sending some of his men over the high passes 'a long and difficult journey', he led the remainder of his troops along the stretch of sea-shore that lies between Phaselis and the approaches to the modern city of Antalya. According to the historian this was a venture that could only be attempted when the wind blew from the N. With a S wind, the route along the shore was impassable. As Alexander left Phaselis, there was a strong wind from the S. However, trusting in the gods and in his own destiny, he set out at the head of his men. Zeus was kind to him. Arrian states: 'the wind turned to the N and made the passage quick and easy'. But his account, which differs from Strabo's, has been questioned by more than one modern historian. George Bean, who discussed the matter with local fishermen, was told that contrary to Arrian's assertion the wind makes little difference to the level of the sea, but that a N wind makes it rough. Bean accepts Strabo's version with minor modifications, i.e. he is of the opinion that Alexander took his troops along the beach where the sea-level permitted this and where the water was too high he made a number of diversions inland.

Perhaps the most recent attempt to follow the shore-line was made by Freya Stark in 1954, while she was researching her book 'Alexander's Path' in Lycia and Pamphylia. Attired in a bathing costume and accompanied by a local girl, she found that she could wade for part of the way, but that there were stretches of deep water where she was obliged to swim. It is unlikely that the mystery associated with Alexander's crossing from Lycia to Pamphylia will ever be solved now as the configuration of this part of the coast has almost certainly changed during the last 2000 years.

21 Antalya

ANTALYA, capital of the province of the same name, is a modern city of 260,000 inhabitants. Its situation on the Gulf of Antalya is one of the finest on Turkey's Mediterranean coast. Clustered around the Yat Limanı are some of the oldest buildings in the city. This area is currently being restored and developed with some imagination by the Ministry for Tourism and Culture. Antalya's shopping centre is bisected by Kenan Evren Bulv. and the Cumhuriyet Cad. (E–W) and Atatürk Cad. and 30 Ağustos Cad. (N–S). The city park, with spectacular views of the Gulf and of the Bey Dağları, is located off 30 Ağustos Cad. Konyaaltı Plajı, a rather stony beach, is 1km W of the city. Antalya's industrial port is located nearby on the road to Kemer. The city's main industries are the processing of sesame and sunflower seeds and of cotton. Antalya is also an important centre for a wide range of agricultural produce including citrus fruit, olives, sugar beet and salad vegetables. The main grain crops of the region are wheat and barley. Antalya has very hot dry summers, when the temperature sometimes reaches 40°C. Winters are warm and wet, with the heaviest rainfall in January. Frosts are almost unknown and snow is only found on the peaks of the Taurus Mountains and the Bey Dağları during the winter months.

Information and Accommodation. The Tourist Information Office in Cumhuriyet Cad., next door to the Turkish Airlines Passenger office, provides detailed, up-to-date information about Antalya and its environs, including hotel and pension prices, restaurants, transport services, car hire, local tour operators and places of cultural interest. It is open Monday to Saturday and also on Sunday during the tourist season.

A wide variety of accommodation is available in Antalya. This ranges from the luxurious *Talya* and *Turban Adalya* hotels to more modest establishments in the old and less fashionable parts of the city, and at Lara Beach (c 12km from the city centre). Full information may be obtained from the Tourist Information Office.

Post Office. The Central Post Office is in Anafartalar Cad.

Banks. Branches of the principal Turkish banks may be found in the city centre in Cumhuriyet Cad., Ali Çetinkaya Cad. and Atatürk Cad.

Transport. Antalya's airport, c 8km to the E, just off the E24, provides connections via İstanbul with many European destinations. There are direct charter flights during the summer season and frequent domestic flights, and services to the Turkish Republic of North Cyprus and to some Middle East countries. A coach from the Turkish Airlines Cargo Terminal in Cumhuriyet Cad. conveys passengers to the airport for a modest charge.

The central bus station is in Kâzim Özalp Cad. There are frequent services to Alanya (2 hours), Perge (¹/₂ hour), Aspendus (1 hour), Side via Manavgat (90 minutes), Ankara, (10 hours), Adana (11 hours), Konya (7 hours), Demre (4 hours), Kaş (5 hours), Fethiye (8 hours), etc. Tickets may be obtained at the bus station and from the town offices of the various companies.

The Dolmuş Garage is situated on Ali Çetinkaya Cad., and provides cheap and rapid transportation both in Antalya and to many of the nearby towns and villages.

Antalya's **museum** which contains an extensive and well-displayed collection of archaeological and ethnographical objects, is at the end of Kenan Evren Bulv. near Konyaaltı Beach.

History. Founded in the 2C BC by Attalus II (160–139 BC), king of Pergamum, and named ATTALEIA in his honour, modern Antalya has few relics of its ancient past. About 158 BC Attalus attempted to subdue the rebellious city of Selge, which was nominally part of the kingdom of Pergamum, and although he failed in his attempt, he managed to conquer a large part of Pamphylia. As Side, the only port of any importance in that province was under the protection of Rome, he was obliged to found the city of Attaleia to obtain an outlet to the Mediterranean. His nephew and successor, Attalus III, (138–133 BC) bequeathed his kingdom to Rome in 133 BC. The bequest did not include Pamphylia, Rough Cilicia and Lycia. Because of its wild and rugged nature and its abundance of small, safe anchorages, Rough Cilicia had long been a haven for pirates who preyed on the coastal trade. Eventually, their activities spread and reached such proportions that Rome was obliged to take action. After a naval expedition against the pirates had only achieved a limited success, Pamphylia, with some surrounding territory, was annexed by the Romans. Direct rule brought few benefits to the inhabitants of the province. A succession of venal and grasping governors enriched themselves at the expense of their subjects and the pirates continued their depredations almost without check. It was not until 67 BC that a successful campaign conducted by Pompey put an end to piracy in that part of the Mediterranean. In AD 130 Hadrian came to Antalya. This visit was commemorated by the erection of a ceremonial arch which still stands. St. Paul visited nearby Perge, but little is known of the early history of Christianity in Antalya. It did not have its own bishop until the 11C.

During the Crusades Antalya was an important staging post for the transportation of soldiers and their supplies to the Holy Land. Briefly occupied by the Selçuk Turks in the 12C and then returned to Byzantine rule, it was reconquered by Giyaseddin Keyhusrev in 1206. During the reign of Yildirim Beyazit it became part of the Ottoman Empire. It remained an Ottoman provincial subdivision until World War I. Then, as part of the spoils of war, it was ceded to Italy in 1918. In 1921 it was liberated by the Turkish army and became a provincial capital in the Turkish Republic.

Travellers. The famous Arab traveller Ibn Battuta visited Antalya in the mid 14C and found it 'a most beautiful city. It covers an immense area and though of vast bulk is one of the most attractive towns to be seen anywhere, besides being exceedingly populous and well laid out. Each section of the inhabitants lives in a separate quarter. The Christian merchants live in a quarter of the town known as the Mina [the Port], and are surrounded by a wall, the gates of which are shut upon them from without at night and during the Friday service. The Greeks, who were its former inhabitants, live by themselves in another quarter, the Jews in another, and the king and his court and mamluks in another, each of these quarters being walled off likewise. The rest of the Muslims live in the main city. Round the whole town and all the quarters mentioned there is another great wall. The town contains many orchards and produces fine fruits, including an admirable kind of apricot, called by them Qamar ad-Din, which has a sweet almond in its kernel. This fruit is dried and exported to Egypt, where it is regarded as a great luxury.' At the time Ibn Battuta visited Antalya it was the most important port in southern Anatolia, particularly in relation to trade with Cyprus and Egypt. Perhaps that is why the lemon is still called 'Adaliya' in Egypt.

In 1671 the Turkish traveller Evliya Çelebi visited Antalya. In his 'Book of Travels' he says the city was 4400m long and enclosed by a wall surmounted by 80 towers and pierced by four great gates. The citadel inside the walls was divided into four districts. A further 22 gates gave access to these districts and to the thousand houses which they contained. The streets were paved. 'Each house has an open-ended verandah built on four high posts where the family sleeps. The cloth market is in the outer suburb. This suburb contains twenty Moslem and four Greek enclaves ... It has one hundred and ninety houses, two hundred shops and more than two hundred fountains whose water comes from the Düden river ... The harbour can accommodate two hundred ships and is protected from the eight winds. The weather in the city is very hot. The bitter oranges, very large lemons, dates, olives, figs, sugar cane and pomegranates are famous. There are vineyards and orchards everywhere. The people of this city, like the people of Anatolia, speak good Turkish. The young men wear Algerian dress. Women are enveloped in broadcloth loose coats and on their heads wear skullcaps covered with entwined white cloth. The people are courteous and givers of alms.'

About 150 years later a British visitor also found Antalya an attractive place. Captain Francis Beaufort of the frigate *Frederickssteen* made a survey of the coast of southern Turkey for the Admiralty in 1811 and 1812. In 'Karamania' he describes Antalya: 'Adalia is beautifully situated round a small harbour; the streets appear to rise behind each other like the seats of a theatre; and on the level summit of the hill, the city is enclosed by a ditch, a double wall, and a series of square towers, about fifty yards asunder ... The gardens round the town are beautiful; the trees are loaded with fruit; every kind of vegetation seemed to be exuberant; and the inhabitants spoke of their corn grounds as more than commonly productive. The soil is deep, and every where intersected by streams loaded with calcareous matter, which, after fertilizing the plain, fall over the cliffs, or turn the corn-mills in their descent to the sea ... Alternate breezes refresh the air in a remarkable manner; for the daily seabreeze sweeps up the western side of the gulf with accumulated strength; and at night, the great northern valley, which appears to traverse the chain of Mt Taurus, conducts the land wind from the cold mountains of the interior. Upon the whole, it would be difficult to select a more charming spot for a city.'

For the eyes of a modern traveller Antalya also had a particular and distinctive beauty. Freya Stark visited the city in the 1950s and in 'Alexander's Path' she enthused on the view over the bay to the Lycian hills. 'In early spring the Bay of Antalya lies under a mist slightly raised above the surface of the water and filled with sunlight, until the warmth of day sucks it up. I would watch it from a slanting little breakfast shop that overhangs the harbour. The six tiled domes of the Seljuk mosque, now the museum, are there in the foreground with a minaret like a bunch of asparagus beside them, rosy as if its bricks had been scrubbed—which indeed they had been, by the Department of Antiquities which has repaired them. Beyond these, brown roofs and the tops of trees push out from hidden gardens; and beyond them a caique might have been moving out from Antalya with the dawn: she would leave a curved trail, marked by the current, as wavering and edgeless as the seasonal pathways made by the feet of flocks; and beyond her and the misty bay, the Chelidonian peninsula spread its tented blue festoons from peak to peak.'

The centre of Antalya is marked by the *Atatürk memorial* in Cumhuriyet Cad. Across the road is the *Vilayet*, the administrative headquarters of the province. From the square by the memorial there is a splendid panoramic view of the city, of the Gulf of Antalya and of the Bey Dağları (the Bey Mountains). On the left and a little below Cumhuriyet Cad. is the **Yivli Minare**, the Fluted Minaret. This structure, which has come to be regarded as the symbol of Antalya, was constructed during the reign of Sultan Alaeddin Keykubad in 1230. Originally attached to a mosque which had been converted from a Byzantine church, the minaret is built on a square base of stone. The body of the minaret is made of brick in eight fluted sections, hence its name. The base and body are decorated with pieces of dark blue tiles. Those on the base bear the words 'Allah' and 'Muhammet'. The minaret is 38m high. The original mosque was destroyed in the 14C and replaced by the building visible today. This has six cupolas supported by columns capped with ancient Ionic and Corinthian capitals. It was built by Mehmet Bey, who also constructed the türbe with the pyramidal roof near the mosque for the

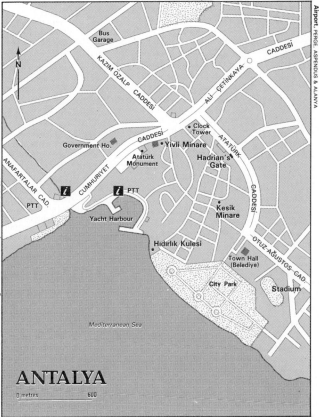

Airport, PERGE, ASPENDOUS & ALANYA

Archaeological Museum Konyaalti Beach & LYCIA

Bus Garage

KAZIM ÖZALP CADDESİ

ALİ ÇETİNKAYA CADDESİ

Clock Tower

CADDESİ

Government Ho.

Yivli Minare

Atatürk Monument

Hadrian's Gate

ATATÜRK

ANAFARTALAR CAD.

CUMHURIYET

i   *i* **PTT**

PTT

Yacht Harbour

Kesik Minare

CADDESİ

Hıdırlık Kulesi

OTUZ AĞUSTOS CAD.

Town Hall (Belediye)

City Park

Stadium

Mediterranean Sea

ANTALYA

0 metres   600

body of his eldest son, who died in 1377. The building adjoining the türbe is a tekke, built in the 18C to house a community of Mevlevi dervishes. Access to the Yivli Minare and to the mosque is by some steep steps which descend from the square to the harbour or from the street which turns sharp right by the clock-tower in Kalekapısı.

To the right of the clock-tower at Kalekapısı is the *Tekeli Mehmet Pasha Mosque*. Built in the 18C by Tekeli Mehmet, it has three cupolas over the central area.

Return to Cumhuriyet Cad. and continue for c 100m before turning right into Atatürk Cad. A short distance along this street on the right is **Hadrian's Gate**. This was built to commemorate the visit by Hadrian to Antalya in AD 130. Constructed of marble, it has three arches with coffered ceilings decorated with rosettes. Four Corinthian columns with granite shafts stand in front of each of the piers. An imaginative restoration by the Turkish authorities, enables us to get a good impression of its original appearance. The gate bore the following inscription: AYTOKPATOPI KAIZAPI (TPAIANΩ) AΔPIANΩ. A portion of this inscription is preserved in the Ashmolean Museum at Oxford. Hadrian's Gate is flanked by towers which are thought to date from the period of the foundation of the city, the 2C BC.

Behind Hadrian's Gate lies a maze of streets that makes up the old town. Ancient houses with overhanging wooden balconies, many in a ruined or semi-dilapidated condition, line the narrow lanes. Sometimes a break in an old wall offers a glimpse of an overgrown garden which contains a few ancient orange trees. Children play happily in streets and lanes, little disturbed by the infrequent traffic. At present this area is undergoing restoration by the Ministry of Tourism and Culture: derelict houses are being painstakingly reconstructed and no buildings in a modern style are permitted.

Following the gentle slope down towards the harbour we reach the *Kesik Minare Camii*, the Truncated Minaret Mosque. Built as a church in the 5C in honour of Mary, it was converted into a mosque in the 13C by Şehzade Korkut, the son of Beyazit II. During this reconstruction a mihrab of cut stone was added. It acquired its name after a bad fire in 1851 damaged the minaret. At present the building is in a ruinous condition.

By turning left here we make our way to the city park. The large building near the entrance is the *Belediye*, the City Hall. During the sweltering days of summer the palm-lined avenues of the park provide a pleasant refuge from the heat and in the evening its tea gardens and belvedere are favourite rendezvous for both visitors and the citizens of Antalya. The cliff-top promenade offers a splendid view of the Gulf of Antalya and of the Bey Mountains of Lycia in the far distance. Popular with children are the small aviary and the funfair located just outside the park near the *Hıdırlık Kulesi*. A Roman building of the 2C AD, this is of a round tower resting on a massive square base. The total height of the building is 13.45m. Various purposes have been ascribed to it—a lighthouse, a fortified structure, a tomb. Its shape and the presence of a carving of fasces (a bundle of rods) the symbol of office of a Roman magistrate, tend to support the third hypothesis. Indeed, most scholars are now of the opinion that it was the tomb of a local dignitary.

From the Hıdırlık Tower follow the road downwards towards the Yat Limanı, the yacht harbour. Just after the office of the Ministry of Tourism the road branches. Take the left fork by the mosque to the tea garden above the S side of the harbour. From there steps lead down to the breakwater. On the left there is a small beach much favoured by local youths, but in view of its proximity to the harbour, bathing here is not recommended. It is also possible to reach the harbour by following the road that runs parallel to the ancient fortification walls, and by turning left at the first main junction.

Following the curve of the yacht harbour we pass the very distinctive *Iskele Camii*, the Harbour Mosque. This building of cut stone has been restored recently. Access to the interior is by a wooden staircase. Immediately in front of this mosque, boats for hire and boats offering sea trips are moored.

The harbour area has been developed by the Ministry of Culture and Tourism, in a very attractive manner. Some of the best restaurants in Antalya are to be found here. In addition there is a post office and a bank, cafés, a barber, souvenir shops, a luxury hotel and a small open-air theatre. Great care has been taken to preserve the character of the area. To dine here by candle-light in one of the restaurants that lie in the shadow of the city's ancient walls is a memorable experience and a pleasant way to end a day's exploration

Antalya Museum. To get to the museum take a dolmuş marked Meteorological Station, Bahçeli or Harbour (Liman) at the stop across the road from the clock-tower at Kalekapısı. (The energetic will find it an easy 20 minutes' walk along Cumhuriyet Cad. and Kenan Evren Bulv.) The museum is on the right-hand side of the road, just after the junction with Piri Reis Cad.

Antalya Museum is open every day except Monday from 8.00 to 12.00 and from 13.30 to 17.00. In addition to the usual facilities there is a small bar which offers light refreshments. At the ticket desk guidebooks to Aspendus, Side, Perge and other sites in the Antalya area, postcards, transparencies and replicas of objects in the museum may be purchased. The following information has been compiled with the assistance of the museum staff.

Room 1 is intended to interest children in history by relating the objects in the museum to everyday life. Examples of ancient pottery and scripts, demonstrations of crafts, and posters and explanatory texts are employed for this purpose.

Room 2 deals with the prehistory of the Antalya region and in particular with the finds from the Karain Cave. This cave is situated 30km NW of Antalya near the village of Yağca, which is 6km from the old Antalya–Burdur road. First excavated by Prof. Dr I. Kılıç Kökten in 1946, only a portion has been explored so far. Artefacts from the Palaeolithic (30,000–10,000 BC), Mesolithic (10,000–6500 BC), Chalcolithic (5300–3000 BC), Bronze (3000–2000 BC) and later ages have been found there. It would appear that at one time the cave was used as a temple. Cases in this room contain examples of hand axes, scrapers made of flint, bone awls, burins, and daggers and spear heads made from antlers. The skull of a Neanderthal child and the skulls and skeletons of Homo Sapiens are on display, also the teeth and bones of extinct animals from the Palaeolithic age. There is a fine example of mobiliary art, the head of a bison or of Elephantus Meridionalis carved in stone. From the Burdur area there is a female fertility figurine from the Chalcolithic period. Bronze Age grave goods from Elmalı-Karataş Semayük include ear-studs, brush handles, bronze pins and spearheads. At the end of the room there is a reconstructed pithos burial from Elmalı and several decorated pots and pithoi.

Joining Rooms 2 and 3 is the Corridor of Short Inscriptions. Two stelae here are of particular interest, one from Perge and one from Aspendus. The stele from Perge, which dates from the 5C BC, is dedicated to Artemis of Perge under her ancient name. 'Klemutas son of Lfaramus of the tribe Wasir Fotas has set up this dedication to Wanasa Preiia Goddess of Perge [as the result of an] order [received in a] dream.' The stele from Aspendus, which dates from the 3C BC, is important as it shows that there was also a temple dedicated to Artemis in that city, and that during the period of domination by the Ptolemies the city enjoyed a remarkable degree of independence. 'When Apollonios, son of Democharis, was demiourgos [governor] and at a full meeting of the ekklesia [assembly], the people of Aspendus took the following decision. Since the city has been honoured by the Pamphylians, Lykcians, Cretans, Greeks and Pisidians who are with Democles and Leonidas and since, like King Ptolemaios they are worthy people and of benefit to our city, they and their children shall receive the title of citizen and benefactor; a stele shall be placed in the temple of Artemis bearing their names and the names of their fathers; if any one of them should so desire, they can be registered with a phyle [tribe]. The cost of this will be paid by the city. This was agreed. Menandros, son of Elisotos of Aspendus. Petrakis, son of Sophanes of Miletos.'

Room 3 contains small works of art. On the left hand side there are two bell kraters and a column krater. The column krater, which comes from the necropolis of Aspendus and dates from the 5C BC, shows three komasts (revellers) dancing vigorously, while holding drinking cups. On the reverse, three youths are depicted arming themselves. On the right-hand wall, there are cases containing figurines from the Mycenaean period; a remarkable terracotta head believed to come from Cyprus and some vases from the Classical period. Note particularly the boy with the hoop and cock (compare this subject with ARV 355,69 in the Ashmolean Museum, Oxford). There are also some cases of jewellery—headbands, earrings, neck-laces, an ivory comb, pins and a decorated bronze mirror. These date from the 4C BC to the 6C AD. Finally, a collection of Classical and Hellenistic lekythoi dating from the 5C to the 3C BC.

Room 4 contains some of the major treasures of the museum. Here in the so-called 'Gallery of the Gods' are displayed statues dis-covered in Perge dating from the 2C AD. They include a resting Mercury, the Egyptian trinity of Serapis, Isis and Harpocrates, Artemis with part of the face and one leg missing, an Athene in good condition, Apollo, Hygeia, Tyche, Aphrodite, a pensive Dioscuros, Artemis, Aphrodite and Nemesis. Appropriately, the display is domi-nated by a fine statue of Zeus.

Room 5 is devoted to small works of art and to objects recovered from the sea. Note in particular the 2C bronze statue of Apollo from Seleucia, the bearded Priapus from Aspendus, the bronze head of Attis from Perge and the bronze statuette of Hercules from Fogla. On the end wall there is a display of amphorae, stone and metal objects and pottery recovered from the sea. These date from the 3C to the 14C AD. Near the entrance to room 6 there is a fine Marsyas, a headless Athena, and a fragment from a pillar bearing a relief of Artemis Pergaea. The latter, which was found in the theatre of Perge, dates from the 2C AD and shows the goddess in the form of a baetyl (sacred stone). At the top there is the head of Artemis, crowned with a polos, above a crescent moon. Below are three scenes of ritual cults. On the right-hand side there is another bust of Artemis, with below the figure of Eros armed with a sword.

Room 6 is dominated by the magnificent statue of a dancer. Behind, in characteristic pose, is a group of the Three Graces. Although room 6 is known as the 'Room of the Emperors' because it contains fine statues of Trajan, Hadrian, and Septimius Severus found at Perge, perhaps its most interesting exhibit is the statue of a woman—Plancia Magna. A dominating figure in 2C AD Perge, she was priestess of Artemis and of the Mother of the Gods and demiourgus. A generous donor, she presented a number of statues depicting various members of the Roman imperial house to her native city about AD 120. The importance of her position is under-lined by the fact that two of the 'founders' of Perge are described on statue bases found in that city as the father and brother of Plancia Magna! Note also the statues of Julia Domna, wife of Septimius Severus and mother of Caracalla and Geta, and of Sabina, the wife of Hadrian.

Room 7 contains some fine sarcophagi from the necropolis of Perge. Immediately inside the entrance there is a striking 3C col-umnar sarcophagus, with a reclining couple, in the Sidamara style. Two 2C sarcophagi are decorated with reliefs showing the labours of Hercules. Note the sculpture form of one of them which was exported illegally to the United States and later returned to Turkey by the Paul Getty Museum. A so-called medallion sarcophagus has sides decorated with winged figures supporting the head of Medusa. Along one wall there are a number of cinerary urns, while another displays several fragments from sarcophagi, one of which depicts a scene from the 'Iliad'. At the rear of the room there is a strange primitive votive stele dedicated to the Twelve Gods of Lycia. This shows 12 armed figures on the upper row with 12 stylised dogs below.

Room 8 a long narrow room to the left of room 7, is devoted to icons from churches in Antalya. All date from the 19C and early 20C. In the case on the left-hand wall there is a series, which relates the life of Christ—Nativity, Presentation in the Temple, Circumcision, Teaching in the Temple, Healing the Blind Man, Speaking with the Samaritan Woman, Transfiguration, Triumphant Entry into Jerusalem, Last Supper, Washing the Feet of his Disciples, Carrying the Cross, Crucifixion and Resurrection. Other icons depict the Virgin and Child, the Evangelists, St. John the Baptist, and St. Nicholas of Myra. There is also a small reliquary containing some of the bones of St. Nicholas (cf. Demre, Rte 19). Note also a portion of the 6C silver treasure of Corydalla (modern Kumluca). This includes ornate silver dishes decorated with crosses. Part of this hoard is in the United States.

Leaving Room 8 we come to the large **Room 9**, the 'Mosaic' room. This contains some fine, if rather damaged, mosaics from Seleucia and Xanthus. A large mosaic from Seleucia is decorated with portrait heads of Solon, Thucydides, Lycurgus, Herodotus, Hesiod, Demosthenes and has Homer's name in the centre. Another, also from Seleucia, shows Orpheus surrounded by wild animals. One of the mosaics from Xanthus depicts Thetis bathing her child, Achilles, in the river Styx to make him invulnerable. Another is decorated with portraits of Eirene, goddess of peace, and Euprepeia, goddess of propriety. On the right-hand wall there is a large 2C disc decorated with a relief of Artemis Pergaea and signs of the Zodiac, from Perge. Note particularly the statue from the Letoön, near Xanthus, which has been painstakingly reconstructed from hundreds of fragments. This once formed part of a shrine dedicated to Leto and her children, Artemis and Apollo, which was damaged in ancient times by fire. Nearby is a 6C ambon decorated with a relief of the Angel Gabriel. Note the Arabic inscription 'Allah' in the roundel on the bottom left. On the wall are two interesting fragments of unknown provenance: one of a male head; the other the arm of a colossal bronze statue. In front of these is a large slab marked out as a gaming board. This was found in the main street in Perge. Evidently such games were very popular, as many similar examples have been found at various sites in Turkey.

Proceeding along the corridor from room 8 we come to **Room 10** which contains the museum's collection of coins. This has a representative selection from Lycia, Pisidia and Pamphylia illustrating the Classic, Hellenistic, Roman, Byzantine, Selçuk and Ottoman periods.

Rooms 11, 12 and 13 are devoted to the museum's ethnograhical collection: 11 contains some very fine examples of Selçuk and Ottoman porcelain; room 12 has a selection of antique weapons and materials connected with the Yürük (nomad) people, regional dresses and embroidery, fragments of old manuscripts, musical instruments, objects from the Abdal Musa Tekkesı and carpets; room 13 and the passage to the entrance hall have some reconstructions of old Antalya houses. Note, particularly, the fine ceiling in the reconstructed room immediately before the exit.

Returning to the entrance hall we pass through a door to the left of the ticket desk into the museum's garden. At this point a pause for refreshment under the shady pergola is indicated. Tea and soft drinks may be obtained from the bar on the left-hand side. Note that there is a public telephone by the door into the garden.

In and around the refreshment area there are some interesting 2C sculptures from Perge and Side. To the right of the door is a fragment with a rearing male goat and bunches of grapes, perhaps part of a Bacchic group. Nearby there are some theatre masks and a headless male statue. Note also the very fine statue of Euphrosyne, one of the Three Graces. This also, alas, lacks its head. From Side there is a sarcophagus elaborately decorated with cupids and garlands. Note the sun dial from Perge. As we advance further into the garden we are faced by a relief showing Artemis, flanked by attendant priests and sacrificial animals. In the colonnade there are several interesting inscriptions. These range from a rather fulsome epitaph to Miletus (Inv,202), to the self-satisfied memorial to one Drungarius Stephanus (Inv,35). This Byzantine period (909–910) inscription begs 'O noble offspring of the brilliant city of Attalus, pray for Drungarious Stephanus (who built this splendid work) exactly like his industrious turn of mind, strong, admirable, enjoyable, in such good time, so that he will be forgiven his sins and escape eternal condemnation'. The nature of his 'splendid work' is not recorded! Also in the colonnade is a 2C fragment from Perge with a vigorous depiction of Bacchus and attendants, and a portion of the pediment from the 2C fountain from Perge.

The antiquities on display in the garden have been arranged with taste and imagination, and backed, as they are, by the striking panorama of Antalya bay and the Bey Dağları provide an aesthetically satisfying end to a visit to the Antalya Museum.

22 Antalya to Side

Total distance c 66km. **Antalya**—E24 16km *Aksu*—(c 2km **Perge**)—(c 8km **Sillyum**)—c 28km *Serik*—(c 5km **Aspendus**)—(c 43km **Selge**)—c 26km **Manavgat**—c 7km **Side**.

Perge and Aspendus are easily reached by using the frequent bus and dolmuş services which link Antalya to Alanya. There are direct buses to Side or you can take a bus to Manavgat, then a dolmuş or taxi. Private transport is recommended for visits to Sillyum and Alarahan, as the alternative is a long walk from the E24. For Selge private transport—preferably a four-wheeled drive vehicle—is necessary. Although the road as far as Beşkonak is in good condition, the last 20km to the site is over a very rough track.

Leave Antalya by the E24, a two-lane, well-surfaced, busy road, and proceed in the direction of Alanya. The E24 crosses the fertile Pamphylian plain, which is ringed to the N by the Taurus mountains, returning to the sea only at the approaches to Alanya. After c 6km, a turning right leads to Antalya's airport. Approximately 10km further, at the village of *Aksu*, a signpost left marks the road 2km to **PERGE**. The site of the ancient city is located c 4km W of the Aksu Çayı, the ancient river Cestrus.

History. Legend states that Perge was founded after the Trojan War by Greek settlers, led by the seers Calchas and Mopsus. Calchas, was the prophet who advised Agamemnon to sacrifice Iphigenia to placate Artemis. Legend also relates that he remained in Asia Minor after the capture of Troy. There he continued to practice divination, until defeated in a contest of prophecy by Mopsus. The persistence of the belief that Calchas and Mopsus were connected with the foundation of Perge is demonstrated by the discovery in 1953 of inscriptions on two 2C AD statue bases. They honour 'The founder Calchas of Argos, son of Thestor' and 'The founder Mopsus of Delphi, son of Apollo'.

Perge enters history properly with the arrival of Alexander the Great in 333 BC. He was welcomed by its citizens, who provided him with guides for his journey from Phaselis to Pamphylia. After the death of Alexander, his empire was divided amongst his generals and Pamphylia was ruled at different times by the Ptolemaic and Seleucid dynasties. In 188 BC the Seleucids were expelled by the Romans, who, having exacted a tribute from the inhabitants, gave the territory to Eumenes II, king of Pergamum. In the 1C BC the Romans, increasingly concerned about the activity of Cilician pirates, sent a force to crush them. Then to maintain their presence in the area, they set up the province of Cilicia. Unfortunately for their subjects, the Roman governors of the new province and their subordinates were corrupt and venal. Verres, who was later prosecuted by Cicero for extortion, robbed the temples of Aspendus and Perge of their statues and votive offerings. In AD 43 Pamphylia was joined with Lycia by Claudius and formally incorporated in the Roman Empire. Under the empire Perge appears to have prospered. It was during this period of stability that many of the city's fine buildings, whose remains may still be seen, were constructed.

Perge was the birthplace of two illustrious men, the mathematician Apollonius (fl. 250–220 BC) and Varus, the 2C AD philosopher, who was known as Stork because of his prominent beak-like nose. Apollonius, known as 'the great geometer', studied at Alexandria. Famous for his work on conic sections, he was the author of several mathematical treatises, seven of which survive. These were used by the astronomers, Ptolemy of Alexander and Kepler, when formulating their theories on the motion of the planets.

Perge was visited by Paul and Barnabas on their first journey. 'After this Paul and his companions took ship from Paphos and made for Perge in Pamphylia; here John left them, and went back to Jerusalem. They passed on from Perge, and reached Pisidian Antioch, where they went and took their seats in the synagogue on the sabbath day. (Acts 13, 13 and 14.) 'They preached the word of the Lord in Perge, and went down to Attalia, taking ship there for Antioch'. (Acts 14, 24.) Although little is known with certainty, it is probable that from the earliest times the city was an important centre for the diffusion of Christianity in Pamphylia. Perge was represented at the Council of Nicaea in 325 by the Metropolitan Callinicus and at the Council of Ephesus in 431 by one of his successors. The flourishing state of the church during the early Byzantine period is evidenced by the presence of two large basilicas. Later, weakened by persistent Arab attacks, Perge began to decline and sometime after the 7C most of the inhabitants moved away. However, there are reports of a small Christian community there as late as 1400.

Pamphylia came under the rule of the Selçuk Turks in 1078 and the Ottomans in 1392. Little is known about the history of Perge during the period from the 14C to the 17C. In 1671 it was visited by the Turkish traveller, Evliya Çelebi. He called it 'the Castle of Teke Hisarı'. This was 'a small rectangular castle situated on a mound. It has seven towers, and a door opening to the S. Behind, there is a fairly high hill. It has no moat. There are no guards, no soldiers ... commandant, or any important official. The place is inhabited only by seventy or eighty households of the Turcoman tribe. They migrate to the summer pastures in July. The castle is not very flourishing, but the district is prosperous and the region fertile.'

Perge, like many ancient sites in Asia Minor, was rediscovered by European travellers in the 19C, when it was visited by Walpole, Fellows, Forbes, Texier, Lanckoronski and others. In 1840 Fellows describes its pleasures, and dangers, in the following terms: 'Continuing my route for eight miles further, I pitched my tent amidst the ruins of Perge; near me was a small encampment of shepherds, who had brought their cattle to pasture amidst the ruins. The first object that strikes the traveller on arriving here is the extreme beauty of the situation of the ancient town, lying between and upon the sides of two hills, with an extensive valley in front, watered by the river Cestrus, and backed by the mountains of the Taurus ... The howling and barking of the jackals and wolves around my tent lasted until daybreak. At seven o'clock Demetrius

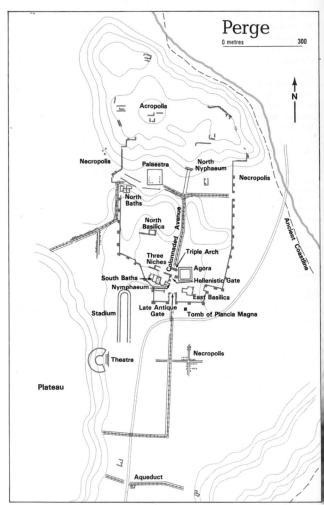

Perge

0 metres   300

Acropolis

Necropolis

Palaestra

North Nyphaeum

Necropolis

North Baths

North Basilica

Colonnaded Avenue

Three Niches

Triple Arch

Agora

South Baths

Hellenistic Gate

Nymphaeum

East Basilica

Late Antique Gate

Tomb of Plancia Magna

Stadium

Theatre

Necropolis

Plateau

Aqueduct

Ancient Coastline

N

returned with his bag of ducks and snipes, and at the same time arrived a present from the neighbouring tents of kymac, milk, eggs, and bread.'

Early colonists looked for a sea-girt peninsula, as at Side, or a flat-topped hill, which could be fortified against their enemies. Perge, Aspendus and Sillyum are examples of cities built on an acropolis. As conditions became more peaceful, these settlements spread out into the surrounding plain, only to retreat back into the citadel in times of danger. The *acropolis* of Perge lies to the N of the site and is clearly visible from the E24.

Approaching from the S, the access road from Aksu passes a low

hill to the right. Excavations in that area have revealed the foundations of a small *Doric prostyle temple*, the only sacred structure so far
discovered in Perge. Some architectural fragments in the Ionic style
which were found nearby suggest that the great temple of Artemis
Pergaea may also have been located there, a situation which would
accord with Strabo's description: 'and near Perge, on a lofty site, to
the temple of Artemis Pergaea, where a general festival is celebrated
every year'. This is echoed by Polemon in the 2C AD. In a work,
preserved in an Arabic translation, he writes: 'Imagine me a city
known as Perge. Here, outside the city, there is a temple of wonderful size, beauty and construction known as the temple of Artemis.'
However, up to the present, all the efforts of archaeologists to locate
the shrine have failed.

Artemis Pergaea, originally the Anatolian deity Vanassa Preiia, Queen of Perge,
later became identified with the Greek goddess of hunting, archery and the
moon. She was worshipped in the form of a baetyl, a block of stone, possibly a
meteorite, crowned with a female bust. There is a fine representation of the
deity in this guise in the Antalya Museum. She was also so depicted on Pergean
coins from the the 2C BC onwards.

Tickets for admission to the site may be purchased from a booth near the
Graeco-Roman theatre. One ticket admits to the theatre, stadium and the main
area of excavation. There is no restaurant at Perge, but soft drinks may
sometimes be purchased at another ticket booth, sited near the car-park at the S
city gate.

Excavations have been conducted at Perge by Turkish archaeologists
over a period of years, first by Professor A. Müfit Mansel and latterly
by Professor Jale Inan. Among the buildings to benefit from their
labours is the **Theatre**, which has been cleared of debris and partly
restored. Built against the hillside, it was capable of seating 14,000
spectators. Originally constructed in the Greek style it was modified
during the Roman period. Its cavea, greater than a semicircle, is
separated from the stage-building by two parodoi. There is a single
diazoma, with 26 stairs above and 13 below. Level with the diazoma
there are two vomitoria, which gave access to the cavea from the
hillside. At the top of the cavea there is a covered gallery, where
spectators could stroll during the intervals between performances or
take shelter from the elements. A parapet designed to protect the
audience during gladiatorial games or wild beast shows separates the
orchestra from the cavea. The stage-building was decorated with a
number of fine reliefs. These depict the river-god, Cestrus, and the
life of Dionysus—his birth from Zeus' thigh, his transportation by
Hermes to Mt Nysa where he was bathed by the nymphs, and his
apotheosis. A late addition to the structure is the nymphaeum, with
five niches for fountains, which was constructed against the outer
wall of the stage-building.

From the covered gallery at the top of the theatre it is possible to
get a clear view of the city's layout. Perge was enclosed with walls on
the E, W and S sides. On the N it was protected by the acropolis. The
walls on the E and W sides date from the 3C BC. The wall on the S
was built in the 4C AD, when the city was extended outside its earlier
limits.

To the NE of the theatre, is one of the finest existing examples of a
Roman Stadium. Constructed during the 2C AD, it has a seating
capacity of 12,000. The open S end was once marked by an arch, all
traces of which have disappeared. The N end is rounded. On the E,
under the seats, there are 30 rooms, 20 of which served as shops.

Some of these bear the name of the owner or of the trade carried on there (cf. theatre at Myra). The other rooms provided access to the arena. Most are now filled with undergrowth and are very difficult to enter.

Head of Medusa, from the theatre (2C AD) at Perge.

A track leads round the N end of the stadium to the car-park and the main entrance to the ancient city. Here there is another ticket booth, where pamphlets, postcards and, sometimes, soft drinks may be purchased.

Immediately to the right of the late *gate* there are the remains of the *Tomb of Plancia Magna* (see Antalya Museum). A benefactress of some distinction, she is mentioned in several inscriptions found in the city. In c AD 120 she caused a number of statues of members of the imperial house to be erected in Perge. These, and a statue of herself, are now exhibited in the Antalya Museum. She was a priestess of Artemis and of the Mother of the Gods and she held the high civic office of demiurgus. Clearly, she belonged to a distinguished and important local family, as her father and brother, M. Plancius Varus and C. Plancius Varus, are listed with Calchas, Mopsus and others as founders of the city. However, the association of their names with the mythical founding fathers probably meant no more than that they had contributed generously to the erection of public buildings in Perge.

Entering the city by the late antique gate the remains of a *Byzantine Basilica* are to the right. To the left are the ruins of a *Nymphaeum*, which was dedicated to Artemis Pergaea, the Emperor Septimius Severus (193–211) and his family. Further to the N a magnificent Corinthian *propylon* of the same period, elaborately decorated with reliefs of Eros, Pan, Dionysus, Medusa, etc., led to a huge baths complex. Nearby, one of three niches housed the statue of Plancia Magna (see above). The **Baths**, which are still being excavated, have the usual succession of frigidarium, tepidarium and caldarium. Their basins, floors and walls were inlaid with marble. Statues of Augustus, Trajan and Hermes which ornamented the rooms are now in the Antalya Museum.

Twin towers, similar to those found at Sillyum and Side, mark Perge's *Hellenistic Gate*. Erected in the 3C BC, this formed part of the city's original defensive system. In the 2C AD, through the generosity of Plancia Magna, a horseshoe-shaped court and an ornamental triple arch were added on the N side of the gate towers. The court was embellished with statues in niches and on a ledge near the ground. The bases of nine of the statues from the ledge were discovered during during excavations carried out in 1954/6. These honoured Perge's founders—Riksos, Labos, Calchas, Machaon, Leonteus, Minyas, Mopsus and M. Plancius Varus and C. Plancius Varus, the father and brother of Plancia Magna.

To the right, beyond the Hellenistic gate, is the 4C AD **Agora**. This consisted of a square 75m by 75m, with shops under a surrounding stoa. In the centre there are the substantial remains of a small circular *temple*, 13.5m in diameter. Perhaps dedicated to Hermes, the patron of merchants, it was crowned by a dome supported by 16 marble pillars. A similar building has been found in Side.

Perge was divided into four by two main arteries. One ran N–S for c 200m from a nymphaeum at the base of the acropolis through the Hellenistic and late gates. The other, which linked the E and W gates, crossed it at right-angles. These *colonnaded streets*, 20m wide, provided the Pergeans with an area where, protected from the weather, they could shop or converse with their friends. A *water-channel* ran down the centre and gently cooled the air. By the side of the N–S street there are a number of *marble columns*, decorated near the top with small reliefs. One shows Artemis, in her Grecian form, carrying a bow and arrows and a torch. Another depicts Apollo, and a third a male togaed figure pouring a libation.

In this street a *carved slab*, marked out for an unknown game, was found. This has three parallel lines of 12 squares. The squares on the outer lines are separated into groups of six by two lozenge shapes, set at an angle to each other. The centre line is similarly divided, but by four lozenge shapes, which form a circle. Evidently the game was popular in antiquity, as several similarly carved slabs have been found at other sites in Turkey. The slab is now in the Antalya Museum.

Almost hidden in the dense undergrowth to the left of the N–S street are the ruins of the *episcopal basilica* (5C). Facing E, with a narthex on the W, the nave was flanked by two side aisles. A large part of the apse remains standing.

At the junction of the two main streets an *arch*, facing E–W and dating from the 2C AD, is being restored. This was erected in honour of Artemis Pergaea and Apollo by two citizens, Demetrius and Apollonius. According to the inscription, Demetrius, a citizen of some importance, was demiurgus, priest of Artemis and gymnasiarch.

The water channels in the two main streets were supplied from a *nymphaeum* at the base of the acropolis. The statue of a river god, probably Cestrus, placed in a central niche, dominated a large basin from which the water flowed. The nymphaeum, which dates from the time of Hadrian (117–138) was richly ornamented with reliefs.

To the W of the nymphaeum, on the right, there are the substantial remains of a building c 76m by 76m which has not yet been excavated. Identified as a *palaestra* by an inscription found there, it was dedicated to the Emperor Claudius (AD 41–54) by C. Julius

Cornutus. The wall overlooking the street, which has several windows, is well preserved.

W of the palaestra, on the left side of the road, in an area heavily overgrown, are the ruins of *Roman baths*, dating from the 3C AD. A courtyard surrounded by columns provides access to a number of parallel chambers.

During excavations conducted by Turkish archaeologists in 1946 a number of elaborately ornamented tombs were found in a *necropolis* outside the W gate. Today little remains to be seen there. The sarcophagi found in the necropolis are exhibited in the Antalya Museum.

Two paths which start near the nymphaeum provide the only way up to the *acropolis*. This takes the form of a plateau of 2500m², 60m above the level of the plain. The acropolis was occupied by the first inhabitants of Perge and again during late Roman and Byzantine times, when the city came under attack from marauding bands. The few ruins remaining there date from the late period of occupation. On the S side of the hill a gateway, now destroyed, controlled access to the acropolis, but there appear to have been no other fortifica tions. Near the site of the gateway is a large vaulted *cistern*, 13.5m².

If the area is not closed for excavation work, an alternative route back to the car-park and the road to Aksu is by way of the E gate. This provides an opportunity to see the Hellenistic city wall, which is in a good state of preservation and is well worth a visit.

Return to *Aksu* and continue on the E24 for c 15km in the direction of Alanya. The acropolis of **SILLYUM** is visible for some time on the left side of the road before the signposted turn-off to the site. This is across the road from a garage, which crowns a small rise. For c 8km follow the reasonably-surfaced minor road. At each fork take the major turning and keep heading towards the acropolis, which is always clearly visible. There are two villages near Sillyum, *Yanköy* to the N and *Asar Köyü* to the SW. The ascent is made from *Asar Köyü*.

At Asar Köyü visitors are frequently approached by villagers who offer to act as guides to the site of the ancient city. It is advisable to accept the offer, as not only will a guide keep the village dogs at bay, but he will help you to avoid the many deep, unmarked and unprotected cisterns on the summit of the acropolis. These constitute a real danger, particularly to children, who should not be allowed to wander alone. The climb to the top of the acropolis, which is more than 200m above sea-level, involves a certain amount of scrambling. As there is no shade on the path and in summer temperatures can be very high, it is advisable to make the ascent early in the day. Taken at a steady pace, the climb should not present any great difficulty to those who are reasonably fit.

Sillyum is a little off the beaten track, and is somewhat overshadowed by its better-known neighbours, Perge, Aspendus and Side, so it does not attract many visitors. However, no discerning traveller should miss the opportunity of exploring the great brooding mass of its acropolis, which crouches menacingly on the Pamphylian plain between the Taurus Mountains and the sea. Exercising a numinous charm, it is most impressive and most moving at sunset. As the light fades, the crumbling remains of its ancient buildings form a stark silhouette against the sky.

A visit to Sillyum requires at least 3 hours. Those who wish to make a more detailed study of the site are usually able to find simple accommodation in Asar Köyü and Yanköy The people of both places, like villagers everywhere in

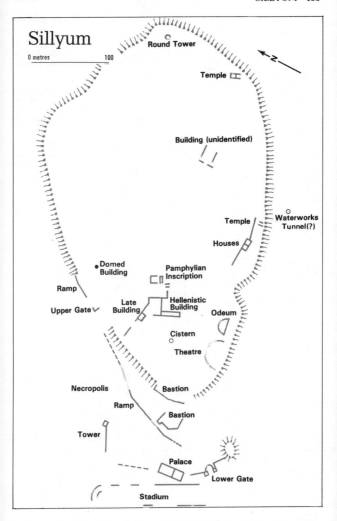

Sillyum

0 metres — 100

Round Tower

Temple

Building (unidentified)

Temple

Waterworks Tunnel(?)

Houses

Domed Building

Pamphylian Inscription

Ramp

Late Building

Hellenistic Building

Upper Gate

Odeum

Cistern

Theatre

Necropolis

Bastion

Ramp

Bastion

Tower

Palace

Lower Gate

Stadium

Turkey, are friendly and hospitable and will often offer a refreshing glass of tea or ayran to visitors. Those who need something more substantial are reminded that the nearest restaurants are in Serik and Antalya. They may wish to bring a picnic lunch to the site.

The summit of the acropolis is covered with pottery sherds and fragments of carved stone dating from all periods. On no account should these be taken from Sillyum. To do so could hinder serious archaeological investigation. One of the unfortunate by-products of tourism in Turkey is an increase in illegal digging and in the production of fake antiquities. Visitors are strongly advised not to buy any such objects or to pick up material from ancient sites. If the artefacts are genuine they could get into serious trouble as, under Turkish law, it is a offence to buy, sell or be in possession of antiquities without permission. Contravention of this law carries very severe penalties. If, on the other hand, the artefacts are fakes, the purchaser will have paid a high price for objects that are valueless.

History. Apart from a brief mention by the pseudo-Scylax, who explored the coast of Asia Minor in the middle of the 4C BC, nothing is known with certainty about Sillyum before the arrival of Alexander the Great in 333 BC. If the ancient legends are to be believed, it was probably founded, like the other cities in Pamphylia, c 1184 BC during the migrations that followed the Trojan War. A statue base found there, inscribed with the name of Mopsus, suggests that, like the Pergeans, the inhabitants of Sillyum honoured that ancient seer and may have believed that their city was founded by him. Certainly the security offered by the high plateau, which may be scaled only on the SW, must have attracted settlers from earliest times.

Sillyum and Termessus were the only cities in S Turkey which successfully withstood Alexander. Arrian describes what happened at Sillyum: 'Alexander left a party of men to occupy Side and then proceeded to Syllium [sic], a fortified town garrisoned by mercenaries and native troops. He was unable, however, to take this place by assault, without regular siege operations, and this fact, combined with a report which he had received during his march, determined him to return to Aspendus.' This report told him that the inhabitants of Aspendus had reneged on an agreement and were fortifying their city. Alexander's swift and unexpected return terrified the Aspendians and they asked for fresh terms. These were granted, but he chastised them by imposing harsher conditions and by taking hostages. He then returned to Perge, studiously ignoring Sillyum on the way.

Presumably Sillyum's history differed little from that of its neighbours during the following centuries. The first coins bearing its name date from the 3C BC. It was mentioned by the geographer, Strabo (64 BC–AD 24), who lists it as one of the cities of Pamphylia. Sillyum was, he said, 40 stades (i.e. c 7km) from the sea. Between 786 and 869 it was joined with Perge to form a metropolitan bishopric. On the *Tabula Peutingeriana*, a map copied in the 13C from a 3C or 4C original, the city was shown as being on the main road from Pergamum to Side. With Alanya, Aspendus and Antalya, Sillyum was occupied during the Selçuk period, when it was known as Yanköy Hisarı.

Leaving the village of Asar, the path climbs gently at first, passing on the left the scanty remains of a large *stadium*. The city's *lower gate*, like those of Perge and Side, consisted of a court and two fortified towers. To the left of the Hellenistic gate is the site of a *Gymnasium*, which later became the bishop's palace. It now serves as a sheepfold.

The acropolis of Sillyum can only be approached from the SW. On the other sides the cliffs rise sheer from the plain. Access to the city was by two ramps. A large stretch of the well-preserved *lower ramp*, which carries a road c 5m wide, is supported by massive buttresses. Above, to the right, are two substantial bastions. The *necropolis* of Sillyum, which was used from the 3C BC to the 6C AD, was sited below, to the left of the road. Most of the existing graves date from the Roman period. To the SW of the necropolis is a roofless, but otherwise well-preserved *tower*, which formed part of the later fortifications.

The *upper city gate* was sited at the point where the two ramps meet. To the SW are three of the most interesting buildings of the ancient city. The most striking is a large late structure, whose upper storey is pierced by several arched windows. S of this is a long narrow *Hellenistic hall*, which may have formed part of a gymnasium. The slots and holes, which were used to close the wooden shutters on the its windows, may still be seen. To the E is a smaller Hellenistic building, which bears on the door jamb an interesting *inscription* dating from c 200 BC. Its 37 lines of text form the longest extant example of the Pamphylian language. This was a Greek dialect which used the Greek alphabet and was not unlike the dialects spoken in Perge and Aspendus. It continued to be used up to the 1C AD, when it appears to have been replaced by the Greek in general use. Unlike the unusual language spoken at Side, which has not yet been deciphered, some words and phrases of the Sillyum inscription can be read, but its precise meaning is not yet known. Decipherment has not been aided by the fact that at some time a substantial section of the text was lost, when a square hole was cut in the door jamb.

Inscription in Pamphylian, c 200 BC, Sillyum.

To the S of these buildings a large part of the cliff has crumbled away, taking with it most of a small *theatre*. Only the top rows of seats remain. E of the theatre there was an odeum, but it, too, has fallen on to the plain. Care should be taken on this part of the plateau, as the cliff-edge is unsafe and landslides are not infrequent. E of the site of the odeum are the remains of some Hellenistic *private houses* and of a small *Hellenistic temple*. Built on a series of terraces connected by steps, the houses were constructed partly of masonry and partly from the living rock. Three walls of the temple, which measured 11m by 7.5m, remain. Masonry from the fourth, the S wall, lies at the bottom of the cliff. Just beyond the temple, gratings in the path mark the site of a long underground *cistern*.

The path, which continues around the cliff-top, offers an excellent view of the Pamphylian plain and of the Taurus Mountains to the N. Apart from a marshy area W of the acropolis, which probably marks the site of lake Capria, mentioned by Strabo ('Geography' 14.4.2), the plain is very fertile. In summer its many villages, surrounded by olive groves and orchards, are linked by the the the white squares of the cotton fields. Near the E edge of the plateau are the ruins of a much repaired *temple* and a *watch-tower*. In the central and NW areas there are many deep *cisterns*, which should be approached with caution. The *domed building* E of the upper city gate may have been used as a mosque during the Selçuk period.

In addition to the path used for the ascent, there are two other routes back to Asar Köyü. One, to the W of the theatre, descends steeply to the area near the lower gate, while another circles the northern ramp to reach the village by way of the tower, the stadium and the gymnasium.

About 300m NE of the lower city gate, at a point on the slope almost directly underneath the Hellenistic houses and temple, there is a disused underground *water channel*. An outer chamber leads to a tunnel c 0.5m wide and c 25m long. This ends in three small rooms linked by narrow passages. Intrepid explorers who wish to examine this construction should carry a light, be of slim build, should not suffer from claustrophobia, and should be prepared for the possibility of a close encounter with snakes or scorpions. According to Bean there is a late inscription in the outer chamber which prays for the salvation of the emperor.

On returning to the E24 continue in the direction of Alanya. After c 13km a left-hand turn leads to the market town of *Serik*. This has supermarkets, banks, a post-office, chemist shops and a number of small restaurants, where simple meals may be obtained. A signpost to the left, c 4km E of Serik, marks the road to the site (5km) of the ancient city of **ASPENDUS**, which is near the modern village of *Belkis*.

Not far from the road junction there is a fine 13C *Selçuk bridge* over the Köprüçay, the ancient Eurymedon. This structure, which is still used, replaced a 2C Roman bridge, whose ruins may be seen in the river-bed a few metres to the N. In ancient times the Eurymedon was navigable as far as Aspendus.

History. Although no archaeological evidence has been found which would indicate that Pamphylia was ever occupied by the Hittites, coins minted in Aspendus between the 6C and 4C BC give the name of the city as *Estwediiys*, which some scholars link with Prince Asitawadi, who is mentioned in a Neo-Hittite text unearthed at Karatepe. He founded a Cilician city in the 9C or 8C BC. The more generally accepted theory is that Aspendus, like Perge and Sillyum, was colonised during the migrations, which followed the Trojan War c 1184 BC. As the name Aspendus is not Greek, but Anatolian, it seems likely that the newcomers did not found the city, but merely took over an existing settlement. The ancient writers offer conflicting versions. Dionysius Periegetes in 'De situ orbis habitabilis' gives the legendary Mopsus as one of the city's founders, while Pomponius Mela ('De Chorographia') states that Aspendus was colonised by the Argives.

During the 6C BC Pamphylia was occupied briefly by Croesus, the King of Lydia. When he was defeated in 546 BC by Cyrus, it came under Persian rule. Pamphylian soldiers fought with Xerxes against the Greeks, but they were not considered very reliable allies. Following the battles of Salamis and Plataea, the Aegean coast came under the control of the Athenians, but Pamphylia, Lycia and Cilicia were still occupied by the Persians. To rectify this situation, in 467 BC the Athenians sent one of their generals, Cimon, at the head of an expeditionary force to the area. Having persuaded the cities of Lycia to support the Greek cause, he came to Aspendus, where Xerxes had gathered a great army. With his ships Cimon attacked the Persians at the mouth of the Eurymedon. The battle, which raged all day, ended in an Athenian victory. The first victory was followed by another. As night fell, Cimon dressed some of his men in the clothes of captured Persians, and, putting them on Persian ships, landed them near the mouth of the river. Deceived and confused by the stratagem, the Persians were routed for the second time in one day. While Cimon's unique double victory earned him a splendid monument in Athens, it had a less welcome result for Aspendus and the other cities of Pamphylia. They were enrolled, more or less compulsorily, in the Delian League, an organisation created to counter the Persian threat. However, it is doubtful if they ever paid their annual dues.

In 404 BC, at the end of the Peloponnesian War, control of the Athenian Empire passed effectively to Sparta. The Athenians, in an attempt to recoup some of the losses incurred during the war, sent an expedition to Asia Minor in 389 BC under the command of Thrasybulus to gather money. To avoid trouble the Aspendians paid up. However, the expedition ended disastrously, as the people of Aspendus, incensed by the bad behaviour of the Athenian soldiers, who had destroyed some of their crops, murdered Thrasybulus in his tent. The Spartans proved to be ineffective rulers and by 386 BC the Asian cities were once more under the control of the Persians. They appointed satraps, who collected the taxes, but otherwise allowed the cities to manage their affairs. Aspendus issued its own coins during this period. However, the flame of revolt still flickered and Aspendus and the other Pamphylian cities, with their governing satraps, rose against the Persians in 365 BC. Defeated by superior forces, they remained under Persian domination until the arrival of Alexander the Great in 334/333 BC.

Welcomed by Perge, Alexander marched towards Aspendus. He was met on the way by envoys, who offered to surrender the city, but who asked him not to leave a garrison there. Alexander agreed to their request, on condition that Aspendus paid him 50 talents and gave him the horses which had been bred for the Persian king. The envoys accepted his terms and Alexander went on to Side and thence to Sillyum. While conducting the siege of Sillyum, he was incensed to hear that the people of Aspendus had refused to honour the terms which he had agreed with their envoys and that they were fortifying the city. Arrian describes what happened next. 'Alexander, as soon as he reached the town, led his men inside the outer wall—now defenceless—and took up his quarters in the deserted town. The shock of Alexander's presence and the sight of his army surrounding them were too much for the people of the town: they sent their spokesmen to him and begged to be allowed their original terms. Alexander, however, in spite of the fact that the position of Aspendus was obviously a strong one and he was not prepared for a protracted siege refused the request.' In addition to the horses, he demanded 100 talents and the surrender of some of the city's leading men as hostages. Aspendus was also to accept a governor appointed by him, to pay an annual tribute to Macedon and to submit its claim to some disputed land to an enquiry.

Anxious to deny Pamphylia and its ports to the Persians, Alexander left it in the hands of his friend, the fleet-commander, Nearchus. After Alexander's death in 323 BC it was ruled by Antigonus Monopthalmos until 301 BC. From then to c 187 BC Pamphylia was, at different times, under the control of the Seleucid kings of Syria and Ptolemaic kings of Egypt. It then passed to the kings of Pergamum. When Attalus III, the last king of Pergamum, bequeathed his kingdom to the Romans, in 133 BC, they formed the Aegean area into the province of Asia. However, they were not interested in Lycia, Pamphylia and Cilicia and only became involved in this region, when pirates began to interfere with their shipping. For the Pamphylians this proved to be a mixed blessing. The consul, Manlius Vulso, extracted 50 talents from Aspendus as protection money. Worse was to follow. When a new Roman province, which included

Pamphylia, was created, its rulers and their subordinates proved to be rapacious and corrupt. Verres assistant to the infamous governor Dolabella who was accused and convicted of theft, was indicted by Cicero in the following terms: 'You are aware, gentlemen, that Aspendus is an old and famous town in Pamphylia, full of fine statuary. I shall not allege that from this town this or that particular statue was removed. My charge is that Verres did not leave one single statue behind; that from temples and public places alike, with the whole of Aspendus looking on, they were all openly loaded on wagons and carted away. Yes, even the famous Harpist of Aspendus, about whom you have often heard the saying that is proverbial among the Greeks ... that "he made his music inside"—him too he carried off.'

With the formation of the Roman Empire matters improved for Pamphylia. In AD 43 it was joined with Lycia to form a new province. However, its cities continued to enjoy a considerable degree of autonomy; Aspendus and several others issued their own coins. Under the Pax Romana the city prospered; most of the buildings visible today were constructed at that time. In the 3C AD the city was granted the status of a neocorus, i.e. the privilege of building a temple dedicated to the worship of the emperor.

Aspendus produced few citizens of note. One, the philosopher Diodorus, affected the unorthodox habits of the Cynics and became notorious for his dirty and unkempt appearance. Apollonius of Tyana, a neo-Pythagorean of the 1C AD, who claimed to have healed the sick and raised the dead, averted a dangerous crisis when he visited Aspendus. He found the chief magistrate, who had not been able to persuade the corn-merchants to release grain which they wanted to sell abroad, clinging to the statue of Tiberius in an effort to avoid being burned to death by an angry crowd of starving citizens. Moved by the tears of the people, Apollonius decided to intervene. He asked the crowd to put their torches on nearby altars. Then, as he was under a vow of silence at the time, he wrote his judgment on a tablet, which the magistrate read to the crowd. According to Philostratus, the biographer of Apollonius, this said: 'Apollonius, to the corn-merchants of Aspendus. The earth in her justice is the mother of all, but you in your injustice have made her mother to yourselves alone, and if you do not stop I will not even let you remain upon her.' Terrified by the words of the mystic, the corn-merchants released the grain and the people were saved from starvation.

Aspendus maintained its importance under the Byzantines, though, unlike Perge and Side, it did not have its own bishop. For ecclesiastical purposes it came under the Metropolitan of Side. Like most cities in Pamphylia and Lycia it suffered considerably during the 7C from raids by the Arabs. In the 13C it was ruled by the Selçuk Turks. During this period the stage-building of the theatre was restored and converted into a palace. From the 15C to the 18C, when it was abandoned, the city was governed by the Ottomans.

At the approach to the site, on the right, are the substantial remains of a Roman baths complex, which dates from the 3C AD. This rectangular structure had the usual arrangement of apodyterium, tepidarium, caldarium and frigidarium. The foundations and upper walls were made of shaped blocks of the local pudding-stone, while the vaults were of brick. Note the terracotta pipes running through the dividing walls.

Approximately 50m SE of the baths are the ruins of the gymnasium, which was also constructed in the 3C AD. The main entrance on the S led to the palaestra. Behind this was a long, narrow rectangular hall used for ceremonial purposes. On the E wall there were statues of the emperor and locable dignitaries. The other rooms were probably used for bathing and for instruction purposes, but, as the building has not been excavated, it is not possible to state this with certainty.

The ruins of Aspendus are scattered widely. To visit the theatre, the aqueduct and the acropolis requires at least a half-day. Refreshments are not available at the site, but there is a small restaurant, much favoured by coach parties, near the river at Belkis and there are others in (9km) Serik, (35km) Manavgat and (36km) Side. Visitors, who bring their own food, may picnic in a pleasantly-shaded park, which borders the river c 2km NE of the site. This has benches,

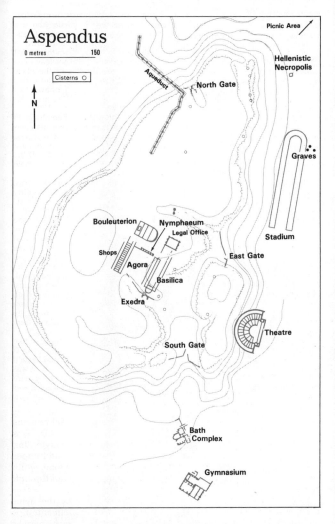

Aspendus

0 metres   150

Cisterns ○

N

Picnic Area

Hellenistic
Necropolis

Aqueduct

North Gate

Graves

Bouleuterion

Nymphaeum

Legal Office

Shops

Stadium

Agora

Basilica

East Gate

Exedra

Theatre

South Gate

Bath
Complex

Gymnasium

tables and barbecue facilities and may be reached by first taking the road that leads N from the car-park and then by following the left bank of the river up stream for a short distance.

The parking-place in front of the theatre has a toilet and wash-room, which usually has running water. Admission tickets, postcards, etc., are sold from a kiosk just inside the theatre entrance. In the right-hand parados there is a small explanatory display about the theatre and its history. There is no museum at Aspendus, but many of the antiquities found there are now in the Antalya Museum, where in addition to those mentioned below, there is a fine limestone stele from the 3C BC, recording the grant of citizenship to a number of foreigners. There are also several coins from Aspendus in the museum's collection. These bear the city's ancient name, 'Estwediiys' (see above), and depicting, on the obverse, a pair of nude wrestlers and, on the reverse, a slinger flanked by a triskeles.

The **Theatre** of Aspendus is the most perfectly preserved Roman theatre in existence. Designed by the architect Zeno during the reign of Marcus Aurelius (AD 161–180), it was given to the city by two brothers, Curtius Crispinus and Curtius Auspicatus. Their dedication of the building to 'the gods of the country and to the Imperial House', partially obscured by arches erected during the Selçuk period, may be seen over the entrances to the stage-building.

Constructed of local pudding-stone, its seats, floors and wall-panels were of marble. The stage-building, which stands to its original height, has five doors and four rows of windows of different sizes. Awnings to protect the spectators were supported by poles held by stone corbels above and below the top-most row of windows. Vaulted paradoi, on each side of the stage-building, and two doors on the hillside, now closed, provided access to the cavea. Today visitors enter by the central door, which faces the car-park.

Apart from some damage, now repaired, to the staircases on the extreme left and right of the cavea and to the vaulted gallery at the top, and the loss of the decoration on the interior wall of the stage-building, the theatre is virtually as it was when first built. The

Part of the cavea of the Roman theatre at Aspendus.

semicircular cavea projects on either side of the stage-building. Its 40 rows of marble seats are divided into cunei by 10 staircases below the single diazoma and 21 above. Over each parados, an area reserved for the city magistrates and other dignitaries may be reached by stairs from the stage-building. Behind the highest row of seats a vaulted gallery offered protection to the spectators during inclement weather. The smaller covered passage behind the diazoma is a constructional feature and was not used by the audience. Several seats, including one near the upper gallery, have the names of individual spectators carved on them—presumably a form of advance booking. The estimated capacity of the theatre is 15,000, though in recent years more than 20,000 have been squeezed in to see Turkish wrestling and song contests.

The inside of the stage-building was elaborately ornamented with about 40 free-standing columns in two rows, Ionic below, Corinthian above. These flanked a series of niches, each of which carried a statue. Today only those parts of the decoration which were attached to the wall remain. In the centre of the large pediment, which had two pairs of columns on each side, there is a *representation of Dionysus* surrounded by floral scrolls. Five doors led to the wooden stage, which stood c 1.5m above the ground and projected c 7m from the stage-building. Smaller doors below the level of the stage were used to admit animals, when the theatre was used for wild-beast shows.

Unlike the Greeks, who concentrated on looking in the theatre—the word *theatron* is derived from *theaomai* to see, the Romans emphasised the importance of hearing—hence 'auditorium'. So, in Aspendus they placed a wooden sounding-board mounted in sloping grooves up on the high side walls of the stage-building to improve the acoustics.

Red zigzag patterns on the walls of the stage-building date from the 13C, when it was used as a palace by the Selçuk Turks. The Antalya Museum has a number of fine tiles from the same period. These, which show birds surrounded by floral patterns, were used to decorate the main theatre structure.

On leaving the theatre, turn left and walk for 100m around the base of the acropolis to the *S gate*. This, the principal entrance to the city, is sited in a ravine that divides the acropolis into two unequal parts. At the point where the path divides, take the left fork. This ascends to a plateau c 60m above sea-level covering c 20 hectares. Although no excavations have been conducted there, surveys suggest that the existing ruins date from the 2C and 3C AD. Almost the whole surface of the plateau is covered with dense vegetation, which make any detailed exploration very difficult.

Where the path reaches the summit there are the substantial remains of a *building*, believed to have been used by orators and philosophers to address their audiences. A semicircular room, crowned by a dome faces the street. Constructed of dressed stone covered with marble slabs, this has five niches which once held statues.

The large open space to the N of this building is the site of the *agora*. The agora was bounded on the E by a basilica, on the N by the bouleuterion and nymphaeum and on the W by shops. Unlike Side and Perge it has no temple in the centre. Care should be taken to avoid a number of cisterns which are concealed by the luxuriant vegetation.

The *shops* form a row of adjoining buildings 70m long, fronted by a stoa. Their dividing walls, constructed of dressed pudding-stone, are pierced with holes for the beams that supported the upper storeys.

Only the foundations of the *basilica* remain. This building, constructed in the 3C AD, was used originally as a hall of justice and
administrative centre. About 105m long and 27m wide, it has a
central nave flanked by two aisles, a form that made it eminently
suitable for conversion into a church in Byzantine times. The aisles
were separated from the nave by rows of columns; some of the bases
may still be seen. Towards the S end, where it passes over the ravine,
the basilica is supported on an arch. Its foundations were made of cut
pudding-stone; the upper walls were of stone and brick. When it
became a church, an apse was added to the S end. At the same time
the vaulted area under the foundations archways turned into a cistern.

At the N end of the basilica three archways provide access to a
square building devoted to legal affairs. Its massive walls 2m thick,
which stand to a height of c 17m, are supported on the E and W by
substantial buttresses. The lower sections are of cut pudding-stone;
the masonry-fill above dates from later restorations. Entrance to the
building was by an arched doorway on the N. Inside, in the centre of
both the E and the W walls there is a large niche, flanked by two
smaller ones. A statue of Hadrian and another of an unknown
woman, which were found nearby, probably came from this building.
They are now displayed in the Antalya Museum.

To the left of the basilica is the *nymphaeum*, one of the most
substantial buildings on the acropolis. Constructed of cut blocks of
pudding-stone, it is 32.5m long, 15m high and 2m wide. The S wall
has two rows of five niches, each covered by a semicircular dome. In
the lower row the central niche served as a doorway; the others were
blocked up. Between the niches free-standing pairs of Corinthian
columns supported a marble entablature, parts of which still remain.
The rest of the rich decoration of marble slabs, which covered the
building, has disappeared.

Water from the aqueduct was delivered to the niches and thence to
a marble basin in front. During the hot, dusty summers, this building,
which was both decorative and practical, must have been much
appreciated by the people of Aspendus.

A rectangular building to the N of the nymphaeum has been
identified by some authorities as the *bouleuterion* and by others as
the *odeum* of Aspendus. As in many Roman cities, it probably
fulfilled both functions; performances of music alternating with
meetings of the Council. Rounded on the E side, it is 38.5m long and
30m wide. Like the annex to the basilica, it was built of worked
blocks of pudding stone and it also bears evidence of repairs carried
out at a late period. On the W, in front of the entrance, there was an
altar and a bema. Holes in the walls indicate that the seats and roof
were made of wood.

By traversing the scrub, it is possible to reach the point near the N
gate, where the aqueduct enters the city. There are the remains of a
number of buildings in this area, but they have not been identified so
far. An alternative route back is by the NE edge of the plateau, where
there are several cisterns. The *Hellenistic necropolis* was sited on the
slope below. Most of the stelae found there bear the name of the
deceased and of his father. Decoration is confined to a simple
pediment with acroteria at the corners and rosettes in the centre.
There are several fine examples in the Antalya Museum.

About 20m N of the bouleuterion a path descends to the site of the
E gate of Aspendus. The remains of the *stadium* are 100m N of this
point. Constructed in the form of an elongated U, open on the S, the
stadium was 215m long and 30m wide. Most of the W section has

collapsed and is buried. The best-preserved part is on the NE corner. Its seats of limestone are supported by walls and vaults of pudding stone. No trace of the main entrance remains; it was probably constructed of wood. Spectators could also enter the stadium from the vaults, some of which, as at Perge, were probably used a shops.

The *Roman necropolis* was to the N and E of the stadium. A number of rock-tombs, which held sarcophagi, may still be seen in this area.

Apart from the theatre, the most interesting monument in Aspendus is the *aqueduct*, which brought water from the Isaurian Mountains in the N. A tremendous feat of engineering, the extant portion stretches for almost 1km over a former marsh and terminates a short distance inside the N gate of the city. A 2C AD inscription, which almost certainly refers to the aqueduct, states that Tiberius Claudius Italicus donated the substantial amount of two million denarii to bring water to Aspendus. Better-preserved than similar aqueducts in the Roman Campagna or in France, it was constructed mainly of cut blocks of pudding-stone with some rubble infill. The section visible today consists of an arched structure 880m long and 15m high, which carried the limestone water pipes, and two pressure towers. The pipe-sections, many of which were used later to construct the Selçuk bridge, were joined by a flange and socket arrangement. On top of the towers, which are $3m^2$ and more than 30m high, an open chamber allowed the air to escape from the conduit, so reducing friction on the water-flow. The towers also permitted the aqueduct to change pressure, when the water arrived in the city.

To get to the N tower, which is 3km from the city, take the road from the car-park as far as the irrigation canal and then turn S along a rough track. For the daring, a staircase provides access to the water-channel. The S tower is 100m NW of the acropolis in the district called Camili. It may be reached by following a track, which starts S of the city, for c 1km.

The oldest necropolis in Aspendus, with burials from the Classical period, is located in the foot-hills to the NW of the city. Grave goods and red-figure vases, dating from the 5C BC, have been found in its tombs. These include a fine Attic krater, which shows three nude komasts on one side and three youths arming themselves on the other. This is now in the Antalya Museum.

Return to the E24 and continue for c 5km in the direction of **Alanya**. To reach **SELGE** take the road on the left signposted Köprülükanyon Millipark and 23km *Beşkonak*.

Selge is one of the most difficult sites in S Turkey to visit. As far as Beşkonak the road is reasonably good. From there to the settlement of *Zerk/Altınkaya*, which occupies the site of the ancient city, there is a very rough track, suitable only for a jeep. Allow a day for the visit, and take provisions, including water, for picnic meals. Also take some warm clothes, as Selge is c 900m above sea-level. The difference between the day-time temperature there and on the coast can be substantial.

At first the road to Beşkonak runs through a pleasant wooded landscape, sometimes approaching, sometimes drawing away from the Eurymedon river. About 5km N of Beşkonak it reaches a restaurant and coffee house, where a pause for refreshment may be made before starting the strenuous climb to Zerk. Where the road forks just beyond the restaurant take the left hand track, signposted

Altınkaya. This leads to a *Roman bridge*, which spans a deep gorge between two cliffs. Across the bridge, turn right on to a minor road that climbs steadily to the village of Zerk. This road's many sharp bends and very rough surface demand careful driving.

The mountain landscape is spectacularly beautiful. Deep gorges clothed in cypress and cedar recede into the distance in ever paler shades of blue. Olive, maple, carob and judas trees crowd the road and only gradually give way to oaks, as the track climbs ever higher. Occasionally the bright green of *styrax officinalis* may be glimpsed through the darker foliage. The Selgians valued this shrub so highly that it appeared on their coins. According to Strabo an aromatic gum which it produced was much in demand in ancient times. It was, and still is used in the manufacture of incense and perfume.

Freya Stark went to Zerk in 1954. Then it had 'fifteen cottages or so scattered among prostrate columns under a Roman theatre in a hollow. It was shallow as a saucer and the ploughed fields filled it, and small pinnacles surrounded it, where temples had stood on easy slopes. Beyond them, the high peaks rose ... Some in light and some in shadow, they had the cold pink mountain glow upon them as we made for an alpine cottage built between the marble shafts of some forgotten public building.' Because of an inadequate water-supply, Zerk was, she found, a poor village. The aqueduct and its terracotta pipes, which had enabled Selge to support a population of 20,000 had long been in ruins. The people of the modern village were obliged to rely on the meagre rainfall and melted snow to grow their crops. However, as is usual in Turkey, their poverty placed no limit on their hospitality.

History. Although generally considered to be a city of Pisidia, Selge, frequently at war with its Pisidian neighbours, looked to Pamphylia for its allies and its models. As early as the 5C BC, it appears to have had a monetary agreement with Aspendus and coins from that period give the city's name as *Estlegiys*, which is not unlike *Estwediiys*, the ancient title of Aspendus. Both words are Anatolian in origin, which suggests that Selge was not founded by Greek immigrants. In Hellenistic times, when it became fashionable to discover Greek ancestry, the Selgians claimed that their city was first settled by Calchas and his followers and later by the Spartans.

In 333 BC, while Alexander the Great was trying to capture Termessus by siege, the Selgians sent him offers of friendship. It is possible that they were motivated by dislike of the Termessians, as it seems unlikely that Alexander would ever have invaded their remote mountainous stronghold. When Alexander raised the siege of Termessus and abandoned his plan to go to Phrygia by that route, he marched N by way of the Pisidian stronghold of Sagalassus. Significantly, the people of that city were also enemies of the Selgians.

The historian Polybius (c 204–122 BC) tells an interesting story of how c 220 BC the vigilance of a goatherd saved Selge from destruction. The city was being besieged by the army of Garsyeris, a general of Syrian origin. He entered into protracted negotiations with the Selgians, who nominated one of their number, Logbasis, to speak for them. Unfortunately, Logbasis was a traitor and he hatched a plan with Garsyeris to surrender the city to him and to his master, Achaeus, the disloyal uncle of Antiochus III (223–187). However, the goatherd, seeing part of the enemy army advance towards the Kesbedion hill while another section moved towards the main gate, gave the alarm. The citizens of Selge rushed to the house of Logbasis and put him and all his family to death. Then, sallying forth, they drove the enemy back and killed 700 of them. Achaeus lifted the siege and the Selgians made peace with him.

Possibly because of its inaccessibility, the Romans took little interest in Selge and the city was able to maintain its independence. For a time it came under the rule of the Galatians, when Antony c 36 BC gave it to their king, Amyntas. Later, with the cities of Pisidia, Selge was incorporated into the Roman Empire. Like their coastal neighbours, the Selgians prospered. In addition to storax gum, they produced an unguent made from the iris. Surprisingly, in view of the altitude, they were also renowned for the olives grown in their territory.

In Byzantine times Selge maintained its status. It was the seat of a bishop, who ranked after Side and before Aspendus and it continued to produce coins up to the end of the 3C AD. Little is known about its history during the centuries that followed. Presumably it began to decline when the irrigation system fell into disrepair and its inhabitants moved down to more temperate regions. Selge was rediscovered by travellers from W Europe in the middle of the 19C, when it was visited by Schönborn and Daniell.

Plans are afoot for a survey and excavation of Selge, so in the future more will be known about the city and its monuments. At present the remains are sparse and visitors go there mainly for the beauty of its situation and for its atmosphere. Many still feel the emotions experienced by Daniell in 1842: 'I came suddenly', he writes, 'in view of a theatre magnificently situated, a stadium, a row of Ionic columns standing, and a square below, which must have been the Agora, though now a corn-field. Standing myself upon a large square platform of ancient pavement, with a beautiful foreground ... I think in all my life I never saw such a mountain view'.

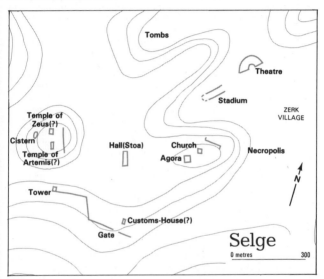

Selge's most striking monument is its **Theatre**, which lies to the NW of the village of Zerk. Partly cut from the natural rock, partly constructed from masonry, it had a capacity of almost 10,000. Like most theatres built in the Greek style, the cavea is greater than a semicircle and, as at Aspendus, it is joined to the stage-building. There are 15 rows of seats above its single diazoma and 30 below. These are divided into cunei by 12 staircases. The stage-building, which is in ruins, had the customary five doors facing the audience.

On a hill to the NW of the theatre there are the remains of three *tombs*. 100m to the SE there is the poorly-preserved *stadium*. The seats on one side are supported by the hill, on the other they rest on arches.

Selge's *agora*, sited on the hill to the S, was a paved area c 45 sq m, open on the S and surrounded by buildings on the N, W and E sides. The ruins of a *Byzantine church* lie nearby. The city's main *necropolis* was on the E side of this hill. Many of the tombs bear an unusual form of decoration, two small circles at the top of a larger circle, which looks like a human face.

About 150m to the W there was a *stoa* 110m long. On the hill to the S there are the ruins of part of the *walls*, which extended for more than 3km around the city. The *main gate* where, perhaps, the Selgians repulsed the attack of Achaeus, is in this stretch of wall.

N of the wall, on the hill believed to be the Kesbedion mentioned by Polybius, are the remains of two *temples*. One was probably dedicated to Zeus, the other, on the basis of an inscription found nearby, has been assigned to Artemis. To the W of the temples there is a large *cistern*, which was filled by rain water and water carried by a channel from the hills situated to the NW of the city. This in turn was fed by an aqueduct, parts of which remain in the high ground above the city.

Many inscriptions have been found in Selge, including a number which show the triskele, the three-legged symbol, which also appeared on the coins of Aspendus. This represented the sun rising at its zenith, and setting, and so the constant renewal of life.

Return to the junction on the E24 for Beşkonak. From here it is c 23km to **Manavgat**, a pleasant market town on the Manavgat Çayı, the ancient river Melas, which has the usual complement of shops and banks.

On the outskirts of Manavgat a road to the left goes first to (4km) *Manavgat Şelale* (Manavgat waterfalls), a beauty-spot much favoured by Turkish as well as foreign visitors. Here, under the pine trees, it is possible to enjoy an excellent lunch of freshly-grilled trout washed down by a dry white wine. Approximately 3km further is Şıhlar. From there it is an easy hour's walk to the site of Seleuceia in Pamphylia.

SELEUCEIA IN PAMPHYLIA was one of many cities named after members of the Syrian Seleucid dynasty. According to Appian, the 2C Roman historian, Seleucus I Nicator (321–280 BC) founded nine cities named after himself. The best known was the Cilician Seleuceia ad Calycadnum, modern Silifke. Its smaller Pamphylian brother was built on a steep hill, inaccessible except from the S. The approach from Şılar is by way of a narrow depression. Just beyond this, to the left, a refreshing spring issues from a cave. Traces of ancient masonry suggest that the spring was known and used in antiquity.

Nearby are the substantial remains of a building which has been identified as a *baths complex*. The walls of its five vaulted rooms, pierced by openings for the water-pipes, stand to a height of more than 9m.

The ruins of a *gate*, flanked by two rectangular towers, mark the entrance to the agora, many of whose buildings are in an excellent state of preservation. A number of the Doric columns of the portico which surrounded it are still standing. On the E, a *market hall* in the form of a line of two-storey shops catches the eye. The lower part is almost undamaged, while much of the upper storey, with its large rectangular windows, remains. Access to the first-floor shops was by a staircase, now destroyed, in the fourth shop from the N. A fine mosaic, showing Orpheus charming the animals, was found in the market hall.

The semicircular building at the S end of the market-hall was probably the city's *bouleuterion*. As at Aspendus, it may also have been used as an odeum. At some time the front portion appears to have been converted, by the addition of a rough wall, into shops.

On the W side of the agora the ground slopes and it was necessary to construct a basement. On the SW corner, where the ground drops sharply away, the wall stands to a height of 15m.

A well-preserved small *temple* is sited to the N of the agora. The city's *necropolis*, which was on the W slope of the hill, has a number of tombs of worked stone.

About 3km from Manavgat there is a signposted turning, just beyond a garage on the right-hand side of the E24, for 4km **SIDE**.

During the summer months most of the long-distance buses on the Antalya–Alanya route call at the resort. Visitors without their own transport can get to Side by dolmuş from Manavgat.

There is a wide range of accommodation in Side. Full information, including prices, about its hotels, motels, pensions, rooms-to-let and restaurants, may be obtained from the *Tourist Information Office*, which is housed in a new building on the left side of the road, c 1km before the village.

Side has become the victim of its own popularity. Originally a small fishing village which was settled by Turkish immigrants from Crete at the end of the 19C, it has been subjected to uncoordinated and unrestricted development, which has destroyed much of its character. Its main street, spoiled by a rash of boutiques and souvenir shops, has become indistinguishable from hundreds of similar tourist traps scattered along the Mediterranean littoral.

Fortunately, the authorities are now correcting earlier mistakes and have imposed strict controls on further development. Fortunately, too, the real Turkey may still be found in Side's quiet side-streets away from its over-commercialised centre, and, in the peace of its ancient ruins and in the beautiful garden of the museum, the spirit of its past lingers on.

A great part of the site of ancient Side has been excavated by Turkish archaeologists working under the direction of Professor Arif Müfit Mansel during the period 1947–67. The fruits of their labours may be seen in Side's museum. Professor Mansel has been succeeded by Professor Jale Inan.

History. Early settlers in S Turkey looked for sites which could be defended easily. In Perge, Sillyum and Aspendus they built on an acropolis, which they fortified and to which they retreated in time of danger. In Side, they found a narrow peninsula, which could be protected on its landward and seaward sides by walls and whose harbour offered both a convenient point of supply and an escape route.

The historian Arrian and the geographer Strabo state that Side was an offshoot of the Aeolian city of Cyme, which was sited to the N of İzmir. Arrian states further that, after they had landed, the colonists forgot their Greek and began to speak an incomprehensible language unrelated to those found in neighbouring cities. Modern authorities believe that the truth behind this picturesque story is more prosaic. They conclude that the settlers from Cyme were not strong enough to impose Greek on the indigenous inhabitants, but were obliged to adopt the Anatolian language which was spoken there.

Evidence of Side's unusual language is provided by the city's name, which means pomegranate and is of Anatolian origin, by coins dating from the 6C BC, and by three 3C BC inscriptions found there. So far this language has not been deciphered, but scholars are hopeful that they will be able to read it one day. Two of the inscriptions, which may be seen in Side's museum, are bilinguals, carrying the text in Sidetan and Greek. Side's unique language appears to have fallen into disuse after the conquest of Asia Minor by Alexander the Great c 333 BC, when Greek became the common language of the new empire.

Unlike other Pamphylian cities, which were colonised by bands of Greek wanderers after the Trojan War, it would appear that the settlers from Cyme came to Side around the 7C BC. What little is known of its early history is derived from the general history of Pamphylia. In the 6C BC the whole area was under the domination of the kings of Lydia until they were defeated by the Persians. Nothing is known about Side during the period of Persian rule. Unlike Aspendus and Sillyum Side welcomed Alexander, and like them was fought over by his successors. Until 218 BC Pamphylia was ruled by the Ptolemies of Egypt, then it came under the control of the Seleucid kings of Syria. Side supported the Seleucids against the rebel Achaeus (see Selge above) and against the Rhodians in 190 BC. Side appears to have avoided falling under the rule of Pergamum, and enjoyed a substantial degree of independence in the middle of the 2C BC. It entered a period of growth and prosperity, becoming one of the most important trading cities in the E Mediterranean and a centre of culture and learning. Unfortunately, its citizens did not always have a very good reputation. When asked to name the most unscrupulous people, the wit Stratonicus replied 'In Pamphylia the men of Phaselis, in the whole world the men of Side'.

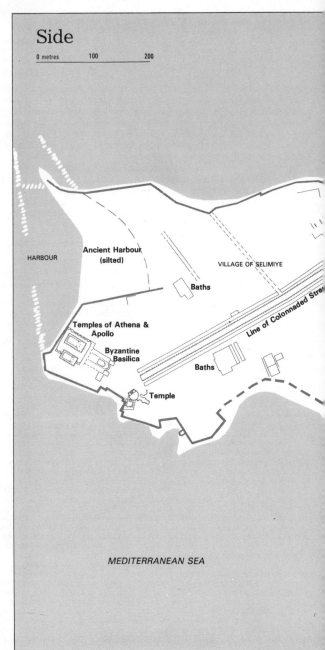

Side

0 metres   100   200

HARBOUR

Ancient Harbour
(silted)

Baths

VILLAGE OF SELIMIYE

Line of Colonnaded Stree

Temples of Athena &
Apollo

Byzantine
Basilica

Baths

Temple

MEDITERRANEAN SEA

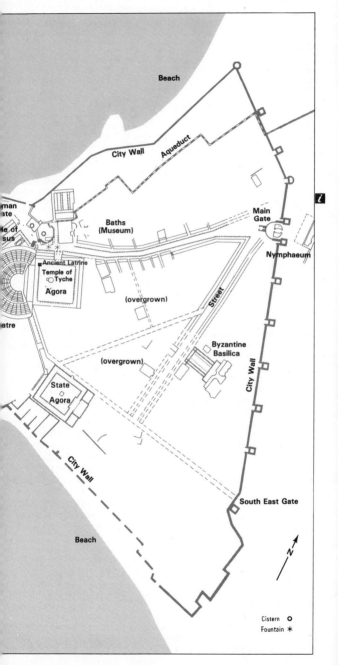

Beach

City Wall

Aqueduct

man
ate

e of
sus

Baths
(Museum)

Main
Gate

Nymphaeum

Ancient Latrine

Temple of
Tyche

Agora

atre

(overgrown)

Street

(overgrown)

Byzantine
Basilica

State
Agora

City Wall

City Wall

South East Gate

Beach

N

Cistern O
Fountain *

According to Strabo, Side became deeply involved with piracy, allowing them to sell their prisoners in the city and to repair their ships in the harbour. Two campaigns in the 1C BC to remove the pirate threat from Cilicia and Pamphylia brought Side under Roman control, and again the city flourished. During the 2C and 3C AD, when it was the seat of the governor, many fine buildings, whose ruins may be seen today, were constructed. The arrival of hostile Isaurian tribes from the N in the 3C brought the first check to this period of prosperity. However, the Sidetans repaired the city's defences and during the reign of Julian (361–363) successfully resisted a siege by the barbarians.

The 5C and 6C were marked by another period of growth. The city walls were extended to enclose a larger area; Side again became an important commercial centre. The seat of a metropolitan bishop, it was famed for its learning and culture. The Arab raids from the 7C onwards put an end to this, its last period of importance. No Byzantine buildings later than the 9C and 10C survive and excavations have revealed the burnt remains of houses destroyed at this time. It would appear that the city's destruction was completed by a number of earthquakes in the 12C. Idrisi, an Arab geographer (fl. c 1150), calls Side 'burnt Antalya' because the inhabitants abandoned the city and moved themselves and their belongings to Antalya. For this reason it was also known sometimes as Eski Antalya, Old Antalya. Pamphylia was captured by the Selçuk Turks in 1148 and by the Ottomans in 1442, but no traces of their occupation have been found in Side. Until it was rediscovered by Beaufort, Daniell and Fellows and other European travellers the 19C, the city disappeared from historical records.

The pleasures and dangers experienced by these early travellers are summed up in an account by Fellows of an evening spent in the neighbourhood of Side. '[I] am now sitting in my tent, surrounded by camels, goats, and cows, the care of the inhabitants of a few tents near me; their fires are blazing, and these, with the light of a full moon, and the various rustic noises of the shepherd's pipe, camels' tinkling bells, frogs croaking, nightingales singing in the trees, and owls hooting from the ruins, and now and then a burst of alarm from all the watch-dogs at the approach of jackals or wolves, give a peculiar effect to the scene; while the open sea before, and the splendid mountains behind, render the scene as picturesque as it is wildly interesting.'

There are few springs or wells in Side, so in Roman times water was brought a distance of 32km to the city from the Dumanlı source near the Melas river. This required an elaborate series of tunnels and channels cut through the rock and, on the lower level, an *aqueduct* supported on arches. Unfortunately, many of the rock-cut galleries, which were fitted with vents to admit air and light are now submerged under the waters of the Oymapınar Dam. However, much of the aqueduct remains and a long stretch may be seen from the approach road to Side. Constructed from shaped blocks of sandstone and pudding stone, the aqueduct entered the city 150m N of the main gate and terminated near the inner gate, close to the theatre. There the water was stored in large cisterns near the baths—now the museum—and then distributed throughout the city by stone and terracotta pipes. During the period of the city's decline in the 3C, this water-supply system fell into disrepair. It was renewed during the reign of Diocletian (284–305) through the generosity of a citizen, Bryonianus Lollianus, and of a number of wealthy foreigners. When during the 11C Side entered its final period of decay, the system could not be maintained and wells were sunk in various parts of the city by the last inhabitants.

One of the structures which was probably supplied by the aqueduct is the 2C AD *nymphaeum*, sited outside the city walls facing the main gate. Similar to the nymphaeum at Aspendus, it consisted of a rectangular wall with projecting wings. Two of the original three storeys remain. The lower storey had three semicircular niches, surmounted by half-domes, which faced a large basin. The whole structure was covered with a facing of marble and decorated with statues and reliefs depicting mythological scenes. Fragments of this decoration lie in front of the nymphaeum on an area once paved with marble slabs. There the Sidetans gathered during the oppressive heat of summer to enjoy and be cooled by the water as it poured into the great marble bowl.

Side's *necropolis* lay outside the city wall in an area now covered by cultivated land. Many of the fine sarcophagi and ostotheks (cinerary urns) discovered by the archaeologists are displayed in the museum. A short distance to the W of the city there are the ruins of a *temple tomb*, which was built in the 2C AD.

The *principal gate* of Side, which faces the nymphaeum, suffered considerable damage when the modern road to the village was constructed. In layout it resembled the city gates at Perge and Sillyum. An outer court, flanked by two towers on the city wall, gave access through a gateway to an inner semicircular court. From there, an inner gate led to one of the principal streets of the city. During a period of peace c AD 200 the original Hellenistic structure was altered considerably. The wall of the semicircular court was covered with marble slabs in which seven niches containing statues were placed. Some of these statues are now displayed in Side's museum.

Side was surrounded on the landward and seaward sides by a *wall* of shaped pudding-stone blocks, erected during the Hellenistic period. Most of the E section is covered by sand and the wall on the S, which faced the sea, has largely disappeared. The best-preserved portion is near the main gate. On the inner side there were three storeys. The bottom storey, partly furnished with arches and pillars, served only to support the upper storeys. In the middle storey there were a number of small rooms, fitted with openings for the discharge of missiles. The top storey had a parapet and a series of look-out points which commanded the landward approaches to the city. The defences were further strengthened by towers placed at irregular intervals. Attention has been drawn by Bean to a curious construction feature for which there is no satisfactory explanation. On the inner side of the wall there is a gap of c 7.5m between the towers, which must have been bridged by planking.

As Side has not been completely excavated, it is not possible to say whether it was laid out in accordance with a formal plan or whether it followed the contours of the land. The modern road covers the colonnaded street which ran from the main gate to the city centre. The area to the right of this street was known as the Quarter of the Great Gate.

On the left lay the Quarter of the Great Guild. A visit to this area, now heavily overgrown and partly buried under sand dunes, will tempt those who are not deterred by a little minor discomfort. They will be rewarded by an opportunity to examine the substantial remains of a *Byzantine basilica* and of Side's *episcopal palace*. These were located near the junction of two streets which joined the main and E gates.

The basilica dates from the 5C and follows the usual plan: it has a central nave flanked by side aisles. To the left of the apse there was a large baptistery, divided into three sections. Three steps led down to the baptismal font, which was located in the centre section. The basilica was attached to the palace on the SE side by a building which is believed to have been a martyrion. The palace, some walls of which remain standing, had a small private chapel with three rows of seats in the apse. Side's ecclesiastical quarter was completed by a large walled garden which lay to the NE of the palace.

A rough path leads from the basilica to the *E gate*. Constructed of shaped blocks of pudding-stone during the Hellenistic period, this opened on to a rectangular courtyard. More than 10,000m³ of sand were cleared by archaeologists to reveal some fine Byzantine mosaics and a number of reliefs. Professor Mansel has suggested that the reliefs, which depict arms and weapons, probably commemorated a victory by the Sidetans over an army from Pergamum in the 2C BC. The reliefs are now displayed in Side's museum.

Continue S until you reach the line of Side's sea-wall and then turn right towards the town. A short walk over the sand-dunes will bring you to the inner walls of the city and the site of the *state agora*. This building has provoked much discussion. It consisted of a large open area surrounded by a colonnade. During the Byzantine period a giant cross stood on a two-level platform in the centre. An elaborately ornamented three-room building filled its E end. The centre room had a timber roof and its walls were covered with sheets of marble. It was decorated, on two levels, with copies of well-known classical Greek statues. These were placed in semicircular domed niches or rested on bases that projected from the wall. Many of the statues were found during the course of the excavations and are now displayed in the museum. One, a headless representation of Nemesis, is in its niche in the SE corner. The room on the S, which was restored by the Byzantines and decorated with a geometric mosaic design, may have been used as a library.

From the state agora a short walk in the direction of the modern road will bring you to Side's *main agora*, the commercial and social centre of the city. It was here that the slave market described by Strabo was probably held. An area c 91 by 94m, it was surrounded on four sides by a stoa, which offered protection from the weather. The modern path passes under the inner walls of the city, which were constructed in the 4C during the period of the barbarian invasions from material salvaged from earlier buildings. This is evidenced by the many column drums which project from the hastily-built wall. Note, too, that the back of the stage-building was incorporated in this late defensive structure.

In the centre of the agora are the ruins of a 2C AD building which has been identified by Professor Mansel as a *Temple of Tyche*, the goddess of fortune. This was a circular cella, resting on a base, surrounded by 12 Corinthian columns and covered by a 12-sided pyramidal roof. Beaufort, who visited Side in 1811/12, saw three of the carved slabs which made up the ceiling of the temple, 'a series of figures that represent some of the signs of the zodiac; Pisces, Aries, Taurus, Gemini and Cancer, were placed in due succession; but the next was a swan, and then the naked figure of a young man'. Unfortunately, these carvings have now disappeared.

Behind the stoa stood some of the city's shops. The largest were on the NE. On either side of the entrance on the NW there was a double row, some of which faced outwards to the street, others inwards to the agora. A number of columns, surmounted by Corinthian capitals, which lined the N side of the stoa, have been re-erected. On the SW, in addition to some shops, which may have offered refreshments to theatre patrons, several rooms provided access to the theatre from the stoa. A fine lavatory in the W corner of the agora near the theatre catered for other bodily needs. Lined with marble panels, it had 24 seats over a water-channel.

On the right-hand side of the modern road the museum of Side (see below) is housed in a restored baths complex, which dates from the 5C AD. To the left of the museum entrance are the ruins of the *triple basin fountain*. This was ornamented with statues placed between the basins. A head of Hermes from one of these statues is in the museum.

The road passes under a *Roman monumental arch*, which may have been surmounted by the quadriga that gave its name to this section of the city. When the inner defensive wall was constructed in the 4C, this arch became the main entrance to the city. For security reasons it was filled in with material taken from other buildings, and a small gate, surmounted by a relieving arch, was placed in its centre. This later addition was dismantled recently, as it was in danger of collapsing.

To the left of the arch there is a *nymphaeum*, composed of a central niche, flanked by two platforms which supported statues. In front was a basin fed by a pipe from the niche. According to its inscription this structure was erected in AD 74 in honour of the Emperors Titus and Vespasian. It was converted into a nymphaeum and moved to its present position some time in the 4C AD, at about the time the inner wall was constructed. Archaeologists restored it to its present state in 1962.

The road bends sharply under the arch, making it a hazardous place for pedestrians and motorists. To the right a path leads down to the beach. On the left are the scant remains of a *temple*. Because of its proximity to the theatre it is believed that this was dedicated to Dionysus. The small pseudo-peripteral building, constructed of lime-stone on a base measuring 7.25 by 17.50m, was built during the Hellenistic period and repaired during the Roman era. Access was provided by steps on the N side. There were four Corinthian columns of red granite in front of the cella.

Side's **Theatre** is one of the most interesting in Turkey. Apart from the stage-building and the orchestra, which have suffered considerable damage, it is in a very good state of repair. Archaeologists are currently clearing and restoring the damaged areas. Constructed during the 2C AD, its shape, greater than a semicircle, suggests that it replaced an earlier Hellenistic building. As the slope was not sufficiently great, most of the auditorium had to be supported by an artificial structure, which stands to a height of 14m. The lower storey is taken up by a vaulted corridor, pierced by passageways. There was a parados at each end of this corridor. The passageways lead to an inner corridor or to rooms, used as shops or storerooms. There was a single diazoma, with 29 rows of seats below and 22 above. The lower section was divided into 11 and the upper section into 24 cunei. The seats in the lower section were reached from the vaulted corridor. However, there was no direct access from the diazoma to the upper section. Interior staircases led to the top of the building, from which spectators descended to their seats. The existing stairs in the upper section are modern and were constructed for the convenience of visitors.

Estimates of the theatre's capacity vary. Beaufort worked it out in the following manner: 'Now supposing that the antients sat as we do, with the legs pendent, and not crossed under them like the modern Greeks and Turks (as Dr Chandler seems to have thought), and therefore taking eighteen inches as sufficient for each person to occupy, this theatre would contain 13,370 persons, when regularly seated; but, in crowded exhibitions, many could sit on the flights of small steps, or could stand on the upper platform, and at the back of the broad Diazomatos ... these may be estimated at 1,870 more, and would together make the enormous aggregate of 15,240 spectators.'

The stage-building, like that of Aspendus, was constructed in the Graeco-Roman style. It had three storeys, which reached a height of c 21m. The central and upper storeys, which formed the background to the stage, were elaborately decorated with statues, niches and friezes. Unfortunately, most of these have been damaged, some by natural causes, some by human action. A series of reliefs, still in position at the back of the stage, are believed to have been mutilated by Christians, when two small chapels were erected in the theatre and the building was used for worship.

In the later Roman period it was customary for theatres to be used not only for the presentation of plays but also to stage fights with wild animals, for gladiatorial contests and naval battles. To enable this to be done in Side, a wall c 2m high was constructed around the orchestra to protect the spectators.

To the right of the theatre is the *bus and dolmuş station* and the *car-park*. Only cars with a special authorisation are permitted to enter the village. Side's main street follows the line of the ancient colon-naded way, which led from the main gate to the harbour. To avoid the modern street's succession of boutiques, restaurants and souvenir shops take the lane on the left that winds around the theatre. At the road junction, the left fork will take you to a fine sandy beach that extends for several kilometres to the E. The right fork leads to the S part of the site where the temples of Men, Athena and Apollo and Side's harbour are located.

At the end of the colonnaded street a semicircular building has been identified as the *Temple of the moon god Men*. Men was an Anatolian deity often associated with Attis. Like Attis he was usually depicted as a handsome youth wearing a Phrygian cap. Among the sites consecrated to his worship was one near Antalya, where mysteries, involving a sacred marriage, were celebrated. His symbols were the pine cone, the peacock and, significantly, the pomegranate. The temple of Men at Side was raised on a base 2m high. Unlike shrines dedicated to the Greek gods, which faced E, access was by a flight of steps on the W side. It has been dated to the end of the 2C AD.

The *two principal temples* of Side, which were dedicated to Athena and to Apollo, were sited on a levelled area near the harbour. Dated to the 2C AD, each was a peripteros in the Corinthian style and had 11 columns on the sides and 6 on the front and on the back. The entrance to the pronaos was flanked by two columns. There was no opisthodomus. Portions of a frieze of Medusa heads, which decorated the temple of Apollo, remain. The construction of a basilica by the Byzantines at a late period completed the destruction of the temples, which were probably in a ruinous condition at that time. Turkish archaeologists are currently engaged in their restoration.

There are substantial remains of the late Byzantine *basilica*, dating from the 5C, which was built to the E of the temples. This followed the customary plan of a central nave, flanked by side aisles. The division was made by two rows of 12 columns constructed from material salvaged from Roman buildings. The apse had a synthronon reached by six marble steps, and sacristies on either side. Later a martyrion was added to the S side. In the 9C or 10C a smaller church was constructed in the centre of the basilica. Much of the buildings remained intact until the 19C, when a large amount of the marble used to decorate then was burned to make lime.

The first *harbour* of Side was constructed during the Hellenistic period on the SE side of the peninsula. It extended as far as the harbour baths complex, which is now some distance from the sea. Surrounded by a quay built of pudding-stone and protected from the SW gales, it played a large part in promoting the city's prosperity. However, it had to be cleared of accumulated silt so frequently that in antiquity any recurring, expensive and difficult task was likened to Side's harbour. By the 5C AD it had become so shallow that it was decided to abandon it and build a new harbour to the NE. This is still used by the local fishermen.

Visitors, who wish to enjoy the great scenic beauty and the antiquities of Side and who want to avoid the excessive commercialism of its centre, can do so by staying in one of the hotels located to the W of the village. The smallest and most comfortable of these is *Cennet Motel*, which is an easy 20-minute walk along the beach from the museum and the theatre.

Side's **Museum** is housed in a restored 5C AD baths complex, sited across the road from the forum. Access is by a narrow, colonnaded street, which led originally to the sea wall. On the left of this street is a kiosk, where tea and cold drinks, postcards, replicas, etc., may be purchased. The street continues to what was originally a courtyard, now a pleasant shaded garden, where sarcophagi, cinerary urns and fragments of antique sculpture lie half-hidden among a profusion of flowering shrubs. Constructed during the last period of Side's prosperity, the building is rectangular in shape and follows the usual plan of a Roman bath. Restored through the initiative of Professor Mansel, who supervised excavations at Side between 1947–67, it contains many of the antiquities discovered by him and his colleagues.

The original entrance to the museum was by two arched doorways, which led from the courtyard to the *frigidarium*, the only unheated room in the baths. Originally roofed, the floor of this room is paved with re-used marble slabs, many bearing inscriptions. Its dominant feature is a large semicircular basin on the NE, which was filled with cold water. Bathers descended into the basin—covered by a dome and lined with marble—by a flight of steps on the left. At the back, three niches which contained statues are set under four large rectangular alcoves. To the left of the basin is a narrow passage-way, through which water was conveyed from the aqueduct.

Along the wall facing the basin are the reliefs depicting arms, which were found at the city's E gate (see above). These are believed to commemorate a victory by the Sidetans over an army from Pergamum in the 2C BC. In the centre of the room are two Roman altars, which were later hollowed out and turned into well-heads. Nearby is a late Hittite column base, dated to the 7C BC, which was discovered near the site of the temples of Apollo and Athena.

A narrow doorway leads to the *sudatorium*, the hottest room in the baths, which was built over a furnace. Now circular in shape, it was originally square. The four niches in the corners contain a selection of small objects found in Side. Note in particular a fine terracotta head.

Continue into the *caldarium*, a rectangular room, which originally had basins at its N and S ends only. Later one large and two small basins were added on the E side. Facing the entrance is a beautifully-composed representation of the *Three Graces*. A favourite subject for artists, they were believed to symbolise beauty, friendship and gentleness. In the centre of the room is a Statue of Hercules, holding the golden apples of the Hesperides. The niches above the basin to the left of the entrance contain Roman copies of Hellenistic statues of a woman and a girl. Along the side of the basin are a number of Roman amphorae, which were recovered from the sea. To the left of the semicircular basins there is a relief of Ixion, King of Thessaly, who was condemned by Zeus to spend eternity bound to a rotating fiery wheel because of his attempted seduction of Hera. Nearby is a statue of the river-god, Melas (the modern Manavgat Çayı). A short 2C BC *inscription in the Sidetan language* (see above), found near the E gate, is displayed near the central semicircular basin. In the basin at the S side of the room there are parts of a 2C AD sarcophagus. The niche in the centre has a headless Nike, the goddess of victory, flanked by representations of Dionysus and Apollo.

In the next room, the *tepidarium*, there is a headless statue of Nike, dated to the 2C AD, which was found in the library in the state agora (see above). In a niche nearby there is a fine statue of Hygeia, the daughter of Asclepius, the god of healing. Note the snake, twined around her arms, which came to be associated with the care and nursing of the sick. An almost complete statue of

Apollo, dating from the 2C AD, is flanked by a head of Apollo and a head of Hermes. The head of Apollo is a Roman copy of the famous Hellenistic original known as the Kassel Apollo. The *head of Hermes*, who is depicted as a pouting, pensive youth, was discovered in the triple-basin nymphaeum near the museum. It was identified as a result of some interesting detective work. Archaeologists believe that in the 3C AD, when Side had become impoverished, a statue of Hermes was taken from another site in the city, suitably altered and in its new persona of Apollo re-erected in the nymphaeum. So far the body of this statue has not been found.

There follows a series of incomplete statues, dating from the Roman period. In a niche on the S side of the room are two 3C AD sphinxes, which were found in the orchestra of the theatre. In the corner is a damaged statue of Demeter. An interesting composite statue of a Roman emperor is in a niche nearby. The head and torso belong to different periods. The body has been dated by the decoration on the armour to the 2C AD, while the head, which is much smaller in proportion, dates from the 4C AD. As in the case of the Hermes' head, it was changed in antiquity. The hair and beard were removed to create a new portrait.

In the centre of the room, there is a Roman 2C AD copy of the famous 5C BC discus thrower and headless statues of Hermes and Ares, the god of war. Amongst other things, Hermes was the guardian of merchants and so no doubt was very popular in a trading city like Side. A well-preserved statue of the god, also found in the area of the triple-basin fountain, stands in a corner of the room. He is shown as a nude, muscular adolescent, carrying a purse in his right hand. He is partly supported on his left by a herm: a plinth, which slopes gradually towards its base, decorated with a bearded head and phallus.

Between two sarcophagi in the centre of the room, there is an altar, ornamented with a bust and two small male figures. All date from the 2C AD. One sarcophagus, discovered in the W necropolis, is decorated with a frieze of children playing musical instruments and preparing for a sacrifice. On the back two griffins face each other. On top there is a headless reclining male figure. The other sarcophagus, from the E necropolis, is ornamented on the sides with

Sarcophagus with Erotes (2C AD), from the East necropolis, Side.

charming, tipsy erotes, who support each other in graceful couples. The cover of this sarcophagus is shaped like a roof. One pediment has a representation of Medusa, the other a round shield.

The last room in the complex was probably the apodyterium. Now roofless, it provides the modern entrance to the museum. It contains a number of inscriptions from various monuments in Side and a giant, headless statue of Nike, which was found near the nymphaeum, which is sited at the principal gate to the city.

Amongst the most interesting antiquities in the garden are two fine sarcophagi. One has two erotes supporting a garland, with a column crater in the centre. On the other side there is an inscription inside a *tabula ansata*. One of its pediments carries a damaged Medusa head. Along the wall there are some architectural fragments from a building near the necropolis. These show Selene, the moon goddess, and Helios, the sun god. Among the Corinthian and Ionic capitals, cinerary urns and fractured reliefs, there is an interesting triangular altar, with representations of a humped bull and a bay tree. This was found in the harbour area, near the temples of Apollo and Athena. A relief from the great baths, showing a procession of sea-creatures bearing gifts to the wedding of Poseidon and Amphitrite, is to be found by the wall on the N side of the garden.

23 Side to Alanya

Total distance c 61km. **Side**—E24/400 c 7km *Manavgat*—(c 9km **Alarahan**)—c 34km *Şarapsa Hanı*—c 20km **Alanya**.

After *Manavgat* the coastal plain begins to narrow. The Taurus Mountains approach the E24 more closely, which now traverses a stretch of very fertile but rather dull countryside. After c 10km road 695 on the left follows a spectacular and winding route over the Irmasan Gedigi (1525m) to c 175km *Beyşehir*. There it joins with road 330 to **Konya** (c 90km; see Rte 26). About 10km further a minor road to the left leads to (9km) Alarahan. There are no refreshment facilities at Alarahan, but a very pleasant picnic could be enjoyed by the river's edge or on the grassy slope under the castle.

Alarahan is a 13C inn, one of a number which lined the ancient road from the Selçuk capital, Konya, to its port at Alanya. These were erected by the sultan to provide travellers and merchants with secure and comfortable overnight resting places. They could store their goods in safety in the inn, stable their animals there, prepare their meals, enjoy a bath in the hamam and recite their evening and morning prayers in the small mosque.

Sited in a beautiful river valley, Alarahan crouches under a protective hillside near the remains of an ancient bridge. A torch is needed to explore its well-preserved interior. At the finely-decorated entrance there was a small *mosque* and quarters for the porter/guard. The han's central chamber is surrounded by a number of small rooms, which were occupied by the travellers. Note the interesting stone brackets, carved in the form of lions' heads, which supported the lamps used to illuminate the interior.

Dominating the head of the valley are the ruins of *Alarakale*, a castle which also dates from the 13C. To reach this building, follow the road to its end. Then, having crossed the vegetable gardens, make your way cautiously along a precarious path that skirts the

river's edge. From there a low-roofed tunnel leads upwards for c
100m to the outer court of the castle. Again a lamp is necessary, as
little light penetrates the passageway. Its sides and roof have many
protuberances and the rudimentary steps are covered with loose
stones. This is not an excursion which will recommend itself to those
worried by claustrophobia or the possibility of a close encounter with
snakes or scorpions.

From the outer court there is a splendid view over the valley. Worn
steps lead by dizzy heights to the second court and thence to the top
of the castle. Above the ruins of the residential quarters there is a
hamam. Note the traces of decoration on its domes. The other
buildings—a ruined palace, servants' quarters and a mosque—are
difficult to reach and contain little of interest to the visitor.

After the Alarahan turn-off, the E24 draws near to the sea once more.
It passes many sandy beaches, some of which have had new hotels
and restaurants constructed near them, while others remain
untouched and undeveloped. Here the landscape changes dramatically. The mountains come closer to the seashore. We leave Pamphylia and enter the ancient province of Cilicia. As if to emphasise
the transition banana plantations appear, an exotic touch among the
citrus groves.

There are the ruins of an unidentified city on both sides of the road
just before c 15km Şarapsa Hanı. This Selçuk inn, on the left of the
E24, was constructed by Sultan Giyaseddin Keyhüsrev II (1236–46)
and, like Alarahan, was another staging post on the ancient road
from Konya to Alanya. In an excellent state of preservation, it
measures 70m by 15m. There was a small *mosque* at the E end.
Unfortunately, it is only possible to admire the exterior of this
building as the farmers, who use it as a store, keep it locked.

At the approaches to c 9km Alanya there is a small well-kept rest-
area to the right of the road. Constructed on a promontory, this has
pleasantly shaded paths, tables and benches, and barbecue pits. No
refreshments are available, but it is an excellent place for a picnic
lunch or dinner. There is a small gravelly beach on one side and the
site is sufficiently far from Alanya for the water to be clean. Parking
at the rest-area is limited and, as it is on a very busy road, great care
should be taken when entering and leaving.

The promontory on which **ALANYA** is built is visible from a
considerable distance to the W of the town. Crowned by its great
Selçuk fortress, it projects majestically into the Mediterranean like a
Turkish version of Gibraltar. Alanya may be divided into two parts:
the older and more interesting section, which nestles under the
protective presence of the fortress, and a ribbon-development of
hotels and shops, which lines the E24. During recent years Alanya
has become one of the most popular tourist resorts on Turkey's
Mediterranean coast. Unfortunately, this has been something of a
mixed blessing. The rash of new, rather characterless hotels along
the shore-line to the E and W of the town add little to its charm.
Fortunately, the older part still retains much of its original
atmosphere and particular Turkish character and this coupled with
Alanya's splendid situation and magnificent climate continues to
make it an attractive and interesting place to visit.

Where the road divides, the right fork leads to Alanya's *Tourist Office*, the
Museum and the W beach. The Tourist Office can provide comprehensive
information about the town's hotels, motels, pensions and restaurants. Most of

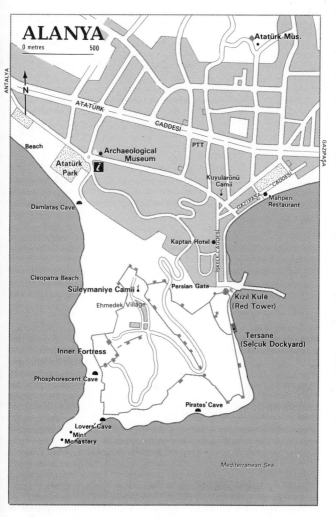

the hotels on the main road, the E24, cater for package-tour groups and offer a reasonable standard of service. However, many visitors prefer to stay in the old part of the town where the comfortable and friendly *Kaptan Hotel* is to be found at İskele Cad. 62. Nearby in Gazi Paşa Cad. there are several restaurants, including the excellent *Mahperi*, which offer a wide range of Turkish dishes. Most of the restaurants have terraces which look towards the harbour, and dinner there on a summer night, under the floodlit battlements of the Selçuk fortress, makes a pleasant end to a day spent exploring the old quarter of the town, visiting the fortress or lazing on the beach.

Most of the principal Turkish *banks* have branches in Alanya. The *Post Office* is located on Atatürk Cad.

Alanya's *bus and dolmuş station* is sited to the W of the town, c 150m off the E24. The principal transport companies provide a free minibus service from the bus station to their offices in the town centre. Some will also pick up passengers from and take them to the principal hotels. Ask the reception clerk at your hotel for details. He will also make reservations on the bus, but not dolmuş, services on your behalf. Taxis may also be hired at the bus station.

There are several travel agencies, which arrange tours to archaeological sites in the neighbourhood and visits further afield. Boat trips may be booked at the harbour to the romantically-named, but historically-suspect, Lovers' Cave, Pirates' Cave and Phosphorescent Cave. Near the Tourist Office on the W side of the town is Damlataş Cave, much visited by rheumatism sufferers, who benefit from its high temperature and high humidity. Although there is no yacht marina on the scale of those at Marmaris or Kuşadası, there are facilities for visiting yachts in the port area. Boutiques and shops in the old quarter offer the usual range of clothes, ceramics, and souvenirs.

Alanya's best beach is on the W side of the promontory, beyond Damlataş Cave, but good bathing may also be had from the beaches off the Gazipaşa road (the E24) on the E outskirts of the town.

History. The site of modern Alanya was occupied in ancient times by the city of CORACESIUM. Apart from a brief mention in the 'Periplus', attributed to geographer Scylax, which records the existence of Alanya in the mid 4C BC, when Cilicia was ruled by the Persians, nothing is known about its early history. However, its commanding and easily-defensible position almost certainly attracted settlers from the earliest times. Remains of a Hellenistic wall may be seen under the Selçuk fortifications that dominate the town. About 197 BC Coracesium was besieged by Antiochus III of Syria. Later the city became the haunt of pirates, one of whom, Diodotus Tryphon, belied his name (Τρυφών means effeminate or wanton) by wresting it from Antiochus VII. Eventually the activities of pirates, who preyed on merchants sailing in Cilician waters, forced the Romans to intervene. Pompey defeated them decisively in 67 BC in a sea-battle off Coracesium and removed this menace from the E Mediterranean for a considerable period. Later Coracesium and the surrounding area were given to Cleoptra by Antony. This was a valuable gift, as timber from the hinterland, a scarce commodity in Egypt, was used by the Egyptians to construct their warships.

Coracesium appears to have had an uneventful existence under the Romans. Apart from the antiquities displayed in the museum, there are no visible remains from that period in the town. Coracesium was probably visited by Trajan, who died in nearby Gazipaşa in August AD 117. During the Byzantine period the city, an episcopal see under Side, changed its name to *Kalonoros*, which means 'beautiful mountain' and variants of this continued to be used in Greek and Italian *portolanos* (pilot manuals) long after the city had fallen to the Turks.

Following the defeat of the Byzantines by the Selçuk Turks at the battle of Manzikert in 1071, Kalonoros was occupied by the Armenians, who ceded it to the Selçuk Sultan Alaeddin Keykubad I c 1221. He called the city *Alaiye*, which means 'city of Ala', a name derived from his title, Alaeddin. He also constructed the citadel and its protective walls and a number of other buildings, which still survive. Under Keykubad, Alaiye became an important cultural and commercial centre, a situation which continued until the 13C, when the Selçuks were ousted by the Karamanid dynasties. Finally, in 1471 the city was captured by an Ottoman army led by the Grand Vizier of Mehmet the Conqueror.

Alaiye was visited by the celebrated Arab traveller, Ibn Battuta, in the middle of the 14C. 'It is inhabited', he wrote, 'by Turkmens, and is visited by the merchants of Cairo, Alexandria and Syria. The district is well-wooded, and wood is exported from there to Alexandria and Damietta, whence it is carried to other cities of Egypt.' Evidently the trade in timber, which had begun under the Romans continued to flourish under the Turks. Three centuries later the Turkish traveller Evliya Çelebi found that, although it had lost some of its former grandeur, Alaiye still possessed many imposing buildings.

One of the first European travellers in modern times to visit Alanya was Captain Francis Beaufort, who surveyed the S coastline of Turkey in 1811/12 for the Admiralty. He received a somewhat mixed reception. A party from his ship, on its way to visit the fortress, was stoned by some boys. Beaufort complained to the Turkish authorities and the culprits were bastinadoed. He found the city, which he identified correctly as the ancient Coracesium, in a very run-down condition: 'Its present importance ... is not great, though capital of a Pashalik: the streets and houses are miserable; there are but few moskes, and they are very mean; there were no signs of commerce; nor can the population exceeded [sic] fifteen hundred, or two thousand at the utmost.'

Apart from the citadel and its surrounding wall, the most striking monument in Alanya is the **Kızıl Kule**, the Red Tower. This is reached by following İskele Cad. from the centre of the old quarter to the point where it turns down to the harbour. One of the first buildings to be constructed by Sultan Keykubad, it dates from 1226. This simple octagonal tower more than 30m high was designed by a Syrian architect from Aleppo. The parapet has openings from which arrows could be shot and missiles dropped on besiegers. The tower served a double purpose: it protected the harbour and the lower reaches of the fortifications. Inside it has five storeys, each of which is divided into eight sections. The central core contains a huge cistern in which sufficient water was stored to meet the needs of the garrison for a long period.

The Kızıl Kule, Alanya.

Restored by the Turkish authorities between 1951/53, it now houses a collection of ethnographical objects. Entry is on the S side by a flight of steps. A small charge is payable. The objects on display include a nomad's tent, a loom and kilims, embroidered garments, and some fine examples of wood-carving. From the top of the tower, which is reached by an open, unprotected, vertiginous stairs, there is a magnificent view of the harbour and the town.

To the left of the Red Tower a path leads to the lower fortification walls. By following a narrow cat-walk for c 200m, it is possible to reach the only remaining Selçuk dockyard in Turkey. At certain points the walls are broken and it is necessary to descend to ground level. The dockyard or **Tersane** consists of five vaulted chambers c 43 by 7.5m open to the sea. An embrasure provides access to the beach, from where it is possible to enter the Tersane. Two small chambers near the entrance on the N probably served as store-rooms or offices. To the S of the Tersane is a large tower, the *Tophane* or arsenal, which protected the Tersane.

Near the Kızıl Kule a narrow lane, which leads S along the promontory, provides access to the many houses which cling to the

512 ALANYA Rte 23

precipitous hillside. In ancient times Alanya possessed only one well, which was located near the Red Tower. The inhabitants' needs were met by huge cisterns, which stored rain water. Of the 400 that once existed a number are still in use.

From the centre of the old quarter of Alanya a steep road snakes upwards for c 3km to the great **fortress** constructed by Keykubad on the summit of the promontory. In the early morning, before it gets too hot, it is an easy and relatively comfortable 40 minutes' walk to the top. Those, who are not tempted by the prospect of some moderate excercise, may hire taxis in the town centre for the single or return journey. There is also a somewhat infrequent dolmuş service. Visitors who compromise and ride to the summit will find the magnificent views of the town and surrounding countryside from the road a more than adequate reward for the slight labour of returning on foot. Below them a vast sector of the Cilician plain, dotted with picturesque villages surrounded by banana plantations and citrus groves, stretches away to the E.

About half-way to the top the road passes under a modern arch by the side of a fine **Double Gate**. For defensive purposes this gate was so constructed that the entrance and exit are at right angles to each other. Inscriptions in Persian date the gate to 1226/31. It was constructed at a point on the lower fortifications, which stretch from the Red Tower to the N fortress at Ehmedek. Here the wall needed to be at its strongest and the defences were reinforced by towers, a second wall and a fosse.

The road continues to the S and then curves upwards towards the **Iç Kale**, the Inner Fortress. At this point several courses of ashlar masonry of the Hellenistic wall, over which the Selçuk fortifications were constructed, may be seen. Visitors not pressed for time may wish to visit *Ehmedek*, where the N part of the fortress was sited and which also served as a residential area during the Selçuk and early Ottoman periods. Today it is a charming village sited among orange groves and clusters of olive trees. It is reached by turning right at the curve into a narrow lane. Inside the fortified area there is a paved court with cisterns. A stairway leads from there to three ruined towers which formed part of the Hellenistic defences. A short distance to the S is the 17C *Süleymaniye Mosque*, a plain box-like building with a much repaired minaret. Beyond the mosque is a ruined bedesten and a caravanserai, now converted into a hotel. This retains its traditional shape of a rectangular courtyard, surrounded by guest rooms. Nearby an interesting building, known as the *Akşebe Türbesi*, contains the tomb of a holy man much honoured by the local people.

A rough path from Ehmedek leads up to the *Inner Fortress*. This can also be reached by continuing on the modern road, bypassing Ehmedek. There is a parking place in front of the main entrance. Admission tickets and postcards may be purchased at that point. Soft drinks (but no food), hand-knitted and crocheted goods are on sale inside. Before entering the inner fortress visitors may like to look at the remains of three buildings on the promontory known as the *Cılvarda Burnu*, which extends S into the sea for c 300m from the hill. The first is a tower, the second a ruin called the *Darphane* (Mint), and the third a small monastery. The monastery may be reached with some difficulty from the sea, but the other buildings are inaccessible to all but the most experienced climbers.

Originally the entrance to the inner fortress was on the E side and it had the customary right-angled bend to delay attackers. Note the painted lozenge decoration high up on the wall inside the modern entrance. The walls enclose a large open space c 180m long, with buildings on all but the W side, where precipitous cliffs drop into the sea. The most striking structure is a small *Byzantine church* dedicated to St. George. Faint traces of frescoes may be seen on the walls and dome. The other buildings are vaulted galleries, which may have served as barracks. There are several large cisterns in the centre near the modern toilet and washroom. A platform overlooking a dizzy drop into the sea is known as Adam Atacağı, the place from which men are thrown, because it is believed that condemned prisoners were obliged to jump from there on to the rocks below. A cynic has observed that any who survived the drop were allowed to go free!

Despite its lurid past the Inner Fortress is now a place of great peace and beauty. The sunsets visible from its walls are spectacular.

The cave of *Damlataş* on the W side of Alanya was discovered by accident in 1948. Now a place of treatment for sufferers from asthma and rheumatism, it is reserved for the sick until 10.00 each day. One of the unfortunate effects of tourism is the rather garish illumination, which has been installed to light its alcoves and natural formations.

Alanya's **Museum**, opened in 1967, is one of the most attractive regional museums in S Turkey. Sited near the Tourist Office and the Damlataş cave, the museum's collection is displayed in the garden and indoors in two large rooms. One contains the archaeological exhibits, the other the ethnographical collection. Many items are labelled in Turkish and English. There is a small entrance fee.

The garden contains various fragments of Roman statuary, some fine cinerary urns, cannon-balls and Islamic tombstones. In the corridor leading to the first room there are some exhibits from the Hatti and Urartian civilisations, coins from Coracesium, Side, Antalya, etc., cinerary urns from Alanya, amphorae, and Hellenistic vases. In the large room to the right there are some fine examples of Roman glass, statuettes of stone, some exquisite terracottas, stelae, bronzes, anchors, amphorae and pottery recovered from the sea. Perhaps the most important exhibits are a small 2C AD bronze of Hercules, a floor mosaic from Syedra with a representation of the Three Graces, bordered by a hunting scene, and the gold treasure recovered from a tomb at Anamurium. The ethnographical collection contains carpets, kilims, weapons, Selçuk tiles, manuscripts and inscriptions, coins and clothing. There is also the reconstruction of a typical 19C room from a house in Alanya.

24 Alanya to Anamur

Total distance c 108km. **Alanya**—E24/400—(c 10km *Laertes*)—c 22km *Syedra*—c 13km *Iotape*—c 9km *Gazipaşa*—(c 2km *Selinus*)—(c 3km *Antiocheia ad Cragum*)—c 34km *Kalediran*—c 30km **Anamur** —(c 6km **Anemurium**).

In antiquity **Alanya** (see Rte 23) was sometimes referred to as 'the gateway to Cilicia'. This province, once the home of bandits, pirates and mercenaries, was divided into *Cilicia Tracheia* (Rugged Cilicia), and *Cilicia Campestris* (Smooth Cilicia). Cilicia Tracheia, the W part of the province, is wild, craggy, and heavily forested and had few settlements of any size; while Cilicia Campestris was made up of the large fertile plain, which is watered by the rivers Seyhan and Ceyhan. Today, little has changed in Rugged Cilicia. The towns are still small and depend largely on fishing and forestry, though the impact of tourism is beginning to be felt in the region.

The road from Alanya to Anamur, a major engineering feat, passes through some of the most beautiful scenery in S Turkey. For much of the way it clings to the side of the Taurus Mountains, offering spectacular views of the rocky coastline far below. Motorists, accustomed to less demanding terrain, may find its many sharp bends intimidating. They will need to exercise great care, as it carries a considerable amount of traffic, including many slow-moving and heavily-laden lorries.

Between Alanya and (44km) Gazipaşa there are the ruins of four ancient cities: Laertes, Syedra, Iotape and Selinus. Although they have been surveyed, they have not been excavated. Their sites are very overgrown and, with the exception of Iotape, are not particularly easy to reach. Consequently, they are visted mainly by specialists. However, their commanding and beautiful situations and the romantic melancholy of their ruins, will attract those travellers who are not deterred by a little physical discomfort.

Syedra, Iotape, and Selinus are mentioned in the works of geographers of the Classical and Byzantine periods, and they are listed in the ancient itineraries. Little is known of their individual histories, but it is probable that they shared the fate of their larger and better-known neighbours. After the arrival of Christianity three of them became episcopal sees, Syedra under the Metropolitan of Pamphylia, Iotape and Selinus under the Metropolitan of Seleucia. In the 12C and 13C they formed part of the Cilician kingdom of Lesser Armenia. Later abandoned, they were not resettled when the population of the area increased in recent times.

For much of the way from Alanya to Gazipaşa the E24 runs parallel to the sea. As far as the turn-off for 25km *Belen*, there are good, clean beaches of shingle and sand. Banana plantations and citrus groves fill every pocket of arable land that flank the road.

To visit **LAERTES**, take a turning to the left, after c 20km from Alanya to the village of *Mahmutlar*. As the site is not easy to find, it is advisable to obtain a guide in the village. From Mahmutlar follow a road suitable for four-wheel drive vehicles only for c 10km in the direction of Hadim Yolu. There is no clearly-defined path to the site. A certain amount of scrambling through thick undergrowth over rocky slopes is necessary. However, the splendid view over the ancient city and southwards to the sea is more than adequate compensation for the effort.

Laertes main claim to fame is that it was the home of Diogenes Laertius, who flourished in the 2C AD. He was the author of a ten volume 'Lives of the Philosophers', a useful if somewhat uncritical work, which is particularly valuable for the information it contains on Epicurus. One of the most striking features of Laertes is its situation. It is built on the slopes of *Cebelireş*, the highest mountain in the region, on a *large terraced area*. On the N edge of this terrace there is an underground construction, the so-called 'house of seven doors', which is believed to have been dedicated to the gods of the underworld. Below are the remains of the theatre and a number of cisterns. Beyond the agora and near the terrace, are the ruins of a large building, which at different times appears to have been used as a palace and as a house.

About 2km further along the E24 are the ruins of ancient SYEDRA. The city was divided into two parts: one near the modern road, the other some considerable distance away (c 90 minute walk) on the mountain-side. Syedra is commemorated by the name of a river to the E of the site, the Sedre Çayı. The city issued coins during the period from Tiberius (AD 14–37) to Gallienus (253–268).

A turning on the left from the E24 leads to the *upper city*. Access is by way of a rocky, overgrown slope. There are several buildings on a large terrace, which is flanked by the remains of the city fortifications. One of the buildings has three chambers, whose walls stand to a height of 10m. Nearby is a house, which has traces of wall paintings. A fine *mosaic* depicting the Three Graces and a hunting scene which was found at Syedra is now in the Alanya Museum.

In the *lower city* there are the remains of a baths complex on the slope of a small hill 100m W of the road. In the necropolis to the E there are many tombs, some of a type found at Iotape and Selinus. Most are in a ruinous condition. One, a barrel-vaulted structure with six niches, has traces of fresco-painting on the interior walls, and the niches are surrounded with a stucco-like decoration of concrete. Again there are splendid views from this site.

About 35km from Alanya the E24 passes through the centre of IOTAPE. Founded by Antiochus IV Epiphanes (175–164 BC), the city was named after his wife, Iotape Philadelphus. It has been identified by inscriptions found on the site. Iotape issued coins from the period of Trajan (AD 98–117) to Valerian (253–260).

Built around a small inlet, the first settlement was almost certainly on the peninsula, which dominates the sea and landward approaches to the city. Later this became the site of Iotape's acropolis. Apart from a fine temple-tomb (now destroyed), which is believed to have dated from the late Hellenistic period, no pre-Roman remains have been found in Iotape.

Although the site is very overgrown, it is possible to examine many of the buildings in the city centre, which lay across the inlet from the acropolis. This residential area was bounded on the N by a ravine, on the S by the sea and on the E by the necropolis. Among the many buildings is a *church*, dedicated to Hagios Georgios Stratelates, and two large barrel-vaulted structures. In the city's necropolis, to the NE of the E24, most of the tombs, which still remain, are in a poor condition. Nearby are the ruins of a *small medieval church*, which bears traces of frescoes on its walls. Among the subjects depicted are the Nativity and a number of saints.

Gazipaşa, formerly known as *Selinty*, a corruption of Selinus, its old name, is 44km from Alanya. It is a sprawling, dusty overgrown village, which serves as a market and administrative centre for the surrounding countryside. There is a small restaurant near the coach station.

On the W outskirts of Gazipaşa, a road to the right leads shortly to SELINUS. The ancient city was built on and around a steep headland, which dominates the landscape. It is crowned with a castle, probably constructed by the Byzantines, but repaired and extended by their Turkish conquerors. In the early 19C Selinus was visited by Captain Francis Beaufort during the course of a survey of the S Turkish coast which he conducted for the Admirality. 'The evening was clear,' he writes in 'Karamania', 'and this spot [the castle] afforded a beautiful prospect. We could trace the coast that had been already explored, to an immense distance; the plain, with its winding rivers and ruins, was spread out like a map at our feet; and behind all, a prodigious ridge of mountains, whose black sides, having already lost the evening sun, formed a singular contrast with their snowy tops. We had a distinct view of the island of Cyprus rising from the southern horizon, though not less than seventy miles distant.'

According to Livy, Selinus was captured by Antiochus III in 197 BC. It is probable that it was fortified by Antiochus IV Epiphanes (175–164 BC), when he founded Iotape and Antiocheia ad Cragum to protect traders from the unwelcome attentions of the pirates and bandits who plagued Cilicia at that time. Archaeological evidence that Selinus was occupied during the late Hellenistic period is provided by the remains of a temple tomb, similar to that found in Iotape. The city issued coins during the reign of Antiochus IV and under the Romans from Trajan (AD 98–117) to Philip the Arab (244–249). When Trajan, exhausted by his campaigns on the E marches of the empire, died here in August 117, Selinus became *Trajanopolis*.

Although much of ancient Selinus has been carried away by the river, some of the ruins described by Beaufort may still be seen. In addition to the remains of the aqueduct which supplied Selinus with water, there is a large *vaulted Roman structure*, which romantics may care to believe formed part of the mausoleum of Trajan. On the side of the hill there are the ruins of a structure which was probably a baths complex, and of a number of tombs. Unlike those found in the neighbouring cities, many of the tombs discovered in Selinus bear inscriptions, usually on their lintels. The area has also yielded a large number of cinerary urns, decorated with garlands, masks and bulls or rams' heads. Near the river there is the outline of an area 80m², which was surrounded by a colonnade. A building nearby has been tentatively identified as a small theatre or an odeum. The line of the ancient fortifications, which ran from the castle to the river, may still be traced. The castle, surrounded by its protective walls and moats, and the large church nearby are not easy to reach, as there is no clearly defined path. However, the view from the summit of the promontory is as striking as it was in Beaufort's day.

From Gazipaşa the E24 turns inland and begins to climb steadily. Then, in a series of sharp curves, it makes its sinuous way along the mountain-side far above the rocky coastline.

To visit ANTIOCHEIA-AD-CRAGUM, take a turning on the right c 20km after Gazipaşa to the village of *Güney*. The ruins of the ancient city, which are spread along the cliff-top, are not outstanding. However, the beauty of their situation and their relative isolation make the diversion worthwhile. To see them all requires about three hours and a good deal of walking. There are many pleasant places on the cliff-top where an alfresco meal may be enjoyed.

Founded by Antiochus IV Epiphanes (175–164 BC) at about the same time as Iotape, Antiochia issued coins from the time of Antoninus Pius (AD 138–161) to Valerian (253–260). In Byzantine times it was the see of a bishop under the Metropolitan of Seleucia. Like the neighbouring cities, it formed part of the Cilician kingdom of Lesser Armenia in the 12C and 13C. In 1332 the Armenians offered the castle to the Knights Hospitallers, as they were no longer able to defend it. It was then known as Antiocheta in Rufine (Papal Bull of John XXII) or Antichia Parva.

The ruins of Antiochia fall into three distinct areas: the city centre and main necropolis, the W necropolis and the citadel. The village of Güney is built over part of the main necropolis, and as a result little remains to be seen. Note the *two monumental tombs* of a type found also in Iotape and Selinus, and the carved stones from various buildings in the ancient city, which have been built into the walls of several of the modern houses.

One of the principal buildings of Antiocheia is to be found on a terrace to the N of the village. This is a large *barrel-vaulted structure* supported by massive buttresses. To the E of this was a colonnade, which led to a terraced area bounded by a ravine. To the N of the colonnade are the ruins of a *triconchos* with a W facing entrance. This measured c 8m by 6.5m. Across the ravine are the ruins of a building, which has been identified as a baths complex.

The *W necropolis* is located on a small peninsula. As well as a number of fine tombs, it has a well-preserved medieval chapel, which bears traces of fresco in a niche on the SW corner, and two cisterns. The tombs, which are all located on the S of the peninsula, date from the Roman period.

The *medieval citadel* is encircled by two walls and is fortified with round and angular towers. At the entrance there is a small chapel built into the outer wall. In the central court is another chapel, a tower and the ruins of an unidentified building. A further group of three small chapels is sited to the W of the citadel.

Approximately 34km from Gazipaşa the E24 reaches sea-level at *Kaledıran*, a name which commemorates ancient CHARADRUS. Described by Strabo as a fortified harbour 'on a rough coast, called Platanistes', today it is a sleepy village surrounded by banana groves and dominated by the ruins of an ancient fortress. After Kaledıran the road rises once more and for a further c 30km makes its tortuous way E, until it descends at last through pine forests to the plain of Anamur.

Silifke and Anamur are the only towns of any size in Rugged Cilicia. **Anamur**, whose name is derived from ἄνεμος, the Greek word for wind, is, appropriatley, a breezy, dusty small town. Although there is little to detain the visitor in Anamur, it is surrounded by places of interest: the medieval castle at Mamure Kalesi; several caves and grottoes; and the ruins of the ancient city of Anemurium. A museum, long-promised, has yet to be completed. However, some artefacts from Anemurium are displayed in the Antalya and Alanya museums.

On the left side of the broad street that climbs steeply to the town-centre from the bus station is the *Tourist Office* and a little further on the *Post Office*. Anamur has the usual collection of banks and shops and there are several reasonably good restaurants near the main square. Dolmuş services to the surrounding villages leave from the town-centre.

Many private houses in Anamur offer simple, clean, cheap accommodation. Ask at the bus station or Tourist Office for details. In summer it is essential to select a room that has effective mosquito-screens on the windows, as the marshes around Anamur produce a plague of these insects. There are several basic hotels in the town and a number on the coast 3km to the S. However, one of the most attractive places in the area is the small *Karan Motel*, c 7km to the E. Far enough from the main road to be quiet and within walking distance of Mamure Kalesi, it has its own private beach and a good restaurant. Most long distance buses stop at the nearby petrol station and there is a somewhat infrequent dolmuş service to and from Anamur.

The ancient city of **ANEMURIUM**, c 6km to the SW of Anamur, is reached by taking the Alanya road for c 4km and by then turning left on to a well-surfaced side road which leads to the site. Anemurium, the most southerly city in Anatolia, has been surveyed and partly excavated by Canadian archaeologists from the universities of Toronto and British Columbia. Restoration, where undertaken, has been limited to preventing further deterioration of the better-preserved structures.

There is a good beach at Anemurium and the sea is free from pollution. While there are no cafés or restaurants at the site, there are many secluded spots where a picnic may be enjoyed.

Because of its favourable situation, Anemurium almost certainly attracted settlers from the earliest times. Sheltered from the prevailing SW winds, only 65km from Cyprus, it must have benefited also from its proximity to the large fertile plain, which lies to the E. Although there are references to Anemurium in the ancient writers as early as the 4C BC, the ruins visible today date from the late Roman, the Byzantine and the medieval periods.

According to Livy, Antiochus III passed by the city in 197 BC on his way to the siege and capture of Selinus. When attacked by tribes from the interior in AD 52, the last Commagene king, Antiochus IV of Commagene, who ruled the Cilician coastal area at that time, came to its rescue. Anemurium issued coins during his reign and under the Romans from Titus (AD 79–81) to Valerian (253–260). It was during the early Roman period, the 1C and 2C AD, that Anemurium, described by Professor Russell, who has directed the Canadian excavations at Anemurium since 1971, as a 'modest market centre in a relatively isolated corner of the ancient world', reached its apogee. This period of prosperity was ended abruptly c AD 260, when Cilicia was invaded by the Persians. Although their stay was comparatively short, further raids by Isaurian tribes from the interior continued to disturb the peace of the city. This necessitated the construction of a new defensive system, which was completed towards the end of the 4C.

Sometime after the arrival of Christianity in Cilicia, Anemurium became an episcopal see under the Metropolitan of Seleucia. Emphasis switched from the construction of public buildings to churches and several were erected in the city. During the 5C and 6C Anemurium's bishops took part in a number of church councils. Like their neighbours in Isauria, the Anemurians adopted the Monophysite heresy, which troubled orthodox Christianity for several centuries and is still accepted by the Coptic, Armenian and Ethiopian churches. This denies the humanity of Christ, teaching that he had but one nature.

During the Byzantine era Anemurium entered a further period of quiet prosperity. This ended suddenly c 580, when the city was devastated by an earthquake, from which it never recovered entirely. The situation was made worse by a further Persian invasion between 610–630 and the arrival of the Arabs in Cyprus in 650. Frequent piratical attacks by Arab pirates caused Anemurium to be abandoned finally in the middle of the 7C, its population moving inland to a safer and less vulnerable area. Part of the site was reoccupied in the 12C and 13C, when Cilicia formed part of the kingdom of Armenia. However, the successors of the Armenians, the Selçuk Karamanoğlu, appear to have ignored Anemurium. They concentrated their attention on the plain to the E, where they constructed the great fortress of Mamure Kalesi. Anemurium became a forgotten city, unknown and neglected until Beaufort and other 19C travellers visited it and wrote about its ruins.

The buildings of Anemurium were constructed from limestone rubble, which was probably covered with marble inlay and stucco. This decorative veneer disappeared a long time ago, so that now, even in bright sunshine, the ruins have a strange, grey, ghostly appearance.

The approach to Anemurium is by way of an extensive ancient necropolis, which was used for many centuries. The tombs range from simple barrel-vaulted chambers to large two-storey constructions. From their decoration and furnishing a good deal of information about the Anemurians and their way of life has been obtained.

Beaufort was greatly impressed by the necropolis, 'we hastened', he wrote, 'to examine a wide field of ruins outside the walls, which had appeared from the top of the cape like the remains of a large city. It was indeed a city, but a city of tombs, a true Necropolis. The contrast between the slight and perishable materials with which the habitations of the living were constructed, and the care and skill which the antients employed to render durable the abodes of the dead, is more than ordinarily impressed upon the mind at this place; for though all the tombs have been long since opened and ransacked, the walls are still sound; whereas of their dwellings not one continues in existence.'

Most tombs were divided into two parts, an inner chamber where the dead were laid, and an anteroom, which was used by visitors, when they came to pray and make offerings to the deceased. Many of the antechambers had mosaic pavements and their walls were decorated with geometric patterns or pictures of flowers, birds, animals and sometimes erotes. A *tomb*, which lies a short distance from the lower aqueduct, has a vault painted with representations of the four seasons, while Hermes in his role as Psychopompos, the conductor of souls, is depicted on one of the walls. The Anemurians appear to have had a very philosophical attitude to death. Professor Russell

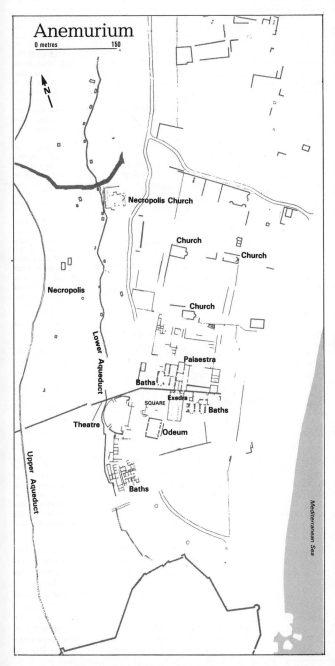

Anemurium

0 metres ————— 150

N

Necropolis Church

Church

Church

Church

Necropolis

Lower Aqueduct

Palaestra

Baths

Exedra

Baths

SQUARE

Theatre

Odeum

Upper Aqueduct

Baths

Mediterranean Sea

describes a tomb with a fresco representing the deceased couple and the laconic inscription ὁ Βίος Ταυτα, 'that's life'.

On the N edge of the necropolis are the ruins of a *church*, which was built c 400 on the remains of a Roman building. In the following century this was replaced by a larger building of basilica form. Cathecumens, who were not admitted to the body of the church until they had been baptised, were able to follow the services from an extension to the N aisle, which had a baptistery at its E end. Like the earlier church, the basilica was decorated with mosaics. On the floor in front of the apse there is a roughly-executed representation of a leopard and kid flanking a palm tree, accompanied by a quotation from Isaiah 11.6: 'And a little child will lead them and the leopard will lie down with the kid'.

Anemurium was supplied with water by two *aqueducts*. These were stone-lined channels cut into the hillside and carried on arches over small ravines. The upper aqueduct supplied the citadel.

To the left of the modern road, just outside the city walls, are the ruins of a large 3C AD *baths complex*. This was raised on a platform which faced a *palaestra*. The total area covered was c 1000m². The palaestra, whose surface was covered with geometric mosaics, was surrounded by colonnades on three sides. The baths, which tried to emulate the great buildings of the Roman province of Asia Minor, betrayed their provincial ethos by the homely exhortation to 'have a good bath' at the entrance, and comment, 'you have had a good bath' at the exit. N of the colonnade was a triconchos (a rectangular building with apses on the N, E and S walls). This had an entrance on the W.

In Byzantine times, when the city fortunes were in decline, short-age of wood for heating and problems about the water-supply produced a change of use in the baths and palaestra. The palaestra was turned into a market and a number of small, poorly-constructed houses were built on its N side. The great halls of the baths were used for various trades like flour milling, lime burning, and as potteries. Smaller baths, more in keeping with the Anemurium's straitened circumstances, were constructed in other parts of the city.

The *theatre* lay on the S side of the city wall. Partly cut out of the hillside, its cavea, 60m in diameter, may still be distinguished. All its seating has disappeared. Beaufort conjectures that this and other building material was taken from Anemurium to Cyprus, 'where art and commerce flourished long after this coast had become the prey of a succession of ruffian conquerors'.

Below the road are the ruins of a building, which has been identified as an *odeum* or *bouleuterion*. It may have served as both. This is 30m long by 20m wide and still has six rows of seats. It was probably roofed.

Beyond the theatre is the best-preserved building in Anemurium. This is another large *baths complex*, which was begun in the 3C AD. A covered stairway, with 30 steps, leads to the entrance on the N side of the building. Most of the vaults remain intact. Fragments of decoration and mosaics from various periods have been found in these baths.

Many of the floors in the private houses in Anemurium were decorated with *mosaics*. These include a winged Victory bearing a palm-branch, a representation of Hermes, and another of Thetis surrounded by various sea creatures. To see these mosaics, ask the Bekçi to remove the sand with which they been covered for their protection.

Visitors with sufficient time, may like to climb to the *citadel* for the sake of the view from this the southernmost point of Anatolia. Cyprus can be seen on a clear day. The citadel was surrounded by a wall, which was fortified with towers and angled recesses. Most of the enclosed area was not inhabited. On the summit there are some ruins from the medieval period. Note in particular a small church and the tower at the intersection of the upper aqueduct and the wall.

A popular EXCURSION from Anamur is to *Köşekbükü Mağarası*. These caves, which are c 15km from Anamur, may be reached by going first to *Kalın Ören* (unexcavated ruins of a Byzantine city here). To reach this village, take the street on the left before the Post Office and then continue on the main road, which traverses a pleasant forested area. Visitors without their own transport may hire taxis at the bus station. As there is no fixed charge for the journey, this should be agreed with the driver before departure. There is a small café near the caves, where light refreshments may be obtained. The caves, which have a constant temperature of 27°C, are believed to be of benefit to asthmatics and infertile women!

25 Anamur to Silifke

Total distance c 121km. **Anamur**—E24 c 7km **Mamure Kalesi**—(c 1.5km *Softa Kalesi*)—c 40km *Aydıncık*—c 51km *Boğsak*—15km *Taşucu*—8km **Silifke**.

The spectacular road between Softa Kalesi and Taşucu—an outstanding engineering feat—progresses in a series of sharp curves over vertiginous drops, a combination which demands very careful driving. It is the main E–W coast road and carries heavy, and sometimes very slow-moving, traffic.

On leaving **Anamur** (see Rte 24) the highway crosses the broad plain E of the town, returning to the coastline once more at (c 7km) **Mamure Kalesi**. This striking building, on the right hand side of the road, is one of the finest medieval castles in S Turkey. Its crenellated walls and towers of many shapes— dodecagonal, square, octagonal, and round—stand to their original height. Surrounded by a shallow moat, which is half-filled with the silt and detritus of centuries, the castle still dominates the E sea and land approaches to Anamur.

A fortress of some kind has stood on this site since the 3C AD. The early construction, enlarged and extended by the Byzantines and the kings of the Cilician kingdom of Armenia, was rased almost to the ground by the Selçuk sultan, Alaeddin Keykubad, who built the present building in the 13C. An inscription over the principal entrance, now walled up, on the W side of the building, refers to this event. The castle was later occupied by the Karamanoğlu dynasty, whose members made further alterations to the structure. In the 16C Mamure Kalesi was captured for the Ottomans and remained in use until the last days of the empire.

When visited by Beaufort in 1811/12 the castle was in a ruinous condition, but substantial repairs and restorations were made to it in the middle of the 19C. Beaufort received a cordial welcome from the Bey, Abdul Muim, who ruled the area, and with his party was able to make a detailed examination of the castle. The Bey, accompanied by a number of his retainers, came down to the shore and spent several hours observing Beaufort's ship with a pocket telescope. However, because of the long swell, he could not be tempted to board HMS *Frederikssteen*.

Mamure Kalesi's era of martial splendour has long departed. Today the castle echoes, not to the sounds of battle, but to the raucous cries

Thirteenth-century Mamure Kalesi near Anamur.

of amorous frogs which inhabit the moat. Boys play football in its great court and girls from the nearby village weave graceful patterns in the air with their spindles, as they watch over the grazing cattle. Only the crash and thunder of waves against the great sea-walls echo the castle's turbulent past.

Admission tickets to Mamure Kalesi may be obtained from a kiosk near the present entrance on the E side of the castle. A pocket torch is necessary for the exploration of the towers and storerooms. There are no refreshment facilities or toilets in the castle. Simple meals, tea, coffee and soft drinks may be obtained from a number of restaurants and coffee-houses nearby. The *Karan Motel* and restaurant are c 1km to the E. There is good bathing at Mamure Kalesi. The beaches and sea are clean and free from pollution and the area is usually uncrowded.

A passage, whose bends and curves were designed to aid the defence of the castle, leads to the towers on the E side. These give a fine view over the surrounding land- and seascape. The principal court is divided by a partially-demolished wall. Near the centre of the castle there is a much-restored mosque. Beyond, to the W, were the quarters of the castle's commander. It is possible to walk around the greater part of the ramparts, but care should be taken in the buildings on the W side, as many are in a ruinous condition. The large vaulted chambers under the ramparts were used as storerooms or arsenals.

Across the road from the castle are the ruins of *Ottoman baths*. These are very overgrown and, according to local gossip, infested with snakes.

Approximately 1km to the E of the Karan Motel there is a picnic area among the pine trees on the right of the road. This adjoins a small, clean pebbly beach.

A rocky pinnacle, c 10km from Mamure Kalesi, is crowned with the ruins of *Softa Kalesi*, the 'Castle of the Fanatics'. Originally the stronghold of bandits who terrorised and robbed coastal traders, it was replaced by the Romans with a guard-post during their drive to suppress brigandage in Cilicia. The structure visible today was constructed by the Byzantines and restored and extended later by the Armenians and the Turks. A substantial effort is needed to get to the castle, within whose walls there is little to see apart from a number of cisterns and the ruins of medieval baths.

The E24 has another spectacular stretch high above the sea for c 40km until it descends once more at the pretty little village of *Aydıncık*. In ancient times this was the site of the Samian colony of CELENDRIS, founded in the 5C BC, whose ruins may be seen near the village. A pleasant point at which to stop, Aydıncık has a small restaurant in the centre and there are several places along the beach where it is possible to picnic.

From Aydıncık to (c 66km) *Taşucu* the E24 first crosses the base of Cape Cavalierè, the modern Ovacık Burnu, and then, entering a relatively fertile area, continues through a series of acute bends to the E part of Rugged Cilicia.

The hamlet of *Boğsak*, on the N shore of an attractive crescent-shaped bay, is an enticing alternative to a Taşucu, which lies c 15km to the E. It has a small motel within a few metres of the sandy beach and one or two simple restaurants. As there are relatively few long-distance buses and local dolmuş services on this stretch of the E24, Boğsak will be of greatest interest to visitors who have their own transport.

Just offshore is *Provençal Island*, so called because it was occupied in the 12C and 13C by the Provençal division of the Knights' Hospitallers of St. John. The Knights were divided into eight groups, of which the first was known as the Langue de Provence. After the fall of Jerusalem in 1290, they moved to Cyprus and also took possession of Rhodes and of a number of castles on the coast of Asia Minor. These served as advanced posts on the fringes of Muslim territory and also provided refuges for Christian slaves. Provençal Island, which has high cliffs on the seaward side, is covered with the ruins of houses, churches and cemeteries. Its summit is crowned with the remains of a citadel. There are no springs on the island, but traces of a number of cisterns have been found.

The promontory to the E of Boğsak is marked by the 14C Turkish castle of *Liman Kalesi*. From there the E24 follows the coastline closely, passing the ruins of two small medieval churches. There are several attractive beaches within a few metres of the road, but not many safe parking places.

Taşucu, the port of Silifke, is a nondescript, characterless, semi-industrialised place. It has a number of modern hotels and expensive restaurants on a strip development, which runs parallel to the main road. There is a daytime ferryboat service from Taşucu to Girne (Kyrenia) in the Turkish Federated Republic of Northern Cyprus. Note, however, that the journey may be made in greater comfort by the car-ferry, which runs on three nights each week from Mersin to **Mağusa** (Famagusta). Details of fares and timetables for both services may be obtained from the Tourist Offices in Silifke and Mersin.

SILIFKE is a sprawling town built along the banks of the Göksu, the ancient Calycadnus. From antiquity it has owed its importance to the fact that it marked the junction between the main route along the S littoral of Asia Minor and a road over the Taurus Mountains to the centre of Anatolia.

The *Tourist Information Office*, on the N side of the bridge at the corner of Atatürk Cad., is one of the best and most efficient in Turkey. Its Director and his small staff deal very capably with enquiries in a variety of languages. Showing great enterprise, they have produced a number of useful booklets and leaflets about Silifke and its environs in English, French and German.

There are courses in Turkish for foreigners in Silifke and an annual festival of the arts. Details may be obtained from the Tourism offices.

Silifke has a number of modest hotels and pensions, but many visitors prefer to stay by the sea at *Taşucu*, 8km to the W, or at (c 15km) *Susanoğlu* and (c 27km) *Kızkalesi* to the E. It is advisable to reserve accommodation some time in advance at all these places, particularly during the summer months. The resorts on Turkey's S coast are very popular with Turkish and foreign visitors and their hotels and pensions tend to be full during the holiday season.

There are several unpretentious restaurants in Silifke. Among the best are the *Piknik* in İnönü Cad. in the town centre and the *Babaoğlu* near the bus station.

The *Post Office* is to be found on the S bank of the Göksu near the bridge. Nearby is the town's main shopping area where branches of the principal Turkish banks are located.

There is a frequent bus-service between Silifke and Taşucu. This starts from a stop near the Post Office. Mainline bus and dolmuş services from the bus station call at Susanoğlu and Kızkalesi.

History. Silifke, the ancient SELEUCEIA AD CALYCADNUM, is named after its founder, Seleucus I Nicator (321–280 BC), a general in the army of Alexander the Great and first king of the Seleucid dynasty of Syria. Anxious to emphasise the family connection with his newly-established kingdom, he was a prodigal creator of cities named after himself and his relatives. According to Appian 'Syriaca' 57, the 2C AD Roman historian, Seleucus founded 16 Antiochs in honour of his father, Antiochus, five Laodiceas named after his mother, four cities in honour of his wives and nine which bore his own name.

Seleucia ad Calycadnum replaced an earlier Greek settlement, founded in the 7C BC. What little is known of the city's history has been gleaned from the events that took place in Cilicia. Like its neighbours, it appears to have enjoyed a period of prosperity under the Romans. From the earliest days of Christianity it was associated with the new religion. St. Thecla, the friend of St. Paul, found sanctuary there. Later it came under the control of the Isaurians, a wild mountain tribe from the interior, which provided two emperors during the Byzantine period, Zeno (474–491) and Leo III (717–741). Although raided frequently by Arab pirates from Cyprus, it continued to be an important port for Christian pilgrims on their way to the Holy Land.

In the 12C Silifke was the scene of an event which affected the Third Crusade dramatically. The Emperor Frederick Barbarossa, who in May 1189 had set out from Germany at the head of a great army to liberate the Holy Land from the Saracens, was drowned on 10 June 1190 in the swift and deep waters of the Saleph, now the Göksu. The way in which he met his death is not known with certainty. Some accounts state that the day was warm and that the emperor was swimming in the river, when suddenly he cried out for help and disappeared. Although his knights rushed to the rescue, when they brought him to the bank he was found to be dead. Other chronicles suggest that he may have fallen from his horse and, a man in his late sixties, he was unable to swim to safety because of the weight of his armour. Whatever the cause, the untimely death of Barbarossa had disastrous consequences for the great enterprise he had undertaken. A part of the army, which had left Germany so proudly a year before, managed to struggle home. A few went on to the Holy Land. The rest perished miserably from plague or were slaughtered by the Turks.

After a brief period under the kings of Lesser Armenia, Silifke passed into the hands of the Selçuk Turks. In turn they were dispossessed by the Karamanoğlu dynasty. Finally, in 1471 the city and its fortress were captured for the Ottomans by Gedik Ahmet Pasha.

During the centuries that followed, Silifke declined greatly in importance, so that by the 19C it had only a handful of inhabitants. Recent years have been marked by a revival in its fortunes brought about by the growth of trade, agriculture and, latterly, by tourism.

Silifke's **Museum** is on the outskirts of the town on the road to Taşucu. On the ground floor there is a fine collection of Persian and Byzantine coins found in the area. Note, in particular, the daric struck during the reign of Darius. There is also an interesting display of

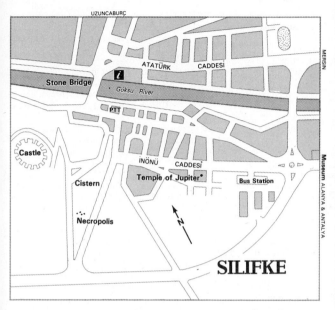

statues, most of which date from the Roman period. Upstairs is exhibited the Gülnar hoard, more than 5000 silver coins of the successors of Alexander minted during the 4C and 3C BC (see below). There are several small bronzes, which were found in the town, near the temple of Zeus, and a number of statuettes dating from the 3C and 4C BC.

In addition, the museum has a large ethnographical collection and a display of statues and sarcophagi in the garden. There may be found the headless, but otherwise almost complete, statue of a Roman emperor or general. This was discovered recently at the new excavations behind the temple of Zeus.

Few traces of Silifke's past are visible today. The Roman bridge across the Göksu, erected by L. Octavius Memor in honour of Vespasian and his sons, Titus and Domitian in AD 77/78, was replaced by the present structure at the end of the 19C.

In İnönü Cad. are the ruins of the impressive 2C AD **Temple of Zeus**. This was a peripteros with 8 by 14 columns in the Corinthian style. The one fluted column which remains standing now supports a stork's nest each spring. A short distance S of the temple is an area which is currently being excavated. Some fine mosaic pavements discovered there are covered with sand for their protection. A Roman statue (see above) from these excavations may be seen in the garden of the Museum.

Silifke has an interesting mosque, *Ulu Cami*, which dates from the Selçuk period. The roof is supported by three arches and there is a dome over the area in front of the mihrab. The mihrab and the entrance are the most ancient parts of the building.

Because of Silifke's strategic situation, the hill which dominates the town was almost certainly fortified from the earliest times. The Byzantines constructed a fortress there in the 7C during the period of the Arab raids. In the 12C, at the end of the First Crusade, the structure visible today was built. Occupied in turn by the Armenians and the Crusaders, it was captured by the Karamanoğlu by trickery towards the end of the 13C. Disguising themselves as Christian merchants, they infiltrated the keep and overcame the defenders. At the end of the 15C it fell into the hands of the Ottomans.

It is an easy walk from the town centre to the **castle**, which stands c 180m above sea-level. Surrounded by a double wall, entrance was by a huge gateway which had a right-angled bend to impede attackers equipped with siege-engines. This was further strengthened by the addition of an iron door in the 15C. Covering a very large area, c 345m by 95m, the castle is in a ruinous condition. Care should be taken in walking in or over the vaulted chambers and in exploring the ramparts. The great breach in the E wall, which provides access today, was made during the Ottoman attack in the 15C.

There are excellent views over Silifke and the surrounding countryside from the ramparts. A number of restaurants near the castle area offer simple refreshments.

At the foot of the castle, to the SE, is a large Byzantine *cistern*, which supplied the upper part of the town with water. Known popularly as *Tekirambarı*, the 'striped granary', it measures 46m long, 23m wide and 12m high. The hardy may descend into its depths by means of a spiral staircase.

Silifke's *necropolis* was located on either side of the road that leads out of the town towards Mut and Konya. Many of the tombs and tombstones bear inscriptions and reliefs. More elaborate funerary monuments are to found in the hills around the town.

The most interesting way to approach *Ayatekla* is by the ancient pilgrims' road, which leads from the S of the town to the shrine. Partly cut through the rock, this road climbs gradually to the hill of c 1km *Meryemlik*.

The most striking feature at Meryemlik is the huge ruined apse of the *basilica* constructed by the Emperor Zeno the Isaurian c 476. The grotto where St. Thecla lived is a few metres to the N. If locked, the key may be obtained from the guardian, who lives in the nearby village. Recently excavated, the basilica had a central nave and side aisles. There were two small chapels, which had altars, on either side of the apse. On the W there was a narrow narthex and on the S a gallery. The walls were lined with marble, the floors were of mosaic and the building was covered with a wooden roof.

Scattered over the summit of the hill are the scant remains of many other constructions—churches, hostels, cisterns and monasteries.

St. Thecla was a friend and follower of St. Paul. Born in Iconium, the modern Konya, she was imprisoned and tortured for her faith. Taking refuge in Silifke, she built a grotto at Meryemlik. Because of the many cures attributed to her, Thecla's fame spread rapidly and contributed to the growth of Christianity in the area. Some accounts state that she lived to a ripe old age, others that she was slain by marauders. She was buried in the grotto. where she had lived and prayed.

Her life is recounted in the apocryphal 'Acts of Paul and Thecla', which was written in the 2C. Described as a member of a noble family, she is said to have broken off her engagement and, dressed as a youth, to have attached herself to St. Paul. Lions, sent to devour her in the arena, lay at her feet refusing to attack her and, when her torturers attempted to burn her to death, the fire could not be lit. St. Thecla's feast is celebrated on 23 September.

For the visitor with a few days to spare there are a number of sites in the surrounding countryside, which merit a visit. To the SW is the *Fortress of Meydancıkkale* not far from the town of *Gülnar*, a pleasant 75km drive from Silifke through a strangely-sculpted limestone landscape. The fortress of

Meydancık is located at the village of *Emir Hacı*, c 9km to the S of the town. French archaeologists working there since 1970 have discovered remains that span the period from the Hittites (second millennium BC) to the Byzantines. The earliest occupation of the fortress, which is sited on a hill linked to the plateau by a ridge, has been dated by a cartouche found there to the time of the Hittite king, Muwattalli (c 1300 BC). There are several stelae and orthostats, much eroded, from that time. The spoil-heap at the base of the cliff has been a fruitful source of artefacts from many periods. Near the road are the ruins of a *Persian palace*, which may have been occupied by a satrap appointed by the Great King as ruler of Cilicia. Reliefs and inscriptions in Aramaic suggest that this building dates from the Achaemenid period (6C BC). Awaiting the archaeologists' spade are the ruins of a Hellenistic city, which covers almost the whole surface of the plateau.

The Gülnar hoard, now in Silifke museum (see above), was discovered in a small palace to the S. This consists of more than 5000 coins of the Diadochi dating from the 3C and 4C BC.

The remains from the period of Byzantine occupation are numerous, but less interesting than those from earlier times.

A shorter excursion from Silifke is to the place where a plaque commemorates the death by drowning in the Göksu of Frederick Barbarossa. This is c 7km from the town, on the right-hand side of the road to Konya (see Rte 26).

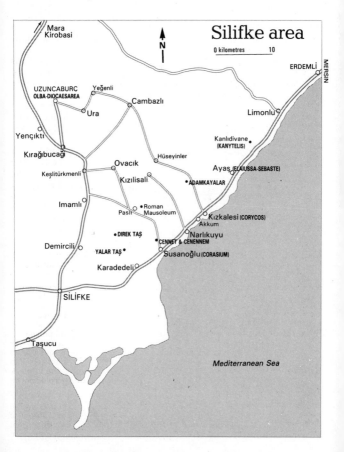

26 Silifke to Konya

Total distance c 252km. **Silifke**—R715 c 7km *Barbarossa
Memorial*—c 76km *Mut* (c 2km *Alahan*)—c 60km **Karaman**—
(c 12km *Canhasan*)—(c 38km *Binbir Kilise*)—(c 26km
Çatalhöyük)— c 109km **Konya**.

Road 715 from Silifke to Konya is one of the most interesting in
Turkey. Physically, it takes the traveller from the fertile plains of the
Mediterranean shore, by way of the high passes of the Taurus
Mountains, to the wide, featureless steppe of Central Anatolia.
Historically, it is a journey through ancient Karamania, that micro-
cosm of Turkish history. The Neolithic inhabitants of Canhasan and
Çatal Hüyük, the Byzantines, the Crusaders, the Karamanids, the
Selçuk and Ottoman Turks are only some of the many races whose
settlements and monuments are scattered across its landscape.
Karamania is a palimpsest from which the history of more than one
culture may be read.

The route, which starts under the high battlements of Silifke's
medieval castle (see above), follows at first the course of the Göksu
river. Then from the depths of a stony gorge it begins a steady climb
through the pine woods that clothe the S slopes of the Taurus range.

Approximately 7km from Silifke in a car-park on the right-hand
side of the road a simple plaque records (in Turkish) that on 10 June
1190, somewhere near this place, the Emperor Frederick Barbarossa
was drowned in the Saleph river (now the Göksu). At the age of 67
this redoubtable warrior, who had brought the German contingent to
the Third Crusade as far as the S shores of Turkey, was, according to
one account, thrown from his horse into the swift-flowing Saleph.
Weighed down by his armour, he perished miserably.

Frederick's followers were demoralised by his death. 'At this point
and at this sad news', one wrote, 'our pen is stilled, and our story
finished.' His body, pickled in a vat of vinegar, was taken to Antioch
where it was buried in the cathedral. The German knights carried a
few of his bones to the Holy Land, which he had sworn to liberate
and which he was destined never to see.

From the sheer cliffs and jagged peaks of the Göksu gorge, road
715 emerges at last into an upland valley, whose austere aspect
presages the arid steppes that lie beyond. At (76km) *Mut*, the ancient
CLAUDIOPOLIS, is the first sizeable town on this route. Here a coffee-
house, pleasantly shaded by a cluster of huge plane trees, provides
an excellent excuse to stop for refreshments. From one of its tables
the unhurried traveller may survey, under the amused and tolerant
gaze of its citizens, the leisurely daily life of the town.

Founded towards the middle of the 1C BC by the priest-ruler of
nearby Olba, Mut's principal monuments are two *türbe*, the 14C
Karamanid *Lal Ağa Camii* and a romantically decayed *fortress*
complete with ruined walls and imposing keep.

From Mut road 715 continues its spectacular course towards
Konya, its many curves taxing the concentration and skill of even the
most experienced drivers. A signpost on the right-hand side, near a
small coffee-house, at a point c 20km from Mut points up a rough
track to 2km *Alahan*. There, perched on a rocky shelf high over the
Göksu, are the ruins of an extremely interesting *Byzantine monastery*. This was first investigated in 1961 by Michael Gough, who was
at that time Director of the British Institute of Archaeology at Ankara.

The monastery had two churches. The first, the Church of the Evangelists, which dates from the end of the 5C, has suffered a considerable amount of damage. Originally this building had three naves separated by rows of Corinthian columns, but it was modified later. Note the fine carving over the main door. In addition to the symbols of the Four Evangelists, there are dramatic representations of the triumph of the angels Gabriel and Michael over two of the ancient pagan religions, Mithraism and the worship of Cybele.

Beyond the ruins of the *baptistery* is the so-called *East church*, which is in a better state of preservation. Dated to the beginning of the 6C, this was also constructed in basiclical form with three naves, one of which was extended by an apse. Note the fine sculptures adorning the doors leading from the narthex to the interior and the slender pillars, which supported the roof. The usual monastery buildings, refectory, kitchens, etc. and the monks' cells, which were cut out of the soft rock, are well preserved.

After Alahan the road, having reached its highest point at the Sertavul Pass (1610m), descends by stages into the great steppe that occupies the centre of Anatolia. In this wild and lonely land the only sign of life is provided by the occasional flock of sheep or goats. Each group of grazing animals is watched over by a patriarchal shepherd, a lonely hierarch in a tent-like cloak, whose acolytes, the fierce, vigilant guard-dogs circling the flocks, keep intruders at bay.

Karaman, at c 48km, is a pleasant green sanctuary, which offers some relief to the eye from the monotonous grey and brown hues of the steppe. This town, the ancient LARENDE, which was founded in the 4C BC, is sited a little way to the right of the main road. From the beginning its commanding position allowed it to control trade between the coast and the interior. Its modern name is derived from a Turcoman tribe, the Karamanids, who captured it from the Selçuks in the middle of the 13C. They founded an emirate, which dominated this part of Turkey—Karamania—for almost 250 years.

Most of Karaman's monuments date from the period of the emirate. One of the most interesting is the *Yunus Emre Camii*, which was constructed c 1349. Dedicated to the famous peasant poet, Yunus Emre, it claims to contain his remains. In the area around the *fortress*, which was built in the 12C by the Selçuks and restored by the Karamanids c 1356, there are a number of mosques and tombs and religious buidings. Visitors not pressed for time may like to visit the *Ak Tekke* which housed a community of Mevlevi dervishes from the time of its completion towards the end of the 14C until the order was abolished in 1925. Note the simple cells where the dervishes lived a life of prayer and contemplation. In the precints of the tekke there are the tombs of several of the early members of the sect.

Karaman has a small *museum* housed in a new building to the S of the Hatuniye Medrese. This contains a selection of finds from the town and sites in the surrounding countryside, in particular from Canhasan. They include objects from the prehistoric, Roman, Byzantine, Selçuk and Karamanid periods. There is also an interesting ethnographic collection.

About 13km to the NE of Karaman is the Chalcolithic site of CANHASAN. Excavations, which took place there between 1961 and 1970, have revealed traces of occupation dating from the end of the sixth millennium BC.

A strong resemblance has been noted between some of the pottery from Canhasan and that found in certain layers of Yümüktepe near Mersin. Both bear distinctive reddish brown geometric patterns. As Canhasan was sited near the route which linked Central Anatolia with the Mediterranean, at the plain of Çukurova, some archaeologists are of the opinion that the pottery found there may have been imported from Yümüktepe.

Apart from the thick mud-brick walls of the rectangular or square houses, which stand to a height of c 3m in places, little remains to be seen at the site. Most of the objects found there are now displayed in the Museum of Anatolian

Civilisations in Ankara and in Karaman's museum. In addition to bulbous polychrome and monotone pots these include stone and clay figures of the Anatolian Mother Goddess, a necklace of stone beads and sea shells, millstones, and some fragmentary wall-paintings.

A more difficult EXCURSION from Karaman is to *Binbir Kilise*, i.e. the Thousand and One Churches, an important monastic site on the lower slopes of Kara Dağ. First go to the hamlet of Maden Şehir, c 38km to the N of Karaman. This may be reached by way of 18km Kılbasan and c 10km Dınek. From the latter village a very rough track leads to the remote valley where the churches are located.

The earliest traces of occupation of the site, which was first examined by Gertrude Bell and Sir William Ramsey in 1905, have been dated to the 4C BC. A small, unfortified settlement, established in a valley at the foot of a steep hill during the Hellenistic and Roman periods, it was abandoned by most of its inhabitants towards the end of the 7C AD, when bands of marauding Arabs swept over S Anatolia. In the middle of the 9C, after the power of the Arabs had been curbed, the settlement was reoccupied and a feverish bout of church building commenced. Most of the churches and monastic foundations in the valley were erected during the next 200 years. Visitors who wish to make a complete tour of all the extant buildings are advised to obtain the services of a guide.

On returning to road 715 continue for c 60km to a turning on the right, which leads to 13km Çumra. The road to c 15km **ÇATALHÖYÜK** may be reached by crossing the railway line, which skirts the NE side of the village.

Çatalhöyük is undoubtedly the most important Neolithic site in Turkey. Discovered by James Mellaart in 1958, excavations were conducted there between 1961 and 1963 and again in 1965. The settlement, which is 900m above sea-level, consisted of a double-mound measuring 275m by 450m and 17m high. No less than ten successive levels of occupation were found at Çatalhöyük. Objects from the lowest levels have been dated to 6500 BC.

The archaeologists were intrigued to discover at the site signs of the first steps towards a planned urban development. The settlement's mud-brick dwellings were built in carefully laid-out blocks. Most of the houses had two rooms and large, airy, well-lit inner courts. Entrance was by ladders through openings in the roof. The inner walls of the rooms were plastered and elaborately decorated with scenes of hunting and religious ceremonies. In a lighter vein the depiction of musicians, dancing girls and acrobats gives some indication of the amusements favoured by the site's Neolithic inhabitants.

Some of the paintings show the bodies of the dead being torn by vultures. It is thought that the bones were collected, covered with a straw mat and buried under the seats which were placed against the walls of the houses. Remains discovered by the archaeologists were in the Hocker position (like a foetus in the womb). Grave goods include wooden cups, stone hatchets and straw baskets.

The presence of many moulded bulls' heads attests to the antiquity of this symbol, which appears repeatedly in Anatolia. Stone and terracotta statuettes of a grotesquely gravid Mother Goddess were found in quantity. Sometimes she appears alone, sometimes in the company of other female deities or she is attended by sacred animals. Weapons included stone maces, clubs, and clay balls to be used in slings. Tools, seeds and animal bones from deer, boar, sheep and goats and extinct wild cattle provide valuable information about the food and agricultural practices of the people who lived there.

As in the case of Canhasan little remains to be seen at the site of

Çatalhöyük. The objects found there are preserved and displayed in the Museum of Anatolian Civilisations at Ankara.

From the junction with the road to Çumra it is an unremarkable 60km journey to **KONYA** (438, 859 inhab.) Road 715 continues in a straight line across the steppe in the S suburbs of the city and enters Konya by the long sweep of Karaman Cad.

Ibn Battuta (1304–69), the celebrated Arab geographer and traveller visited Konya c 1333. In the book describing his journeys in Anatolia he wrote: 'It is a large town with fine buildings and has many streams and fruit-gardens. The streets are exceedingly broad, and the bazaars admirably planned, with each craft in a bazaar of its own. It is said that this city was built by Alexander.'

Today Konya is a bustling, noisy town, filled with chaotic, unruly traffic, a place where buses and lorries compete for space—not always successfully—with carts drawn by lively, high-stepping horses. However, there are still reminders of that green oasis which so delighted earlier visitors. Its fine Selçuk buildings continue to refresh the eye and revive the spirit of travellers wearied by the long hours which they have spent crossing the great Anatolian plain.

Unfortunately, industrial development has encircled Konya with a belt of hideous buildings. The grey concrete factories lining the great boulevards which carry traffic to the centre are a poor introduction to a town of such historic importance. However, the reflective traveller might see that this juxtaposition of beauty and ugliness is in character, as Konya is a place of extremes, of violent contrasts. In summer the temperature sometimes rises as high as 38° C and the sun is blotted out for days by violent duststorms; while during the winter icy winds bring deep falls of snow from the steppes.

Undoubtedly, Konya's greatest attraction is its association with the mystic Jalal ad-Din ar-Rumi, better known as Mevlana. Throughout the year, but especially between 9 and 17 December when the Festival of the Dancing Dervishes is held, pilgrims in their thousands flock to Konya to visit the Mevlana Tekke, where the sage is buried, and to witness performances of the Sema.

There are several hotels in Konya which are registered with the Ministry of Culture and Tourism. However, accommodation in the town is limited and is often difficult to obtain. Reservations should be made well in advance, especially during the period of the Dervish festival. Full information about accommodation may be obtained from the *Tourism Information Office* at Mevlana Cad. 21. Tickets for the Mevlana Festival are sold at the Municipal Information Office, which is located on the other side of the boulevard.

Konya has always been an important centre of communications and there are frequent bus services to Ankara, İstanbul, İzmir, to the cities on the Mediterranean coast, and to E Turkey. The non-stop luxury bus services to Ankara are highly recommended. Konya is also on the Turkish Railways network. There is a morning train to İstanbul, which has first class coaches and a dining car. There is no direct train service to Ankara. Konya has no airport.

History. Ibn Battuta was misinformed (see above). Long before the time of Alexander there were people living on the site of Alaeddin Parkı, which is in the centre of the modern town. A limited excavation conducted there has revealed traces of occupation from the Chalcolithic period (third millennium BC). Later the settlement came under the control of the Hittites. From them it passed to the Phrygians who believed that it was the first place to be settled after the great flood. According to the Greeks the city obtained its name, EIKONION (Latin, *Iconium*), from an icon or image of Perseus holding the Gorgon's head, which stood before the main gate.

The Phrygians were followed by the Lydians and the Persians. After Alexander broke the power of Darius at the battles of Granicus and Issus, Iconium

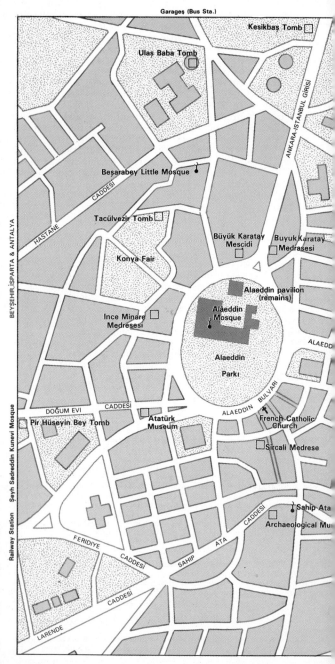

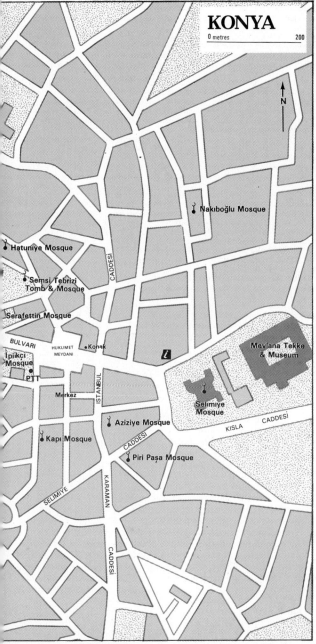

KONYA

0 metres — 200

N

Nakıboğlu Mosque

Hatuniye Mosque

Şemsi Tebrizi
Tomb & Mosque

Şerafettin Mosque

BULVARI

HUKUMET
MEYDANI

Konak

İplikçi
Mosque

PTT

Merkez

CADDESİ

İSTANBUL

Mevlana Tekke
& Museum

Selimiye
Mosque

KIŞLA   CADDESİ

Aziziye Mosque

Kapı Mosque

CADDESİ

Piri Paşa Mosque

SELİMİYE

KARAMAN

CADDESİ

MERSİN & KARAMAN

and the surrounding territory was absorbed in his empire. Following the death of Alexander it fell into the hands of Lysimachus, one of his ablest generals. Subsequently, possession of the city was disputed by the Seleucids and the Attalids of Pergamum. When Attalus III died in 133 BC, he bequeathed his kingdom, which included Iconium, to Rome. The city appears to have prospered under the rule of its new masters. During the Imperial period, perhaps in an attempt to curry favour, it changed its name twice—first, in AD 41, to Claudiconium in honour of Claudius and later to Colonia Aelia Hadriana Augusta Iconiensium as a compliment to Hadrian.

According to the Acts of the Apostles, Iconium was visited by St. Paul and St. Barnabas. They preached in the synagogue and their message attracted the attention of many Jews and gentiles. However, some dissident Jews spoke against them and the city was divided about the new faith. When Paul and his companions heard that their adversaries were plotting to stone them, they fled to Lystra and Derbe for safety.

The apocryphal 'Acts of Paul and Thecla' contains some additional information about the apostle's stay in Iconium. A catechumen named Thecla, who lived in that city, pestered him to baptise her. For some reason this request caused an outcry and they were brought before the tribunal. Paul was condemned to be beaten and exiled from the city and it was ordered that Thecla suffer death by burning. However, an opportune shower put out the fire and saved her life. Nothing daunted by this narrow escape from death, Thecla dressed herself as a boy and followed Paul to Antioch. There she came to the attention of the authorities once more and was sentenced, this time to be thrown to the lions. She managed to escape from this punishment also and, perhaps, having learned her lesson at last, withdrew to Seleucia (Silifke). There she lived out the remainder of her days in a convent, which she had founded. (See above.) It has been suggested that Thecla's persistence, which caused Paul so much trouble, may have been the cause of the apostle's alleged anti-feminist bias.

During the Byzantine period Iconium was an episcopal see. Like most of south and central Anatolia the city suffered badly from Arab raids during the period from the 7C to the 9C. First attacked by the Selçuks in 1069, the city was taken by them a century later. As the capital of the Sultanate of Rum it enjoyed a period of great prosperity under Selçuk rule and was enriched by the erection of many splendid buildings. Apart from two brief periods when it came under the control of the Crusaders—Barbarossa stopped briefly in 1190—it remained in Selçuk hands until their defeat by the Mongols at the battle of Kösedağ in 1242. From the Mongols it passed to the Karamanid dynasty. They were the rulers of the city when Ibn Battuta visited it c 1333. Konya was captured by Mehmet II in 1467 and from that time onward it formed part of the Ottoman Empire.

A tour of Konya requires a full day. The best starting-point is in the centre of the town at Alaeddin Parki. On the NE side of the park, is **Alaeddin Camii**, the biggest of the town's Selçuk mosques. This is a complicated, rambling structure, which was begun c 1150 and completed 70 years later. The entrance on the E side leads to a large rectangular prayer hall, which was built by Sultan Alaeddin Key-kubad I (1219–36). It has a flat timbered roof, which is supported by 42 antique columns crowned with Roman and Byzantine capitals. The domed area beyond the hall was started by Mesud I (1116–56) and completed by his son Kiliç Arslan II (1156–88). Note the beau-tifully-carved ebony mimber (c 1155), regarded by many experts as one of the finest examples of Selçuk art. To the W is a hall divided into four irregularly-shaped aisles. This is believed to have been completed during the reign of Keykavus I (1210–19). To the N is an octagonal türbe built by Alaeddin Keykubad. The decagonal türbe beside it contains the tomb of its builder, Kiliç Arslan II. It also holds the remains of seven other sultans, including those of Keyhusrev III (1264–83), the last Selçuk ruler of the Sultanate of Rum.

A tower forming part of the defensive wall, which surrounded the area now occupied by the park, may be seen to the N of the mosque. This, the so-called *Alaeddin Köşkü* (kiosk), was used as a royal residence during the reign of the last years of Selçuk rule. It is protected from the elements by a modern concrete roof.

On leaving the park, cross the road to the **Büyük Karatay Medresesi**, which is named after its founder, Celaleddin Karatay. This remarkable ruler of Greek origin, having occupied high office under two sultans, was appointed regent at a time when the stability and very existence of the sultanate was threatened by the Mongol invaders. The medrese, which was completed c 1251, was repaired in 1955 and now houses a magnificent collection of tiles. Particularly rich in specimens of the fine glazed faience, which was used to decorate the interiors of buildings during the Selçuk era, its range covers all periods from the 13C to the 18C. Note particularly the wall-tiles from a palace built by Alaeddin Keykubad I on the W shore of Beyşehir Lake at Kubab-abab (now Hoyran). These have representations of people and animals on brilliantly-coloured glazed stars, octagons, squares, crosses and tiles of many other shapes.

The İnce Minare Medresesi, completed c 1267, Konya.

The doorway of the medrese is ornamented with intricately carved designs and inlays of blue and white marble. Above the entrance is an inscription in Cufic script of some of the sayings of the Prophet. The dome of the principal chamber is covered with a pattern of blue and gold tiles, which represents a firmament resplendent with the sun and stars. Below the dome is an inscription in Cufic of a verse from the Koran. On the pendentives are written, also in Cufic, the names of Abu-Bekr, Omar, Othman and Ali, the first four caliphs of Islam. The türbe of Celaleddin Karatay opens off the central chamber.

The constitution of the medrese required that the students be selected from one of the four Sünni divisions of Islam and that the scholar and his assistant be from the Hanefi division. Another rule stated that study should be held every day except Tuesday and Friday.

On the W side of the park is the *İnce Minare Medresesi*, the Medrese of the Slender Minaret. The minaret, which is covered with an elaborate design of blue and red tiles, was badly damaged by lightning in 1901 and is less than half its original height. With its adjoining mosque (now in ruins) it was the gift of one of the most prolific builders of his day, the Emir Sahip Ata Fahrettin Ali. It was completed c 1267 to the design of an architect named Keluk, son of Abdullah. Repaired in 1956, the medrese has been reopened as a museum of stone and wood carving.

A highly decorated entrance leads to a court containing inscriptions and gravestones of the Selçuk and Karamanid periods from the Konya region. In the principal room there are a number of splendid reliefs from the castle built by Alaeddin Keykubad I in 1221. These include representations of lions, an elephant, fish, a rhinoceros, human beings and mythical beasts including dragons, a two-headed eagle, and a harpy. In addition to windows and doors from the Selçuk period there are many finely-carved examples of Ottoman furniture.

On the S side of the park take the Ressam Sami Sokağı to the *Sirçalı Medrese*. This, the so-called Glazed Medrese, was founded by Badr al-Din Muslih in 1242. Rescued from its semi-ruinous condition it was reopened in 1960 as a museum of tombstones from the Selçuk, Karamanid and Ottoman periods. In an alley nearby is an interesting example of Karamanid architecture, the *Hasbey Darülhafızı*, which dates from 1421. Here students were taught to memorise the Koran.

Further along Ressam Sami Sokağı is the *Sahip Ata foundation*. The gift of Sahip Ata Fahrettin Ali, who founded the İnce Minare Medresesi, this contains a mescit (small mosque), a türbe, a hanikah (oratory) and a hamam. Completed in 1258, it was also the work of the architect Keluk, son of Abdullah. The türbe, which is decorated with mosaic tiles, contains the sarcopahgi of the founder, his daughter, sons, and grandsons. A passage from the hanikah leads to a vaulted burial chamber under the türbe.

Nearby is Konya's **Archaeological Museum**. Opened in 1962, this contains a rich collection of objects from the Prehistoric era to the end of the Byzantine period. All were found in Konya or in the surrounding countryside. They are displayed in the courtyard, garden and in a number of pavilions. In the garden and first pavilion are statues, grave stelae, sarcophagi, inscriptions, altars and architectural fragments from the Classical to the Byzantine eras. In most cases the provenance of the exhibits is not known.

The second pavilion contains the museum's greatest treasure, a 3C AD sarcophagus in the Sidamara style, which was found in 1958 near the village of Yunuslar (Tiberiapolis). Finely-carved friezes on the sides portray the twelve labours of Hercules. The hero is shown fighting the Nemean lion, killing the Hydra of Lerna, capturing the Erymanthian boar, killing the Cerynitian Hind, removing the Stymphalian birds, obtaining the Amazon's girdle, cleansing the Augean stables, capturing the Cretan bull, seizing the mares of Diomedes, fighting the brigand Geryon, bringing Cerberus from Hades, and stealing the Golden Apples of the Hesperides. On one of the short sides of the sarcophagus there is a representation of the deceased. Other exhibits from ancient Isauria and Lycaonia in this pavilion include incriptions, statues, and a large collection of objects in bronze and marble.

The Selimye Mosque, 16C, Konya.

The third pavilion is devoted to exhibits from the Prehistoric, Hittite and Phrygian periods. These include pottery, stone and metal objects, seals, jewellery, and statuettes and come mainly from Canhasan and Çatalhöyük.

On returning to the park take the third street on the right, Alaeddin Bulv. Just before the Post Office at Hükümet Meyd. is the İplikçi Camii, a much restored mosque, which dates from the 12C. To the left of its attractively-carved mihrab there are some traces of a 13C mosaic.

The large mosque on the other side of the square is the Şerafettin Camii, which also has received much attention from restorers. Just before Mevlana Cad. a warren of small streets on the right leads to Konya's bazaar. At the W extremity of the bazaar is the Azizye Camii, notable for the extravagant, almost rococo, style of its architecture and decoration.

At the end of Mevlana Bulv., in front of Mevlana Tekke, is the large Selimiye Camii. This Ottoman mosque is believed to date from the reign of Selim II the Sot (1566–74).

The **Mevlana Tekke** is, without a doubt, the most important monument in Konya. It contains the tombs of the mystic philosopher and theologian, Mevlana Celaleddın-i-Rumi and of his father Bahaeddin Veled. Perhaps the most important Islamic shrine in Turkey, it brings thousands of devout pilgrims to Konya each year.

Mevlana was born in Balkh (Bakhtri in Persian, the capital of ancient Bactria) in Afghanistan c 1207. His father, Bahaeddin Veled, was a distinguished teacher who, because of his great learning, had been honoured with the title of Sültan, ül-Ulema, Lord of Scholars.

Balkh has been exposed to many different cultural and religious influences. Before the advent of Islam, the Zoroastrian Magi, the Hellenistic philosophers of the Seleucids, Christian missionaries and Buddhist sages had all left their mark on the city. It has been suggested that this heady mixture of beliefs may have produced an atmosphere of speculation and enquiry in Balkh. If so, it may explain Mevlana's spiritual and intellectual development.

Many legends and stories are told about the young Mevlana. One day, while playing with other children, he disappeared into the sky. When he returned 'greatly altered in complexion' he talked about a 'legion of beings clothed in green mantles', who had shown him many strange and mysterious things of a celestial nature.

Possibly because of the threat offered by the approaching Mongol armies, Bahaeddin decided to take his family away from Balkh. They went first to Nishapur, then to Baghdad, Kufa, Mecca, Medina, Jerusalem, Damascus and Aleppo. After spending some time there Bahaeddin felt drawn to Anatolia. His little caravan journeyed to Malatya, Erzincan, Sivas, Kayseri, Niğde and finally to Karaman in 1221. There they stayed for seven years and there Mevlana was married in 1225.

Alaeddin Keykubad, the ruler of Konya, learning that the famous teacher Bahaeddin Veled from Balkh was in Karaman, implored him to come to Konya. Bahaeddin finally acceded to the sultan's request in 1228 and he taught in Konya until his death in 1231. Mevlana took his father's place and quickly established a reputation for scholarship. His speciality was canonical jurisprudence, but he had an extensive knowledge of all branches of philosophy and was well-read in the works of the Greek classical authors.

An event of great importance occurred in November 1244. Riding his donkey home from the medrese in the company of a group of admiring students Mevlana was accosted by a ragged dervish who proceeded to ask him a number of searching questions. This was the man known as Shams Tabrizi in Persian (Sun of Tabriz) or Şems in Turkish. Şems and Mevlana quickly became close friends and spent days and weeks closeted together in philosophical discussion. Mevlana abandoned his teaching and appeared rarely in public. This caused jealousy and anger among his students and friends who began to put it about that he had been bewitched by an evil sorcerer. Perhaps in response to this pressure, in February 1246 Şems disappeared as suddenly and as mysteriously as he had appeared.

Mevlana was heartbroken at the loss of his friend. When he discovered after making many enquiries that Şems was in Damascus, he begged him to return to Konya. Şems did so eventually and the two men resumed their friendship and their discussions. To draw him more into his family, Mevalana gave his adopted daughter, Kimya Hatun, to Şems in marriage. However, before long fresh plots were hatched against Şems and this time Mevlana's younger son, Alaeddin Çelebi, was induced to join the conspirators. One dark night in December 1247 Şems disappeared and was never seen again. It is probable that he was murdered by his enemies. Mevlana could not be comforted. He tried to come to terms with his grief by writing poetry about Şems. 'Oh my soul's essence, how did you hide yourself from me?' Hoping that Şems had returned to Damascus, Mevlana searched for him there, but the two sages were destined never to meet again.

With the help of other companions Mevlana continued his philosophical speculations. The Sufic seed planted by Şems germinated and flourished with their help and encouragement. One of his friends, Çelebi Hüsamettin, inspired Mevlana to write his greatest work, the 'Mesnevi'. This collection of more than 25,000 poems fills six volumes. As an exposition of his philosophy it had a great effect on his followers. It was studied in schools, which were established specially for that purpose.

By 1273 it became evident that Mevlana's health was beginning to fail. In December of that year a great cold settled on Konya and he began to sink rapidly. To his weeping friends and followers Mevlana spoke constantly of the longing which he felt for his forthcoming union with God. He called his approaching death 'şeb-i-arus', the night of union.

Mevlana died on 17 December 1273. He was held in such esteem that members of all races and creeds mourned his passing. Jews, Christians and pagans were with their Islamic brothers in his funeral procession, which took a whole day to pass through Konya. Mevlana was buried near his father and a türbe was erected to shelter their sarcophagi.

The followers of the mystic philosopher decided to continue to study his teaching and they appointed Çelebi Hüsamettin as his successor. When he died, Mevlana's son, Sultan Veled, became head of the order. It was Veled who was mainly responsible for formulating and popularising his father's teachings. Soon other tekkes were established, first in various parts of Anatolia then in countries as far away as Egypt. In time the Mehlevi order acquired royal recognition, so that when a new sultan came to the throne, he received the sword of state from the Çelebi Efendi, the head of the Mehlevis.

In 1925, when the Islamic mystic orders were abolished by the Government of the Turkish Republic, the Mehlevi order lost possession of its convents and its numbers declined. However, in recent years public performances of the sema have recommenced. The best known and most widely attended are those held in Konya in December each year, on the anniversary of Mevlana's death.

After the supression of the Mehlevi order the Mevlana Tekke was converted into a museum. Originally the site was occupied by a garden, which was given to Mevlana's father as a gift by Alaeddin Keykubad I. Bahaeddin Veled was buried there and later Mevlana was laid to rest by his side. At first a simple türbe housed the two sarcophagi. In 1397 the striking cylindrical spire, divided into 16 sections, was constructed by Emir Alaeddin Ali. This was covered with turquoise-coloured tiles which have been replaced from time to time.

In front of the türbe there is a spacious courtyard with a şadirvan in the centre. On the left-hand side are rooms built by Murat III in 1584 to house the dervishes. A number of these have been refurbished to show them as they were, when occupied by members of the community. In others a collection of Selçuk, Karamanid and Ottoman fabrics and carpets is displayed. On the S side of the courtyard are the kitchens, where food for the dervishes and their guests was prepared. The fountain to the right of the entrance was known as Şebi Arus, the Night of Union, in memory of Mevlana's death. Each year on 17 December, after the members of the tekke had eaten their evening meal, they performed the sema around this pool. The four türbe at the extreme right date from the 16C and contain the sarcophagi of various Karamanid and Ottoman high officials of state.

Over the door to the mausoleum the following is written in Persian:

'This station is the Mecca of all dervishes.
What is lacking in them is here completed
Whoever came here unfulfilled was here made whole.'

An ante-room was used by the dervishes to read passages from the Koran. It now contains examples of the work of some well-known Ottoman calligraphers. These include Mustafa Rakım, Izzet, Mahmud Celaleddin and Hamid. A door of walnut covered with silver plaques, which was presented to the tekke by Hasan Paşa in 1559 leads to the main chamber of the tekke, the Huzuri-i Pir, the Presence of the Saint. The tomb of Mevlana and of his son, Sultan Veled, are under the green dome. They are covered with richly-embroidered tapestry presented by Sultan Abdulhamid II in 1894. The silver lattice-work grill surrounding Mevlana's tomb was given to the tekke by Mahmud Paşa, Governor of Maraş in 1597. The plaque fixed to it is inscribed with a poem in Turkish by the celebrated poet Mani. Below the grill is the silver threshold, where the dervishes made their obeisances to their founder. On the W side are the tombs of Mevlana's wife and children and some of his descendants. On a dais are six tombs arranged in two rows of three. Here were laid to rest the Horasan Erler, the Horosan Men, dervishes from Balkh, who came with Bahaeddin Veled and his family to Konya.

This area contains some early manuscripts of the Mesnevi, the Divan by Sultan Veled and other early writings. The famous April Cup, a beautiful bronze bowl, decorated with damascene figures and ornamented in gold and silver, is also kept here. This was given by the Mongol Sultan Ebu Said Bahadir Han to the tekke in 1333. The bowl was used to collect the spring rain, which was believed to have curative properties. Prayers were said over it, the tip of Mevlana's turban was placed in it, and then it was offered to pilgrims.

On the N of the tekke are two large domed chambers. One of these, which served as a mescit (small mosque), now contains a collection of beautifully-illuminated Korans. Note especially a tiny version of the sacred book, which is decorated with exquisitely-executed miniature ornamentation. In the area between the mescit and the semahane there are two carved walnut lecterns from the Selçuk period.

The other chamber was the semahane, the room where the dervishes performed the sema. Dating from the reign of Süleyman the Magnificent (1520–66), this now houses a selection of the instruments used to accompany the dance—the ney (reed flute), rebab (a stringed instrument similar to a violin), tef (hand drum) and tambur (lute). Some of Mevlana's garments are also preserved here.

The dervishes no longer dance in the semahane. The sema is now held in the gymnasium of a high-school in another part of Konya. Presented as an exhibition of folklore, for many of those who attend it is nothing more. However there are others for whom it continues to be a moving religious experience. The dervishes, who take part in the sema today, live in the world, they are bus mechanics or teachers or schoolboys. They are no longer obliged to submit to the extended novitiate and strict discipline, which existed in the past. Yet, when they dance, the air becomes charged with a feeling of great spirituality and the spectators forget the bleak setting in which the sema is being held and are no longer conscious of the icy temperature and discomfort of the unheated arena.

At the sema the dervish wears a white jacket over a long white skirt (tennure), which represents his burial garment. These are covered by a voluminous black cloak (khirka), which represents his tomb. On his head is a conical brown felt hat (sikke), representing his tombstone. Around his waist is a long girdle of cloth and on his feet are high slippers of soft, pliable leather. The sheik's costume differs only from that of the dervishes in that his sikke is encircled by a black band.

The ceremony begins with a prayer and a sura from the Koran. This is followed by a plaintive melody on the ney. Before beginning their dance, the dervishes bow to the sheik and kiss his hand. Then, letting fall their black cloaks to symbolise their escape from the tomb and their readiness to dance for God, they begin to turn slowly. Each dervish raises his right arm above his head with the palm facing upwards, while turning his left hand downwards. This indicates his willingness to receive God's grace and blessing and to pass it on to the world.

Then, as the dancers begin to move faster and faster and their garments billow outwards, it seems that the hall is full of large white flowers opening in the sunlight. Mevlana believed that the sema enabled his followers to reach out and touch the Infinite. He did not restrict his teaching to the dervishes. The way of enlightenment was open to everyone. He wrote:

'Come, come again, and again ...
Come, be you unbeliever, idolator or fire
worshipper ...
Our hearth is not the threshold of despair
Even if you have broken your vow of
repentance a hundred times
Come again.'

27 Silifke to Uzuncaburç

Total distance c 32km. **Silifke**—7km *Demircili / Imbrigon*—c 25km **Uzuncaburç**—(4km *Ura*).

One of the most interesting excursions from **Silifke** (see Rte 25) is to the archaeological sites at Demircili, Uzuncaburç—the ancient city of Olba/Diocaesarea— and Ura, three villages high up in the foot-hills of the Taurus Mountains. Allow a full day for this visit. There are no restaurants in the villages, but there are plenty of pleasant picnic places en route. You may be invited to eat with one of the village families or with the Yürük people (Turcoman nomads), who are renowned for their hospitality and for the welcome they extend to strangers.

Visitors without their own transport can get to Uzuncaburç and the other villages by dolmuş. They leave—usually early in the morning—from Atatürk Square, near the bridge over the Göksu. There is also a bus at about midday from the same place, which returns to Silifke the next day. As a rule, it is possible to find overnight accommodation in the villages, an arrrangement which will suit visitors wishing to make a leisurely examination of the sites.

From the N bank of the Göksu take the Mara (Kırobası) road, which is well-surfaced, if rather narrow. This climbs steadily, affording fine views over the town and surrounding countryside. Soon it enters a forest of pine and laurel and continues upwards through a series of sharp bends to 7km *Demircili*.

This modern village, built over the ancient settlement of IMBRIOGON, has six well-preserved Roman mausolea. A short distance from the village school, on the right-hand side of the road, is the *Lower Mausoleum* (5.3m by 4.25m by 6.25m). The two central columns and the architrave have fallen to the ground. Two columns attached to the side walls are crowned with Corinthian capitals. Beyond the columns is the empty burial-chamber. On the wall at the back is a console which may have supported a statue of the deceased. The mausoleum's pediment has a circular relief, much eroded. There are a several graves, carved from the rock, in front of the building.

Directly across the road are further remains of the ancient settlement. A 5m-long column, which has fallen to the ground, is flanked by the Corinthian capital which once surmounted it. W of the column there are two empty sarcophagi on a stone base. Nearby lie the lids, where they were left by the tomb-robbers. To the NE are the ruins of the *Three Storey Mausoleum*, whose W wall still stands. A door on the S led to a dark underground chamber and another on the W to the upper storey.

About 500m to the N there is an interesting pair of *mausolea*. The building on the left measures 5m by 6m by 6m. Supported in the front by stone blocks, its handsome Corinthian columns lead the eye upwards to a frieze, decorated with a pattern of acanthus leaves and a cornice ornamented with geometric designs.

The building on the right, which has two storeys, is 4m by 4m by 7.5m. It is the only mausoleum in Demircili where sarcophagi were found. The lower chamber, which is carved from the rock, is fronted by four Ionic columns 2.3m high. The entrance to the chamber on the right-hand side is blocked with fallen masonry. The upper floor has four fluted columns in the Corinthian style which support a pediment decorated with a damaged relief. Inside were three sarcophagi, 1m by 2m by 1m, arranged along the side walls. The lid of the sarcophagus on the left is decorated with a lion couchant carved in high relief. The sarcophagus in the centre has an inscription picked out in red and a male head flanked by two female figures on the front and two lions facing each other on the lid. The sarcophagus on the right has been destroyed. Only the base and a few fragments of the lid remain. In view of the size of the sarcophagi, they must have been placed in the burial chamber before the tomb was completed. Two consoles, which may have supported busts of the deceased, are fixed to the side walls.

The *Upper Mausoleum* of Demircili, located on the right-hand side of the road near the outskirts of the village, measures 4.5m by 4m by 7.5m and has two storeys. The lower storey is carved from the rock and is fronted by four Ionic columns c 2.6m high. The entrance to the empty burial chamber is c 1m behind the columns. Behind four Corinthian columns an arched entrance 2.75m high provided access to the upper burial chamber, also empty. Fragments of the pediment, which has been completely destroyed, lie on the ground in front of the tomb.

The sixth *mausoleum*, which betrays some orientalising influences, is some distance to the E of the village. Apart from damage to the SW corner and S face, it is in a good state of preservation. Measuring 4m by 4m by 8.5m, it has a pyramid-shaped roof which was probably surmounted by a statue of the deceased. There is no trace of a burial inside.

On leaving Demircili, continue for c 21km to Kırağıbucağı, where (4km) **Uzuncaburç**, the site of OLBA/DIOCAESAREA, is signposted to the right.

If you require accommodation in Uzuncaburç, it is advisable to seek assistance from the Bekçi at the site, from one of the teachers at the school or from the proprietor of the village coffee-house. You might also try the small pension, *Burç Pansiyon*, near the temple of Tyche. In addition to tea and coffee the village Kahve offers soft drinks and some of the specialities of the region: *kenger kahvesi* (coffee made from the fruit of the acanthus) and *pekmez* (boiled, concentrated grape juice).

Uzuncaburç is well-known for the excellent quality of its handicrafts, especially rugs (*çul*), saddle-bags, *meşe külü* (soap made from oak ash) and needlework. A large village of 3000 inhabitants, it has primary and secondary schools, a health-centre and a detachment of gendarmerie. Surrounded by rich pastures, where the yürük people graze their herds during the summer, it is an important farming and agricultural centre.

Although the people of Uzuncaburç are accustomed to receiving visitors in their village, they have not been tainted by mass-tourism. Strangers will be welcomed with the traditional hospitality and kindness found in villages all over Turkey.

Uzuncaburç
(Olba/Diocaesarea)

Far from the debilitating heat and the crowded resorts on the coast, Uzuncaburç is an exhilarating place to visit in the summer. In the clear mountain air, more than 1000m above sea-level, one explores with zest the ruins of Olba/Diocaesarea, arguably one of the most interesting ancient cities in Cilicia.

History. After the death of Alexander the Great in 323 BC, control of Rugged Cilicia was disputed by the Seleucid dynasty of Syria and the Ptolemies of Egypt. By 300 BC Seleucus I Nicator (321–280 BC) appears to have consolidated his hold on the area. At about that time he founded the city of Seleucia ad Calycadnum (Silifke) and built the temple of Zeus at Olba. According to Strabo, Olba is derived from the Greek word ὄλβος (happy), perhaps a reference to the disposition and temperament of its citizens.

At the end of the 3C and beginning of the 2C BC Olba was governed by a dynasty of priest-kings, the Teukrides. It is not known when or under what circumstances this dynasty was established, but it appears to have had more than a local importance. The discovery of a dedicatory inscription to Zeus Olbios on a fortified Hellenistic tower at Elaeusa/Sebaste suggests that the rule of the Teukrides extended at one time as far as the coast. They suffered a period of temporary eclipse between 150 BC and 50 BC, possibly as the result of a revolt or an invasion, but had recovered power by AD 17. Apparently they were not regarded as posing a threat to Roman authority as they continued to rule the area when Cilicia came under the control of the Romans in the early part of the 1C. Olba changed its name during the reign of Vespasian (AD 69–79) to Diocaesarea and was so known from then onwards. During the Byzantine period its temples were preserved by being turned into churches. Later Olba/ Diocaesarea entered a period of decline from which it never recovered. For centuries it remained an obscure, almost forgotten village in the foothills of the Taurus Mountains.

Interest in Olba/Diocaesarea was revived by the publication of Victor Langlois' 'Voyage dans la Cilicie et dans les montagnes du Taurus' in 1861. In 1890 the area was visited by an English scholar, Thomas Bent, and later by the Austrians, Rudolf, Heberdey and Wilhelm. Important research by Herzfeld at the beginning of this century is contained in 'Monumenta Asiae Minoris Antiqua'. In 1925 Keil and Wilhelm of the American Society for Archaeological Research in Asia Minor examined the ruins of the city and published their findings.

Apart from a striking Hellenistic pyramid-roofed tomb on the S approaches of Uzuncaburç, the ruins of Olba/Diocaesarea are contained in a fairly compact area near the modern village. The *tomb*, which crowns a hill c 1200m above sea-level, measures 5m by 5m by 16m. Constructed from stone blocks without mortar, it has a plain architrave 10m from the ground. This is surmounted by a frieze bearing metopes and triglyphs in the Doric style. The pyramid-shaped roof supported a platform on which a statue of the deceased was placed. Entrance to the burial chamber was by way of a cleverly concealed door, which, unfortunately, was discovered at some period by tomb-robbers. There is no sarcophagus. Inhumation took place under the stone floor. For safety reasons entrance to the tomb is forbidden.

To the S of the modern village-centre was a colonnaded street which continued the line of the ancient paved road linking Corycus (now Kizkalesi), Ura and Olba with Seleucia. Five limestone columns, crowned by Corinthian capitals, of a Roman *monumental arch* which spanned this street, remain in place. Half-way up the columns, which are 6.75m tall and 1m in diameter, there are consoles on which statues were placed. This unfortunate practice, which may have originated in the Middle East, breaks the line of the column in an unpleasant, abrupt way. Other examples of the style may be seen at Pompeiopolis (see Rte 28).

To the left of road are the ruins of the *Roman theatre*, which, according to an inscription found there, was built during the joint reign of Marcus Aurelius (161–180) and Lucius Verus (161–169). Entrance from the street was by a vomitorium. The cavea, which had a capacity of 2500, was supported at the back by a stone wall. No trace of the stage-building remains.

On the right-hand side of the road are the remains of a *Roman nymphaeum* which was linked to the city's water supply system. The channels through which the water flowed into the basin are still visible.

During the Roman period a system was installed which brought water 20km from the Lamas river to Diocaesarea through channels and tunnels cut into the rock. This ancient system, supplemented by the winter's rain and snow stored in ancient cisterns, still provides Uzuncaburç and a number of other villages with fresh water.

On the left-hand side of the road, in the centre of a vegetable garden, are the imposing ruins of the *Temple of Zeus Olbius*. This, a

Hellenistic tower at Uzuncaburç.

peripteros of 6 by 12 columns of the Corinthian order which measures c 40m by 21m, is in a good state of preservation. In 1958 the stylobate and crepidoma were cleared of debris by the Directorate General of Antiquities and Museums. It has the distinction of being the earliest known example in Asia Minor of a temple of the Corinthian order, tradition ascribing its foundation to Seleucus I Nicator (321–281) towards the beginning of the 3C BC. Of the 30 standing columns four still have their capitals. Each column is c 10m tall and has a diameter of 1.5m. The architrave has largely disappeared.

When the temple was turned into a church, an apse (now removed) was added to the E end, and the columns, on three sides, were pared to permit the construction of walls and doorways. At the same time the original ceiling was removed and a wooden roof put in its place. The inside faces of the columns show that the building was seriously damaged by fire at some stage.

In the temenos is a sarcophagus, a number of reliefs and some architectural fragments. Note the defensive wall on the street-side of the sanctuary, which was designed to protect the temple and its treasures from marauders and thieves. To the S of the temple are the ruins of a building which may have been a gymnasium. It is believed to date from the Roman period.

Returning to the road and proceeding towards the W end of the site, we reach the ruins of the *Roman Temple of Tyche*.

Tyche, the Greek goddess of chance or fortune, was the daughter of Oceanus or Zeus and Tethys. She was particularly popular during the Hellenistic era, when she was first accorded the status of a goddess. During the Roman period Tyche was often equated with the ancient Latin deity Fortuna.

The temple of Tyche had an interesting plan. The square cella, which contained the cult-statue of the goddess, was c 34m behind a row of 6 columns surmounted by Corinthian capitals, which supported an architrave. Five of the columns survive. Each has a shaft made from a single piece of imported granite, and is 5.5m high and 0.65m in diameter. According to an inscription on the architrave, the temple was the gift of one Oppius and of his wife, Kyria. It has been dated, by the inscription and the style of the Corinthian capitals, to the end of the 1C AD.

To the right of the temple of Tyche a short colonnaded street (with only the bases of the columns remaining) leads to the *NW gate* of the city. This well-preserved, late Roman structure, which was joined to the city's defensive wall, is 31.5m long, 12m at its highest point, and 1.15m wide. There are four consoles or brackets on which statues were placed, two on the inner and two on the outer face of the wall near the central arch. An inscription, to the right of this arch, states that the gate was constructed during the reign of the E Roman Emperor Arcadius (395–408) and of the W Roman Emperor Honorius (395–423). These youthful and unskilled rulers, the sons of Theodosius the Great, were largely dominated by their regents. They reigned at a time of insecurity and uncertainty. The E Empire was under threat from the Ostrogoths and the Huns and many of its cities erected walls for their protection against the barbarian hordes.

The *necropolis* of Olba/Diocaesarea lies in a valley to the N of the modern village. It may be reached by following the road from the coffee-house, which passes the bust of Atatürk and the secondary school. There were interments during the Hellenistic, Roman and Byzantine periods. These ranged from individual burials in sarcophagi, graves carved from the rock, and family mausolea in caves, which contain several tombs. Most of the sarcophagi are similar in style. A number bear inscriptions in Greek. During the Byzantine period a mortuary church was erected in the necroplis.

To visit the last and, perhaps, the most striking monument of the ancient city, it is necessary to return to the village centre and walk a short distance to the E. The *Hellenistic tower*, which gives the village its modern name—Uzuncaburç means high tower—is 12.5m by 15.5m by c 22.5m. Apparently constructed as a watch-tower and for defensive purposes, it has five storeys. Its importance to the inhabitants of Olba/Diocaesarea may be judged from the fact that it appeared, as a symbol of the city, on its coins. Like some of the other buildings it bears traces of damage by fire and was heavily restored at various perods. An inscription in Greek on the S side, near the entrance, appears to refer to some repair or refurbishment of the building in the latter part of the 3C AD.

The tower is in urgent need of repair and restoration. Some of its walls bulge ominously. Because of its dangerous condition, entry to the structure is strictly forbidden.

Note the ingenious device near the tower which was used to control the flow and pressure of the water brought from the Lamas river and to direct it to various parts of the city.

During the Byzantine era, when the temple of Zeus was converted into a Christian basilica, a number of other churches were constructed in Diocaesarea. The ruins of two of these lie to the S of the theatre, while in the area of the Hellenistic tower are the remains of the Stephanos church.

To get to 4km *Ura* take the road which runs from the left of the theatre in a SE direction. The ancient settlement, which contains evidence of occupation during the Roman and Byzantine periods, was built on the slope of a hill, whose summit is 1100m above sea-level. Some authorities believe that it was a dependency of Olba/Diocaesarea, while others suggest that it was the original site of Olba.

On the outskirts of the modern village, to the right of the road near the primary school, are several architectural fragments—a column 5m high and another, which lies in pieces on the ground. The entrance to the school is composed of three ancient stone blocks, which measure 2.25m by 2.25m. In the centre of the modern settlement, which lies in the valley, are several coffee-houses where the visitor may stop for refreshment. Across the road are the ruins of a *Byzantine church*.

At the base of the hill to the SE of the coffee-house are the remains of a *Roman nymphaeum*. Surrounded by a 12m-high wall, it received water from the Lamas river. Nearby are the ruins of the *theatre*. Access to this building, which has not been excavated, was by two doors 1.6m wide.

The ancient settlement, which was on the slope of the hill, is marked by the remains of houses, cisterns, watch-towers and a church. There are also several *mausolea*, including a fine specimen made of cut stone blocks which measures 8m by 6m. To the S lies a necropolis and a ruined church. On the NE slope of the hill are two *watch-towers* which commanded a clear view over the valley and the aqueduct, on which the city depended for its water-supply. The stone blocks of the watch-towers, which measure 1m by 0.5m, are pierced with observation holes. According to an inscription, the *aqueduct* was constructed during the reign of the Septimius Severus (193–211). Water was conveyed in a U-shaped channel over an arched structure c 150m long and 25m high.

To the N of the aqueduct are the remains of some ancient buildings. In one of these there are several basins which could be filled with water from the aqueduct. A small movable stone block controlled the supply.

The road to the Yeğenli village is flanked by another necropolis. Note the two fine *sarcophagi* near the road-sign which are decorated with garlands and a representation of Eros.

28 Silifke to Mersin

Total distance c 72km. **Silifke**—E24 7km *Karadedli*—5km *Susanoğlu*—(17km *Türkmenuşağı Paslı*)—5km *Narlikuyu*—(c 2km **Cennet** and *Cehennem*)—3km *Akkum*—(c 7km **Adamkayalar**)—(12km *Cambazlı*)—5km *Kizkalesi*—3km *Ayaş*—(c 4km **Kanlıdivane**)—14km Erdemli—23km *Mezitli* (2km *Viranşehir / Soli/ Pompeiopolis*)—11km **Mersin**.
All distances are approximate.

E of **Silifke** (see Rte 25) the E24 continues across a rather featureless plain 7km to *Karadedeli*. This is a new village populated by former nomads who used to live in tents on the slopes of the Taurus Mountains. Now an agricultural centre of some importance, it is well-known for its woven rugs and saddle-bags which are produced in traditonal patterns. There are the ruins of a Byzantine church near the village.

The road returns to the sea at the pretty village of 5km *Susanoğlu*. This has several small pensions and simple restaurants. A good place to spend a few relaxing days on the beach, it is also a useful centre for visiting the many ancient sites around Silifke.

Near the village the ruins of ancient CORASIUM, founded c AD 375 by Flavius Uranius, Governor of Isauria. There are the substantial

remains of fortifications, churches, stones, baths and two necropolises, all of which were constructed during the period from the
beginning of the 5C AD to the 8C AD.

About 17km N of Susanoğlu, near the village of *Paslı*, there is an interesting 2C
Roman *temple-tomb*. The village has no restaurant but there are several places
en route where it is possible to picnic. The Yürük people, who live near the
tomb, are well-known for the welcome which they extend to visitors, whom they
frequently invite to their homes for a meal. (It would be impolite to offer
payment for any hospitality of this kind.)
    The dirt road from the coast, which climbs steadily, first through olive-groves
and then through pine plantations, demands careful driving. Continue through
Türkmenuşağı to Paslı. As the tomb is some distance from the road and is not
easy to find it is advisable to take a guide from the very helpful Serin family. He
will also keep at bay the fierce guard-dogs which protect the villagers' herds!
    The tomb, which was built near the ancient paved road linking Corycus with
Seleucia, is in an excellent state of preservation. It has four double columns
surmounted by a decorated pediment. Consoles or brackets, which may have
supported statues, project from the columns. In the burial chamber there were
two sarcophagi, both of which have been destroyed. The names of those buried
in the tomb are not known.
    On the left-hand exterior wall there is the relief of a large, erect *phallus*. Local
tradition, which equates virility with courage, has given the building its popular
name, the Temple-Tomb of the Great King. It is also known as the Priapus
Tomb.
    Priapus, a god of Phrygian origin, enjoyed great popularity during the
Hellenistic and Roman eras. The son of Aphrodite and Dionysus or, as some
claim, of Aphrodite and Zeus, he possessed a phallus as large as the rest of his
body. The worship of Priapus spread from Lampsacus on the Hellespont to the
whole of the ancient world. The donkey, an animal notorious for its lust, was
sacrificed in his honour. As the god of fertility and growth, his garlanded
ithyphallic image watched over fields and gardens. He was also credited with
the ability to ward off the evil eye and to neutralise the spells of the envious. In
literature he was honoured especially by the Bucolic Poets. Moschus, who lived
in Syracuse c 150 BC, wrote: 'Your sudden end, sweet Bion, was matter of
weeping even unto Apollo; the Satyrs did lament you, and every Priapus made
you his moan in sable garb.' The Romans, too, honoured him. The 'Carmina
Priapea', a collection of 80 poems which dates from the 1C AD, celebrates this
lusty god. Even after Christianity had triumphed and most pagan practices had
been suppressed, Priapus was not forgotten in Asia Minor. With Pan and the
Satyrs he continued to preside over country matters!
    To the right of the tomb there is a deep, uncovered cistern, 5m wide, 20m long
and 8m deep. Nearby, among other relics of the past are two large cylindrical
stones used for crushing olives and a carved slab, which carries a brief
inscription in Greek.

After leaving Susanoğlu the road follows the coastline, passing on
the way a number of small bays, which offer excellent swimming. At
5km *Narlikuyu* (the Well of the Pomegranate) there are several good,
if rather expensive, restaurants. Their speciality is fish, which is
served grilled, fried or baked with 'buğulama', a mouth-watering
vegetable sauce.
    A small building at the entrance to the village, the Kızlar Hamamı
or Bath of the Maidens, shelters a 4C AD Roman *mosaic* portraying
the Charites. Better known as the Three Graces, Euphrosyne, Aglaia
and Thalia, they were minor goddesses usually associated with
Aphrodite. First mentioned in Homeric times, they personified
beauty, gentleness and friendship. Depicted in the usual manner as
beautiful, nude female figures, in this mosaic they are surrounded by
fluttering doves and partridges. According to an inscription, the
mosaic came from the bath of Poimenius, who claims to have been
the friend of emperors and governor of the Sacred Islands (the
Princes' Islands in the Sea of Marmara).
    At Narlikuyu a subterranean river empties into the bay, pushing
the salt water back, so that animals wade into the sea to slake

their thirst. This river is believed to come from *Cennet Deresi*, the Valley of Paradise, which lies a short distance inland. Its water is much colder than the sea, a fact which provides an unpleasant surprise for the unsuspecting bather.

According to Strabo, the *Corycian Cave* where the monster Typhon was born, is to be found in this part of Cilicia. Modern scholars are of the opinion that this cave may be identified with the gigantic chasm known today as **Cennet Deresi** (the Valley of Heaven). This is c 2km inland from Narlikuyu.

Typhon, a chthonic deity, was the fruit of the incestuous union of Tartarus with his mother Gaia. He had a hundred serpentine heads which roared like a bull, barked like a dog and spoke the language of the gods. Having disputed control of the world unsuccessfully with Zeus, he was defeated by him and buried under Mt Etna. However, according to Hesiod, Typhon was confined in the depths of the underworld with the Titans, where he fathered harmful winds like the typhoon which is named after him. Some accounts identify him with Seth who killed Osiris. Before his defeat by Zeus, he mated with Echidna, a coupling which produced the Chimaera, the Sphinx, the Sow of Crommyon, the Nemean Lion and the eagle that tormented Prometheus. Typhon is usually portrayed as a many-headed snake-like creature. The early Christians identified him with the devil, a belief later accepted by the Muslims.

Cennet Deresi is a natural pit 200m long and 70m deep. Because of the effort required, it is best explored in the cool of the early morning or the late afternoon. Visitors, who have not brought a pocket-torch, may hire a lamp near the entrance. More than 450 steps lead down to a small grassy plateau. At the far end there is an exquisite 5C **Byzantine church** dedicated to the Virgin Mary. This had an apse flanked by two domed sacristies and was probably covered with a pitched wooden roof. The apse and side walls were decorated with some fine frescoes. Unfortunately, in recent years mindless vandals have almost completely obliterated these with their graffiti. Unless the authorities take action soon to protect the frescoes, nothing will remain and a precious piece of history will be lost forever.

To visit the area below the church you will need a lamp. A rudimentary path leads downwards for c 200m to a huge cavern. This was believed to be the abode of Typhon. At the rear, a river known locally as the 'Stream of Paradise' disappears through a gap in the floor with a thunderous roar. It will reappear in the sea at Narlikuyu 2km away (see above).

The bushes at Cennet Deresi are covered with pieces of cloth, as symbols of the wishes of those who placed them there.

Cehennem Deresi, c 75m E of Cennet, with precipitous sides 120m deep, is accessible only to experienced rock-climbers. Still regarded as one of the entrances to hell, the bushes here are festooned with scraps of cloth to keep at bay the evil spirits believed to dwell in the cave.

A road from the left of the car-park leads to *Dilek Mağarası* (the Cave of Wishes), which also forms part of the Corycian Cave group. Less interesting than Cennet or Cehennem, it is being developed as a tourist attraction. Many visitors come to this cave because of its reputation for alleviating the symptoms of asthma.

NE of the chasm is a *Hellenistic peribolos*, which encloses a 5C church. It is probable that the pagan sanctuary, which dates from the 3C or 2C BC, was dedicated to Zeus Corycius.

From Narlikuyu to 5km Kizkalesi the road, now always close to the sea, passes a number of small, clean beaches. One of the most attractive of these is at 4km *Akkum*, where there are several good pensions and an excellent small restaurant, *Mola 33*.

Between Akkum and Kizkalesi a rough track on the left leads to one of the most interesting and least visited sites in Cilicia. Known as **Adamkayalar** (the Cliff of Men), it is c 7km from the coast road.

The track climbs steadily into the hills, offering magnificent views of a coastline littered with the ruins of ancient cities. Away to the right, on higher ground, are the remains of a 1C building, which may have formed part of an early Christian settlement, and a perfectly-preserved Roman tomb.

After c 8km look out for a sign on the left which points to Adamkayalar. From the track it is necessary to proceed on foot for c 1km following the route marked by red stripes. Adamkayalar is a large Roman necropolis of the 1C AD. The

Roman rock-tombs at Adamkayalar near Silifke.

tombs, cut from a terraced rock-face, bear reliefs of the deceased. Some recline on couches, others are depicted as armed warriors. A few are accompanied by their wives. The reliefs, executed with a rough naivety, are believed to commemorate the rulers of the small town which lies nearby.

Visitors with sufficient time may like to continue N by way of Hüseyinler to c 12km *Cambazlı* where there are the ruins of a Byzantine church. Instead of returning by the same route to the coast it is possible to do so via Keşlitürkmenli, Demircili and Silifke.

Kızkalesi is a small resort, popular with Turkish and foreign holiday-makers. It has several fine sandy beaches, a number of hotels, including the excellent *Hotel Kaya*, and some small, clean pensions. Like all the holiday resorts in this area, Kızkalesi attracts large numbers of visitors in the summer, so it is often very difficult to get accommodation at that time of the year.

At Kızkalesi there are two of the fairytale *castles* which ornament the S Turkish coastline. One is sited at the end of a narrow promontory, the other is on a rocky islet c 150m out to sea. Kızkalesi, which means the Maiden's Castle, acquired its name from the legend about the princess who was kept in isolation in one of the castles for her own safety. The prophecy that she would meet an untimely death from a snake bite was fulfilled when one day a basket of figs containing a hidden viper was brought to her castle-chamber.

The real history of the Corycian castles is scarcely less dramatic than the legend. An Armenian inscription on the outer castle states that they were constructed in the 12C, when the area formed part of the Cilician Kingdom of Armenia. Originally connected by a causeway or jetty the castles were built to protect the city and port of Corycus.

After the defeat of the Byzantine army by the Selçuk Turks at the battle of Manzikert in 1071 many Armenians settled in Cilicia. About 1080 two nobles, Ruben and Oshin, established dynasties in the Taurus Mountains. Their successors increased the territory controlled by them, largely at the expense of the Byzantines, so that by 1132 Sis, Anavarza, Adana and Tarsus were under Rubenid control. In 1199 Leo II the Great (1187–1219), the friend and ally of the German emperor, Frederick Barbarossa (see Silifke, Rte 25), was crowned king of Armenia in Tarsus in the presence of the Papal Legate, Cardinal Conrad von Wittelsbach.

Under Leo, the Cilician Kingdom of Armenia absorbed many western influences. In close contact with Crusader families, it developed trading links with the Venetians and Genoese. The Armenian language was strongly influenced by French. Control of the kingdom passed from the Rubenids to one of the descendants of Oshin, Hethoum I (1226–69). He and his successors allied themselves with the Mongols against the Mamelukes of Egypt who were beginning to pose a threat to the Levant. In the 14C the kingdom went to one of the Lusignan dynasty of Cyprus, but by then the end was near. The Mamelukes continued to advance. By 1359 Adana, Tarsus and most of the Cilician plain was in their hands. The Corycian castles fell into the hands of Peter I of Cyprus in 1361. The capital, Sis, and the king, Leo VI were captured by the Mamelukes in 1375. Ransomed, Leo VI died in exile in Paris in 1393 and was buried in St. Denis, where his monument still stands. The title King of Armenia went to the Cypriot James I. Through one of his descendants it passed to the House of Savoy. However, by this time Armenia had ceased to exist as a separate state.

The *land castle* was constructed largely from material taken from the ancient city of Corycus. The walls contain many broken columns, some of which are laid in regular courses. One tower has a complete Roman door which may have been taken from a tomb. A building of considerable strength, it was protected by a moat connected to the sea by a rock-cut channel 10m deep, and by a double wall flanked by towers. Several reservoirs assured an adequate water-supply for the garrison.

Access to the interior is from the sandy beach on the W. A breach leads through the first defensive wall to an area that is very overgrown and filled with debris. By proceeding carefully it is possible to reach a gate which led to the causeway or jetty linking the two castles. Continue along the ramparts to the E where from a ruined tower the hardy may get a fine view of the sea, of the interior of the castle and of the surrounding countryside. Three churches inside the castle have traces of faded frescoes on their walls.

Few images are more romantic than that of the *sea castle* of Kızkalesi mirrored in the calm waters of the harbour at sunset. Remote and unreal, it floats between sea and sky, nearer to the world of legendary maidens than that of the warring factions of Crusaders, Armenians and Mamelukes who fought and perished for its possession. Today visitors are conveyed to it by boats, which leave the beach W of the land castle at frequent intervals. The journey takes 20 minutes.

The walls of this stronghold, which is in a better state of preservation than the land castle, are 3m thick and 8m high. Roughly triangular in shape it has towers at each corner 20m high, with five turrets in between. Entry is by a door at the E end, the keystone of which is decorated with a finely-carved cross. Above the door there are two inscriptions in Armenian which give the date of the castle's construction as 1151 during the reign of Hetoum I. A stone stairway leads to one of the towers, from where there is a splendid view of the whole structure. It is possible to make a circuit of the ramparts, which have been repaired recently in part. Note the reservoirs hollowed from the rock and the ruins of a small church in the centre of the keep.

Across the road from the land castle are the ruins of the city of CORYCUS. Here the remains of tombs, baths, churches and private houses are scattered in wild confusion over the hillside. For the most part they are covered in tangled vegetation, which makes any detailed examination very difficult. Many of the tombs are decorated with reliefs. According to the inscriptions people of all occupations were buried there—cobblers, goldsmiths, fruiterers, shipbuilders, weavers and midwives. Note, in particular, the crude 4C AD carving of an armed warrior which may be found at the end of a field flanking the main road. Headless now, he stands stiffly, legs apart, with his left hand resting lightly on his sword-hilt.

Visitors from Beaufort onward have been struck by the profusion of ancient ruins on the coastline between Corycus and Ayaş. Writing in 'Karamania' he commented: 'the shore presents a continued scene of ruins, all of which being white, and relieved by the dark wooded hills behind them, give to the country an appearance of splendour and populousness, that serves only, on nearer approach, to heighten the contrast with its real poverty and degradation.'

At *Ayaş*, 3km to the E of Kizkalesi, are the extensive ruins of the city of ELAEUSA/SEBASTE. There is a coffee-house on the right of the E24 where vistors with their own transport may park. This is also a stopping place for dolmuş and long-distance bus services.

History. Some authorities identify Elaeusa with *Vilusa*, a town mentioned in Hittite records which date from c 1400 BC. However, the first concrete proof of the city's existence is provided by a tetradrachm issued in the late 2C or early 1C BC. This gives the city's name and bears a representation of a female deity holding a rudder, presumably a reference to Elaeusa's importance as a maritime trading centre.

When Pompey cleared the pirates from Cilicia in 67 BC, many of its inhabitants were settled in other areas, some as far away as S Italy. Virgil recalls this event in the following lines:

'Beneath the towers of a Calabrian town,
Where dark Galaesus waters yellow fields,
I once beheld an old Cilician
Who owned a paltry patch of unclaimed land'

In the 1C BC the area around Elaeusa was controlled by Tarcondimotus Philantonius, a dynast from E Cilicia. Later, c 20 BC, it was given by Augustus to Archelaus I of Cappadocia. In gratitude he renamed the city *Sebaste*, the Greek for Augustus, in honour of his imperial patron. According to Strabo, Archelaus built a palace there. He may also have enlarged the city, as on his coins he describes himself as a builder. In AD 38 Sebaste came under the control of Antiochus I of Commagene and his wife, Iotape.

Later Sebaste became an episcopal see in the province of Cilicia Prima. Its bishop attended the Council of Chalcedon in AD 451. Little is known of the city's subsequent history under the Byzantines and the Turks.

Elaeusa's original settlement was on an island, which in the course of time was joined, through silting, to the mainland. The N end of the peninsula thus formed has been separated from the rest of the city by the main road. The island site, which is much overgrown, may be reached from the beach to the E of the coffee-house. It shelters the remains of a Byzantine basilica.

Perhaps the most interesting monument in Elaeusa/Sebaste is a *Roman temple* which was built on the S end of a headland at the SW of the bay. To the NW of this building there was a terrace 100m wide, while on the E several smaller terraces supported a number of tombs and heroa. The temple was a peripteros with 6 by 12 columns in the Corinthian order. The stylobate, 17.6m by 32.9m, is paved with stone slabs. Only five of the columns now stand higher than their bases. With the temple of Zeus Olbius at Uzuncaburç it ranks as one of the best-preserved Classical temples in Cilicia.

Towards the end of the 5C a small church, measuring 11.35m by 7.30m, was built inside the temple. This was frequently done, partly to save construction costs and partly to affirm Christianity's victory over paganism. A crudely-executed mosaic in the apse, depicting birds and animals in a setting of paradise, is reminiscent of earlier mosaics of Orpheus charming the animals.

The city's necropolis was sited to the N of the modern road. Terraces there support row after row of heroa, while the road to the inland site of Çatı Ören is lined by sarcophagi.

About 3.5km E of Ayaş a road on the left leads to 4km **Kanlıdivane**, perhaps the strangest site in Cilicia. Known in ancient times as KANYTELIS or NEAPOLIS, it has not been excavated and much of what has been said about it is based on folklore and conjecture.

To appreciate to the full the evocative atmosphere of Kanlıdivane, visit it at twilight, when the shadows lengthen in the necropolis and the great cliffs of the central chasm are stained with scarlet. Then it is possible to understand the meaning of its Turkish name. Kanlıdivane means the 'crazy place of blood', because it is believed that condemned criminals were thrown into the chasm, there to be devoured by wild animals.

There are no refreshment facilities at Kanlıdivane as it is little visited even during the holiday season. There are, however, several places where you may picnic—if you are not overwhelmed by your surroundings.

History. Kanlıdivane, probably founded during the Hellenistic era, was almost certainly a dependency of Olba. The ruins visible today are almost all from the Roman and Byzantine periods. The Byzantine town is believed to have been founded about the time of Theodosius II (408–450). Sufficiently far away from the coast to be unaffected by the Arab raids, it appears to have enjoyed a long period of prosperity. After the capture of the Cilician coastal area by the Selçuk Turks, at the beginning of the 13C, Kanlıdivane entered a period of decline from which it never recovered. It was virtually forgotten until the accounts of 19C travellers, like Victor Langlois, brought it once more to the notice of scholars.

Near the parking area are the substantial ruins of a *tower*, 17m by 15m by 9.25m, which was used to guard the approaches to the city. Some authorities believe that the carving of a triskele above the entrance is proof that this was built when the city was ruled by Olba. Others maintain that it was constructed during the Roman period. It certainly antedates the Byzantine era, when it was repaired and reinforced. To the left of the tower are the remains of a large Byzantine *church*. Like all the churches at Kanlıdivane, it was constructed in the form of a basilica with a nave flanked by side aisles. Its walls, which stand to c 10m are pierced by well-preserved doorways.

On the S wall of the chasm there is an interesting *relief* which is believed to date from the 3C BC, the period of Olbian domination. This may be examined by descending into the chasm at a point W of the tower where there has been a landslide. The relief, sited in a recess, c 4m by 2m, is executed in a crude, naive style. It is surmounted by an inscription written in Greek letters which is partly worn away. It shows six figures, two male and four female. Their identity is not known; they may be members of the Olbian priestly dynasty. (See Uzuncaburç, Rte 27.) Seated on a tribune at the right-hand side of the relief there is a male figure, clothed in a toga. He holds his right hand across his breast. By his side sits a female figure. To the left there are four younger persons, a man wearing a toga, and three females. The female figures are also depicted with their right hands across their breasts. This relief is faced by another on the NW wall of the pit. Set somewhat lower down, it shows the standing figure of an armed warrior dressed in a Roman-style tunic with his left hand resting lightly on his sword.

To the left of the path, which encircles the chasm, there is a small Muslim cemetery, which is still in use. Beyond the cemetery are the ruins of a church and of buildings which are believed to have been occupied by a monastic community. Note in particular the fine vaulted *cistern*. To the right of the path, on a terrace overlooking the chasm, are the remains of a small *temple*. The path terminates in a plateau occupied by a large *church*, which is in a good state of repair. The apse, choir and the lower part of the doorway remain. Note the inscription above the entrance. To the N of the church are the ruins of a *temple-tomb* which, like most funerary monuments in the area, was desecrated at some time by grave-robbers. There are fine views of the city's ruins and of the great pit in its centre from this plateau.

To the E, half-hidden by a tangled mass of vegetation, there are the remains of many buildings, including a number of churches. Some of these ruins are now used as shelters by the nomad shepherds who graze their flocks near the site. Care should be taken in exploring this area, as it contains several cisterns whose entrances are partly or entirely covered by the dense undergrowth.

Kanlıdivane is surrounded by ancient cemeteries. *Tombs*, many of which date from the Roman period, are scattered across the hillsides. A number bear representations of the deceased: soldiers in armour; men reclining on couches; women in graceful poses. There are several good examples on the approach road from the S. Unfortunately, all have been robbed, and most are partly covered by the thorny scrub which makes exploration difficult.

A short distance after the turning for Kanlidivane, the E24 crosses the *Lamas Çayi*, the ancient Lamas, at the village of Limonlu. This river was regarded by Strabo as the boundary between Rugged and Smooth Cilicia. Just beyond the Lamus the remains of the *aqueducts* that brought water from the Taurus Mountains to Kanytelis / Neapolis, Elaeusa/Sebaste and Corycus may be seen on the left-hand side of the road.

In the Middle Ages the Lamus separated two warring and incompatible worlds. Gibbon relates how Christian and Muslim captives were exchanged on the bridge over the river in the 9C. When they reached their own lines, the Arabs cried out 'Allah Akbar', which the Christians countered with a lusty 'Kyrie Eleison'.

At this point the foothills of the Taurus Mountains give way to the great plain that extends E to Adana and beyond. Lacking the variety and the ancient ruins which make the journey across Pamphylia and Rough Cilicia so interesting, Smooth Cilicia (Cilicia Campestris) does not tempt the traveller to linger. In summer a sea of green rice fields, relieved only by the white squares of the cotton plantations, it swelters under a fierce and unrelenting sun. In winter, swept by cold winds from the Taurus Mountains, it is equally uninviting.

The E24 between the Lamas river and Mersin carries a good deal of commercial traffic and follows a relatively straight course across the plain. At 14km *Erdemli*, the only town of any size before Mersin, there is a pleasant camping site, *Erdemli Çamlığı*, set in a pine grove on the right. Open all the year round this has a buffet, electricity and running water.

At 23km the village of Mezitli, a turning on the right leads to 2km **Viranşehir**, where the city of SOLI/POMPEIOPOLIS was sited.

The village of Viranşehir has developed into a small resort much frequented by the people of Mersin. Near the rather uninviting beach of grey sand and mud, there are several motels and camping places. Because of its proximity to the city, the sea at Viranşehir is unlikely to be free from pollution.

History. Founded by the Rhodians c 700 BC, Soli was one of the oldest settlements in Rugged Cilicia. In 83 BC the Armenian king Tigranes the Great (94–55 BC) captured the city during the campaign that won him the Syrian monarchy. His kingdom then extended from the Euphrates to the Mediterranean. Tigranes moved the inhabitants of Soli to his capital, Tigranocerta, on the Tigris. However, after Pompey had defeated and routed the Cilician pirates at the battle of Coracesium (modern Alanya) in 67 BC, Tigranes offered him his submission. Pompey built a new city at Soli, and in gratitude its citizens named this foundation Pompeiopolis.

In antiquity the people of Soli were reputed to speak such a barbarous form of Greek that the word σολοικισμός was coined from the name of their city to describe it. It is from this that the English word solecism is derived. An unsupported tradition relates that Alexander the Great was so angered by the failure of Soli to preserve the purity of the Greek language that he imposed heavy penalties on its citizens. However, according to Arrian, its citizens were fined, not for bad grammar, but for their support of the Persian cause (see above).

Soli/Pompeiopolis, which is believed to have had a population of 250,000 at one time, was almost completely destroyed by an earthquake in the 6C AD, hence its Turkish name Vıranşehir, city in ruins. Perhaps the most imposing monument to remain from the past is the line of 37 *columns*, on the right of the road which leads to the sea. These columns, some of whose capitals are ornamented with human figures and mythological animals, formed part of a colonnaded street c 450m long and 10m wide constructed in the 2C or 3C AD. Each column has a bracket or console which supported a bronze statute (cf. Uzuncaburç, Rte 27).

Beaufort was impressed by this colonnade as an architectural feature, though critical of the workmanship and design. In 'Karamania', he wrote: 'the stone of which they [the columns] are composed is too coarse to admit of much delicacy in the workmanship, and the taste of the architect seems to have been as corrupt as the execution. Some are Corinthian, others are of the composite order; even their proportions vary; the design of the foliage differs in capitals of the same order; and between the volutes of some, are placed the human bust, or figures of animals and other meretricious ornaments.' It would seem that Soli's lapses in taste were not confined to grammar!

In the marshy ground around the colonnade there are the ruins of several unidentified buildings and a number of cisterns. In Beaufort's time Soli still boasted the remains of the theatre, the city walls, an aqueduct and a prodigality of tombs scattered in the surrounding countryside. There was also 'a beautiful harbour, or basin, with parallel sides, and circular ends; it is', he wrote, 'entirely artificial, being formed by surrounding walls, or moles, which are fifty feet in thickness, and seven in height.' Today traces of the mole, which protected the ancient harbour may still be seen.

There has been no systematic exploration or excavation of the ruins of Soli. It may be that, when this is done, further evidence of the city's past may be discovered.

From Metzitli to 11km **Mersin** (see Rte 29) the E24 is bordered by new hotels, restaurants and apartment houses, which are being built to attract tourists to the area. These offer an attractive alternative to those who wish to spend some time in Mersin, but not in the city centre.

29 Mersin to Adana

Total distance 67km. **Mersin**—E24 29km—**Tarsus**—38km **Adana** (c 50km *Karataş / Megarsus*).

The history of **Mersin** (314,105 inhab.) may be traced back to the Hittite era. However, the modern city retains little evidence of its past and most visitors who stay there use it as a base for excursions to places of interest in the surrounding countryside or as a staging-post on journeys in SE Turkey.

When Beaufort sailed along the S Turkish coast in 1811/12, Mersin was a hamlet of a few miserable huts on the shore. Today it is Turkey's largest port on the Mediterranean. An important trading centre, it now handles much of the produce from Çukurova. Linked by the E24 with the cities on the W Mediterranean littoral and with Adana and other large centres to the E, it also has good communications with Central Anatolia through the Cilician Gates. There is a night ferry service to **Gazi Mağusa** (Famagusta) in N Cyprus and frequent boat services to other Mediterranean ports.

The city has been well planned. It has wide boulevards and on the seafront there are attractive formal gardens full of exotic plants. In the centre and on the E24 towards Mezitli and Viranşehir (see Rte 28) there are several good hotels and restaurants. However, despite strenuous efforts to turn it into a tourist centre, Mersin's future appears to be linked firmly with commerce. The plumes of smoke that float across the city from the industrial area to the E, disfiguring the blue Mediterranean sky, are vivid reminders of that fact.

Information and Accommodation. The Tourist Information Office is sited near the docks, beyond the seafront gardens, in İnönü Bulv. Information may also be obtained there about restaurants in the city, transport services (including the ferry-boats to Cyprus) and places of interest in İçel (Mersin) province. There is a wide range of accommodation in Mersin, from the excellent, if rather high-priced, *Mersin Oteli*, Gümrük Meyd. 112, to inexpensive pensions. Full details may be obtained from the Tourist Information Office.

Post Office and Banks. Mersin's principal post office is a few doors from the Mersin Oteli in Gümrük Meyd. Branches of the principal Turkish banks may also be found throughout the city.

Transport. Mersin is linked by train to 29km Tarsus and 67km Adana. From Adana there are services to all the cities on Turkish Railways network. The nearest airport is at Adana, from where there are frequent internal flights by Turkish Airlines. International connections may be made through *Ankara* and *İstanbul*. City buses, including those to *Mezitli* and *Viranşehir*, and dolmuş services for destinations in the city and environs leave from stops near the Tourist Information Office. Long distance buses depart from the new bus station on the N outskirts of the city.

Museums. At present there is no museum in Mersin. However, it is planned to erect a building in the city centre which will house an ethnographical collection and archaeological finds from the area. These include a hoard of coins and numerous architectural fragments. At present some artefacts from Mersin are displayed in the Adana Archaeological Museum.

The earliest traces of occupation were found in a mound, *Yümüktepe*, on the W outskirts of the city. This may be reached by bus from the city centre. A site more for the enthusiast or specialist than the casual observer, it is now largely covered by a rather run-down municipal park. Excavations made at Yümüktepe by Professor Garstang of the Universtiy of Liverpool have revealed 23 levels of occupation, the earliest of which dates from c 6300 BC. Sherds and earthenware link it with Çatalhöyük and Canhasan and with the N Syrian sites of Byblos and Ras Shamara. Fortified towards 4500 BC, Yümüktepe was abandoned c 3200 BC and reoccupied c 1200 later during the Middle Bronze Age. There are traces of habitation by the Hittites and by Greeks of the Geometric period, for whom it marked an important staging-post on the coastal road. Roman, Byzantine and Selçuk remains found near the summit of the hill suggest that it continued to be occupied until the 16C. At present many of the objects found at Yümüktepe are displayed in the Adana Archaeological Museum.

From Mersin eastwards there is a substantial increase in traffic on the E24, as it is used by many commercial vehicles on their way to and from the port. Passing through an unattractive stretch of landscape, pockmarked with industrial development, it is with some relief that the traveller turns left off the main road to 29km Tarsus.

Although **TARSUS** now has few reminders of its long and turbulent history, the old houses, rambling streets and flower-filled gardens of the city combine to produce an effect that is difficult to resist. Tarsus wears its ruins with a charming air of insouciance that disarms and stifles criticism. However sceptical one feels, there is an urge to believe that on an autumn day in 41 BC Cleopatra came through this crumbling gateway to meet Mark Antony or that St. Paul once quenched his thirst at that unremarkable well.

History. The origins of Tarsus are lost in legend. According to an Islamic tradition it was established by Seth, the son of Adam. Excavations prove that it existed during the Early Bronze Age (between 3000 and 2500 BC). A fortified settlement c 2500 BC, it was then the capital of a minor kingdom. Its position on the coast S of the Cilician Gates enabled it to control trade between Syria and Egypt to the S and E and settlements all over Anatolia. Imported artefacts found there, from these countries and from Cyprus and Mespotamia, testify to its importance in this trade route.

Greek settlers from Argos, attracted no doubt by its commercial reputation, founded a colony at Tarsus in the 12C BC. Captured by the Assyrians towards the end of the 8C BC, it revolted and was rased to the ground by Sennacherib (705–681 BC) in 696 BC. Xenophon came here in 400 BC during the course of his famous and unsuccessful expedition to put Cyrus on the throne of Persia. He describes it as being a rich and powerful city, which was governed by a king named Synnesis.

Alexander the Great came to Tarsus in 333 BC and fell seriously ill, because, the ancient historians maintained, he had bathed in the icy waters of the

Cydnus. It is possible, however, that he contracted a fever in the malaria-ridden plains around the city. After the death of Alexander, Tarsus came under the control of Seleucus Nicator, King of Syria (c 321–281 BC). By the 2C BC it was an important centre of learning and it had also acquired a large Jewish community. With the remainder of Cilicia the city was occupied for a time by Tigranes the Great (94–55 BC) and it also attracted the attention of the pirates who had begun to prey on the coastal trade. After Pompey defeated the pirates in 67 BC, Tarsus and the rest of Cilicia came under Roman rule. Cicero, who was one of the first Roman governors of Cilicia, lived here from 51–50 BC. Julius Caesar visited the city in 47 BC.

In 41 BC Tarsus was the scene of one of the most romantic encounters in antiquity. Cleopatra, queen of Egypt, came to the city to meet Mark Antony, the 'triple pillar of the world' whom she 'transformed into strumpet's fool'. Shakespeare, drawing on the account in Plutarch, describes her arrival as follows:

'The barge she sat in, like a burnish'd throne,
Burn'd on the water: the poop was beaten gold,
Purple the sails, and so perfumed that
The winds were love-sick with them; the oars were silver
Which to the tune of flutes kept stroke, and made
The water which they beat to follow faster,
As amorous of their strokes. For her own person,
It beggar'd all description: she did lie
In her pavilion, cloth of gold, of tissue,
O'er picturing that Venus where we see
The fancy outwork nature; on each side her
Stood pretty dimpled boys, like smiling Cupids,
With divers-colour'd fans, whose wind did seem
To glow the delicate cheeks which they did cool,
And what they undid did.'

About 46 years after this fateful meeting, Saul, the future St. Paul, was born in Tarsus. A Jew by birth he was also a Roman citizen. After his dramatic conversion on the road to Damascus he was obliged to flee from persecution in Damascus and Jerusalem and he returned for a time to his native city. Though it is not recorded in the Bible, it seems likely that he visited Tarsus also during his missionary journeys to Galatia and Phrygia. Certainly Paul's pride in his native city is reflected in his statement to the Roman Commandant in Jerusalem. 'I am a Jew, a Tarsian from Cilicia, a citizen of no mean city.' Tarsus soon became an important Christian centre and three of the great councils of the church were held here—in 431, 435 and 1177.

After a period of prosperity under the Byzantines, the fortunes of Tarsus suffered a reverse in 641, when it was sacked by the Arabs. During the centuries that followed the city had many rulers. The Arabs held it until it was recaptured by Nicephorus Phocas in 965. In 1087 it was taken by the Selçuk Turks. Ten years later during the First Crusade it was recaptured by Christian forces under Baldwin and Tancred, who placed a Byzantine garrison there. From 1132–1375 Tarsus was part of the Cilician kingdom of Armenia. In 1199 Leo II was crowned here by the Papal Legate, Cardinal Conrad von Wittelsbach. Pillaged twice by the Arabs towards the end of the 13C, it was taken by the Mamelukes in 1359. Finally, in 1515 it came under Ottoman rule.

When Beaufort came to Tarsus in 1812, he received a cool welcome from the governor and his officers were rudely treated by the populace. It was then a city of several thousand inhabitants and had a number of 'respectable looking moskes' and well-stocked bazaars. However, apart from the governor's residence, its houses were small and wretched.

At the entrance to the city there is the *Kancık Kapısı*, the Gate of the Bitch. This is also known as Cleopatra's Gate or St. Paul's Gate, though it has no known links with either. It was probably a portal in the ancient city-walls which gave access to the harbour.

A short distance from Kancık Kapısı is Tarsus American College, a junior and senior high school for Turkish boys and girls which was established in 1888. Under the grounds of this building lie the foundations of a 1C AD Roman hippodrome.

Near the vegetable market in the city centre is an ancient spring which romantics have labelled *St. Paul's Well*. The guardian will assure you that the saint often drank there and that its waters have remarkable curative properties. About 1m below ground level, it is surrounded by Roman paving. There are plans to excavate the area and restore the well to its original state.

Also in the city centre are the ruins of a Roman building which may have been a bath. By the side of this building is *Kilise Cami* which was built over a 14C Armenian church dedicated to St. Peter. According to an Islamic legend, the prophet Daniel is buried under a stream which flows close to the nearby Makam Cami.

The **Museum** of Tarsus, Tahakhane Mah., 155 Sok., No. 1, is housed in the Kulat Paş Medrese, built in 1570. Each cell is devoted to a particular subject. In the courtyard there is a fine *Roman sarcophagus*, decorated with erotes and garlands. The apse at the end houses an *Assyrian* or *late Hittite stele*, with representations of the sun-god and moon-goddess in roundels and a male figure between two lions. Nearby is a *Urartian urn*. Note the beautifully carved *mihrab*, which dates from c 1600. Against the left-hand wall is a mysterious *graffito*, which depicts a figure of indeterminate sex partially encircled by a snake. Popular tradition has given it the name of King of the Snakes, but its subject, period and provenance are unknown.

In the ethnographical collection are Ottoman-period illuminated Korans, hamam shoes, silver head-covers and silver belts and buckles. Note the Ottoman gravestones, many of which are elaborately carved.

The museum has a fine collection of Greek, Roman and Byzantine coins and some interesting jewellery including a 2C AD gold diadem from Tarsus and Roman rings and bracelets.

Near the museum is *Ulu Cami*, which was constructed in the 16C on the site of the Cathedral of St. Paul. Following the customary plan of mosques of that time, it is rectangular in shape, with a length three times its width. Inside are the tombs of the Caliph Mamoun, of Seth son of Noah, and of Lokman Hekim. (The tomb of Seth may have been an early Christian shrine.) Near Ulu Cami is *Kirk Kaşik*, a covered market, which dates from the same period as the mosque. It has been restored recently.

Outside the medieval city walls, to the E, there is a remarkable construction called Donuktaş, the *Frozen Stones*. Unfortunately, it is hidden in a maze of tiny streets and is not easy to find without the help of a guide. Popular tradition asserts that it was the tomb of the Assyrian Sardanapalus, who perished at the siege of Nineveh in 612 BC. In fact, it is almost certainly the core-wall of a Graeco-Roman temple which has lost the marble slabs that once ornamented it. It may have been dedicated to Tarz who gave his name to the city.

To the NW of the city is Gözlükule, a *tumulus*, which has been excavated by the University of Princeton. Its layers have revealed remains that date from the Bronze Age to the 16C AD. These include baths and a portico from the Hellenistic period and part of a Roman theatre. From the top of the tumulus there is a fine view of the plain that stretches S from Tarsus to the sea. This was once covered by the lake called Rhegma which Strabo states formed the harbour of Tarsus, where Cleopatra disembarked from her golden barge.

As part of a scheme to prevent flooding of the city, the Emperor Justinian (527–565), had a *bridge* constructed on the Tarsus river, the ancient Cydnus. Repaired and restored during the Ottoman period, it is still in use.

Pleasant EXCURSIONS from Tarsus may be made up the valley of the Cydnus and to a eucalyptus forest on the outskirts of the town. The banks of the river, which here descends in a series of rapids, are favourite places for summer picnics. The eucalyptus forest abounds in game, especially wild boar. All are protected by law and may not be hunted.

Between Tarsus and (38km) Adana the E24 passes through an area, formerly dependant on agriculture, which is rapidly becoming industrialised. As it approaches Adana, traffic density increases. Everything from slow-moving bullock-carts to heavily laden lorries may be encountered on this section of road.

A wide boulevard leads to the centre of Turkey's fourth largest city, **ADANA** (776,000 inhab.). The provincial capital, it derives its wealth from the vast Çukurova Plain and from its strategic position near the junction of the main E–W highway with the route through the Cilician Gates to central Anatolia. Pleasantly laid-out along the banks of the Seyhan river, the ancient Sarus, the city is surrounded by gardens and citrus groves which lend to it a pleasant feeling of *rus in urbe*.

Information and Accommodation. The Tourist Information Office is at Atatürk Cad. 13. Adana offers a wide choice of accommodation. At the top end is the expensive, but excellent, *Büyük Sürmeli*. There are several medium-priced hotels, including the recently refurbished *İnci Oteli*, Kurtuluş Cad. For the budget-conscious traveller a large number of inexpensive pensions offer varying degrees of comfort and service. Some of the city's best restaurants are in the hotels, but there are many others, particularly in the area near Ulu Cami, which specialise in regional dishes like Adana Kebab. Full information about hotels and restaurants in Adana and the surrounding area may be obtained from the Tourist Information Office.

Post Office and Banks. Adana's principal post office is located near the Kemeraltı mosque in the city centre. There are branches of the main Turkish banks in various parts of the city.

Transport. Adana has good road, rail, and air connections. There are coach services by the E24 W to *Alanya* and *Antalya* and by way of Gaziantep to E Turkey, also by the E5 S to Antayka and N, via the Cilician Gates, to *Ankara*. For travellers who are not in a hurry there are comfortable, long-distance train services, including a nightly sleeper to Ankara. THY provides connections with all the principal Turkish cities and, via Ankara and *İstanbul*, with destinations abroad.

History. The origins of Adana are shrouded in legend. Its name is supposed to be derived from Adanos, son of Uranus, who is credited with having founded the city c 1000 BC. It was probably the *Danunas*, the city of the Hittite king Asitawadda, which is mentioned on an inscription found at Karatepe, 125km to the NE (see Rte 30).

From its earliest days it sheltered a colony of Greek traders and it had important commercial relations with a number of countries in the Middle East. According to the Bible (I Kings 10.28), Solomon imported horses from the plain of Coa (Çukurova). Conquered by the Assyrian Sargon II c 712 BC, the area later came under Persian control.

Until the Hellenistic period, Adana was overshadowed by its larger and more important neighbour, Tarsus. It enjoyed a period of prosperity under the Seleucid Antiochus IV Epiphanes (175–164 BC), who renamed it Antiocheia on the Sarus. When Cilicia came under Roman rule in the 1C BC the strategic and economic importance of Adana's location was soon recognised. During the reign of Hadrian (117–138) a stone bridge, which is still used, was constructed over the Sarus (Seyhan).

In the centuries that followed, Adana changed hands frequently. Like its neighbours it was conquered by the Arabs and became part of a chain of fortified outposts on the frontier with Byzantium. In the 11C the city came, successively, under the rule of the Selçuks and the Armenians. It fell into the hands of the Mamelukes in the 14C, when they overran the Cilician Kingdom of Armenia. Finally, in 1515, during the reign of Selim I, Adana was captured by the Ottoman Turks.

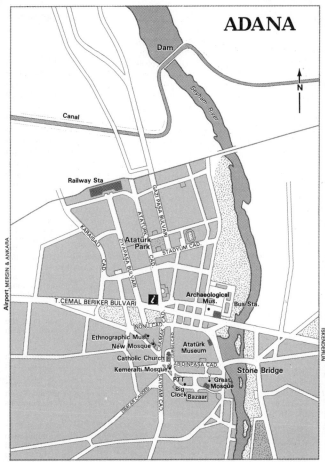

Adana's **Archaeological Museum**, in Fuzuli Cad. near the Seyhan River, has an excellent collection of artefacts most of which were found in the city and surrounding countryside. Unfortunately, only a few bear labels giving dates, and provenance. Apart from a short leaflet in somewhat fractured English, there is no published information available about the collection.

The garden surrounding the building contains a selection of architectural fragments, stelae and funerary monuments from various periods. In the entrance hall there is the so-called *Achilles sarcophagus* from Tarsus which dates from the 2C AD. The long sides are decorated with scenes from the 'Iliad': the dead Hector, Priam before Achilles, Hermes and Briseis, the dead Patroclus. At the ends there are representations of a sphinx and of a griffin. Nearby is a 4C BC *anthropoid sarcophagus* which was found at Soli but came originally from Sidon in Phoenicia. This takes the form of a figure of indeterminate sex with long hair. Three *Roman cinerary urns* from near Adana contain human remains. On the wall to the right there is a large fragment of a *statue* from Kadirli which is believed to depict a Roman senator.

Just inside the door of the room to the right are two lead *coffins*, which date from c 1400. One has the representation of a seven-branched candlestick on the inside. Note the large sections of *Roman and Byzantine mosaics* from Adana mounted on the wall nearby. A fine *Hittite stele* from Maraş shows a male figure standing on a bull's back holding an axe. In the centre of the room there is a large *bronze statue* of a Roman senator which was found in the sea at Karataş. This has been skillfully restored by Turkish archaeologists. On the end wall is a 2C AD *mosaic* from Adana. This shows two erotes, one fighting an animal, the other holding a bow. The two large *bronze bowls* are Roman, as is the substantial fragment of a *statue of Bes*. On the landing upstairs there are several late period funerary stelae and cases of *Roman glass*. Note also the fine *female head* with an oriental-type headdress.

Apart from a large mosaic from Adana, which may depict Orpheus, the rooms on the first floor are devoted to a display of ceramics, terracottas, bronzes and coins. Among the Roman bronzes there are two fine *figurines of Mithras*, one wearing a curious cloak. There are also busts of Ares, Zeus, Apollo, Aphrodite, Tyche and Pan. A *bronze Hittite figure* is fitted with a detachable gold mask. Objects found in 1972 at Anazarbus in a 2C or 3C AD sarcophagus include a marble bust, glass rod, bone needle, glass bottles and glass hairpins, gold earrings and a ring, and a pottery lamp. Among the jewellery there is an *iron seal ring* set with a red agate, which bears a representation of Augustus. There is a large selection of *gold grave goods*, including a circlet of leaves which was placed on the head of the deceased, and a crown. Among a fine display of seals from many periods and locations there an interesting group of *Hittite seals* from Tarsus.

The **Ethnographical Museum** is located in the city centre, near the Adana Hotel in a former church. In addition to the usual collection of costumes, household objects, jewellery, musical instruments, carpets and kilims, there is an excellent reconstruction of a nomads' tent. Note also the fine display of copies of the Koran and of traditional embroidery.

When Atatürk visited Adana in 1923 and 1925, he stayed in the former palace of Suphi Paşa. This building, located near the Seyhan, has been turned into a *Museum* to commemorate his visits.

Adana's most striking reminder of the past is the **Taş Köprü**, the Stone Bridge, which spans the river Seyhan (the ancient Sarus). An inscription in Adana's Archaeological Museum suggests that it was constructed by the engineer named Auxentius in the reign of Hadrian. Akurgal, however, proposes that it may have been built by Auxentius, 'comes et mechanicus', who was known as a constructor of bridges in Rome c AD 384. The bridge was restored by Justinian in the 6C, by the Caliph Memoun, the son of Haroun-al-Rashid, in the 9C, and several times under Ottoman rule. Until the the beginning of this century a toll had to be paid by those who crossed it. Secured in the past by strong gates at either end, the Taş Köprü is 300m long and 13m high. Three of its 21 arches have been filled in. At one time the Seyhan was navigable as far as Taş Köprü. However, the water-level of the river has been lowered by the construction of two dams upstream and this is no longer possible. A pleasant evening walk, particularly during the fierce heat of Adana's summer, is from Taş Köprü to the lower dam, a distance of c 1.5km.

Adana is rich in examples of Islamic art. In the centre of the city at the back of of Abidin Paşa Cad., is the 16C *Ulu Camii* (Great Mosque). Constructed by members of the Ramazan family in a style found frequently in N Syria, the outside is decorated with black and white marble. The mihrab is surrounded by a band of the same marble and ornamented with ceramic tiles from Kütahya and İznik. In a park nearby is the tomb of the well-known Turkish poet Ziya Paşa. To the rear of Ulu Camii is the small 15C Akça Mesçidi. Two examples of old houses are the late 15C Harem Dairesi and Selamlik Dairesi which were built by Halil Bey, a distinguished member of the Ramazan family who initiated the construction of Ulu Camii (see above). Much loved by the people of Adana is the late Ottoman *clock tower*. Built of brick, its stark, simple lines are reminiscent of the medieval watch-towers of San Gimignano.

A visit to the *artificial lake*, created by the upper dam on the Seyhan river, provides a diversion which is particularly welcome during the oppressive heat of Adana's summer. Sited to the N of the city this is easily reached by the road to c 10km Cıraklı and c 35km Çatalan. At the lake there are facilities for boating and a number of pleasant picnic sites.

To the S of the city, road 815 traverses the fertile, if monotonous, Cilician plain to reach the sea at 50km *Karataş*. This has been identified as the site of MEGARSUS which was visited by Alexander the Great in 333 BC. Here, according to Arrian, he sacrificed to the 'local Athene'.

On the outskirts of the modern village are the remains of ancient walls and baths, while a short distance from the shore there are some submerged ruins. A fine bronze statue, believed to be a representation of a Roman senator, was found in the sea off Karataş. It is now in the Adana Archaeological Museum (see above).

About 2km to the E of Karataş there is a pleasant camping area sited in a small wood, but the modern village has few attractions. The surrounding coastline is dull, the beaches are muddy and not very clean. Interest in this part of Cilicia springs from its historical associations. Alexander came to Megarsus at a critical moment in his campaign against the Persians and it was from here that he went on to his decisive encounter with Darius at Issus.

A short distance inland on the Pyramus river, the modern Ceyhan Nehri, the site of MALLUS has been located. Here Alexander sacrificed to the ghost of the seer and demi-god Amphilochus, who was, according to Strabo, the son of Alcmaeon and Manto. With his half-brother Mopsus, also a famous soothsayer, he founded a dream oracle at Mallus. Later they quarrelled over who should rule the town and, engaging in single combat, each fell by his brother's hand. They were buried at Megarsus but their animosity continued after death. The tombs of the soothsayers were so placed that one could not be seen from the other! (Strabo, 'Geography' 14.516.)

Alexander settled some local political problems at Mallus. He also remitted the tribute, which the town paid to Darius, as it was a colony of Argus and he claimed descent from the Argive Heracleidae. Today nothing remains of this ancient settlement. All its stones have been carted away to be used in the construction of the modern village of Kızıltahta.

30 Excursions from Adana

A. Yılan Kalesi, Anavarza (Anazarbus), Kadirli and Karatape

Total distance c 169km. **Adana**—E24/E5 c 25km—(c 3km **Yakapınar**, formerly Misis, ancient *Mopsuetia*)—(c 10km *Sirkeli*)—(c 3km **Yılan Kalesi**)—(c 3km *Ceyhan*)—R817 (c 4km **Anavarza / *Anazarbus***)—c 12km *Çukurköprü*—c 15km **Kadirli / *Flaviopolis*—** c 21km **Karatepe**—c 18km *Bodrum / Hierapolis Castabala*—c 3km **Toprakkale**— c 75km **Adana**.

This excursion, which takes in the Hittite, Roman, Crusader and Armenian sites around Adana, is aimed at visitors who have their own transport. It can be covered in one day, but a fuller and more rewarding examination of the sites requires at least two days. As accommodation outside Adana is not easy to find, it is advisable to use that city as a base. There are restaurants at Ceyhan and Kadirli and light refreshments may be obtainable at or near the other sites. However, there are many places on the route where it is possible to have a pleasant picnic.

All of these sites may be reached by some form of public transport, bus or dolmuş, possibly supplemented by taxis. However, this will certainly be at the cost of much wasted time as connections between the various towns and villages are neither frequent nor reliable.

Cross the Taş Köprü and leave Adana by the E24/E5 in the direction of Ceyhan. After c 25km a turn to the right leads to the village of (38km) **Yakapınar**, formerly known as *Misis*. In ancient times it was called MOPSUESTIA from the tradition that it was founded by Mopsus.

History. According to the legend Mopsus fled with a group of followers from Troy after its capture by the Greeks. In addition to Mallus and Mopsuestia, he is credited with having established a number of other cities in Asia Minor. An interesting link with this traditional belief is provided by an inscription at Karatepe (c 60km to the NE). This states that the Hittite king Asitawada, who reigned in the late 9C or early 8C BC, claimed descent from Mopsus. The presence of Hittites in the region of Mopsuestia is proved by the discovery of a 13C BC relief of King Muwattalli at nearby Sirkeli.

After the death of Alexander the Great, Mopsuestia became part of the Seleucid kingdom of Syria and, to flatter its conquerors, called itself for a time Seleucia. Later it passed into the hands of the Romans and reverted to its old name. However, the Mopseustians were always ready to change when it was to their advantage. During the reign of Hadrian (117–138), the town took his name. Not surprisingly, under the Pax Romana it enjoyed a period of considerable affluence. After the coming of Christianity to the area it became an episcopal see.

In the 7C and 8C, when the Arabs ravaged Cilicia, Mopsuestia suffered badly from their raids. During the centuries that followed, it shared the fate of its neighbours. At various times it was ruled by the Byzantines, Arabs, Armenians, Crusaders, Mamelukes and Turks. To the Crusaders it was known as Mamistra. It was under its walls that the bloody, fratricidal encounter between Baldwin and Tancred, which so disgraced the First Crusade, took place in 1097. Because of the Roman bridge over the Pyramus (Ceyhan Nehri) at Mamistra and, as an important stronghold on the route to Syria, its possession was frequently disputed by both the various Christian factions and by the Muslims. About 1134 it was captured by the Armenian Leo I, but retaken shortly afterwards by the Byzantines under John Comnenus. In 1158 Manuel I Comnenus received the submission of Reginald de Chatillon, who had ravaged Cyprus, at Mamistra. From 1173 onwards, after Mleh's victory over the Byzantines, it was again in Armenian hands. Despite all the turmoil, it continued to be an important trading post until the late 14C. The Genoese and other European merchants established depots there and bartered for goods brought overland by caravan from the Far East. With the rest of Cilicia, Mamistra came under Ottoman rule in 1515, when it was captured by Selim the Grim (1512–1520).

Today there are few traces of the past at Yakapınar. When Victor Langlois visited Cilicia in 1852 and 1853, the *Roman bridge* over the Pyramus bore a cippus commemorating a soldier of the XVI legion, who had served in Cilicia, Lycia and Palestine. This bridge, which was repaired by Justinian (527–565), was badly damaged by a flood in 1717 and again after the battle of Beylan in 1832.

There are also the ruins of theatre, of a temple of Apollo, and of an aqueduct from the Graeco-Roman period. From the Christian era there is a fine 4C *mosaic* which depicts Noah's Ark surrounded by a decorative border of animals. This, found some years ago in an orange grove near the village, is believed to have ornamented the floor of a Byzantine basilica. For conservation reasons this structure is not open to the public at present. Although Mamistra was an episcopal see during the Byzantine period and the Venetians are known to have had a church there, no other Christian buildings have been found so far.

The Ottoman period is represented by a caravanserai and a small mosque near the bridge.

To see the Hittite relief at 10km *Sirkeli*, take the old road from Yakapınar to Ceyhan. The *relief*, which shows King Muwattalli (c 1315–1282 BC), is on a rock by the Ceyhan Nehri. Muwattalli defeated the pharaoh Rameses II at the battle of Kadesh (1285 BC) and made the Hittite Empire into a formidable power, which rivalled Egypt in importance. It is known that he moved from Hattusa to a new capital called Dattassa, which so far has not been discovered. Because of this relief, some scholars believe that Dattassa may have been located at Sirkeli.

From Yakapınar return to the E24 and continue in the direction of Ceyhan. After c 8km a striking medieval castle, **Yılan Kalesi**, comes into view on the S skyline. At 12km turn to the right and proceed for c 3km across the valley to a parking place on the spur just below the castle.

The medieval name of this castle is unknown. It has not been possible to link either its Turkish name, which means the Castle of the Snake, or its Kurdish name *Shah Meran*, King of Snakes, with any of those in the baronial lists or in medieval chronicles. In popular mythology it was believed to be the home of a tyrant with magical powers, a medieval version of Typhon, who was part-man and part-snake. Serpents came at his bidding and he used them to enforce his will. Finally, he was slain at Tarsus where he had gone to kidnap the daughter of the king of that city. Another legend relates that the castle was never captured, but that it had to be abandoned, as it was infested with snakes. Both stories probably originate from a misinterpretation of a relief over the main gateway. This shows a majestic seated figure holding sceptre-like objects, which somewhat resembles snakes.

Yılan Kalesi is sited strategically on a ridge which dominates both the road from Adana and the Armenian capital Sis, the modern Kozan, and a wide stretch of the Pyramus river. An examination of its design and structure has suggested that it was built by the Armenian Crown Prince Leo, later Leo III (1270–89), sometime before his capture by the Arabs in 1266. A rough path leads upwards from the car-park to the outer fortifications. From there onwards the going is difficult, as to get to the castle's only entrance it is necessary to clamber over a confused mass of huge boulders. Reaching upwards for hand-holds that are out of sight, one remembers the castle's name with some misgivings. However, there appear to be few snakes now in Yılan Kalesi. As a rule, the only reptiles visible are the sun-loving lizards, which gaze fearlessly at visitors and wait until the last moment before disappearing into cracks in the ancient masonry.

The castle gatehouse is guarded by two projecting towers. Facing the relief over the entrance (see above) is another, which bears the representation of a rampant lion. The theory that the castle was built by a prince and not a king is based on the fact that neither the seated figure nor the lion are crowned.

To assist the defenders, access to the interior of the castle was by a passage at right angles to the gateway. This opens on to a large court which was probably used to shelter the local inhabitants in times of danger. A cistern, which still bears traces of its waterproof coating, ensured an adequate supply of water for the defenders. Opening from the ramparts there are a number of vaulted chambers which may have served as storerooms or quarters for the garrison. There are the remains of a small chapel and the more substantial lodgings of the castle's commander. From the walls there are fine views

S over the Pyramus river, the modern Ceyhan Nehri, and N to the distant Taurus Mountains.

In the late evening, when the towers and ramparts of Yılan Kalesi turn red in the light of the setting sun, and the shadows, gather at its feet, this castle becomes both a symbol and a reminder of the turbulent history of the Cilician Kingdom of Armenia. After the Mamelukes had defeated the Armenians and captured Crown Prince Leo in 1266, they roamed, unchecked, pillaging and ravaging the cities and towns of the plain. 'Sis [the capital] and its chief church were given to the flames, the tombs of the kings and princes violated, and their bones torn from this last resting place, burned, and scattered to the winds.'

Ten years later Leo succeeded Hetoum I as king of Armenia and in desperation turned to the Mongols for help. It was too late. The Mamelukes could not be stopped. In 1281 he joined with the Mongols in an invasion of Syria, but their combined armies were defeated at Homs by a Mameluke force under the command of Sultan Kalavun. Leo had to sue for peace. In 1285 this was granted on crushing conditions. The Armenians undertook to pay an annual tribute of 1,000,000 dirhams and promised that they would not build any more castles.

On returning to the E24, continue in the direction of (5km) Ceyhan, which is reached by a turning on the right. **Ceyhan** (55,000 inhab.) is a bustling market town for the agricultural produce of the surrounding countryside. Apart from being a useful centre for visiting E Cilicia it has little to interest the traveller.

Unless you intend to visit Ceyhan, take the left turn from the E24 on to R817, signposted Kozan and Kadirli. After c 23km turn right on to a narrow, dusty track, which leads to the village of c 4km *Anavarza*, which is dominated by the great **fortress of Anazarbus**. This raises a long limestone escarpment which measures 4.5km N–S and rises in places to a height of 200m. An area much subject to earthquakes—it suffered a particularly severe shock in 1945—it also has a very capricious climate. Thunder storms in June are not at all unknown.

History. The history of Anazarbus has been pieced together from a variety of sources. Coins, inscriptions and an examination of its ancient remains have all helped to provide a picture of its past. Attempts have been made to identify the city with a place called Kundu which revolted in the mid 7C BC against Assyria. However, the first hard evidence about Anazarbus is provided by coins which have been dated to the 1C BC. Research by the English archaeologist Michael Gough suggests that the city's name, which is not Greek, may be derived from the Persian *nabarza*, which means unconquered and is an adjective frequently applied to Mithras. Anazarbus was probably first applied to the escarpment and the buildings on it and later to the lower city.

Two inscriptions found in Anazarbus support the theory that it formed part of the realm of Tarcondimotus, who c 52 BC ruled a large part of the Cilician plain from nearby Hieropolis Castabala. In 19 BC Tarcondimotus II renamed Anazarbus *Caesarea* or *Caesarea by Anazarbus* as a sign of gratitude to Augustus, who had restored his kingdom to him. The city probably came under direct Roman rule during the reign of Claudius (AD 41–54).

By the reign of Domitian (AD 81–96) the office of demiurgus existed in Anazarbus. In 207 it began to call itself a metropolis and from then on appears to have had equal status with Tarsus. A commemorative coin was issued in 221, when it enjoyed the dubious honour of having the notorious and dissolute Emperor Elagabalus as one of its two demiurgi.

Little is known about what happened in the city during the late Roman and Byzantine periods. It became the principal city of Cilicia Secunda during the reign of Theodosius II (408–450). Twice in the following century it suffered severe earthquake damage and changed its name, first to Justinopolis and then to Justinianopolis, perhaps as a mark of gratitude for imperial assistance received after the disasters.

When the Arab raids began, the city's isolated position on the frontier of Byzantine territory made it particularly vulnerable. From the late 8C to the late 10C it was in Arab hands. During this period the fortifications of *Ayn Zarba*, as it had become known, were improved twice; first by Haroun al Rashid in 796 and then by the Hamdanids in the 10C. After a brief period of occupation by the Byzantines, it passed to the Armenians and Toros I made it his capital in 1100. It retained that status for almost a century, but when the centre of power moved first to Tarsus and then to Sis, Anazarbus began to decline. When the Mamelukes finally swept away the Cilician Kingdom of Armenia in 1375, the city was abandoned and was never reoccupied.

A number of antiquities found in the city are preserved in the courtyard of the bekçi's house which is in the centre of the modern village of Anavarza. These include some fine *mosaics*, one of which shows Thetis with dolphins, late Roman *sarcophagi* and *funerary stelae*. The bekçi, who has a fund of information about the site, will sometimes entertain visitors with his comments on his little collection. He will also indicate the best and safest way to get to the summit of the escarpment. If possible, anyone wishing to visit the castle should take a guide from the village, as parts of the enceintes are dangerous.

The remains in the lower city fall into three main sections—those to the right of the dirt road, which passes through the artificial cleft in the escarpment, those on the W slope of the escarpment, and those in the large area enclosed by the city walls.

The most striking ruin to the right of this road is the *stadium*, which measures 410m by 64m. At the principal entrance on the SW there are a few damaged cornice blocks and part of the pilaster. On the SE side spectators sat in two stands cut from the rock-face. Above the top level of seats, holes cut into the rock probably held beams, which supported vela to protect spectators from the weather. The spina in the centre of the track is well preserved. There is no trace of the seating on the NW side of the stadium. It is probable that wooden stands were used there. A very worn inscription on the front of the SW stand has been dated to the 3C or 4C AD.

Above the stadium and to the S are sarcophagi and a number of rock-tombs. About 100m to the SW, part of the *ancient road* to Mopsuestia may be seen. To ensure that it was not flooded during the winter, this was built on a causeway. Traces of an *amphitheatre* lie c 150m to the E of the road. As far as can be judged from the small part remaining, this formed an elliptical structure measuring c 60m by 80m, which backed on to the rockface. When the amphitheatre was used for wild beast shows, the animals were probably brought into the arena through the underground passage on the W side which is now largely filled with debris.

The *artificial cleft*, 250m long and 4–5m wide, which divides the escarpment is thought to date from the late Roman or early Byzantine period. The road, which passes through the cleft, probably connected Anazarbus with Flaviopolis, modern Kadirli, and Hieropolis Castabala. It was carried by a Roman bridge, now ruined, over the the Sumbas Çayı, c 1.5km to the E. In the cleft there are several 4C tombs and sarcophagi cut from the rock-face. There is also an inscription which quotes the opening words of the 46th psalm, 'God is our refuge and stronghold'. This probably relates to the earthquakes which devastated Anazarbus so often, as the prayer continues, 'sovereign aid he has brought us in the hour of peril. Not for us to be afraid, though earth should tumble about us, and the hills be carried away into the depths of the sea'. If so, it is a moving reflection of the strong faith of the Christians of Anazarbus at those times, when their city was visited by frequent natural disasters.

To the N of the cleft are the remains of the *theatre* which is in a very ruinous condition. This had a diameter of c 60m and was free-standing on the S, where the retaining wall of the cavea was supported by concrete piers that reduce in height. On the N it was built into the hill. At each side of the cavea there was a covered parados. Most of the scaena has disappeared. Because of the poor general state of preservation of the theatre it is impossible to determine its seating arrangement or capacity.

Above the theatre there are several *sarcophagi* and two interesting *reliefs*. One, first described by J.T. Bent in 1890, shows four nude athletes in a palaestra: one youth is doing a handstand with the help of a companion. Their exercises are presided over by a clothed figure, presumably the gymnasiarch, who holds a wreath and a palm branch. The other depicts a winged deity, who stands on the back of a dolphin while holding a funerary inscription above his head.

Continue around the base of the escarpment to a stretch of the *city wall* which is well-preserved. About 250m to the N of this is the *cave* where Bent discovered a dedication made in AD 153 by the priestess Regina to the gods of the city, Zeus, Hera Gamelia and Ares. He describes its location as being high up in an almost inaccessible cave in a mountain behind Anazarba. The inscription is on the the upper surface of the S wall of the outer part of the cave. Access to the cave, which is c 30m above ground-level, is not easy. Care should be taken, particularly on the descent.

At the bottom of the escarpment, c 500km N of the cave with the dedication, is the *rock-tomb of the two eunuchs* (Furies' Tomb). They were the servants of Queen Julia the Younger, sister of Philopator, who died in AD 17. An inscription over the tomb, which has been partly erased, appears to invoke a curse on anyone who disturbs it.

To the W of this tomb are the substantial remains of the principal *aqueduct* which is believed to date from the time of Domitian. This supplied the city with water from the upper reaches of the Sumbas river. S of the aqueduct, towards the centre of the area enclosed by the walls, are the ruins of a church and of a baths complex. The *church*, dedicated to the Apostles, was an early Byzantine basilica. The *baths*, which were also constructed during the Byzantine period, measured c 40m by 25m. About half of the area was taken up by the vaulted frigidarium on the W, the remainder being divided between the tepidarium in the SE and the calidarium in the NE corner of the complex.

From the baths walk S for c 700m to the substantial remains of the *triumphal arch* which is believed to date from the time of Septimius Severus (193–211). This measures c 30m by 9m. The height of the central arch is c 10.5m and that of the side arches 7m. The arch is constructed of concrete faced with ashlar and, on the upper area, tufa. Elaborately decorated with columns and pilasters of the Corinthian order, its three arches are linked by an internal vaulted corridor.

Visitors who have the time and the energy to go to the castle, should return to the theatre. From there rock-cut steps lead up to the first enceinte. This is an easy climb and worth the effort. There is a splendid view from the ridge over the walled lower city and the surrounding countryside.

The fortified area stretches for c 700m along the escarpment. It is

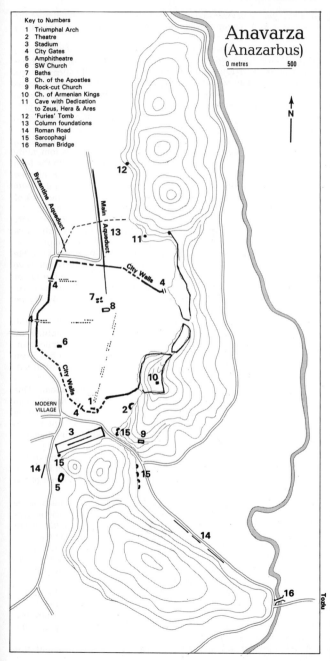

Key to Numbers
1 Triumphal Arch
2 Theatre
3 Stadium
4 City Gates
5 Amphitheatre
6 SW Church
7 Baths
8 Ch. of the Apostles
9 Rock-cut Church
10 Ch. of Armenian Kings
11 Cave with Dedication
   to Zeus, Hera & Ares
12 'Furies' Tomb
13 Column foundations
14 Roman Road
15 Sarcophagi
16 Roman Bridge

Anavarza
(Anazarbus)

0 metres   500

divided into three sections: the first enceinte, where the garrison was quartered and where the city's inhabitants took refuge in time of danger; a three-storied tower, and the second enceinte.

Entrance to the *first enceinte* is by a gateway at the W end of the S wall. This is believed to date from the 8C, when Anazarbus was occupied by the Arabs under Haroun al-Raschid. The stretch of wall to the E of the gate, which has four defensive towers, was constructed by the Armenians. Access to the semicircular towers is provided by doors raised c 1m above the ground. Their dusty interiors are dimly lit by arrow slits. Wooden beams, which have disappeared, supported an upper floor. Towards the SE corner of the wall there was a primitive toilet.

Flights of steps lead to the battlements where there is a parapet 1m wide protected by a curtain wall. Most of the E defensive wall, which is in a ruinous condition, dates from the Byzantine period. The W side of the enceinte was never walled as, sloping at a steep angle, it soon becomes a cliff that drops sheer into the plain.

In the SE corner of the first enceinte are the ruins of the *Church of the Armenian kings*. This building, measuring 13m by 9.6m, had a central nave flanked by two aisles. There were three narrow windows at the E end, three on N wall and one on the W and S.

Around the top of the wall there was inscription in Armenian, part of which was still intact when Victor Langlois visited the castle in the mid-19C. Much of this has fallen down and has been damaged in the intervening period. Among prayers 'for the health of my children; in memory of my parents ...' he found a memorial to an unknown nephew of Leo I named Ochin and another, dating from 1188, which mentions Rupen III. This was the Rupen who, according to the chroniclers, went to Antioch, towards the end of his life, 'for orgies with evil women', but instead was seized and imprisoned there by Bohemond III. Presumably chastened by this experience, he gave the throne to his younger brother Leo. When released from captivity, he retired to a monastery near Sis in 1187, where he died within the year.

The interior of the church was covered with frescoes. Langlois comments on the well-preserved representations of saints of the Armenian church which he saw there. Unfortunately, these have suffered much damage from the weather and some have been defaced deliberately. It is still just possible to make out the the figure of Christ Pantocrator on the dome.

To the NE of the church is the outline of a small Byzantine chapel. Gough reports having found an empty burial vault to the SW.

To the N of the first enceinte, the escarpment narrows dramatically. A gap 15m wide, which presumably was spanned by a bridge, separated it from a three-storied *Armenian tower*. This gap is not easy to cross and many visitors find it too daunting and abandon their tour of the fortress at this point. According to an inscription in Armenian, the tower was erected in 1188, just after Rupen's brother, Leo II, came to the throne.

Access to the *second enceinte* is no easier. It is separated from the tower by a gap c 4m wide, whose base has been shaped artificially so that it slopes to the precipice on the W and the cliff on the E. Great care should be observed in crossing over.

The oldest buildings in the castle are to be found in the second enceinte. Many have been damaged, perhaps by earthquakes, during the course of the centuries and it is difficult to determine their purpose. There are several cisterns, the ruins of a small Armenian chapel, a postern and vaulted passages.

Gough describes a long, narrow room 12m by 7m on the W side of the second enceinte. This has a blackened patch on the ceiling, the only place in the castle which provides evidence of artificial lighting. The room also has a large window on the W wall with a terrifying view. 'Its sill is at the same level as the present floor ... the cliff overhangs slightly at this point, and there is nothing to be seen between it [the window] and the plain, except the eagles below, circling about their nests in the rock.'

On returning to the main road continue N to c 12km Çukurköprü. There turn right for c 15km *Kadirli*, the ancient FLAVIOPOLIS. One of the few visible remains of the city's past is *Ala Camii*, a former Christian basilica, built on the foundations of a Roman temple, which was later turned into a mosque. It has now been deconsecrated. Ask for directions as there are no signs.

Leave Kadirli by the Andırn road. On the outskirts of the town take a right-hand turn which is signposted to c 21km **Karatepe**. Careful driving is required as although it has a good surface this road is very narrow in parts and has many bends. Climbing steadily for most of the way, it reveals pleasant vistas of the surrounding countryside.

Karatepe is on a slight, pine-clad eminence that projects into a modern artificial lake produced by the construction of a dam on the Ceyhan Nehri. Its situation and lay-out combine to make it one of the most attractive sites in Cilicia. Near the entrance there is a small tourist pavilion where light refreshments may be obtained. The authorities plan to provide facilities for camping in the area.

Excavations have been conducted for more than 20 years at Karatepe by Professors Bossert, Alkım and Çambel. The site has been turned into an open-air museum, and the finds are displayed where they were discovered. Because it is still being excavated and has not been published photography is not permitted at Karatepe. Cameras must be left with the bekçi at the entrance.

History. The Hittites, a people of Indo-European origin, conquered a large area of central Anatolia towards the beginning of the second millennium BC. Hattusas, the modern Boğazköy, on the Halys river was their capital. Towards 1640 BC they extended their influence to S Anatolia and N Syria. Eventually, this brought them into conflict with the Egyptians, whom they defeated decisively at the battle of Kadesh in 1285 BC.

The first phase of Hittite civilisation came to a comparatively sudden end towards 1200 BC. Its downfall is usually attributed to an onslaught mounted by that mysterious race known to the Egyptians as the Sea Peoples. They are blamed not only for the destruction of the Hittite Empire and the reduction of Egyptian influence in the Middle East, but for the overthrow of the Mycenaeans and the creation of widespread chaos throughout the Levant.

With the destruction of the empire, Hittite influence did not come an end. A number of petty kingdoms, whose rulers had Hittite names, sprang up in Syria and in the area of the Taurus Mountains. One of these, located in Cilicia, had an interesting link with Greek legends. According to a text of the 8C BC Asitawada, the ruler of neo-Hittite Karatepe, described himself as belonging to the 'House of Mps'. Mps is usually taken to be the same as Mopsus, the legendary founder of Mopsuestia and a number of other cities in Asia Minor. (See above.) The orthostats, described below, display signs of Greek influence and some of the inscriptions on them refer to a people called Danuna and Danauna. They may have been the Danaoi mentioned by Homer, who took the side of the Achaeans in the Trojan War. This theory is supported to some extent by the discovery by Myres in 1903 in Troy I of fragments of pottery, which he described as Anatolian. Similar pottery has been found at Karatepe.

About 500 years after the fall of their empire, the extinction of the Hittites as a political force was completed. One by one the neo-Hittite kingdoms were overthrown by the Assyrians and their peoples merged with other races.

A path leads upwards through the pine woods to the gate of the *palace*. This was surrounded by a defensive wall c 1km in circumference, which was pierced by gateways guarded by lions and sphinxes. Karatepe was the summer palace of King Asitawada and there are a number of orthostats which illustrate in a delightfully informal way the relaxed atmosphere of his court. The king is portrayed at dinner. Holding a meat patty in his left hand, he leans forward to take a loaf of bread from a bowl. Two attendants gently fan the air to cool him. More food, including roast hare and other meats, fruit and drink, is being brought from the kitchens. On the lower part of the slab servants lead an ox and a lamb to the palace for the feast. During the meal musicians with lyres play for the king's entertainment.

Daily life at the court of Asitawada is illustrated by a number of naturalistic tableaux. A monkey crouches half-hidden under the king's table, bears perform a shambling dance, the grotesque god Bes carries two monkeys on his shoulders, birds of prey peck at a dead hare, warriors display their arms, and a mother leans forward protectively to suckle her child.

A path to the right leads across the promontory to the *lower gate* of the palace. Like the principal entrance this is also protected by lions and sphinxes. The orthostats here carry a number of inscriptions in hieroglyphic Hittite on the right hand side and in old Phoenician on the left. This enabled the archaeologists to decipher the Hittite texts. Note the particularly fine representation of a ship. From the lower gate take the path above the lake and follow the circuit of the ancient walls back to the entrance.

A large part of the enjoyment derived from a visit to Karatepe comes from the beauty of its surroundings and from the imaginative way in which the archaeologists have displayed their finds. A summer picnic in the shade of its pine wood is an agreeable way to end the visit and to prepare the traveller for the next stage of the journey. It is also a reminder of the pleasures once enjoyed there by its founder Asitawada.

About 5km to the NE is another ancient site, DOMUZTEPE. In addition to remains contemporaneous with those of Karatepe, 8C BC, it has two layers of occupation dated to c 9C BC. These bear traces of destruction by fire. A 7C BC gateway is decorated with sculptures taken from a much earlier building. The site appears to have been occupied also during the Hellenistic and Roman periods.

On leaving Karatepe take the first turning on the left along a rough track for c 10km. On reaching the main road, turn right and continue for c 15km to the dam at Çevdetiye Köyü. Follow the track, which runs parallel with the canal for c 5km, and then turn right on to the main road. On the left, a short distance before Toprakkale Köyü, are the ruins of HIERAPOLIS CASTABALA, known today as *Bodrum*.

History. Curtius relates that Alexander the Great joined forces with Parmenion at Hierapolis Castabala in 333 BC. However, it seems more likely that they met on the S part of Castabala territory and that Parmenion visited the city during his exploratory patrols in the N passes of the Cilician plain. After they had marched S towards Issus, Darius followed them with his army. Freya Stark, paraphrasing Curtius, provides an imaginative description of the exotic spectacle created by the Persian army as it passed under the walls of Castabala. 'The fire altars were carried across the pass and the young men in red cloaks marched before him [Darius]; and those who led the chariot and the horses of the sun; and the twelve nations; and the Immortals with their apples, in sleeved tunics and gold; and the King's relatives that surrounded his high car; and the thirty thousand footmen and the four hundred horses; and the six hundred mules and three hundred camels with money; and the chariots of the mother and wife, the women and children behind.'

Three hundred years later, Castabala was an insignificant principality in Cilicia which achieved brief fame in 31 BC, when its king, Tarcondimotus, was killed at the battle of Actium opposing Octavian. Augustus appears to have borne no grudge as he later confirmed Tarcondimotus II as its ruler. However, the dynasty did not prosper, it appears to have died out in the early 1C AD.

The ruins of Castabala have not been excavated and in summer they lie partly covered by fields of corn. A ragged *colonnade*, some of the standing columns still crowned with their Corinthian capitals and bearing the same unsightly brackets found at Pompeiopolis and Olba, straddles the plain at the foot of the acropolis. From a later period there are the walls and choirs of churches. On the right-hand side of the road are the remains of the *theatre* and of a *baths complex*.

It has not been possible to identify positively the *castle* of Castabala—a successor to the fortress which witnessed the passage of Darius' army—with any of those which appear on the list of Cilician barons compiled in 1198. It may have been constructed by the Armenians in the 13C or, as others claim, by the Knights of St. John to guard the route through Syria to the Holy Land. Separated from the nearby hill by a gap 5m wide made in ancient times, its ruined towers and broken walls, home of countless sun-worshipping lizards, are rarely visited today. However, its peaceful appearance belies a violent history. It may have been here that Stephen, brother of Thoros II, was boiled alive by the Greek garrison in 1164.

About 3km to the S **Toprakkale**, constructed of volcanic rock, sits menacingly on a low hill at the point where two of S Turkey's busiest roads, the E24 and the E5, diverge. In the Middle Ages, *Til Hamdoun*, as it was known, was one of the most important castles in Cilicia, as its strategic situation allowed it to control the traffic through Maraş and Antep to the E and down through Alexandretta (İskenderun) and Antioch (Antakya) to the S. On a clear day it is possible to see Anazarbus and even Sis from Toprakkale.

Like all the castles and cities in the area, it changed hands frequently. In 1151 it was occupied by the Armenians under Thoros II. In 1158 it was captured by the Byzantines under Manuel Comnenus. In 1185 it was delivered to the son of the Crusader Tancred, Boehmond of Antioch, as part of the ransom of Rupen (see above). Later it was regained by the Armenians under Leo II. He had established good relations with the Hospitallers (the Knights of St. John of Jerusalem) and placed the castle in their hands. In 1266 it came under the control of the Mamelukes, but was recaptured by the Armenians. In 1337 it was surrendered by Leo V to the Mamelukes and from then onwards it appears to have been abandoned.

Care should be taken in visiting Toprakkale as parts of the ruins, particularly the roofs of the vaulted chambers, are in an unsafe condition. There are also many deep cisterns, which are unprotected.

Toprakkale is protected by a double enceinte which measures c 100m by 70m. Originally constructed by the Byzantines, it was rebuilt by Armenian masons for the Hospitallers. Modelled on Krak of the Knights in Syria, it was almost impregnable. The inner bailey was protected by an ingenious series of defences, while its garrison was able to deliver a concentrated and highly directional stream of arrows from the inner and outer enceintes. Specially constructed embrasures in the curtain walls, and later in the towers and battlements, were often shaped at the base to increase the archer's field of fire. On the W there was a large thinly-walled enclosure which was added at a late period. This may have been used as temporary quarters for refugees or reinforcements to the garrison.

Access to the castle is by a minor road which is signposted in the village. From the car-park walk up a track that leads towards a doorway on the N side. There, a great gap in the wall leads first to a large vaulted chamber and then to a central courtyard which is much overgrown. In this area there are several cisterns which are partially covered by vegetation.

From the courtyard it is possible to mount the battlements which give excellent views over the Cilician plain. On the SW, in an area protected by the inner and outer defences, the commander of the castle had his quarters. Underneath the battlements large vaulted rooms, which could be entered from the inner ward of the castle, provided lodgings for the garrison and were also used as storerooms and arsenals.

On completing the visit to Toprakkale, return to 75km **Adana** (see Rte 29) by the E24/E5.

B. Kozan

Round trip c 162km. **Adana**—E24/E5 c 35km Ceyhan road junction—R817 c 46km **Kozan / Sis**.

To visit **Kozan**, ancient SIS, capital of the Cilician Kingdom of Armenia, leave Adana by the E24/E5 and continue as far as the turning for *Ceyhan*. Here take road 817, signposted Kadirli and Kozan, and at c 29km *Çukurköprü* take the left-hand turning to 17km Kozan (see also Rte 30A).

The great fortress, constructed by Leo II (1187–1219), still dominates the town. Built on a long ridge that projects from the Taurus Mountains into the Cilician plain, it controlled an important trade and communications route from the coast to the interior.

History. The Armenians were not the first to appreciate the strategic value of Sis. A Byzantine stronghold in the 9C, it was captured by the Abassids who enlarged it and improved its defences. During his great campaign against the Arabs, the town and castle were recaptured by Nicephorus Phocas in 962. Occupied by the Armenians for the first time under Thoros I (1102–29), Sis was retaken by John Comnenus. In 1114 a great earthquake centred on Maraş did considerable damage to the cities of Cilicia, including Sis. The town later fell into Armenian hands again and was capital of Armenia from 1162 until 1375. It had its share of violence and drama. In 1225 Philip, son of Bohemond IV of Antioch and king for three years only, was first imprisoned and then poisoned there. In 1309 heretics, who refused to 'accept water in the chalice and other religious innovations', were brutally punished by Oshin in Sis.

However, the last days of the Armenian capital were, perhaps, its most dramatic. Leo VI and his wife, Margaret of Soissons, were crowned in Sis on 14 September 1374. Leo's reign was brief. Mameluke forces, encouraged by a traitorous Armenian called Achot, who had become a Muslim in Egypt, were soon camped outside the walls. A contemporary chronicler voices the despair felt by many in the Levant when the lower town was sacked: 'Who can recount the tragedy that my eyes witnessed, for I saw the bright sun, the stars and the moon fall down.' In the castle the resolution of the defenders was weakened by a shortage of supplies and the fear of approaching famine. Traitors attempted to seize the king, but he made a dramatic escape by rope down into the castle moat. However, further resistance was fruitless and Leo capitulated. News of the victory produced great rejoicing in Cairo. The drums beat without ceasing for three days.

Leo and his family were taken in chains to Egypt, but later were ransomed. Then for many years, like an unwelcome ghost, he haunted the courts of Europe in a hopeless quest for aid to recover his lost kingdom. Leo, the last king of the Cilician kingdom of Armenia, died in Paris in 1393. He was buried in St. Denis, where his monument may still be seen.

Having sacked the town, the Mamelukes dismantled the castle. As time passed it fell into ruin and many of its stones were taken to build a new town.

Sis was visited in the mid 19C by Langlois and at the beginning of the 20C by Lohmann. In 1901, in the Armenian church, Lohmann saw the throne of Leo II which was ornamented with the carving of a double eagle. This has since disappeared.

Apart from the ruins of the castle, there are few reminders of the past in Kozan. Stretching for c 900m along a narrow ridge high above the town, the design of the castle was adapted to the shape of the escarpment. Where the cliffs are low, walls and towers crowned with continuous rows of machicolations were constructed. Otherwise the builders relied on the protection provided by natural features. As it is surrounded by steep rocky slopes where siege engines could only be used with difficulty, its walls are slimmer than those of contemporary Crusader castles which occupy more vulnerable positions.

Access to the castle is by a narrow path on the E side. On the right, to the N of the entrance, a spacious court, now heavily overgrown, provided shelter for the townspeople in time of danger. Near the W wall there is a large, vaulted *underground cistern*. Among the brushwood are the ruins of the garrison's quarters.

S of the entrance two gates lead, by way of narrow corridors, to the the inner keep of the castle where the *royal apartments* were sited. These terminate in a strongly fortified tower which fills the whole width of the escarpment and drops sheer to a deep rock-cut moat. The S enceinte is separated from the rest of the castle by this moat.

Even in its ruined state the castle of Sis is one of the most striking medieval buildings in Cilicia. Sadly, it attracts few visitors today. Not many are willing to make the journey to Kozan to examine its remains and ponder on its turbulent history.

Those with sufficient time and fortitude may wish to extend their excursion by going c 20km to the NE to *Fehratlı*, where there are the ruins of a small Roman sanctuary and an unusual Assyrian relief. This is believed to depict Shalmaneser III (858–824 BC), who led several expeditions against Babylonia, Anatolia and Syria. He is depicted, arms raised, facing some religious symbols.

31   Adana to İskenderun

Total distance c 124km. **Adana** E5/E24—75km *Toprakkale*—c 7km *Epiphania*—19km *Dörtyol*—4km *Yakacık / Baiae*—9km *Saraseki*—10km **İskenderun** (c 32km *Uluçınar*).

Leave **Adana** (see Rte 29) by the E5/E24 and continue for c 75km to *Toprakkale*, where the roads divide. A right-hand turn takes the E5 S to Dörtyol, İskenderun and Antakya.

For thousands of years the strip of land that separates the Amanus

Mountains from the sea has been an important trade route linking
Anatolia with Syria and the lands to the S. It has also seen the
passage of the armies of many conquerors. In 333 BC Persian might
and Greek valour met here in a battle that made a significant change
to world history. Thirteen centuries later Tancred led his band of
Crusaders through the Amanus Gates and the Pillars of Jonah, to
Syria, the Lebanon and Palestine in the first of many vain, idealistic
and blood-stained attempts to liberate the holy places of Christendom.

After c 7km, where a turning on the left leads to *Yeşilkent*, a few
ruined walls and the broken arches of an aqueduct on the right-hand
side of the road mark the site of EPIPHANIA. This city was founded c
175 BC by one of the strangest of the Seleucid kings, Antiochus IV
Epiphanes (175–164), sometimes known as Antiochus the Mad.

After spending 12 years as a hostage in Rome, he succeeded his
brother Seleucus IV Philopator. Shortly after his return to Syria,
Antiochus embarked on a series of military adventures which met
with varying degrees of success. In an attempt to unite his Greek,
Macedonian and Syrian subjects he declared himself to be Theos
Epiphanes, 'god made manifest'. His efforts to establish the worship
of the Greek gods in Jerusalem provoked a successful revolt led by
Mattathias and his sons, the Maccabees.

The sleepy town of 19km *Dörtyol* is the nearest modern settlement
to the site of one of the great battles of the ancient world.

Here, on the **Plain of Issus**, Alexander the Great and Darius, King of Persia, had
their fateful encounter on a winter's day in 333 BC. The location of the
battlefield has not been identified with certainty. It is known that the Persians
had drawn up their army on the steep banks of a river, which most modern
historians believe to have been the Payas. However, during the intervening
centuries the three rivers which cross the plain at this point, have almost
certainly changed their courses and may have deepened their beds. Consequently, it is very likely that both the configuration and height of their banks are
different today.

Alexander marched S along the coast as far as the Pillars of Jonah in search of
Darius, who had been camped at Sochoi on the other side of the Amanus
Mountains. However, the king had left this encampment and had taken his
army N towards Cilicia. When he discovered that Alexander had gone to the S,
Darius followed him and took up a position behind him on the Plain of Issus.
Alexander was informed by his scouts of the Persians' new location. So, early on
a cold November morning, after a dreadful night of gales and rain during which
he offered sacrifice to Thetis, the mother of his great hero, Achilles, he turned
his army around and marched N to meet the king.

Darius, accompanied by his family and his courtiers, had an army of 30,000
cavalry, 60,000 Cardaces, the equivalent of the Greek epheboi, and 10,000
Greek mercenaries. Alexander faced this formidable force with fewer than
35,000 men. He and the Companions were on the right near the mountains. In
the centre there were Foot Companions and Shield Bearers and the left flank by
the sea was covered by Parmenion and the cavalry.

The battle was confused and bloody. Its turning point was a daring charge by
Alexander and the Companions against the centre of the Persian army, where
the king was directing the battle. Darius panicked. Then he fled in his chariot
followed by part of his army. According to Arrian 'he led the race for safety'.
This is the scene depicted in the famous mosaic in Naples Museum.

The king kept to his chariot until, as Arrian relates, 'he was forced to abandon
it when ravines and other obstructions barred his way; then, dropping his shield
and stripping off his candys—and even leaving his bow in the war chariot—he
leapt upon a horse and rode for his life. Darkness soon closed in; and that alone
saved him from from falling into the hands of Alexander, who, while daylight
held, relentlessly pressed the pursuit; but when there was no longer light
enough to see what he was coming to, he turned back—but not without taking
possession of Darius' chariot together with his shield, mantle and bow.' He also
took more valuable booty. In Darius' headquarters he found the king's wife, his

infant son, his mother and his sisters. Alexander treated them with the courtesy due to their rank.

According to Callisthenes, the Persian casualties at Issus were 110,000 dead against a loss of 302 Macedonians. The great army of Darius was scattered to the winds. Some of his soldiers had fled with him, others had gone N into Cappadocia, others again to Egypt and Cyprus. The way to the S was open for Alexander.

Today the Plain of Issus is a pleasant, fertile region of orchards and citrus groves. Bounded on the E by the green slopes and deep ravines of the Amanus Mountains and by a low, bleak coastline on the W, it is bisected by the narrow, busy line of the E5, as it pursues its charmless way S.

At 4km *Yakacık* (formerly Payas) ruined columns mark the site of the Seleucid city of BAIAE. A small fort overlooking the sea was constructed by Ibrahim Khan-Zadek in the time of Süleyman II and restored in the 19C. Olive groves shelter a 16C mosque and bedesten. Unfortunately, the charm of the site is greatly reduced by its proximity to a large modern industrial complex.

About 9km to the S is *Saraseki*. Here were the the *Pillars of Jonah*, a pass which guarded the approaches to Syria. It was here that Alexander came in his search for Darius. (See Battle of Issus above.)

A *tower*, which may have been part of a Seleucid customs post, is popularly known as Baba Yunus, as it is believed that Jonah was delivered from the belly of the whale on a nearby beach. There are also the ruins of a *castle*, which some authorities have identified with the medieval Castrum Puellarum, or Castle of Godfrey of Lortet. Apart from a ruined tower by the entrance, which may be Frankish, the visible remains date from the Ottoman period.

10 km from Yakacık, the modern city of **İskenderun** (125,000 inhab.), formerly known as ALEXANDRETTA, is a busy commercial centre and an important trading port with a fine harbour. Sheltered by the verdant slopes by Mt Amanus, the modern Kızıl Dağ, it has a pleasant cosmopolitan air. An agreeable place to spend a few restful days, it has several good hotels and restaurants along the seafront. However, apart from its name (İskender is the Turkish for Alexander) the city retains few traces of its ancient past.

Information about accommodation, restaurants, transportation etc. in Iskenderun may be obtained from the *Tourist Information Office* in Atatürk Bulv. No. 49/B. Branches of the principal Turkish banks are located in the business and commercial quarter nearby.

History. To celebrate his triumph, Alexander dedicated altars to Zeus, Athena and Heracles on the banks of the river Payas. In imitation of his father's practice, he further commanded that a city, Alexandria ad Issum, be founded to commemorate his great victory over the Persians.

Under the Seleucids, and later the Romans, the city enjoyed a modest degree of prosperity. Two factors limited its expansion. As a port it could not compete with Seleucia ad Pieria, which was nearer to Antioch, and, because of its proximity to marshy ground and the absence of cleansing winds, it had an unhealthy climate.

Captured by the Arabs in the 7C, it was ruled by a Selçuk vassal in 1097 at the time of the First Crusade. Until the middle of the 13C it suffered the same fate as Antioch. At different times it was under Frankish, Byzantine, Armenian and Arab control. Finally, in the 16C it became part of the Ottoman Empire.

According to Langlois, Alexandretta had developed a considerable commercial importance by the mid-19C, despite its dangerous climate. It was the port of Aleppo and had attracted a number of European consular and shipping agents. Apart from the ruins of a castle built by Ibn Aly Daoud, during the caliphate of Vasik, the city had no ancient remains.

Occupied by French and British troops towards the end of World War I, it later became the Sancak of Alexandretta, a special administrative region. In 1939, with the rest of the Hatay province, it was returned to Turkey.

A pleasant EXCURSION from İskenderun is to 32km *Uluçınar*, the former Arsuz. There are frequent dolmuş services from the centre of İskenderun. Travellers with their own transport should take the E5 in the direction of Antakya and then turn right on to road 817. This follows the seashore for most of the way. Bathing here is not recommended as the beaches are pebbly and the sea is not always free from pollution.

Uluçınar, now a sleepy little village, occupies the site of the city of RHOSUS (or Rhosopolis), built by the Seleucids c 300 BC. It was mentioned by Strabo. In Byzantine times an episcopal see, there are a few traces of its past on a hill to the SE.

A rough track, not recommended for cars, continues S to *Hınzır Burnu*, where there are the ruins of a Crusader fortress which belonged to the La Roche family. Attacked by Saladin in 1188, it was later occupied by the Templars who held it until 1267, when they were ousted by the Mamelukes.

The principal charm of Uluçınar is derived more from its relaxed atmosphere than from its historical associations. To stand on the bridge over the small river and watch the fishermen land their catch, to swim from its clean beach, or to enjoy an excellent meal on the terrace of the *Arsuz Hotel* overlooking the sea, will be sufficient reward for all but the most demanding traveller.

32 İskenderun to Antakya

Total distance 57km. **İskenderun**—13km *Belen*—(c 4km *Bakras / Baghras*)—E5 44km **Antakya**.

There are frequent coach services from İskenderun to Antakya. The journey takes about two hours. Travellers who are not in a hurry may like to stop at (13km) *Belen* for lunch or to sample the waters of its spa. From Belen the road climbs steadily to the pass (500m) known in ancient times as the PYLAE SYRIAE, the Syrian Gates. They were of great strategic importance, as all traffic between Alexandretta and Antioch over the Amanus Mountains had to go through them.

About 20km from Belen a turning to the right leads to the 4km *Castle of Bakras*, formerly Baghras. This is sited at the end of a narrow valley on a hillside behind the modern village. The old road from Alexandretta and Belen to Antioch descended through this valley.

There are references in the works of Strabo, Pliny and Ptolemy to a settlement in this area called *Pagrai* or *Pagras* and in the 5C AD there was a σταθμός (station) there. This was a resting place for soldiers or travellers on a main road. After the Arab conquest of the region in the 7C AD the first stronghold was constructed at Baghras. It was used to mount attacks against the Byzantines and to prevent counter incursions by them.

Destroyed by Tancred during the First Crusade, Baghras was the subject of a fierce battle in 1156 at Alexandretta between the prince of Antioch and the Templars on one side and Thoros, ruler of the Cilician Kingdom of Armenia on the other. Known to the Crusaders as Gaston or Gastrim, the castle was a keypoint in the Templars' defensive system. Captured by Saladin in 1188, its possession was frequently disputed by the Templars, the Armenians and the Arabs. After the destruction of the Cilician Kingdom of Armenia in the 14C, it remained in Arab hands until it was captured by the Ottomans at the beginning of the 16C.

The castle occupies an area c 120m by 100m. It was surrounded by a double enceinte. Entrance was by a *gate-tower* on the NE corner which overlooked the precipitous N slope of the hill. In the interior a ramp led to a complex of rooms and buildings on several levels. These were dominated by a large *pentagonal structure* (possibly a stable) and a *chapel*. The garrison's water supply was ensured by a substantial *cistern* under the chapel and an *aqueduct* which entered the keep in the SW corner. In spite of the damage created by several earthquakes and the removal of large quantities of worked stone for building purposes in modern times, the ruins of Baghras are substantial. This interesting castle is well worth a visit.

From Bakras the E5, passing Amikgölü, Lake Amik, on the left, continues across the plain to 30km **ANTAKYA** (in the province of Hatay) the ancient ANTIOCHEIA AD ORONTEM. Antakya (109,000 inhab.) is a pleasant, compact city, oddly reminiscent of a French resort in the foothlls of the Alps. This may be due to its wide boulevards and steep-banked river and, of course, some lingering traces of the inter-war French mandate. It also has something Arabic in its make-up. This is made evident by its environs and the fact that many of its inhabitants are equally fluent in Arabic and Turkish.

Information and Accommodation. Information about accommodation, restaurants and transport in and around Antakya may be obtained from the Tourism Office at Vali Ürgen Meyd., Atatürk Cad. 41. A number of new hotels have been built in the city, but many visitors still prefer to stay in the pleasant hill-suburb of Harbiye, ancient Daphne, 9km to the S on road 825. The Hidro at Harbiye, with its atmosphere of comfortable informality and French-style unpredictable plumbing, is specially recommended (see below).

All of the main Turkish **banks** have branches in the business and commercial quarter on the right bank of the Orontes (Asi). The main **Post Office** and the **Hatay Museum** are near the bridge in the same part of the town.

History. Founded by Seleucus I Nicator (321–281) c 300 BC and named after his father, Antioch's first inhabitants were a mixture of local people and Graeco-Macedonian settlers. Many of these, including more than 5000 Macedonian and Athenian ex-soldiers, came from the nearby city of Antigonea, the short-lived creation of Antigonous I Monophthalmos (382–301 BC). The new city became the capital of an empire which at the time of the death of Seleucus extended from Macedonia to the borders of India.

Called Tetrapolis by Strabo because of its division into four self-contained areas, its great wealth attracted artists from many countries. Eutychides of Sicyon, the pupil of Lysippus, made a famous bronze statue of Tyche, the Goddess of Fortune for Antioch. One of the best known representations of the female form in antiquity, this statue is known only from a heavily-restored Roman copy in the Vatican Museum and from coins. The goddess was shown seated on Mt Sipylus, wearing a turreted crown which represented the city's fortifications. She held the palm of victory in her right hand, while resting one foot on the river-god Orontes; Seleucus I and Antiochus I placed a wreath on her head.

Because of its position on the Silk Road, the city helped to popularise the use of this material throughout the Hellenic world. Surrounded by wealth and luxury the inhabitants of Antioch soon developed such a sybaritic, self-indulgent life-style that it acquired an unequalled reputation for licence and decadence.

The Seleucid Empire was ended by the invasion of the Armenian, Tigranes the Great (94–56 BC) in 83 BC. In 64 BC Antioch was created capital of the Roman province of Syria by Pompey and under the Pax Romana its wealth and power increased. Only Rome and Alexandria surpassed it in importance.

Among the many foreigners in Antioch there was a large community of Jews. Their numbers were greatly increased during the reign of Antiochus IV Epiphanes (175–164), when the troubles in Judaea forced many to take refuge in Syria (see above). Accustomed to living among unbelievers, some used the Septuagint, the Greek translation of the Bible, in their synagogues. Jewish beliefs permeated non-Jewish society and, as a result, many gentiles in Antioch were familiar with Jewish ethical and spiritual values. It is hardly surprising, therefore, that Christianity soon made a large number of converts. As they included both Jews and Gentiles, the concept of a universal church whose members called themselves Christians began in Antioch. Şt. Peter lived for a time here and St. Paul and St. Barnabas used the city as a missionary centre. Under Diocletian the Christians of Antioch suffered grievously. Many of their churches were destroyed.

Later the city was not only an important centre for the diffusion of orthodox Christianity but also of heresy. Arius and Eusebius, who promoted the heretical doctrine that Christ is not co-substantial with the Father, were educated and, according to some historians, infected with their unorthodox beliefs in Antioch. Condemned by the Council of Nicaea in 325, Arianism continued to trouble the church until the end of the 4C. However, Antioch was also the city of Ignatius, famous for his expositive letters on Christian doctrine written to Polycarp and it was the birthplace c 345 of St. John Chrysostom, the great Patriarch of Constantinople.

Under the Byzantines Antioch continued to prosper. Filled with beautiful buildings and a centre of intellectual ferment, it challenged both new and old Rome. In the 6C it suffered two devastating blows. It was badly damaged by an earthquake, which killed more than 200,000 of its inhabitants, and it was captured and burned to the ground by the Persians. Rebuilt by Justinian, it was taken again by the Persians and then by the Arabs, who had overrun Syria.

Antioch remained in Arab hands until 969, when the Byzantine Nicephorus II Phocas recaptured it. In 1084 a new group of conquerors, the Selçuks, appeared on the scene. The Crusaders under Boehmund took it in 1098 and made it the capital of the principality of Antioch. The city remained in Christian hands until 1268, when a Mameluke army under Baibars rased it to the ground.

Antioch never recovered from this blow. In 1516 it was captured by the Ottomans under Selim II the Sot. The centuries that followed were marked by

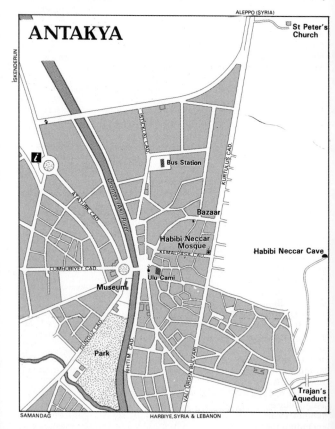

decay and decline. It became little more than a village inhabited by a few hundred people, who lived in a cluster of miserable huts surrounded by the ruins of ancient splendour.

Ruled briefly by the Egyptian Mehmet Ali from 1831–40 it came under French jurisdiction after World War I. In 1939, as the result of a plebicite, with the Sancak of Alexandretta, Antakya was returned to Turkey.

Apart from the city walls, a Roman aqueduct, some mysterious reliefs and the Church of St. Peter few traces of ancient Antioch are visible today. The clearest impression of its past glories may be obtained from the wonderful collection of late Roman and Byzantine mosaics in the **Museum**. These were found in Antakya, at Harbiye (ancient Daphne), and in various sites in the surrounding countryside.

The museum is located in the city centre near the Orontes. Opened for the first time in 1948, it was enlarged in 1973. The collection was reorganised and reclassified and the museum in its present form opened its doors to the public again in December 1974. The rich collection is well lit and imaginatively displayed. Allow at least two hours for your visit. Details of current opening times and admission charges may be obtained from the Tourism Information Office.

The following are some of the more interesting exhibits. **Entry hall**. Two fine *statues of Venus*. One found at Mağaracık near Samandağı, dating from the 1C AD, shows the goddess seated on a rock with her left hand resting on an amphora. The other from Antioch, a *crouching Venus*, 1C or 2C AD, is a Roman copy of a Greek original.

Room 1. Mosaics from Daphne: *Narcissus* by a stream (2C AD); the *Four Seasons* (2C AD) includes the *Calydonian Boar Hunt* and *Paris and Helen, Hippolytus and Phaedra*; the *Bird Mosaic* (5C AD); *Personification of Ge, Pegasus and the Nymphs* (3C AD); the *Triumph of Dionysus* 2C AD; the *Handing over of Chryseis*; a *Ceremony of Isis*. Mosaics from Antioch: *Personification of Soteria (Salvation)* (5C AD), *Iphigenia in Aulis* (3C AD) and the *Judgement of Paris* (2C AD). Statues and statuettes: a Roman *Faun; Hygeia* (3C AD) and *Fortuna* (2C AD).

Room 2. Mosaics from Daphne: *a theatre scene; Narcissus and Echo*; and the *Buffet Mosaic*, which shows the rape of Ganymede with Zeus in the guise of an eagle. All 3C AD.

Room 3. Mosaic from Daphne: *Oceanus and Thetis* (4C AD). Mosaics from Antioch: the *priapic happy hunchback* and *negro fisherman*; the *infant Hercules strangling serpents* and the *attack on the evil eye*. All 2C AD.

Room 4. Mosaics from Antioch: *Oceanus and Thetis* (2C AD); the *jugglers* (4C AD); the *drunken Dionysus*; Mosaics from Tarsus: *Zeus and Ganymede; Dionysiac subject; Orpheus charming the beasts*. All 3C AD. Mosaics from Daphne: *Satyr and Hermaphrodite; Apollo and Daphne*. Both (3C AD). Statues: *Hades*, Roman; relief *head of Thetis* (4C AD). Both from Kapısuyu.

Hall. Mosaics from Daphne: *Summer*; the *sundial*. Both 4C AD. Mosaic from Antakya: *Dionysus* (2C AD). **Room 5**. On the wall at the entrance: four *funeral stelae in the style of Palmyra*. All 3C AD. In this room are displayed Mitanni, Assyrian, Hittite and post-Hittite artefacts found in four mounds in the Amik plain. They include *altars, idols*, and *reliefs* dating from the 15C to the 7C BC.

Room 6. Small objects found near Antioch. These date from the Palaeolitic age to the Islamic era. Note especially the Roman bronzes (one of *Tyche*; see above) and a number of small statues and busts, including the fine head of an *ephebe*, found at İskenderun. There is also a collection of coins dating from the 5C BC to the Ottoman period.

Portico and Garden. A number of Roman sarcophagi from various locations; and mosaics from Daphne, İskenderun and Seleucia ad Pieria.

Antakya's main thoroughfare, the Kurtuluş Cad., follows the line of a magnificent colonnaded street that divided the centre of ancient Antioch. Traces of this were discovered during the course of excavations carried out in the 1930s. Approximately 10m wide and 4km from N to S it had ceremonial arches at either end and a large circular forum in the centre. After the city was almost completely destroyed by earthquakes in the 6C, this great artery was partially rebuilt by Justinian.

In the Kurtuluş Cad. is the *Mosque of Habib Neccar*. Originally a Crusader church, it was converted into a mosque after the city was captured by the Muslims. The minaret was added in the 17C. It contains a number of interesting tombs.

The ruins of a *Roman aqueduct* built in the reign of Trajan (98–117) may be found near the city hospital. It is known today as the Memikli bridge.

St. Peter's Church, Antakya.

To visit the *Church of St. Peter*, cross the Orontes (Asi) and turn left along Rıhtım Cad. Then continue on road 420 in the direction of Reyhanlı and Aleppo for c 2km. A turning to the right leads up to the church, which is in a grotto cut out of the hillside.

The Christians of Antioch, fearful of persecution, met secretly in this church for prayer and worship. It is known that St. Peter was in the city between 47 and 54, and according to an ancient tradition he preached and taught here. The present façade dates from the period in the 11C and 12C when Antioch was in Christian hands. The mosaic floors, which have suffered some damage, are much older, dating from the 4C or 5C. On the left side of the apse there is an opening, now partially blocked, which, legend related, was used by the congregation to escape in times of danger. A pious tradition asserts that the water, which flows from a fissure in the wall, is blessed and has curative properties.

Mass is celebrated in the church on 29 June, the feast day of St. Peter and St. Paul, and at a number of other times during the year.

About 200m to the NW of the church there is a mysterious *relief*. This is reached by scrambling up the hillside on the left to a small artificial terrace. The relief, cut into the cliff face, is of a veiled person, who gazes steadily and menacingly over the city.

Nothing is known with certainty about either the subject or the date of this monument. According to an account in a 6C chronicle, it dates from the reign of Antiochus IV Epiphanes (175–164 BC), the king who claimed to be Theos Epiphanes, god made manifest. It is believed to represent Charon, who ferried the dead across the Styx to Hades and it may have been carved at a time when Antioch was being devastated by plague. The smaller draped figure nearby perhaps depicts the king.

To visit the *fortifications* of Antioch, continue on road 420 in the direction of Aleppo for c 5km. Then turn to the right on to a side road, which winds sinuously up the E slope of Mt Sipylus for c 10km. The earliest surviving portions of the walls date from the time of Theodosius (AD 378–395), but they were repaired, enlarged and extended many times during the succeeding centuries. Access to the section, which ran along the crest of the mountain is made difficult by dense vegetation. However, a splendid view of Antakya and the Orontes valley may be obtained from a modern viewing platform which has been constructed near a thoughtfully-sited parking space.

A *castle*, which formed part of the fortifications, was constructed by Nicephorus Phocas c 969. Refurbished by Basil II in the 11C, it remained largely untouched until the 19C. Then, during the occupation of Antakya by the Egyptians, it was stripped of its much of cut stone. This was used both by the invaders and the local people to construct new buildings.

To visit 22km *Açcana Höyük*, formerly known as Alalakh, continue on road 420 towards Reyhanlı. Excavations conducted here between 1937–48 have revealed 17 separate levels of occupation dating from the Chalcolithic period, c 4500 BC to c 1200 BC.

Remains of two palaces were found in the tell, which was the site of the capital of the kingdom of Mukish. One dating from c 1785 BC, was constructed by the Hittite Yarim-Lim, the other built by Nigme-Pa, dates from the 15C BC. Possession of the city was contested on several occasions by the Egyptians and it was sacked by Ramesses II in 1285.

A number of objects found in the tell are displayed in the Hatay Museum in Antakya. These include two idols carved from basalt, one male, one female; a 15C BC basalt altar; a 15C BC dolomite ram's head and a 13C BC fresco from a Hittite palace.

33 Excursions from Antakya

A. Yayladağı, via Harbiye, Cursat and Çatbaşı

Total distance c 40km. **Antakya**—R825 9km **Harbiye**—R825 (c 3km *Cursat*—(c 2km Şenköy/*Çatbaşı*)—31km *Yayladağı*.

For the visits to Çatbaşı and Yayladağı it is advisable to take guides from the villages. Before going to Yayladağı, check with the Tourist Information Office in Antakya about *any restrictions* on visiting the frontier area.

One of Antakya's greatest assets is its proximity to (9km) **Harbiye** a picturesque village in the hills S of the city. Occupying the site of ancient DAPHNE, Harbiye may be reached by taking road 825 in the direction of Yayladağı. There are frequent dolmuş services from the city centre.

In the summer residents of Antakya go to Daphne frequently to enjoy its cool breezes and wander through the laurel groves escaping, however briefly, from the stifling heat of the city.

History. The importance of Daphne in ancient times may be gauged by the fact that the great city of Antioch was sometimes called Epidaphne: near Daphne. This beautiful gorge with its cascades, its shaded groves of laurel and brooding cypress has many legends told about it. Here, the ancients believed, the youth Cyparissus accidentally killed his pet stag and, grieving over its death, was turned by Apollo into a cypress tree. Here, too, it was said Paris delivered his fateful judgment. In the groves of Daphne he gave the golden apple to Aphrodite and by doing so set in train the chain of events that led to the Trojan War.

Perhaps the best known legend concerns Apollo's pursuit of the nymph Daphne, the daughter of the river god Peneus. Apollo had mocked Eros and for his pains was struck by one of the love god's golden arrows. Seeing Daphne he was captivated by her beauty and fell madly in love. Unfortunately, Eros had transfixed her heart with a lead-tipped arrow, so making her incapable of loving anyone.

Pursued by Apollo, she was seized by him on the banks of her father's river. Desperately she prayed for deliverance and Peneus, hearing her plea for help, turned her into a laurel tree which took root on the river bank. From then on the laurel was called daphne in memory of the nymph. Apollo, saddened by his loss, decorated his lyre with a wreath of daphne and, as god of music, decreed that thenceforth prize-winning musicians should be crowned with laurel. (One of the best known representations of the story of Apollo and Daphne, which has inspired many artists, is the painting ascribed to the 15C Florentine artists Antonio and Piero del Pollaiuolo in the National Gallery in London.)

Apollo's infatuation with Daphne was commemorated in a temple erected there in his honour by Seleucus I. This temple contained a famous statue of the god (the Apollo Citharoedos) by the celebrated Athenian sculptor, Bryaxis, which has been lost and is now known only from coins and from Roman copies in Florence and Naples. Other members of the Olympian pantheon, Artemis, Aphrodite and Zeus also had their sanctuaries at Daphne. Antiochus IV Epiphanes, who ordered the construction of the temple of Zeus at Daphne, instituted the Olympic Games of Antioch and built a stadium for them there, where not only athletic events took place, but plays, music and poetry were also performed.

The Romans displayed a similar enthusiasm for this suburb of Antioch. Indeed it became so notorious that for a time it was declared off-limits for the Roman army! In addition to theatres and fine public buildings, they built luxurious villas and created elaborate gardens amongst its laurel groves. Under their rule it had a reputation for luxurious and licentious living which it had begun to acquire under the Seleucids.

With the arrival of Christianity the fortunes of Daphne began to decline. Apart from a short period during the reign of Julian the Apostate (361–363), when paganism enjoyed a temporary revival, ancient rituals were allowed to lapse and temples everywhere fell into decay. In Daphne the temple of Apollo was destroyed by fire, an incident for which the Christians were blamed by Julian. The devastation produced by the Persians in the 6C and the Arab raids in the 7C and their subsequent occupation of Antioch and the surrounding countryside reduced Daphne to the status of an impoverished village. It never recovered its former glory.

Today there are no visible remains of Daphne's past. All the great buildings have disappeared and of the formal gardens there is no trace. The gorge is once more a wild and untamed place. Water cascades through natural channels and laurels and cypresses grow where their seeds have fallen. Perhaps as a wilderness it is as beautiful, evocative and numinous as it was in the days of the Seleucids or the Romans.

Continue S on road 825 in the direction of Yayladağ. After c 8km a turning to the right leads to the *Castle of Cursat* (Qalat az Zaw), which is now in a ruinous condition. Built on a narrow plateau protected by deep river valleys this fortress fulfilled the same function as Bakras to the N. It defended the S approaches to Antioch. Fought over by many armies and factions, it was captured, after a long siege, by the Mamelukes in 1275.

As access is difficult, allow two to three hours for the visit.

About 10km to the S of Cursat a track to the left leads to the village of *Senköy*. From there, with the help of a guide, it is possible to visit the *reliefs of Karabar* located near *Çatbaşı*. Dating from the 8C BC, when the area was under Assyrian rule, one depicts a bearded god imparting his blessing, the other a suppliant and a god, surrounded by symbols of divinity.

A further 13km brings the traveller to *Yayladağı*, the last Turkish village before the border with Syria. Nearby is Djebel Akra (1759m), the ancient Mt Cassius. Regarded as sacred from the earliest times—the Hittites had a sanctuary on the summit—it was the site of the temple of Zeus Cassius. Seleucus I Nicator (321–281) sacrificed there before deciding on the site of Seleuceia ad Pieria, the port of Antioch (see below).

No trace of the temple remains. Excavations suggest that it may lie under the foundations of the ruined Monastery of St. Barlaam which dates from the 5C. Anyone intending to climb the mountain should employ a guide and obtain any permits required from the local and civil military authorities. Initial enquiries should be made to the Tourist Office in Antakya.

B.   Seleuceia ad Piera

Total distance c 32km. **Antakya**—28km *Samandağ*—c 4km *Çevlik /
Seleuceia ad Piera.*

The inhabitants of Antakya seek refreshing summer breezes and relaxation at 28km *Samandağ*, a small seaside resort sited to the N of the mouth of the Orontes. Nestling picturesquely among olive groves and big trees, it also attracts many visitors who wish to examine the remains of nearby Seleuceia ad Pieria and Al Mina.

On a mountain peak to the left of the road, c 20km from Antakya, are the ruins of two *churches*, which were built in honour of St. Simeon Stylites the Younger (521–592). In imitation of the better-known St. Simeon Stylites the Elder (fl. 390), while still a child Simeon the Younger embraced a life of prayer and fasting and ascended a column where he spent the rest of his life. Pillar saints, like the two Simeons, played an important part in the history of the early church. Great crowds came to hear them preach and both the civil and ecclesiastical authorities were much influenced by their views.

The ruins of SELEUCEIA AD PIERIA are c 4km to the N of Samnadağ, near the village of Çevlik.

History. Seleuceia ad Pieria was founded by Seleucus I Nicator (321–281) in 300 BC as the port for his new capital Antioch. According to legend, he chose the site while sacrificing to Zeus on Mt Cassius. An eagle snatched part of the sacrificial victim and carried it N to the place where the new town was built.

A prosperous trading centre under the Seleucids, it continued to flourish when Antioch became the capital of the Roman province of Syria. Goods were shipped from here to Rome and other parts in the empire. St. Paul and St. Barnabas sailed from Seleuceia to Cyprus c 47–49 on their first missionary journey (Acts 13–14).

The port, badly damaged by the earthquake which devastated Antioch in 526, entered a period of decline under the Byzantines. This continued after the Arab conquest of Syria in the mid 7C, when it became known as Soueidiyeh. On March 19 1148 Louis VII of France, one of the leaders of the Second Crusade, who had sailed from Attaleia (Antalya), with part of his army, arrived at Seleuceia or St. Simeon, as it was known by the Crusaders. Here he was greeted warmly by Raymond, prince of Antioch.

After the sack of Antioch by the Mamelukes in 1268, Seleuceia seems to have been abandoned. It appears no more on the pages of history.

Today Seleuceia ad Pieria, like Harbiye, is visited more for the beauty of its setting and for its historical associations than for its ruins. Apart from an impressive underground water-channel, few traces of its past remain. The town was built partly on a rocky promontory which projects from the foothills of Musa Dağı and partly on a small plain at its foot. Its port was created by the enlargement of a natural basin which had been formed by a fast-flowing stream. To prevent flooding, a dam and an artificial water-course were commenced during the reigns of Vespasian (69–79) and Titus (79–81) and completed in the 2C under the Antonines. The river was diverted into an *underground channel* c 1400m long, whose construction is commemorated by two inscriptions carved on its walls. A formidable engineering achievement, the work was done by legionaries, sailors and prisoners from Judea.

In an area called Beşikli Cave there are several *rock-tombs*, some of which bear low reliefs. In the upper part of Seleuceia there are the insignificant remains of a gateway and of two temples, one of which, constructed in the Doric style, was dedicated to Zeus. The acropolis was surrounded by walls dating from the Hellenistic period.

In 1936–37 Sir Leonard Woolley excavated a site known as **Al Mina** at the mouth of the Orontes river (Asi), which had been inhabited from before the 9C BC to the end of the 4C BC. On the basis of the pottery which he found there Woolley distinguished ten separate levels of occupation. From the archaeological evidence it is clear that Al Mina was an important emporium where both Greek and Syrian traders lived and worked side by side. Their homes and warehouses have been laid bare by the excavators' trowel. The principal product offered by the Greeks appears to have been pottery. It is not clear what they obtained in exchange—some authorities suggest metals, perhaps iron and copper.

However, trading posts like Al Mina did more than facilitate the exchange of goods. They were almost certainly channels through which ideas, skills, and artistic influences flowed. It is probable that the adoption of orientalising motifs like the palmette, lotus and sphinx by Greek potters may be traced to emporia like Al Mina. In turn there is evidence that local pottery was affected by Greek taste and style.

It is even possible that the Greeks acquired their alphabet through trading contacts of the kind provided by Al Mina. Herodotus states (Book 5. 58) that they learned writing from the Phoenicians, a suggestion supported by their term for the letters of the alphabet, *phoinikeia*, the Phoenician things. Some of the oldest Greek inscriptions have been found in Euboea and the Euboeans were probably the first Greek traders to come to Al Mina. Their pottery has been discovered by the archaeologists in levels IX and VIII (late 9C BC) of the site. Some of the later Greek pottery found there bears graffiti in Aramaic.

Al Mina declined in importance towards the end of the 4C BC. It is not clear whether this was due to the activities of Ptolemy Soter I or commercial competition from the new port of Seleucia ad Pieria (see above), which was located c 7km to the N. Woolley suggests that the population of Al Mina and Sabouni may have been removed by force to the new city by Seleucus.

The fortunes of Al Mina enjoyed a brief revival during the Crusades, but later the settlement sank once again into obscurity and neglect. According to recent visitors to the site, few traces remain of the buildings laid bare by Woolley during the course of his excavations. It now requires a considerable effort of imagination to visualise them in their original state. However, the excellent display of artefacts from Al Mina in the Ashmolean Museum, Oxford, is a lasting reminder of the discoveries made by the archaeologist and his colleagues at this remote site in SE Turkey more than 50 years ago.

INDEX

Modern place names are in bold type and ancient place names in Roman capitals. The names of eminent persons are in italics.

NOTES

NOTES

NOTES

NOTES

NOTES

NOTES